COOPERATION AND COMPETITION
AMONG PRIMITIVE PEOPLES

# COOPERATION

## AND

# COMPETITION AMONG

# PRIMITIVE PEOPLES

EDITED BY
MARGARET MEAD

BEACON PRESS BOSTON

# PREFACE TO THE BEACON PRESS EDITION

When I was asked to prepare this book, which was written in 1935, published in 1937, and which went out of print in 1954, it presented me with a dilemma quite new and different from the problem of reprinting, for example, *Coming of Age in Samoa*[1], written a decade before. This was in many respects a pioneer effort. The venture of which it was a part was a new form of co-operative research — the phrase "interdisciplinary research" had not yet been invented. The book grew out of anthropological research resulting from a new kind of cooperation between graduate students, young field workers, and older field workers. It was a first attempt to think about the very complex and knotty problems of cultural character and social structure. Unlike a report on a piece of field work, which stands forever as a valuable record if carried out with fidelity to the scientific canons of the day, an adventure in theory which really relies on materials and is not merely imposed upon them is, in one sense, only as good as the original materials. In this case there were no original materials, no data collected on the questions we set out to answer. We had to create these materials somehow, in New York, in the middle of the depression with a minuscule budget.

What is valuable about this book, aside from the intrinsic usefulness of chapters prepared in relation to one another and on a common theme, is, I believe, the sense of research process which those who are just developing an interest in anthropology can find here. It is not only an account of how it *was* done, in much greater detail than is usually given, but it remains still an account of how a comparative study of this kind *can be done*. Fifty years from now, if the processes of modernization continue to spread over the face of the earth, scientists who wish to ask *new questions* of ethnological materials will be in much the same

[1]Margaret Mead, *Coming of Age in Samoa,* William Morrow and Company, Inc., New York, 1928.

position that we were in 1935 — although for quite different reasons. Then, it was because there were neither funds nor trained anthropologists available to send expeditions out to answer the question posed by an interdisciplinary committee: "to provide a report on the possible contribution of ethnological material to the planning of research in competitive and cooperative habits." In the year 2010 we will still be asking new questions, questions raised by the other human sciences, questions grown urgent in the light of new forms of social organization — on this earth and perhaps on other planets. There will be no primitive peoples left to study: there will be a few anthropologists who studied primitive cultures in their youth, who can be asked to help reorganize the existing materials in a way that may be fruitful. There will probably be no one alive who was in my position when I organized this research by using my own fresh field materials from my last three expeditions to provide a way of looking at published materials, collected by older or inaccessible ethnologists, on cultures which have since disintegrated.

It is in this sense that *Cooperation and Competition Among Primitive Peoples* provides a model to think with and a corrective for the usual "survey of the ethnological literature," in which odds and ends and titbits of Human Relations Area File cards are assembled, out of context, to provide "research leads." Today, as in 1935, there still is a lack of understanding of what cultural relativism means in anthropology — not, as vulgarly understood, that all *ethics* are relative, but that *any* item of cultural behavior must be understood in relation to the culture from which it comes, and that, torn out of its context, it is meaningless. So, in 1935, I was instructed by a member of the interdisciplinary committee to do a survey of about twelve cultures — without any "of this nonsense that anthropologists are always insisting upon, about 'whole cultures,' just do cooperative and competitive habits in about a dozen cultures." There were funds available for one senior anthropologist for about three months. We had to devise a way of doing whole cultures to the best of our ability. The procedure is described in detail in the body of this book.

These chapters are not to be treated as source material on the various peoples concerned. They are not primary materials but are organized, interpretive statements, all pointed to a common problem and related to each other. For basic data on any of these cultures, the reader is referred to the bibliographies, those used then, and those published since, which are provided in the Additional Notes to Chapters and Bibliographies (p. 529).

The book has been reproduced exactly as it was originally published, as any alterations would intrude inappropriately into a whole operation that was finished long ago. The group who did the original work are scattered: two of them, Buell Quain and Bernard Mishkin, who went on to field work in the Pacific and South America, are dead. Each of the living authors has been asked to provide corrective or expansive notes on his own chapter. For consultation help on bibliography and changes of emphasis, I want to thank Harold Conklin on the Ifugao, Peter Vayda on the Maori, William Fenton on the Iroquois, Helen Codere on the Kwakiutl, Ruth Bunzel on the Zuni, and Geoffrey Gorer on psychological theory.

If we were to organize a new seminar on Cooperation and Competition, we would not revise these materials but would be able to stand, not only on our own structure, but also on the great volume of work in this field which has been done in the last twenty-five years, since I sat in a mountain village in Bali and read a review by a senior colleague, which included the sentence: "If the long 'interpretative statement' had been written by anyone but a proved member of the faith*, it would be regarded as almost undiluted bunkum."[2]

Fortunately, we introduced very little jargon. We used the definitions of *cooperative* and *competitive* behavior provided by the committee, found it necessary to distinguish between *individual* and *collective* behavior, and used two concepts from contemporary psychoanalytically oriented social science — that of *ego strength* and *a sense of security,* and the words *guilt* and *shame, internal* and *external sanctions* with specified meanings. To understand the discussion, these now outmoded usages must be kept firmly in mind, or the reader will feel as confused as did Milton Singer trying to mix the first tentative gropings in 1935

*Young field workers take note: Always bring back some voluminous materials in categories of research that are already recognized as significant — like tobacco drying, or string figures.

[2] *American Anthropologist,* N.S., Vol. 39, October-December, 1937, No. 4 (Part 1), pp. 710-711. For reply see *American Anthropologist,* N.S., Vol. 40, July-September, 1938, No. 3, pp. 530-531.

with the sophistication of 1953.[3] Theory cannot be read back-
wards. It is as much a task to place oneself intellectually
twenty-five years back as it is to place oneself within another
culture, and it is an activity which is equally anthropological in
the intellectual elasticity it requires.[4] But if one learns to do
this, then the struggles of an earlier age become available at
another level, and as students learn from the history of the
natural sciences, so also they can learn from the youth of the
human sciences. I believe that youth has a quality of its own
— whether it be chronological youth, or the youth of a science,
or the youth of a particular new approach, freshness, eagerness,
dizzy excitement and black despair speak to each other across
the boundaries of the years.

MARGARET MEAD

*American Museum of Natural History*
*New York, 1961*

---

[3]Gerhard Piers and Milton B. Singer, *Shame and Guilt: A Psychoanalytic
and Cultural Study,* Charles Thomas, Springfield, Illinois, 1953.

[4]Because I believe it is so important to know more about how it all began,
I have helped organize fuller statements elsewhere. See Margaret Mead,
*An Anthropologist at Work, Writings of Ruth Benedict,* Houghton Mifflin
Company, Boston, 1959. Margaret Mead, "Apprenticeship Under Boas" in
*The Anthropology of Franz Boas,* edited by Walter Goldschmidt, Memoir
No. 89 of the American Anthropological Association, Vol. 6, No. 5, Part 2,
October 1959, pp. 29-45. Margaret Mead and Ruth Bunzel, *The Golden Age
of American Anthropology,* George Braziller, Inc., New York, 1960.

# PREFACE

These studies were prepared as a survey of the possible contribution of ethnological material to the planning of research in
competitive and cooperative habits. They were undertaken
at the request of the Subcommittee on Competitive Cooperative
Habits of the Committee on Personality and Culture of the
Social Science Research Council. As this was the first attempt to
assemble material upon primitive societies as a background for
planning research in this field in our own society, I followed two
principles in the selection of the material to be covered. The
material was chosen to show the range and possibilities of various
kinds of ethnological sources available for such research; it was
focused on cultures that appeared to be relevant to the problem
in hand.

The range of literature includes:

1. Old published sources describing cultures now greatly
altered by white contact without supplementary material from
recent field work (Maori).

2. Comparatively recent published material in which no
consultation with the field workers was possible (Ifugao and
Amassalik Eskimo).

3. Published and unpublished material which has been collected over a considerable period of time and at different stages
of acculturation. Here it was possible to consult ethnologists
who have worked and still are working in these cultures (Kwakiutl, Zuni, Iroquois).

4. A culture now greatly altered but about which we have
a few old records, a contemporary unpublished study of cultural
change, and the manuscript of a trained member of the tribe who
was accessible also for questioning, and for which there were
some observations made by a psychologist (Dakota).

5. Studies prepared by field workers for this investigation.[1]

[1] Certain omissions must be explained. Dobuan society was omitted
because Dr. Ruth Benedict's restatement, *Patterns of Culture*, Chap. V
(Houghton Mifflin Company, Boston, 1934), of Dr. Fortune's material

By interpreting in this rather broad way a mandate to examine what ethnological literature had to contribute, it was hoped to demonstrate the relative richness of the various kinds of sources. It will immediately be evident that there are a multitude of questions which the summaries of old literature leave unanswered and on which it is impossible to obtain further information. The time and effort spent in reworking published sources is as great as when field workers organize their own materials in response to a new inquiry. Therefore, if this kind of examination of ethnological literature is to be frequently undertaken, the most promising lead would seem to be to regard the field worker as the source rather than published material that has been organized to some other point. Such a method would be much quicker and more economical than sending special research workers into the field, so that, wherever only a small fund was available, maximum results could be obtained.

This inquiry was conducted as a seminar. Associated with me were four graduate students in the Department of Anthropology at Columbia University, Irving Goldman, Jeannette Mirsky, Buell Quain, and Bernard Mishkin, and two postdoctorates, May Mandelbaum Edel and Ruth Landes. We worked simultaneously upon our several cultures and met to discuss preliminary results and frame further working hypotheses.

In the Introduction is a list of the guiding questions which were prepared at the beginning of the research. Our

---

was already organized to the point of the Dobuan obsessional fantasy competition, and the original materials on Dobu (Dr. Reo Fortune, *Sorcerers of Dobu*, E. P. Dutton & Co., Inc., New York, 1932) are already published in one volume organized to modern anthropological interests. Prof. Malinowski's data on the Trobriands was also omitted because the published material is clearly organized. In addition, the account of agricultural economics of the Trobriands had not yet appeared; the two volumes of *Coral Gardens* (George Allen and Unwin, London, 1935) appeared the following autumn. Dr. Ian Hogbin's study of Ontong Java, *Law and Order in Polynesia* (Harcourt Brace & Company, New York, 1934), was omitted because it duplicated the Samoan material to some extent. Australian material would have been extremely relevant to the study of the relationship of competitive habits to scarcity of food supply. However, pending Prof. Lloyd Warner's publication of his Australian monograph, there was no published material that seemed adequate. It would also have been desirable to have included more African studies but published materials were not available.

definitions and conclusions emerged slowly as we worked over the analyses.

Each contributor is responsible only for his own contribution, although in many cases he may have contributed much insight on the subject of one or more of the other cultures. For the Introduction and the Interpretative Statement I alone am responsible. Most of my associates were able to criticize and add to it in the original form in which it was prepared for the Committee in May, 1934; but three of them were away in the field when it was finally revised and prepared for publication. While, therefore, I have made every effort to do no violence to any individual's interpretation of his own culture, I may very easily have shifted an emphasis here and altered a relationship there. For the theoretical assumptions upon which my interpretations are based, I alone am responsible. Neither the Introduction nor the Interpretative Statement should be regarded, therefore, as comprising any other part of the study.

This book, then, consists of individual studies of thirteen cultures and of the attempt of one individual, myself, to organize and interpret what I consider the more important matters stressed in these thirteen studies. Each one of my six collaborators would probably have presented a different interpretative statement. Mine is presented here because I was asked by the Committee to make such a statement. But each study may be regarded as a separate unit, standing on its own feet and important in its own right. Should any reader disagree with the interpretation, the separate studies remain for his consideration, offering ample material for a different analysis. At the same time, the material has the advantage of having been organized from one point of view. The student in search of primitive materials is usually asked either to read great monographs on different tribes, or else to accept colorless condensations of unweighted statements about a diversity of tribes. In this study he can gain an insight into the comparative method by following the same clues through contrasting types of primitive material. It is to be hoped that in this way he will come to realize the advantage of submitting all generalizations about human nature to the comparative test.

Furthermore, each study is sufficiently independent of each other study so that it can be used alone, and there are some studies that are more illuminating on certain aspects of culture than others. Students of economics will find the Manus, Ifugao, and Zuni most interesting; students of education will find more material in the Arapesh, Samoans, Zuni, and Dobuans; and those who are specially interested in political science will find the Bathonga, Samoa, and Iroquois studies most useful.

The book as a unit, with the Introduction and Interpretative Statement, may be used as the basis for a systematic approach to the problems of culture and personality.

The group was guided by a common but loose frame of reference. It seemed more desirable to follow the emphases in the diverse materials rather than to constrict the material to fit a given mold. Each individual's research was informed and enriched by the conclusions that every other worker drew in the course of his research. This method seemed best suited to obtain a maximum contribution from each member and a maximum integration of the material.

Our special thanks are due to several anthropologists who have given most generously of their time and materials to this research. Dr. Ruth Benedict assumed part of the task of supervision and planning and provided criticism of the Zuni, Kwakiutl, and Dakota studies. Dr. Ruth Bunzel permitted the use of her exceedingly valuable manuscript upon Zuni economics, without which this study would have been most impoverished, and also contributed specific criticisms and suggestions. Mr. William Fenton not only furnished us with unpublished materials and spent many hours with Mr. Quain working over the problem, but also obtained new field material from one of his informants among the Iroquois. Dr. Scudder Mekeel permitted us to consult his unpublished manuscript on the Dakota and generously answered special questions that arose in the course of the study. Miss Ella Deloria's unpublished manuscript and detailed material on special points provided the basis for the study of the Dakota. Dr. Otto Klineberg was kind enough to read the Dakota study and comment upon it from his experience in doing psychological testing among the Dakota. In developing the theoretical background from which I have interpreted these materials, I am particularly indebted to Prof. A. R. Radcliffe-Brown, Dr. Erich Fromm, Dr. John Dollard, and Dr. A. Edel. Thanks are due to Dr. Clark

*PREFACE*

Wissler, who has approved the expenditure of time necessary for me to participate in and supervise this study, and to the Departments of Anthropology and Psychology of Columbia University, who contributed facilities for mimeographing the preliminary edition.

NEW YORK, N. Y.,
*November*, 1936.

# Contents

# CONTENTS

# COOPERATION AND COMPETITION AMONG PRIMITIVE PEOPLES

## INTRODUCTION

### by MARGARET MEAD

This book differs from the ordinary textbook. It is an attempt to describe a piece of research which is just begun; a stage in thinking which is tentative, experimental, inconclusive, but which is hopefully pointed in a direction which will make better thinking possible. This volume is the result of an exploratory piece of research, and for the reader to get the most out of it, it will be necessary to follow the work through from the beginning and to see how ideas changed and developed as the material was handled. In order that the reader may be party to the research problem, each step must be noted: why this research was undertaken, how it was carried on, and why it was worked on as it was.

The term *culture and personality* has come into prominence in the social sciences as a focusing point for bringing together the findings of several disciplines which were all dealing with different aspects of the socialized human being. Those who feel that the term represents a legitimate field of research hope that it will act in this way. Biologists will be asked to deal not merely with the total physiology of the human individual but will pay special attention to what Dr. Dollard has called the "socially relevant biological factors," those parts of the organism whose responses are most significantly responsive to and elaborated by social conditioning. So the biologist would be asked to turn from a recording of physiological changes in the stomach, and to take into consideration the whole mechanism by which hunger is transformed into appetite, so that the organism responds not merely to internal physiological changes, but also to a time rhythm imposed from without, and to a selection of foods which

1

tradition has declared to be desirable. From the psychologist, this approach demands an orientation in two directions: that in every hypothesis made about an individual, he take into account the biological basis on the one hand and the cultural conditioning on the other. This does not mean that he must cease to postulate hypotheses which are consistent upon the psychological level, but that such hypotheses must be firmly attached to both the biological underpinning and the cultural conditioning which shapes the individual at every turn. From the psychiatrist, it asks that he cease to see each case of individual breakdown either in isolation, as a function of that one individual's past, or as a symptom only of physiological malfunctioning, or only of social malfunctioning. In other words, the culture and personality approach asks that the psychiatrist should not reduce all cases of mental disease purely to the status of breakdowns resulting from known lesions; that he should not refer them purely to faulty glandular functioning; or at the other extreme, that he should not regard the nonfunctioning of an individual purely as the result of his social conditioning, or of his peculiar social position in a given social situation. From the student of culture this approach demands that he cease to consider exclusively the patterned interrelations of items of social behavior. The student of culture must grapple with several problems which he has traditionally ignored. He must give due consideration to the details of the way in which the new organism is added to the group, and also to a particularistic and detailed attempt to follow given individuals' life histories, so that he may see the way in which a given type of culture is laid down in the human organism. The sociologist is asked, first, to add to his traditional discussion of groups and group behavior a more thoroughgoing recognition that this group behavior is tremendously subject to the specific pattern laid down by the culture within which it takes place. Second, that he make specific allowance for the interaction within group situations of identified individuals with organisms which have been specifically conditioned throughout their life histories. Third, that he recognize each such constellation of individuals as unique.

The culture and personality approach, then, demands that these separate disciplines cease to abstract certain aspects of human life and study them without reference to the whole individual, and to the numbers of whole individuals who make up any group. It insists that there is a common meeting ground where the hypotheses of each discipline can be tested out and made relevant to a more genuine social science.

This is the hypothesis, but now came the question of how to proceed with it. Since 1927 various groups have been grappling with the problem, defining the issues, breaking the ground.[1] The Social Science Research Council has been actively interested in developing, as one of its areas of concentration, the field of personality and culture. A brief history of its activities in this field is found in the various annual reports of the Council and particularly in a recent report of the Subcommittee on Cooperative and Competitive Habits under the auspices of which the present work was carried on. This committee, composed of Profs. Mark May, chairman, Gardner Murphy, and Gordon Allport, undertook the task of determining the boundaries of scientific knowledge concerning cooperation and competition as a special phase of the larger field of personality and culture. This survey included contributions from the field of child psychology, qualitative and quantitative adult psychology, psychoanalysis, sociology, and anthropology. I was asked to supervise the survey of ethnological literature and to report on at least twelve cultures.

This history should be held firmly in mind. A group of psychologists, accepting the premise that the concept of culture and personality outlined above was a valid one, were asking me and my associates: "What does the literature on primitive peoples yield on the subject of competitive and cooperative habits which throws light on the problem of culture and personality?" We were responsible both to the psychologists who

[1] *Proceedings First Colloquium on Personality Investigation, held under the Auspices of the American Psychiatric Association, Committee on Relations in the Social Sciences, December 1–2, 1928, New York City,* Lord Baltimore Press, Baltimore, Maryland, 1928.

*Proceedings Second Colloquium on Personality Investigation, held under the Joint Auspices of the American Psychiatric Association, Committee on Relations of Psychiatry and the Social Sciences, and of the Social Science Research Council, November 29–30, 1929, New York City,* Johns Hopkins Press, Baltimore, Maryland, 1930.

*Report of the Committee on Personality and Culture of the Social Science Research Council, Agenda for Meetings of the Social Science Research Council and the Committee on Problems and Policy, September,* 1934. (Mimeographed.)

asked for specific materials and to the fundamental hypotheses of our own discipline. Therefore several considerations guided me in setting up the plan. As the committee wished to know what the literature yielded, it was necessary to sample various types of literature. This was done, but this gives very uneven results and the sketchy studies of the Maori and the Iroquois must be judged with this situation in mind. Since this was an exploratory study it seemed worth while to try out a new approach to the literature, and to go not only to published sources but to research workers who could reorganize their original notes in the light of this special problem. So five of these studies[1] are written by field workers in response to the stimulation of the specific problem. In three others[2] the work was done where it was possible to consult the field workers themselves and in one case[3] it was possible to consult extensively a trained Indian woman belonging to the tribe. This further presents an opportunity to judge the likelihood of answering a new problem from published sources on primitive peoples. Because so many social theorists from the time of Herbert Spencer down to the present day have done this very thing—asked a question and expected published sources of most uneven merit and incompatible orientation to answer that question—it is worth while to look closely at these studies from this point of view. These studies will show the difference between the old type of ethnology, in which customs were recorded without any reference to the given persons who carried them or without specifying the one tribe among many which practiced them, and the new type, in which the ethnologist studies the same group of people as they interact in a set of defined and limited social situations. These studies will make patently clear the kind of material obtained by reconstructing a social system which is now practically dead,[4] and how unsatisfactory this is as compared with the study of a living culture.[5] These studies will illustrate how the failure to record the cultural patterning of the educational process leaves the student completely in the dark as to

[1] Bachiga, Ojibwa, Manus, Arapesh, and Samoa.
[2] Zuni, Kwakiutl, Iroquois.
[3] Dakota.
[4] Especially Maori and Iroquois.
[5] Especially Manus and Arapesh.

*how* the members of each generation were made into the individuals whose behavior is recorded. A realization of all these differences, shortcomings, and omissions in published sources should provide the reader with a body of criticism when confronted with social theories based upon an irresponsible quoting from all kinds and degrees of primitive materials.

In planning the research I was guided by the desire to have as many types of culture represented as possible: large and small political units, different levels of technology, patriarchal and matriarchal institutions, different economic institutions, etc. Then the very practical issue of which students were available, here in New York, in the winter of 1934–1935, gave a further skewing to the problem. If this research had been done in London rather than in New York, Africa would have been more fully represented. If I had not been directing it and writing three of the studies myself, the South Seas would have been less fully represented.

So the history of this research may be taken as a bit of evidence on what forces shape and determine the pieces of research which are presented so neatly as finished products in textbooks. A new movement for the integration of the sciences dealing with human relations, which owes most of its impetus to Mr. Laurence K. Frank, Prof. Edward Sapir, and Dr. Harry Stack Sullivan; my participation in the Hanover Seminar of Human Relations; the fact that the study was done in New York and therefore drew on Columbia University students who had worked on certain underlying common hypotheses—all served to shape and to limit its final form.

In planning the research I made two assumptions.

1. No fact about the behavior of the members of a group which share a common culture, and are in greater or less degree members of a given society, is relevant out of its context. For example, the mere recording of the fact that a group of men were accustomed to build a canoe together would have no comparative significance, unless one knew: the sociological constitution of the group who build these canoes, the way in which this canoe-building group fitted into the total social structure, the articulate ends for which each individual in that group was working, the sanctions which lay behind their working together, and the extent to which this group activity, whether it was

6 COOPERATION AND COMPETITIONCOOPERATION AND COMPETITION

defined as cooperative or merely as collective, was representative of the usual behavior of members of the society. One would, furthermore, have to know the nature of the material environment within which the group got its livelihood and the existing state of technology. In order to answer these questions, it was impossible merely to skim through the ethnographic data picking out matters which looked as if they could be classified under the headings of competition and cooperation. It became necessary to analyze each culture as a whole so that each of these orders of facts occupied a significant position in reference to a cultural constellation which has been considered as a whole.

2. To understand personality it is necessary to study character formation. What is the mechanism by which the newborn individual is transformed into a more or less adequate adult representative of his culture through the operation of cultural agencies? To lay a background for the study of the relationship between competitive and cooperative behavior, and the problem of culture and personality, it is therefore necessary to know not only what the form of the culture is which dictates certain forms of adult behavior and interdicts others, but also how this adult personality is formed in the long process of building the cultureless infant into the adult. Where materials on the educational process are lacking, the problem of personality and culture cannot really be attacked at all; it can only be sketched in, and to some extent delimited. For instance, if we know of a culture in which wife lending is a recognized and socially sanctioned form of behavior, we can say that no theory of male jealousy is admissable which assumes the impossibility of producing individuals able to lend their wives with every appearance of equanimity. But without details of the educational process from early infancy to adulthood, we would still have no idea of how such a type of male personality was produced. For several of the cultures discussed in this book we have only the first type of information. We know that certain kinds of unusual and striking behavior were characteristic of the average adult in the group which the ethnologist studied. We know, furthermore, that this type of behavior has been characteristic of the human carriers of that culture for some time, because it is reflected in linguistic usage, in proverb, in folklore, in ritual, in institutionalized forms which take some time to develop.

But we neither know why such behavior is found institutionalized in these cultural forms, nor how the character of each individual carrier of the culture is developed so that he will reenact and perpetuate these forms. From such materials as we have on the Iroquois and the Maori, for instance, we can only discuss patterns of culture at their most institutional level. Because these patterns were originally derived from observation of items of behavior of human beings, we can guess, using our knowledge of the common organic basis of human nature, at the nature of the middle term, the formation of character. But we cannot even guess profitably. These descriptions must remain representative of a certain order of ethnological inquiry, which, while it yields valuable material on comparative social forms, begs the particular question which we wish to ask.

In those cases in which we have not only information about the characteristic behavior of adults but also a description of the educational process by which those adult characters are formed, we may then ask how much we can expect to know about the problem of culture and personality. And here again we must recognize very definite limitations. When we are told that Zuni parents reproach their children if they behave in a childish way, and that Samoan parents reproach their children if they behave in an adult way, and we are furthermore given descriptions of the characteristic behavior of Zuni adults and of Samoan adults, we can assume that we are dealing here with a set of related facts. If Zuni parents—as a rule—treat their children in a certain way, and Zuni children—as a rule—grow up to behave in a certain way, we can assume that the method of education, within the total Zuni cultural scheme, is related to the adult character. But we cannot assume that the Zuni character could not be formed in other ways. We cannot assume that these items in the Zuni educational process which have so far been observed and recorded are the most significant items. Furthermore, we cannot assume that if all these items of parental behavior could be incorporated whole in the educational program of some people whose total culture was very different from the Zuni, that the same character formation would result. We have in such a case, I believe, been able to describe another dimension of the cultural process, but we are still describing it from the outside because we are dealing with how individuals, exposed to certain educational forms, within a given total cultural setting, will behave *on the average*. We build our picture from a series of cross sections. We know how one set of infants are carried in blankets, how another set of three-year-olds are rebuked for overeating, how another set of twelve-year-olds are initiated, and finally how a still different group of adults behave. But to put the matter at its crudest and simplest, we do not know how the rank order of any individual has changed at different age levels. We know there are infants who cry a great deal and adults who are very voluble. But we do not know, and we cannot, conclusively, find out, from this kind of research, whether it is the infant who cried the *most* who talks the most, or the infant who cried the least, or merely the infant for whom vocalization was not a conspicuous infantile problem. We may be able to describe the behavior of each age group with such precision that in a homogeneous and slowly changing culture, an investigator a hundred years hence would find the same relationships holding good, the infants responding—on the average—in the same way to being carried in blankets, the novices responding—on the average—in the same way to their initiation. Our information would be valid. It would not be guesswork as long as we recognized that we were still making sociological generalizations, that we were describing and predicting the behavior of the average individual and not of any given named individual. We would be saying that this culture, in order successfully to adapt succeeding generations of human infants to its forms, works in such and such a manner.

From the psychological committee we had the following definitions:

*Competition:* the act of seeking or endeavoring to gain what another is endeavoring to gain at the same time.

*Cooperation:* the act of working together to one end. We are interested in competitive and cooperative *habits*, not in competition and cooperation in the abstract.

*Habit:* a usual or customary mode of action.

With these definitions, we started to explore our sources, published materials, manuscripts, or field notes. As a partial guide I prepared this list.

## POINTS TO WATCH FOR

*In the Study of Economics.*—Watch closely the correspondence between the group habits and the actual economic conditions, that is, the amount of genuine environmentally determined social cooperation which is necessary. Do they use boats needing several people to build them, to man them? Try to estimate the extent to which environment dictates cooperation, and at what ages, in what activities, etc., so that later you can form a judgment on whether this factor is important in dictating habits in other spheres. For instance, are the customary occupations of women solitary or social as compared with the men? Distinguish carefully between individual activities performed in groups —as when a group of women meet to weave mats together, and activities which require each member of the group actually to contribute to one end, as in a drive of game or fish. (In mat weaving, for instance, the women may meet to make mats for the dowry of the chief's daughter; they are engaged in social cooperation, but there is nothing in the actual work they are doing which dictates cooperation, and in fact each one may compete with the other to make the best mat, or work the fastest.) When an activity does require group effort, as a fishing drive, is the contribution of individual effort assessed individually so that the actively existing cooperation is given no social expression? (*E.g.* when four men fish in the canoe which belongs to each man, and the owner of the canoe receives two-fifths of the catch, each other man a fifth; or when the fish is devoted without comment to some communal purpose.) How many differential skills are involved in the economic life? Is a high quality of skill demanded in any particular activity? Is it socially recognized? Is there a different organization of behavior in the activities demanding skill and those which do not?

Is the food supply plentiful, seasonal, unreliable? Does the acquisition of food depend upon skill, luck, foresight, aggressiveness in securing a share of a fixed supply? Is the absence of cooperative effort, or the absence of a partner in cooperative effort, such as a wife or parents, economically penalized in the society? Are other materials besides food—such as wood, clay, metal— limited in supply, difficult to secure, etc.?

Is the community self-contained?   Is there division of labor?
Is there dependence on trade?   How is the trading situation
organized: cooperation between members of the community as
over against members of other communities, or cooperation
between trade partners, *across* community lines?   Is this
extended to groups?   Among manufactured articles how much
differentiation is there between the items of a given type, in value,
beauty, etc.?   What considerations are used to evoke trade,
free barter, compulsive barter (where one object will be traded
only for another of a particular type): magical compulsion,
maintenance of alliances, etc.?

What are the property arrangements?   Here note particularly
whether individuals own a share of ground, but not a definite
piece of ground, etc.   Does one inherit property, or the right to
share in a cooperative agricultural group, etc.?   What are the
rules in regard to newly created property as over against old
property?   What are the proportions between old property
which is inherited and new property which an individual can
create by skill, industry, social manipulation, etc?   Is property
perishable?

What is the position of the skilled worker?   Is he set apart,
given different rewards from others?   Do skilled workers compete or cooperate among themselves?

What is the nature of the economic activity?   Does it require
long-time planning, unremitting daily activity?   Does a sick
man fall inevitably behind?   Are misfortunes individual—like
the loss of a valuable fishing trap—or communal in incidence, as
a crop failure?   Can you estimate the time spent in different
kinds of activities, cooperative and competitive?

*In the Study of the Social Organization.*—In studying the *kinship system*, what situations are structurally set up which are
relevant to the inquiry?   What is the defined status of brothers,
of cross-cousins, of brothers-in-law, of affinal relatives?   Are
certain fixed relationships selected as cooperative or competitive?   Is the kinship structure such that an individual behaves
in contrasting and specific ways toward different relatives, *e.g.*,
does he cooperate with everyone he calls "relative" or does he
cooperate with his brother-in-law and compete with his cross-
cousin?   How are the sanctions arranged in such relationships,
*e.g.*, does the society insist upon the relationship which is struc-

turally most competitive being characterized by superficially cooperative behavior, etc.? Try to assess the degree to which the structure of the kinship system determines that an individual behave in a given way, at different periods in his life, *e.g.*, before and after marriage, toward different individuals all the time, or toward the same individuals at different times. That is, does the social structure permit him to take his behavior clues from personality choices, from fixed and unchanging kinship positions, from a temporal or social situation? Are these different roles in any way compensatory, *e.g.*, as when the same individuals can occupy reversed status relationships in different social situations? To what extent does the kinship structure, in its economic and other ramifications, suppress individual activity, or deny genuine personality alignments, *e.g.*, must one have one's most important cooperative life with one's brother-in-law, whether or not he is skilled or inept, lazy or industrious? If the kinship basis has been modified to give play to personality, how has it been done? Is kinship used as a scheme for extending cooperative activity? When choice is made between cooperation with different personalities in the society, is it phrased in structural kinship terms? Which is primary, structure in determining behavior, or behavior in determining the recognition of structure, *e.g.*, as one cooperates with a man because one calls him cross-cousin, or as one selects, from a distantly related group, a man to call cross-cousin because one wants to cooperate with him? To what extent does the kinship system define perpetuity situations, groups which must cooperate through several generations, status as between children of parents related in a given way, etc., and how does this function? To what extent does the kinship structure reinforce, contravene, or crosscut other solidarities in the society, such as age, sex, occupation, rank, etc.?

*In Examining the Political Structure.*—To what extent is it integrated with other forms of power? Is the leader also the chief magician or the best hunter, or a member of a ranking family? How fixed is the political structure? Does the individual who wishes to alter it, alter the structure or does he change his position in a fixed structure? To what aims is political activity directed, power, prestige, of the individual or the group? What are the routes to political power?

*In the Social Structure.*—Note the characteristic behavior in age, sex, occupational, ranking groups, the functioning of clans, dual organizations, moieties; the amount of conflict and cross-cutting. Does one set of interests and of loyalties compete with other interests and loyalties in the individual or is he permitted an integrated social life? (Compare societies where membership in family, clan, and state are all parts of one hierarchy, and societies where society membership and claims are independent of, or conflict with, clan membership.) From considerations of this sort several kinds of result may be obtained; it may be found that a kind of behavior dictated by one group is interdicted in another; that instead of the individual being able to establish and hold to one consistent set of habits toward other people, within a fixed or variable pattern he may be constrained continually to alter his behavior; his conceptualization of competition may be very much affected by the competition of different loyalties for his attention, etc. Is intragroup cooperation stressed with intergroup competition as an end?

*In Working Out the View of Life.*—What are the aims of (a) social existence, (b) individual existence, (c) are they identified or placed in opposition? Is subordination of the individual to the group phrased as ennobling the individual; is the group symbolized by an individual leader, or chief? How is the aim of the group phrased, *e.g.*, as fertility, power over environment, power over other tribes, subsistence, health, perpetuation of a past tradition, provision of a place for the next generation? Whatever the main end, do people compete for it or cooperate to get it together?

How are the ends of the individual phrased? Is there only one course which is honored? If several, do they involve the same kind of behavior? Are there several fields with different kinds of behavior, as art, war, politics, in which different inter-relationships between individuals and different personality roles are required, or several acceptable versions of one role, *e.g.*, is everyone rated as a good, bad, or indifferent hunter and that is all? For what does the individual strive, *e.g.*, power, skill, security, peace, honor? in what departments of life—political, economic, warfare, love, family life, art, religion? What means does he use, his own labor, skill, intelligence, energy, manipulation of other people through leading, dominating, originating, intimidating, inspiring, etc.? (In the course of defining the role of the leaders, the roles of the followers will also appear.)

What is the theory of personality, especially in relation to competition and cooperation? Is education conceived of as molding the personality, as stimulating it, as suppressing undesirable features? On what kind of behavior is the moral valuation placed? Are people conceived of as competing in order to cooperate or cooperating in order to compete? Are the sanctions internally or externally administered, *e.g.*, are they self-administered, or are external sanctions like sorcery, supernatural chastisement, or law necessary? If there are external sanctions, against what proportion of the community is it necessary to use them (*e.g.*, compare the amount of actual law enforcement which we expend on traffic violations and on theft).

What is the pace of life? What is its peak? Can the goal be reached young, at middle age, only in old age, after death, never? Does having passed the peak mean that one is no longer honored? Is competition limited to one period of life, as before one gets a wife, or does it continue through life? How limited is the reward of a given competitive effort to the field in which the competition takes place, *e.g.*, can counting coup in war be translated to every other field of activity, membership in societies, chieftainship, right to joke at a party, or must each activity be competed in all over again, as in Dobu? Is every field of life included in a competitive scheme, or a cooperative scheme, or are there fields which are exempt, as a midwife in Samoa is exempt from competition and a leader in Arapesh is specifically exempted from overcooperation? How has the culture phrased the different activities of life, such as winning distinction in war, getting a wife, making a fence or a garden? Do men compete for an object, for a position, or for an increasing relative status? Is the orientation of the individual in any activity specifically toward the rival, toward the goal or toward success as an ideal, or toward activity for its own sake? Is there any opposition between work and play in relation to cooperation and competition? How much displacement of individual competitive behavior is there upon the gods, on a national ideal, etc.?

*In Studying the Educational Process.*—What is the suckling situation? Does the child have to fight for its food? Are child

and mother opposed or cooperating? Are the two parents
opposed in attitude toward the child? Do they compete for the
child's attention? What is the relationship between siblings,
in regard to order of birth, sex, age, etc.? Is the child taught to
defend itself, contest, compare its record with others, beat its
own record? Does the child spend most of its time in children's
groups, or with older people? Is the child's personality commented upon and fostered, or set into an age or sex or class
pattern? How are children treated who struggle and quarrel?
Is a child given a thing when it cries for it? What are the
rules of the children's group, bullying, protecting, girls versus
boys, etc.? What games are played: games with sides, imitative
of adult activity, games with an "it"? Do the adults supervise
or stimulate the play? Which kind of play do they encourage
and which kind disapprove? To what degree do children take
other children or adults as models? To what extent does success
in one situation contradict or reinforce success in another? Can
the small swift child play with his own age group in running
games, but win success in the small children's play in wrestling
games? How many different kinds of play are there? Compare the habits which the children's world enforces, the habits
which the adults enforce in children by the encouragement of
some and the suppression of others, and the habits which are
displayed in adult life? Are they congruent or contradictory?
Can the interrelationships set up between individual children,
one sex, or both sexes, prevail through life, or does residential
mobility of one or both sexes prevent this?

I furthermore prepared a brief study of Manus so that the
members of the Committee could criticize it, and so that it with
their criticisms could serve as a sort of model upon which the
organization of the materials could be based. The working group
then met periodically in a seminar to discuss results and to refine
and develop hypotheses. No member of this group, including
myself, knew where the research would lead. The most dis-
cernible bias was a slight leaning toward a dependence upon the
environmental factor, an expectation that scarcity of food or
materials, or technological practices which required collective
activity might have a determining influence. The nature of the
material environment and the details of the technological

procedures of the different primitive peoples were therefore put down as two of the chief subjects for our research. A third subject was the structure of the society and a fourth was education. If these four emphases are examined it will be seen that they involve four possible conclusions: (1) that competitive and cooperative behavior are primarily responses on the part of the human organisms to a situation which is set up by the natural environment itself. This would be based upon a hypothesis which regards man as primarily a craving organism who will compete with other organisms only to satisfy a desire for an object of which there is a limited supply. ~~Even in this possibility, there is the recognition of a social factor in cooperation, for we did not fall back on an instinct of cooperation such as may be postulated for the social insects.~~ (2) That competitive and cooperative habits might be fixed in the members of any social group by the nature of their technology, so that people who habitually pulled together in a big canoe, or hauled as a group at a big log, would also be cooperative in aspects of their lives where these technological factors did not operate. The hypothesis upon which this expectation is based looks toward the kind of overdeterminism which is characteristic of so many historical interpretations of social forms. That is, that the way in which men make their living accounts for their marriage forms and their religious beliefs. It would postulate that certain habits, themselves culturally determined, are nevertheless more important than other habits, and will in fact determine them. (3) That the social structure of the society is the most dynamic factor, the forms which govern the interrelations of individuals in the group, the way in which that group life is defined, and the resulting presence or absence of group goals. (4) That the most determinative factor is the educational system and that by examining this with care we might find forms of education which seemed necessary to the formation either of a competitive character structure or of a cooperative character structure. We might possibly be able to go beyond this simple congruence between a form of education and a character structure, and even suggest why certain educational forms did develop certain types of character structure.

As we worked along on these assumptions several points became clear. In the first place, we found it necessary to emphasize that the terms *cooperative* and *competitive* were not opposites, as they are so loosely used in popular speech. To make our analysis complete we had to add a third category which we called *individualistic* behavior, that is, behavior in which the individual strives toward his goal without reference to others. It is necessary for the student to keep this definition of *individualistic* in mind. It must not be confused with "rugged individualism," or given the aura of exploitation of others, or aggression toward others, which surrounds the word in current speech. We furthermore found it necessary to distinguish between *collective* activity and *individual* activity, terms that refer only to modes of overt behavior but not to goals. This second classification is purely objective and does not take into consideration the motives of the participants, whereas the first, that of cooperative, competitive, and individualistic behavior, is defined in terms of the major motivation of the participant. So a man who hunts alone in the bush in order to contribute his kill to a communal feast is engaged in an individual activity inasmuch as he is working alone, but he is nevertheless engaged in a cooperative enterprise. By making this distinction it was possible for us to examine each social system with a view to determining whether the presence of collective situations made for the greater prevalence of cooperative motivations, etc.

Another distinction became clear as we went on working. We found that we could accept the definition of competitive and cooperative behavior as given, and that these concepts were sufficiently abstract to use in reference to different cultures, but that the concepts *noncompetitive* and *noncooperative* behavior could not be so used. It was necessary to make quite clear that any act could be classified as noncompetitive or noncooperative only *after* the fields of competition and cooperation had been defined in that culture. They therefore did not have cross-cultural meaning. The recognition of this fact led us far toward the most basic conclusion which comes out of this research: that competitive and cooperative behavior on the part of individual members of a society is fundamentally conditioned by the total social emphasis of that society, that the goals for which individuals will work are culturally determined and are not the response of the organism to an external, culturally undefined situation, like a simple scarcity of food.

We had recognized at the start that it was necessary to keep in mind Folsom's distinction between *competition* and *rivalry:* that whereas competition was behavior oriented toward a goal in which the other competitors for that goal were secondary, rivalry was behavior oriented toward another human being, whose worsting was the primary goal, and the object or position for which they competed was secondary. As our understanding of the problem became more precise, we found it necessary to make a somewhat similar distinction between *cooperation* and *helpfulness.* In cooperation, the goal is shared and it is the relationship to the goal which holds the cooperating individuals together; in helpfulness, the goal is shared only through the relationship of the helpers to the individual whose goal it actually is. The emphasis is on the relationship to that individual, not upon the goal itself. So, if two men, each of whom wants a shark, go shark fishing and as each shark appears each one goes after it because he wants the shark, this is individualistic behavior. But if two men are rivals, and when a shark appears, each one goes after it because he wants to beat his rival and be the one who got the shark, this is primarily rivalry and only secondarily competition. If, however, the aim of the fishing is to catch the largest number of sharks, and, as each shark appears, each fisherman attempts to get it in order to attain the goal which can be obtained only by outdistancing all others and preventing the others from attaining the goal, this is true competition. In the same way, if two men go hunting in the bush and each kills the animals which he sees, which he will then dispose of himself, for his own ends, this is individualistic behavior. If both hunt either together or alone in order to obtain meat for a feast in which both are interested, this is cooperation. But if the object of the hunt is to obtain meat for a feast which one of the two men will give, and the other man merely goes with him and helps him because he wishes to promote the other's ends, this is helpfulness.

It is perhaps necessary to define here the way in which the term *culture* is used. *Culture* means human culture, the whole complex of traditional behavior which has been developed by the human race and is successively learned by each generation. *A culture* is less precise. It can mean the forms of traditional behavior which are characteristic of a certain society, or of a group of societies, or of a certain race, or of a certain area, or of a certain period of time.   So it is possible to speak of Zuni culture, by which we mean the culture which is shared by all the members of Zuni society.   Or we can speak of American Indian culture, in which we should properly include not only the culture which was characteristic of American Indians at the time of the discovery of America, but such aspects of their behavior as their adjustment to reservation life or their attitude toward the white man's alcohol.   Or, third, we could speak of the culture of the inhabitants of the North American continent, in which case we should include not only Indians but also the traditional culture of all the inhabitants of this continent at any selected period in time.   This latter use of the term has greatest value when our attention is focused upon the relationship between the behavior of the inhabitants and the natural environment.   Last, we could speak of the culture of the Middle Ages, in which we should include the then existing traditional behavior of all the peoples of the world at, say, A.D. 1200.   But it is always necessary to particularize the term culture, if we wish to speak of *a culture* at all.   In the following pages, in the descriptions of the culture of Arapesh, Manus, Zuni, Samoa, Iroquois, Bachiga, Eskimo, and Dakota, the culture is that of a given society at a given time in history, whose members inhabited a known area. For the Ifugao, the Kwakiutl, the Bathonga, and the Maori, the culture is that of a group of more or less autonomous societies whose cultures were very much alike.   The greatest contrast lies probably between the Manus and the Maori.   All the statements upon Manus culture are based upon the behavior of the two hundred and ten individual members of the village of Peri, in the year 1928–1929, which was observed simultaneously by Dr. Fortune and myself.   The description of the Maori, on the other hand, represents observations over a period of about 125 years. It is a composite drawn from a great number of tribes which occupied such contrasting environments over the entire area of New Zealand that they can be classified into eight different culture areas, that is, territories occupied by groups of tribes whose common culture differed in characteristic ways from the culture of other tribes of New Zealand.   Now there is no theoretical objection to a point-by-point comparison between a culture shared by a society of one hundred and a culture shared by a society of a hundred thousand persons, provided we are quite sure that in each case the items which we are comparing were characterisitic of each culture at one definite period. But in accounts such as those of the Maori, the observations were made on many different tribes by different observers at different times, and cannot be compared except in a highly speculative way, and for suggestive purposes only, with the culture of the village of Peri, of the Manus people, in 1928–1929.

Progress in this whole field of culture and personality seems to be very definitely associated with pinning our data down more and more in time and space, so that each observational item can be referred to named identifiable individuals or groups. Continued observations should be made so that more and more data are accumulated on the same human organism, over time, or on the same human organisms at a given time, or best of all on a *group* of human organisms who remain together over time.

This is as far as we had gone in our thinking when the thirteen studies were completed. For the reader to continue to participate in the spirit of this research, the next step is to read these studies in the light of the problem set, the methods used, the definitions adopted. With this data and a history of how the material came to be assembled, those who are interested in the field of culture and personality are free to draw their own conclusions and make their own interpretations regarding the problem of competitive and cooperative habits. In what terms are we to think of the individual who acts in one of these ways? How are we to give proper weight to his biological inheritance? How shall we handle the motives which are a combination of his hereditary temperament and the character structure which the educational system of his culture has developed in him? What is the relationship in which he stands to his material environment and to the techniques which he uses to control it? What cognizance shall we take of his being a member of a society of a certain size and composition at a given period in history? These are some of the problems.

# CHAPTER I

## THE ARAPESH OF NEW GUINEA

### *by* MARGARET MEAD

The Arapesh are a Papuan-speaking people who inhabit a section of land which extends from the Pacific Coast over the triple range of the Prince Alexander Mountains down to the edge of the grass plains which are drained by the Sepik River. The people, who number some seven or eight thousand in all, are divided into three main groups in terms of geographical position and relative exposure to outside influences. The Beach Arapesh live in large villages, and have been extensively influenced by trade relationships with the Melanesian peoples of the islands adjacent to the coast. The Mountain Arapesh live a scattered, seminomadic life within narrow geographical limits in the precipitous, inclement mountains which separate the beach from the interior. The Plains Arapesh occupy the low foothills of the Sepik grass plains, living, like the Beach Arapesh, in large villages. They are most strongly influenced by the Abelem, a warlike, head-hunting people of the Sepik plain.

The bulk of this study was carried out among the Mountain people,[1] using Alitoa, the largest village in the mountain region, as a base. Eighty-seven people had a direct residence claim there which, however, they exercised only on special occasions.

The Mountain Arapesh are without any form of political organization. They have no name for themselves, nor have their neighbors any name for them. Among themselves they distinguish by name small locality groups, varying from 150 to 250 people. Each of these groups has a guardian supernatural, a

---

[1] Informants were used from both Beach and Plains, and Dr. Fortune made short expeditions into each territory. All generalizations may be taken to apply to the Mountain Arapesh unless otherwise stated, and illustrations from the Beach and the Plains will be used only when it is necessary to clarify a point or throw it into relief.

*marsalai*, who in the form of a giant snake or reptile lives in a quicksand or water hole or steep declivity.

The most effective unit in Arapesh is the localized paternal clan, which seldom numbers more than six or seven adult male members. Each clan has either a marsalai or a share in a marsalai, the other share belonging to a clan in the opposite dual division. The clan has also hamlet ground, within which individuals own house sites; it has hunting bush, territory which is usually divided into smaller units for different lineages, and it owns gardening land, which is again formally assigned to members of different lineages but which in case of death is most likely to revert to the clan at large. All land, consequently, with the exception of the marsalai site, which is always a particularly undesirable spot, is actually owned by individuals, or pairs of individuals, but may be spoken of as belonging either to those individuals or to the whole clan, because in Arapesh terminology and feeling the emphasis of the word *belong* is reversed. People are conceived as *belonging to* the land and the trees planted upon the land; the land is not conceived as *belonging to* them. The land is inhabited, not only by the marsalai but by the ghosts of dead clan members and their wives.[1] The ghosts stay in the marsalai place, or wander about in the bush, and must be spoken to whenever a man comes on the land. A clan member must never fail to announce himself to his ancestors or he may expect the marsalai to punish his disrespect by a small landslide, a wind which will damage his house, or by some other minor physical disaster. And a newcomer, not a member of the clan, must be specifically introduced to the ghosts and commended to their care. The sanctity of the marsalai places is further emphasized by specific tabus against the intrusion of pregnant women, menstruating women, or people who have recently had sexual relations.

When the Arapesh go beyond their own locality, whether toward the Beach, the Plains, or the tribes beyond, each man must follow an inherited path. There are three networks of such paths along which the members of different lineages walk from hamlet to hamlet. The people using these paths have their safety guaranteed under the pledge of safety given by the presence in each hamlet of a hereditary trade friend who is called "brother." Along these roads all the articles which are traded

[1] The ghosts of wives are not thought to return to their fathers' place.

in to the Arapesh come—bows and arrows (they themselves
know only how to restring a bow and to retip the simplest arrow),
stone tools (they themselves know only how to haft a stone adz
when the hafting has decayed or the handle is broken), baskets
(they themselves plait only the simplest and least efficient form
of palm-leaf baskets), and ornaments of shell and dogs' teeth.
These come from the Beach.  From the Plains come pots, net
bags (they themselves make only a few small coarse unadorned
ones), shell rings (which are used as currency and in marriage
exchanges), spears, more stone tools, cassowary daggers and
knives, lime gourds, and lime spatulas.  All this importation
is phrased as gift giving between devoted friends.  The Mountain
people only manufacture a few objects, and these—simple net
bags, wooden plates, coconut shell spoons,* wooden pillows, taro
pounders,* grass skirts,* bark-cloth loincloths,* belts, arm bands
and leglets, hair bands, simple cassowary bone daggers, a simple
kind of spear—are none of them, with the exception of the few
objects starred, sufficient for their own use.  For their tools, their
weapons, their cooking utensils, their currency, their ornaments,
they are entirely dependent upon importation.  Without manufactures of their own, and without an agricultural surplus, their
only possible contribution to this trading chain is labor, the
labor (trade) of "walking about to find rings."  A Mountain
man will go a day's journey in one direction, receive the gift of a
locally manufactured object, walk two days in the opposite
direction and present this object to a friend in a region where it
has a scarcity value.  He receives a gift in payment, part of
which he keeps, part of which, or its equivalent, must eventually
be passed along to the Beach friend.  This is the general principle
of Arapesh trade, but because of the absence of any attempt to
keep accounts, and the absence of direct exchange on the spot,
the emphasis is upon the friendliness and kindness of the giver,
and the joy and gratitude of the receiver.  It is often a most
uneconomic procedure; people even walk in the wrong direction
and so obtain no profit.  Along these hereditary paths also pass
puppies, little pigs, bits of magic, and personal body leavings
which are used for sorcery.

From the Beach the Mountain Arapesh receive also the elaborate dance complexes—songs, steps, masks, costumes, charms,
tabus, etc.—to purchase which many people band together,

sometimes all the hamlets of a locality. Their whole association with the Beach is one of pleasant anticipation of the luxuries and refinements of life, the only unpleasantness arising when the Beach people come into the mountains following the trail of some bit of personal leavings which has been sent into the Plains to be used for sorcery. Although individual trading is usually in manufactured objects—including shell rings—it is occasionally in tobacco, feathers, little pigs, little dogs, and sago worked in the mountains; of the last, however, the Mountain people have a most inadequate supply. For the purchase of large dance complexes, pigs are taken down from the mountain villages to the Beach.

The Plainsmen are hedged in between the mountains and the Abelam-speaking people. Their land is very limited. They are exposed to the forays of warlike neighbors. They have a desperately inadequate food supply, little timber for building, and only a small amount of game. The only manufactures which they can use for trade are shell rings which they make by laboriously grinding down giant clam shells. These shells come from the beach and in order to obtain them the Plainsmen either have to pay high trade rates, or walk through the unfriendly Mountain people—this, however, they do by virtue of their reputation as dangerous sorcerers.

The territory of the Mountain people is thus threaded through by roads upon which individuals walk by virtue of a hereditary right, which is reinforced on the part of the Beach people by the benefits they bring, on the part of the Plains people by the threat of death which they carry with them.

Although this mountain country has no definite borders which may be defended, it nevertheless offers the Mountain Arapesh fair sanctuary from any large invasion. The region is damp and cold; the soil is thin and subject to landslides; and there is hardly any level land. The game—cassowary, tree kangaroo, wallaby, follanger, bush pigs (escaped domestic pigs), bandicoot, and rats—is scarce and scattered. The roads are slippery. The streams are many and often impassable. The bush is inhospitable and yields little vegetable food upon which a hostile and invading group could feed. Furthermore, this territory of theirs is not coveted by their neighbors, who prefer walking through inhabited country so that they will not have to carry food.

The energies of the Mountain people are devoted to obtaining food, building shelter, and walking about from Beach to Plains to obtain tools, implements, utensils, and the refinements of life. The chief emphasis is upon food. The Arapesh place their major dependence on taro, which is predominantly women's work, and is a continuous crop, many varieties having to be planted back from the green tops as soon as they are harvested. Taro, however, is not a crop which can be kept and is not so suitable for feasts as yams and sago. Yam cultivation is men's work, and throughout this part of New Guinea is closely associated with the men's cults. Only a very inferior variety of yam can be grown in the mountains, but yams are relied upon for feasts and as food that can be stored. Sago is scarce, and is planted in one generation for the next. It is used only for feasts, forming a part of the average family's diet about one tenth of the time. Yams appear in the diet about one sixth of the time. The people also plant banana gardens, and raise various forms of greens which they use to season their carbohydrate diet in the absence of meat, and for both meat and greens they use the same general term, meaning a *garnish*. Coconut palms are also planted near hamlet sites but they are scarce and are under tabus most of the year in order to save enough coconuts for feasts. After a feast the nuts form part of the diet of the community for some weeks. The government of New Guinea, in working out a minimum diet for laborers on plantations, has specified as the minimum seven pounds of taro or yams per day, and a pound of meat a week. The Arapesh adult consumes on an average about three pounds of taro or yams a day, and four to five ounces of protein a week, which includes grubs, caterpillars, small rats, lizards, etc. They are conspicuously undernourished; the children show marked rachitic signs and a great number of the people are actually emaciated. Their economic scarcity, however, is of a different order from that of a hunting people like the Ojibwa—while they face years of undernourishment, they do not face the possibility of actual death through starvation.

Their houses are very simple. They are built on piles, walled with plates of sago bark and thatched with sago leaves, which are sewn by the men, though this is women's work in many localities. Smaller huts are built on the ground. With the exception of raising the ridgepole of a large house thirty feet long and twenty feet wide, of which there will be but three or four in any given area, housebuilding is a task which a man can perform for himself.  A man makes his own bark-cloth G-string, and a woman makes her own pair of aprons from shredded sago palm leaves.  In gardening the big trees are not cut down, the branches are merely lopped off to let in light, so that in preparing a garden plot there is no need for more than one man to do the work; similarly, fencing is done with saplings which an adolescent boy can cut.  In sago working, a well-grown boy can cut down the tree, and an adolescent girl can quite adequately work the sago.  Hunting is usually practiced in pairs for companionship, but the most successful hunter in the locality hunted either alone or with his nine-year-old son.  The methods of hunting consist in trapping and snaring, the use of hunting bags, and finding animals in hollow trees or asleep in trees.  The various traps and pitfalls can be constructed by one man.  There is no hunting in which a group drives the animals.  Rather the emphasis is upon waiting in the right place, and game will fall into one's traps, get caught in one's snares, or appear before one's eyes, when it can be killed with spear or bow and arrow.  Nowhere is there a technological need for more than one person's labor.

The division of labor between the sexes is an artificial one. Women cook, except for feasts; men hunt because the reproductive capacities of women are inimical to hunting.  Women tend the taro gardens, men the yam.  These roles represent not so much an adjustment to environmental conditions as a cultural expression of beliefs concerning the different kinds of potency in men and women.

The Arapesh, like the rest of the tribes in this region of New Guinea, have clans, dual divisions, infant betrothal, and formal economic obligations which must be observed between families related in marriage.  Though the Arapesh have modified the functioning of these formal units in their own way, it is necessary in order to understand their life to have a clear idea of these items of their social structure.

The social organization provides that groups of patrilineally related kin live together in a clan-owned hamlet, in which each has a house site.  On this site coconut palms, betel palms, medicinal, culinary, and magical herbs, herbs used in dyeing, etc., are grown.  Gardening is carried on in clan-owned garden land which is so extensive that rotation of crops is possible over fifteen- to twenty-year periods. Hunting is carried on in clan-owned bush which is left undisturbed by gardening, and is presided over by the clan marsalai. The clan has certain powers over its members. The ancestral ghosts that inhabit the marsalai places are subject to the importunities of elder clansmen, male or female, and may be invoked against younger and recalcitrant members of the clan, and also against the children of women of the clan who have married out of it, to bring about barrenness or death of children, if it is women who are cursed. The clan holds other rights, also, over the women whom it permits to marry into other clans; each child who is born is made of the blood of its mother's clan, and must be paid for, and for any of its blood that is shed—the cutting of a boil, a girl's blood when she is scarified at puberty, a wound in battle—a payment must be made to the men of the mother's clan.

By the existence of two dual organizations, to one or the other of which each clan belongs, the social organization provides for two further kinds of activity, the initiation of boys and exchange feasts. These dual organizations exist mainly as fictions, and the membership has become confused, but they express, structurally, the need of larger groups than the clan in the initiation ceremonies into the men's cult, Tamberan, and in the formal exchange feasts between groups.[1]

The social organization further provides for certain fixed relationships between affinal relatives which are perpetuated into the first descendant generation. Girls, at the age of six or seven, are betrothed to adolescent boys and go to live in the households of their future husbands who, with their fathers and mothers, "grow" their small wives by contributing the food which makes their bodies. This is the principal claim which the clan of the husband has upon the wife, a claim which will be invoked in case she runs away, in future attitudes toward her children, and in demanding repayment if, as a widow, she marries outside the clan of her deceased husband. The claim of the husband's clan is further explicitly validated by the payment of a few rings to the parents of the bride, and the exchange of some eight to ten more rings for other rings of a similar value with her other male rela-

[1] Although such exchanges actually take place within one side, the dual division is used as a ground plan for the exchange.

tives, and by frequent presents of meat, in which the husband's people should always give a little more meat than the wife's people. This economic relationship, begun between the contracting parents-in-law, is perpetuated between brothers-in-law, who exchange presents of meat with each other, and it culminates in initiation ceremonies for the children, in which a large feast must be made to the mother's brother in the name of the sister's son, and in death payments by a woman's son when she dies. At each of these, a man is said to be paying his mother's brother *and* his sister's son. Actually in each case the payment is due to only one side, and the other payment is a repayment; a man who is giving a funeral feast for his mother pays his mother's brother, but he also pays his sister's son, because he owes him return gifts for a feast in the past in which he—as mother's brother—received gifts. In all such payments to the wife's clan and the mother's clan, a group of clan brothers are supposed to act together, each contributing from his resources for the benefit of the member concerned.

Arapesh society therefore explicitly relies upon groups of male kin who live, garden, and hunt together, pay heavily for the women whom they absorb into their organization, both by feeding them as children and by maintaining gift obligations to their kin thereafter. If such a structure were observed in practice—as it is in many primitive societies, notably Dobu—we would have an example of small, politically autonomous groups cooperating within themselves and within definite territorial limits in maintaining order, and the economic obligations of individual members to outside groups similarly organized. This cooperation would be enforced by the ancestral ghosts, a sanction which is theoretically present.

Actually the functioning of Arapesh society is of a very different order than that implied in their structural arrangements. The Arapesh minimize blood position, inalienable membership in any given group, or fixed association with any piece of land. Even in the use of kinship terms, instead of conceiving the self as occupying a fixed position in a genealogical scheme, on the basis of which kinship terms are applied to other related persons, the Arapesh make an individual choice in each instance, conceiving the application of a kinship term to be a personal matter, depending in many cases on whom one "helps," that is, through whom one is counting the relationship at the moment. All economic activities are conducted in small groups which work together in terms of personal ties between members and without more than lip service to the clan structure. Each man is a member of from two to six working groups—those who belong to only two are the very old, who are practically out of the active structure. An active man with two wives may have more than six groups in which he works—with relatives of his own and of both his wives.

These gardening groups consist indifferently of blood or affinal relatives; of men who count their kinship through their mothers or through their fathers. They are sometimes organized about one individual, who may or may not be the host on whose land the garden is located, or they may show a chain form of organization in which *B* joins the group to be with his mother's brother *A*, then *C*, the parallel cousin of *B*, will follow *B*, and his two sister's sons, *D* and *E*, may come to be with him. The groups break up from year to year in the same haphazard fashion; sometimes two or three men will leave and join another constellation, sometimes two or three will drop out of a common constellation and not work together during the coming year. Occasionally an old or stubborn person will plant his major crop in one spot and, while he may welcome others, will not join them at a distance. The garden magic for these crops is sometimes performed by a member of the group, if he happens to know it;[1] otherwise some relative of a member of the group will be called in. One magical operation will do for the entire garden. Although only one of their number, himself or through a relative, need actually contribute the necessary knowledge, the gardening group all work together in collecting the essential magical leaves, and this may take as long as two days.

In each garden, a man stakes out a section in which he plants his own seeds and here he and his wife garden and ultimately reap their harvest. If the crop is taro, he will harvest it for his own family, or to contribute it to another family. If it is an ordinary yam crop, all the wives of all his different working companions will be asked to help with the harvest and will be given sixty or seventy pounds of yams when they go home. A working group will clear and fence and plant together, but the fence which

[1] Magic is inherited, is very seldom paid for, and which child inherits is usually due to demonstrated memory capacity or special ability.

surrounds the plot is the only group contribution to the enterprise. The small hut which stands on the ground is usually constructed by the man whose land it is, very probably with the assistance of an entirely different group of relatives and connections than those with whom he is at present gardening and who will sleep in the hut. There is no group harvest by the working group, but instead, if a man is particularly successful with his garden plots, which are scattered among several working groups, he may give a feast based upon the yams which he has grown in each of those places.

This use of a yam surplus, accumulated in various gardens, perhaps some five to eight miles apart, is called making an *abullu* and is typical of Arapesh attitudes toward food. The fortunate man, who thinks he has a large surplus, will consult his elders, or they themselves may tell him that his supply is sufficient. He then gathers all his yams in one place, brightly paints them in lots of ninety-six each, spreads them out on a long piece of rattan which will be kept as a measure of their number, piles them into a "mountain," and after he and a series of associates—brothers, cousins, brothers-in-law, etc.—have gathered together enough meat, he gives a large feast to which most of the locality come, and members of adjacent and related hamlets. Each guest family brings gifts, mainly meat, but also net bags, plates, etc., and takes away a part of the piled up yams to use as seed, seed from which the maker of the abullu can never eat again. He has the honor of having given the abullu, symbolized by the length of the rattan cord, and his gardening luck has increased the food supply of the community. Although this is always phrased positively—that a man is "permitted" to make an abullu—it is actually an effective measure against any one man's accumulating wealth disproportionate to the wealth accumulated by others.

Sago working groups do not follow the same lines as gardening groups, since they are more definitely influenced by the location of the sago palm trees. Each clump—a mother tree and a series of clustering daughter palms—is named and owned individually. Although a man will usually own a series of clumps close together, this may not be the case. The palms are planted by a father for each of his sons, but where he will plant them is often determined by the fact that he is working sago with some relative at that time. So while a man is helping his brother-in-law work sago, they may both set out some sago shoots for their sons. When the cross-cousins are grown their sago will be located side by side, and they will perhaps work together. Sometimes also a man who owns much sago will say to a relative who owns less and who is engaged with him in preparations for a feast, "Go and work my sago for this feast, and then we will both contribute it to the feast." This is the nearest approach to benefits from capital which is found in the society, and is part of a general preparation for a feast. The owner of the sago may be a skilled hunter letting someone less skilled in hunting work his sago, while he secures the meat; or the young people of two or three households may be sent together to the palms of one household to work sago for the feast.

Coconut palms and betel palms are planted not on one's own hereditary house site, but on the house sites of one's brothers, one's uncles, one's brothers-in-law, one's mother's brothers, so that a man may often live many miles from most of his palm trees. This is not, however, because he is living at his own hamlet site, for the same disregard of actual ownership is shown in residence, each hamlet being composed of an arbitrary and haphazard association of kin, who may be grouped around one man to whom they are variously related, or each one may be there because of some personal association with one member of the group. In each case, the right to build a house on the house site, or to use the house of another, has been explicitly accorded from individual to individual, but without payment of any kind. In case of exceedingly nonstructural residence arrangements, when two men who are explicitly and ceremonially opposed to each other in formal meat exchanges between dual organizations—to be discussed below—live in the same hamlet, in the course of controversy the fact that one man does not belong there but is a guest may be mentioned, but this is more frequently invoked by the guest who threatens to leave than by the host who requests him to do so.

In the care of pigs, the same diffuse, scattered method is followed. People do not feed their own pigs, but give them to others to feed. Those who feed the pig are called its parents, and when the pig is finally used by its owner in a feast, the return which is made for the pig is partially shared with the parents, and sometimes even with the grandparents of the pig.

A typical Arapesh man, therefore, is living, for at least part of the time (for each man lives in two or more hamlets, as well as in the garden huts, huts near the hunting bush, and huts near his sago palms) on land which does not belong to him. Around the house door are pigs which his wife is feeding but which belong either to one of her relatives or to one of his. Beside the house are coconut and betel palms which belong to still other people and the fruit of which he will never touch without the permission of the owner or of someone who has been accorded the disposal of the fruit by the owner. He hunts on bush land belonging to a brother-in-law or cousin at least part of this hunting time, and the rest of the time he is joined by others on his bush, if he has some. He works his sago in others' sago clumps as well as in his own. Of the personal property in his house, that which is of any permanent value, like large pots, well-carved plates, good spears, has already been assigned to his sons, even though they are only toddling children. His own pig or pigs are far away in other hamlets; his palm trees are scattered three miles in one direction, two in another; his sago palms are still further scattered; and his garden patches lie here and there, mostly on the lands of others.

If there is meat on his smoking rack over the fire, it is either meat which was killed by another—a brother, a brother-in-law, a sister's son, etc.—and has been given to him, in which case he and his family may eat it; or it is meat which he himself has killed and which he is smoking to give away to someone else, for to eat one's own kill, even though it be only a small bird, is a crime to which only the morally—which usually means in Arapesh mentally—deficient will stoop. If the house in which he is living is nominally his, it will have been constructed in part at least from the posts and planks of other people's houses, which have been dismantled or temporarily deserted, and from which he has borrowed timber. He will not cut his rafters to fit his house, if they are too long, because they may be needed later for someone else's house which is of a different shape or size.

This, then, is the picture of a man's ordinary economic affiliations, crosscutting every defined line of geography and blood kinship, based upon personal ties between individuals, which serve to tangle the members of each group into many other groups, and to blur every possible distinction between groups which would make possible either permanent and exclusive cooperation or sustained hostility to the outsider. All these activities, in which a man is helped by others, either by their actual contribution of work or materials, as in housebuilding or pig feeding, or by their presence in the working group, as in gardening, hunting, and sago working, are initiated by someone in the group; the helpers respond, going from a garden here to sago working there, to hunting on the third day, the next two days accompanying a brother on a trading trip in which they have no interest of their own and merely go as company, etc. Only about a tenth of an average man's time is taken up with initiating enterprises in which he invokes others' help—for the other nine-tenths he is following leads which come from many different groups.

We must now turn from the organization of everyday economic life to the organization of large-scale feasts. Here again, no matter how large the undertaking, it is phrased as one individual acting for a hamlet, or even sometimes for a cluster of hamlets, taking the responsibility of organization, while the others merely help him. It is a chain organization grouped around a leader who is called the *trunk* or *base* of the enterprise. The organization of feasts makes a man a "big man," but the Arapesh conceive this as an onerous duty which is forced upon him by community recognition of his ability to organize and lead, a duty which he fulfills without real enthusiasm and from which one retires as soon as one's first child reaches adolescence. In addition to organizing specific feasts centering about initiation, the exhumation of the bones of the dead, or the importation of some ceremonial dance complex from the Beach, the "big men" stand in a continuous exchange relationship with exchange partners, theoretically members of the opposite moiety, and always members of a different clan. These exchange partners call each other *buanyin*, are hereditary, usually in the male line, but not necessarily in the direct line. Old buanyin partnerships which have been unsatisfactory, that is, unequally matched, may be abandoned and new ones founded at any time. Such new ones again become hereditary. The buanyin relationship is modeled upon the relationship of brothers-in-law and the relationship which continues from it in the next generation, the cross-cousin relationship. Buanyins are conceived as members of autonomous

groups, and engage in exchanges one with the other. But whereas
between relatives and between trade friends, cost accounting,
dunning, reproaching in economic terms are regarded as disgrace-
ful, between buanyins there is a frank accounting system. Each
one is expected to initiate exchanges with the other, and they are
expected to insult one another publicly and to goad one another
on to economic activity. The major exchanges between buanyins
are of meat, and an exchange is initiated usually by the present
to one of the buanyins of big game—wild pig or cassowary—or
a domestic pig which has been trussed to a pole ready to be killed.
If the man who now has become the temporary owner of the
meat does not wish to use it, he gives it to his buanyin. He
cannot refuse it, and will owe a return of the same amount to his
buanyin in the future. If he has no pig or game with which to
repay, he will have to rear domestic pigs in order to return the
gift. Giving meat to a buanyin is therefore a way of banking.
When a man receives this large present of meat from his buanyin,
he in turn distributes it to his relatives, who are thus obligated
to help him make returns to his buanyin when necessary.
Buanyins give each other feasts, at which neither buanyin eats,
but each distributes food to his helping friends and relatives.
Buanyins do not compete with each other, rather they keep
each other up to the mark. They cooperate in maintaining a
more rapid large-scale turnover of food than would otherwise
occur in the community. It is a cooperative activity in which
each man has a distinct role to play, and his buanyin ceremonially
goads him toward the successful discharge of this role.

A man who is to be the trunk of a feast in reckoning his resources
counts on his buanyin for the repayment of the debts which the
latter owes him. During the year to three years while he is preparing for the feast, he will strive to accumulate more credit with
his buanyin. Some of his relatives will help him directly and
informally, and others more formally as subordinates called
"dogs." A trunk usually selects four of these latter, each of
whom is, or is on his way to becoming a "big man." The trunk
gives a series of feasts to the dogs, at each of which he cuts up a
specified number of pigs—seldom more than one—a fourth of
which is given to each dog, who in turn distributes it among his
helpers together with the cooked carbohydrates and the dry
uncooked sago which accompany the offering. There are three

such feasts, and the same men are the dogs in each.   When the time for the final feast is set, each dog gives back a whole pig, representing the three-quarters of a pig which he has received, plus the other food.   The trunk thus has all his negotiable wealth in his hands at once, and exchanges it either for dance ceremonial or for other pigs, or arranges for a return feast in another community which has similarly been organized around a trunk.

The Arapesh, in case of quarrels and dissensions, very seldom resort to physical violence.   Instead the injured person turns to sorcery, or if both individuals feel injured both may use sorcery. Body leavings (dirt) are stolen and sent to the Plain sorcerers. The quarrel is subsequently healed, and no further payment is sent the sorcerers, who retain the dirt, however, and collect black-mail payments on it.   When the man dies whose dirt has been stolen, even if it is ten years later, the professional enemy sorcerers are blamed and not the man who delivered the dirt into their hands.   Quarrels between groups of individuals are always phrased as being a protestation against a friend's injury—the abduction of his wife or the loss of a strayed pig.   The active part in defending the injured man is more appropriately taken by his cross-cousins, his mother's brother, his brothers-in-law, or his buanyins, than by his clan brothers, who, because they are a little more closely identified with him in terms of property and inheritance, might be regarded as fighting for themselves as well as for their injured relative.   Indignation of any magnitude is permitted only on behalf of another.   One's own indignation over an injury may be correctly expressed only in further injury to oneself.   An angry man may actually cut down his own trees, destroy his own house, his pots or plates or rings, but he cannot inflict such injury directly upon the property of another.

Many quarrels are concerned with pigs.   A pig may have strayed into someone else's garden or bush, or it may have been killed by a hunter in mistake for a bush pig.   If the killing of the pig is an accident, the killer sends for the owner and tells him to come and get it.   If the owner does so, and then uses the pig to feast his buanyin or to give to his brother-in-law, there is no further trouble; but if he refuses, a quarrel may follow.   A trespassing pig may be intentionally killed only after a whole group of related men have assented in order of rank.   If the whole group agree, the pig may be killed, and a part is eaten by each one, who thus commits himself to defend the act if a group comes with the pig's owner to demand redress.

Quarrels over women are more complicated. In most unilaterally organized societies, the kin of the woman retain a protective claim upon her, and take her part if she is badly treated; the fear of their anger is a direct sanction which she can invoke against her husband. But the Arapesh tend to group brothers-in-law in as warm and close a relationship as brothers. This means that a man cannot protect his sister against her husband, any more than he can help his own brother's wife to escape. One tie is as strong as the other.[1] This attitude is explicitly recognized in the only formulation about incest which I could obtain from the old men. I asked what they would say to a son who proposed an incestuous relationship to his sister, and they said, "What is the matter with you? Sleep with your sister? But don't you want a brother-in-law? With whom will you garden, with whom will you hunt, with whom will you visit?" The assumption is that the wife is firmly incorporated into her husband's family and so unites her brother to her husband.

If a woman is unhappy in her marriage, therefore, and wishes to run away, her kin will not take her part, or if they do, they can do it only secretly. Her desertion must be publicly staged as an abduction by a new husband. The relatives of the new husband then become involved in defending the theft of the woman.

When such a theft occurs it is often accompanied only by angry words, but sometimes two hostile groups meet, first to argue and later, if some excitable person throws a spear, to fight. The Arapesh have no pattern of real warfare. There are no rewards given to the homicide, as so commonly in this region; he is viewed a little askance and must be put through certain protective rites by other men who have killed. If in one of the small fights he kills a close relative, a mother's brother, for instance, as does occasionally happen, it is no occasion for blood feud. The people say, surely his mother's brother had been subjected to sorcery which drew the spear of his sister's son toward him, for surely no sister's son would be willing to kill his mother's brother. The killer is commiserated with and allowed to mourn at the funeral. If the killing takes place between more distant relatives, between

[1] See case of Agilpwe in Margaret Mead, *Sex and Temperament*, pp. 159–160.

whom the warm feeling is not so clear, the killer may have to flee the locality forever.

Significantly there is no offensive war magic, but only protective magic to be used in case one is drawn into a fight over a pig or a woman. But these fights between temporary groups of outraged persons are not perpetuated into permanent enmity, because each member of each group is connected with members of the opposite group through as many different ties. The allegiance of each individual is always to another individual, and through him to others, rather than to any formal group.

The whole society is a vast network of personal relationships, of temporary companionships and alliances, and there is nowhere an effective closed group which demands internal cooperation from its members and maintains its position by hostility to outsiders. Hostility to rank outsiders the Arapesh do feel, but each man does not feel hostile to the same outsiders; men from the Plains, whom one family may regard with terror as sorcerers, may be the special trade friends of their nearest neighbors, and so must be given sanctuary. The "roads," the lines of trade friends which stretch into the society from every side, threading it through and through with lines of mutual help and friendliness, serve to blur any real sense of territorial barriers. Furthermore, there is no local group, not even the clan itself, which maintains its solidarity by demanding absolute allegiance from the individual. Residence and working groups crosscut clan lines, marriages and feasting plans crosscut hamlet and locality lines, and all these are couched in terms of person-to-person relationships.

Though these person-to-person relationships are all helpful and friendly, very few of them are in any material sense cooperative. A group of men make a garden together, but each plants his own seed, which he will dispose of as he wishes in accordance with the rules of distribution. A man builds a large house and all his friends and relatives help him and he feasts them in gratitude for their help. The house is his. They claim no share in it. Even when a man organizes a large feast, it is his responsibility. When he buys a dance from the Beach he feasts others, who help him in gratitude for food received, but it is he who has bought the dance for the community.

In only a very few instances is there genuine cooperation and these are mostly in the interests of the Tamberan cult. Even when a small hamlet initiates one or two boys, a house must be built into which the Tamberan, impersonated by the sacred flutes, can enter, and on this house all the members of that residence group will work. It may in some slight sense be said to belong to all of them, although they say it belongs to the trunk of the feast. When a larger initiation feast is given, in which some fifteen or twenty boys from several localities are initiated, each hamlet involved will make a definite contribution in work and wealth to the ceremony, in the rites of which they will all share. These ceremonies take place only about once every six or seven years, and the same locality will hold one only once in a lifetime. The task of collecting enough food to feed so many people for such a long time is a staggering one, and it takes a very long time to organize large groups along such very personal lines.

But if with this rare exception the people do not cooperate toward a common material goal, working together for a store of food or on a house which will belong to all, this is not because there is any objection to cooperation. Cooperation does occur sporadically, as when two brothers hunt together to give the meat to the same feast, or when two men build a house together. But enforced cooperation is replaced in Arapesh by active helpfulness to individuals, a low valuation of the self in relation to the ends of others, and above all by the devotion of the entire people to a common non-material ideal. The knowledge that the brother for whom one hunts, the cousin for whose roof one is sewing thatch, the uncle for whom one is cutting sago, are all of them like oneself devoted selflessly to the same way of life is the bond which makes men work together, helping one another. The end toward which every Arapesh works is the growth of the next generation. As a means to that growth he values the growth of pigs and yams and palm trees to feed the children that they may be many and strong and not leave the land and the ghosts of the ancestors desolate. In the interests of this end, men call upon each other for help, and may even chide one another for being lazy and unmindful of gardening. The buanyin insults his buanyin that food may be accumulated and feasts given; the old men exhort the unwilling young man to take upon himself the responsibility of organizing ceremonies which are important for the happiness and growth of the community. In the interests of health and growth, men demand of their trade friends the necessities of life, or demand that those who know a certain path into the Plains accompany them upon a search for the dirt of a sick relative. Each request has behind it the dignity of devotion; no ambitious man is subordinating others to his ends, requiring that others bask in his favor or work for him because he is rich and can pay them; each man is invoking the sanction of a common ideal. So although almost every act of an Arapesh is performed as an individual service in a person-to-person relationship, all the acts form a pattern of non-material cooperation toward a common goal.

This cooperation toward the goal of growth is particularly well exemplified in the behavior of the men and women in the Tamberan cult. This cult is a symbol of the men's power. From its mysteries women and children are excluded, and into it at puberty boys are initiated with incision, a meal of the old men's blood, running the gauntlet, beating with nettles, ceremonial tabus and bathings during a segregation period of several months. This ceremony in many parts of New Guinea is symbolic of hostility between the sexes, and of hostility between the older men and the young boys. The Arapesh have converted it into a ceremony of growth, a ceremony essential to preserving the fundamental plot of the society, the antithesis between women's reproductivity and all sex activity on the one hand, and man's food getting powers on the other. This separation is as essential to the women as it is to the men. The men protect the women by guarding their secrets, just as the women protect the men and the yams and the children by segregating themselves during menstruation and at childbirth. The young boys are not made to feel that they are excluded from this male cult. They will be taken in as soon as they are old enough, and many a stripling is actually admitted to the secrets and the feast before he has been properly initiated. A ceremony of exclusion has been rephrased as a ceremony of growth, and all the hazing characteristic of the ceremony has been turned into hygienic performances for the growth of the novices.

In the same way, the relationship between the old and the young, between the parent generation whose power is just waning and the son generation whose power is still waxing, has been phrased as one of mutual helpfulness and care. Food is divided into two categories: food for children and the old, and food for those of reproductive years—some yams for one, some for the other; the yellow fellanger for the middle years, the white for children and old men, etc.  On the Plains all young people are excluded from eating any meat, even caterpillars, until after they have borne children, but the Mountain people have phrased meat as an available relish in which all share.

The puberty of an oldest child is a sign that the father may retire from active life.  There is no contest between father and son over women, in spite of the presence of polygamy, because from the time the oldest son is ten or so, the father's whole interest is turned toward getting him a wife.  Indeed young men of thirty are often engaged in helping aging male relatives provide for their sons, so that a man of thirty may be helping financially to get a wife for a boy of eighteen.  For this help he expects no return.

The growing generation is bound to members of the last generation by the fact that the latter have fed them, that they have "made their bodies."  This fact can be used by a father to chide a disobedient son, by a husband to hasten the lagging footsteps of a desultory wife, by any older man to a young man who has been hasty or importunate: "I grew the yams, I worked the sago, I grew the pigs, I killed the game which went to making your body.  How is it that you can behave thus?"  This strongest of ties—feeding, and in return for food, gratitude—is repeated over and over again, between a man and all who help him in any enterprise, between trade friends, between a trunk and his dogs.

With early betrothal and residence in her husband's family, the husband and wife relationship repeats the parent-child pattern. The child wife calls her husband's brother by his kinship terms, and she learns to depend upon all the members of his group. When one of his brother's wives enters the home as a widow, ideally the two still cooperate.  If they do not, as is the case if the second wife is a runaway Plains woman, or a too young widow, or if the first wife is out of favor with her husband, etc., the husband will build a house for each.  Most co-wives, however, sleep in the same house, share the housework, and take care of one another's children.  Even if at first polygamy is a little stormy, wives tend to get on better as the years go on.  A man's brother and cousins cooperate with him in helping him buy his wife and in growing her.

The division of labor between the sexes is not rigid.   Women as a rule cook for the household, fetch firewood, weed and harvest taro, raise bananas and greens, search for wild greens and grubs, clean the village, carry burdens on the trails.   Men hunt, make their hunting snares, plant and harvest yams, build houses, climb coconut trees, do a little woodcarving and painting.   Both sexes may carry, both take care of the children, both cook, the men for feasts, the women more for the household, just as the women bring the wood for cooking, the men for the feast fireplaces.   Both cooperate in making the child, which is conceived as being built up through six weeks to two months of steady intercourse after the first signs of pregnancy are noted.   The child is a product of mother's blood and father's semen in equal parts.   The care of the child after birth is also one in which the two parents cooperate in observing sexual tabus and in sleeping on each side of the child to make it grow.

## THE IDEAL PERSONALITY

The Arapesh ideal man is one who shows an all-round capacity for devotion to the community ends, one who is able and willing to lead in spite of a native dislike for leadership, one who is hospitable, wise, gentle, unquarrelsome, and intelligent in the sense that he is able to understand the ends of his society and to carry them out.   It is such a one whom they describe when they speak of one "whose ears are open and whose throat is open." He is able to hear and to understand and to speak in order that things may be done.   Such a man is valued far above the man who shows special skills.   The Arapesh attitude toward all special skills is one of tolerance, of mild admiration.   A man may choose to hunt, or to go far abroad trading, to carve, or to paint.   Every man must garden to some extent, but while one man may plant two crops in four years, another may plant every year.   The boy who wishes to hunt seeks out some hunter to teach him; the man who wishes to paint or carve simply begins to do so.   There is no apprenticeship worthy of note in art, and the Arapesh always feel that other tribes' creations are intrinsically superior to their own. With each generation new models are traded in from the Beach or the Plains; an artist here or there copies them, and then the style dies.   The society has no objection to the practice of individual ends, but it has no special rewards for them.   Some months after death the bones of men who have been much admired are dug up and kept by their descendants and relatives, for use in magic—gardening, hunting, and protective war magic. I took a census of which bones had been dug up and kept, against a census of late members of the locality, and found that they were those of Arapesh of all-round character. The hunting specialist who had not been a "good" man would not have his bones used for hunting magic.

There is, however, no hierarchy of leaders, no competition between leaders. It is said that there are never enough individuals who will take responsibility, that the community is happiest which has most big men. There is no way in which the big men are ranked, no common denominator of greatness by means of which men within one locality compare themselves. There is only one rivalry situation institutionalized in Arapesh, and this is between men of different localities who have been on opposite sides in a small fight and have felt each other to be personal opponents. Such men may declare that henceforth they will be *ano'in*. Usually one man makes the announcement among his own group, and rumor carries it to the man he has dubbed a rival. The other may take up the challenge if he wishes. The challenge runs: "He defeated me. He kept that woman (or some similar cause over which a fight was waged). Henceforth we will be ano'in. I will stay in my place. He will stay in his. I will grow yams. He will grow yams. I will kill game. He will kill game. I will raise pigs, he will raise pigs. I will be big. He will be big. I will watch him. He will watch me." Such ano'in never meet again, and their children in turn call each other ano'in. If these children are boys, they can joke together; if they are boy and girl it is considered appropriate for them to marry. (Marriage is always regarded as a peacemaking move, for between affinal relatives there can be no real enmity.) This one isolated institution, which has practically no cultural reverberations, is a refuge for those who, in spite of the training which their culture has given them, are still competitive and likely to see insult in another's triumph.

## SANCTIONS

The community has very few well-developed sanctions, partly because there is no concept that proper social behavior is difficult or that it needs to be enforced.   There is a series of sanctions which may be used within personal relationships which are normally characterized by warmth and interchange of food: an angry man who feels a relative has been unhelpful and unresponsive to his wishes may tie a mnemonic knot in a draceana leaf, which means that he or she will never eat with the other person again.   This tabu remains in force until the man who set it up looses it by giving a feast to the other person.   It is very seldom resorted to, but more often threatened or ostentatiously deliberated over by disgruntled persons.   Buanyins may dissolve their relationships forever by placing a wooden bowl set about with herbs in the feast place.   A man who wishes to declare that his wife is unfit to feed pigs, because she has let so many pigs entrusted to her die, may set up a special sign outside her door, thus making the matter public and avoiding a private brawl.

For disciplining individuals who habitually get into brawls and difficulties, the Arapesh device is to punish the one who is injured, or if both are injured, to punish both.   This punishment is meted out as an extension of the claims of the mother's kin to any loss of blood on the part of a child of a woman of their clan.   Not only cuts and bruises, but being publicly subjected to obscenity or abuse, falls into this pattern, and the mother's brother, or mother's brother's son, or a buanyin, may set in motion the forces of the community against an injured man. If the emphasis is upon the injury to the body, the mother's brothers, etc., will merely demand gifts from him; if the emphasis is upon the loss of dignity which he has sustained in public, they may gather together all the men who happen to be available, take the sacred flutes which represent the Tamberan, and go and play the man and his wife off the premises, cut down a tree or so, and scatter the leaves in his house.   The object of this community discipline will then flee to some relatives or friends at a distance and not return until he has a pig to feast the Tamberan, i.e., the men's group.   But all these sanctions are against the individual who provokes anger.   Against the violent man, the man who is possessive, high-tempered, jealous, distrustful, the Arapesh have no effective sanctions, if such a man is also intelligent.   The less intelligent men of this sort tend to be marooned in the bush looking after pigs, and are almost forcibly kept away from group occasions. The community regards them as a definite liability, and their care a necessity. If any one of these men takes refuge in running amok,[1] the Arapesh treatment is to give such a man, without his knowledge, soup in which dog dung has been mixed, and then later tell him that he has eaten it. Any shock of this sort seems adequate to curb such violent hostile behavior.

In the discipline of intelligent men whose character formation is faulty in its adaptation to the Arapesh mild and kindly ends, the Arapesh are hampered. They believe that aggressiveness in men is something which must be fostered, shaped into a likeness to real aggressiveness. When they are occasionally confronted with an aggressive man who has also become a "big man" they are completely confused.[2]

The sanction for an ordered attention to life lies in the theory of the incompatibility of sex and growth and black magic, each one of which is incompatible with the other. As growth is the most valued, this incompatibility is powerful in inducing men to have no formal traffic in sorcery. For the Mountain people such traffic means either sending or carrying people's dirt to the Plains sorcerers, who if they have been paid sufficiently will use it to cause the victims' disease or death, or themselves practicing mild forms of sore-producing sorcery. No death-dealing sorcery is practiced by the Mountain Arapesh themselves; occasionally individuals attempt to import sorcery arts, but in each case they are forced to give them up.

No one is sufficiently afraid of sorcery so that such fear generally deters him from any act. The average Arapesh does not threaten sorcery and there is never an admission that sorcery is planned. Theft of dirt is always considered an impulse of an aggrieved moment, and the act is always subsequently disowned. Only in the relationships between the sexes is sorcery used as a sanction. In the occasional cases when a man makes overtures to another's neglected wife and urges her to run away with him, he will have intercourse with her as an earnest of his honorable intentions, thus leaving with her his semen, the most

---

[1] A very mild form of the familiar Malay seizure, in which the aim is not to kill and be killed, but merely to terrify others by one's violent behavior and apparent complete lack of attention.

[2] See *Sex and Temperament*, p. 147.

potent of all dirt.   If he does not fulfill his promises he is risking
sorcery, and this is invoked as a definite sanction against affairs
with strange women, especially the Plains women, who are
actively sexed and accustomed to take the initiative.

Another sanction sometimes invoked is the curse of an elder
relative.   It is unimportant because the group of elder relatives
has such slight social cohesiveness, but it is occasionally used by a
violent and aberrant person.   The mother's brother's curse has
been rendered nugatory as compared to its use by other tribes of
the area because among the Arapesh the same mother's brother
who put it on need not be the one to remove it.

## EDUCATION

No Arapesh child which is unwanted by its parents is permitted
to live.   If the child is a girl, and the couple already have several
girls, it may be killed so that a boy may be born all the sooner.   If
there is any disagreement between the parents, the infant is
killed, because it is essential to the child's growth that both
father and mother should actively cooperate in the observance
of the lactation tabu.   The newborn infant which is to be kept is
washed by the mother, who also fastens the cord, and is immediately put to the breast.   The father brings his pillow and sleeps
beside the mother.   He is in native phrase "in bed having a
baby," and the one Arapesh word for bearing a child is used
indiscriminately of either parent.   Until the child can walk, the
father must sleep beside it and have no sex relations either with
the mother or another wife.   Both father and mother hold the
baby and care for its needs, the father staying home specifically
to care for the child if the mother has an errand away from the
village.   The suckling situation is one in which the mother as
well as the child delights.   The child is permitted to suckle all
day, and as it grows older and the mother has to leave it behind
when she goes on short trips, she makes up for her absence by
suckling it for hours.   Nevertheless these increasing absences of
the mother—and in the small groups there is very often no nursing
mother to suckle the child in her absence—leave the child desolate
and rebellious and seem to lay a basis for the child's later temper
tantrums when food is refused it, and, later still, tantrums when
anything is refused it.

The child is kept in a net bag curved close to the mother's body; it is held in the arms a great deal of the time; its crying is always hushed against its mother's breast; and even after children have been weaned for several years, the mother gives them the dry breast if they are frightened or in pain. As the mother feeds her child, she commends the whole world to it: "This is your grandmother, this is your aunt, she will give you food. She is good, good, good." Monotonously, all relatives, and even the pigs and the dogs, are so commended to the child until every relationship term comes to carry a definite affect of warmth and security and reassurance. As the child gets a little older, two and a half or three, it begins to hear how dangerous the *waribim*, the inland Plains sorcerers, are, to feel its parents clutch it tighter, to catch the tenseness in their voices when there are arrogant demanding Plainsmen in the village. By the time a child is six or seven it is given a small basket if a boy, a small bag if a girl, in which to hide all its own personal dirt and half-gnawed bones and odds and ends of food; later it will bury them, lest the sorcerers steal the dirt. So a groundwork for fear of sorcery is laid, and in adult life, if any loving and friendly relative refuses an individual a request, the childhood situation seems to be reinstated—the traumatic absences of the mother and the fear of the stranger—so that the injured person resorts compulsively to sorcery, sorcery which he or she later disavows, and for the ultimate outcome of which the Plainsmen's cupidity is finally blamed.

Only this dismay at what he interprets as withdrawal of affection disturbs the peacefulness of the child's development. For the rest, children tumble contentedly about near their mothers, never encouraged to venture far, discouraged from crawling and walking too early. The child learns before it is weaned to play with its lips in a large number of highly stylized ways, among which thumb sucking does not appear, and amuses itself when it is part of an adult group by sitting passively bubbling its lips. Girls continue this practice until marriage, boys until puberty, and it is culturally standardized as a symbol of irresponsible childhood. Masturbation is not indulged in, and is frowned upon by the Arapesh. Children are given no training except in language, but in this the parents take a great deal of specific interest and insist upon grammatical correctness in the use of the thirteen noun classes. For the rest, the development of children is left to slow imitation of older children; they are not forced toward efficiency in any way, although they are often permitted to try tasks for which their skill is inadequate, and the parent has to intervene to help them out. They are given anything they cry for and are permitted to break their mothers' beads or scatter their plaiting materials. If the parents have something which they do not want the child to touch, they hide it.

Little children are given a great amount of demonstrative affection by everyone, and respond very quickly to a caress, crawling or tagging after the last person who has tickled or patted them. This habit makes it easy for the parents to hand children of four or five from one relative to another, and, in passing from one small family group to another, the child's experience of kind pairs of parents is reinforced.

Fighting between little children is never permitted. The contestants will be carried in opposite directions by their elders, and then permitted to vent their rage by rolling in the dirt, scratching or biting themselves, or tearing at their own bodies. Anything with which they could injure others—like firewood—is carefully removed out of reach. Over and over again the point is made that one may injure oneself if one wishes, but one must not hurt others.

In training children to care for the property of others, the emphasis is not upon "mine and thine," but rather upon being careful of the property of others: "That is grandfather's. Hold it carefully. Don't break it. It is your grandfather's." This running comment, which elder women make to children from two to five years old, goes on as an undertone of gentle recommendation.

There is no children's group. The shifting residence and small size of the hamlet groups tend to keep groups of children from gathering except at feasts, when they are so interested in the adult activities and so cramped for space in the tiny villages that they never play games of their own. What games are known—and fewer games are known the higher one goes in the mountains—are games which imitate animals, or in which all the children squat and hold each other's waists and represent a snake, or a game of cutting sago in which one child is carried in the arms of the others as a present of sago. These games are the simple, noncompetitive games of our kindergarten types.[1] The pattern behavior of children is to tag about after adults all day long, helping according to their skills. The little girl is given a carrying bag before she can walk steadily, the small boy a tiny bow and arrow. Their daytimes are spent with adults, and when there is a dance, the women dance with the small children of one to three years of age on their shoulders, and here again the pattern of being a passive part of adult life is reinforced. When the adults are gathered together, sitting about in the open place, the children tend to sit about, too, bubbling their lips. No training given them insists upon initiative, upon control of the environment. Emphasis is always upon dependence upon others, responsiveness to the requests of others, activity peripheral to the activity of adults.

When the children are six or seven, the education of the two sexes becomes socially differentiated. The girl is betrothed and goes to live part of the time with her parents-in-law, and all the members of her husband's kin group become parent substitutes. She has learned to carry and she becomes more and more a working member of the community, joining a group of other girls only when some carrying job like harvesting or collecting firewood for a feast is on foot. All her most socialized activities are associated with work, and with being too tired to talk at nightfall to her best chum, whom she may not have seen for two or three months. In adult life the women prefer the small group in the tiny hamlet or garden to a large feast group, as if they still associated crowds with hard work. The little girl bends to her tasks earlier than the little boy and seldom indulges in temper tantrums after five or six, though the boy may continue them up to the age of twelve or thirteen.

The boy's work experience is typically as a companion of one older boy or man, hunting, trapping, searching in the bush for rattan or magical herbs. His infrequent association with other boys of his own age is a holiday matter. They may shoot lizards together for sport, or sit and sing songs, or play at small pantomimic games. The men throughout life continue to be a little more gregarious than the women.

---

[1] In the last two or three years, football, played with a lime fruit, has been introduced, and the small boys play it enthusiastically when they get together, but with frequent tears and refusals to play and violent rages.

Puberty interrupts the girl's life only for the five days of her first menstrual seclusion and slight scarification. She has been in and out of the menstrual hut since childhood and is not in any way afraid of it, but settles down to the hygienic measures which the older women teach her—observing food tabus and thrusting rolled nettles into her vulva in order to make herself grow. Boys learn, before puberty, from older boys, a corresponding ritual of cutting the phallus to let out "the bad blood" which may accumulate from eating forbidden food or any careless handling of the genitals. Without a tabu being set up upon casual warm contact between the sexes, both sexes are taught that precocious sex activity is harmful to growth, and they have been firmly taught that growing oneself is the main task of an adolescent girl or boy. The only chaperonage which the society recognizes is the need of chaperoning a pair who have lived in the same house as betrothed spouses for six or eight years. They should not consummate their marriage until they have fully attained their growth, and at that time chaperonage is withdrawn. But in a situation which has not been defined as sexual it is not felt that any chaperonage is called for.

The existence of polygamy always means possible rivalry between men for available women. This the Arapesh meet in certain definite ways. The way in which rivalry between the older and younger generation is met has already been discussed. Between brothers, all of whom have helped to grow a young wife, there is occasional rivalry, as when Wabe[1] and his brother solved their dilemma by exchanging wives. The only violent outbursts over women arise in the case of widows. If a widow refuses to marry the logical heir, and he resents it, he may resort to sorcery threats. The Arapesh picture as their ideal a young wife devoted to an older husband, to which couple, later, an older benevolent widow may be added; and any actual marital disaffection greatly distresses them. Deaths at the wrong ages also are complicating, and they have no adequate mechanism to deal with such cases. In first marriages, although the parents of boys always feel some anxiety for fear they will not obtain a wife for their son, all little girls are eligible. But if a boy has "grown" his wife and she dies, it is not a simple matter to get another wife of a suitable age. Here again feelings are hurt. Nowhere in the entire educational

---

[1] See *Sex and Temperament*, pp. 125–130.

system is there any training which enables an individual to bear any kind of rejection or refusal with equanimity.

There is another aspect of the Arapesh educational system which shows how completely the Arapesh rely upon person-to-person relationships. All ritual acts are associated with a large number of special herbs and also with various ritual performances. These are never taught by an adult who knows them to young people in a group. Only as the need arises is the younger person taught by the older. So a boy whose sister is not yet adolescent and whose young wife has not yet reached puberty has no idea what herbs and foods should be used or what the procedure is. When his sister or his wife reach puberty his father will tell him. The woman in her first childbirth relies for help and information on the last woman among her immediate associates who has borne a child. When a man wishes to marry a widow, which is dangerous, he goes for instruction to another man who has married a widow. It is the same with making an abullu. The tradition passes at the moment when it is needed from one who has gone through the experience to one who will now go through it. There is no sense of accumulated knowledge which is taught to all. And because of their scattered living there are slight opportunities to see ritual performed. All this enhances the young men's sense of dependence upon their individual elders: "If our older men should die, what would we do? Who would instruct us? How could we know what to do?" Life has been presented to them as a series of emergencies for which they are not expected to prepare but merely to trust to the beneficent common purposes of their elders.

## SUMMARY

The Arapesh are a society within which cooperation toward a general cherishing conserving goal is obtained through the ramification of helpfulness within person-to-person ties rather than by any allegiance to closed groups or by any resort to rivalry or competition between groups. The multiplicity of these person-to-person ties prevents any boundaries being set up either to the groups with common language, which are crosscut with trade relationships, to the localities, which are crosscut with affinal, residence, and working-group ties, or to the biological family itself, so close are the ties of each spouse to the relatives of the other.   Conspicuous also is the diffuseness of the goal set up by the society, the number of ways in which a satisfactory functioning may be attained, the freedom left to the individual to choose or reject a skill, the lack of any single scale by which success can be measured.[1]

### Bibliography

MEAD, MARGARET: "Arapesh Education."   An article which forms part of the mimeographed materials prepared for the Hanover Seminar on Human Relations.

———: *Sex and Temperament in Three Primitive Societies*, William Morrow & Company, Inc., New York, 1935.

[1] The only one which I found was using the bones of the dead.   About this the people themselves were completely inarticulate.

# CHAPTER II

## THE ESKIMO OF GREENLAND

### *by* JEANNETTE MIRSKY

In 1884 there were 371 Ammassalik Eskimos. They are an Eskimo group who inhabit and recognize as their home territory that long stretch of the east Greenland coast extending from the 65th to the 68th degree of latitude. The name is used by the Eskimo further south to indicate all those people within that district who go to a certain spot from the middle of May to the middle of June to hunt ammassat (capelins). The spot where the capelin run occurs is within the Ammassalik fiord, but there are no permanent dwelling places there.

The east coast of Greenland has, geographically, a specific character, though it conforms in general to the rest of the arctic regions, and this is an important consideration in any discussion of its inhabitants. The coast line cuts a slim path between the high mountains which back on the great Ice-Cap and the east Greenland Sea; it is cut by deep fiords on whose banks berry bushes and edible herbs grow luxuriantly during the short summer season; it has jutting capes in whose lee are waters protected from the masses of pack ice; and it is still further protected by islands. This protection offered by islands, capes, and fiords is needed, for past that shore flows the enormous drift ice carried by the east Greenland current. At the mouths of the fiords and on certain banks off the islands are the breeding places of the large seals. The east Greenland Sea is one of the greatest sealing grounds in the arctic, and its terrible pack ice has helped to save the natural resources from total extermination at the hands of the European sealing fleets. A factor which plays a determining role in the very life of the Ammassalik is the state of the *storis*. This is the name given to the drift ice. As a rule the whole coast is free from ice for some few weeks in August or September. Then the pack again becomes heavy and by November the floes freeze solidly together into fields of great size, which become immovably fixed and pressed into ridges along the coast. As gales sweep over this frozen sea the masses of ice are broken up and set into violent motion, and as the gale subsides they re-form. About this time the winter ice covers the fiords and may unite with the drift ice, although there is usually a strip of open water left, several miles wide and running parallel with the shore. In April the stamp of winter is complete, the ice stretches to the horizon, only to diminish as warm weather brings the open water closer and as the swells again break the pack to pieces. Whereas this is the usual state of affairs, it is not an invariable one. Alternatively either the ice can remain fixed to the coast throughout the whole winter, the sea ice joined to the fiord ice—in which case there is no hunting, and famine ensues; or the ice may not come in close enough to the land and then the breakers are so wild that ice cannot form, the seals are not forced to specific breathing holes, and the hunters' search is fruitless. The economy of the Ammassalik depends entirely on the sea and the currents and the ice.

## Economic Background

The Ammassalik look to the sea, for from the sea come their food, their clothes, their shelter, and their main means of intercommunication. The western drift of the Arctic Ocean brings Siberian driftwood to their treeless land. The sea washes up pumice stone used in preparing the hides. Though the land provides them with a certain amount of food—foxes, birds, berries, herbs (the hare, the reindeer, and the musk ox have long disappeared from their district)—they depend practically entirely on the skin, flesh, and blubber of the seal, the walrus, the bear, the narwhal, etc. The different kinds of seal are their great staple. They use it for food, its fat furnishes them with light and heat, its skin gives them clothes, wall coverings for their winter houses and for their summer tents; seal-skins are used in kayaks (men's boat) and umiaks (women's boat), for bags, for harpoon lines, dog traces; the sinew is used for sewing thread; the guts are pieced together for waterproof kayak suits and translucent windowpanes. From the ivory and bones of these animals are fashioned many tools, weapons, and implements. The driftwood is used in housebuilding, to make the frame for their kayaks and umiaks, for boxes, water tubs, and urine tubs, for shafts for harpoons and lances, for snow knives, sledges, and the scoops with which the capelins are caught.

The Ammassalik have a vast territory at their disposal and they are well aware of it, knowing in detail the uninhabited coast line to the north of them as well as the various settlements to the south. But they are concentrated around the three large fiords of Sermilik, Ammassalik, and Sermiligak. In winter they live in settlements, each of which consists of one long house, and these are scattered along the shores of these three fiords, some only a few miles apart, some completely isolated.[1] Neither the place nor the composition of these settlements remains the same winter after winter. People live together because of preference, and thus settlements may be made up of families who are related to each other—brothers and their families, or an elderly couple and several of their married sons and daughters and their families—or just friends and their families. The people live in the winter houses from the end of September to the end of April. Then the settlements break up into individual small family units who spend the other months living in tents, moving about from place to place. It is during the summer hunting season, when they move freely about, that plans are made for the following winter's settlements, who is to live with whom and where.

Property among the Ammassalik consists in food, dogs, blubber, house parts and tents, sledges, kayaks and umiaks and their accessories, hunting weapons—harpoons, lances, darts, throwing sticks, floats, fishing scoops, dredges, snares, slings, etc.—men's knives, saws, hammers, bow drills, and other tools, women's knives, scraping boards, needles and awls, twisting and plaiting implements, household utensils—skin bags used for storage, fire-making implements, lamps, drying frames, cooking pots and accessories, water and urine tubs, dishes and plates and spoons and ladles, trinket boxes and chests—clothing, headdress, bracelets, combs, back-scratchers, buckles, beads, snow goggles, amulets, masks, drums, dolls, and toys. All these things are owned individually by the man or woman or child who makes or

---

[1] In 1884–1885 there were four settlements in Sermilik fiord; one had 58 persons, two had 31, and one had 12. In Ammassalik fiord there were seven inhabited houses: one had 47 inhabitants, one had 37, and one each with 35, 34, 28, 25, and 19. In Sermiligak fiord there was only one settlement of 14 persons.

uses them and most of them are of a perishable nature. Each man is expected to be a hunter and his own manufacturer of weapons, tools, and implements; it is necessary for a man to have a woman in order to complete the picture of domestic economy. In order to exist it is imperative that there be cooperation between a man and a woman; their tasks complement each other's nicely, and in some instances overlap, but because of this complementary cooperation a couple is entirely self-sufficing.

Men and women have their own field of work. The man takes the initiative in the struggle for existence, not only in getting a wife—which generally takes on the aspects of a kind of robbery— but also in providing the food for the family by hunting the marine animals, and in deciding where the family shall live in summer and winter. He makes his hunting and working implements himself, and this is the basis for ownership. Every youth and man owns a kayak. The man also makes the tools and utensils and adornments used and owned by the women in their work and in the common household tasks. The women's work consists of skinning the animals brought in by the man and cutting up the meat. Upon them rests the complicated and difficult routine needed to convert the densely furred and fatty skins into leather suitable for use in clothes, boot soles, boat and tent coverings, dog harness, whips, harpoon lines, bags, sheaths, and needlecases. She also nurses the children, looks after the lamps, the cooking, the drying of wet clothes, the rubbing and drying and mending of all the boots; she sews the prepared seal-skins into coverings for the kayak and umiak and assists the man in stretching the skins securely over the wood frame; she coop-erates in the housebuilding in the autumn and in the tent raising in the spring; she rows the umiak and takes part in the capelin fishing, drying and preparing the scooped-up fish for winter storage. In addition during the autumn the women harvest the wild berries and edible herbs and gather the mussels and small seafood to be found along the shore.

The division of labor is thus clearly marked between the sexes, yet there is no prohibition against a woman being a hunter.[1] Each couple is at once the producer of the means of subsistence and of the necessary raw materials, the manufacturer of the finished product, and the direct consumer. Each couple is thus

[1] See Case 10.

a completely self-sufficing unit and the struggle for existence is continuous, precarious, and dependent on factors outside the individual's control. Property consists of the basic needs of food, clothing, and shelter and the means of procuring those, and is for the most part perishable and barely above the subsistence level. In consequence wealth is fairly evenly distributed among the people. But within this equality there is a variation depending on individual ability. An angakok (shaman) is likely to have more possessions, obtained as fees for his services. But in general inequalities are not of quantity but of quality. So a man will not have two kayaks, but a skillful workman may have a better kayak than a less skillful one; a more skillful and enterprising hunter will have more to eat; everyone has clothes, but some will be made of skins that are worked and sewed and decorated by a more skilled woman; etc. Another factor in addition to the limitations set by the environment and the technology that tends to equalize the domestic economy and keep all property at the same level of distribution is the mobile life of the Amassalik. Were it possible to accumulate large surpluses they would only prove a serious problem in their mobile summer life, and mobility is dictated by their pursuit of game.

It is important to remember that the Ammassalik depend largely upon seals and other blubbery sea mammals for their food, clothing, light, and heat and that, though the coastal waters are rich in these animals, it is impossible for them to accumulate great stores of food. And even were they able to, they have no way of preserving the meat and blubber from year to year. At the best they can keep food for a few weeks or months without spoiling. Therefore, when hunting is good, they eat plentifully; when continued bad weather makes hunting impossible they have sufficient stores of meat and blubber to last them several weeks; but if conditions are unfavorable for any protracted period then starvation faces them. These famine times are frequent enough for them to have a recognized way of behavior during such times, but unless otherwise specified, this discussion will not deal with their life as lived during times of great stress.

The technology of the Ammassalik reflects individualism in the procuring of animals and the manufacturing of articles. Whatever is possible for one person to handle is done alone, though two or more persons may cooperate in a task because it is pleas-

anter and easier. Thus cooperation is found principally in the
whale hunts and shark roundups (formerly in reindeer and
musk-ox drives), and to a lesser degree in the building and
organizing of their winter houses. Yet within this cooperative
framework an extraordinary amount of individualistic play is
found. There are no rewards for certain individuals within the
group enterprise, and this rules out any competitive element.
In a whale hunt several men paddle out together in an umiak,
one or all may harpoon, and when the whale is dead they tow it
back to land, where the entire community shares in the kill. In
a shark roundup, men, women, and children unite to secure as
much of the school as possible: they all dig the hole in the ice, the
women and children run up and down along the edge of the hole
and shriek to attract the sharks to the surface, where they are
harpooned by the men. In the reindeer drives the women and
children set up the stone walls and drive the herd between these
to a narrow spot where the hunters lie concealed. All these are
cooperative enterprises in which the work and the rewards are
shared by the whole community. These contrast strongly with
the salmon fishing, the capelin hunting, and the berrying, in
which several persons carry on the same work at the same time
and at the same place without any cooperation or help. Each
man works alone for his own end and the fact that other men are
similarly engaged around him does not make the work cooperative. It is an individualistic note in the face of an environmental
setting which indicates cooperation. During the summer, when
the people are living alone in small family units, whatever a man
or woman collects is for his own family's use at that time and is
part of the provisions he brings with him when he becomes part
of the settlement in the fall. A good hunter or a man with many
rolls of dried capelins is an asset to any settlement. And yet
whether a man hunts by and for himself or with and for a group he
uses the same tools, weapons, and implements. There is no
specialization of roles in the cooperative ventures: any man can
handle any phase of the work since each is master of all the
needed techniques.

This is one of the factors that make it possible to understand
the amount of individualism allowed within the winter long house.
The winter settlements may be thought of as a federation of free
and sovereign states, composed of members who can join or not

at will, who are free to leave at any time, and who, while they are within the federation, retain a maximum of their individual rights. During the summer hunting season arrangements are made, purely on preference, as to who shall constitute the personnel of each house, and where they shall live. There is no competition for such house sites, for the territory is vast and there are a great number of vacant house sites whose old walls of turf and stone may be used to advantage. The house itself consists of one room, varying in size from twenty-four to fifty feet in length, depending on the number of families to be accommodated. It is built close to the sea, toward which the door and windows face. The walls support a ridgepole, a piece of heavy driftwood, and this is further supported by wooden props. Along the back part of the house runs a wooden platform six feet wide that is the living quarters for the families. The props that support the roof also divide this platform into stalls, each of which is occupied by a family and which are partitioned off from the adjacent stalls by skin hangings. (In a stall six feet wide by four feet long a man, his two wives, and six children live.) Skin hangings are also used to line the inside of the entire house, and to pad the living platform. The platforms are used as beds by night and as the workroom for the women during the day. The unmarried men, big boys, and casual guests sleep on narrow benches which run under the windows on the opposite side of the house. Alongside the stall every family has its own lamp over which the cooking is done and the clothes and boots are dried out. Each woman cooks food in her own pot. Under the platform are kept the skin bags and wooden boxes which contain the family's tools and utensils. Outside the house each hunter has a stand on which his kayak rests. The picture given by such settlements is similar to that presented by a *wagon-lit*. The housemates cooperate to build the common outside covering, and the food brought in is for the communal stores. But except for the containing walls of turf and stone the different parts are individually owned and contributed: the ridgepole, the props, the planks for the platform, the skin wall and platform coverings. The food, which is mainly acquired by individual efforts, is put into a common storeroom, though the skins are individually owned and used. In handling the food each woman cooks her own share in her own pot over her own lamp and then hands the prepared meat and soup around for all to share.  (This may be an expression of individuality in cooking or it may be due to the fact that there is no cooking pot which would be large enough for the whole group and still be transportable, or that it would take too long to cook such a big potful over a blubber lamp.)   Each house has several communal urine tubs but each family within the house has its private one. The latter are used for individual washing purposes—the women are constantly washing their hair in urine—but the stale urine is collected in the large group urine tubs for all the women to use in tanning the animal skins.   Each compartment is a separate unit.   Its occupants can, for the most part, do as they please while they are on the *wagon-lit* and they can get off at any place they choose.   Only when hunting is bad and the supply of food and blubber is short—when the environment forces it—do the members cooperate more fully.   Then only one lamp is lit, only one pot used.   At such times, though, no person or family is obliged to remain within the group.   In times of scarcity a man is free to leave whenever he pleases.   This freedom makes intelligible the chief role of the "headman," whose authority is limited to acting as host when strangers arrive and to determining the division and arrangement of the stalls within the house.

In the entire arrangement of the winter settlement, which for the Ammassalik is the peak of cooperative activity, there is present no factor of competition since there is no limitation on either the territory or the house sites available or in preferable stall locations, and there is no obligation to become part of any group or to remain a part of a group so entered.   There is a minimum of cooperation demanded or required.   There is a maximal amount of individuality expressed in the living arrangements, the securing and cooking of food, and the ownership of everything except the walls which were originally made use of.

Outside these cooperative activities, the Ammassalik have only one hunting technique that requires the work of more than a single hunter.   In the *ittuarteq* method of hunting seals two hunters must work in close harmony.   It is used in the winter when the ice has become so thick that it is difficult to see the seal's breathing holes.   A spot is chosen in the vicinity of a strong current where, owing to the rise and fall of water under the ice, fissures have formed.   Through these the light penetrates and attracts the seals.   There two holes are cut, one large

enough for a man to lie in, the other just big enough to accommodate a harpoon. Inside the larger hole a hunter peers into the
water, watching for seals, while the other man manipulates the
harpoon, which is tipped with pieces of white bone to lure
the animals. When the lookout sees a seal opposite the point
of the harpoon he gives an emphatic but cautious cry, at which
the other man strikes. Then the men widen the hole and haul
the seal up. With this method a pair of lucky hunters might
catch six or seven seals a day.

All the other hunting methods require a single hunter. Whenever there is open water seals, walrus, narwhals, etc., are hunted
from a kayak. Though two or more men might go out together,
each in his own kayak, it is more common for a man to go out
alone. To them kayaking implies a solitary venture, and so
well is this understood that a good kayaker must be able to right
himself by his own efforts when his kayak capsizes. When ice
covers the fiord the commonest method is for a hunter to locate
a seal hole and wait until the animal comes there to breathe.
Since a seal has several holes it may be hours before the hunter's
patience is rewarded. In the spring seals come up on the ice to
sleep and sun themselves and then the hunter crawls slowly and
carefully until he is within striking distance of his prey. Bears
are met with in both summer and winter and they are attacked
either from a kayak or sledge, or on foot. In securing small
game—foxes, birds, etc.—traps and snares are set by individuals,
usually boys.

The everyday routine methods of hunting are, therfore, an
individual activity. All other routine affairs are similarly carried
on. Except for those things in which a wife helps her husband, a
man makes and decorates all the tools, weapons, and implements
which he needs in order to exist. The bow drill used by the men
to drill holes in bone and wood is manipulated by one person;
the hands are used to pull the bow back and forth while the
round stick which it turns is held firmly in place by means of a
mouth grip.

In the tasks performed by the women there is the same individualistic note. Cooperation exists between the adult women
of a family; between co-wives, a wife and a mother-in-law, a wife
and an unmarried sister-in-law, but such cooperation is not
implicit in the tasks. Two women carrying out their share of

the domestic economy can be considered as the equivalent of one extraordinary woman, a supercapable wife. It is better to have two women to take care of the game brought in by a capable hunter, but it is not compulsory to have more than one. Even the umiak is better rowed if there are two women rowers, but it can be rowed by one. That two women handling the female side of the domestic economy may be equated with the work of one very capable woman is seen in the fact that when a man has two wives there is still but one lamp used for light, heat, and cooking though in the winter house each family tends its own lamp. There is nothing in the raw materials they handle or the articles they make that cannot be accomplished by one woman.

In the preparation of a skin a woman first cuts away the layer of blubber, then cuts away the slimy membrane next to the skin, and then scrapes it thoroughly clean. When this is done it is put on a stretcher, where it dries. Then it is tanned by being soaked in a large tub of stale urine, washed out in sea water, stretched, and dried, and is finally ready to be made into clothing, coverings, thongs, boots, etc. The sinews of the bear and narwhal, by being kept moist in the mouth and made pliable by being rubbed against the cheek, furnish the sewing thread. The great art of the Ammassalik seamstresses is to make watertight seams, and every women learns that. All the tools used by women in their work are owned by them though they are made by the men. Possessing the necessary skill and owning her tools, a woman is not only a capable craftsman but she is fully equipped and ready to set up "shop" anywhere she pleases and to cooperate with any man. This fact must be constantly borne in mind to understand the freedom with which the individual woman can move about in the social setting. Every man must have a wife as an economic partner and it is desirable for him to have two such partners. A hunter is seriously handicapped if he has no wife, and if he has two he need be only inconvenienced if one of his wives leaves him.

There is no organized trade, but bartering is carried on. Bartering can include everything from a wife to a bone dart; it can be a permanent transaction or a temporary exchange. It is carried on in much the same informal way that small boys "swap" picture cards, marbles, and knives. The transactions vary with the individual and the article to be exchanged. In one instance two men had exchanged their wives and other possessions at the same time, the wives being just one on a list of items exchanged. When the time came to return what had been traded one of the men refused to return the wife because he did not want to have to return the other objects which he had acquired at the same time.[1]

## SOCIAL STRUCTURE

The same strong sense of individualism that characterizes the technology and economics of the Ammassalik is markedly present in their social structure. They have no political unity, no organized leadership, no social stratification. They have no complicated relationship system nor any set of kinship attitudes that defines by its terms the rights and obligations obtaining among its members. There is no set residence. The biological family constitutes the only recognized bond. With each new marriage a new household is set up so that a family of adults does not function as a group. Every adult may be thought of as a sovereign state dealing with other such sovereign states and answerable to no one but itself. Children are cared for and protected as long as they are unable to do so for themselves; but they take over adult patterns as soon as they are physically and physiologically able.

A few bonds unite the Ammassalik among themselves and set them off as a group from their neighbors. They use the same dialect, they are natives of the same territory, and they have a way of life that is slightly different from other Eskimo. The Ammassalik have *not* certain widespread Eskimo traits. Here we do not find hospitality wrestling matches, we do not find group ritual, they do not practice female infanticide, they do not substitute the murderer for the man he murdered, there are no *angakut* (shamans) contests. The absence of the first of these traits may be due to the fact that the Ammassalik are a small group who meet once a year during the capelin season. Each person is well known and there is no necessity of having contests in order to place a newcomer in the hierarchy of strength. This fact may also explain the lack of angakut contests. This eliminates the competitive element that is so characteristic of the other Eskimo angakut. The very cooperative religious custom of communal confessions which the Central Eskimo have are also lacking here.

[1] See *Meddelelser om Grønland*, Vol. 39, p. 69.

On the other hand the Ammassalik have the institution of the juridical drum songs, a mechanism that can be used to settle any conflicting claims within the community (see below, p. 68).

The attitude of suspicion and slander that exists between the Ammassalik and their nearest neighbors, the southeastern Greenlanders, is the same within the Ammassalik group.  The attitude contrasts strikingly with their behavior.  To all persons, whether in the group or outside the group, they behave hospitably, extending this hospitality to include food as well as shelter, enemies as well as friends.  The widespread Eskimo pattern of including sex in the hospitality pattern, of a man offering his wife to a guest, is here carried on under the guise of the game of "Putting Out the Lamps," which may be played whether a guest is present or not. But a good host is one who always has the lamps extinguished in the evening when there are guests in the house.  In this game both the married and the unmarried take part and complete liberty prevails.  (The incest tabus which do not permit intercourse between parent and child or between siblings still hold.) Under cover of darkness a man may take any woman as his sex partner.  In the summer when the family unit is small and light lasts far into the night the game is not played.  Then two men will formally exchange wives, or an unmarried man will try and steal another's wife.

Under this pattern of extended hospitality runs the ever present note of suspicion and slander.  It is present between the group as a whole and the outsiders, between members of one settlement and all other settlements, and between an individual and the rest of the group.  The lack of political unity is carried to such extremes, the marked individualistic nature of the people is so opposed to the slightest suggestion of cohesion, that the same attitudes and feelings are found intratribally as well as intertribally.

There is no organized leadership, but there are recognized leaders.  An outstanding hunter, a powerful angakok, a skillful drum singer—individual differences within the same field of endeavor are known and casually rated.  But there is no "best" hunter, or "most powerful" angakok, or "most skillful" singer; there is no set point, no limit to what a role demands, and each man rolls up his own score for his own satisfaction and to his own interest.  Leadership, such as it is, is ephemeral.  A man's standing as a successful hunter may vary from season to season, depending on his luck as well as his skill, and since prestige depends on how well a person is doing, not on how well a person has done, a man whose best days are past will not be so important as one who is in the full vigor of his prime. It is this ephemeral quality and the stressing of individualism that tend to preclude social stratification.

Their kinship system is similar to ours; bilateral, counting sex, generation, and direct and collateral descent. A man, his wife or wives, and their children constitute the family. The man and woman unite their efforts to take care of themselves and of the immature children (the man may be the real or foster father, the woman the real or foster mother) and together they form a social and economic unit, a household, within which the young are cared for. But even within this small, closely related group there is a complete allowance for individuality. There is no set attitude that prevails between such fundamentally close relationships as parent and child, siblings, and the conjugal pair. There is a complete tolerance for the role the individual chooses to take in any of these relationships. A father may provide for his son, and this is the usual picture, but he may also abandon him; a mother may aid her daughter in getting a husband or may compete for her daughter's husband; a son may look out for his mother or he may not see her from one year to the next and be indifferent to her fate; siblings may live together and work together or they may be members of different settlements and strangers to one another. Marriage, which is extraordinarily brittle, cannot be said to have any norm of conduct as regards the conjugal pair; it is only when there are children born to a couple that there is a tendency toward stability; but even then the picture presented by the married couple is as varied as the number of marriages (see the case histories). This minimal kinship structure gives free play to the individuality of the persons within that structure. The high incidence of foster parents may be an important factor in giving this wide variation within the kinship structure, but it cannot be the cause of it since both real and foster relatives behave in the same way.

There is no set residence. We have seen how the Ammassalik spend the winter months in settlements which consist of one house each. The housemates can be relatives or merely friends or both, who decide to pass the winter together. As a general rule old house walls which are vacant and plentiful are used rather than new ones being built. But it is not necessary for such old sites to be used. A group may decide to try out an entirely new region, and so a number of families may go as much as eighty miles away,[1] to try out new hunting grounds. Though the sites for the settlements are permanent, the houses are not. When spring comes it is impossible to live in the houses. They are flooded as the ground thaws and the snow melts, and the skins used in the roofing become useless from constant wetting. The environment forces the change from winter to summer living quarters. But even so it would be possible for the same group to return year after year to live with each other were this congenial to the individuals. It would seem rather that this enforced change is utilized in a manner compatible with their strong sense of individuality. A family will go where they want to, not where they are expected to because of blood ties or habit. This annually renewed chance to shift about further separates the adult members of the same family.

The following outline illustrates the way closely related families are spread out among the different inhabited places:

$A$ and $B$ are brothers of $C$ and $D$, who are their sisters.

$A$ lives at Umivil with his wife, a married daughter, two sons, two daughters, and a married niece who has one child.

$B$ and $C$ live at Tasiusarsik with a married daughter and a son and daughter of $B$; $C$, who is a widow, has her married son and his four sons and two daughters.

$D$ lives at Sermiligak. She is a widow. With her live her two married sons, each of whom had one child, two daughters, and one son.

$C$'s other children: one married son lives at Sermilik; he has two children. One married daughter lives at Norsit with a married daughter and her child, four sons, and an unmarried daughter. One married son lives at Norajik with his child. One married daughter lives at Kangarsik with her child.

In all there were fifty-six persons in these related families, in which there were thirteen married couples whose spouses were alive and living with them. They were scattered over seven different settlements. During the summer, when the people live

[1] See "Dead House at Nualik," *Meddelelser om Grønland*, Vol. 39, p. 69.

in tents and move about from hunting ground to hunting ground, there is an even greater individual initiative in the matter of residence. A family is free to make a long trip to the south-eastern group, and such a trip may last from two to four years.

With such a loose social structure the economic activities which stress the all-round ability of each man to get a living and the self-sufficiency of the conjugal pair harmonize completely. A man behaves toward other people as he wants to, whether they are related or not. Kinship does not demand any set patterns of behavior. Residence in a group exacts the minimal amount of cooperation and this lasts only while a man is a member of a group. The suspicion and slander that exist between settlements are also present between members of the same settlement. In the social as well as the economic pictures there is a very great accent on individualism.

It is absolutely necessary that a man marry. As soon as a youth is able to support a wife he is in a position to marry. Since supporting a wife depends directly on a boy's hunting ability, and since boys are trained to hunt seriously from the age of ten on, it often happens that boys marry at a very tender age. Marriage implies getting a woman to complete the unit of domestic economy. The chief incentive to marriage is to have a wife to look after a man's things and dress his game, and so a mother will urge her son to marry because "she can scarcely see to sew any longer." This sometimes leads to very strange unions with a young man married to a woman old enough to be his mother.[1] No man no matter how old he is can be without a wife, and in looking at the census we find that while there are widows there are no unmarried widowers. A widow can help out in her son's household, but she will only help out, she will not carry the full load of the work. A skillful and lucky hunter will actually be in need of two wives, for one woman is overwhelmed by the amount of work to be done. A second wife may also be taken so that a man can have two rowers to propel the umiak.[2] In taking a second wife a man is not supposed to take a sister of his first wife, nor to marry the mother after having been married to her daughter, but instances of both occur. Complete sex freedom exists before and after marriage. Marriage is deeply

[1] See Case 4.
[2] See Case 5.

rooted in economic necessity and can be divided into two component factors; on the one hand a woman is a sex partner, and on the other an economic partner. In securing a sex partner a man does not have to marry. Any man who wants to may participate in the game of "Putting Out the Lamps," and a man has access to the unmarried girls and the temporarily unattached women. Both during the winter and during the summer a man's sexual wants can be easily gratified. If a man is married he can take advantage of the opportunities stated above and, in addition, he is free to exchange his wife with another man for as long as both want to.[1] This whole pattern is congruent with the individualism that is characteristic of other activities; and in addition there is a slight note of helpfulness that pervades this sex field. A man whose wife fails to conceive and who is desirous of having children may call upon an angakok to cure her of her "sickness." The treatment consists of the angakok's journeying to the moon, whence a child is thrown down to the wife, who thus becomes pregnant, and as a reward for having made such an arduous trip the angakok has the right to have intercourse with the wife. That the treatment consists of both the angakok's journey and his copulating with the wife can be seen in the alternate method, which is to urge the wife to have intercourse with other men in order that she may conceive.[2] Exclusive sexual prerogatives do not seem to be the cause for competitive claims.

There is competition, however, in securing a wife as an economic partner. In this competition there does not appear to be rivalry for a particular woman. Rather, there is a constant scrambling around for any woman if she is desirable. If she is attractive that is pleasant but not necessary. (Desirability is not phrased in terms of beauty or youth or family, etc., it is rather how skillful a worker, how fruitful a woman, how cooperative a partner a woman is. This allows, except in the instance of childbearing, women of all ages to be sought after, it increases to the limit the number of women a man has to choose from.) Competition enters into this acquiring of female economic partners because there is a limited number of women available— though there are 114 women to every 100 men—because of the economic drive to get a wife, because polygamy exists (all the

[1] See Case 21.
[2] See Case 8.

good hunters try to get two wives to handle the game they bring in), and because marriages are brittle.[1] The actual securing of a wife is simple and direct. There are no preliminaries, no prerequisites, either social or financial. A young man may give the father a payment in the shape of a harpoon, or knife, etc., for the privilege of marrying his pretty daughter; but often a father will give a present to a skillful hunter in order that the latter will marry his daughter; but by far the greater number of marriages are concluded by the simple act of a man's taking a woman, whether it be from her father or her husband. Women are taken by force, with the rewards going to the most powerful man.[2] The economic character of the marriage is stressed in the reasons for which a woman is divorced. Unfaithfulness plays a small part. It is rather because she is a bad housekeeper, because she is a bad or negligent seamstress, because she eats too much. A man will divorce and leave his wife even though at the time she is pregnant or has children. While it is true that women are taken by force and kept or left at will, women are not cowed. There is as much freedom of choice for the women as for the men. A woman may take the initiative in the game of "Putting Out the Lamps," or in getting a desirable husband,[3] or she may leave her husband because she wants to go to another settlement, or because he has abused her. The securing of wives is the focal point around which competition centers.[4]

Since marriage is easily entered and as easily left, and since it is almost obligatory for adults to be married, it is regarded lightly and it is nothing for a young man or woman in the early twenties to have been party to five, six, or seven marriages. Marriages assume a more stable aspect when there are children born to a couple, but the children are no guarantee of stability. The whole field of marriage—outside the competitive securing of wives—reflects the individualistic note. A man is at liberty to treat his wife as he wants, and the range of attitudes goes from caressing to beating and stabbing, from devotion to desertion;

[1] See Cases 1, 3, 4, 5, 22.
[2] See Case 22.
[3] See Cases 5, 7.
[4] A reference to the cases of Pitiga (3), Igsiavik (4), Sanimuinak (5), Angmalilik (7), and Papik (22) will bring out this competitive scrambling for wives, the factors that are relevant to the competition, and the extraordinary brittleness of marriage.

and reciprocally a wife can "take it or leave it." Marriages are as varied as the people themselves.

Another factor that tends to keep the competition for wives in a constant state of flux is the high death rate among the hunters. Of the thirteen deaths reported during ten months among the Ammassalik all but three were men; of these ten, seven were twenty years and older. Any such death, with its consequent widowing tends to focus the competitive struggle and to carry in its train a whole series of marital readjustments.

Women are the primary source of quarrels, and such quarrels are carried on between individuals in a variety of ways. They may lead to murder, to revenge by theft, or to a drum match. Quarrels may occur between a man and his wife, between two men, or between two women. In any case there is no attempt on the part of outsiders to interfere in any way. It is quite ordinary to read such an account of a conjugal quarrel. "When Piutek saw the new wife she became angry and began to scold her husband. He flew into a passion, seized hold of her hair, and thumped her back and face with his clenched fists. Finally he stabbed her in the knee so that the blood spurted out. As is usual in such cases the other inmates of the house looked on with perfect composure at this connubial quarrel."[1] There are no cases reported, however, of death resulting from such quarrels. Killing a spouse as a way out of an unsatisfactory or unpleasant marriage does not occur. Likewise there is no instance of a woman killing anyone, though women may fight physically or verbally in a drum match.

Drum matches are held both summer and winter. While this is a juridical procedure and a method of settling disputes, yet it conforms to the wider social pattern of singing songs for pleasure. (In fact old drum-match songs constitute part of the repertory of songs sung during the long winter nights.) Both men and women may sing, but they must do so in the traditional style which governs every expression, tone, sound, and movement, and those who cannot master the style are ashamed to sing or touch the drum. A match of this kind is not settled in one encounter, but is carried on for years, the parties taking turns visiting one another. For each new meeting the parties prepare and practice new songs, in which the crimes are vastly exaggerated, or, if they

[1] See Case 5.

can find no new material that is suitable, they may father new crimes on their opponents or reproach them for deeds which may have been merely intended but never committed. They can enumerate the faults of the opponent's family living and dead. The opponents stand facing one another. They sing one at a time while the other party stands quietly and listens. The singer mocks the other in a number of ways, by snorting and breathing right in his face, by butting him with his forehead so that he tumbles over. The listener accepts this with the greatest composure and even laughs mockingly to show the audience his indifference. When the singer is about to butt him he shuts his eyes and advances his head to receive the blow. The match can thus go on all night, each man taking turns in beating the drum and singing but otherwise not budging from the spot. In the intervals between songs and before and after the match, the opponents do not show the slightest sign of their hostility but appear to be friendly. This is carried on before a large audience which follows every word and movement with keen enjoyment. A man has often several drum matches going on at the same time and, if during the years in which a match is going on one of the parties dies, the survivor prides himself on it and boasts of this fact to others. The same pattern that is found in these juridical drum matches is found in matches similarly carried·on just for pleasure. In fact drum matches are the chief pastime of the Ammassalik.[1]

Drum songs are never sung, as on the west coast of Greenland, to taunt a man with his incompetence as a hunter, or accuse someone of laziness or cowardice. They arise from a competitive situation, a man's taking another's wife, which may be obscured under a charge of stealing food, poisoning a man, using a dead relative's name, etc. They start out in a competitive mood, each competitor striving to gain a definite point, to swing the opinion of the onlookers to his side in the same way that a debate in our society is carried on.[2] But from this competitive start

[1] See Cases 2, 3, 4, 8.

[2] But once having obtained the approval of the community, that is all that is secured, for there is nothing the community can do besides give its approval. Neither the approval or the disapproval of the group carries with it any weight. A man can do whatever he pleases, and the more powerful he is, the freer he is to fly in the face of public opinion. Winning the approval of the group carries with it no social sanction.

the drum matches, after a long inconclusive series of events in which the initial hostility gets lost in a pleasant social pastime, degenerate into a cooperative act in which the two principals and the onlookers all enjoy the "show."

Theft itself does not seem to lead to a drum match, though it may be included with other items to furnish the material in the matches whose original cause was tied up with the competition for wives.

Murder is of frequent occurrence. The lack of social forms makes it possible for a man to murder within the group without having any punishment visited on him. There is no blood feud, no retaliatory act, either physical or magical, no substitutive procedure, no purification rite, nothing. The man remains within the group and people are careful not to provoke so powerful a person. At the most his act can furnish material for a drum song. He is accepted realistically. In 1884 there were three murderers within the Ammassalik group. All were young men and angakut and they moved freely about. Not even murder alters the hospitality pattern. One young man who had killed his stepfather because the latter abused his mother "wanders all about the fiord, and even comes on visits by sledge and boat to the near relations of the murdered man. He is spoken of with dread, but not on account of the murder, but because as an angakok he has robbed so many souls from people who afterwards died."[1] The two other murders were done because in one case a brother resented the harsh way his sister was treated by her husband when she broke a tabu; and in the other case a man killed his father-in-law, after he had been divorced from the man's daughter, because the older man had frightened him badly years before.

Religion among the Ammassalik is a highly individual affair carried on by angakut, each of whom has one or more spirit helpers who act as messengers and help him to get in touch with the spirit world. The religion centers about obtaining the means of subsistence and curing the sick. Any person of either sex may become an angakok, and the only differentiation among the various practitioners is based on personality traits, the acclaim going to the most fearless, the most adroit and cunning. There is a slight amount of cooperation needed to become

[1] See Case 7.

an angakok. One must be taught by an established angakok how to go out to a lonely spot and there to rub a small stone on the top of a large stone for three days until this brings out the spirit of the rock. This procedure is repeated at different times during the next three or four years, during which time the disciple enters into communion with different spirits who become his *tartoks*, servants. Once a person has been instructed, the whole matter again becomes a personal affair. The angakut perform according to the shamanistic pattern of being securely bound, going into a trance in which their spirits speak and make their presence felt through them and making journeys to the moon, to the depths of the ocean, etc. They are all good ventriloquists and sleight-of-hand artists. Most of these séances are performed for the pleasure of it. In cases of illness the angakok goes into a trance to find out what has happened to the soul of the sick person—for all sickness can be traced to some harm which has happened to the soul, its having been abducted by an evil spirit, its having gotten lost, etc.—and if possible bring it back to the body. Such services are paid for in sledges, dogs, harpoon points, etc., ostensibly to the tartok who served the angakok in effecting a cure, but through the angakok who controls it. Except for the small amount of help given in instructing an aspiring angakok, angakokism is consistently devoid of cooperation or competition; it is individualistic.

The one time when there is a maximum of cooperation within the society is in times of famine, which occur only in winter. Then we find the individualistic stress that characterizes the winter settlements giving way to a certain cooperation motivated by the desire to live. Forced to extremes by the environment, the Ammassalik will cooperate. To conserve the blubber needed for heat and light, only one or two lamps will burn for all the housemates, and cooking will be communally done and shared. But even in the face of this anyone is free to step outside the settlement and go to another, or to try to fend for himself. It is only as long as they choose to remain together, and the choice is open and free for each person to make, that they cooperate. Famine must be distinguished from "times of fast." The latter occur when there is a scarcity of seal meat though there may be plenty of other food. But when the pack ice is a solid mass for many weeks and hunting is impossible and the food is used up,

that is famine. First the dogs are eaten. (Holm, the ethnologist, was unable to make long dog-sledge trips because the
previous winter most of the dogs had been sacrificed during a long
lean period, and there were very few dogs available for driving.)
Then, if the famine continues, the living are forced to eat the
dead. They face this possibility quite realistically. They dread
it and those who have been forced to it shrink from speaking of
it,[1] but it does not drive them insane, they are not reproached for
having been cannibals. When Kunit, a man whose wife and
mother-in-law survived a terrible famine by eating the dead
children, had this fact hurled at him in a drum match, the two
women were made so miserable that they burst into tears. The
onlookers thought this was a needlessly cruel point for his opponent to bring up. As if to fortify this realistic acceptance of the
inevitable there are tales told of people who grew so fond of
human meat that they longed to taste it again.

In accordance with the theory that persons are adult as soon
as they can maintain their part in the domestic economy, they
remain an integral part of the group as long as they are able to
carry on their tasks. Because of the high death rate among the
men and the strenuous life they lead, old men are few. The
Ammassalik do not, as the Central Eskimo do, consider a man
dead when he is too old to hunt and ceremonially wall him up to
die, but a very sick person who seems moribund will be thrown
into the sea to avoid the necessity of handling his dead body.
Of the six old men, between fifty and sixty, all but one were still
good hunters, the remaining one had two capable sons who chose
to look after their father. An elderly woman can still carry on
her work, but this feeling against an individual remaining alive
past the days of his usefulness is explicit in the case of a man who
told his mother-in-law that she was so old she was of no use in the
world and that she might as well be dead. After hearing this
she threw herself into the sea.[2] It is this attitude of being unable
to provide for oneself or being past the useful age that is directly
reflected in the position of the orphan. The orphan in tales and
in fact is hungry, ragged, and abused. He may be killed,[3] or
abandoned; he is without strength in a society that values it above

[1] See Case 6.
[2] See Case 13.
[3] See Case 17.

all else, without power where a powerful personality is a distinguishing mark, without any skill where skill is necesssary to
maintain life itself.

The position of the old, the young, the unplaced is the same:
they are set over against the mature independent adult upon
whom they are wholly dependent for food, clothing, and shelter.
It depends on that adult what their life shall be, if they are allowed
to live; and the treatment accorded them is a personal matter,
has no group sanction, and varies from individual to individual,
case to case.

In a society that allows such free uncensored expression to the
individual, the question of the deviant would prove an interesting
study. Unfortunately, the material on that aspect of the Ammassalik is lacking. No study was undertaken with that in view.
There is only one case reported that might be even remotely
considered in this light.[1] In this case Utuak, a man with two
wives and seven children, had been a successful hunter and had
aspired to become an angakok. Failing in the latter and subsequently failing in his hunting ability, the stand he took was one
of violent agnosticism towards angakokism. At the same time
he was so mortally afraid of the angakut that he would not go
out hunting alone lest they kill him. This obsession had reduced
him to the position where he lived on the charity of Kutuluk,
an important hunter. How long he remained in that position,
how long Kutuluk tolerated the great burden of Utuak and his
family, what subsequently became of him—all these questions
are not answered. Yet Utuak was well on the way to being
a deviant.

## THE IDEAL PERSONALITY

The Ammassalik ideal man is one who is outstanding in skill,
in strength, in power, a man who expresses his personality fully
and without being deterred by economic, social, or supernatural
sanctions. Such a man can take what he wants without fear, he
can do as he pleases without being checked or ostracized, he is at
once a terror and a pride. Such outstanding men are not
classified, rated, and compared one with another; there is no set
number of such individuals allowed; each stands out clearly and
when they compete they afford pleasure to the whole group.

[1] See Case 19.

Prestige is a direct reflection of a powerful personality. And having set this as an ideal the Ammassalik accept all behavior by which such an individual manifests his greatness: violence, arrogance, aggressiveness. The society with its self-sufficient economic base and its loose social structure is constructed like a man's hunting shirt, it fits him snugly for warmth and yet it is loose enough so that a sudden violent movement will not catch the hunter or pull the sleeve out.

The Ammassalik give all the rewards to those who are skillful in hunting, angakokism, or drum singing. With that as a basis a man is free to act as he pleases. The successful hunter or angakok can get two wives and he is welcomed as a son-in-law, a husband, and a housemate. The skillful drum singer who is inventive, a capable artist, and a clever composer may steal, murder, slander, etc., and yet win the community's approval by his superior ability in a drum match. These are the three avenues in which a man may become outstanding. And if he has any of the skills necessary to advance along any of these lines and the personality to distinguish him, then he, with other such men, stands out from the common group. (In the case of Utuak, above, it might be phrased that he had the personality without having the necessary skill to validate it and thus missed attaining the position he craved.) But there is no competition among the big men for such high positions. Any number of men, all those who qualify by virtue of their skill and personality traits, can be termed important. The community is elastic and individual enough to allow each man to think of himself as important and the only check on this is in those cases when one man has cut across the path of another; then the one who does not yield is the more important. And yet there is no open phrasing of competition. A man can show his bigness by going far away from everyone else and there maintaining himself and his family. The one time when competition does explicitly enter the social picture, the drum match, it quickly loses its character and becomes a game in which neither side wants to win, in which both are united in continuing the game and enjoying it.

The injection of strong personality, as an ideal, in a highly individualistic group is here carried out so that one proof of a man's power is seen in his disregard of customs and tabus. One way that people knew Avgo was a very powerful angakok was the way in which he married his mother-in-law while still married to her daughter.

Success and the attainment of prestige depend directly on a person's skill and personality alone. Conversely a person who has neither skill nor a marked personality to exploit with the sanction of his skill is the despised one, the butt of his fellows. Such a role is traditionally and factually taken by the orphan.

## EDUCATION

Among the Ammassalik, children are greatly desired. Both male and female children are welcome since the one means future hunters and the other means hunters' partners. No sickly child, or one without a mother, is allowed to live, and in times of stress it is understood that children must be sacrificed before their parents, because even if they were kept alive by any such gesture they would be unable to cope with the environment and would quickly succumb. They are an investment that is not allowed to become a liability. It is essential to the infant's very life that cooperation exist between the parents in raising it. (There are exceptional cases in which a father or mother will desert, and then unless a foster parent replaces the runaway in the household economy, the child will be abandoned to die.[1]) There is no conflict between the welfare of the child and the practice of exchanging wives.[2]

As soon as a baby is born and washed the mother dips her finger in water and passes it over the baby's lips. Thus with its first breath a child is introduced to the sea on whose bounty its life depends. The mother, whose duties keep her at home, takes complete care of the child and is on hand to nurse the child whenever it cries. A great number of "Petting Songs" sung by the mother to her infant or young child indicate a warm, cherishing, tender attitude. If the mother goes out of the house or tent she carries her child with her strapped securely on her back and kept warm between her fur blouse and her own body. A child suckles until it is past two, but when it is only a few months old it gets additional food, meat that the mother has first masticated thoroughly. Love and attention are given the child the first time it wears a little shirt, the mother kissing the child's breast,

[1] See Cases 16, 17.
[2] See Case 21.

shoulder, hips and navel in order that the child may be healthy. This is continued each time its shirt is put on until it is able to walk.

Again, when the child cuts its first tooth, it is the center of attention. This pattern of giving the child some mark of attention when it first performs some act that marks a stage on the road to adulthood is observed when a boy gets his first kayak, when he is about twelve years old, and when he brings home his first large game. There are, however, no rites to mark a girl's first menses or a boy's puberty. Children are never punished, no matter how refractory they may be. (Among the Coppermine Eskimo to the west the reason given for such tolerance on the part of the parents is that a child is the reincarnation of someone newly dead and that his desire for something is not a childish whim but the expression of this reborn soul. Thus the children are not refractory, it is rather that the parents do not understand what the veteran soul wants. Hence it is better to humor the child.) There was only one instance noted of a child being punished. Then it was on the occasion of a violent crying fit. The child was taken outside and laid on the snow until it quieted down.

The child is brought up in the midst of the household. It goes from the small summer tent to a larger winter house, but wherever it goes it is an intimate part of the family; it sees its mother at work, it awaits its father's return with food, it watches as the father makes his tools and implements, it listens to the adult conversation, it hears the songs that are sung and the tales that are told on long winter nights, it goes with the mother when she goes berrying or visiting or to a drum match, it sleeps under the same cover as its parents. During the summer the child learns to play by itself or with a group. In the winter it may have children its own age around it, or it may not, and this factor varies as the groups do. Most of the children's games are imitative ones that can be played alone or with others: hunting, rowing in kayaks and umiaks. They make figures of stone to represent kayaks, umiaks, tents, and houses. In their games they carry out the same pattern they have seen in adult activities. All the situations which they create in play are reflections of those they have seen or heard about. The small boys make hunting implements and show an extraordinary skill in making the models, with which they practice shooting and harpooning.

A boy usually gets his own kayak, made for him by his father, when he is about twelve. One boy who had received a kayak when he was ten had within three years caught thirty seals. Little girls are given dolls to play with and to dress. Each girl usually has about four and they are named for couples whom the girls know. The games in which these dolls figure are also imitative of adult activity, and usually the dolls are made to dance and sing in the manner appropriate to drum matches. The dolls are so realistically made that if a child is born to the couple for whom the dolls are named, a baby doll is inserted in the mother doll's fur blouse. The children themselves own all their toys.

By the time a boy is thirteen to fifteen he has become quite adept at making tools and implements and has learned the technique of hunting. From that time on it is a matter of constant practice. The transition from play to adult occupations is made early and follows a consistent training. The same is true of girls, and by the time they are this age they are able to do excellent sewing.

Within a tent or house the adults wear only a *natit*, a G-string. Children go about quite naked in the houses and tents until they are almost grown up and do not put on the natit until they are fifteen or sixteen. As soon as a youth puts on a natit, the women begin to smile at him and he is ready for marriage. When the girls put on their natit, they also put up their hair in a topknot as a sign that they are ready for marriage. Neither boy nor girl needs any further preparation for marriage. Each can carry on the work that is required of him; they have liberal sex knowledge, for there is no privacy achieved or desired in sex; they have no social structure to learn, no formalized ritual. They are as they are and that is the way the society takes them.

## Summary

The Ammassalik have achieved a society that is highly individualistic. Each couple is a self-sufficing economic unit in a community with a minimum of social forms, and there are no effective social sanctions to regulate murder, competition for women, or economic activities. There are occasions for cooperation which are implicit in their relations with the environment, but when they occur actual cooperation is minimized. There are occasions for competition, and competition occurs realistically as conflict for the only fixed goods which are limited in their otherwise limitless environment—women to serve as economic partners. It is competition that is without rivalry. The one place where rivalry occurs is in the juridical drum songs, and these quickly lose that aspect and tend to become pleasant, sociable affairs which all enjoy. The society sets up no one goal, and a man can attain importance as a skillful hunter, or angakok, or drum singer if he also has the proper arrogant personality traits. Social cohesion is at a minimum. There is no social coercion, no judgment is passed, and no man's importance is considered relative to that of another. Within this open field an individual is allowed a latitude few societies could tolerate.

*Bibliography*

BOAS, FRANZ: "The Central Eskimo," *Report of the Bureau of American Ethnology*, Vol. 6.
THALBITZER, W. (editor): *Meddelelser om Grønland*, Vols. 39 and 40.

### CASE HISTORIES
### CASE 1

Ukutiak is a shrewd lively man of about thirty-five. His wife died from some chest ailment. Two weeks later he left his house for another settlement with the intention of marrying a rather young girl. As he was dragging her out of the house she hurt her leg, and he had to go back home with his errand unaccomplished. A few days later he married Perkitigsak's former second wife. She had left the latter when he was ill and appeared likely to go mad (delirious). A short while after this Ukutiak visited the ethnologist and behaved like one crazed with grief. He kept referring to the great amount of weeping he had done upon his wife's death. He said repeatedly, "Did we not pity him, who was now left all alone?" Then he spoke of his new wife and praised her needlework. Upon leaving he said that since he had observed all the necessary customs on this his first visit since his wife's death, the next time he called he would be free to smile. When we (the ethnologists) paid him a visit in his tent a few days later we found him in high spirits. He was quite charmed with his new wife, whom he kept caressing in a most intimate manner (pp. 77–79).[1]

### CASE 2

This story has been handed down as a legend.
Ariagsuak was having a drum match with a friend of his. Just as his friend was having new clothes sewn for him because he wanted to make the journey to visit Ariagsuak, the latter died. The survivor, nothing daunted,

[1] All these case histories are from Thalbitzer, Vol. 39.

carried out his original plans and set out for Ariagsuak's dwelling. His party consisted of four umiaks. As they approached Ariagsuak's house they sang out from the umiaks, and then the drum singer said, "Ariagsuak, though one of us dies, shall we still have our drum matches?" It was still in the house but the grave stones began to move. And then the people in the umiaks saw Ariagsuak come down from the sky, go to the grave from which the stone had moved, take out a shoulder-blade for a drum and a thigh bone for a drumstick (pp. 290).

The drum match was to continue after death, as it had for so many years before death took one of the contestants.

## CASE 3

He is twenty-eight and has been married three times before, but each time for only a few months. He divorced his first two wives because they did not keep his boots in order. His third wife wanted to go on a trip north-ward with her family, and Pitiga would not consent to it. She went and he divorced her. One day he saw the wife of Maratuk outside the house. Urged by his brother-in-law, Pitiga took her by force and made her his wife. It was for this reason that Maratuk challenged him to a drum match. According to Pitiga, Maratuk had stolen a seal from him. This fact was at once his defense, justification, and rebuttal. This is his song,
"I was afeard when I heard thou wouldst challenge me to a drum dance, ah! ja! ja! etc. (Between each verse)
Thou jeerest at me because thou deemest I am too unskillful!
Thou wouldst challenge me to a drum dance because I am alone, and thou deemest I am unskillful!
Oh! how forgetful thou art, though! It is very bad to be so forgetful!
Dost thou remember the time when thou couldst not live with others and we received thee into our house? and now thou will challenge me to a drum dance!
Why were we so foolish to take thee in and give thee a place in our house!
Thou didst bring us no good, thou didst take up room, eat from us, steal from us!" (pp. 301–302).

Previously Pitiga had taken the gall of a dead man and cast it on the spot where a girl had urinated. He did this as punishment for her refusal to lie with him. She died a short time after (p. 101).

## CASE 4

Igsiavik was a young man of twenty-two. His first wife had died after he had divorced her. His second wife, an elderly woman, he was divorced from when her former husband insisted that she return to him. Igsiavik cried when this happened. (She afterward married another man.) Last winter Igsiavik married Avgo's daughter. But one day, about six months later, when they were capelin fishing she ran away from him. (She then married Ipatikajik.) Igsaivik got his fourth wife by robbing Misuar-nianga (aged twenty) of his wife Jatuak while the latter were capelin fishing. Jatuak is eighteen, the daughter of Kutuluk, and was Misuarnianga's second wife. She had tired of him and would not let him touch her; but he still wanted her. This was the state of affairs when Igsiavik took her. For this Misuarnianga challenged Igsiavik to a drum dance. By this time they had already had many encounters, had sung at each other many times.

Misuarnianga then married a girl of seventeen, Aguluk, whom he stabbed with a knife in the thigh. She too had shrunk from him when he tried to touch her, and went with Igsiavik's brother when he took her. When Misuarnianga's "house father," who was his uncle, rebuked him, he went to another uncle in another settlement. He remained single for six months. Then he married Utukulok, aged twenty-two, who after seven marriages was without a husband. This marriage lasted but a short while, for Utukulok returned to her husband No. 6, whom she preferred above all others, when he showed he was willing to take her back.

After having been married four times, Misuarnianga could no longer get a wife because there were no more available women in the district. He later remarried Aguluk, his third wife, whom Igsiavik's brother had left because she ate up too much of his provisions.

Ipatikajik, who was twenty-five, and had taken Igsiavik's third wife from him, had previously been married to Misuarnianga's mother. (Her death had terminated that marriage.) Because he had taken Igsiavik's wife, the latter had challenged Ipatikajik to a drum match. When these contestants met, Misuarnianga substituted for Ipatikajik, his former stepfather, who, he says, is unable to sing. The real reason is that his stepfather has no new material left to use in a song against Igsiavik. In the song Misuarnianga sang he accused Igsaivik of having tried to murder a certain man.

*Igsiavik's song in reply:* (There are cries of Ah, ja, ja, etc., interspersed.)

"Thou art very fond of him and thou consortest much with him. When thou singest thou must take him around the neck, look on him, and be good to him. (Igsiavik put a stick edgewise in his opponent's mouth.)

"I cannot help my opponent not being able to sing or bring forth his voice. (He put a block of wood in his opponent's mouth and pretended to sew the mouth shut.)

"What shall we do with my opponent? He can neither sing anything, nor bring forth his voice. Since one cannot hear him, I had better stretch out his mouth and try to make it larger. (He stretched his opponent's mouth to the sides with his fingers, crammed it full of blubber, then gagged it with a stick.)

"My opponent has much to say against me. He says I wanted to do Akenatsiak a hurt and would have slain him. When we came hither from the south, it was thou who didst first challenge Akenatsiak to a drum match. (He put a thong in his opponent's mouth and tied it up under the rafters.)

"I would not have done a hurt to Akenatsiak nor slain him, and I know not why I should have done such a thing.

"It must be no doubt because we are both after his (Ipatikajik) wife that he accuses me of it.

"When he sings at me again I shall also sing at him again."

This is part of the song given. The whole song lasted an hour. Each time Igsiavik mocked Misuarnianga between the verses by playing those tricks on him, the latter showed his indifference by encouraging the onlookers to shout and laugh at him (p. 303).

Sanimuinak, a man of thirty, was an angakok and a smart hunter. Last spring he had two wives. For one of them, Piutek, he had given her father a knife. He had been married to her for several years and had had two sons with her. Amakotak, the other wife, was taken from him soon after marriage by Uitinak in revenge for Sanimuinak's having been the one to urge Ingmalukuluk to take Uitinak's former wife (she was Piutek's sister). According to Uitinak this was done because he failed to catch anything for five days. When Uitinak found his wife had gone he was approached by Amakotak's mother who urged him to take her daughter away from Sanimuinak who, she said, could not support two wives. Amakotak was willing to leave Sanimuinak because he habitually scolded and abused her, and such conduct had made both her and her mother angry and restive. So Amakotak left him for Uitinak.

Sanimuinak was in the habit of making visits when provisions were low at home, and from one of these he unexpectedly brought back a new wife, Utukulok. (See Case 4.) He was her seventh husband. She had left her sixth husband because she had, by her violent impatience, killed the child she was about to deliver and had, for this, been made to feel like a second wife. She had also been accused of being a witch and of having collected human sinews with which to kill her husband. Sanimuinak had won her at the game of "Putting out the Lamps," and had carried her off, apparently by force.

When Piutek saw the new wife she was very angry and began to scold her husband. He flew into a rage, beat her, and even stabbed her in the knee. As usual the other inmates of the house watched this connubial quarrel with perfect equanimity. The new wife, Utukulok, retreated to the stall of a distant family. The next day Sanimuinak went off to a near-by place to eat some narwhal flesh, a delicacy, leaving his wives to make it up between them. Sanimuinak's mother scolded Utukulok, who still clung to her corner though she had slept with Sanimuinak that night, while Piutek watched her mother-in-law approvingly. The old woman accused the girl of having been repudiated by her previous husband and, to escape from an unpleasant situation, had begged Sanimuinak to take her with him. She also said, "There is no room for that long creature here and for that matter she has no business to be here." (Sanimuinak's stall was four feet long.) But by the time the husband returned, several days later, amicable relations had been restored and they were all living peacefully in the stall.

Sanimuinak told the ethnologist that Utukulok was his foster daughter, not his second wife. A few days later Sanimuinak with Piutek visited the ethnologist. He started to tell how he had performed tornak incantations to cure his new "foster daughter" of a chest ailment. At this an amicable dispute ensued between the couple, Piutek maintaining that her husband was lying, that Utukulok was his wife. After much protesting Sanimiunak admitted it, and said that he had taken her so that he might have her to help row his umiak when he traveled south next summer.  He was embarrassed when Piutek described the beating he had given her.  The relations between them were most friendly.  It seemed almost as though Sanimiunak regretted having taken a second wife.

A few days later Utukulok seized the chance to leave Sanimuinak and travel with some visitors to another settlement.  There she immediately married a young man (Misuarnianga).  This eighth marriage of hers lasted but three weeks, when she left to go back to her sixth husband.  This man took her back because she told him that she had missed him so she could not sleep at night.

A few days after Utukulok had left Sanimuinak, his housemate Pitiga caught him trying to get hold of his wife.  Pitiga is now Sanimuinak's enemy and watches him covertly (pp. 71–73).

## CASE 6

In the winter of 1881–1882 there lived in one house Kunit, an angakok, his parents and his wife, Aistiva, and their two children.  Aistiva's mother and her husband, two nearly grown-up sons, two nearly grown-up daughters, and three small children.  Also Aistiva's sister and her husband (a cousin of Kutuluk) and their two children.  There were nineteen in all, divided into four families with five hunters.  For a while there was no hunting and all the food on hand was used up.  Kunit went to another settlement to get aid, but his return was cut off.  His parents were the first to die and were thrown into the sea.  Kutuluk's cousin went for aid but froze to death on his way back.  Spring came.  The survivors were in great extremity.  There was no blubber left for fuel to keep them warm.  One by one they died.  During April the survivors ate the dead in order to keep alive.  When Kunit finally reached them there was only Aistiva and her mother left.  The latter had joined in eating her husband, eight of her children, and four grandchildren (pp. 131–132).

In the spring of 1892–1893, the Eskimo found a house in Ammassalik fiord where all the inhabitants were dead.  It contained the bodies of Kunit, his wife, four children, and his wife's mother.  Since there was food around it was evident that they had not died of starvation.  It was supposed that they had been scared to death by the angry souls of the people who had been eaten by Kunit's wife and mother-in-law during a famine ten years previous.  "The souls had evidently made their appearance and frightened them to death" (p. 675).

## CASE 7

Angmalilik was Maratuk's mother.  (He was one of the outstanding angakut in the community.)  She had married a man much younger than herself who beat her constantly because she was unfaithful and a bad housekeeper.  To punish his stepfather for such treatment to his mother, Maratuk killed him.  It happened thus.  Maratuk and his cousin Sanimuinak were out in their kaiaks when they met the stepfather.  Maratuk thrust his harpoon at him, striking him in the loins.  The stepfather shrieked and tried to escape, but Sanimuinak killed him by harpooning him in his back.

Then Angmalilik seduced Avgo, a very great angakok, into marrying her although one of his wives was her own daughter. The daughter was so wrought up over her mother's action that she drowned herself.

Toward the end of February Avgo, Angamalilik, his new second wife, and several others started on a long trip to visit Holm. This hard trip exhausted Angmalilik, and she was forced to rest while the others pushed on to the nearest settlement. From there they went back to fetch her with a sledge and found her badly frozen. Her legs and thighs were so badly frozen that she was forced to stay at the settlement for six weeks. In that house lived the kin of her husband, whom her son had murdered! As soon as it was possible to travel, Maratuk made a long and arduous journey to take his invalided mother back home. It was also risky for him to walk thus right into the camp of his enemies.

Later, because her legs were still so swollen with frost, Angmalilik got tired of life and drowned herself (pp. 64–65).

### CASE 8

Drum song of Tigajak or the man who desired to have a son.

A man who was unable to get his wife with child, urged her to have intercourse with other men in order that she might become pregnant. When she did so, her husband became jealous and began to beat her. The man she had had intercourse with challenged the husband to a drum match and sang:
"In warm weather when I am among women I must go with my drawers down,

People who can't get sons, should not think of lying with women.

Thou saidst to her that she should seek intercourse with other men that she might have children.

But when she lay with other men, thou nevertheless didst become jealous and beat her!

Thou art not the only one who owns her, so thou shouldst not beat her! ah ja! ja!" (pp. 303–304).

### CASE 9

The ethnologists were asked by the mother of Uitinak's pretty young wife to lay our hands on her abdomen in the hope that it would help her conceive, since both women were afraid that Uitinak would leave the girl because she was childless (p. 70).

### CASE 10

At Imarsavik (Southeast Greenland) there were twenty-five persons with only five hunters. The fathers, therefore, trained their daughters to hunt seals from the kaiak. A girl of twenty owned a kaiak and was a famous hunter. She was the only child of a man who was a dwarf. Another girl, who had three sisters but no brothers, also owned a kaiak and her younger sister was going to get one soon. These girls behaved and dressed like men, and they were treated by the other inhabitants as though they were. When offered presents, they did not choose any of the things women fancied, but took rather iron arrowpoints and knives (p. 76, note).

## Case 11

Extreme dread of touching a corpse is extended to include those who are in a desperate, possibly fatal accident.

Suirkak's kaiak capsized one day just as he was about to land. His father and several others who were near by made no attempt to rescue him, though it might have meant no more than giving him a paddle to grab as he floundered in the deep water (p. 75).

## Case 12

Tigajak's sister, upon her return to Ammassalik after an absence of several years, went to live with strangers instead of with her father. This action so grieved him that he deliberately slept outdoors so that he might get sick. He accomplished his own end (p. 147).

## Case 13

A man reproached his mother-in-law with being so old that she was of no use in the world. He told her he could not understand why she did not die. After that she threw herself into the sea (p. 147).

## Case 14

Dead house at Nualik.

The objects brought back from the dead house at Nualik were shown to the people at Ammassalik. They recognized them as belonging to a man who with some other families had journeyed northward about ten years before. Nothing had been heard of them since. Circumstances pointed to the fact that these thirty Eskimo had been overcome by some catastrophe—hunger or poisoning from rotten meat. The settlement they had started was about eighty miles from their native district (pp. 323, 346–347).

## Case 15

This child is the son of Utuak (Case 19).

A thirteen-year-old lad had already caught thirty seals, the first at ten. His father, who was not such a good hunter and had a large family—two wives and seven children—stole a kaiak for this eldest son from another boy who lived in another settlement (p. 64).

## Case 16

Ilinguaki had living with him his wife and, in addition, Apusuk, an elderly woman who had been discarded as wife some years back because an illness had left her marked with huge scars. Apusuk submitted to her fate, was fond of Ilinguaki, and adored his children by a former marriage, to whom she acted as foster mother (p. 68).

### Case 17

Perkiligsak was the most skillful hunter on his fiord. He poisoned his brother's son. Perkiligsak had lived in a tent during the summer with his brother. The latter left, abandoning his son. People said the household was large enough without the boy, and therefore Perkiligsak had put him to death (pp. 102–103).

### Case 18

Avgo (see Case 7) was feared and hated by all, yet powerful enough to stay a whole month in the midst of his enemies. He was accused of killing people both actually and magically and taking what he wanted. The only good trait he had was his affection for his children: he paid visits to two divorced wives in order to keep in touch with his children. He and Maratuk having committed several crimes, did not feel safe where they were and so they moved with their families to Sermiligak fiord. When Holm said he was going there to visit these two men, all the people warned him against it. When they saw their advice was disregarded they asked him to rid the world of these two bad men by shooting them (pp. 142–143, 146).

### Case 19

Utuak, a man with two wives and seven children, had once been an able hunter. He had tried to become an angakok, but had not received the necessary supernatural sanction and had become violently agnostic. When his hunting skill failed him, he went to the angakut for help; this too was fruitless. More than ever he was a disbeliever in angakokism. At the same time he lived in terror of their vengeance. Thus when Avgo and Maratuk were said to be going to Sermiligak fiord (see Case 18) where Utuak lived, the latter was so alarmed that he fled precipitously, leaving his umiak behind. Avgo took his umiak immediately. Today Utuak lives on the charity of Kutuluk and dares not go out hunting alone for fear of some angakok's vengeance (pp. 142–143).

### Case 20

Adliortortuk, who lived far inside the Ammassalik fiord, caught a narwhal. As is customary he shared his catch with the inmates of his house, his neighbors, and all strangers who came on visits. And that winter, when there had been no communication between his place and a near-by one, he undertook a long, very tiring trip to the place where his married sister lived. He went thirty-two miles, over hard country, in the face of a bitter wind to carry her a large parcel of meat (p. 142).

### Case 21

Holm gave Simiok a present for his child. The next day he returned and asked for a similar present, saying that he had slept that night with Amatinguak's wife, who lived in another place on the fiord. She had a little child which he now regarded as his own, just as his own was, strictly speaking, now Amatinguak's (p. 69).

## Case 22

Papik was a skillful and highly esteemed hunter.   Patuak was a younger man and no match for Papik in skill or strength.   Papik saw Patuak's young wife and desired her.   He went to where the young couple were living, taking an empty kaiak with him.   He landed, went up the shore to their tent, and without any fuss took the wife out of her tent.   He carried her to the kaiak, put her in the empty one, and paddled off with her.   Patuak was forced to be content with the loss of his wife, since Papik was so much the stronger (p. 67).

# CHAPTER III

## THE OJIBWA OF CANADA[1]

### by RUTH LANDES

The Ojibwa described in this account live in woodland and lake country at the Manitou Reserve, on the Rainy River, in southwest Ontario, on the international boundary. Manitou Reserve represents the aggregate population of seven villages, which prior to 1914 were scattered along the Canadian side of the Rainy River. In 1914 the government assembled them on the one reserve, compelling the independent, quasi-hostile local groups to assume the appearance of a single local group. In 1931–1932 there were some 230 persons living on the reserve.

The Ojibwa are hunters of big game and fur animals, and game is scarce in this part of Canada. It is probable that this is an aboriginal condition, though it has been aggravated by white settlement. All accounts of old Ojibwa life are shadowed by fear of starvation, and each man hunts for himself, alone on his trails, the hunters scattering as widely as possible in order to make the most of the thin supply of game. The household of wife and children who depend upon the man's hunting lives in complete isolation during the winter season (November-March), and households come together in village life only during certain summer months. Then three to fifteen families live for a time in close proximity, but there is no village organization. It is a time of games and ceremonies, but each family lives to itself alone.

The chief economic resource is game. Fur animals are used partly for food, but chiefly for trade with the Hudson Bay Company. Big game is used for food; the sinews are used for sewing thread; the large internal organs are used for sacks; the hide is used for moccasins, snowshoes, and children's bows, and people in the more isolated districts wore hide garments up to thirty years ago.

[1] This work is based on my own field work the results of which have not yet been published.

Hunting is done chiefly by men; hunting, they say, is a male occupation.   On his isolated estate, the husband hunts as though he were alone in the world.   He does not think of securing more game than his neighbor—rather, he has no neighbors.   Surrounding him at inaccessible distances are fellow Ojibwa all trying to keep off starvation.   Each hunter is absolutely self-dependent, never giving thought to aiding or competing with the hunters of other households.   Stories of starvation are innumerable, both in myth and in life histories, and their nightmare demon, the *windigo*, is a personification of death or insanity from constantly threatening starvation.

Every man owns privately the hunting grounds where he alone may hunt and trap.   A man stakes out his trapping territory in one or more places, and the territory cannot be crossed without permission under pain of death at sight.   The boundaries of the grounds are clearly marked by blazed trees, trails, traps, and a hunter's shack.   A land with such "improvements" upon it is tabu to all but the owner.   The trespasser can be killed by the owner's shooting at him, or by the bad medicine which the owner lays on the trails.   This medicine may simply cripple the legs of the trespasser, but this is for the time being a fate worse than death.

The absoluteness of individual ownership excludes even the closest relatives.   The closest relatives are those who are members of the same domicile.   One domicile may include persons who are terminologically unrelated or only distantly related, but those in one house are considered closer than relatives who live in other domiciles.   Children generally share the domicile of the parents.   They are forbidden the use of the trapping grounds unless they have formally asked permission, and likewise a father cannot use his son's trapping grounds without the son's consent. Even a wife rarely goes on her husband's trails unless he has requested her to accompany him.

Permission to use someone else's estate may be asked and granted by the owner.   Permission is of several sorts.   The owner sometimes stakes out large trapping grounds and conserves the resident fur animals, such as beaver, so carefully that in some seasons he may have a great number.   Then he may invite his son, or son-in-law, or friend, or father-in-law, to trap with him, the guest's catch remaining the guest's own private property. Or an owner, having staked out a new trapping area and finding himself unable to use the old, may lend the use of the old grounds to guests of his choice. Sometimes a family starving on its own grounds will go to an owner and request the limited use of the owner's trapping grounds, and this the owner usually grants. Even when several trappers work on one territory, they work independently, as though isolated on their own grounds. A competitive attitude is ruled out at the start by the conditions of the permission, which state precisely the limits of a guest's activity and the length of time he may stay. The host likes to supply his guest with the traps because this automatically limits the scale of the guest's operations; he also assigns trails. The guest must faithfully observe the conditions of the agreement.

One reason that a man may choose to invite guests upon his land is to provide company for the lonely evenings. The men usually camp together, and at night eat and enjoy the first smoke of the day together. Winter nights are the great storytelling times. The cooperation between the men is bounded by this sociability, and by the maintenance of public order on the grounds. Never more than three men are together on the grounds; and under ordinary hunting conditions even this number would be fatal.

A man acquires trapping grounds in several ways. He may stake unclaimed land. He may own property that has been given him as a gift, and property that has been given him as a death-bed bequest. If the man is seen to use the property regularly, his ownership will never be disputed, and on his death-bed he will have the right to pass it to whomsoever he pleases. Even if the land lies idle for years, it will still belong to the man who used it last, but people will begin to inquire about his intentions. These inquiries lead to permission to use the land, and perhaps to ultimate transfer.

However he has come by the land, a man owns the property outright, and in his individual name only. Relatives have no claim upon a man's land. He transfers it when he pleases and to whom he pleases. Relatives and friends do not compete for a man's affections in order to gain his land. One reason may be that people meet too seldom and too briefly to cultivate such rivalry. Another may be that there is no scarcity of land, and game is equally scarce everywhere. In fact, owners are so seldom asked for land that some forget to bequeath it.

A man also has winter fishing places which he owns in the same fashion as the trapping grounds. The winter fishing holes are on a body of water upon or near the trapping grounds. The man fishes alone. He cuts a small hole in the ice and crouches over it, covering himself and the hole with a blanket or a tiny birch-bark wigwam. He has a lance and a lantern— formerly, a cedar-bark torch. He attracts the fish with the lantern and then spears them with his lance.

The summer fishing is quite different. In summer, there is no private ownership of fishing places. The firstcomer claims a particular site, to which he has rights for the length of his stay only. The natural conditions that govern this difference in ownership are obvious, for in summer the waters are crowded with spawning fish. Of recent years, Manitou has been suffering a shortage of fish due to the pollution of the water by white settlements, but the Ojibwa have not yet altered their rules regarding summer fishing. At Ponemah, however, the neighboring American village, summer fishing sites are privately owned, owing perhaps to Ponemah's closer contact with white settlers. However, the fishing, in summer and winter alike, is conducted in the same individualist fashion. Each man fishes for himself, even if a son or a father is fishing a few feet away. A certain competitiveness appears in summer which is lacking in winter, when a man hunts all alone in the world. This competition expresses itself in bandying words, and sometimes in vandalism, like the cutting or sinking of a neighbor's nets. The suspected culprit is punished in kind.

The game and fish that a man catches in winter are his private property. When he returns with them to the lodge, after a few days or weeks on the trail, he decides what to do with them. When he sets certain furs aside for trading, no one in the household can claim them. If he hands other furs to his wife, or daughter, or son, these belong to them to do with as they see fit. When he gives game to his wife, this too becomes his wife's, and he has lost all claim to it. It is never said that a man gives game to his wife for her use in making food and clothing for the family; but they phrase it that a man gives game to his wife and that therefore the game belongs to her to do with as she pleases. And the average husband never questions his wife about its disposal.

The wife now employs "her" property in the manufacture of food and clothing. She gives the finished product to her husband, immature children, and herself. When these gifts have been given, they become the property of the recipients.

Thus the Ojibwa phrase an objectively cooperative economy in the most individualistic terms. The man hunts alone on his isolated trails; the wife works alone in the wigwam, with the occasional assistance of her children or elderly mother; and they exchange the products of their work.

The woman is engaged in many more tasks than the man, and does them alone, though she is surrounded and occasionally aided by her young children. Besides cooking and making clothing, she cures meat and fish; sets out fish nets; traps rabbits; embroiders with porcupine quills or beads; tans leather; prepares bark for roofing and mats; dries sinews for thread; rolls native twine; brews native dyes; cleans and mends her and her husband's utensils; makes bark utensils for herself; weaves fish nets, mats, and rabbit robes; makes the necessary sacrifices when her husband has killed bear and moose. The products of her labor are enjoyed by the family, so that the wife, viewed objectively, is working for the domicile. But the native phrasing is that the wife owns the product of her work, and distributes it as she pleases.

The division of labor is primarily sexual, and regardless of age. A couple is supposed to be, and ordinarily is, self-sufficient. A couple is man and wife; but before young people are married, a couple may consist of brother and sister. The boy, taught by his father, will have his own trapping trails; he will bring his catch to the parental wigwam, where it will be transferred to his adolescent sister, who in her turn has been taught by her mother and grandmother.

The division of labor assigns domestic and relatively sedentary work to women, and the active, nondomestic work like hunting and trapping to men. But man and his activities are thought to be more important than woman and her work. So the division of labor is not the cooperation of individuals possessing equal status, but the cooperation of unequal individuals. Tremendous cultural pressure is massed behind this status distinction between men and women, a pressure which commences at the hour of birth. A man is continuously stimulated by his desire for prestige; a woman has no such incentive.

About the middle of March when the snow begins to melt, each family moves to its maple-sugar groves. Maple-sugar manufacture is considered chiefly woman's work, though men may cooperate in tapping the trees; and many women own groves upon which they work with their husbands. The person who taps a maple "owns" the gash and the sap which drips from it. Only he, or she, may remove it. Then he, or she, brings it to the great vats where the sap is boiling. The vats are owned by the woman, the housekeeper. When the sap is brought to the vats, it is given to the woman, who now owns it. Man and wife, whichever happens to be near, take turns at stirring the boiling liquid. Usually it is the wife. Sometimes she undertakes all the work, and the man spends these days in trapping. Just as men sometimes invite guests upon their trapping estates, so they invite families to work their maple estates. At sugar time, however, guests are far more usual than they are in winter. There are many maple groves, and some people have hundreds of trees upon their estates. The trees are all owned by one person, the man or the wife, and the grown children work in the capacity of guests. In addition to the children who have the status of guests, another household may be invited. This outside household usually lives under the same roof as the host's household. The birch-bark wigwam is furnished by the women of both households, and each woman owns her contribution. Each family occupies its own half of the wigwam, and the housekeeping of each half is conducted independently. The guest's work on the groves is conducted as independently as the housekeeping. The host stipulates the number of hours a day his guests may work, the number of trees, draining pans, and vats that may be used. So far as possible, the host tries to supply his guest with the utensils needed, for this will automatically limit the guest's work. All that such a guest produces for himself is his own property.

If no cooperation exists between a host and his guest, between a man and his neighbors, it is not surprising to find that there is no competition. A man claims as large a grove as he thinks he can handle, and is satisfied with the results. Nor does he think of working faster or more productively than his neighbor. The conditions of the host's permission prevent open competition.

Occasionally workers on a grove will cooperate, though this is not common. This is generally the case when the workers are women, and no men are about. Thus, one widow invited her sisters to share her grove. The women, two of whom had children, pooled all their operations and divided the finished products. These women were unusual for their spirit of mutual cooperation, though they were haughtily individualistic toward others. They shared their trapping trails and fishing places also, though they nevertheless preserved the fundamental forms of owning their land and property individually.

During this season, when people live closer together, the hosts and guests enjoy themselves immensely. The wives work side by side and gossip together. The children scamper together through the woods. The men loll about at night in the center of the wigwam, the place of honor, smoke, and tell stories. People from neighboring groves sometimes visit one another in the evenings. At the close of the sugar season, or during the village season, different families make their arrangements for the next season, which are based solely on personal preference.

The sugar season ends late in May, when the snow is off the ground, and the earth is thawing. Then each family moves to the traditional village site. A village is a group of households that collect about some body of water where there is fishing and berrying. Aboriginal villages, in prereservation days, consisted of from three to fifteen families. In Canada, the families in these villages were always closely related. The nucleus of the village would be an old couple surrounded by their married sons and daughters. These would be joined either temporarily or permanently by other relatives. Friends might also come. However, no outsiders could take up residence and stay unless they were welcome to the original settlers. This attitude in the village approximates that of a landowner who, having rights over his lands, may or may not grant permission to use them.

It must be stressed that the village is not a political unit. It is not a unit of any sort. It is an aggregate of households that are mutually independent, but that have been drawn together through desire for sociability. A family is allowed to come and go at will.

The summer activities are berry picking and fishing, and, for housewives, the trapping of rabbits. Berry and fishing sites are not privately owned. The firstcomer claims the site for the length of time he remains on the spot. The berries and fish appear inexhaustible to the Ojibwa, and, consistent with this view of the abundance of these natural resources, there is no urge to stake out private claims. I do not know of any Indians who have ever tried to do so. This absence of private property in berry patches and fishing places is the more impressive because of the high value placed upon these articles of food. Berries are preserved and hoarded for religious ceremonials and for winter use, and sturgeon, whitefish, and pike are considered the kings of fish, and are honored in the oldest myths as well as in the latest idioms of conversation. They are considered the equals of beaver and lynx.

The Canadian attitude toward berry and fishing sites must be contrasted with that of the Minnesota village, Ponemah, only ninety miles to the south, where there is terrific competition over the best berry patches. The berries are sold to the white market, and men, women, and children all work at berry picking, and the wealthier families hire assistants. However, even in Ponemah there is no ownership of berry patches by private individuals. The Indians are not allowed off the reservation, so the patches are viewed as village property, to portions of which the firstcomers each season make claim. As a result of this, pickers from other villages or reservations are violently resented, and blows are frequent. The summer fishing sites, however, are owned privately, just as are groves and trapping grounds, and the produce is sold to the commercial market. Competition is so keen in Minnesota that trespassing on fishing sites and acts of vandalism occur.

In Canada the attitude is that berry picking is women's work. Mother and daughter go out picking together; often a mother or a grown girl goes picking alone. While the women pick berries, the men lounge about, smoking, drinking, talking. They may rehearse their supernatural techniques. They may look for herbs or bark. Whatever they do is dictated by their individual whims, for the summer, even more than the spring, is vacation time for men. The woman returns with the berries she has spent hours in picking, and they are "hers." She prepares them for food, however, and the food is eaten by husband and children. If a woman decides to sell some of her berries to another Indian household or to a neighboring white family, she has a perfect right to do so, and to keep the price she receives. But this is not done regularly.

There are, or were, relatively few polygynous marriages among the Ojibwa. But among those that persisted and where the women were friendly, the several wives of a man might pick berries in company. Among such women, according to reports, there was neither competition nor cooperation in the job at hand. Each woman picked as though she were alone in the world. The women picked together because they desired company, or because they feared a rumored kidnaper.

Summer fishing is carried on by men and women, though the women fish more than the men. The wife sets out her net. Sometimes she is assisted by an adolescent daughter, sometimes by her husband. But she can manage very well alone, and often works in solitude. She hauls in her fish the next morning, and spreads the net to dry. Then at twilight she sets the net out again. Even when households neighbor one another, the women and men of the separate domiciles set out their nets individually, at the same time joking and talking together.

Nets usually belong to the woman because she makes them. However, she lends her nets to her husband if he asks for them. To that extent he is a "guest" of his wife, for he has no rights over the net beyond the conditions under which he borrows it. The catch, if he has set out the net, belongs to him, but whether the fish is husband's or wife's, they go into the pot, and all in the family are invited to eat.

Dances occur in the summer, during the village period, because at that time many people are available and because it is easy to travel. Most curing, especially the elaborate MIde or Grand Medicine ceremonial, also takes place in the summer, because then many doctors are at hand, and many patients.

By the middle of August, the village breaks up, and each family moves to the rice beds. The firstcomer at a rice-harvesting site claims the site. At some of the richer rice beds, a number of families may be working alongside one another, but they never cooperate; each couple works individually. The man poles the boat, and his wife knocks off the heads of rice. The canoe is usually owned by the man, for he made it. The rice is sometimes said to be owned by the woman, for she harvested it; sometimes it is said to be owned by the man and the woman, for the man helped in poling the boat. The couple cooperates in the succeeding stages of parching the rice grains in the sun and by the fire; the man treads the rice to loosen the chaff; later the woman winnows and stores the rice. Each stage, and the rice worked at each stage, is owned by the worker. However, if any part of the rice is sold, it is usually sold by the woman. The money belongs to her, to use as she likes. It is unlikely, however, that a woman would sell rice if her husband objected strenuously, not because she felt his authority, but because she would choose to avoid ill-feeling in the household. Again, a cooperative situation is phrased individualistically.

Since a number of families, each eager for their own supplies of rice, crowd around a desirable rice bed, it would appear that such a situation might become competitive. The rice beds are very near the international boundary, extending north and a few hundred miles south of it. The people who gather around these beds, particularly those on the American side, have developed an organization that is designed to mute competition. An old experienced man is chosen by common consent to set the hours of work, and to announce when the rice bed must be closed to additional families. The leader has no executive authority, and anyone can flout him, but no one does. A flouter finds it more fruitful to migrate to another rice bed. The Canadian beds are now too sparse to attract many harvesters, and the more ambitious go to their relatives in the United States to join them on their rice-making expeditions. In those rice villages which are organized under a leader, while cutthroat competition is avoided, nevertheless there is still no real cooperation. Each couple is out for itself. Each pair knows what minimum of rice it must harvest, and what maximum it can manage. No display of rice is ever made. Competitiveness, like cooperativeness, may be more highly developed on the American than on the Canadian side, because a small white market for the purchase of wild rice is appearing.

Rice harvesting and manufacture lasts about a month. Toward the middle and end of September, the individual families move away, en route to their winter estates. On the way, each family halts at various lakes to hunt migrating ducks. The meat is used as food; down feathers are sometimes saved for future use in costumery; the skin is frequently prepared as a sack. By November each family is isolated on its own winter hunting grounds.

Property, as we have seen, is individually owned. The test of ownership comes when a person asks for the loan of something. A man cannot lend his wife's net; a woman cannot lend her husband's horse. When a poor person requests a charitable gift of fish, only the one who caught the fish can give it away. The borrower must be referred to the owner.

People who come to borrow are often granted their requests, provided they are likely to respect the conditions of the loan. It is difficult to refuse the request of a borrower because of the practice and fear of sorcery. A borrower who has been refused will feel shamed and will retaliate at one time or another by practicing sorcery upon the one who refused. On the other hand, any violation of the conditions of a loan would be highly resented, and I know of no cases where such conditions have been violated. Sometimes drunken people seize property without requesting permission. Sturgeon became drunk one night and took his son's boat without notice. In his drunken state he abandoned the boat down the river. The boat was missing for days before the culprit was discovered. However, no words were exchanged because "John isn't one to throw lip to anyone, and certainly not to his father." But there was a deep undercurrent of resentment on the part of John's family.

The property that above all else confers power upon the possessor is supernatural, and it is hardly too strong to call the Ojibwa owner of such power a sorcerer. Each local group is dominated by such men—and, sometimes, women. They are influential in forming war parties, in organizing the *ogima* or "Chief" dance and the MIde ceremonial, and they are solicited as curers and diviners. Their supernatural powers are owned and employed in a fashion that strictly parallels the ownership and use of material property. That is, they are owned by individuals who have absolute rights over them. Supernatural powers are secured in four ways, the way depending upon the specific supernatural power desired. Some powers are secured by vision, and others by purchase, while rights to certain limited powers are validated by experience only, and other ownership rights are validated by a combination of vision and purchase. Vision powers are secured by a person, typically male, who goes out alone to supplicate the supernatural. Alone, he passes days of hunger and thirst, yearning for the realization of his hopes. If he is successful, he is vouchsafed a vision which is given him in the most personal terms: the supernatural benefactor says, "My grandchild [or brother or sweetheart or any other relationship term which has emotional significance], I have taken pity upon you. [This is a very respectful phrase, not a patronizing one.] I have seen you in your sufferings, and I have taken pity upon you. I will give you something to amuse yourself with." And then a moving panorama unfolds in which the visionary sees what he will, henceforth, be able to practice. He may see an act of divining, or a successful hunt or warpath. What he sees in his vision will come to pass. The gift, even when a doctoring gift, need not be used for the good of the people, though a few individuals say that they believe doctors receive their gifts in order to help the people. (I have never heard a doctor say this about himself.) It is given with the recommendation that it "amuse" the beneficiary. The guardian spirit is not thought of as philanthropically minded. The beneficiary knows that his guardian expects a return for his gift, that is, periodical offerings of tobacco. Indeed, the relationship is one of purchaser and seller. The individual supernatural sells his powerful wares to individual supplicants in return for a periodic payment of tobacco. It is explained that the supernaturals love the tobacco found in the human world. If the visionary has secured powers of curing and divining, he and his client enter into a relationship which duplicates that conceived as existing between a guardian spirit and the beneficiary. The doctor is sent for by the client and arrives at the latter's wigwam. Before he undertakes a cure, he is given plugs of tobacco by his client, and new blankets and calico, perhaps furs, are spread before him. He receives his fee in advance. This fee must be sent in part, and the rest displayed, to the doctor's guardian spirit. If this is not done, the doctor may find himself deserted by his guardian in the middle of his cure. After the terms of the contract between doctor and guardian have been fulfilled, then the contract between doctor and client can be fulfilled and the curing, or divining, ensues.

From the doctor's viewpoint, he is giving out wares in exchange for value received. He never thinks cooperatively, except in certain circumstances when a man treats a dearly loved friend or relative like a wife or child. From the client's viewpoint, he is receiving wares or services in exchange for what he pays. The case is treated on no other merits than this. Maggie said, "The [sucking doctor] used to give you four days for so many blankets and dishes; but now they are getting so they give you only three days." Thus, the objectively cooperative arrangement between beneficiary and guardian spirit, between client and doctor, is couched in the most individualistic terms.

Powers like MIde curing and evil formulas like love medicine are secured by purchase. The owner, who secured his possession by previous purchase, has the right to sell his knowledge to a solicitor. He can conduct this sale an infinite number of times, for he never forfeits title to his possession by selling his knowledge. The amount of knowledge that he passes on at any one occasion depends upon the price offered.

Ownership rights, validated by experience only, are used by an individual in the earlier stages of midwifery, and in the conduct of a funeral. Public opinion recognizes the title by employing the qualified person. This form and kind of ownership is open to all who care to qualify. Since the title is secured without payment, the services are not paid for in advance, nor is the sum standardized. The functionary is paid at the end of his performance, and paid whatever the beneficiary cares to give. This, too, is a situation that is objectively cooperative, but is phrased in individualistic terms.

The sucking-doctor practice is validated by a combination of vision and purchase. The technique of sucking and like techniques are secured by vision. But certain herbal prescriptions are used which may only be secured by purchase from other sucking doctors. The securing and exercise of these property rights are the same as in those described above.

Women are admitted to the ownership and practice of all the forms of supernatural property except divining, and in the MIde hierarchy of powers they are allowed the ownership and practice of all but the very highest rank of power. The debarring of women is not thought to be the function of any competitive attitude, but of a precaution due to the maleficence of menstrual discharges. A few strong female characters have ignored the barrier and secured recognition as MIde practitioners of the highest rank. No woman seems to have done the same in divining.

Supernatural powers are the all-important means to influence and prestige among the Ojibwa. The close relatives of a powerful MIde shaman often obtain instruction from him, and well-known shamans are often related. This does not mean that opportunities of acquiring religious property are restricted to relatives. It means only that relatives, because they tend to live closer together than nonrelatives (as in the summer village, and as guests on the maple groves), have better opportunities than outsiders for acquiring such property. But all salable forms of property (as MIde instruction, charms) are transferred to any outsider who has the price. A vision is a form of property which is not transferable, but the pursuit is open to all, and most people have visions of varying character.

A person's rights of arbitrary disposal of his property are exemplified again and again in extreme cases. Ben Spence disliked his wife, and when he died he left her nothing. He stated on his deathbed, before witnesses, that he desired all his livestock and his house to be transferred to his young daughter, to be used by her at her discretion. Mrs. Spence's second husband was very fond of her, and left her all his property. When Mrs. Spence died, she left nothing to her third husband, nor to her daughter by her first husband, but she left all to her adopted daughter, who was a white girl married to a white man. Another man was deserted by his wife shortly before his death. Upon his deathbed he stated that his deserting wife had no claims upon him, and that all he owned, cabin, furniture, horse, and trapping grounds, was to go to his elderly mother. Bombay left his valuable shamanistic paraphernalia, a gun, a canoe, and his trapping grounds to his wife; to his son, Sam, he left a sacred hand drum, a gun, and some man's clothing; to his son-in-law he left certain trapping grounds that this son-in-law had wanted. Old Medicine ordered that his paraphernalia be burned after his death. His trapping grounds lay fallow, since he had appointed no one to succeed him, and they can be claimed by the first-comer. When Madeleine Bones died, she left her pension to her baby, not to her husband or her grandmother.

Also, a person has rights of arbitrary disposal over his own self, and these cannot be disputed. A number of persons at one time or another contemplate suicide. Some momentary distress will incite them—such as a mother's scolding of a girl, the loss of a husband's affection, the death of relatives—but a momentary encouragement, like the appearance of a new lover, or a mother's soothing voice, will dissuade them. Some people do commit suicide. Others, who are afflicted with characteristic windigo insanity, order themselves burned either before or after death, and no one can gainsay them. Mrs. Cochran felt that she was becoming windigo: the people around her looked like beavers and she wanted to eat them. So she ordered her brother-in-law to strait-jacket her, stun her with an ax, and then set fire to her and her tent. While this was done, her husband and children looked on, for she had an undisputed right to dispose of herself as she chose.

While a person is acting individualistically in outlining his will, he assumes that his witnesses will cooperate with him in executing it. This is usually the case, though in some instances the will is slighted. Madeleine Bones's grandmother, Mrs. Blackbird, was notorious for her disregard of deathbed bequests. When her daughter died, having willed that her husband should inherit her property, Mrs. Blackbird simply ignored the will and seized the house and furniture that her daughter had left. When her mild-mannered son-in-law protested that some things at least should go to him, Mrs. Blackbird overruled him, and Bones stepped aside. Mrs. Blackbird did the same when her granddaughter Madeleine Bones died, and Madeleine's widowed husband, also, could not resist the old lady's formidable insistence.

There are no cases of true group ownership. Within the past fifty years the bands now assembled on the Manitou Reserve have been buying dance ceremonies from the Dakota Sioux and the American Ojibwa. The various dances are referred to as band owned. But the briefest examination shows that a dance is not owned by a band, but that constituent elements of the dance are owned each by individual members of the band. It will be remembered that the present bands represent the aboriginal villages, the old native local groups. It seems that during the truces between the Ojibwa and the Sioux, the latter came on visits to Ojibwa villages, and made "gifts" of Dakota dances to the chief men in the Ojibwa villages. Thus the Ojibwa received the Give-away and the Rabbit dances. However, the Ojibwa have no gift concept;[1] everything is exchanged through purchase and sale. So when a Sioux visitor gave Sturgeon, of the Manitou village, a dance, Sturgeon had to make a handsome return. He did not feel that his poor possessions would suffice, and called upon his fellow villagers to contribute to the pile that had to be accumulated for the return gift. All did contribute. Thereby each contributor became a part owner in the dance, and had a voice in its performance. Again, an objectively cooperative situation was transferred into an individualistic one.

## SOCIAL STRUCTURE

The largest local group, the village, is no more than a neighborhood. It is not united by any formal structure. Each local group acquires a certain tenuous coherence on account of its hostility toward other local groups. Ojibwa life may be thought of as resting on three orders of hostility. All Ojibwa-speaking persons feel a major hostility toward those of alien speech, epitomized by the Dakota Sioux. Next in order is the hostility that exists between different local groups of Ojibwa, and the third is the hostility felt by any household toward another, whether or not of the same village. Thus, the group feeling foisted upon a village by the fact of its separateness from other villages is constantly threatened by the latent hostilities of its constituent households. Politically and economically the Ojibwa are an atomistic society. Functionally, the household is the irreducible unit; but in the cultural thought, the individual person is the unit.

The very kinship terminology isolates the domestic household relatives from other relatives. The terms for mother, father, son, daughter, are applied only within the biological family, while all other terms are widely classificatory. This linguistic fact is strikingly consistent with the physical, economic, political,

---

[1] Except that bequests are made on the deathbed. Also, individuals irregularly and whimsically and privately give gifts to people they like. So one may give some relative or loved friend a gift of vegetables or maple sugar. Sometimes trapping grounds are discarded in the form of giving the title to another, as to a son-in-law or father.

and affective separateness of the domestic relatives from all other people.

In northwestern parts of Ontario and in southeast Manitoba, about Buffalo Point, the parents of one domestic household try to marry their child to the child of that other domestic household which is least hostile to it. Prescriptively, this latter household is that of a parent's sibling of opposite sex: that is, the child of a mother's brother, or of a father's sister, is sought in marriage. And the kinship terminology makes these identifications. That is, the term for "cross-cousin of opposite sex" is the only term for "sweetheart"; the term for "cross-cousin of same sex" minus an affix is the only term for "sibling-in-law of the same sex"; the term for "cross-cousin of opposite sex" minus an affix is the term for "sibling-in-law of opposite sex"; the term for "father's sister" minus an affix is the term for "mother-in-law," but the former term (with affix) is preferred. The same equations are made for "mother's brother" and "father-in-law"; for "cross-niece" and "daughter-in-law"; for "cross-nephew" and "son-in-law." Siblings of opposite sex are prescriptively the most loyally devoted of relatives; indeed before they marry, the brother and sister cooperate economically, as do man and wife. The family of a man's sister is doubly bound to the family of the man, for terminologically, and often actually, the sister's husband is "brother" to the man's wife. And the family of a woman's brother is also doubly bound to the family of the woman, for again the brother's wife is "sister" to the woman's husband. Cross-cousins are trained from the day of birth to behave toward one another as prospective mates; and all courting behavior between persons who are unrelated but eligible in marriage is patterned after the conduct of cross-cousins.

Despite the prescribed friendship and affection existing between households of cross-cousins, a strong feeling of self-consciousness and even of hostility exists. For when cross-cousins meet, they must try to embarrass one another. They "joke" one another, making the most vulgar allegations, by their standards as well as ours. But being "kind" relatives, no one can take offense. Cross-cousins who do not joke in this way are considered boorish, as not playing the social game. On the other hand, a person's behavior toward his prospective parents-in-law is characterized by the most painstaking respect, the most punctilious diffidence, the greatest efforts to avoid giving offense.   And a person behaves in the same way toward his prospective child-in-law (cross-niece and cross-nephew).

At the Manitou there is a blanket tabu on marriage between all relatives, which means that cross-cousin marriage, also, is forbidden.   But this seems a recent development, a consequence of contact with the Dakota Sioux.   Nevertheless the categories of relationship are just the same, and the corresponding behavior is the same.

It is well recognized that parents have the right to arrange marriage for their children.   Either parents, but usually the parents of the boy, make initial gifts to the father of the other. Then the couple is considered betrothed, and shortly become married by sleeping together in the wigwam of the girl's parents. Parents have various reasons for proposing a marriage.   Sometimes they want to cement a friendship with another family, regardless of relationship ties.   Sometimes the desired child-in-law possesses valuable abilities, such as industriousness or supernatural power.   More rarely, they see a budding romance between their child and the other.

In most cases the child has the right to refuse the arrangement made by his parents.   The one exception occurs when the prospective spouse of a girl, or the prospective parent-in-law of a child, are sorcerers.   Then the child can refuse only under pain of horrible disease and death which she incurs because of the humiliation put upon the prospective groom.   Even so, some girls refuse.   Children also refuse the marriage arrangements of the parents when these arrangements conflict with their private inclinations.   Sentimental and romantic love are valued tremendously, and marriage is supposed to be the fulfillment of this attraction.

Marriage is short- or long-lived according to the private inclinations of one or both partners.   But most marriages are fairly short and very stormy.   Spouses kick and beat one another, use abusive language, desert one another, and, if they choose, reunite.   Since each household is independent of every other, no one has the right to interfere with the course of marital relations.   Sometimes people quietly desert spouses with whom they have always gotten along well, because they have fallen violently in love again.   These postmarital loves are sometimes highly romantic, devoted, and permanent affairs; the earlier marriage is broken up and the new household established.

If the deserted person is a man, he usually feels his humiliation keenly, and devotes his energies to retaliation. A deserted woman, also, feels terribly humiliated but seldom attempts retaliation. Usually she quietly remarries. A man may pursue his wife even if he is not in love with her, and try to coax her back, for he believes that she has left him because she finds him undesirable, and this slight he cannot endure. If she refuses he usually swears to injure her. One shaman for several years tried to win back his wife, who had left him after ten years of marriage. Then he threatened her with his sorcery. Soon she became paralyzed and remained helpless for nine years. If a wife has gone off with a lover, or has at some time remarried, a deserted husband tries to injure both the woman and the man. Often he tries to kill the man, for he knows that this will hurt the woman, who obviously prefers the second to him. It will also show that he is superior, and has more power than his rival. Marsh Woman deserted her first husband. Later he pursued her and her second husband. At the end of ten years he succeeded in killing Marsh Woman's second husband by sorcery. Then he forced Marsh Woman to live with him. He wanted to show her that he was not a man to be easily dismissed. One night, some time later, Marsh Woman split his skull open.

The attitude of the husband was not strictly competitive. He wished to murder his rival and take back his wife in order to restore his self-esteem, rather than because he desired his wife for herself.

One woman who was deserted by her husband but, as is conventional among women, who did not attempt overt retaliation expressed herself as follows when her husband wished to return to her: "You made me so ashamed when you left me! People thought that you left me because you did not want me any more. They thought I must be a loose woman! I never want to see you any more. Go away and forget that you ever knew me. When I see you it reminds me of my shame. I don't want to see you or any other man. If I was not good enough for you, no decent man can want me. Oh . . . you made me so ashamed! Go away!'

Polygyny was allowed, but seldom practiced, in spite of the fact that the men, many of whom were killed in war, must have been fewer in number than the women. When a man came home with a second wife, the first wife almost always deserted him. Since marriage was supposed to be, and generally was, contracted in response to a personal attraction, the choice of a second wife appeared to the first wife as a humiliating announcement that she had lost her hold on her husband. She would leave, and there was no way to bring her back. One woman bargained with her husband that she would remain with him if he sent back the second wife, which he did. Even the second wife does not like a polygynous marriage, and may have married the man not knowing that he was already married.

That certain polygynous marriages persist where the wives are not lovemates of their husbands, does not conflict with this romantic viewpoint. If a shaman had cured a girl of a dangerous illness, had "given life to her" through the power of his guardian spirits, he might receive her in payment of his priceless services. The first wife might resent the marriage, but she still endured it, recognizing that it was inevitable. The first wife herself might have been the price of a curing, a wife who knew that she could never desert because she owed her life to her husband, because he held her life in his hand. When co-wives were all of this price-for-a-curing status, the marriage persisted, and individual disruptive attitudes were muted.

There are a few plural marriages, conspicuous through the generations, that persist even though the husband had taken a second wife for love. The first wife, in such cases, is indifferent to the shame of lost love, and prefers the quiet continuance of old habits. One or two such wives were completely displaced sexually by the second wife, but even continued to be friendly with the favorite wife.

Plural marriage among the Ojibwa is not a cooperative arrangement but a difficult concession to a man's desire to display his individual superiority. With the stress on romantic, selective, possessive love, and upon a self-conscious individualism, it is indeed a feat for a man to carry out a polygynous marriage. More than one wife is of no economic aid to an Ojibwa man, but a great economic drain. Each wife and her children have to be supported independently. Even when three wives live under one roof, the wigwam is partitioned into three apartments, and all the housekeeping details are triplicated. Co-wives do not take care of one another's children except in very exceptional cases, and a man has to hunt and trap to get meat and furs for all his wives and children. His sons are of no aid to him, for as soon as they are old enough to hunt and trap effectively, they go off on their own. As his wives die, the husband has to pay compensation money to the sib of each deceased wife.

Marriage is regulated in part by bilateral kinship and in part by the gens organization formulations. Certain localities still practice the cross-cousin form of marriage, but prohibit marriage between all other classes of relatives; and at Manitou there is a blanket tabu upon all marriage between relatives. Actually incestuous marriages are common enough through all the categories of kinship, except between parents and offspring and between siblings. And these incestuous marriages persist, owing to the independence and self-sufficiency of the domestic household. Sexual intercourse, moreover, occurs between individuals of all categories. This laxness cannot be interpreted as cultural breakdown. It probably was common, as even the Indians say, in the days of cultural vigor, owing to the extremely high premium placed on individual whim and on an individual's choice of his own course of action.

Besides relatives, sibmates are also forbidden to marry, being classed as siblings. But also within this category incestuous marriages occur, motivated by the same individualistic drives. There is no effective penalty for incest. Caustic remarks are passed behind the principals' backs, but nothing further.

The sib extends its supervision of the marriage arrangements to regulating the behavior of the surviving spouse of a deceased sibmate. The sib of the deceased states that the survivor "destroyed" the deceased and therefore must compensate the sib of the deceased. Compensation must be made in a considerable amount of real wealth, and until this debt is paid, the debtor spouse is supposed to be the property of the creditor sib. It is supposed to take two to four years before a debtor can collect sufficient wealth to clear himself or herself; and if it takes less than two years, the debtor is regarded askance as one who is overeager to forget the deceased. While a debtor, a person is supposed to mourn greatly, dress shabbily, keep his hair unkempt, and be indifferent to the opposite sex. One who dresses well during this period, and who flirts, is penalized drastically by the creditor sib, specifically, by the domestic family relatives of the deceased who are of the latter's sib.  The punishment is to strip the offender of his or her fine clothes, gash him or her on the face and body, and damage his or her property.  If the debtor marries before paying his debt, the same punishment is inflicted.  Thus, John Gane married while yet a debtor, and had the poor judgment to visit with his new wife the village of the sibmates of his deceased first spouse.  The father's brother of the deceased crept into Gane's wigwam during the night, stripped the blanket off the couple, stood them up naked, gashed their blankets and clothes, tore Gane's hair, and ripped their canoe.

Many individuals neglect the debtor obligations.  A few simply ignore them.  Some widows and widowers cannot unaided assemble sufficient wealth.  Others fall in love or have sexual relations and illegitimate children during the mourning season.  Some dislike the parents of the deceased, or dislike the deceased, and so are not interested in honoring the creditor family by deferring to the debtor obligations.

Although many persons ignore the debtor obligations, knowing the consequences and putting up with them, there is no weakening of the view that sib debts ought to be paid, and that a delinquent should be punished.  The very avenging creditors may themselves be delinquent debtors in other relationships.

The sib functions in general are slighted whenever private interests dictate.  Thus the sib categories often conflict violently with the categories of kinship.  For example, in the kinship system, mother's brother is a "great respect" relative, a potential father-in-law, but according to the gentile formula, he is a "sweetheart," a prospective spouse, because he is not a sibmate (Ojibwa have patrilineal gentes) but belongs to another sib. Consequently people who are closely related to one another sometimes choose to ignore their gentile affiliations and obligations.  However, individuals will recognize sib ties when such recognition satisfies desired ends.  Thus, a girl who chose to discourage the attentions of a distant cross-cousin, or prescriptive sweetheart, told him that they were sibmates, i.e., siblings and ineligible to marry.  On the Manitou, where there is a blanket tabu on marriage between relatives, Maggi made a great point of the fact that Philip, her fourth degree cross-cousin, was not of her sib and therefore could marry her.

The sib functions not only to supervise the mourning of the spouse of its deceased sibmate, and to collect the debt, but also to arrange for the remarriage of the survivor to a sibmate of the deceased. That is, the survivor is supposed to remarry in obedience to sib-prescribed rules of levirate and sororate. A person who has paid the debt in a satisfactory manner is automatically given in marriage to a sibling of the deceased, and if the widowed person objects, he or she is punished summarily. Some people do object. Today, since the government has forbidden polygyny, the objectors find themselves in a more comfortable position. People object to the compulsory marriage for the same reason that a young person objects to the marriage proposed by parents,—that is, because the prescribed marriage does not satisfy their individual inclinations. Since a goodly proportion of the people do not pay the sib debt, they are automatically debarred from remarriage by levirate or sororate. And since some people who have paid the debt refuse the conventional remarriage, it may be seen that a considerable number of the Ojibwa flout their own institutional arrangements. They are individualistic even in the face of culturally required behavior.

Most delinquent sib debtors take their punishment in good part, but some resent it. It may be assumed that those who take their punishment quietly understand the meaning of the sib's actions, understand their own delinquency, and to the extent of accepting their punishment cooperate with the sib. It may, also be assumed that those who resent sib action choose to ignore their obligations in the interests of personal preferences. One woman left her husband's village shortly after his death because she disliked her husband's parents and sisters. About two years later she returned to visit her husband's grave; her sisters-in-law beat her and damaged her canoe and luggage. She felt ashamed before the onlookers and swore to revenge herself upon the creditor sib. Shortly afterward, she remarried without paying her debt. She married a man who was a powerful shaman, and she persuaded him to punish her sisters-in-law shamanistically. As the years passed, it was learned that sister-in-law after sister-in-law fell ill and then died.

Outright murder does not appear to be common. Slashings frequently result from summer hostilities, but do not culminate in murder. Grievances are nursed by one or both individuals and avenged shamanistically, by sending bad medicine omens, winter starvation, and attacks of paralysis. When a person dies of winter starvation, or of some insanity, the suspected sorcerer is alleged to be the murderer. Murder might, also, result from trespass upon trapping grounds. From the viewpoint of the owner, such killing was deserved; from the viewpoint of the victim's family, this was murder.

Murder, like death on the warpath, was avenged by a close relative of the deceased, regardless of sib. The relatives who feel close to one another are those who have lived in the same household. Consequently a person's avengers are either his parents, his spouse, or his siblings. Some people ignore such a responsibility; others hasten to accept it. Those who ignore it are not penalized in any way; nor are those who observe it rewarded.

## War Party

When a man has a vision depicting success on the warpath, he sends out invitations to the men in the village inviting them to attend a "smoker" in his wigwam. When they arrive, he tells them of his vision, and requests volunteers to follow him on the warpath. Those men volunteer who trust his reputation as a warrior and visionary, and agree to train for war through the following year. They seek visions, and then repeat their visions to the self-appointed captain to secure his approval. The next summer they meet and train again. The men rejected by the captain are supposed to be debarred from the expedition, for their presence, unempowered by the supernatural, will threaten the safety of the entire party. Actually, any man who cares to flout the captain, does so. One man with a buffalo guardian spirit was turned down, as it was said that in the battle he would loom as large as a buffalo and be a target for the enemy. He went along, however, and was injured. In the criticisms made of him, he was not condemned for disobeying the captain, but for having ventured forth with so little power. Women were debarred from war, because the evil effect of their menses would injure the strength and guns of the warriors. But one famous young Amazon trained secretly, and appeared when the party was already at the edge of the prairies. She recited her vision, and all saw that she had the greatest power of all. She secured the greatest honors and supplanted the captain. The captain simply had to give way to a better man, although this "man" was a ritually excluded woman. In this way the cooperative structure of the war party is shattered. Each warrior is unmindful of his comrades, has no duties regarding them, and is intent only on increasing his own power to the highest degree of effectiveness. He spends his rest periods talking to supernaturals, fasting and thirsting, and in "making his dream so real that he can almost see it." If he is a novice, he smears charcoal about his eyes and sits apart from the rest. At the charge, there is no military formation, and no plan of battle; each warrior fights for himself. Two coups are counted on a vanquished enemy. Upon the return of the party, if they have been victorious, all sing songs; if they have met defeat, they cry. At the victory dance, the warriors are shown admiration, according to their feats on the warpath. Those who have acquitted themselves bravely acquire feathers, and the bravest—who is not necessarily the captain—is sometimes presented with a virgin bride. A man who has successfully captained a war party adds to his personal reputation and is facilitated in organizing a future party.

## MIDEWIWIN

The MIde or Grand Medicine ceremony is considered to be extremely potent in curing illness. Objectively, it is a society of curers who have acquired their powers through purchase. Each individual in the society has been instructed separately, and has paid separately for his instruction. Moreover, each individual functions separately. When a patient calls upon a MIde shaman for a cure, the shaman responds in the same way that a sucking doctor or diviner would. The MIde shaman goes to his client as an individual, regardless of his MIde colleagues. The client offers the shaman tobacco and goods, and the shaman communes with the supernaturals associated with the MIde practice. Then he commences to cure the patient. The cure lasts for several days, a length of time which depends on the number of times the patient has been cured through MIdewiwin (mystic ritual) before, and on the size of the fee. The shaman who has been called may require some of his MIde colleagues to assist him, the number varying with the complications of the cure. The patient empowers him to select his assistants, and the shaman then proceeds to hire each one individually. These shamans do not act together as a body, but each one who has been instructed in some specific MIde technique is hired on account of his special ability. Each individual therefore works alone, at the task for which he has been paid in advance.

Membership in the MIdewiwin is a source of great and much feared supernatural power, and influential men become the chief shamans in the ceremony. People know that these men have great MIde powers, bulwarked by powers of other sorts, and that they want to conduct MIde ceremonies. If ignored or crossed, such powerful men will cast dour looks that threaten sorcery on the patient who slights them. So the greatest MIde leaders, and those in constant demand, are not always those who effect the most numerous cures, but those who have the greatest reputation for sorcery and evil temper.

Every MIde practitioner, both the chief shaman and his assistants, is paid separately by the patient. His fee is displayed before a cure is attempted. The fees are graduated according to the importance of the practitioner in the cure. The chief shaman receives the most, the next chief receives less, and so forth. Whatever the fee may be, it remains the private property of the recipient. Since each household is self-sufficient in everything but curing and divining, wealth is relatively stationary. So the dreaded MIde sorcerers are hated not only for their suspected practice of evil, but also because they monopolize the real wealth of the community.

Chief George was notorious in this respect. He died about 1927. He appears to have been a markedly capable person, and possessed all of the twenty-odd abilities allotted to men. This meant that he was preeminently powerful, threatened his fellows with sorcery, and practiced bad medicine. He desired power over others, and he was greedy for material wealth. As a consequence, George did all the curing and divining for the people of his village. Lesser personalities with the same ambitions had to content themselves with his leavings, or depart for another village. He was so feared that few shamans dared to enter shamanistic combat with him when he insulted them with slighting remarks. A patient would call him if he thought his illness was mild enough to be cured by the sucking technique. If this failed, divination would be attempted. And of course George would be called to do that. Through George, the divining supernaturals would diagnose that the ailment could be cured only by MIdewiwin. George would be asked to conduct the ceremony. If the first ceremony failed, another had to be attempted, for the MIde is the most powerful of all therapeutic measures. Ceremonies would be given in successive years until the patient was cured, with George as the chief officiant. If the patient died before he was cured, then a ghost MIdewiwin had to be held, a ceremony that cured the soul of the deceased on its journey to the next world. And George conducted that. George, also, divined for war parties, and for hunting. As his power over the people increased, he fell into the habit of dictating the nature and quantity of the fees he desired. When a patient sent for him, he would fall into a trance before the messenger and say, "The *manido* [supernatural] requests a raincoat and a dozen boxes of snuff, and a gun. . . . " He taught MIde knowledge to his wife and daughters so that they could act as his assistants. Therefore in George's village, all the wealth came to be concentrated not in the hands of a few households, but in the hands of one only.

Billy M'Ginnis tried to do the same at Manitou. He was successful for some years. Then his wife, little daughters, and brother died one after another. People said, "His power must have left him if his relatives die. He must be practicing bad medicine, and it has returned and killed his own relatives, and now he is not strong enough to cure them. And if he has power, why did he send for the white doctor?" Billy was in such despair that he threw away his paraphernalia. He stripped himself of the promise of his youth and "became a coward." Just as he had assumed powers on his own initiative, and had felt that he had measured up to them, so now he felt that he had fallen short.

Influential persons who are known or suspected to be sorcerers are recognized in more general ways than in being deferred to professionally. People cower physically before them, shrink away, hush their talk, straighten their faces lest the shaman suspect some intended offense in their behavior. A child's casual laugh might be interpreted as ridicule by a shaman. Once a girl and her mother were walking along a road and passed close to where a shaman lay dozing in the grass. They were joking and talking. Yet because of their laughter the shaman became furious and muttered, "I'll get you! I'll get you!" And the woman soon showed the effects of evil medicine; her mouth became "twisted" and she became incontinent of urine. One boy became paralyzed shortly after a shaman chose to be offended by his careless laugh. It is perfectly consistent with this attitude that laughing, particularly on the part of women, is not loud but light. Paralysis, incontinence, twisted mouth, and windigo insanity are sent by shamans who have been offended by casual behavior.

Girls, especially, are taught to be careful of shamans, for the sight of an attractive girl may excite a shaman's lust. Then he will try to attack and "ruin" her, or solicit her in marriage. No girl can refuse a shaman without inviting the most dread sorcery on herself and her family.

The shaman's exquisite sensitiveness to slights, real or imaginary, is intelligible to the people because it is only an accentuation of the sensitiveness felt by every person. A person spends the greater part of his life in the small company of his domestic family, and is highly unused to association with others. It is a trial to a man to be easy over long periods even with his wife, and divorces are exceedingly numerous. Different households, even in the same village, are potentially hostile to one another. This is true even when the members of the different domiciles are closely related, like father and son. The people of other domiciles are strangers, outsiders, for they do not share their economic life or daily intimacies. This tension between the members of different households expresses itself in a personal self-consciousness. A person from one household meeting someone from another will wonder to himself: how do I impress him? does he realize how powerful, or how weak, I am? what is the meaning of his smile? Day after day, when such people meet, they commence their intercourse with a blank look, gaze off at the horizon, and sigh "E. . . !" They smoke their pipes or cigarettes, or chew their quids of snuff, and then gradually, carefully, casual remarks are passed. When they know each other better, and come to like each other, a thin, slight, but—because of its break in the polite impassiveness—unmistakable smile lights the face. Only heedless young men, those who drink, dance, and have no powers, are foolish enough to guffaw at one another. Women behave similarly, though with less reserve. They are not so sensitive about their self-esteem as men.

The hostility between domiciles manifests itself clearly in the games that take place during the village period. The games include games of chance (moccasin game, hand game, Indian dice of plumstones, cup-and-ball) and of skill (lacrosse, foot races, squaw hockey, throwing snow sticks), all of them gambling games. All games, except lacrosse and squaw hockey, are played during the winter by the inmates of each wigwam. At that time, when each human being is valued for his company and is, besides, a trusted member of the family, games are played in an atmosphere of gaiety and good fellowship. They cheer the tired hunter during his brief rest periods; they while away long winter nights for the stay-at-homes—the old grandparents, the very young children, and the mother. But during the summer, games provoke tension. Games include large numbers of people. Opposing sides are aligned by draw, or on a basis of age, or of localization in the village, or hosts versus visitors, etc. Then the two sides play to win, not to have a good time as they do in winter. Each individual wants to show his superiority. This attitude is familiar to us as existing between opponents. But besides this, the desire of each person to display his own ability, to win the admiration of others, affects the relationship of members of the same side. Defeat in a game—whether suffered at the hands of opponents, or felt subjectively in the light of a colleague's superior play—is difficult to bear. The defeated one feels shamed, as though the other's victory were a pointed comment on his own inadequacy. Consequently, blood is frequently drawn. Shahboyez was a Paul Bunyan in talent and accomplishments. Once when he was visiting his father-in-law with his wives, he was invited to take part in a moccasin game. He did, and played brilliantly, to the chagrin of all. His brother-in-law, who could not bear the humiliation of defeat, drew his knife and plunged it between Shahboyez' collarbones. Shahboyez was spirited away from the village and his life was saved, though he always remained a cripple. It was reported that then his brother-in-law tried long-distance sorcery upon him. The duel was kept up past Shahboyez' early death. For upon his deathbed, Shahboyez said that he bore no grievance against the man who had stabbed him, but that he loved his little brother-in-law and desired his company on the long ghost journey. And four days later, his brother-in-law died.

In games, women play with the same ferocity as men. Indeed the values attached to games are the same for men and women, though the sexes rarely play together. Both men and women secure visions giving them supernatural powers in play, and both gamble for high stakes and personal prestige. Both feel that their self-respect is involved; both are ready to revenge themselves for their humiliation with knife and sorcery.

Half-sky was famous for her skill in foot races and squaw hockey. She defeated men and women alike. More than once a humiliated female opponent had cut her face and neck. Half-sky's reaction was scorn and pleasure. She knew that the bitterness of her rivals was testimony to her own superiority. The time came, however, when a female rival hired a sorcerer to injure Half-sky, and she went about for several years with "worms eating her nose." Then she had her nose cured, and returned with the determination to avenge herself. She did. But her fierceness and unflagging success acted like a boomerang. Women refused to play on her side, for she gave no one a chance. They resented her incomparable superiority. She simply had to withdraw from play, because no one would play with or against her. Indeed women expressed themselves as feeling humiliated by her very appearance.

In this way competitive games develop into duels between individuals. The dueling pair may be on the same or opposite side. When a pair reaches the private dueling stage, they are no longer competing as lacrosse or racing rivals. The humiliated person, who initiates the duel, is trying to wipe out the shame that threatens his self-esteem. The successful person at first tries to defend himself; then, as in the case of Half-sky and of Shahboyez, he attempts revenge.

## EDUCATION

The child is born into the small world bounded by the members of the domestic family. This family includes the parents, immature children, sometimes elderly grandparents, an aunt or uncle, and sometimes a son-in-law or daughter-in-law. For six months of the year, this is all the society that a child knows, and during the remainder of the year family ties are emphasized by the words and attitudes with which his family distinguishes itself from other households.

From the moment of birth, the child is trained to be an adult. The people feel that a helpless person is a suicidal drain, so near do they consider themselves to the subsistence level. Therefore a child must be made competent as soon as possible.

The typical values of competence appear in the training of the male child. He must be given powers and attitudes of self-reliance. He must be taught to forage for himself, to have initiative and mental and physical fortitude. He must be kept free of illness. He must possess private property.

A day or two after birth a naming feast is held. To this the parents invite men and women who are known to have received visions empowering them to name a person. This naming carries with it supernatural strength; the child is named after the supernatural events of a vision, and therefore given a bit of the power connected with the vision. The naming is also an earnest that the supernaturals of the names will look with kindliness upon the child, and the parents rejoice that fewer of the universal powers are hostile to the child. Plaything tokens of the namers' visions are given to the child beneficiary, and through them the child is introduced to the values of the adult world.

The child is told that the token—a tiny cane, signifying long years of life; a tiny gun, signifying hunting success; a tiny bow and arrow, signifying success on the warpath—has been vouchsafed by a supernatural. Then the ideology of the vision pursuit is told, and repeated, and repeated. When he gets older, at the age of four or five years, the neutral character of the recommendation is switched, and the boy is told that he must seek a vision for himself, "to learn what to do with his life." In his natural state he is "empty" of qualities. He must develop a personality and abilities by soliciting the supernaturals to drop abilities into his "emptiness." The boy's face is smeared with charcoal, and he is sent out without breakfast to play with his siblings or village mates. The very young child is made to abstain from one meal a day at intervals that are graduated to the fanaticism of the parents. The common fasting period is in the winter. Between eight and ten years, the child may fast a couple of times a week, for several weeks on end. It is insisted that he fast for knowledge and abilities or he will be helpless in the struggle for life.   At puberty the village boys are sent out on a joint fast, to seek the great vision.

The vision is exceedingly personal property, and as such must not be revealed casually.   It is a compact between the beneficiary and the supernatural, and therefore references to it should be confined to consultations with the supernatural.   If a child seems about to discuss his vision with his father, the latter will halt him, saying, "This is yours.   You must keep it close to you. Do not talk about it.   But think about it.   Make it so real to yourself that you can almost touch it and hear it."   So the child who has once dreamed vividly continues to dream.

The parents' cooperative teacher relationship to the child continues until the child marries.   The parents advise the child of the symbols of good supernaturals and of bad supernaturals, how to accept a vision, and when to reject a vision.   Withal, the individualistic values are stressed, for the parents never cease to remind the child that he must not communicate his vision; if he does, his power will be gone.

The years devoted to the vision pursuit are also devoted to the techniques of hunting, trapping, and fishing.   Either father or mother teaches the child to throw a stone accurately, to use a peashooter and a small bow and arrow.   The day the child bags his first bit of game, whether deliberately or accidentally, he is given extravagant praise.   Leonard Wilson at three years was idly casting stones, and accidentally struck a bird.   His father shrieked excitedly, "Our son has killed a bird!   Our son has killed a bird!"   The fact that the bird had been killed accidentally did not alter the fact that the boy had ability, indeed the accident appeared to make this argument the stronger.   The neighbors were invited and a feast was given.   Experienced hunters recited their deeds, and promised the patronage of their supernaturals to the sleepy little boy.   When he was about nine years old, he trapped a beaver, and that entailed another feast.   At sixteen or seventeen, he killed a moose, and that brought more celebration. Other boys who kill their first duck, or their first sturgeon, are honored by their parents.   A boy's life is full of never-ending incentives to personal achievement.   As the boy becomes older and stronger, his father takes him with him on his trails, and teaches him to shoot, to cruise the forest, to be a woodsman.   He teaches him the variety of traps.   And he also points out the profit and pleasure of owning private trails. He teaches him that these trails are his, the father's, private property, and that others are forbidden to use them without permission, under pain of death. He tells the boy that the very traps and gun and shells he uses belong to another, that is, to his father. Then when the boy has caught some furs, the father sells the pelts for him, taking him along to watch the sale, in exchange for gun, traps, shells. And as soon as the boy feels himself competent, he strikes his own trails. Albert Wilson had his own trails when he was twelve years old, but this seems to have been precociously young. The usual age is between fifteen and seventeen years. The boys strike their trails just adjacent to the grounds of the father. Sometimes they live with the father in the cabin on his trapping trails, and go forth daily to their own grounds. Sometimes they build their own wigwams, where they stay a few nights at a time. At certain intervals, once a week or once every two weeks, the boy returns with pelts and meat to the family lodge, where his elder unmarried sister cures them. So, from the day of birth, the boy has been taught to be an individualist.

During the years that her brother is being trained to be an adult, the girl has been undergoing similar experiences, though in a far less intense fashion. She, too, has had a naming feast, but the stress upon its vocational significance is much less. Something is usually said about fertility and easy childbirth, but this is not very important. The chief purpose of a girl's naming feast seems to be to cure her of impending or actual illness. Typically, the girl is not urged to fast for a vision, though she hears constant talk about the vision pursuits of brothers and father. If she is so inclined, and if she is a lonely or suffering child, she "dreams" spontaneously. Sometimes, when a girl is the only child, she is treated like a boy in all respects, and therefore is sent out to dream. Indeed, her parents do not think of her as fundamentally different from a boy; she is simply the second-best possibility. At menstruation, however, some weak analogy is made with the boy's puberty fast by insisting that when the girl goes into her isolated menstrual hut, she must try to seek a vision. But few girls obtain visions. First, they are not physiologically conditioned through fasting and thirsting. They are given poor food, it is true, from the belief that the world supply of fresh food will be injured if a menstruating girl eats of it, but still they are given enough to satisfy their hunger.   They are also given drink, and they can make a fire to keep themselves warm. Postclimacteric women visit them to teach them the significance of the ceremonial, that it makes them desirable and eligible in marriage, that they are now women, not girls, and that in their seclusion they must perfect their handicraft abilities.   If several girls are undergoing the ceremony, they visit one another, and have a good time.   They play with the idea that they are dangerous to men and babies, and practice strewing the leaves that are a warning to these vulnerable persons.   Also, parties of boys and young men coming through the forest ignore the traditional barricades, and visit the girls, sometimes sleeping with them. Indeed, the menstruating girl is distracted from the vision pursuit as much as possible.

At the time when the little boy is learning to throw stones accurately, the little girl is simply toddling around after her mother or grandmother.   She watches them set nets, tan, and do beadwork.   She is shooed from participation in the dangerous occupations like setting the nets and boiling the maple sugar. But gradually, by imperceptible stages, she is allowed small portions of the work, and by the time she is nine or ten years old she is competent to aid in the women's work.   She is also employed as her father's or stepfather's aid in poling or paddling the canoe on duck and moose hunts.   She is developing abilities, but more than that she is developing an attitude of cooperation in a subordinate capacity.   She is not yet given any drives toward independent work or toward owning private property.

But when her brother has reached the stage where he is a competent trapper and hunter and owns his own grounds and trails, new vistas open for the girl.   Her mother tells her that she must work the hides and meat brought by her brother, just as her mother works the hides and meat brought by her father.   In other words, she is now to commence the womanly role of working in partnership with a man.   Of course, she has yet to be taught much; and in the first years she secures help from her mother and grandmother.   All this help is tacit, however, for the job is said to be the girl's.   At this late date—late, that is, by contrast with the boy's training—the girl is furnished with certain incentives.   She hears the work of various women in tanning and beadwork compared.   She discovers that there is a women's world, closed to men or ignored by them, with its own standards of excellence. And as the girl continues with her work, she learns that during the village season, when women of different domiciles visit one another, they display their handiwork casually but for approval; and that at dances they also display their skill in women's crafts, for the gorgeous costumes of the men are the work of their women. In this way, through gossip, visiting, and dances, a woman's fame as a worker gets noised abroad and she acquires a certain informal renown. Some women take to "dreaming" about their work. Maggi, a great beadworker, often dreams about beadwork patterns. Another woman dreamed of a new style of cutting moccasins. But a woman never acquires the ceremonial and titular rewards of a man or of a boy.

Some girls are reared like boys. This is often the case when there are no boys in the family, and the father takes his daughter as his companion. Sometimes this happens when a girl is the particular favorite of her father. Or a woman, long widowed, may have developed the masculine arts of hunting, trading, and fishing, and rear her daughter in the same way. There is a considerable group of girls and women who like to live alone or in the company of another woman. These girls have to develop certain masculine techniques in order to maintain themselves. Not all these women are permanent bachelors, but they live alone for as long as they choose. Women who have learned male hunting techniques and male attitudes regarding private property also have visions pertinent to men's work; while at the same time they are skilled in women's work. Such women are given the same recognition as men. Female shamans are solicited to cure and teach men and women alike, and female warriors are given the male title of "brave."

While the vocational training of boys and girls is so disparate, they go through the same experiences in learning games. It is in this sphere that adult men and women are nearly equal with respect to motivations and standards of ability. During the winter time, the brothers and sisters who live in the isolated family wigwam play the same games regardless of sex. Many a boy admits that his sister has beaten him in foot races. They play alike for stakes, and place their self-respect upon the excellence of their performances in play. Boys and girls secure the same visions for success in gambling and foot racing, etc. They play in company with the older people of the lodge, as pupils. During the village period, where there are more children, the boys and girls play separate games according to sex; but despite the difference of sex, the same standards hold for both groups.

There is a double standard of morals concerning premarital chastity. Boys are allowed complete freedom, but girls are supposed to be chaste. However, a single standard actually obtains, for the girls are not supervised, except for rare instances, and then not always effectively. During the summer, the children play together in mixed groups, and part of their play is the imitation of the intimate behavior of adults. Girls are supposed to be passive, and boys are supposed to pursue them. The game of love is a tremendously important preoccupation, and is enriched with songs, music, tales of ascetic and faithful devotion, of suicides, and even of visions.

At the time of her first menstruation, a girl is reminded that she must be chaste. However, the childhood habits, and the insistence of boys and men, nullify this caution, and almost every girl bears one or more illegitimate children. These early years condition the behavior of most women for the rest of their lives. They never cease to feel that it is wrong to make love outside of marriage, but most women do just that. In their quiet way, by submitting to the romantic appeals of men, they fly in the face of their conventions. Repeatedly they ignore or defy the convention, make illicit love, and bear illicit children, even during the mourning period of widowhood.

Individualistic ideals for boys are correlated with pride. A boy is taught not only to become a competent hunter, but to feel that his self-respect depends upon the successful outcome of his hunting. Also in wooing, he views the girl of his desire as he views game: he says that he "hunts" her. If she refuses him, his pride is injured and he is shamed. A man seldom considers that a woman is entitled to her personal choice; he feels only that his choice, his individual ambition, must be satisfied. A boy is taught by older boys and by young men that he, and not the girl, must take the initiative in romantic advances and must force the outcome. So in adult life, it is men who have elaborated the extremes of pride and of shame; while in women the development of these is muted, and so they are manifested very unevenly. Girls who have borne illegitimate children and have been abandoned by lovers are shamed, but not overwhelmed by shame, and they adjust quietly and adequately. It is the brother, overwhelmed by the shame of his sister, who flees to a strange locality where he may forget.

Little positive attention is paid to the role of women in Ojibwa. While boys are encouraged to fast for visions, to concentrate upon becoming great shamans, hunters, and warriors, and are lauded at every advance made, girls are simply ignored. If girls, influenced indirectly and spontaneously by the highly charged environment, pick up some of the talents of men and boys, they are not actively discouraged, but they are not praised. So most women show the motivations and attitudes of the typical man, but in a greatly lessened form. On the other hand, many more individual exceptions appear among women than among men. Women are the great unspecialized group, and can take up different kinds of behavior; while men are the highly specialized group. Having few or no stakes in the culture, individual women behave in highly variable ways, relative to other women and to their own conduct of an earlier date. A man's motives are stereotyped, and consistent from one period of his life to another, but this cannot be said for women. For example, a typical man always resents being deserted by a wife, regardless of his personal feeling for the wife. A woman may or may not resent desertion, and her attitude at one time of her life may contradict the attitude of an earlier or later date. A man typically punishes the wife who has humiliated him by deserting him; a woman may or may not attempt punishment, and the object of her punishment (whether her husband or his paramour) is variable. A man aspires for renown in the male activities of shamanism, hunting, and war, in all or in some of these; and loses status if he is permanently unsuccessful. A woman is supposed to be confined to the domestic routine, which is without status. But if she cares to she may cultivate male pursuits and achieve masculine rewards. Some women do slowly come to the realization that they prefer male occupations, or take these up in addition to female ones. Some women make male occupations a life ambition, other take them up at one time of life and drop them at another, perhaps to resume them again. Their course is not prejudiced by any cultural judgment, but is largely influenced by personal inclination. Some women transfer male drive to female work (securing visions about midwifery, bead-work, striving for excellence in performance so as to shame another); others do not.

## Summary of Competition and Cooperation and Individualistic Emphases

*Individualistic.*—The domestic household is independent, and in winter completely isolated. The man's economic occupations are isolated, and under his sole direction. Woman's economic occupations are also individual, but her children play about her, and her mother may be living with her, working at her own tasks but keeping her company. Spouses own everything individually; there is no common property as a result of marriage. All property is transferred by the owner to any individual or at any time that he pleases. The transfer follows no institutional lines, only lines of personal affection or private interests. Marriage is sentimental, and reflects personal choice. Polygyny is highly unpopular. Marriage is so private that incestuous unions are frequent and survive. One reason for the survival of these marriages is the complete independence and self-sufficiency of the household. Divorce and remarriage are common, as well as remarriage to the divorced spouse. From earliest infancy children are trained to become adults so that all their conduct is adult in miniature. Boys trap alone, seek small game alone, own private property, seek visions alone. Young girls have no such clear-cut training. The relation between supernatural patron and beneficiary is not viewed as a cooperative one, but as one of individual bargain and sale. The supernatural patron sells his gift in exchange for tobacco. The shaman treats his patient in the same way, for value received. His primary motivation is not to outdo or cooperate with another, but simply to fulfill a job which he likes, and to show off his power exhibitionistically.

The lone economic household and the hunter's lone pursuit of game in the winter are perfectly consistent with the game resources of the region. For there is little game, and at any locality hunting or trapping cannot be carried on by more than one man. The household which is fed by the proceeds of one man's hunting must of necessity be small. Labor is divided between husband and wife. The husband goes out hunting alone; the woman attends to her household tasks alone.

The same economic isolation is carried over into spring sugar making. Despite the fact that people live near together, and a few couples may even live under the same roof, each family works independently, and husband and wife work separately at different stages of the manufacture.

The independent household continues through the summer, when many households live near together but pick berries and fish independently. Also, the same division of work between man and wife continues. The man hunts and traps and lances fish alone. The woman picks berries, sets rabbit traps, sets fish nets, cures meat and animal hides alone.

The independent household continues through the fall rice making. During the harvesting, the husband and wife work together, but through all other stages, each works independently.

*Competitive.*—Institutionalized competition appears in games, which are organized into competitive sides. This arrangement works out when members of the domestic household play together, as during the winter; but fails during the summer, when members of different households play together. In the latter situation, pride inevitably becomes a factor. When a man's self-esteem is pricked by another, the game becomes secondary to the conflict of personalities.

In individual instances, but not institutionally, there is competition in love: several women over a man, or two men over a woman. In such competition pride-shame soon dominates the situation.

Individuals sometimes assume competitive attitudes in the village season when displaying or talking about beadwork, tanning, amount of furs, etc. In rare cases, this competitiveness blooms into a motivation which becomes confused with pride.

All persons and households mistrust one another, for reasons of pride. In guarding his pride, a person verges upon competition with others who are guarding their own pride.

*Cooperative.*—The economic household is objectively, but not subjectively, cooperative: the husband provides raw materials, and the wife manufactures them. Parents teach their children, but the teaching is phrased as a right of the individual. Simultaneous economic cooperation between husband and wife occurs when the man poles the canoe in which his wife sits, harvesting the rice. All cooperation usually is limited to a lodge, not between lodges.[1]

Members of the same side in a game cooperate, but prideful resentments crop up and disrupt the cooperation. The war party is supposed to be cooperative, with the captain having central powers. But each warrior actually exercises the right of overriding the captain's authority at his individual discretion; so the war party is reduced to an aggregate of individual warriors, each one interested only in ascertaining the fact that he can achieve distinction, regardless of whether or not others do. Polygyny reduces itself to monogyny in the same way, by the will of one of the wives. Parents are supposed to arrange the marriages of their children, but this occurs in a minority of cases, and usually in deference to the wishes of the young couple. In most cases the young couple arrange their own marriage, or carry out an affair which does not result in marriage. Dances obtained by villagers from the Sioux are cooperatively owned; but each individual villager views himself as owning a portion of the dance, and not as a member of a collective body. The village council is a cooperative body: this consists of the men who gather for gossip either spontaneously or at the specific invitation of any man. It gathers usually to discuss the boys' puberty fast, sometimes to plan a war party, occasionally to plan a return gift for a Dakota dance. But the council has no authority, and any person may dissent with impunity. The council has no officers.

[1] However, people of different households sometimes borrow tools (or other property) from one another during the village season. A person can lend only his own tools, etc., and a borrowed thing has first to be requested, and borrowed under stipulated conditions. Trapping grounds are loaned to needy families in the same way, but under the most rigid restrictions.

# CHAPTER IV

# THE BACHIGA OF EAST AFRICA

## by MAY MANDELBAUM EDEL

The Bachiga[1] live in the mountainous highlands of western Uganda, just north of Ruanda.  They keep some domesticated animals.  Essentially they are agriculturists.  Before the recent advent of the British, they were very warlike and highly anarchistic.  Their contacts with other people were primarily through warfare, though there was also some trade.  They differ from their neighbors chiefly in that they are less integrated politically and lack the intricate caste system common in this region.  It is also probable that their marked individualism is peculiar to them.  Individualism is the keynote of Bachiga social and economic life.  It affects even the family structure. This emphasis is particularly striking in contrast with the cooperativeness of the Bathonga, who share so many cultural institutions and traits with them.

The Bachiga consider themselves members of one tribe, speaking the same language, subscribing to the same customs, and inhabiting a single region, but there is no centralized authority, and they present no unity to the outside world.  The largest organized social units among the Bachiga are the patrilineal clans, of which there are about thirty.  They are autonomous, and are constantly at war with one another.  They vary greatly in size, and some number several thousand members.

[1] According to the spelling adopted by the African Institute, the tribal name would appear as Ciga.  This account is based upon my own field work, the results of which have not yet been published.  I spent the whole of 1933 among the Bachiga, but part of the time was devoted to work which referred only indirectly to the culture.  I stayed in a native village, and carried on my research in the native tongue.  The hamlet in which I lived consisted of the households of fifteen adult males, and there were as many again in the two adjoining hamlets which were part of the same community. Some of these people I knew intimately, and with most of the others I was on terms of friendship.  Most religious practices were in abeyance during my stay because of a government ban.

127

The clans are local groupings, though many of them have subdivisions in several different parts of the country, and in every village live some individuals not members of the local clan. Although the reasons for leaving one's own relatives may be many, it is difficult to gain acceptance among strangers. However, this desertion of one group for another is quite frequent, and is evidence that the clan itself is not a highly integrated unit.

Feud is the keynote of interclan relationships. For the murder of a fellow clansman, vengeance must be exacted, upon the murderer himself or upon any one of his relatives. This is carried to an extreme, and any stranger may be killed on the grounds that there may be some forgotten and still unrequited killing on the part of his clan, or on the suspicion that he may perhaps himself be about to take revenge for some such crime against his clan. This situation is aggravated by the fact that exploits in war are the subject of public boasting. War between the clans used to be common. This was caused by conflicts arising out of cattle stealing, and by the need of growing clans for additional territory. The forms of fighting ranged all the way from the ambushing of a lone stranger to pitched battles fought by prearrangement on the boundary of the warring clans, and raids in which unsuspecting villages were pillaged and sacked.

Certain clans never took part in fighting. These are known as the Abashe. They have various extraordinary roles to play. When the two families are from different parts of the country, they act as proxies for the parents of a girl in some of the marriage rites. With them a wounded man might safely take refuge. Today, since overt hostilities have ceased and traveling is safe, their role has largely disappeared.

Relationships between members of different clans are not necessarily warlike. Certain interclan institutions guarantee this. One is the pact of ritual blood brotherhood. In this two individuals take an oath of mutual protection, swallowing a small amount of each other's blood. It is believed that this blood will swell up and kill anyone who breaks such an oath. This relationship is considered closer and more trustworthy than actual brotherhood. This makes it possible for a man to travel in strange territory with a certain amount of safety, and it assures him of a friendly, hospitable, and cooperative trade friend. The choice of a pact brother lies with the individual and is not determined by existing clan alliances. Whatever trade there is is carried on through pact brothers. Markets have always existed, but until very recently they were rare and unfrequented, because in the absence of any peaceful policing authority they were places of danger.

The institution of the pact brother is important even today in connection with the interclan bonds set up by marriages. Clans are exogamous, and the complicated marriage negotiations require a go-between. Affinal ties, however, do not bind two clans together, but only the two families concerned. The preferred marriage is that of a man with a girl from his mother's clan, but this actually happens in only a small proportion of cases. For the most part choice is dictated by other considerations, such as ownership of cattle, or personal friendship between individuals of the two families. The kin of the wife expect the young husband to fulfill certain obligations of respect for her parents. He may talk to his sisters-in-law, and even tease them, as they are potential mates. The extension of these attitudes beyond the bride's own family is very slight. A woman coming to dwell permanently among her husband's kin has more widely ramifying obligations, but it is toward the actual parents and brothers of her husband that they are most sharply defined. Even the ties between a woman's children and her own relatives are of a familial rather than a clan nature.

The clan has very few functions. It defines the limits of relationship beyond which marriage is allowed. Its members have a common food tabu, but as this is often shared with other clans it is not a very significant bond. The clan has no central organization and no unifying authority. It is made up of a varying number of autonomous subdivisions which tend to split off and to become in their turn separate clans.

These subdivisions, like the clan itself, are paternal lineages, but they are smaller than the true clan and made up of closer relatives. Sometimes these subdivisions are friendly and some share the same villages. But others are as inimical as separate clans. A peace rite which includes the payment of wergild exists as a possible way of terminating intraclan feuds, but it can be used only when the families particularly concerned agree to it.

These clan subdivisions have more social functions than the clan. The leaders of the latter are for the most part only the great men, warriors or priests, of some particular lineage, whose personal prestige is so great that it extends beyond the family. It is within this paternal lineage that murder is prohibited under penalty of burial alive with the corpse of the victim. This penalty must be exacted on account of the belief that any member of the family who eats with the fratricide will contract leprosy. And it is within this group that the responsibility for avenging a murder falls. In warfare, the group involved is often only the lineage and it also usually settles newly conquered land. It also plays a social role in marriage, not an economic one; that is confined to the small family and the individual. It is the girls of the groom's paternal lineage who welcome the bride, and it is the girls of the bride's who bid her farewell. The members of the lineage must spend four days at the kraal of the deceased after a funeral, and in religion we find that group rites which involve relatives outside the immediate family are functions of this group, not of the entire clan.

But even this formal subdivision of the clan is not a thoroughly integrated unit. In a great many respects each kraal is independent. Each household, resident in a number of huts facing upon a central compound, and recognizing one man as its head, is made up of a father and his adult sons with all their wives. Even when sons set up establishments of their own, these are usually adjacent and remain subsidiary. No man may build a home of his own during his father's life except with his express permission. A father must obtain a first wife for each of his sons and give him land for his wife to work. In return the son, however mature, obeys his father and owes him certain specific duties. He must present him with a share of all the beer he brews, and of every animal he kills, and each year he must give him a share of the first fruits of various crops. In addition his wife must do some work in the fields of her mother-in-law. To enforce these obligations there are sanctions, the strongest of which is the threat of the parental deathbed curse, which makes a man a pariah by heaping maledictions not only upon him but also upon anyone rash enough to associate with him.

The large polygynous household is the basic unit of Bachiga society. In many respects it operates as a group. A father and his sons with their families may leave their relatives to live among strangers. In some parts of the country, especially the forests of the northwest, there are virtually no villages, and each such family group forms a settlement by itself. Even where there are more compact groups of houses, there is no village organization of any sort, either structural or political. Members may leave at any time, and newcomers are comparatively free to join it. The household is also a religious unit. The father as its head makes offerings for all his family to the gods, the rain maker, the ancestors. Economically, too, there is considerable cooperation within this group. Since men's and women's tasks are distinct, some measure of cooperation is imperative. A father looks to his children for the performance of chores, especially help in herding. Sometimes a group of younger brothers will go through a special rite at the marriage of one of them which entitles them all to free access to the wife even before she has borne her first child (which is otherwise forbidden).

Economically, the hut is an independent unit within the kraal. This is true not only of the domestic economy of the sons, but of the various wives as well. Each woman has a separate hut, her own fields and granaries. Women cannot claim property in their own right, but some things are for their use and for their children. In this limited sense even a cow may belong to one of the wives, so long as she remains part of that family. Each woman reaps and stores her own crops, which she uses in feeding her children, and each wife cooks for her husband as though she alone were responsible for his food. The attitude is individualistic, and there is not even that competitive striving we find among rival hostesses of the same circle in our society. The husband is allowed no favorites. He must spend two nights at the home of each of his wives in fixed order, and share all gifts equally among them. Even the chief wife (who is here always the first wife) has only very limited special privileges. She occupies the hut opposite the gate, and commands some show of respect from her co-wives. No wife is penalized for faults such as inability to weave. Only laziness with regard to agriculture or cooking is regarded as a really serious fault.

The individualism within the family becomes very marked after the death of the father. His wives are apportioned among his sons, and a new set of houses is built. Only such of a man's property as was not associated with some particular wife is equally distributed. The rest goes to the new husband or the children of the particular widow who owned it. The oldest son is officially head of the whole family in place of his father. He supervises the distribution of the inheritance, makes arrangements for marriages, negotiates with the ancestral spirits and the priests, etc. However, the unity of the group of brothers is often not very long preserved. Brothers usually live in separate, though often neighboring, houses, and serious quarrels and litigations are not exceptional. The Bachiga recognize that the relationship between brothers, which should be a friendly and helpful one, has no important sanctions to make it so. Thefts and sometimes even murders occur between brothers. Several particularly unfortunate effects of this lack of strong cohesion are the possibility for cheating and cruelty on the part of the older brothers; and the common neglect of orphans who, though adopted by close relatives, are not necessarily assured adequate care.

For example, two brothers live in adjoining compounds. In that of the younger there is the hut of a younger girl and boy, children of the same father by another mother. Originally, as was proper, they had lived with the older brother. He had used their cattle to get himself a wife, and she had torn down their house for firewood. Because they were so cruelly treated, the younger brother had voluntarily taken over their care. Similarly, married sisters sometimes persuade their husbands to allow orphaned younger brothers to live with them, when they are neglected by others.

The religious life of the Bachiga may be briefly summarized. For the most part religion is a family affair, the head of the household making offerings to the ancestral spirits on behalf of all its members, as the diviners order. There are diviners practicing many different techniques. They are consulted principally in case of illness, to decide what sort of spirit is at fault and what is to be done about it. There are other specialists as well. There are powerful individuals with knowledge of herbal medicines who control mysterious nonhuman spirits, often in the form of snakes, which they can call upon to plague and even to kill enemies. This black magic is a socially acceptable kind, not to be confused with sorcery, which is forbidden. The magician is expected to use his power only against an offender, when hired to do so by those injured. He uses it particularly in the punishment of unidentified thieves and wives who have disappeared. There are also rain makers, whose positions are hereditary. Their power depends upon knowledge of charms and also upon their relations with their own familial spirits. Most important of all are the priests, whose power comes by direct personal inspiration from powerful spirits. These can make people ill and even kill them, and it is the priest alone who can intervene and present the layman's placatory offering.

The relationship among these practitioners as well as their economic and social position I shall discuss later. It is enough to indicate that they are not an organized group, and do not cooperate with each other. What is interesting from our point of view is that, in practically every case, the individual who consults a diviner or makes an offering to a priest is engaged in an activity which is primarily personal, having to do with an illness or other danger to himself or some member of his immediate family. The only group religious activities of which I could obtain an adequate account were annual offerings to the rain makers, and through the priests to their spirits. In both of these, although offerings were made by many at one time, the ends were personal for all the participants. They were concerned with warding off from themselves, possible evils such as lack of rain or illness, and had no special relation to each other as members of the same congregation. There was another set of religious observances which was moribund even before the British ban. What little I could find out about this suggests that it was more genuinely communal.

When we turn from the essentially individualistic character of the social structure and religion to the realm of technology, we find a similar situation. Most techniques demand no special group participation. When the relevant activities are, as sometimes occurs, collectively organized, we find not true cooperation, but helpfulness, or else at least that the individuals concerned have an individual stake which is of major importance. It is only within the family that we find true division of labor and sharing.

Bachiga livelihood depends upon agriculture, cattle keeping, hunting, and the practice of various specialized skills—ironworking, pottery, basketry, and woodwork. Yams and potatoes are harvested throughout the year, but the other foods are seasonal. The dry season, after the millet harvest, is normally a period of great plenty. Beer is brewed, marriages and other feasts take place, and the women, upon whom falls the bulk of the agricultural work, enjoy comparative leisure. Most communities are on the whole self-supporting. There have always been a few standard imports—belts from the pygmies, and bamboo—but as a rule trade occurs only when it is necessary, as the result of a lean harvest, to eke out the food supply.

Gardening demands the cooperation of men and women. The initial clearing of the fields is men's work, the subsequent labor is primarily women's, though men will help too. Sometimes a man plants a garden and tends it entirely by himself. A woman is usually aided by her own young children, but they are encouraged to undertake the care of small independent plots as soon as possible. Even when a garden is the concern of more than one person they do not necessarily work at it together. Group work parties do occur. These are not carried out by any system of rotation or mutual help, but rather are organized by particular individuals who have butter or an excess of food with which to pay the workers. This does not account for more than a very small share of the work, because all are busy in their own gardens at much the same time.

There is one partial limitation upon individualism in gardening. In some parts of the country it is thought best to group gardens together, and for everyone to start work on them at about the same time. This is due to a fear of marauders, wild pigs, birds, and voracious insects, dangers which are best met by sharing, and so lessening, the risk.

Herds, too, are for the most part individually tended. Cattle are less important here than in other, more pastoral, cultures of East Africa. The herds are not very large, and the rhythm of life is not regulated by their needs. A father usually sends his cattle out in charge of one of his children, son or daughter, and often several of these children will spend the day herding together. But each night the cattle are separated, and brought to the kraals of their respective owners. This is done even when, as sometimes happens, several men, with a few cows and no children, band together to engage a cowherd. An alliance of this sort, like all others among the Bachiga, is arranged to meet the particular circumstances. It does not necessarily involve people who stand to each other in any defined relationship.

There are some rather complicated joint ventures with regard to cows. All these involve a basic individualism. If a man has only one cow he may find it simplest to entrust it to someone else's care. There are traditional rules for the obligations involved. The herdsman has the right to a share in the milk and offspring of the cow. This arrangement is disliked, for no Bachiga feels that another can be safely trusted. Sometimes men may purchase an animal jointly, and in that case there are prescribed rules for the distribution of its calves. There is rarely any attempt to build up a joint herd. Sometimes a father and son will do so.

Hunting is often a joint activity, although it can also be undertaken separately. Usually when dogs, and always when nets, are used, several men can hunt together. It is all carefully prearranged. Certain tabus are observed the night before, and the hunters set out together at the sound of a horn. But there is individualism even in this group venture. Each man receives at the end of the day precisely the share which his own efforts and luck have brought him. All those whose dogs effectively started animals later slain receive a certain share, those who speared the game get a definite portion of it, etc., according to the rules, which are complex and definite and rigidly adhered to, so that dispute is largely avoided. For example, on one occasion when an animal was killed by stumbling over the cloak of an old man sunning himself by the bank of a river, the hunters who had been pursuing it had to allow him the rights of the killer. Should there be rival claimants, tests are resorted to. Each may be challenged to feed a portion of the disputed meat to one of his dogs. It is believed that this will harm the one whose master falsified his claim. Despite its cooperative framework, with different roles assigned to various participants, the whole situation seems to be a competitive one, with each man striving to be the first to wound and kill. The goals are both profit and glory. Unfortunately, I can shed no more direct light on the forces at work, because hunting was under a temporary ban during the time I was there. The one hunt I witnessed was very irregular. A buck came near the village and was driven into the lake. Canoes were hurriedly launched and efforts were made to stun it by blows over the head. The large, excited audience on shore was torn between applause and fear that the whole procedure was illegal, "stealing from the government," in spite of the fact that no spears were used.  Certainly there was keen, good-humored rivalry among the huntsmen, but the whole was too abnormal to give any insight into the usual practice of hunting.

Housebuilding is another technique in which group activity may play a part.  A house is built of a circle of stakes thrust into the ground to which at intervals withes are bound horizontally. The roof, spiraling to a point at the top, is joined to these.  The whole is then thatched with bundles of dried reeds or grass. Whenever an important member of a family dies, the house must be torn down and a new one built on a fresh site.  It is possible, however, to use some of the old materials again.  If this is done, speed in rebuilding is important.  A house can be built in a day with the assistance of neighbors and relatives.  Sometimes an entirely new house is built in this way.  The work is initiated by a particular individual, who secures the help of others by feasting them.  He must brew quantities of beer, and at the conclusion of the day's work there is drinking and singing in the new house.

The lack of organization in such proceedings is typical of most Bachiga attempts to work together.  There are usually too many people present, children dash about underfoot, and there is much shouting and occasional quarreling.  For most of the people the group activity is essentially a gala social event.  In the same way, when a group of people work together on a field, they take a long time off to regale themselves at noon, at the expense of the owner of the field, who must feed them.  And there is so little order that it is not uncommon for a person to be hit accidentally by another's hoe.  It is only in paddling a canoe that real cooperation is achieved.  This is accomplished by the singing of songs, most of which are borrowed from Ruanda.  In any case paddling is important only to the relatively few who happen to live on the shore of the lake.

All other activities are essentially individualistic.  This is especially true for the women.  As we have seen, each runs her own household separately even if her husband has other wives; cooking is done on the hearth within the hut, and food is stored separately.  But in spite of the institutionalized independence of their activities, and in spite of the fact that any ties which bind them are slight, supported neither by blood nor common upbringing, we often find among the women of a village a high degree of casual helpfulness. They like to hold each other's babies, to shell peas in each other's yards, and to work on each other's baskets. Their efforts support the cultural emphasis on hospitality. They must grind the grain and cook the gruel. But these joint activities are not cooperation towards a common goal. However much the women may help as a group toward giving a feast, they are doing so merely as friends to the giver, and the feast is given only by the latter. This individualism is clearly shown in the arrangements for beer at a party. Neighbors do not contribute. The beer is made by the wives of the man giving the party, but each keeps her brewing apart from the rest, and the guests drink each wife's beer in her own hut.

The work of the specialist again presents a picture of individualism. There are no craft guilds. Not even the blacksmiths form a class apart. Persons skilled in the various crafts are found scattered through the villages. Artisans learn during their apprenticeship either to their fathers or to distant relatives with whom they go to live. Occasionally a grown man sets himself to learn a skill, which he masters in the same fashion, sometimes even going to a famous stranger for training. The fact that the son commonly follows his father in the practice of a craft is not phrased as inheritance. The son of a smith may inherit from his father the implements of his craft, but if he is lazy or inept he will not know how to use them. The apprenticeship system incidentally affords a means whereby even assistance is individualistic, for the helper of the blacksmith, for example, is most often someone who wants to learn the technique himself.

The labor of the specialist at his chosen craft is not a full-time occupation. Like any other man, he depends for his livelihood upon the produce of his garden. He and his wife are busy with household chores. However, he does sell the products of his skill, usually at his own home rather than in the markets. Values are lower at a market, for the seller is there only under the duress of difficult circumstances, and so the advantage lies with the purchaser. At home the seller can demand much more. The buyer-seller relationship clearly involves competition.

But this abrogation of typical Bachiga individualism is not further elaborated in trading. There is no competition between craftsmen. A group of villages has normally only one smith, and carpentry and other such skills are too slightly remunerative to stimulate competition. Nor are the Bachiga sufficiently interested in craftsmanship to compete in terms of skill. The only situation which may have developed competition was between the various diviners, of whom there were a great number, each noted for some special method or ability. Unfortunately the present ban on the old religious activity makes it impossible to tell to what extent they may have been conscious of joint exploitation of a limited clientele.

Other aspects of economics are as individualistic as the organization of production. Property holding, for example, is vested in individuals, and especially in heads of kraals.

This is true even of land. Although the clan is a local unit, or at least has subdivisions which are local, these groups do not communally own all the land which is "theirs." Some of it is used in common by the group for raising cattle, hunting, and gathering firewood. But it would be truer to Bachiga concepts to consider this land as unowned, much as frontier land was in our own history. Local residents who are not clansmates—few because of the strict immigration rules—have exactly the same rights as anyone else to land. The purposes for which land ownership is deemed necessary are housebuilding and agriculture. For these separate claims may be staked on undivided land within the environs of a village, or on unused land in the wilderness, or on land acquired by driving out the clan originally living there.

Individually owned land is treated like any other individually owned property. Its control is in the hands of the owner, who is a male family head. He has the right to use it and to refuse it to others. He may rent it or sell it outright. This is not done very often. In most localities there is so much land that there are large unclaimed tracts. In spite of this, aggressive disputes over land do occur. Sometimes these are about the precise location of boundaries. There are generally plenty of witnesses to help settle such questions. More often the disputes involve the damage of growing crops by cattle. Exact repayment must be made for any damage done.

There is one more important complex in which the land question may play a part. Land becomes scarce when a clan or lineage, whose domain is limited to a series of hills and valleys, grows much larger. A group will then split off to find new homes. Either they may seek out unclaimed parts of the wilderness, or they may attempt to attack and drive out their neighbors. If they are successful, such acquired land will be divided among individual claimants. It is only in such extreme cases that there is competition over land.

Tools and implements may be said alternatively to belong to the family or to particular individuals within it. Each daughter may have her own hoe, and various children their own separate drinking cups. Each house must have a full set of furnishings for its master, a stool, meat bowl, eating baskets, and so forth. Certain household possessions are commonly spoken of as the property of the wife, like the cooking pots, though actually she has only limited disposal of them. There are certain minimum requirements for every home. An important one of these is the hoe. To be without one is to be in a very awkward position, because a new one is expensive and it cannot be homemade. But there is no group of the dispossessed. The necessities are few and easily obtained. It is always possible for a man to find someone among his friends from whom he can borrow the curved knife he needs to cut materials for housebuilding. Materials for making baskets are also easily come by. Even though property like canoes is privately owned, this does not make an enormous economic difference. A man may not borrow anyone's canoe without his specific permission, but there are almost always several canoes about, so that should one man be ungracious, it is easy enough to find another who is not. There is no idea of renting out tools, though the lake-shore people do exact hire for ferrying.

There is some limitation upon the individual owner in the fact that there is an emphasis upon hospitality and generosity with regard to food. As with any other merely socially approved pattern among the Bachiga, there are many who disregard it, preferring to do without the measure of social esteem it brings. Such an individual and the members of his family would still be called upon to play their parts in marriages, and would need to show up at funerals of relatives, etc. The person who chooses to hoard may be stigmatized as a thief, but this is by no means a rare distinction.

There is a great difference in the amount of property possessed by various individuals among the Bachiga. For the most part this means merely that those who have more can consume more, and that in this they will be helped by others. There is no special prestige attached to plenty.

Having claim to a stretch of land somewhat larger than one's neighbor's claim does not constitute wealth by Bachiga standards, though to be landless is to be indeed poor. Having better or more available fields may mean a larger yield, but more important than this is the amount of labor a man and his wives expend, and the action of locusts and hail, rain, and sun. Besides, producing a large amount of food does not in any case make a household wealthy. "He grew good crops" does not mean that others are not assured of at least a sufficiency. And in famine years all are likely to be in the same straits. It is only then that food becomes, in a real sense, a commodity, to be exchanged for other things. Otherwise, though food may be used to buy a hoe or a few day's help in the fields, it will not readily purchase animals, and these alone belong to the category of what the Bachiga recognize as wealth.

The distinction is clearly drawn linguistically between possessions which are merely a means to present satisfactions, and "wealth," which is property intrinsically worth owning. There are concrete advantages to be derived from the possession of cattle, but there is in addition prestige attached to possessing them in considerable numbers. It represents one of the goals which the Bachiga select for approval, though not for universal striving.

The chief advantage in the possession of cattle lies in their use in the bride price. The father of the bride must be paid in cattle, sheep, and goats, by the groom or his father. No one else is economically involved in this transaction, which is ceremoniously conducted in the presence of many witnesses. The size of the bride price reflects the dignity of the girl's family. Daughters are, however, not viewed as commodities. The bride's father, if he is a man of honor, who must appear generous however ill he can afford to, must send with his daughter gifts which may amount to a considerable proportion of the bride price. These go to the groom and pass to his children by this particular wife. They may be used as bride price for her sons. In addition, there is a sharp distinction drawn between marrying a daughter off acceptably, demanding the largest possible recognition of her worth and one's own, and selling her outright because of need, as sometimes happens in times of famine. In the latter case the father is himself the suitor, and he therefore receives much less for her than would normally be the case. The girl is a legal wife, but her position lacks the usual safeguards, for her family cannot support her welfare by threat of divorce. Having used the cattle they were so direly driven to acquire, they cannot return them to her husband. The only proper use of cattle received in bride price is for the purchase of another wife, whence they can, if necessary, be called back.

Having many wives is in itself distinctly valuable. A wife is a good investment, for your grain may be burned and your cattle stolen by raiding enemies, but a wife can be trusted to look after herself. A wife is also the major source of a family's subsistence, for it is she who does most of the work in the fields. In addition to this, many wives means the possibility of many daughters, who in their turn will bring cattle to augment the herd.

In addition to their major role in the bride price, cattle are valued for specific material ends. Their possession, for example, means plenty of butter, which is essential as an ointment, if not as a food. Butter is so precious it can be used to hire laborers for an occasional day's work in the fields, as fee for the jeweler, or to purchase other foods in times of famine. Also, a large number of animals in one herd means that an animal can be butchered when there is need of a skin for clothing. This, incidentally, creates a supply of meat, though animals are seldom slain in order to be eaten except for an important feast. Beef is not subject to the demands of generosity, but is so valuable that it is sold rather than given away.

But the possession of relatively few cattle will satisfy these ends. Having greater wealth than one's fellow does not mean very sweeping differences in the standard of living. Wives of a man of substance must go daily to the fields, like those of any other man, his sons are busy caring for the cattle and carrying on the various other occupations of young men. They have an advantage over the sons of poorer men in that they are able to marry earlier, but this again depends on the relative number of sons and daughters in a family as well as the wealth of the father.

A rich man also has more butter and food for hiring helpers, but these are too seldom available to accomplish the bulk of the work. There are also some slaves, but they have never been very common, and in any case they produce little more than they consume. There are more female slaves than male. They are assigned to particular wives, in whose houses they sleep and whose household tasks they help lighten.

The wealthy head of a household is himself, of course, relieved of the necessity of doing any kind of work. He can afford to sit back and take his ease, and drink quantities of beer. But so, to a great extent, can any middle-aged man, whose children are sufficiently grown up to be trusted with responsibility, and whose wives are not lazy. What is important, then, is to have enough cattle to marry two or three wives, and have a self-supporting household of one's own, and children to assure oneself of a comfortable old age. Independence, not wealth, is the prime desideratum. Failure to achieve it is real failure, whereas "poverty" is accepted with a shrug. To be master of one's own household, it is imperative to be married. Aside from slaves, dependents are those who are still bachelors, who must rely for certain services upon others, or perform them for themselves at the risk of being looked down upon for doing women's work. There is no conception of the fact that had everyone the means to buy wives there would then be a shortage of women. This system tends to postpone the marriage age for many men and so to make polygyny possible. Access to a woman is allowed many men other than her husband, and I have never heard of this being the cause of the breakup of a home. It is considered dangerous only if the man is a stranger. Adultery in such cases is punished severely.

But there are many ways, other than having wealth, for acquiring glory in the eyes of one's fellows. Wealth itself, as a matter of fact, without generous hospitality, brings one only scorn. And is not hospitality itself a possibility for anyone who grows crops energetically, and has wives to brew beer for his guests?

A man must have a wife. This desire serves as a drive for acquiring cattle. To turn one's other possessions or talents into cattle, which belong to a separate economic order, is neither easy nor common, but it is possible, as will be seen in the following account of methods of acquiring wealth.

Inheritance is one of the possible ways of getting wealth. This is not so important as it might seem, because for the most part a man of wealth has many children among whom his herds must be divided.

Another method is to bind oneself as a servant to a wealthy man. This means that one lives in his house, and tends his cattle, or does some similar task. Faithful service of this sort is not paid for in wages, but may be well rewarded. The servant is a member of the family, and should his master have no sons he may inherit. But this is the only way in which working for others can serve to increase a man's wealth. Otherwise it may be carried on sporadically, and at the expense of one's own work. At most it can be used to supply little luxuries, like butter or extra beer. Even today most men use the numerous opportunities for paid work only as a means to such spending, and not to buy cattle, unless they are interested in getting a wife.

Most other activities are equally unlikely to bring wealth. The successful hunter gets sport and some prestige, and the meat and skins of the animals he kills. But such meat, though important to a people to whom meat is both a favorite food and a rare treat, brings no material reward, for custom dictates that it be divided among friends and family. Only those specialists who trade upon fear of the supernatural can hope to turn their talents into wealth.

There has always been one direct means of acquiring cattle, by stealing them. So long as the thief restricts his activities to strangers, and is successful, he is not looked upon askance, even though stealing is itself disapproved.

One man of my acquaintance had the ingenuity to try to become wealthy in a very original fashion. Most of the Bachiga, despite their delight in smoking, raise too little tobacco to satisfy their needs. This man grew tobacco for sale until he had enough to purchase a calf. His success did not act as a spur. As a calf had been his goal, he stopped raising tobacco. Nor is there any systematic advantage taken of the fact that the Banyaruanda, who are settled about Kabale township, do not raise crops and are ready to purchase food. This is in spite of the fact that this way of raising money is readily turned to when funds are necessary for the annual head tax.

As a matter of fact the failure to utilize these means of acquiring extra cattle is perfectly intelligible. In the first place, luck plays a major role in determining whether cattle will thrive and multiply, or whether they will perish, just as luck determines whether one's children will be girls and so bring wealth into the family, or boys whose brides must be bought for them. And then there is not the imperative drive there might be if satisfaction were measured solely in these terms. This is far from the case. One of the most interesting and significant points about the ideals of the Bachiga is their diversity, and the variety of achievements which are open to the individual.

Bravery is one of the more important means of acquiring prestige. The right to boast of war exploits one must have in order to cut a satisfactory figure at a beer party. But one is not limited to one's own deeds; one may use the exploits of one's ancestors and other members of the family. These boasts are to a considerable extent literary forms rather than factual accounts. I do not know to what degree competition enters into their recital and to what degree each man attempts to outdo his fellows. In any case it is clear that the person to whom killing is uncongenial may avoid it. Even the ghost of your own brother may be laid by someone else's valor. Of course the recognized coward runs the risk of being treated as such, and plundered with impunity. But a large family of close relatives helps to insure him against this danger. And though war names are valued as praise nicknames, there are other qualities which nicknames can single out for praise—he who has beautiful hands, or runs well, or argues shrewdly, etc. In particular, quarrelsomeness must never be confused with the love of fighting honorable battles, for the former trait is foolish and unfortunate, and it may prevent a man from playing a leading role among his fellows.

Some individuals, because of their prowess in war and other personal qualities, such as generosity and a capacity of leadership, have held positions of prestige and power. Others are looked up to for their calmness of temper and soundness of judgment, so that their opinions are sought and their decisions respected. The prestige which comes with wealth is certainly not greater than these. As a matter of fact, wealth is intricately related to personal achievement. It is more accurate to view wealth as the result of achievement, rather than as the source and guarantee of power. The man of great wealth can make one special use of his wealth which itself exemplifies this. When a man is very wealthy, he can practice direct patronage, and give a suitor a cow. In return he expects fealty. The grateful recipient must bring him frequent gifts of beer, and when a calf is born to the cow, it is suitable that it be given to his benefactor. Failure to give such tangible evidence of one's appreciation is rebellion and rebellion is a reflection on the power of the donor. Very few of the Bachiga are wealthy enough and strong enough to risk such a practice, which they have learned from the nobles of neighboring Ruanda. It is clear, then, that wealth can bring its possessor followers only if they are bound to him by fear as well as gratitude. And it is, as we shall see, the same fearsomeness which itself brings wealth.

Foremost among those who have had the means and the power to behave in this lordly fashion are the spirit-inspired priests of whom we have spoken. They are held in great awe and, before the coming of the British, held what little political authority there was. Disputes were brought them for settlement, and their judgments were generally obeyed, partly through fear of supernatural sanctions, and partly through fear of the followers of the priests. Such men, when sent to seize a sheep which a man had been ordered to pay as compensation and had failed to give up, were very likely to take more than the sheep. His position in society gave the priest both the incentive and the means for the accumulation of wealth. Like the Ruanda chiefs after whom their behavior was modeled, the priests demanded heavy annual tribute. They could also demand such cattle or girls as attracted them, in the name of their supernatural spirits. They lived in state. Leopard skins, double-headed spears, and various other such insignia, modeled again after the attributes of Ruanda royalty, were exclusively for priestly use. They even held court, entertaining satellites with beer and the dancing of youths and maidens summoned for the purpose. They had large numbers of wives, some of whom were purchased in the ordinary fashion, others who were presented to them. And there was usually a sufficient surplus so that they could give wives to their loyal followers.

Not all priests rose to such positions of power. A priest's calling comes by inspiration. The fact that such supernatural calls have tended historically to follow patrilineal lines of descent is not formally acknowledged. Even the son of a priest can become a priest only if, after the death of his father, the spirit comes to him. Theoretically, anyone may be so inspired, women as well as men, but women must have the priestly offices performed for them by their husbands. Allegiance to a priest does not follow clan or community lines. It is determined by the effectiveness conceded his spirits in causing illness. Some spirits of this sort only bother their own hosts. Whether other illnesses are laid to their account depends upon the diviners, who are diagnosticians. It is evident that there is room here for real competition, but I have no knowledge of the extent to which it was actually practiced. Certainly the role of the diviner cannot have been a conscious one. He was only a fairly well-paid technician, and the fact that he did not use his position to further his own ends makes it clear that he cannot have been the conscious tool of the priests. The diviners admit their subordinate position, and even make offerings through the priests to the spirits which they represent, lest the spirits withdraw the favor of allowing them to interpret.

There were a few other positions which controlled power and wealth. One was that of the rain maker, who was universally feared and respected. He and the priest recognized and respected each other's sphere of influence. Other medicine men, who performed curative and also destructive magic, had varying status. In most cases they were less important and less wealthy than the priests. Their positions were on the whole coexistent rather than subject to rivalry. But in at least one clan, no priest was ever able to attain a foothold. It is highly probable that there was some connection between this and the fact that the war leader, and most powerful man of that clan, was also a famous medicine man. This may have had some weight, conscious or not, with the diviners, who could easily have refused to recognize possible rivals.

One point at any rate is clear. There was certainly scope for the expression of a drive for power on the part of some individuals, and there were sufficient goals and means for realizing them to minimize competition, although competition in unstereotyped forms was certainly present. The same sort of thing is evident even under changed modern conditions, where an individual occasionally may resort to bribery, lies, or other trickery, to assure himself of some coveted chieftainship, the position today which alone offers similar opportunities.

In spite of the lack of any goals which it is imperative to achieve, and a general lack of emphasis upon competitive prestige, personal achievement of some sort is intensely important to the Bachiga, though it may be satisfied by a diversity of goals. The Bachiga are exceedingly headstrong. The average man can brook no authority he does not fear, but he will capitulate to an authority he fears with an amazing lack of opposition. Personal grudges find their expression readily in violent animosity, taking such forms as murder and house burning. Insults are actively resented, and quarreling is very common. Betting is another indication of delight in winning. Even when nothing of value is wagered, remarks are often cast as though there were. Showing off, boasting of one's own exploits in any sphere, calling attention to one's own ability, are all accepted forms of self-expression. Dancing is a good illustration of this. In dancing, everyone tries to do a praiseworthy dance and to show off his skill. But custom allows everyone to dance differently, so that everyone may in fact be excelling in his own particular step.

The system of education, or rather the lack of it, in which children grow up is such as to provide a base for the kind of individualism which we find among the adults, and to develop very marked individual differences in personality and ability.

Unless the mother becomes pregnant again, no attempt is made to wean a child, who does not stop being nursed till he is three or four years old. The situation, which the mother enjoys, is a warm and friendly one. In other ways the infant's contacts are friendly. Others are at hand to carry, fondle, and kiss him. He is carried on his mother's back or in her arms, and sleeps cradled next to her at night.

A mother always indulges her children. Some are spoilt, and the tendency to favoritism is marked. But all of them have a great deal of freedom. The preferences of a child are consulted even about important matters. A youngster of three may elect to live in his grandmother's home, and this would be sufficient grounds for letting him do so. "I refuse," is a favorite answer by a young child when sent out on a chore by its mother. "I can't punish him," she will explain lamely when she returns from fetching water herself, "he might not love me, or he might run away and sleep out in the bush." The latter was the explanation for failure to beat a very malicious child who liked to throw stones with marked precision at other children.

Instead of punishment, threats are used, and the children are allowed to develop fear of various bogeys, either imaginary, or real, such as the co-wife of the mother. Sometimes a beating by the father is threatened, but this rarely materializes. The child's relation to his father is a close one. Little children are often completely devoted to their fathers, and delight in going about after them. However, I do not know of any cases of rivalry for the child's love between a mother and father, although the situation would seem to allow for this at least as an unpatterned possibility. Neither parent is much of a taskmaster. I have seen a man grin with delight when his two-year-old daughter called him a filthy name.

No specific training or instruction is given children, except in manners. A little girl is taught to sit modestly, and children are expected to know how to receive a guest, that it is wrong to grab food, and how to eat delicately with two fingers. Errors in such points are corrected by nagging, but also by the teasing of the other children, and perfection is expected of eight-year-old girls and ten-year-old boys.

General and special techniques, however, must be acquired by the child on its own initiative. Going to the fields with its mother, it learns to wield a hoe, and a boy early tags after the herdboys and learns their ways. A girl of eight or nine may start making a basket if she wants to, and may put it aside indefinitely if she loses interest or is discouraged. A girl may never even make such an attempt. Any such endeavor is praised. All assumption of responsibility must come from the child but always meets extravagant approval. The precocious child is talked of and acclaimed. The one who fails, or fails to try, is not helped over his or her difficulties in any way, but he is not made to suffer any humiliation.

The same lack of compulsion is seen in all fields. The child is not expecially urged to learn social or religious lore, and the varying extent to which this is mastered is very great. Encouragement and praise are given, but the laggard is not shamed, even in the form of invidious comparisons. Each child does his best according to his own inclination, and there is no set pattern to which he must conform. But he is allowed to call attention to any excellences or imagined excellences on his part, and bragging is the rule for children.

In character training we find likewise that there is no one mold to which everyone must be fitted. Personality is treated as a fixed attribute, as evident in a tiny child as in an adult. Any scolding, therefore, which is given a child is not seriously directed toward its correction. If a child refuses to coo delightedly at everyone, and to allow itself to be slung by the arm from one person to another at a gathering, then it is said to be bad-tempered. It will become a mean, sulky person. A child's refusal to share a bit of food with everyone around will cause it to be dubbed a thief, stinginess and thieving being identified. Obviously the constant use of these terms will tend to develop these very characteristics. There is no idea of trying to train the child to attain the ideal character—generous, brave, not quarrelsome, energetic, and trustworthy. Instead, there is praise for those who achieve it and a shrug for the rest.

The effect of this is clearly seen in the adults. Many women, for example, have no knowledge of so simple and important a craft as basketry. Technical excellence is not fostered, nor is it apparent in performance. There is complete tolerance for individual differences in skill and interests, and acceptance even of widely variant behavior. A man known for his lack of generosity is none the less privileged to share in the community life, and even a lazy woman is not necessarily divorced. Social disapproval is almost completely ineffective as a sanction, at least for the men.

If a child lives away from home his position is not very different, though the responsibilities of maturity may in this case be thrust upon him a little earlier. In any case as the child grows older obedience is forced upon him. Even a boy who has early in life taken the initiative, and worked for his own bride price, cannot conduct his own marriage negotiations. A girl is similarly bound to go to the husband to whom her father presents her. Her only choice is to run away to some total stranger, which involves considerable discomfort and some risk. A father uses the threat of failing to provide a husband for her, so that she will be forced to run off, as a means of coercion. Fear is the only means of control which has been developed by the Bachiga, and is the only one which is practical. The only really effective prohibitions are those which carry specific sanctions stronger than the temptation. This is true for adults as well as children. In spite of the fact that she knows that should she become pregnant she runs the risk of death, a girl will allow herself to be seduced by a clan brother, if he convinces her he has medicine which will insure its not being found out. Grown children may be beaten, though little ones never are. A girl who stays out late, a headstrong boy who wishes to choose his own bride, may even be tied to a tree in the center of the courtyard and left there for several hours. Today this is not often resorted to for fear of government interference, but an exaggerated fear of the father is still customary and expressed, especially by girls.

Children's play habits also conform to adult attitudes. The play group is small, and heterogeneous. Large groups usually come together only on adult occasions, and then the children either join the dancing or sit quietly by. Only the more daring of them dash about on their own concerns. In the play group for the most part the children carry on individual games, one singing and hopping while another builds a little mound and a third parades about in some elaborate imagining. The very young are usually tolerated by their elders, and the group may number children of very disparate ages. Among the children whom I saw most frequently, there was no special fixity to the groups and, since each child was self-engrossed, there was little leadership. It is possible that there are different forms among the children when they are herding cattle, but I have no information about this.

There are certain competitive games played by children. Dart throwing and racing are known, though they are not very popular. Sometimes also the children join in a really cooperative venture, such as going off together to make bird traps. Children's activities are not interfered with at all by the adults, except that the latter may call them away to do chores. Violent quarrels are allowed so long as they do not disturb the conversation of the elders.

Sex division develops early. Girls leave the play group younger than boys, and generally play a more important role in the labors of the family. Boys soon learn to idle while their sisters work.

The unmarried girls who are near or just past puberty form groups of their own, and usually fast friendships develop between pairs of girls. All they can do is to work at the same time and next to each other, but not actually together. The only activities in which they can both join are dancing and gathering grass for a feast. These friendships are doomed to dissolution upon the marriage of either of the two. Once a girl is married she can never really be intimate with her erstwhile comrades, even when visiting her old home.

A girl's sex attitudes are developed quite early. Her first lesson is in sitting modestly. She is forced to change many of her ways with the approach of puberty. She must give up eating the meat of sheep or goats, and be shy in the presence of male strangers. She must give up her tomboy ways, lest they become habits she cannot readily break and so disgrace her after marriage. Her father and brothers chaperon her rigidly. All this is in preparation for marriage to a total stranger, involving a disagreeable, lengthy, and very trying ceremony culminating in institutionalized rape.

The boys' introduction to sex is quite different. It is casual and gradual. The women married to his older brothers are accessible to him, and they live in the same village. Full maturity is conceived as coming to him gradually. After marriage, he continues for a time to live in his mother's house, and when he finally establishes a home of his own, it is under his father's protection and with the latter's help. Practice of "medicine," initiation into cults, all such things take place much later, for no man is considered really intellectually mature and thoroughly responsible until he is at least thirty.

There is a conspicuous lack of any behavior in childhood guaranteed to establish respect for one's elder brothers. So long as they are of the same generation, brothers treat each other as equals, and it is just as likely to be the younger who dominates, particularly as a baby is so commonly petted and spoiled by his parents and by older children. This is of course rather different when ages of brothers are very disparate. In such case the younger has the same attitude toward his brother as he should have toward all his elders, one of respect. However, since this is untrained even with regard to parents and grandparents, it amounts in most cases to little more than a few verbal forms.

This is true of the adult picture as well. Relatively greater age theoretically brings respect, but this is overridden in many ways. The really old are consistently honored and not a little feared. A man with a family is assured of a respected and secure old age. For the childless, however, there are likely to be grave difficulties. An old woman usually must continue her labors in the fields, as her daughters are married. It is only if she is a widow with many daughters-in-law that she can in some measure take her ease.

The young on the other hand are in a position of subservience. A man is dependent upon his father or some chosen master for a wife. However, as we have seen, marriage is more important than chronological age. A bachelor cannot be independent, for he has not a woman of his own to grow his food. And the age at which marriage occurs is for the men extremely variable, anywhere from before puberty to long past maturity.

At every point of Bachiga culture there is a marked individualism. Sociability and informal helpfulness are common, but except for the small family and pact brothers, there are no units practicing cooperation. Individualism is apparent in collective activity and is manifested even in the family, within which there is room for personal differences and independent action. Structurally this is reflected in the lack of political integration and in the tendency of families and of clans to break up. Competition is not a clearly organized and standardized pattern of behavior, but is present at least in the desire for personal glory. In many ways the culture is organized in such a fashion as to minimize the competitive effects of the recognized traits clearly seen in the love of boasting and of betting. There is leadership, but no man need be a follower, except to a limited extent of a priest; there is success, but no stigma attached to failure. No man's gain is another man's loss, and there are no social forms to make it seem so. Ability is lauded and encouraged, but no individual submission is required even in the acceptance of authority, no accomplishments are demanded, and there is no social emphasis upon comparing favorably with others. Women are of course dependent upon their husbands, but within a more limited range their activities, too, are individualistic and their personalities only slightly less so than the men's. These patterns are consistent in the various phases of Bachiga life, and the system of education both expresses and perpetuates them.

# CHAPTER V

## THE IFUGAO OF THE PHILIPPINE ISLANDS

### by IRVING GOLDMAN

The interior of Northern Luzon is one of the most isolated regions in the Philippines. Towering mountains, rugged hills, and dense forests have made it relatively inaccessible to foreign intrusion. It is this country that the Ifugao, a brown-skinned Malaysian people, inhabit. A population of 130,000 live scattered through the many valleys and mountain pockets over a total area of no more than 750 square miles. Yet villages are generally small, each with from six to twelve houses clustered around the base of a mountain, close to the precious rice fields. Between villages of even adjacent valleys there is little contact, for vertical distances are great. Moreover though the Ifugao are generally at peace with their fellow men in the same valley, blood feuds and warfare mark the relations between more distant neighbors. Thus, isolated from external contacts, cut off in large measure from their own tribesmen, the Ifugao live in compact groups, composed mainly of their own kin. They cultivate with scrupulous care the rice fields that cling to the mountain face in an intricate system of terraces, as their most valued possessions. Tending vegetable gardens and sweet-potato plots, hunting, and some animal husbandry take up the balance of their food-getting energies. A living is wrested with difficulty from the mountainous but fertile soil. The climate is tropical and precipitation heavy[1] but uncertain. Rain at the wrong season ruins crops.[2] It is not a healthful climate and illness is frequent.

The problems of economic scarcity, coupled with an elaborate system of loans for which usurious interest rates are charged, have

---

[1] The average rainfall is between 100 to 125 inches a year. R. F. Barton, *Ifugao Economics*, p. 388.

[2] The season in which rice is raised is very uncertain as to rainfall. In 1912 there was only one-fourth the average yield due to drought. Barton, *op. cit.*, p. 405.

served to produce an economic and social stratification in Ifugao society based on the ownership of rice land.    Political authority is entirely lacking.    The bilateral family to which the individual bears a deep-rooted allegiance is the social nucleus.    In all disputes kinsmen act as one; and when no compromise can be reached the final legal sanction is the lance.    Religion pervades all activities of any importance, with no little share of the food supply of the community being destroyed in the endless sacrifices to the numerous deities and ancestor spirits of the Ifugao pantheon.

## ECONOMIC BACKGROUND

Rice is the most valued food.    It is the most nourishing, and can be made into a wine which is indispensable to religious ceremonial and to social festivity.    The ownership of rice fields is taken as a measure of social status.    Yet because of factors mainly inherent in the physical environment and partly due to conditions set up by the economic structure, rice is not the chief food of the Ifugao family.    In the first place, "land in areas of considerable extent suitable for rice culture is scarce, or requires long irrigation ditches and concerted labor for its development; requirements the Ifugao's social and economic requirements cannot meet."[1]    Then again, the division of the land into small holdings is not very productive, for rats, wild pigs, monkeys, and deer wreak havoc with the border fields.    Nor is the method of turning the soil with narrow wooden blades highly efficient. Nevertheless to an admirable extent the Ifugao have mastered the agronomical and technological requirements for the cultivation of rice.

Rice fields are owned and cultivated by men and women of a household.[2]    In the division of labor between the sexes the principle of the hardest work for the men and the most work for the women is adhered to.    The men construct the terraces. Stone and earth are banked up to a height that may reach twenty feet, forming a terrace that may be only eleven feet wide.    Into

---

[1] Barton, *op. cit.*, p. 405.

[2] A household consists of husband and wife, and their unmarried children. In a wealthy family servants and slaves form an additional group in the household.

this terrace, formed as a shallow ditch, is run a stream of water in which tons of clay have been poured; the settling of the clay forms a tight subsoil that prevents seepage. Topsoil is added by the same process. In this way the men of each family construct their segment of a field. Only the wealthier families can afford to hire outside labor. If an irrigation ditch is to be dug it will also be done by the menfolk of a single household. Others desiring to use the water from that ditch purchase an interest in it. The upkeep of the ditch then becomes an equal burden on all, and all share the water according to their needs.

The planting and care of the growing rice is women's work. Carefully they transplant the young rice shoots into the rich nitrogenous mounds,[1] and carefully they watch the plants grow for nine months until harvest, pruning the shoots, picking the weeds. It is arduous back-straining work in the hot tropical sun, and groups of women cooperate to do the fields of one and then of another. At harvest time, men, women, and children work together in the fields in an atmosphere of high spirits and gaiety not a little heightened by the liberal consumption of rice wine.[2] The entire able-bodied community works together, each family in its own field. In the larger fields of the wealthy hired laborers work side by side with their employers,[3] diligently cutting the stems with short hand blades.[4]

---

[1] The Ifugao method of heaping up the earth with the decaying vegetable matter serves to maintain the soil at a high level of fertility.

[2] "Harvest time is a highly festive period for all classes. For the old men and women in their capacity as priests and priestesses it is a continuous round of feasting and drinking with real picnic food and inexhaustible jars of rice wine. For the poor who have lived principally on *camotes* [sweet potatoes] during the month preceding it is a time when they gorge themselves on rice and meat-rice and meat every day." Barton, *op. cit.*, p. 404.

[3] Agricultural labor is considered dignified, and even the wealthy, if they have time, do not hestiate to do their share of work in the rice fields.

[4] "All this work [weeding and caring for the rice crops], under a flaming tropical sun, that not only beats directly on the worker but is reflected back to him from the flooded field, is arduous. It can best be done by groups, and the Ifugaos cooperate to do now the fields of one and later, another; they lighten its drudgery by working and singing together. If you should be passing through a terraced area during the growing season, you would see groups of six to fifteen women going over the fields, wearing thick home-woven bodices to protect their back." Barton, *The Half-way Sun*, p. 61.

*Camotes* (sweet potatoes) are despised as a food, but represent, nevertheless, 42 per cent of the total food supply.[1] It is one of the mainstays of the poor, whose rice supply, if they own land, rarely lasts from harvest to harvest. Camotes require less care and less fertile land in their cultivation than does rice. Unclaimed ground on the side of a hill that is heavily overgrown with *runo* grass is cleared by the men of the family and the camotes sown. The women do the rest. After three years or so, the field, having lost its fertility, is abandoned until, when it has again been overgrown with grass and weeds, it is reclaimed by another family. To understand the disrepute in which the native camote is held one must recognize that the camote grown by the Ifugao is decidedly inferior in food value to rice.[2]

Chickens, pigs, and carabao (buffalo) are important primarily in religious sacrifices and only secondarily as food;[3] and since sacrifice plays so prominent a role in Ifugao life, the animals are in great demand and thus highly valued. Livestock are the coin with which the coveted rice land is bought; and in the elaborate system of lending, borrowing, and sale developed by the natives the animals are used as the chief negotiable property.

During the idle period between the rice harvest, ending in July, and spading time, beginning in October or November, the men in those regions where game is available go hunting.[4]

[1] The following table gives the percentages of the eight basic foods used by the Ifugao:

| | | |
|---|---|---:|
| Agriculture | | 84.0 |
| Hunting and fowling | | 0.45 |
| Fishing | | 0.8 |
| Univalves | | 8.0 |
| Insect foods | | 0.05 |
| Wild vegetable foods | | 0.1 |
| Total per cent of wild foods | 9.4 | |
| Animal culture | 4.2 | |
| Camotes | 42.0 | |
| Rice | 32.0 | |

Barton, *Ifugao Economics*, p. 398.

[2] Dr. Margaret Mead has informed me that seven to eight pounds of camotes are equivalent in their food value to one and a half pounds of rice.

[3] Animal sacrifices are eaten by the priests and the petitioners.

[4] "The number of animals killed in a year is great. Annangu, a hunter of Kiangan, has fifty skulls of deer and wild pigs in his house. He has been hunting less than three years." Barton, *Ifugao Economics*, p. 393.

A party of men with dogs is organized to follow the game—wild pigs, deer, and wild carabao—through the forest and grassy hills. Two to ten men form a hunting party. Generally, there are many more dogs. Armed with spears, the men spread out over an area waiting for the dogs to drive the game toward them. When the kill has been made, the flesh is divided on the basis of the number of dogs each man contributed. The spearer of the animal demands and gets a share larger than that which would fall to him if he had not thrown the decisive weapon.

Besides this collective method of hunting, there are more individualistic ways of catching game. Nets are set up across trees to ensnare bats; larger animals are caught in pitfalls. A spear set on a powerful spring is highly effective for catching the wild hog, though being dangerous to other hunters it is not much used.

Vegetables grown in gardens by the women, fruit from family-owned fruit trees,[1] and fish and clams that are free for the taking, round out the Ifugao diet. Fish are "sowed" in the flooded rice fields during the rainy season. Within three or four months the spawn are well grown; and the owners of the fields invite their friends and relatives to fish. Men, women, and children catch the fish in small hand nets. The *ginga*, a univalve shellfish, is so plentiful that it is not sold. Anyone may go to any rice field and pick as many as he desires. This shellfish is an article of diet four nights out of five[2] in the houses of the wealthy as well as the poor.

Each Ifugao family is more or less a self-contained unit and manufactures its own items for its own uses. Still, in regions troubled by density of population manufacturing tends to become centralized.[3] There are men who support their families to a great extent by manufacturing such items as curios, cloths, spears, baskets, long knives, and in regions where potter's clay is available, clay pots. However, demand for such items does not appear to be great, and the maker almost invariably has to seek his own

---

[1] Ownership of a fruit tree does not necessarily extend to the land upon which it grows. Generally no ownership claims are put upon that land.

[2] Barton, *Ifugao Economics*, p. 396.

[3] In those regions where, because of the extreme limitation of land, a good part of the population is landless, manufacturing becomes almost the sole occupation of certain families and their sole source of livelihood.

market. Certainly "nobody in Ifugao expects to get rich and nobody does get rich through manufacturing."[1]

Nevertheless barter had a large place in the economic scheme in the old days and still has. It not infrequently happened that for ten days' work ten men would be given one woven breechclout between them. Since the clout could not be divided, one of the men would purchase it from the other nine, paying them in rice. But in general barter was not well organized. For instance three or four death blankets are generally traded for a jar, and yet an Ifugao owning the necessary blankets and wishing a jar might have difficulty in finding a man who had a jar and wanted the blankets; such a man generally traded his goods for rice or pigs, as these were most negotiable.

A not uncommon form of trade was in slaves. The Ifugao acted as middleman, selling the slaves to their Christianized neighbors on the west. But in the main it was a risky business and was engaged in primarily by landless young men seeking their fortunes.

From the preceding statements of the Ifugao's adjustments to the environmental demands involved in his struggle for subsistence, certain clear-cut principles running consistently through the entire range of social relationships can be derived. The organization of agriculture, particularly rice culture, reveals rather clearly the essentially atomistic structure of Ifugao society. In an enterprise where "concerted labor" would seem to be environmentally required, the size of the cooperating group is limited to the family. Each family pursues its own individualistic ends in the endeavor to accumulate great stores of rice even at the expense of impoverishing a section of the population. The owners of border tracts, for example, are left to suffer the ravages of animal pests on their fields; those who own the inside fields are protected at their expense. Individual misfortune is faced by the individual, or more properly, by the individual and his near kinsmen. Where the physical environment allows no other solution, as in the use of mountain spring water for irrigation, cooperative adjustment is extended beyond the family. But even in this instance the limited cooperative mechanism[2] is

---

[1] Barton, *Ifugao Economics*, p. 424.

[2] Once the arrangement with regard to irrigation (as described on p. 155) has been reached "no rice field may be established to interfere with the

employed to further, in a more efficient manner, individualistic (family) ends. As in our own capitalistic society, so in Ifugao the chief return in economic goods is to capital rather than to labor. Workers in the rice fields at harvest time are paiḍ a small fixed sum,[1] the bulk of the rice going to the landowner.

The same pattern of cooperating for individualistic ends is manifest in hunting. Men combine to exploit the natural environment more adequately, but the division of the game is neither equal nor based on need. The "pay off" is in terms of the number of dogs contributed, or as we would call it, on the basis of capital investment, with a bonus for the spearer. In brief, the individual in Ifugao cooperates within his family group;[2] family groups are competitive among themselves; and such groups may cooperate when necessity demands, cooperation being directed toward individualistic ends. With property held in great esteem, the rewards of the culture go only to those holding property. Except then for a limited range of intergroup cooperation, the behavior characteristic of Ifugao economic relations is competitive. Family is organized against family in a dueling situation that is reflected in practically every aspect of social behavior.

The confluence of a system of usury and conditions of economic shortage, the latter influenced by environmental and cultural factors, has resulted, in Ifugao, in the production of a type of feudalistic structure closely akin to the European model. Land is limited and, in many regions where population pressure is

---

water supply of an already existing field, nor may water which has been flowing to a field be diverted." Barton, *Ifugao Law*, p. 60.

[1] Ten men getting a single breechclout among them for ten days' work.

[2] The sex division of labor within a family group follows:

| *Men* | *Women* | *Either* |
|---|---|---|
| spading fields | basket making | spading fields |
| (except in Kiangan) | planting rice | (only in Kiangan) |
| getting wood | care of growing rice | cooking |
| all work in wood | weaving | harvesting |
| pot burning | pot molding | caring for baby |
| blacksmithing | camote culture | carrying rice to granary |
| rice field construction | (in Kiangan) | camote culture |
| basket making | | (except in Kiangan) |

Barton, *Ifugao Economics*, p. 423.

marked, concentrated in the hands of a few families.[1] The remaining families possess on the average scarcely enough rice-field acreage to yield the barest subsistence.[2] By the time the next harvest has come around, these marginal producers have already depleted their rice stores and are forced to borrow from the wealthy families at exorbitant interest rates. Rates range from 100 per cent for a loan of a few weeks to a year, to 200 and 300 per cent and so on for each additional year the debt is not repaid. Thus, even under the best conditions, many families are driven to indebtedness. But there are many more factors operating to produce shortage. The vagaries of climate and animal pests limit the harvest yield, and such conditions affect even the more well-to-do.[3] In addition, there is the heavy drain on animal stock by sacrifice. The Ifugao believe that all fortune and misfortune are imposed by the activity of a host of supernaturals, which must be appeased and petitioned—in their own phrasing "bribed"—with animal offerings. Illness, which is common, is one of the more frequent occasions for sacrifice. When old age comes on with its attendant ill-health, one field after the other is sold to purchase the livestock needed for sacrifice, until even the most prosperous are driven to the wall.[4] Eco-

[1] Where the total amount of irrigable land is limited, it is concentrated in the hands of a few men. In Lepanto, Benguet, and Bontok where this is true a feudal system is in force. Barton, *Ifugao Economics*, p. 412.

[2] Holdings of rice land in Kiangan district. Census of three villages:

| | |
|---|---:|
| No. families | 109 |
| Population | 444 |
| No. houses | 122 |
| No. families holding 2 acres | 20 |
| 1–2 acres | 40 |
| 1 acre | 40 |
| 0 acre | 9 |

The wealthiest family in these villages had less than twelve acres. Barton, *Ifugao Economics*, p. 412.

[3] See note 2, p. 153, for crop failure due to drought. See also case of Guadde of Maggok, Barton, *Ifugao Economics*, p. 415, for illustration of some of the factors making for the decline of an individual from a position of wealth.

[4] "In proportion to the Ifugao's wealth he does more borrowing than any other people with whom I am acquainted. Most of his borrowing has no connection with any economic principle. Instead most of it finds a motivation in religion." Barton, *Ifugao Economics*, p. 425.

nomic fortunes may thus fluctuate, but the net result is the enrichment of a small landowning class that is never "caught short," and the utter impoverishment and possibly eventual enslavement of the landless. Between these classes is a middle class desperately struggling to climb to higher status on the one hand, and desperately struggling to avoid falling into bondage on the other. Because land is limited, the struggle is all the sharper—the wealth of one family being necessarily obtained at the expense of another segment of the population. This situation is in accordance with the strongly competitive tone of Ifugao society.

## SOCIAL STRUCTURE

As in our own society where social status is generally correlated with economic position, so in Ifugao the influence and social esteem which an individual can achieve is dependent upon the amount of property—rice land, chickens, pigs, carabao—he owns and can control. True, the extent to which class lines are observed varies in each province, but even where such distinctions are weakest they operate decisively in the choice of a mate. In all provinces, socioeconomic classes are named.

At the apex of society, toward which only a limited number can strive, is the *kadangyang* class, the very wealthy, who have validated their position by giving elaborate and costly feasts to their poorer neighbors, and who have acquired, either by inheritance or by having constructed at great expense, the insigne of office, a huge lounging bench. A kadangyang must come of kadangyang blood. But it is a caste position which is validated actually by economic considerations. For in Ifugao, where ancestors are counted back seven or more generations, there are few families that cannot claim kadangyang blood. The power which a kadangyang wields is based on the great wealth he controls. He is like a banker in our culture in this respect. A good part of the community is in debt to him. Should he be involved in a dispute he can call on numerous kinsmen to support his cause with arms. But his power and prestige are more frequently used in the settlement of disputes, in which he serves as arbitrator.

The middle class, the *notumok*, includes the bulk of the population. The notumok are the landowners, who at one extreme are wealthy enough to lend pigs and rice to the needy at high interest and thus accumulate enough property to join the kadangyang, and at the other are a sort of lower middle class producing almost enough rice to last until the next harvest. The latter are the marginal producers, always in debt, always struggling to keep from sinking deeper, to keep from being dropped into the abyss of the landless. The basic orientation of the upper middle class is to rise higher, that of the lower middle class to maintain the *status quo*.

At the very bottom of the social and economic scale are the despised *nowatwat*, the landless. From this class are drawn the wage laborers, the servants, the slaves, and the tenant group. They share no stake in the struggle for status but are content to eke out a meager subsistence in whatever way possible. In a feudal order the nowatwat are the serfs.

The effectiveness with which the individual can function in the complex commercial structure of borrowing and lending, and the endless litigation that ensues, depends largely upon the economic condition of his family and the support it will give him. For this reason the "family unit is the most precious thing in all Ifugao social life."[1] It is a powerfully cohesive unit cooperatively organized and sanctioned by custom and the necessity to contend with other families, similarly organized, for the things they hold most valuable. The individual lacking a family, the orphan, the bastard, the adopted child, is heavily penalized in the economic game.[2] Loyalties are only between kin, and there can be no ties of friendship[3] or any obligations due to friendship that will in any way interfere with the primary kinship obligations.

The family is organized as an institution to perpetuate the existing property relationships, to preserve and if possible enhance an estate that has descended through many generations in the face of a hostile social setup. To this end are geared its

[1] Barton, *Ifugao Law*, p. 63.

[2] Thus, in inheritance, for example, a bastard will inherit only half the property providing there are no other children, the other half going to those who would normally inherit if there were no children. In relation to a legitimate child a bastard is considered a younger child. An adopted child is similarly put in an unfavored position unless he has some kin to support his claim to the property. If an adopted child is related to only one spouse he inherits from that one only. Barton, *Ifugao Law*, p. 51.

[3] There is no institution of friendship in Ifugao.

structural principles. The rules of inheritance, the strongly phrased family unity, are well adapted to meet a competitive situation.

We are familiar with the principle of primogeniture in its Western setting, in which the eldest son inherits the bulk of his father's estate. The Ifugao make this property shift earlier. At some undefined time when the children are quite young the parents decide to make assignment of the family property to them. The rice fields and family heirlooms[1] are apportioned among them with the greater part of the land going to the eldest boy or girl. At this early stage, though, the assignment is provisional; nevertheless it is highly important as a preparatory step for the marriage of the children. It is a statement to the outside group of the economic condition of the children in a culture where economic condition (allowing for exceptional circumstances) is the sole basis upon which a marriage can be arranged. The parents (actually the father) are still managers of the estate; they can still draw on the assigned property to meet such contingencies as sacrifice in time of illness, debts, fines, indemnities. (At the death of either parent a funeral feast must be provided.) They are waiting the time when the children will marry and leave the household, the time when the estate will be fully transferred to the children and they, the parents, having brought their social career to a climax with the arrangement of the children's marriage, can retire from the active scene. At this point the eldest son or daughter becomes the new manager of the estate, the family "center." The parents serve as advisers, or devote themselves to religion. They have done their share by passing on a heritage that goes on in perpetuity from generation to generation, with the younger generation picking up the gauntlet of battle as soon as it is able.[2] In this way the family property is preserved.

The Ifugao make primogeniture meet two demands: to keep the landed estate as undivided as possible, and to maintain the family unity. By passing the bulk of the estate to the eldest

[1] Family heirlooms are gold neck ornaments, rice-wine jars, glass beads, and brass Chinese gongs and have high sentiment as well as economic value.

[2] Children also inherit debts. See case of Pitch Pine vs. Eagle of debts descending through generation after generation. Barton, *The Half-way Sun*, pp. 65–87.

child, and if necessary the entire estate,[1] the property remains essentially intact; and what is probably even more important, the child who has inherited the bulk of the land is in a position to make an advantageous marriage, and by combining two estates, to enhance the value of the family property. The second demand is met by centering the economic responsibility of the family in the hands of the holder of the largest parcel of property. The family "center" is obligated to assist his younger brothers and sisters when they become involved in debt or need a pig for sacrifice.[2] They form a family constellation with the center as the spearhead for the commercial transactions and litigations of the economic world. Beyond the immediate family the same unifying ties are supposed to exist, and with near kin they do. But on the whole the more distant the relationship of a kinsman, the more remote is the possibility of his lending assistance. When distant kinsmen do unite, however, the motives are realistic. Each expects a reciprocal benefit at some future date. One great source of power for the wealthy is the number of relatives they can muster if need be. Because a rich kinsman can be counted on for financial assistance (and the wealthy are always making gifts to their distant and near kin), he is a great asset to the family and must be supported. Yet it would be incorrect to suggest that considerations of wealth underly family unity. Where close kin are concerned, motives of sentiment, of family pride, may transcend other interests. For example no kinsman may proceed against another for any cause unless it be sorcery.[3] Nevertheless, whatever drives there may be, family unity is essential in Ifugao economics.

Kinship ties are of course affected by marriage in a society where the father's and mother's line are of equal importance. The union of members of two families brings in line a new host of relatives on both sides with the result that two brothers, if they

[1] If a family has only one rice field it is not divided but given to the eldest child.

[2] "The mutual duty of kinsfolk and relatives, each individual to every other of the same family, regardless of sex, is to advise, assist and support in all controversies and altercations with members of other groups or families." Barton, *Ifugao Law*, p. 92.

[3] Sorcery is the gravest of all offenses in Ifugao. The use of sorcery against any kinsman is taken as a grave threat to family unity; it is treachery of the highest order.

marry into different families, will be allied to different sets of kinsmen. For the Ifugao such a situation is a difficult one. Siblings above all owe their allegiance primarily to one another and to their own kinsmen. Affinal relatives are still strangers. In effect a marriage is no more than an alliance between members of two families, an alliance that at its strongest may give way to the more imperative demands of family ties. Its basis is not in emotion but in economics; marriage effects the merging of two estates and is as much a commercial and political[1] arrangement as the alliance between two royal houses in Europe. The amount of bickering and formal exchanges that go on during marriage arrangements reflects the importance of such alliances. It is striking that even the very poor, the landless, must validate or legitimatize their marriage by a series of exchanges even if the amount of property involved is but nominal.[2]

With regard to property, the relations between the spouses are also in the nature of an alliance. Until there are offspring, the property which each has contributed is still considered as belonging to the respective families. In the event of divorce, which is not infrequent, each withdraws his or her share. Should the spouses die childless, the property which each has contributed goes back to the original families. Only when there are children to inherit is the property really merged and the two affinal lines joined. Equality in property control is also correlated with a broader equality in the relationship between husband and wife. They both have joint and equal rights in all property acquired after marriage; they are both involved in any sale or mortgaging of such property. They have equal authority in the household.

In the absence of any centralized political authority, relations between families, in view of their frequently conflicting interests, are constrained to a highly formalized system of customary procedure. The principles of this legal system serve further to throw into relief the basic principles upon which Ifugao society

[1] I have used the term "political" here in reference to the custom of settling a feud between two families by arranging a marriage between them. As already mentioned, there is no political structure in Ifugao.

[2] The organization of marriage around property concepts is also characteristic of the Kwakiutl Indians (see pp. 313 *ff.*). It is significant to note the very marked resemblances between the marriage customs of two cultures geographically so far apart, yet in their particular orientation so close.

is constructed. The greatest concern of law is with disputes over property, the occasions for these being many. There are disputes over loans, over sales, over violations of marriage contracts, over land boundaries, etc. In none of these disputes does the individual stand alone. Kin are responsible for all crimes, debts, and civil injuries in proportion to the closeness of their relationship to the principal. Hence in a dispute kinsmen rally together so that family is actively aligned against family. To facilitate the adjustments of disputes a prominent and powerful man, generally a kadangyang, is employed by the offended party to act as an impartial mediator. His recommendations are accepted, not necessarily, as among the Indians of the southwest pueblos, because the Ifugao are willing to accept any peaceable solution, but because the mediator—the *monkalun* as he is called—has his prestige at stake in effecting a settlement.[1] Any party that may be in an obdurate mood after the preliminary overtures have been made may find itself faced with the danger of physical violence from the combined forces of the kinsmen of the monkalun and of the contending party. So a settlement is usually effected, but not without bickering and endless palaver. For to accede too quickly to a demand is to exhibit a weakness that may later prove costly. For the same reason, the plaintiff in a suit must not show himself too ready to accept anything less than the full settlement. Barton has put the situation: "An Ifugao's pride as well as self-interest demand that he collect debts due him and punish crimes against himself. . . . Let there be but one debt owed him which he makes no effort to collect; let there be but one insult offered him that goes unpunished, and in the drunken babbling attendant upon every feast or social occasion, he will hear himself accused of cowardice and called a woman."[2] On the other hand he must not accept punishment too meekly, settle too quickly, or pay an exorbitant fine. If he can beat down the demands usually exacted in his case he gains in prestige. "It is the part of the accused to dally with danger for a time . . . and at least accede to the best terms he can get, if they be within reason."[3]

[1] For a typical controversy, see case of Eagle vs. Pitch Pine in Barton, *The Half-way Sun*, pp. 65–87.
[2] Barton, *Ifugao Law*, p. 95.
[3] *Ibid.*

The prominent role of force in a dispute tends to place the poor in a less favorable position than the rich. One means of ascertaining guilt is by ordeal. An accepted form of ordeal involves the pressing of a hot bolo against the palm of each of the litigants on the theory that if a man is innocent the knife held by an "impartial" monkalun will not injure him. In a case narrated by Barton[1] a poor man who challenged a wealthy person to this ordeal was worsted because the monkalun was bribed. This happened to be a special case, because had the poor man chosen the hot-water ordeal[2] he might have been given a more "objective" trial. In a dispute over property the poor man lacking the support of a large body of kinsmen is again at a disadvantage and must accept the terms offered without much debate.[3]

In the levying of fines and indemnities for wrongdoing, class distinctions play a somewhat different role. The Ifugao on the one hand demand a fine according to the ability of the defendant to pay; rich men are expected to pay heavier fines than the poor. On the other hand, an offense against a rich man is more reprehensible than a like offense against a member of the poorer class. In a clash between classes a sum intermediate between that which each class member would normally pay is demanded.[4]

One other method of settling a dispute remains to be described. This too is a dueling method in a very literal sense. To settle cases of disputed rice-field boundaries wrestling bouts are ordinarily resorted to.[5] The disputants must be evenly matched or

---

[1] Barton, *The Half-way Sun*, pp. 87–89.

[2] In the hot-water ordeal the litigants are required to fetch a pebble from the bottom of a twelve-inch jaw, filled with boiling water, without undue haste.

[3] A man refusing to pay a fine or indemnity may have it seized by force if necessary. The creditor may enter the house of the debtor when the latter is away and seize the value of the fine, leaving an identification of himself to signify his intent. He generally leaves behind a knife, a scabbard, or a blanket. Such a seizure may be perpetrated against a rich man but is always dangerous.

Another method of collecting a debt is for the creditor to descend upon his debtor in company with a group of his powerful kinsmen as unwelcome guests and stay there consuming his store of goods until the debt is paid, Barton, *Ifugao Law*, p. 103, Section 136.

[4] *Ibid.*, p. 67.

[5] *Ibid.*

champions representing them are chosen. In the company of a crowd of kinsmen of both sides the wrestlers take their positions at the mid-point of the disputed boundary. Each tries to throw the other beyond the confines of his own field, for at the point where a wrestler falls the new boundaries are fixed. A monkalun serves as umpire. Kinsmen may sometimes engage in such duels, but they do so in a very friendly way.

In the prosecution of criminal cases the same principles are employed as in civil cases. In only two instances, murder and sorcery, is the death penalty exacted by the kin of the injured. Of these sorcery is the more frequent. It is another means of carrying on hostilities against an enemy. Though witchcraft is sometimes used by a sorcerer on one of his own kinsmen, it is more frequently used against distant enemies. The most common form of sorcery is the *ayak,* or soul stealing, a series of ceremonies in which the sorcerer calls to a feast the ancestral spirits of some man whom he desires to bewitch together with a number of maleficent spirits and deities. He bribes these to bring him in the form of a bottle fly or a dragon fly the soul of his victim. When this insect comes to drink the rice wine that has been set for it, it is caught and imprisoned, and the enemy, having been deprived of his soul, dies.

The intentional killing of a person must be avenged by the victim's kinsmen. Thus a killing always leads to a blood feud that may continue *ad infinitum.*[1] Other offenses such as theft, rape, arson, insult, adultery[2] are punishable by the payment of an indemnity to the injured.

The avenging of a murder has been institutionalized in head-hunting. It must be understood that murder rarely occurs among families living in the same valley, and, when it does take place, public pressure is sufficiently great to prevent a blood feud from starting. But to avenge a death attributed to someone from over the mountains, from another valley, is one of the noblest deeds an Ifugao can accomplish. It gives him great

[1] Since no Ifugao undertakes any but the most elementary acts without consulting the other members of his family, all kinsmen of a murderer are held responsible for the crime.

[2] Adultery discovered *in flagrante* is punishable by death if the guilty persons are murdered on the spot. In other cases the guilty person pays a heavy fine. A married man, *e.g.,* must pay a fine to the kin of his wife, who have been outraged, and to the injured husband.

prestige; it is a blessing for the whole community. "The individual goes head-hunting to gain distinction, obtain vengeance, ingratiate himself with the women or to secure a change of luck or surcease from grief. Head-hunting enables him to marry a wealthier girl than himself. It greatly helps toward the career of monkalun. Also it lessens the expenditure of gifts to the girl's kin when one takes a wife."[1]

Head-hunting is rarely an individual undertaking. A small party of six to ten men form an expedition and proceed with as much precaution as possible to avoid danger to themselves. The victim is ambushed and speared. All then scramble for the head.[2] When they are a safe distance from the enemy territory, the head-hunting party gives a loud shriek of victory as a signal that a head has been taken. The village that has lost a head is stricken with the greatest grief. Men and women clamor for vengeance. The decapitated victim is brought back to the village and insulted and maligned to excite his soul to vengeance. It is not long before the men, stung into action by the reproaches of the women, organize a retaliatory expedition. In this way the blood feud goes on interminably.

Religion is closely integrated with the ideals of the culture and plays a major role in all social activities. The Ifugao does not seek from his gods release from mundane existence or contact with great supernatural power. His desires are simpler. He would greet wealth, many children, and success against his enemies. To achieve these blessings he bribes the gods with animal sacrifices; he repeats long ritual myths that will force the gods to act for him. If his gods are troublesome and afflict him with illness or destroy his rice crops, they can be bribed with rice wine and animal sacrifices. In religion as in other spheres the wealthy are the more blessed and their wealth is due to the good offices of the gods. They can make the heaviest sacrifices. For that reason the wealthy make the best priests, and, though the tendency is for each family to have its own priestly body, the old men and women, a wealthy priest is called to officiate in a serious conflict. The priests are not paid for their offices, but they are given all the rice wine and meat they can eat.

[1] Barton, *The Half-way Sun*, p. 197.

[2] The one who actually takes the skull is privileged to carry it back to the village. His is the greatest glory. However, each man shares in the prestige of merely having been on a head-hunt.

## EDUCATION[1]

At a very early age children are cautioned against any but the most formal relations with their siblings of opposite sex, or with their near relatives of opposite sex. When at the age of three or four, the children go to live in the village dormitories, houses where the unmarried live. Brothers and sisters are placed in different dormitories. Though living away from home the children are required to assist their parents in the fields and the house. Corporal punishment is rare.

Attitudes toward property must be taught at an early age, for the child soon begins to look at the family property as his own and is prepared to defend his interests in that property.[2]

## ROLE PLAYED BY THE INDIVIDUAL IN THE SOCIETY

The role allowed the individual in Ifugae is one that is limited by two very decisive factors, the economic status of his parents and his relative age position in the family. Within the fixed range set by these conditions he can more or less modify his position depending upon his personality. But in the main the culture has set up external conditions that only the exceptional person can alter. Theoretically the sexes are treated with equality. Women inherit property. They may even act as the family center. But since a woman is not prepared to fight to defend her interests her cultural role is more or less a passive one.

To analyze the position of the individual without reference to his socioeconomic class is no more valid in Ifugao than such an analysis would be in our own culture. I have, therefore, reconstructed hypothetical life histories of individuals within each of the three major socioeconomic groups.

A family in the nowatwat poverty-stricken class has few economic opportunities. It owns no rice land and lives on camotes, shellfish, hunting, and from what little rice the husband

---

[1] Except for a few scattered and casual remarks the subject of child life is barely touched on in the only available literature on the Ifugao.

[2] Barton cites the case of a son who killed his father because the latter to pay gambling debts had mortgaged off some of the family fields and made no effort to retrieve them. The punishment was socially recognized and the boy had consulted his kinsmen and had gained their sanction before proceeding with the deed. Barton, *Ifugao Law*, p. 107.

There is no further mention of gambling in the literature.

and wife may earn by working during the harvest in the rice fields of the upper classes. Possibly, the man will be urged by his wife to manufacture a basket or a spear to trade for rice. At best, existence is at the subsistence level. When there is illness or some other misfortune, a chicken or a pig must be sacrificed to the gods. But if the family does not possess a pig, and if there are no kinsmen to lend them one, they are forced to borrow from the kadangyang or from some middle-class family. With the high rates of interest repayment is well-nigh impossible, so the parents mortgage their child to the creditor and extend the debt. In the end the child will be enslaved by the creditor in full payment.

Or the family may lease a quarter acre of land from a landlord, and become tenant farmers. Under this arrangement the landlord supplies the land and half the seed. At harvest time the rice is divided equally between landlord and tenant. But if in the meantime the unfortunate tenant has borrowed rice from the landlord this is deducted from the crop with the usual 100 per cent interest. The status of the tenant is no better than that of the lowliest serf on the medieval manor.

What can be the horizon of a child born to a nowatwat family? At the age of three or four the children go to live in the village dormitory. The small boy learns to snare birds and small game to supplement the food in the house. When grown up he works in the rice fields alongside his father as a laborer. Should his father fall badly into debt he will bond his son out as a servant.[1] In this condition he has the hope and the possibility that his master will be generous enough to provide him with the cost of a marriage feast when he has chosen his bride. Then the young man and his bride can settle down to the routine of tenant farming, with the chances that their children will grow up in bondage to some master.[2] Should a boy escape being bonded out as a slave by his father he is in effect no better off. Lacking property he has little chance to marry. In the dormitory he may enter into clandestine relations with some girl, but no girl of any status will admit him as a lover.[3] With no better prospect

[1] The selling or bonding out of children in payment of debt was formerly extremely common. Barton, *Ifugao Economics*, p. 419.

[2] *Ibid.*

[3] Barton tells the following incident in this connection: A young man knocked at the door of a dormitory and asked to be admitted. When the

offering itself the young man enters into voluntary bondage to someone he hopes will be a kind master. Possibly he is treated as a member of the family, but always his master has the power of life and death over him.

For a girl of the nowatwat class conditions are a bit brighter. Women are always an economic asset. They work in the fields. Some young man, possibly a younger son of a middle-class family, will marry her if he lacks the property essential to marriage with a girl of his own class.

Lacking all stake in the culture the poor are often driven to desperate acts. An aggressive man can make himself feared by his more wealthy neighbors, who may dread his wrath.

The middle class, the owners of land, exemplify most completely the various dynamics of economic life. In the lower economic level, an average middle-class family will own a small plot of rice land, possibly an acre or less. The rice will barely last from harvest until harvest. They supplement this meager supply with camotes and hunting. About a month or so before the rice crop ripens, the family finds it necessary to borrow rice. At the harvest it will repay the debt with the interest. Illness is a greater misfortune than lack of rice. Animals must be had for sacrifice and a field is mortgaged. The only hope of social advancement is that the oldest child will marry well. If a boy, he will go on a head-hunting expedition and thus gain prestige and a reputation for valor, qualities which will compensate largely for his deficiency in land. He may accumulate some property on his own account by partaking in the dangerous slave trade. His success depends largely on his valor and aggressiveness. He must also be shrewd and cautious to avoid getting involved in disputes that might bring a heavy fine upon him. The role of a girl is again more passive. She waits for her parents to arrange an advantageous marriage for her with the chances that if she is scrupulous in her choice of lovers her social condition will be advanced. For younger sons inheriting no land and

door was not opened he drew his Jew's harp and played a plaintive tune and sang a love song to one of the girls in the house. But she disdained him and complained that he was lazy, came from poor stock, of a family that had no fields and never had any. She confessed that she had no estate herself, but her eldest brother had, and one of her grandfathers had been a kadangyang. Barton, *The Half-way Sun*, p. 49.

very little other property the social outlook is little better than that for the nowatwat youth, except to the extent that the prestige of coming from a family with land helps him get a bride.

The upper middle class, the wealthy landowners, those producing more than enough rice for their subsistence needs and lending out the surplus at high interest rates, are motivated by one drive—to become kadangyang or to make their children kadangyang. To this end vast quantities of clouts,[1] women's skirts, rice-wine jars, and iron pots together with great supplies of food and rice wine are collected. The former items are to be used as gifts to the kin of the bride, the latter will form the basis of the great *uyauwe* feast, at which the kadangyang status is validated.

At an early age, the children are withdrawn from the village dormitory for fear they might ruin their chances of an aristocratic marriage by getting involved in some sexual indiscretion.[2] The children of the very wealthy are wed early. If for example a first son is born to a wealthy family, his parents look about for some wealthy family to which a girl has been born. The kinsmen of both families then agree to a betrothal of their children. After much bickering back and forth the amount of property that will be settled on each child is decided, and negotiations continue for the final marriage. For the parents, the marriage will be the climax of a successful career of shrewd economic dealing, it will mean the realization of their fondest dreams. Their child is to be made a kadangyang. The importance with which such a marriage is regarded is indicated by the circumspect care with which all the negotiations are conducted. At each of the four stages necessary to complete a marriage, omens are consulted. Should the gods prove themselves unfriendly then the whole matter is dropped. Finally, all is ready; property and food have been accumulated and the great uyauwe feast, a public festival, is held. Gifts are distributed to the kin of the girl.

As a kadangyang the youth must show himself worthy of his rank. He must acquire a reputation for courage and resoluteness that will be a valuable asset to him in his commercial affairs,

[1] Cloth breechclouts woven by the women.
[2] See Barton, *Ifugao Economics*, p. 53.

that will permit him in later life to become a monkalun.[1]  He must likewise be shrewd in his business dealings, collecting all debts due him, protecting his investments.  Thus he will become more powerful and an enviable figure in the community.  His distant kinsmen will rally around him as a great family center and contribute appreciably to his power.  If he is wise he distributes gifts judiciously among them to cement their support.[2]  As a wealthy and powerful man, the kadangyang can take two or three wives, an action that none but the most powerful would dare.  The kadangyang is only the more envied for this violation of custom.

The vagaries of Ifugao life, however, make no man's position certain.  Inevitably illness afflicts him, and his carefully accumulated stock of animals, his many rice fields, begin to flow through the sieve of sacrifice.  Further his children are now grown and his fields are divided among them.  He has lavished a great deal on feasts which he must give at intervals if the villagers are to respect him.  His wealth may have been used to elevate a child to kadangyang.[3]

As a younger son of a kadangyang or of a wealthy family, he inherits a few fields, but is not raised to kadangyang status automatically by his parents.  He must fight his own way to fortune.  A head-hunt will give him the prestige necessary to permit him to marry higher than his economic state, and at least he can depend upon his children to become kadangyang.

## IDEALS OF THE CULTURE

The male Ifugao is motivated by the drive for wealth in property and the power and prestige that go with it.  To attain this end he must be aggressive and valorous but above all shrewd.  "One of the fine points in buying consists of an insidious hospitality on the part of the purchaser which gets the seller and his

[1] In any commercial dealing the Ifugao is liable to run up against a situation calling for the display of force.  The man who has demonstrated his valor by engaging in a head-hunt is more likely to be feared and his wishes respected.

[2] In the disputes that may arise in the ordinary course of commercial activity the man with the strongest family backing stands the best chance of success.  To this extent the cementing of family ties to include distant kinsmen may be crucial.

[3] See case of Guadde of Maggok, Barton, *Ifugao Economics*, p. 415.

kin drunk so that they forget some of their perquisites."[1] In their economy of a fixed and limited supply the Ifugao honor those who can accumulate the most even at the expense of their neighbors. The man of wealth, the kadangyang, may take two or even three wives and be envied, though monogamy is the cultural pattern. A lesser man would be hounded to death for daring such a thing. On the other hand, the man of wealth must not be stingy. If he is to maintain his status as a kadangyang he must continually redistribute some of his wealth in a series of elaborate and costly feasts to the populace. Along with and fitting into the economic framework of desire for wealth is the Ifugao emphasis on pride. The man who is slow to avenge a kinsman's death is stung into action by his sister's giving him her skirt to wear. It is pride as well as business necessity that drives an Ifugao to bear down on his debtor or to resist a creditor. What the Ifugao fears most is loss of face.

I might add here parenthetically that the Ifugao disorder of running amok seems to be related in the one instance that Barton describes to "hurt feelings." An Ifugao laborer who had applied for a leave of absence to visit home and had been denied permission ran amok two days later, killing three men and stabbing the foreman. According to the reports of other laborers he had complained for some days past of being in a state of *higa*, a "painful mood."

## INTEGRATION OF CULTURE

The emphasis upon property and upon wealth and the competitive forms associated with that emphasis run consistently through every aspect of Ifugao social relations. In religion, the favors of the gods must be bought with bribes, and the wealthy as exhibiting the greatest supernatural blessings are the most effective priests. In law, most of the disputes center about property or the collecting of loans. Marriage is but another phase of the economic struggle, serving as a means for joining two parcels of valuable rice land.

## CONCLUSIONS

*Technology.*—In the construction of rice terraces the Ifugao are *noncooperative* to the extent that the joint effort required to build

[1] Barton, *Ifugao Law*, p. 48.

these terraces is limited to the men of a single household.   In the opinion of Barton[1] more extended group labor would result in greater productivity.

Collective use of and collective responsibility for the maintenance of the irrigation ditches are based upon a purchased interest in the ditch, and the cooperative venture is directed toward individualistic ends in that the rice is shared only by members of the household.

Work in the fields such as weeding the rice is organized cooperatively among all the women of the village.   Groups of women cooperate to do now the fields of one and later of another.   By working and singing together they lighten the arduousness of the work under the hot sun.[2]

At harvest, household units work together with additional assistance of hired laborers.   Individual hand implements are used with the result that each person works by himself.

Limited household cooperation is also expressed in camote culture and in the care of pigs and chickens.

Hunting is cooperative, with two to ten men forming a party and pooling their dogs.   The end result though, is entirely individualistic, with the division of the game on the basis of capital investment rather than of effort.   The use of snares and pitfalls for catching game is entirely individualistic.

Gardening is individualistic; the women of each household do all the work by themselves with some assistance from the little girls.   The food is also used only within the household unit.

Catching of fish from flooded rice fields is done individualistically with individualistic ends.   However, the action of the owners of the field in sowing the fish is cooperative.   Shellfish, very commonly used as food, are taken individualistically.

For the most part, each household is a self-contained unit with regard to manufacturing.   The manufacturing process seems to be individualized.   Cooperation between various villages or households in terms of barter is limited mainly to pottery under conditions of environmental necessity.

*Economic Relations.*—Ownership of land: land is considered as belonging to a family line but is under the control of husband

[1] *Ifugao Economics*, p. 405.

[2] Barton, *The Half-way Sun*, p. 61.

and wife. In effect, land is individually owned by a household in its linear extensions. The products of the land are individually used.

Ownership of other property: pigs, chickens, carabao, and family heirlooms are individually owned. Here, too, the linear extensions of the household are included in the ownership. The use of this property may be shared only among members of the household and to a lesser extent among the very near kin of the collateral lines.

Between members of different families there is strong competition for the accumulation of property. Competition for property is the basis of practically all interfamilial relations. It might be said that all property owners are, outside the phrased family obligations, rivals.

The strong rivalry for property is expressed in the unusually high interest rates charged for loans.

The socioeconomic class stratification is another expression of the strongly competitive struggle for property.

*Social Structure.*—Members of a household are always cooperative in technological as well as in property relations. Members within the bilateral extensions of the family group are in the use and manipulation of property noncompetitive, and in cases of interfamilial disputes cooperative. Between members of different families there may, to a limited extent, exist some cooperative arrangements, as in hunting, head-hunting, weeding of the rice fields, where environmental conditions call for a cooperative effort. But essentially their relations are competitive. Friendship across family lines is strictly limited.

The rule of primogeniture in inheritance, by which the younger children are left landless, might lead to attitudes of resentment, but strong family unity tends to limit this. Rivalry among siblings and first cousins is strictly curtailed by the demands of the culture that they assist one another. There is no interest charged for loans between siblings and near relatives.

Marriage unites two families and limits competition between them. Blood feuds that might have existed between families are ended after a marriage. However, the essentially competitive organization at the basis of interfamilial relations is illustrated by the conceptualization of marriage as merely an alliance, in which each of the spouses owes primary allegiance to his or her own family group. The union of the families is only fully expressed in the next generation.

The legal system reflects the competitive emphasis in the culture. In every case, the final sanction is the lance. Litigations are conducted between families, with the greatest chance of success going to the family that can marshal the greatest array of kinsmen. Procedure is competitive even in a literal sense. Land disputes are settled by wrestling. Before a settlement is reached each family as a point of honor strives to beat down demands and to uphold its own demands.

Though relations between families within the same district are competitive with regard to property, relations between families of different districts are distinctly hostile. The blood feuds are based on points of honor, prestige, and supernatural well-being. In that sense they are competitive.

Head-hunting expeditions are cooperatively organized from the standpoint of insuring safety and success, but the results of the head-hunt are both cooperatively and individualistically distributed. The taker of the head, who exhibits the skull in his house, gains most in prestige. All members of the expedition share in the prestige. The entire community shares in the supernatural blessing which the taking of an enemy head brings. The prestige which the individual obtains he uses to further his own property interests.

Religion is individualistically organized. Each family by its own sacrifices seeks to add to its own welfare. Poor families unable to sacrifice much are correspondingly neglected by the gods. The wealthy are the most blessed.

*The Individual.*—The personality traits required of the individual to compete successfully for the rewards of wealth and status are aggressiveness and shrewdness.

In the landless class the possibility of competing is almost entirely restricted. In the landowning class, on the other hand, habits of aggressive competition are most valuable. For an eldest son of a middle-class family, for example, shrewdness in manipulating his property plus an aggressive insistence on his rights will frequently bring success. A younger son can compensate for his property deficiency by a strong show of aggressiveness and courage.

Only toward his own near kin is the individual required to exhibit habits of noncompetitiveness and, when occasion demands, cooperativeness.

In conclusion, it is clear that from the preceding analysis of the organization of competitive, cooperative, or individualistic habit patterns of the Ifugao the culture is predominantly oriented toward competitiveness. In every situation the individual is required to display two sets of contrasting behavior patterns: toward his own kinsmen cooperative, or at least noncompetitive, patterns; toward nonrelatives competitive, or at best noncooperative, patterns. But the effect of a cooperatively constructed family group is to render more effective interfamilial competition.[1]

*Bibliography*

BARTON, R. F.: *The Half-way Sun*, Brewer, Warren & Putnam, Inc., New York, 1930.

————: *Ifugao Economics*, University of California Publications in American Archeology and Ethnology, Vol. 15, No. 5, 1922.

————: *Ifugao Law*, University of California Publications in American Archeology and Ethnology, Vol. 15, No. 1, 1922.

[1] For personal accounts see *The Half-way Sun*, pp. 65–87; *Ifugao Economics*, pp. 53, 415.

# CHAPTER VI

## THE KWAKIUTL INDIANS OF VANCOUVER ISLAND

*by* IRVING GOLDMAN

Along the narrow strip of indented coast line stretching from Juan de Fuca Strait to Yakutat Bay live a number of Indian tribes differing among themselves in speech and physical characteristics but sharing a highly distinctive culture. Among these are the Kwakiutl. Hemmed in by rugged mountains and dense forest on the east the Kwakiutl have been crowded onto the beach, where they build their large plank houses. They wrest their living mainly from the sea, using salmon, candlefish, halibut, and mountain goat as the main items of diet. No land is cultivated, but the Indians pick wild berries and seeds from family-owned grounds and tend small clover gardens. Some animals are hunted in restricted and family-owned hunting areas. From the forest comes the red cedar used in the construction of houses, the large seagoing canoes, the richly carved boxes, and totem poles. On the whole, in comparison with the rest of the continent, the Kwakiutl are rich in material goods. Food is plentiful. In aboriginal days the Kwakiutl must have numbered from 10,000 to 20,000, but epidemics have twice decimated the population until in 1904 they numbered no more than 2,000.[1]

Upon an economic base of comparative plenty, the Kwakiutl have developed a system of economic exchanges that bears little relation to the problem of existence. Property is accumulated only to be redistributed or destroyed in a game in which prestige and self-glorification are raised to an egomaniacal pitch. More important even than material property as counters of prestige are the jealously guarded honorific names, titles, family traditions, and ceremonial prerogatives. Material property is valued only to the extent that it can procure or validate these prerogatives and names. The social structure reflects the great valuation of immaterial property in Kwakiutl life.

[1] A. L. Kroeber in *Encyclopaedia Britannica*, 13th edition.

The Kwakiutl are composed of a great many tribes that are subdivided into bilateral family lines—the *numaym*[1]—the members of which claim descent from some mythical ancestor. The chiefly family within each numaym has its own history dating from a supernatural ancestor. The striking emphasis is upon rank. All tribes, numayms, and families are graded according to a strict pattern.[2] Within the tribe each individual is further classified as a nobleman, commoner, or slave, but the latter group, being for the most part made up of captives in war, are of no importance in the social structure. The nobility are the first-born of families of rank; the commoners are the younger sons and daughters. At the head of each numaym is a chief, one coming from a chiefly line. This chief possesses a certain limited political power.

Religion, too, is subordinated to the drive for rank and prestige, contact with the supernatural during the important winter religious ceremonials being based upon strictly owned, inherited, or otherwise validated prerogatives.

## ECONOMIC BACKGROUND

In a region renowned for the abundance of its sea life, the principal economic pursuit of the Kwakiutl is fishing. Sea lions and seals are harpooned, the barbed point of the harpoon being attached either to a floating bladder or to the stern of the canoe. Cod and halibut are angled for with hook and line; salmon are caught in traps and in fish weirs placed in the rivers or swept up in nets dragged between two canoes. In addition to the fish that are caught by men, a variety of mollusks are gathered by the women.[3]

The organization of fishing within the numaym is[4] essentially individualistic, though sometimes a group of brothers cooperate in fishing. Half the catch is given to the chief of the numaym to be distributed by him to all who need food during the winter,

[1] The numaym also includes individuals, not members of the bilateral family group, who have been given or purchased names belonging to the numaym.

[2] Originally all were equal.

[3] Franz Boas, "Social Organization and Secret Societies of the Kwakiutl Indians," p. 318.

[4] The present tense is used for narrative purposes only. The account refers to aboriginal conditions in the old days.

when economic life is suspended.   It is always the responsibility of the chief to provide for his people when they are in need.   The other half is used to feed the household of the men who caught the fish.   The same distribution of the catch occurs even in those frequent cases when a number of canoes are needed to surround a school of porpoises to prevent their escape, but the usual method is individualistic—a man and his steersman hunt the porpoises alone.   In salmon fishing, hunting, and berry picking also the members of a household pay a percentage of the food taken to their chief and use the rest for themselves.   By paying this tax each member of the numaym is contributing to a communal food supply to be drawn upon by all.

Members of a numaym cooperate also in the ownership and exclusive use of hunting, fishing, and berry-picking territory. Even fishing rights in the sea are rigidly marked by sighting against two landmarks.   Certain rivers belong entirely to a numaym, others to a tribe.   Trespass on such territory is forbidden, and the aggressor may be killed.   These strictly maintained property rights are not related to any kind of food shortage.   On the contrary the Kwakiutl are economically very well off and are not faced with the necessity for competing for a limited food supply.[1]

Only a relatively small proportion of the Kwakiutl's time is devoted to food getting.   "The great occupation of the men, aside from hunting and fishing, was wood working."[2]   The most time-consuming activity of the women is not the household routine or the gathering of berries but the making of baskets, mats, and cedar-bark blankets, property that is used in the formal distributions around which every significant aspect of Kwakiutl civilization is oriented.   Woodworking is the great skilled craft on the Northwest Coast.   The men can construct, out of a single cedar trunk, huge seagoing canoes holding sixty persons.   With skillfully directed wedges, they split tar logs into planks to be used in house construction and in making beautifully carved boxes.   Logs are carved into huge totem poles.

In all this work skilled labor is required, and when a chief desires to have a house built or a totem pole carved he hires a

[1] The tribes living up the inlets and deeper in the interior were sometimes faced by famine.

[2] Ruth Benedict, *Patterns of Culture*, p. 174.

number of skilled workers. A great many men are hired to build a house, each of whom is given a specific task, some to lay rafters, some to adz planks, some to dig holes into which the house posts are set. In one description of house construction cited by Boas[1] the following division of labor was followed: Fourteen men were hired to chop down the trees and prepare the different kinds of lumber. One man was hired to get the thick posts, two to chop down one beam apiece, two to chop down two posts each, two men each to hew one side bar, two men to chop seven rafters apiece. Each was paid ten pairs of blankets for this work. For chopping roof beams and retaining planks, each of the other five men hired was paid five pairs of blankets. All chop down the cedar trees together and peel the bark. The men hired to do the same task work together, assisting one another. When this work is done, the logs are hauled through the water and rolled up the beach to the house of the chief who has ordered the construction. Then the chief hires six adzers, two from each of the three Kwakiutl tribes, and the latter hire from among their relatives the men they wish to assist them. Others are hired to dig the four post holes. The adzers are given ten pairs of blankets apiece, and the hole diggers five pairs apiece. After about eight days of labor the house is completed. For the carving of the house posts special carvers are employed and paid 200 blankets for four posts. Only a single pair of blankets is given to each pair of the laborers who bring up the logs to be carved.

Thus, in every construction requiring the labor of a number of men the work is collectively organized. To the extent that the workers are all drawn from the same numaym and are working at the command of the chief the ends are cooperative too. Under present conditions, workers are drawn from different numayms and are attracted primarily by the promise of wages. In food getting, on the other hand, the emphasis is primarily individualistic both as to means and ends.

## SOCIAL STRUCTURE

All the social relations among the Kwakiutl are keyed to the principle of rank, and each individual of any status in the com-

[1] Boas, "Contributions to the Ethnology of the Kwakiutl," pp. 311 *ff*.

munity is motivated by an obsessive drive for prestige. The social stratification, which in Ifugao is based on the ownership of rice fields, is, on the Northwest Coast, carried to an extreme degree in terms not of material goods but of prerogatives.

The peoples speaking the Kwakiutl dialect are divided into a number of tribes, each with a head chief and each arranged in a hierarchical order of rank and possessing certain crests and privileges obtained from the supernaturals. Each tribe is further subdivided into a number of family lines claiming descent from a mythical ancestor and cherishing a specific tradition. These family lines, the numayms, are also graded in rank. In addition, the individuals composing the numaym are divided into a nobility and common people. A slave class consisting of individuals taken captive in war or purchased does not form an integral part of the numaym, the slaves being regarded as property. The organization of the numaym is such that only a limited number of families are recognized.[1] Thus, the numaym possesses a fixed number of noble titles descending always in a strict line of primogeniture. The bearers of these names and the privileges that are attached to them form the nobility. All others are despised commoners. But the members of the nobility are not equal in rank. They are ranged in a hierarchy of nobility in the same way as their ancestors were supposed to have been ranked.[2] At festivals, at the great distributions of property, at the potlatches, whenever the nobility gather, this order of rank is strictly followed.

The possession of a title, however, does not in itself give the individual social prestige. Each claim to nobility must be validated by the distribution of property, blankets, boxes, and by the giving of feasts during which great quantities of valuable oil are conspicuously destroyed. Above all, an individual gains prestige by crushing a rival. It is this intense rivalry that is at the heart of Kwakiutl social relations. Property is given to a rival which he must repay with a 100 per cent interest. If he cannot meet this payment, he is crushed and loses in social status. Similarly, when a feast has been given to a rival, this rival must

---

[1] Boas, "Social Organization and Secret Societies of the Kwakiutl Indians," p. 338.

[2] *Ibid.*, p. 339.

counter by giving a more elaborate and costly feast or lose in status. It is a war in which property is the weapon.[1]

There is, however, another aspect to the strongly phrased property-exchange rivalries between individuals. Such rivalries are frequently conducted on a friendship basis; for the chiefs who habitually potlatch one another are actually alternating in raising one another's prestige. It is when the perpetually rising scale of exchanges reaches a critical crescendo in which the financial capacities of the rivals are taxed to the utmost that the friendship is converted into snarling enmity.

As the numaym is the unit which owns land and fishing rights, so it is the noncompetitive and frequently cooperative unit in property "wars." Originally the numaym was a village community,[2] the members occupying large square wooden houses in which four families lived in the manner of our modern apartment houses. That is, each family occupied one corner of the house, prepared its individually owned food supply over individual fires. There were, in other words, four individual households within each house, with a tendency for a group of married sons with their wives and children to live together. Each family occupied a corner of the house according to its degree of nobility.[3] Theoretically only the eldest child inherited the family names and the privileges of nobility, the rest being commoners,[4] so that a household presented a cross-section of Kwakiutl society. A number of such houses comprised a village.

The organization of the numaym becomes clearer from a discussion of the principles of inheritance. Fundamentally a numaym consists of a fixed number of names and privileges that were originally obtained by some ancestor from the supernaturals after a series of adventures. It is probable that at some earlier time the number of names was much less than it is now, owing

[1] *Ibid.*, p. 343. "Formerly feats of bravery counted as well as distributions of property, but nowadays, as the Indians say, 'rivals fight with property only.'"

[2] *Ibid.*, p. 334.

[3] Boas, from lecture notes.

[4] It is obvious that if strict primogeniture were adhered to in the inheritance of names, in the course of time all the names would tend to pile upon one individual. This of course is not actually the case. In practice second-born children are also given important names that entitle them to noble rank.

to the piling up of names on one person. At present, there are in many numayms more names than persons to use them, but since each name within the numaym occupies a fixed position in a hierarchy of rank only certain individuals can inherit the most honored names, the first-born. Other children receive the more common names and thus fall into the ranks of the commoners. In addition to the names the individual receives from the father, there is another class of names that come from the mother's side through the maternal grandfather. That is, a man at marriage is entrusted with a dowry of names and titles by his father-in-law. The son-in-law may not use these names himself but must pass them to his children, although the strong individualistic stress of the Kwakiutl actually allows the son-in-law a much wider latitude in disposing of these names. He may give them to the children from another marriage, for example. Thus the individual may belong to two numayms, by virtue of the fact that he has claim to names that have come from both the numaym of his father and that of his maternal grandfather. Women inherit as men. A first-born daughter of a noble family takes on a man's name and socially plays a man's role, but she ceases to potlatch when her first-born child comes of age.

As a result of the strong emphasis upon primogeniture the noblest names within the numaym tend to descend along the line of the first-born, while the less noble names are held by the other family lines. The system, however, is complicated by the fact that another line of names descends through the maternal line, so that what might have developed into a rigid social stratification under a unilateral system of inheritance is much more diffuse. Nevertheless, within any given generation, all the names are ranged in a hierarchy of rank from the most noble name, which gives the individual rights to chieftainship, to the most unprivileged name. Further, when an individual takes on a name he assumes in his person all the greatness of his ancestors, whom he is thought to be impersonating. Therefore when a man passes his name to his heir he necessarily relinquishes all rights to its use.[1]

A similar condition of primogeniture has been described for the Ifugao, but unfortunately no information was available with

[1] Boas, "Social Organizations and Secret Societies of the Kwakiutl Indians," p. 338.

regard to the attitudes of the younger members of a fraternity, the disinherited, toward their more fortunate senior brothers. Among the Kwakiutl there are a number of instances of hostility between brothers. Since a younger brother inherits the names and privileges of his elder brother if the latter should die without an heir, he may seek his death by sorcery.[1] A younger brother may exult because he has shamed his older brother. On the other hand, an older brother may loan his name and dance privileges to a younger brother providing the latter can demonstrate his economic fitness for the names by giving a potlatch. Competition between brothers may also be avoided by the younger one's leaving the numaym of his father to go to the numaym of his mother. Dr. Boas[2] cites the case of two brothers the older of whom, when he grew up, took the seat of his father as well as the office of assembler of the tribes during the winter ceremonial. The younger brother became sick at heart, for he had wanted to take the latter privilege from his father. When the older refused to give up this position, the younger brother went to his mother's numaym and took the office of assembler there.

Although the oldest children inherit the bulk of the names and honorific privileges, the Kwakiutl leave at least one honorific office to the youngest son, the position of counter and tally keeper of the dishes used at a feast given to many tribes. Curiously this office passes to the youngest because they are considered to be clever, whereas the oldest children are thought likely to be foolish.[3]

Whatever rivalry exists between brothers is always indirectly expressed. In the socially recognized form of rivalry, in the potlatch, brothers do not compete against one another. Nor do members of the same numaym fight against one another with property. For if one is to gain the full prestige of having vanquished a rival that rival must be a worthy opponent. A nobleman does not compete with a commoner. He competes only

[1] Boas, "Ethnology of the Kwakiutl," *35th Annual Report of the Bureau of American Ethnology,* Part 2, p. 1358. "It is said that the younger brother often bewitches his elder brother that he may die quickly, because the younger brother wishes to take the seat of the elder brother."

[2] Boas, "Contributions to the Ethnology of the Kwakiutl," p. 61.

[3] *Ibid.,* p. 58.

with another nobleman of similar rank. This equation is carried to the point where the numayms are "perpetually pitted against each other according to their rank."[1] In intertribal rivalry only certain tribes are traditionally paired off as worthy rivals.

The Kwakiutl numaym functions cooperatively in interfamily conflicts in a fashion somewhat similar to the Ifugao family. The great property distributions of the Kwakiutl are between numayms and often between tribes. In these, though the chief of the numaym or the head chief of the tribe is the figure-head of the potlatch, he is assisted by all his numaym or tribal colleagues, whom he calls upon for property.[2] It is the chief who gains the greatest prestige in "flattening" his rival, but the glory is shared collectively by the tribe in somewhat the same manner as a college student body shares in the achievements of its football team.

Before proceeding with the discussion of rivalry for prestige it is necessary to familiarize the reader with the basic economic mechanism behind this competition. The Kwakiutl are a people of great wealth and they consider it honorable to amass a fortune. But it is not hoarding they are interested in. Wealth, such as blankets, boxes, and copper plates, is used in a game of rising in rank, of validating honorific titles and privileges.[1] Upon the occasion of taking on a name a man distributes a considerable quantity of blankets among the men of another numaym in the presence of the entire community. The recipients are obligated to accept the property and must be prepared to repay it at the end of the year with 100 per cent interest. Such men probably have property out at interest, which they call in at the end of the year to meet their payments. Should a man be unable to repay he is "flattened" and falls in social status. The victor, on the other hand, rises another rung in the social ladder. With each successful potlatch a man accumulates more renown as well as more property with which to conduct even greater potlatches. With prestige the driving motive in Kwakiutl society and with the basic intent of the potlatch the crushing of a rival, these property bouts take on a fiercely competitive tone.

[1] Boas, "Social Organization . . . of the Kwakiutl Indians," p. 343.
[2] Benedict, *op. cit.*, p. 184.

The standard of value in the potlatch is the blanket, at present worth about fifty cents. The Kwakiutl also make use of bills of much higher denomination, called coppers. These are etched, shieldlike plates of copper with a T-ridge hammered on the lower half. Though they have little intrinsic value each copper represents thousands of blankets, its value being determined by the amount paid for it when it was last sold. Since each buyer makes it a point to pay more than the previous value of the copper, its denomination is increasingly higher. Thus one such copper was reported as worth 7,500 blankets.[1] Because of the high value of the copper its purchase brings the buyer distinction, but in addition, since he will have paid for it more than the last purchaser, it is a demonstration of his superiority.

Coppers are offered for sale to a chief of a rival numaym or to a rival tribe.[2] It is a challenge which the rival must accept or admit defeat. More than a challenge to an individual chief, it is a challenge to his numaym or tribe, who stand to gain or lose collectively depending upon whether the price for the copper can be met or not. All assist their chief with loans of blankets, the amount each contributes being in direct ratio to his nobility. Thus where the man next to the chief in rank gives one hundred blankets, a commoner may give only five. Nor do all the members of the numaym expect the chief to return the blankets that have been given for a potlatch, although generally these are returned with interest the day after the copper has been purchased.[3]

The motives, the intense rivalries that mark the sale of a copper, are clearly portrayed in the following account of a copper potlatch between a chief of the Kwakiutl tribe and the chief of the Mamaleleqala, a neighboring tribe.[4] Preparations for the transaction had been made far in advance, and invitations to the tribes had been sent out. The copper was offered at a great feast given by the chief of the Mamaleleqala.

"Now take care, great tribe! This great copper has a high price; its name is Maxtsolum (the-one-before-whom-all-are-ashamed). Now I am going to lay it down before you,

[1] *Ibid.*, p. 344.
[2] *Ibid.*, p. 342.
[3] Boas, "Ethnology of the Kwakiutl," p. 1341.
[4] Boas, "Social Organization . . . of the Kwakiutl Indians," pp. 346 *ff*.

Kwakiutl." The copper was laid down before the chief, who offered to buy. Shortly afterward he invited all the tribes to a feast at which he would buy the copper. When all were assembled on the beach, the Kwakiutl chief made an offer of 1,000 blankets for the copper. These were counted out and piled high against a measuring pole. Then the chief rose and spoke: "Tribes, I buy this copper with these 1,000 blankets. I shall not give any more unless the chiefs of the tribes ask for more, wa! That is my speech, Chiefs of the Kwakiutl." He sat down and the seller of the copper arose and spoke, "Ya, Owaxtalagilis! are your words true? Did you say it was enough?" He turned to his tribe and called upon Chief Olsiwit to speak.

"Are those your words, Kwakiutl? Did you say this was all that you were going to give for the copper? . . . Do you think you have finished? Now take care, Kwakiutl! You, Chief, give twenty times ten pairs more so there will be two hundred more." Owaxtalagilis ordered two hundred more blankets to be paid out. But this was just a beginning. Another noble of the Mamaleleqala spoke. "You were not provident when you resolved to buy this great copper. My heart is well inclined toward you, Chief! You have not finished; you will give more. The price of the copper must correspond to my greatness, and I ask forty times ten blankets. . . . "

"Yes, Chief, your speech was good. You have no pity," replied Owaxtalagilis. His retainer counted out another four hundred blankets. When this was done Owaxtalagilis spoke again: "Wa, wa! I say it is enough, Mamaleleqala. Now you have seen my name. This is my name. This is the weight of my name. This mountain of blankets rises through our heaven. My name is the name of the Kwakiutl, and you cannot do as we do, tribes. When you do it you finish just as soon as you reach a thousand blankets. Now look out! later on I shall ask you to buy from me. Tribes! I do not look forward to the time when you shall buy from me. . . . That is what I say for all of you from whom coppers may be bought by the chiefs of these our rivals, the Mamaleleqala, wa, wa!"

But still another chief of the Mamaleleqala rose and demanded another thousand blankets to cover the greatness of his name. Thus, 2,600 blankets were piled on the beach. The Mamaleleqala chief lay down on the beach and covered himself with his blanket as though he were insulted. So six hundred more blankets were added. Then the chief selling the copper rose and said, "Now take care, Mamaleleqala! Now I take that price for the copper. Now give the boxes into which we may put the blankets. We need fifty boxes and each will be worth five pairs of blankets." Owaxtalagilis showed his greatness by doubling that amount.

Calling upon all thirteen chiefs of the Mamaleleqala to rise and face the Kwakiutl chief, the seller of the copper spoke: "This, Kwakiutl, is the strength of the Mamaleleqala. These whom you see here are your rivals. These are the ones who have the great coppers which have names, and therefore it is hard work for you to rival them. Look out, Chiefs of the Mamaleleqala, in case they should bring us the copper which we now sold, that one of you may take it up at once, or else we must be shamed. That is what I say, Chiefs of the Mamaleleqala. Wa, Wa!" Owaxtalagilis now had three hundred more blankets brought out with which "to adorn the chiefs." The price was thus accepted at four thousand pairs of blankets. But Owaxtalagilis was not yet finished. "You take the price too soon," he said. "You must think poorly of me, Chief! I am a Kwakiutl; I am one of those from whom all your tribes all over the world took their names. Now you give up before I finished trading with you, Mamaleleqala. You must always stand beneath us, wa, wa!" With a final gesture of superiority the Kwakiutl chief added two hundred blankets, bringing the total price to four thousand and two hundred blankets.

The purchase of a valuable copper adds prestige to the name of the individual, but it is an important economic investment as well, for at the next sale the copper will bring an even higher price. The economic motives are, however, only incidental in potlatching, as is indicated by the fact that one gains even greater prestige by destroying property.[1] As in the sale of a copper, the destruction of a copper is a challenge which the rival must meet with the destruction of one of an equal or greater value.

Another form which the destruction of property may take is a feast given to a rival at which enormous quantities of valuable

[1] "The rivalry between chiefs finds its strongest expression in the destruction of property." *Ibid.*, p. 353.

candlefish oil are destroyed in the fire.  It is at these feasts that the intense rivalry that is at the crux of Kwakiutl social relations frequently breaks out into open enmity.  The rival guests are seated before the fire into which oil pours from a "vomiter beam" in the ceiling.  The flames scorch the guests and even ignite the roof beams, but the guests may not move, they must appear unconcerned—or admit defeat.  During the feast the retainers of the guest chief sing songs of unrestrained praise about him.

"Our great famous chief is known even outside the world, O! he is the highest Chief of all. . . . Do not let our chief rise too high.  Do not let him destroy too much property, else we shall be made like broken pieces of copper by the great breaker of coppers, the great splitter of coppers, the great chief who throws coppers into the water, the great one who cannot be surpassed by anybody, the one surmounting all chiefs."[1]

The host is no less vehement in his scathing attack on his rival.  He sings songs of bitter abuse.  To add to the effect of the song an effigy of the rival is set up near the fire.  He is portrayed as thin, his ribs bursting through his skin, with a pitiable beseeching attitude.  "What will my rival say again?" the host sings, "that spider woman, what will he pretend to do next?  The words of that spider woman do not go a straight way. Will he not brag that he is going to give away canoes, that he is going to break coppers, that he is going to give a grease feast? . . . Nothing will satisfy you; but sometimes I treated you so roughly that you begged for mercy.  Do you know what you will be like?  You will be like an old dog, and you will spread your legs before me when I get excited.  You did so when I broke the great coppers. . . . This I throw into your face, you whom I always tried to vanquish; whom I have maltreated; who does not dare to stand erect when I am eating; the chief whom every weak man, even, tries to vanquish."[2]

When the grease is passed around to the guests, the rival if he has given a greater feast refuses to take the proffered ladle but rushes out of the house to get a copper which he strikes against one of the house posts, an act equivalent to striking the host in the face.  The latter may forestall this by tying a copper to each of the four house posts.  Then the rival breaks his own copper

[1] *Ibid.*, p. 355.
[2] *Ibid.*, p. 356.

and gives it to the host.[1]  Such contests once entered upon may continue indefinitely with even greater displays of ostentatious destruction and with an ever rising pitch of hostility between the rivals.  The conflict between the rival chiefs Fast Runner and Throw Away[2] is an excellent example of the extremes of destruction that are indulged in by two contestants for prestige.

Even marriage among the Kwakiutl is phrased as a conflict for prestige.[3]  When a chief des res to take a wife he calls his numaym together "to make war against all the daughters of the chiefs," to "make war against the tribes."  Marriage is the most important means of obtaining honorific crests and dance privileges.  It was pointed out previously that certain numaym names and crests descend through the son-in-law to the grandchild.  The son-in-law may not display or make use of the prerogatives except at the time when he first receives them but holds them in trust for his son when the latter comes of age.  Thus, it is not the bride that a man pays for at marriage but the prerogatives that go with her.  In this respect a marriage is conducted along precisely the same lines as the sale of a copper.  Both for the father-in-law and for the son-in-law marriage represents a climactic point, an occasion for displaying their high rank by indulging in an elaborate potlatch.  And like the purchase of a copper the marriage transaction evokes a display of hostility between the parties.  The prospective son-in-law and his party of nobles armed with blankets and coppers descend upon the house of the bride's father to overwhelm him with property.  Often a sham battle between the retainers of both sides takes place in which people may be killed.  Or the father-in-law may make the party of the suitor run a gauntlet of flaming torches, or eat before a blazing and scorching fire.  As for a copper, the price for the bride, that is for the prerogatives that go with her, is bid higher and higher as each of the nobles brings forward blankets "to lift the bride from the floor."[4]

[1] *Ibid.*, p. 355.

[2] For the contest of Fast Runner and Thrown Away, see Benedict, *op. cit.*, pp. 197–200.

[3] Boas, "Social Organization . . . of the Kwakiutl Indians," p. 358. "Marriage among the Kwakiutl must be considered a purchase, which is conducted on the same principles as the purchase of a copper."

[4] Boas, "Social Organization . . . of the Kwakiutl Indians." From description of marriage, pp. 359–366.

The payment of the bride price does not at all complete the marriage transaction.[1]  When a child is born the father-in-law repays part of the bride price by bestowing some of the names and a quantity of property upon it.  By doing this he is "dressing" his daughter and thus elevating her rank.  Should he delay this property transaction it would be considered shameful.  After two or more children have been born the father-in-law has repaid the entire amount with 300 per cent interest.  Now he has returned the potlatch, and the marriage is considered annulled. The father has redeemed his daughter.  She may or may not continue to stay with her husband.  But rather than have his wife stay with him unpaid for, the husband makes another payment and the cycle of potlatching is resumed.  With each payment the bride gains in rank until after four payments have been made, *i.e.*, in four marriages, she attains real greatness. The payments are a symbol of her husband's wealth and of his regard for her.  These property exchanges between son-in-law and father-in-law contribute to their prestige so that the relationship between them may be friendly.  But it is not always so. In one case a man whose father-in-law was slow in ceding the promised dowry of numaym crests and property had an image made of his wife and in the presence of the assembled tribe fastened a weight around it and threw it into the sea.  In this way he shamed his wife, and through her, her father.  The marriage was broken off.[2]

Conflict over a marriage may arise in still another way.  The numaym crests and names are greatly valued and the members of the numaym may be outraged at the thought that these valuable numaym possessions should pass to a rival chief. Jealous warfare may result, and in one particular instance the tribe, from which the father-in-law had originally obtained certain ceremonial dances, angered that these were now to pass to a rival chief, killed the father-in-law and many of his friends to prevent the passage of the dance.[3]  Some of the southern tribes of the Kwakiutl value their clan privileges so highly that they practice clan endogamy to prevent the loss of

[1] *Ibid.*, p. 359.

[2] *Ibid.*, p. 366.

[3] Boas, "Ethnology of the Kwakiutl," p. 1030; cited by Benedict, *op. cit.*, p. 207.

valuable prerogatives. However, the Kwakiutl numayms are exogamous. A chief who has no daughter to whose children he can pass the numaym names arranged a marriage between a part of his own body and a son-in-law and by this means insures the continuity of the name.[1]

For a younger son, a commoner without status, marriage may afford an opportunity to acquire names and privileges that will raise his rank, though this is not easy. A princess loses in status if she marries below her rank, and the nobility resent any attempt of a commoner to establish himself on a level with them. Besides, a commoner cannot usually accumulate enough property to provide the expensive potlatch. Marriages in which the formal payments are not paid are not recognized, the Indians calling such arrangements "sticking together like dogs." Commoners are therefore for the most part restricted to marrying commoners. Since they cannot obtain names through marriage they may simply invent them,[2] though of course invented names have no status. Wealthy and powerful men, on the other hand, may take a number of wives and, with each wife, new valuable names and privileges.

Properly speaking, competition for a mate among the Kwakiutl is a competition for names. Such competition actually is limited by the fact that only individuals of relatively the same rank marry. In any event powerful individuals would have the first choice of a mate—and the prerogatives transferred in marriage—in a family of wealth. The strong equation of rank that operates in the transfer of a copper sets a firm limitation upon the range of choice the individual can make in chosing a mate and keeps, more or less effectively, individuals of low rank from rising above their status.

Besides marriage the Kwakiutl recognize murder as an equally valid method of adding to one's privilege and rank.[3] A man claims as his own all the names and special privileges of his victim. Some of the most valued of these are the winter ceremonial dances. If a man met the owner of a dance and killed him, he could assume the right to give the dance himself. A

[1] Boas, "Social Organization . . . of the Kwakiutl Indians," p. 359.

[2] See history of a slave numaym in Boas, "Ethnology of the Kwakiutl," Vol. 2, pp. 1093 *ff*.

[3] Benedict, *op. cit.*, p. 210.

commoner would hardly avail himself of this method of rising in status unless he had enough property to validate his assumption of the dance prerogatives. In the past, a number of wars were conducted primarily to increase the number of tribal names, crests, and dances.

Thus, every aspect of Kwakiutl life is oriented to the basic drive for prestige, which is maintained and augmented by the possession of two types of property, the nonmaterial—traditional histories, names, songs, special privileges such as the right to give a particular dance or the right to tie a dancer to a post—and the material—blankets, boxes, canoes, coppers. Neither property has much value without the other. A man might conceivably amass a fortune in blankets and coppers but, unless he had claims to nobility, material wealth would not carry him far. The situation is closely analagous to the one in our own culture, where in "society," wealthy families with "background" try to exclude the newly rich, while on the other hand pauperized families with background are handicapped by their lack of wealth. Among the Kwakiutl the latter condition is relatively rare, for the conditions of potlatching are such that once given a start—as the children of the nobility are—the accumulation of wealth becomes almost inevitable. In one essential respect Kwakiutl potlatching differs from economic exchange in many societies: the stakes are always above and beyond subsistence requirements. As has been mentioned previously, food is held collectively by the numaym and the chief is responsible for feeding his people. Even such property as blankets may be used cooperatively in the competition between tribes or numayms. But while collective notions may have entered into the use of material property, the paraphernalia of nobility are strictly individualistic.

Congruent with the strongly individualistic tone of Kwakiutl society is the absence of any strongly centralized political authority or any legal structure.[1] The position of chief is mainly honorific and relatively devoid of political authority. A chief, as coming from a noble family in which the chieftainship is hereditary, is the spearhead of intertribal and inter-numaym rivalry because his are the highest names and the most honored prerogatives. At the head of all the numayms is the great chief

[1] The material on law is from lecture notes by Franz Boas.

of the tribe, honored because by birth he is the highest ranking individual in the tribe. His functions, too, are nonpolitical except that he may be instrumental in organizing a competitive potlatch with a rival tribe. In general the authority of a chief in legal matters is nonspecific. On many occasions, as when a chief wishes to give a potlatch to the tribes or to take a wife, he consults the other members of the numaym or calls together the other chiefs of the tribe. But, as has already been shown, the men called together have an economic and prestige stake in the transaction.

The numaym, on the other hand, has a number of regulatory powers over its own members since it can refuse to support a projected marriage or a potlatch. In addition the members of the numaym can check a chief who becomes overbearing and too autocratic; they can kill him without incurring the vengeance of any united chiefly class. The murder of the chief falls in line with the attitudes of the culture, which though permitting the individual great leeway in expressing his personal glory nevertheless draw the line at overdoing. A chief may become so arrogant and no more.

For disputes within the group, action is taken only by the principals involved. Trespassers on numaym property may be killed by any member of the numaym, the action being individualistic and spontaneous. The Kwakiutl regard murder as an affront to their prestige, as a shameful happening that must be wiped out by the murder of some other individual not necessarily related to the murderer. In contrast to the situation in many other tribes a death puts the individual into a sullen mood, and calls for the death of another individual from another tribe or numaym so that another family may be made to feel the shame of grief. As in a potlatch, all the men of a numaym cooperate to avenge by blood the murder of one of their members, for the honor and prestige of the entire numaym is affected as well as that of the particular family of the victim. The following case of the murder of a chief by a commoner well illustrates the basic attitudes surrounding homicide:

The chief of the numaym Gexsum was killed by a commoner, Muled, of another numaym. The mother of the dead chief called his numaym together, and it was decided at this meeting to wash off with blood the disgrace that had been brought upon the numaym by Muled. It was decided further that if they could not find Muled they should kill his elder brother.

However, Muled knowing that they were after him kept his door bolted. But the chiefs of all the tribes kept on the watch for him and finally he was killed, not by a member of the dead chief's numaym but by some other man. The murdered chief's mother rewarded the avenger of her son's death with a slave. However, the honor of the numaym was hardly vindicated. Rather it was even more disgraced because not only was Muled a commoner, but the chief had been avenged by an outsider who had been given a slave, so that the numaym Gexsum lost both a chief and a slave while the rival numaym had lost only a commoner. Therefore the numaym Gexsum stood beaten by the numaym of Muled.[1]

It is theoretically possible, and it does occur, for a murderer to compound the murder. This is a disgrace that will hound the murderer's family for generations. Only the weak-minded pay an indemnity. For in all disputes the Kwakiutl recognize only two possible outcomes, victory or defeat, and compromise, as a sign of weakness, is defeat. The emphasis upon rank is reflected in their law of vengeance in that the death of a nobleman is required to avenge the murder of a member of the nobility, while the murder of a commoner is avenged by the death of another commoner. In the case just mentioned, the entire numaym of the murdered chief united to avenge his murder. But information is lacking as to whether the murder of a low-caste commoner would have produced the same result.

As the secular organization of the Kwakiutl is built around rivalry for prestige and the display of honorific prerogatives, so is the religious. Among the Pueblo Indians of the Southwest religious performances are collectively performed for the collective good. Kwakiutl ceremonialism, on the other hand, though calling for collective participation is directed entirely toward individualistic ends. Ceremonial dances are owned like coppers, and may be given only by the rightful owner to demonstrate his nobility. Moreover, consistent with the emphasis upon rank, each of the dances is ranked in a hierarchical system. It is these dances, which confer the most valued Kwakiutl preroga-

[1] Boas, "Ethnology of the Kwakiutl," pp. 1360 *ff*.

tives, that are obtained through inheritance from the mother's line or through the murder of the previous owner.

A widespread characteristic of North American religion is the contact of the individual with a personal guardian spirit from whom he obtains certain supernatural powers. Generally the kind of spirit encountered by the individual and the kind of blessing it will give him depends on chance. Among the Kwakiutl the young man prepares to meet only that spirit to which he is entitled by birth. For the obtaining of a guardian spirit is the supernatural validation of the ceremonial dance which he has inherited, the dance being the dramatic performance of the myth relating to the acquisition of the spirit.[1] Thus, when a man has killed the owner of a dance he is immediately seized by the spirit associated with the dance. When a man has obtained a dance through marriage, he passes it to his son when the latter comes of age. The taking over of the dance is an initiation for the young man. In this case, too, the youth must await a seizure from the spirit associated with his dance.

In general, the religious organization of the Kwakiutl parallels the secular. As there are titles of nobility so are there recognized hierarchical distinctions in the use and ownership of religious prerogatives. The year is divided into two halves, the summer, when the secular social organization is in use, and the winter, when the entire social organization is dropped and a new organization based upon membership in religious societies is in force. With the ushering in of the winter ceremonial season new rank alignments are set up according to the greatness of the name a man holds as a member of a religious society. This does not imply, however, that there is any marked change in the status of the individual from the secular to the ceremonial season. Because of the method of inheriting the winter ceremonial religious prerogatives, these tend to become concentrated in the noble families. Religious prerogatives are but another aspect of the nobility and power of an individual of rank.

The classification of individuals into commoners and nobility in the secular organization is paralleled in the winter ceremonial organization by the grouping of the religious societies into two groups, the seals, comprising the highest ranking societies,

[1] Boas, "Social Organization . . . of the Kwakiutl Indians," p. 396. The material presented here on religion is from this article.

and the *quequtsa*, the societies of lower rank. In the latter group belong all those individuals, men and women, who have not been initiated into one of the seal societies or who have relinquished to their sons their seats in the ranking societies. Between the seals and the quequtsa there is a formalized hostility. "The seals when excited attack and torment the quequtsa; the latter, on the other hand, tease and torment the members of the seal society."[1]

But not only does Kwakiutl religion reflect the stress upon rank in the culture, it serves as one of the most important mediums of prestige rivalry. Most of the dances are shown during the feasts given to rivals, and many are given in connection with the distribution of property.[2] The great occasion, however, for the giving of a ceremonial dance is at the initiation of a boy when he has reached the age of ten or twelve. At this time the boy's maternal grandfather, who has promised at the marriage of his daughter to transfer his membership in one of the religious societies to one of her children, undertakes in conjunction with the donor's son-in-law, the boy's father, to initiate the boy into one of the lower societies. From this society the boy is elevated by successive initiations, each marked by a great distribution of property, until he becomes a member of the highest ranking society. Like the assumption of any other prerogative, initiation into a society must be validated by the distribution of property at a great feast to which all the members of the tribe are invited. And the higher the rank of the society the more property is required, so that only men of wealth can initiate their sons and grandsons into the ranking societies. Moreover, the privilege of joining a society depends upon inheritance.

Among the Zuni Indians of the Southwest ceremonial performances are essentially mild and sober in tone. In sharp contrast the Indians of the Northwest Coast make ecstatic frenzy the high point of their religious ceremonies. The chief dancer, at least, is expected to become violent, to froth at the mouth, to break into an ecstatic fit in which he threatens to do violence and must be restrained by men who have the hereditary privilege of doing so. Dancers who make mistakes in the ritual fall down as though dead and are attacked by the other dancers. In such cases

[1] *Ibid.*, p. 420.
[2] *Ibid.*, p. 436.

the entire initiation may have to be repeated at great expense. Strikingly, in the initiation of a dancer into the Cannibal society, which is ranked highest, frenzy is carried to its furthest pitch.

The Cannibal Spirit, the supernatural patron of the Cannibal society, is a mythical monster who lives on the corpses of men supplied him by two supernatural servants. He instills in the initiate a mad craving for human flesh. But Kwakiutl cannibalism is by no means the epicurean cannibalism of certain tribes in Africa or Oceania.[1] On the contrary the eating of human flesh is highly abhorrent to the Indians. But precisely because of this abhorrence the rite is all the more powerful.

Soon after the property arrangements for the initiation have been made, and the chiefs of the tribe have investigated the financial condition of the men sponsoring the initiation, the initiate disappears into the woods, where he remains fasting for three or four months so that he may be emaciated. During this period he appears once in the village and takes back with him a female relative, a member of the Cannibal society, who must fetch food for him. Finally he returns to the village in a violent ecstasy and moves to attack all the people in sight, crying for human flesh. But his Cannibal society attendants surround him and attempt to pacify him. They offer him their flesh to bite. Sometimes the initiate returns from the woods carrying a corpse in his arms which also excites him in his lust for human flesh. At one point in the ceremony the initiate, who is running about like a madman, must be lured into the ceremonial house by his female coinitiate, who, naked, carries the corpse into the house and places it by the fire. Then all the old Cannibal members who have been outside the house jump down from the roof and rush in through the door. They are all naked and dance around in high excitement. The master of ceremonies, also a hereditary position of privilege, divides the flesh among the Cannibals. On very great occasions a slave is killed and eaten and substituted for a corpse of one previously dead. After the ceremony the initiate must indemnify by a distribution of property those whom he has bitten and the owner of the slaves who have been killed. After the ceremony because of the great contamination from eating human flesh the initiate remains in isolation for four months under numerous tabus about eating

[1] Benedict, *op. cit.*, p. 178.

and drinking.    Traditionally even after this period he is supposed
to remain continent, and abstain from working and gambling.

Although the initiation of the Cannibal is the occasion for the
highest display of violent frenzy and of the most valued privileges,
all other societies down to those of lowest rank fit into the same
general pattern.    In each the initiate succumbs to ecstasy and
must be exorcised before he can return to normal life.    In each
it is the group of individuals comprising the society who cooperate
in the exorcism.

As over against the thoroughly collective and truly cooperative
ceremonial organization of the Zuni, Kwakiutl ceremonialism
is fundamentally individualistic and almost always competitive.
In a sense the members of a society cooperate to exorcise their
fellow initiate, but the motives are individualistic, for the
concern of each member is to display his own special prerogatives
whether it be that of carrying the corpse for the initiate or
bringing in shredded cedar bark for him to wipe his face on.

As the relations between man and man among the Kwakiutl
are marked by aggressiveness, so are the relations between men
and the supernaturals.    The Kwakiutl do not make themselves
humble before their gods.    In mythology, the hero boldly seeks
out the god and demands his supernatural powers, or he kills
the supernatural to gain his power.    And when the gods inflict
misfortune, the Kwakiutl insult and shame them, calling them
slaves, the highest affront the Kwakiutl can pay.[1]

The Kwakiutl make use of still another aspect of religion in
their drive for prestige.    By becoming a religious practitioner
a man can obtain valuable prerogatives without inheriting them
and without buying them.[2]    A person cured from a severe illness
can become a shaman and show his power by curing someone
else.    He, too, must validate this power by distributing property.
But once installed as a shaman the individual makes the same
use of his special prerogatives as the noble.    Each shaman
holds up the supernatural pretensions of his rival to ridicule
and strives in contests of power to defeat his rival and so to shame
him.    Thus every cure that a shaman undertakes is viewed com-
petitively and failure means defeat in the same terms as failure
to match a property distribution means defeat.    The vehemence

[1] *Ibid.*, p. 221.
[2] *Ibid.*, p. 211.

of the rivalry is carried to a point where a group of shamans may organize to kill a successful competitor, and the competition is also directly expressed whenever a group of them match their powers in a single cure. If the victor is killed by his unsuccessful rivals, his death is never avenged. This strong rivalry between shamans may reflect an earlier condition when each chief of a numaym had his own shaman to assist him in his inter-numaym rivalries.

Part of the stock in trade of each shaman is his assortment of tricks, which he guards zealously against detection. To have one of his subterfuges uncovered is equivalent to defeat by a rival. The shaman to whom this happens gives up his practice. He goes mad or dies of shame.

For his cures a shaman is paid a fee according to the rank of the family of the sick person. The wealth he accumulates in this way he uses, like any secular chief, in potlatches to validate each assumption of a new power. Shamanism is a back-door method of rising in status. Yet the fact that shamanistic tricks must be taught suggests that the power must be trans-mitted from individual to individual through purchase or through inheritance.

## EDUCATION

The individual among the Kwakiutl is fitted very early into the competitive pattern. A child when a year old has its hair singed, and, after the father has distributed some small gifts to the tribe, the child takes on its first name.[1] A few years later the father distributes more property among the unmarried young men of the tribe, and so validates the second name. It is not until he is ten or twelve, however, that the boy begins to distribute property in his own behalf. When this time comes, all the members of the numaym assist him with the loan of blankets which of course the boy must repay at the end of a year with 100 per cent interest. But if the boy has collected 100 blankets he distributes these among his friends, who are obliged to repay him at the end of a month at double the usual interest, so that the boy may now have amassed 300 blankets,

[1] Boas, "Contributions to the Ethnology of the Kwakiutl," p. 112. All material on the acquisition of names in this section is from this article, pp. 112–132.

of which he owes 200.  By loaning out these blankets he can
proceed to give a feast and distribute goods in a potlatch, and so
take a potlatch name, the mark of an adult.

At this time the boy's father gives up his seat in the numaym
in favor of his son and retires among the old men.  The event of
the investiture of the heir is an occasion for the giving of a
feast and a potlatch.  Now the boy who has been helped all
along by the members of his numaym is pitted in his first competition with boys from other numayms and exhorted to do his
utmost to outdo his rival.

As soon as he has accumulated a quantity of blankets the boy
can advance another step in status by undertaking the purchase
of a copper.  He starts by purchasing a part interest in one of
the cheaper coppers with an older friend.  The latter makes the
purchase and announces the boy as his partner.  When he has
accumulated enough property to repay with interest the debt
to his partner the boy becomes full owner of the copper and can
proceed to offer it for sale to a rival.

Along with the names which the boy inherits and assumes at
each potlatch he gives, he inherits from his maternal grandfather
certain dance privileges entitling him to membership in one of
the many ranking religious societies.  The initiation into such a
society has already been described.  It is the high point of the
boy's passage into adulthood.

This training in the manipulation of property and potlatch
rivalry is typical of the nobility.  Younger sons of nobles and
sons of commoners having no status in the culture are scorned
by the first-born children of the nobility.  A chief will encourage
his son to throw stones at the young commoners so that the
young prince may learn early the proper attitudes of contempt
toward his social inferiors.[1]  Children who do not inherit any
of the prerogatives of nobility are also encouraged to give potlatches, but in the rigid equation of rank among the Kwakiutl
a commoner could potlatch only with a commoner.  To that
extent the education of the commoner follows the same general
line as that for the nobility.  The commoners of course may not
potlatch with as much property as the more noble members of
the community, but the man who gives away five blankets values
that privilege just as much as the one who may distribute

[1] Boas, from lecture notes.

thousands.  Like a haughty chief he makes the same grandiloquent speeches and expresses the same contempt for his rivals.

The first-born daughter of a nobleman exercises by the rights
of primogeniture all the social functions of a man.  Each name
that she assumes is the occasion for a great potlatch in her honor
in which her father enhances his status another step.  At
puberty, the girl is secluded for four days, though without any
severe restrictions.  After a period of purification her father
gives a potlatch in which the boards of the house are given away
and the girl takes one of the names from her mother's family.[1]
At this period the girl is expected to learn a number of household
tasks.  Copper rings are placed on her ankles to impede her
actions while she is learning the required number of tasks.

## The Role Played by the Individual in the Culture

Public behavior on the Northwest Coast is dominated by the
need of the individual to demonstrate his greatness over against
his rivals.  A man seeks great wealth not as an end in itself but
as a weapon to crush a rival.  By the humbling of his rival the
individual builds up his own prestige.  In that respect, Kwakiutl
society is warlike, and the greatest rewards of society in terms of
individual glorification go to the man who has conquered with
property and by a display of privileges his most powerful rivals.

A man not only must establish his own individual prestige, but
must extend his greatness to his children and grandchildren.
To accomplish this a man assists his son in potlatching, he is
careful to arrange an advantageous marriage for his children,
he is punctual in making return payments after the birth of his
daughter's first child so that she may not be shamed.

Consistent with the cultural demands placed upon it, the
personality of the individual reacts in a manner that we would
classify clinically as paranoid.  The grandiloquent speeches made
by the retainers of the chief at a potlatch may be characterized
in our own cultural terms as megalomania.  But for the Kwakiutl
this unabashed boasting is culturally accepted and formalized.
It is necessary to stress very strongly the fact that the Kwakiutl
are not paranoid in terms of abnormal psychology.  In reacting
to their own environment they do not lack the sense of orientation
that is so strikingly absent in the individual classified as abnor-

[1] Boas, "Current Beliefs of the Kwakiutl Indians," p. 209.

mal.  Kwakiutl society in contrast to many other cultures permits great latitude to the individual both in his attempts to secure individual aggrandizement and in his expression of self-importance—but always with the provision that he must not overdo it.

In keeping with these formalized self-glorification sentiments is the correlated quick reaction to the sentiment of shame.   When a young prince capsized in a canoe, his father felt it necessary to wipe out the shame of this trivial accident with the distribution of property.[1]

Actually the wiping out of a shame, since it is an occasion for a potlatch, is another means of rising in status.   It is a demonstration of superiority.   A chief quarreled with his wife so loudly that people came to see.   When the chief noticed that all the Kwakiutl were gathered about his house he stopped quarreling with his wife and said, "Thank you, Kwakiutl, that you have come to see how we are quarreling.   Now take everything in the house and all the roof boards of my house."   Left with nothing but the blankets on their bodies the chief and his wife went to live in another house.   Of course the chief was not left poverty-stricken.   Every bit of property taken out of the house and every roof board at the next distribution of property had to be repaid him with interest.[2]

Among the Zuni Indians of the Southwest shame is the major social sanction but the reaction to it is relatively mild.   Suicide is unknown.   On the Northwest Coast, on the other hand, an individual unable to show himself superior to a situation that has shamed him commits suicide or "dies of shame."   The chief who discovered that his eldest son had married the common daughter of a youngest son died of shame, not because the marriage was considered incestuous but because his son had been tricked into a low marriage.   Similarly a shaman whose tricks are discovered will die of shame.   In a milder form the response to frustration is sulking.   A constantly recurring incident in the myths of the Kwakiutl is of a boy who when reproached by his mother for refusing to marry lies down on the bed and for four days refuses to stir or to take nourishment.   Then he rises and goes out of the house into the woods where, through a series of

[1] Boas, "Contributions to Ethnology of the Kwakiutl," p. 132.
[2] Boas, "Ethnology of the Kwakiutl," p. 1358.

adventures with supernaturals, he obtains supernatural privileges and a totem pole and thus puts his parents to shame.[1]

Death puts the Kwakiutl in a vicious temper and from his intensely egocentric position he feels that others must be made to suffer too. This is equivalent in our own culture to the reaction of a petty executive who having been taken to task by a superior vents his emotions on his inferiors. In a parallel situation the Kwakiutl demands that another person be killed to atone for a death in his own family. When the son of a chief died the father called out that another must go with him, and so with two other men of the numaym he went to another village and entering the house of a chief announced, "My prince died today and you will go with him." Then the men fired, killing the chief and wounding two others in the house. When the father of the dead boy returned home with his crew, "they felt good."[2]

What is accepted behavior for a chief or a nobleman is, however, denied the commoners. A low-caste man may give small feasts to which the chiefs would come and he also gives away property at potlatches of others, but he must not aspire too high. It is impossible to overemphasize the antagonism with which the nobility regard the newly rich. The slave who acquired a copper from his daughters was threatened with death. In the same way, a commoner who dared to set himself up with the chiefs and to compete with them was threatened. In one instance a number of chiefs banded together to crush a commoner in an extravagant potlatch.[3] The commoner's place is primarily on the side lines. He lends blankets to the chiefs when they prepare to wage a great intertribal potlatch and he is present at all feasts and potlatches. Yet each commoner in his own right and within the limits imposed upon him by his lack of noble prerogatives behaves in precisely the same way as a chief. Kwakiutl society is permeated to the core with the urge for personal glory. And with few exceptions each individual follows the road that has been laid out for him by his ancestors.

Yet Kwakiutl society is not so rigid a caste society as some of the northern tribes where privileges descend in a fixed unilateral

[1] Boas, "Social Organization . . . of the Kwakiutl," p. 412.
[2] Boas, "Ethnology of the Kwakiutl." *Ibid.*, p. 138.
[3] *Ibid.*, pp. 110 *ff.*

line from generation to generation. There are three sources from which the Kwakiutl individual can derive privileges: from the line of his father, from the line of his mother, and from his father-in-law. It is true that he may not use the privileges obtained from the latter source, but the fact that he is able to manipulate them and that he has paid for them as he pays for a copper gives him added status. In addition the individual is judged by the zest with which he conducts a potlatch and by his skillful manipulation of opportunities for distributing property. We may thus visualize the individual as occupying a fixed point on a sloping line of rank but oscillating within a relatively narrow orbit in prestige, the first line representing his rank in terms of his inheritance of names, and the variable orbit his skillful use of the opportunities given him by the conditions of inheritance.

### Integration of Culture

Public behavior in Kwakiutl society is integrated around a basic pattern of individualistic rivalry. Food for the most part is individually obtained and used, although the giving of presents of food to a chief in return for his acceptance of the responsibility of feeding the group in time of need is clearly a cooperative feature of food getting. The numaym functions cooperatively in the financing of a great potlatch. But the numaym as a unit functions over against outsiders as an individualistic and rivalrous group. The emphasis upon rank and prestige rivalry is consistently reflected in social relations, in marriage, in religion, and in law.[1]

*Bibliography*

Benedict, Ruth F.: *Patterns of Culture*, Houghton Mifflin Company, Boston, 1934.

Boas, Franz: "Contributions to the Ethnology of the Kwakiutl," *Columbia University Contributions to Anthropology*, Vol. 3, New York, 1925.

————: "Current Beliefs of the Kwakiutl Indians," *Journal of American Folk-lore*, Vol. 45, No. 176, pp. 177–260, April–June, 1932.

[1] For case histories see:

    Boas, "Contributions to the Ethnology of the Kwakiutl," pp. 71–93, 93, 97.

    Boas, "Ethnology of the Kwakiutl," pp. 1093 *ff*.

    Benedict, *op. cit.*, p. 197.

————: "Ethnology of the Kwakiutl," *35th Annual Report of the Bureau of American Ethnology*, Part 2, Washington, D. C., 1921.

————: "Religion of the Kwakiutl," *Columbia University Contributions to Anthropology*, Vol. 10, Part 2, New York, 1930.

————: "Social Organization and Secret Societies of the Kwakiutl Indians," *Report of the United States National Museum for* 1895, pp. 311–738, Washington, D. C., 1897.

# CHAPTER VII

## THE MANUS OF THE ADMIRALTY ISLANDS

### *by* MARGARET MEAD

The Manus are a sea-dwelling, fishing people who occupy villages built on piles in the shallow lagoons along the south coast of the Great Admiralty Island. They also occupy villages in the shelter of some of the smaller islands of the southern section of the Admiralty Archipelago. They practice no agriculture, and, with the exception of some families in the village of Peri, own no sago swamps. Their land is limited to a few rough coral outcrops and platforms of coral rubble which they have painstakingly built up in their villages. These serve as platforms for large gatherings and as workshops for economic activities requiring space, such as canoe building and fish-trap building. Their entire economic dependence is upon fishing and trade. Their fish is exchanged in daily or triweekly markets with near-by agricultural and sago-working land dwellers. They rely upon trade to obtain manufactured articles from more distant sections of the archipelago. The Admiralty Archipelago contains some 30,000 people, belonging to three major cultural divisions. Within these are many local tribal divisions, each of which has a particular economic pursuit. Thus obsidian is mined and worked into spears and knives on the island of Lou, wooden plates are made by certain of the Usiai tribes of the main island, etc. The whole archipelago is threaded together into a network of interdependence and exchange. The Manus canoes play the major part in this exchange on the south coast. They serve as carriers for the southern region because they have almost entirely prevented other peoples from owning or operating canoes. (There is another group of canoe people on the north coast who exercise a similar function and with whom the Manus had occasional warlike clashes when they ventured into their trading and fishing grounds.)

The part which the Manus play in this localization of industry in the Admiralties is limited to providing fish for a selected market among adjacent peoples, to carrying goods in canoes from the small islands to the large. One Manus village, Mbuke, which is too far from any agricultural neighbors to trade fish, relies upon manufacturing and trading pots instead. Otherwise the Manus merely manufacture their own houses and canoes—the materials for which they have to trade from the land people—their own ornaments and scanty clothing—two aprons of shredded sago leaves for the women, and a bark-cloth G-string for the men. For everything else, pots, baskets, wooden bowls and plates, spears, bast, fish nets, wooden beds, currency—which consists of worked shell and of dogs' teeth—they are dependent upon trade.

The trade dependency between the fishing and agricultural communities is very great, and cooperation between them against another similar combination of Manus fishers and other-tribal land people sometimes occurs even in case of war.

The Manus tribe, which is a cultural and linguistic unit, consists of some two thousand people. They are scattered in eleven completely autonomous villages. Because the village is the largest administrative unit found among them the Manus can be said to have no political unity. But there are many interrelationships between individuals of different villages, such relationships being based on intermarriages and the ties resulting from these intermarriages. There are occasional intervillage relationships, when one village undertakes to give a feast to which it invites all the members of another village. Such events are rare, however, and occur only about once in a generation in any given village. Although they lack political unity, the Manus recognize themselves as a people with a language and a culture distinct from their neighbors. They speak of themselves as *yoya Manus* (we, exclusive, Manus) and discuss with much interest the small differences in custom and dialect which vary from village to village. Because of this similarity of culture and the importance of kinship ties it is possible for an individual, or a family, or a clan to leave one village and live in another where they have relatives.

Thus while the village is the largest effective unit, its constitution varies over time. It is not a closed group in which individuals live from birth until death. Nor is there any way in which the Manus, as a whole, present a united front to the surrounding peoples, who speak different languages and are characterized by different cultures. War was not only permissible between Manus villages, but sometimes occurred between two divisions of the same village, in which case the defeated section moved away. The ties which bind an individual to his own village are primarily those which bind him to his own paternal clan. These ties are enforced by the ghosts of the clan, who are interested in keeping the clan together. But this sanction is not strong enough to oblige an individual to stay in a village. The forces by which an individual is outlawed from a village are the concerted, informal action of the other inhabitants, not any such formal procedure as occurs for instance in Samoa.

Without land, without any farinaceous food, dependent upon barter for the very tools and utensils with which they earn their livelihood, the Manus are up against an exacting environment. Accumulated wealth, in the form of currency, cannot release them from continual labor in their extravillage relationships. The whole system of foreign trade in the Admiralty is organized on compulsive barter: fish must be traded for taro, sago for coconuts, areca nut and the pepper leaf which is chewed with it for the pulverized lime which is a third essential ingredient of areca-nut chewing, etc. By this device, each community is assured that every other community will produce a sufficient surplus of the particular food or manufactured product which the other communities need. The Manus have a technique for smoking fish which somewhat lessens the need for daily fishing to obtain their farinaceous foods; but smoked fish keeps only a week to ten days and is no more than a palliative in the situation. Whereas the Manus are not up against the threat of starvation, like the Eskimo or Ojibwa, their situation is analogous to that of a low-paid worker in our society during a period of maximum employment. They always have a good supply of food and manufactured objects, but each individual must work to live. The Manus have developed a prodigious amount of social energy to meet this exacting environmental situation with the result that they, most disadvantageously placed of all the tribes in that part of the archipelago, are nevertheless the richest and have the highest standard of living.

## THE FUNCTIONING OF THE SOCIETY

To discuss the functioning of a Manus village, it is first necessary to state the social structure, the background of ideas, with which each generation of Manus men work out the local group economy.

The village unit is an aggregate of loosely organized paternal exogamic clans, all bound together by mutual economic obligations incurred through marriage between their members. These obligations are enforced by the spirits of the dead. Manus is an open society in which each individual has manifold and unique relationships in and outside his village. The prosperity or state of depression of a given community depends upon the organizing force and ability of leading individuals. The actions of these leading individuals—highly individualistic and dependent upon personality to an unusual degree—can be understood only if we first consider the following concepts with which they work: the basic importance of kinship, reckoned bilaterally; the concept of hereditary rank; the system of economic obligations between affinal relatives; the localization of industry; and the belief that the ghosts of dead members of the relationship group continue to influence the affairs of the living members of that group. All these cultural forms are widespread over this part of Oceania, but the particular phrasing they have been given in Manus is thoroughly congruent with the dominant attitude of this society.

Kinship is reckoned bilaterally and carries with it obligations of the blood kin to help one another and to cooperate in undertakings which are regarded as pertaining to the whole group. In Manus these mutual obligations between kin are expressed specifically in a strong brother-sister tie which is conceived as one of mutual aid and interdependence. The brother-sister relationship is extended in various ways to include practically any contemporary male relative of the women, either matrilineal or patrilineal. This feeling of interdependence is handed down from such siblings to their children. It therefore tends to override the boundaries of the patrilineal group, the localized gentes in which the Manus are organized.

This interdependence is expressed in the right of a man to take a wife for his son from the group to which his mother belonged.

That is, a male of the sister's lineage has the right to demand a wife from the line of his grandmother's brother. In Manus women are thought of as scarce and the right to demand a wife is an important prerogative. The right itself has behind it the sanction of a curse which the descendants of the women of the clan can invoke against the descendants of the men. According to this right it is the children of cross-cousins who marry, and it is male cross-cousins who, as the contracting parents to this marriage, become involved in a great number of mutual obligations. Thus, by the provisions of the kinship system, each adult male would be involved in a series of affinal exchanges, in which he would be called upon to contribute perishable goods if he is on the bride's side and imperishable wealth if he is on the bridegroom's side. These exchanges he would make, in the name of his own marriage, with his brother-in-law, and, in the name of his child's marriage, with his cross-cousin. Were the kinship system adhered to in these exchanges, it would mean that a man's position depended upon birth, since the size of the exchanges he could make would be entirely dependent upon the economic possessions of the designated relatives, his brother-in-law and his cross-cousin. For exchanges must be equal. In order, however, to allow an individual full rein for his capabilities, that he should not be confined and restricted by the accident of birth, the Manus, while still giving lip service to the kinship system, carry out another, more congenial, arrangement of affinal exchange.

Recognition within the community goes to a man in terms of the amount of wealth which has passed through his hands. The only way in which such manipulation of wealth can be arranged is in terms of affinal relationships. The Manus have therefore built up these affinal exchanges to enormous heights, ten thousand dogs' teeth sometimes being given in one exchange. A man's obligation to exchange valuables in the name of his own and his children's marriages has been translated into a system by which a man may assume the responsibility for as many marriages of younger people or contemporaries as he wishes. He may include within the circle of his operations his own kin, real and adopted, his wife's kin, real and adopted, and sometimes relatives even further removed. By divorcing the actual financing of a marriage from the direct kinship tie, it is possible for two vigorous and enterprising men to become exchange partners in marriages. This allows for each to put forth a maximum amount of energy and display. Not only those who finance the marriage but also the marrying pair usually are persons not really related to one another, as Manus formal arrangements require. By a series of fictions it is possible for a rich man to arrange marriages for young boys and girls within his circle of influence to young girls and boys within the circle of influence of some worthy exchange partner. They regard it as adoption, and it is extremely prevalent in Manus for a wealthy man to adopt a child either in infancy or later.

By this very widespread usage of adoption, in which a wealthy man assumes the responsibility for arranging the marriage payment for a boy or girl, the Manus have overridden the blood tie in favor of economic cooperation. A man who works with another man as an assistant or as a collaborator is closer to him than his blood brother who works with someone else. The importance of this tie of immediate cooperation is shown by the fact that the religious sanctions (ghosts) take cognizance of it. Where the ghosts in other groups punish someone who ignores a blood tie, in Manus punishment is as frequently directed against failure to follow lines of economic cooperation.

Congruent with this modification of kinship to further their social and economic life they have introduced the idea of individual responsibility for debt. Under the characteristic Oceanic picture of affinal exchanges, two kin groups exchange with each other, and within each group the lazy and the inefficient can be coerced only by pressure from within. If they fail to do their share, pressure is exerted upon them by the relatives with whom they are supposed to cooperate. Under the Manus system, each affinal exchange is organized by a leader, and he puts in and receives the largest payment and the major part of the prestige. His associates all act as individuals: each man is responsible for contributing his share and for returning his own debts contracted in the exchange. It is an individual matter between a man and his exchange partner on the opposite side of the exchange. In Manus there is no external pressure, each man participates and exerts himself as his ambitions compel him to. Debtor and creditor are conceived as the most intimately connected individuals in Manus. The one is regarded as cooperating with the other in an endless endeavor to engage in as many economic activities as possible.

This emphasis on an unceasing manipulation of goods has permeated the concept of rank. This has remained untouched in just one respect. In each old village there is a family which holds the hereditary right to furnish the *luluai*, the war leader of the village. His position in times of peace is honorific and lacks any administrative authority except as he may attempt either to institute or to participate in intervillage feasts. In these instances all the members of his village act with him along the same lines which the members of a kin group follow in cooperating with their economic leader. In Manus the difference between families which are of high rank, *lapan*, and families which are of low rank, *lau*, forms the basis for defining the relationship between a rich leader and his less wealthy followers. Thus a poor lapan may have to cooperate in a group led by a rich lau. Successive validations of position by participation in large-scale economic events, combined with advantageous marriages, serve in time to elevate a lau family to lapan rank. The outward manifestations of this rank are merely a matter of verbal usage and the exercise of a few formal prerogatives, such as putting more dogs' teeth on a string. Thus the rank idea has given form to the distinction between rich and poor, and the classification between men of importance and men of lack of importance is no longer based upon birth.

There are three incentives which operate to make a man assume leadership. First, there is the prestige accruing from participation in conspicuous financial operations. Second, there is the power which such a man has over the younger men whose marriages he has financed and who are forced to work for him for several years after their marriages. Third, there is the social pressure which occurs when an individual's ability to lead and dominate his siblings and contemporaries designates him as the logical heir of some economic leader in his widely reckoned kin groupings.[1] These incentives are not ranked; one may operate more strongly in one case, an other in another.

The pace of life in a given Manus village, the amount of goods in circulation, and therefore the actual amount of goods in

---

[1] See Mead, Margaret, *Growing Up in New Guinea*, pp. 135–142.

existence[1] depend upon the number of leaders in that village.
It varies with their enterprise, intelligence, and aggressiveness,
and the number of their kin whose cooperation they can enlist.
There is no fixed structure, no fixed number of events in a year, no
certainty about the number of marriages that will be validated
with a minimal display and exchange of property, nor how many
girls will have conspicuous first-menstruation ceremonies. Even
in a community possessing a great number of enterprising leaders
not a tithe of the possible occasions for conspicuous exchanges
of wealth is ever utilized. And this is so even when the same
economic goods can be used over and over again. For each time
a pig or a canoe load of sago changes hands it counts, so that a
pig may change hands three or four times in one morning. No
limitation on land, or on local trading, holds the Manus down;
in their canoes they can range far afield for new supplies; there
are always more fish to be had by more fishing; any number of
grass skirts and pots can be manufactured at need.

The forces which keep this continuous game of exchanging
going are several: In the first place, no one can ever retire on
his laurels. Every economic reward of leadership is expressed
dynamically, "I have done and I am doing." The control of
the leader over the young men whose marriages he has financed
and is financing exists only so long as they are unable to assume
the burden of financing their own affinal exchanges. It is not
that they owe him interest on past expenditures, they are his
dependents by virtue of the existence of continuing expenditures,
expenditures which, it is true, were begun in their childhood.
Since all these exchanges operate over a credit period of a
month to several years, it is impossible for any individual ever to
get out of the chain of debt and retire with a fixed position.
This condition operates to make anyone who has once been
involved in the game stay in. The minute that a man is no longer
an active participant he loses all standing in the community, and
may even be taunted with the fact that he was once a big man.
Someone else must always take up the chain of debt, as each

---

[1] As an illustration of the way this works a local trader (white) has started
buying sago in one village. He pays in money with which the natives buy
beads. The beads are made into belts, which are used in exchanges which
require more sago in return for them, so more sago is traded, and again more
beads bought.

link is dropped, and the person who takes it up receives the prestige, while the man who through age or infirmity has dropped it receives only ignominy. A man who has grown old or sick or blind, and boasts of his former exploits, is laughed at if he can no longer meet his debts. To avoid this a man drives himself so hard that he dies in his early middle age. It is rare for a man to live to see his first grandchild.

The second of the forces behind this game of continuous exchange is the fact that the affinal exchange system with its long-time credit is the principal mechanism for distributing goods within the village, and between Manus villages. This stands in opposition to the institutions of the market and trade friends which exist between the Manus and their other-tribal trade connections and which operate on very short-time credit.

Except for the daily fishing and market trading, cooking, bringing water, building the small canoes, manufacturing the fishing gear, and making ornaments (mainly bead and gum work), no economic activity in Manus is performed by the family group merely for its own use. Oil is made to use in an exchange, sago is bought to use in an exchange, grass skirts are made in large quantities to use in an exchange. The constant circulation of the imperishable valuables creates debts which must be met by fishing, trading, and manufacturing; the community relies upon using, eating, and wearing goods which have been distributed in this indirect manner.

Every community in Manus presents the picture of an uneven skyline: a few leaders standing out against the sky and giving form and definition to the immediate situation. The position of each leader is dependent upon the number of other leaders in the community. If the standard is high, his standard must be higher. Thus each leader goads each other leader, both as his partner in economic transactions and as a measure of his own success. No one is primarily interested in humiliating others, but only in maintaining his own position. A man can maintain his own position only if those who owe him debts pay them. As a man pays his debts, his prestige is automatically enhanced, and the race goes on. The ferocity with which those who are no longer able to keep up are sometimes abused reflects the desperate position into which anyone who cannot pay his debts puts all his creditors. It is not an expression of the superiority of those who are still in the race. So each man is matched against the *pace* of the group; his position is a function of it.

A survey of the adult male population of a Manus village shows three major divisions: leaders; their dependents and followers (these include the young men whose marriages the leader is financing, and the group of unenterprising dependent relatives who are also attached to him); and a group called "independents." These last are men who are neither dependents of any leader nor make any attempt to lead. The leaders spend all their time, except during the big monthly fishing drives, in making financial and trading arrangements. Their households are supported by the fishing of the young men whose marriages they are financing. The young dependents work to support their own households and those of their leaders, and also to get a foothold in the exchange system, for through that route lies emancipation. The older dependent men fish for themselves, sometimes make a slight daily contribution to their leaders, and work hard to make a showing at a big exchange. The independents fish for themselves and sometimes conduct very minor affinal exchanges; often they are skilled in specialized fishing techniques, like the use of traps. This picture must be borne in mind in order to understand the educational system.

Women in Manus also participate in this economic game, but usually not on so large a scale as men. Theoretically the wives of important exchange partners become exchange partners, and actually women operate and control a considerable body of debt. Their daily economic contribution consists of reef fishing for shellfish and small fish, bringing wood and water (the collection of firewood is also part of the system of affinal exchange), making grass skirts and beadwork, helping in the manufacture of lime, and cooking. But aside from this regular contribution, they also operate as individuals in the exchange system, having men as exchange partners almost as often as women. The sanction which lies behind the proper exercise of wealth and acts as a compulsion to make each man maintain or improve upon the economic standing which he has once attained is here a religious one and is in the hands of the ghosts.

Each Manus household is governed by a ghost of a recently dead male relative. In conception this ghost is a father, but a son may actually be raised to this position after death. The skull of the ghost is kept in the house and presides over the moral and economic life of the household. He punishes sex offenses, scandalmongering, obscenity, failure to pay debts, failure to help relatives, and failure to keep one's house in repair. For derelictions in these duties, he sends illness and misfortune. The cause of his anger may be ascertained, first by a male diviner[1] and then by séances with a female medium. Through her control she communicates with the ghost and learns of what he disapproves and the conditions upon which he will permit the sick person to recover. The ghost is expected to protect his ward from the malice of the ghosts of other households. Therefore if a male ward dies, his Sir Ghost[2] is conceived as having failed in his duty; he is evicted and the ghost of the newly dead takes his place.

The supervision of the Sir Ghost of a leader includes all the younger or dependent males who cooperate with his ward. Thus they have two Sir Ghosts to chastise them should they fail to cooperate. The séances are more frequently cast in terms of failure to help a relative than of failure to pay a debt. This phrasing of ghostly anger is characteristic of Oceania; but because of the individual responsibility of each member of an exchanging group, ghostly anger actually becomes the sanction behind the payment of debts and therefore behind the active continuance of the system.

Through their function as mediums women also affect the economic life. In this they closely follow the general trend of public opinion, as do the diviners. The diviners work in the daytime whereas a medium can work only at night, so that the divination is usually held first. In both divinations and séances the emphasis is upon some recent failure of a man to meet his obligations or upon some sex offense. It must be emphasized that there are not enough sex offenses to provide explanations for all the illness and death, so that sex offenses have been extended to include a chance physical contact in a crowd, or a too gay jesting between jesting relatives when there is no economic sin to explain an illness.[3]

[1] The diviner is usually someone within the immediate relationship circle.

[2] Sir Ghost is the term used to distinguish the particular ghost who presides over his particular ward's household; to all other men he is merely a ghost.

[3] In all the cases which Mr. Fortune collected there is not a single proved case of adultery committed by a married woman. There was one case of

## THE EARLY TRAINING

From the time a child is born, emphasis is laid upon respect for property, shame, and physical efficiency. Mother and father, aunts and uncles, and cousins of each kin group compete with each other for the child's allegiance. The child is made to feel that it is valuable, that it is an object of extreme solicitude and desire on the part of older people.

An extreme respect for things, the wickedness of stealing or breaking or losing any material object is early instilled into the child. This is accomplished by a reiterated training in *mine* and *thine*, by continually emphasizing both concepts. In addition to these attitudes toward property, a child is required to preserve the sex tabus and to make every effort to be successful and efficient, never to be stupid or clumsy.

Children are not taught to compete with each other, one child's record is not compared with that of another child. But each child is continually held to a merciless regime of improving upon its own record, of putting forth evey inch of energy and skill possible. In the children's games tests of skill and speed are emphasized and assiduously practiced. Young children of both sexes are forever competing in throwing darts, in foot races, in canoe races. Here the effect to achieve success is the dominant note: the child is trying to win, rather than trying to beat. Chosen companions are those over whom a victory is an accomplishment, not those whom it is easy and therefore uninteresting and dull to conquer.

In the children's group, the relative dominance and submission among the boys is very noticeable.[1] This is less marked among the girls, as the normal constellations are continually being disturbed by the exigencies of the avoidance tabus which are enjoined upon betrothed girls. But the small boys take on and keep the behavior which characterizes their fathers, whose constant companions they are during the first six years of their lives. Sons of important, successful men tend to be aggressive and dominating. Sons of men who, while not yet successful, are none the less aggressive and assured, take up a middle position. Sons of the

---

premarital relationship in Peri and one in the village of Taui during our stay in Manus.

[1] For further details see Mead, *op. cit.*, pp. 135–142.

very young and dependent men and of the men who have no pretensions to leadership or success are of a more recessive, less assured and less dominating personality type. These individual differences are partially based upon this early conditioning rather than upon inheritance of characteristics. For there is a close correspondence between the socioeconomic status of the father and the behavior of the child. Furthermore, there is a closer correspondence in this respect between foster parents and foster children than between those children and their own parents. Differences in intelligence between the children appear early and are noted and commented on. Thus in early childhood play the personality traits are already obvious and carry the relative aggressiveness and energy over into adult life. Very few men, and these usually men of low fiber, ever go to live in their wives' villages. As a result the relative positions which are set up in early boyhood continue throughout life. These early established interrelationships have a holding power upon all the individuals concerned. There is no example of an individual who as an adolescent or as an adult could enter a new group and work out his position there for himself or who could change his relative position in his age group.

This large children's group[1] is very important since it includes all the children of the community from the age of four to twelve and the young unmarried men. This wider group serves to blunt the importance of sibling rivalry within the home and over-shadows home interests. Among themselves children boast and compete in terms of their own capabilities and achievements; they do not invoke the wealth, position, or status of their parents. Parents sometimes take violent part in quarrels which start between children, but the children take no part in adult quarrels. Here again the child's valuation of the importance of his own swiftness, skill, intelligence, or physical prowess is reinforced by adult interest, but he is not asked to sink his own self-interest in defending others.

The absence of any ownership of property cuts off the children's world from that of the adults. The children see the adult world as one in which people are driven by anxiety and ghosts to an endless round of labor. They do not look upon it as desirable or something to which they wish to attain.

[1] For details see *ibid.*, pp. 143–149.

During adolescence, the energies of the young men are not directed toward any communally useful work. All that is required of them is that they make no inroads upon the young girls of the community, all of whom are now safely betrothed. As these engagements are the pivotal points upon which the economic superstructure of the community hangs, they must be preserved at any cost. The pairs of betrothed young people are forbidden even to mention each other's names, and an elaborate framework of tabus surrounds their relationship with each other's relatives. Betrothals are usually not terminated by marriage until the boy, and often the girl, is over twenty. The older adolescent boys are found to be efficient, energetic, and anxious to show their capabilities; they are heavily weighted with a respect for property and a sense of shame about sex, but they are without sense of obligation to anyone. They are permitted no role in relation to the women of the community, but are allowed to raid enemy communities to obtain a prostitute. The man who actually captures her can exact fees from the others, but she is essentially a group prostitute. The young unmarried men of a community are united by the common possession of a captured woman, whom they share. She forms a bond of interest among them all, and she is vigorously hated by all the women in the community, from whom she has to be constantly guarded lest they succeed in killing her.

This group share a common clubhouse and a common mistress and their tobacco and betel nut passes freely from hand to hand. From this merry roistering life, on the borders of society, one young man after another is withdrawn to marry, now that his financial backer has the necessary collection of property for the marriage exchange ready.[1] For the young man's life of hearty self-expression and comradeliness is now substituted a virtual economic slavery. He is held to his financial backer by shame because he has not paid for his wife. It is shameful to enjoy a wife until a man has paid his backers for her.

A man who has not begun to assume the economic burden of his marriage by making the subsequent payments for his wife must go about shy, silent, and ashamed, fishing, fetching, and carrying for his financial backer. From this position he works furiously to extricate himself. He fishes, trades, makes canoes,

[1] For details see *ibid.*, pp. 206–209.

etc., for himself, as well as for his patron, so that he himself will be able to make the necessary payments when his first child is born.    Only if he can take over the whole burden of these payments is he regarded as independent.

During this period of early marriage the whole emphasis is again individualistic.    A man's one aim is to get out from under. He is not concerned with what other young men are doing, for what they do is not relevant to his problem.    He is competing for no prize.    He is working merely to accummulate enough property and enough credit to regain his freedom.    In this he is better off to the extent that he can command the quiet, more or less unofficial help of his brothers-in-law and his brothers and cousins.    They will go fishing with him, they will help him build a canoe.    He and his brother-in-law are bound together by a common aim and tie: each wishes to get out of economic bondage so that they may become *vis-à-vis* in validating the payments which center about the sister of one, the wife of the other.    So these years are characterized by this desperate race for freedom. One's eye is upon an individualistic goal, not upon any competitor or rival.

One route to freedom is to begin cooperating in a small way with some other economic backer besides one's own.    A man adds his contributions to other exchanges, and so banks his credits, which may be called in later to pay off obligations. Though such young men frequently divide their allegiance between their own backers and one or more others, there is the ghost-administered sanction that they will be supernaturally chastised should they fail the head of their own group, who holds the father or elder brother position toward them.

During these years, then, a man's efforts are directed toward his own ends, which can be obtained by cooperating with others. He barters service for service with young men of his own age and invests in other leaders' operations.    Finally he emerges from his obscurity; he himself is able to conduct a small exchange. Henceforth the ghosts recognize him as a functioning unit in his society.    He will be chastised for not paying his debts, for not participating in his relatives' and associates' exchanges, but it will be on more of a footing of equality.

Some men never reach this stage.    They continue to depend upon the leadership and financing of others, until even as old men, when their wives die, the death payments have to be made by other people. The other people, the sons or heirs or the original backers perhaps, continue to finance them because the ghosts[1] insist upon the economic validation of the more important *rites de passage.*

The men who never reach the stage of conduting even very small exchanges in their own names are regarded as failures. They are often given more or less abusive nicknames and are bullied by their successful relatives. The failures include the very stupid and thc se individuals who show markedly abnormal traits.[2] There are records of more marked maladjustment, of individuals who became hobos and wandered in canoes from community to community doing no work at all. These failures do just enough work to keep their families fed, and their children are frequently adopted by more successful people.

The young men of about thirty can be divided into the three main groups. First, there are those who will continue in a position of economic dependence and subsidiary cooperation with some leader, who is often but not necessarily the man who backed their marriages. Second, there are those who will step out of the round of exchange and become independent fishermen with no ambition beyond providing for their families. Third, there are those who will become leaders. In the first group are those who are not intelligent or aggressive enough to become leaders or to whom a position in which they exchange economic help and loyalty for economic direction and provision for their children is temperamentally congenial. To these men the Manus ideal of continuous exchange of valuables is thoroughly satisfactory. In the second group are the men who do not respond to the Manus ideal of an endless race after success. These men value independence and frequently are good craftsmen, but they are without the personality traits necessary for Manus leadership. They lack an ability to plan, aggressiveness, energy, a good memory, and some facility in public speaking. These independents simply step out of the game altogether. Their children's marriages are

---

[1] The ghosts' insistence is, of course, the insistence exercised by the diviners and mediums who perpetuate the catalogue of sins for which illness is the punishment.

[2] Two failures included a man who was subject to cataleptic seizures and a man who alternated between fits of rage and compulsive behavior.

either provided for with a minimum of ceremony or become pivots for some leader's activities; but they themselves do not become heavily involved. They continue to fish every day and go to market to trade their fish for other food. Their houses are small and unpretentious. They have made subsistence and not success an ideal.

Those who are to be leaders are destined for the position very early in terms of their relative position to other children of their age. A prominent leader will frequently select such a young man from among his temporary dependents to be his heir. But this is not a position for which individuals compete; too little property is bequeathed at death to give any individual a prominent position. If there are two potential leaders in the following of an older man they may both become leaders after his death.

## PERSONALITIES OF THE DIFFERENT TYPES

*The Leaders.*—In the village of Peri every man of outstanding personality, which expressed itself in dealing with other people in aggressive initiating terms, was a leader. There was, however, some variation. Talikai, the new luluai, and Tchanan, the leader of Kalat,[1] were both reserved, aristocratic men, arrogant, uncommunicative, given neither to bluster nor boasting. Talikai, the new luluai, came from the leading family of the leading clan of his village, and did not show the same kind of personality traits which made men of lesser lineage successful. Without the backing of his strong kin group his cold reserve and shyness would probably have prevented his becoming a leader. When we entered the village, he sent his adopted son and putative heir to be one of our boys; he himself, however, hardly ever came to the house, and when he did, remained on the most distant and formal terms. Tchanan was a man of very similar type, reserved and formal. His arrogance he derived from his rank and he depended upon the cooperation of the more aggressive but stupider Sanau to maintain his position in the village. When there was need for quarreling over an exchange, it was Sanau who did it while Tchanan preserved his aloofness. His position was even more

[1] See Mead, *op. cit.*, Appendix V; also "Kinship in the Admiralty Islands," pp. 207–209.

markedly dependent upon rank than Talidai's, although it was his mother's gens with which he cooperated.

Ngamel, the third leader in Peri, was slight, smaller than any other leader, and very intelligent. His position depended partly on his rank as a member of Peri clan and partly on the cooperation of Pwisieu, an adopted brother. Pwisieu belonged to an extinct gens and had not been adopted early enough to become thoroughly incorporated into Peri.

Paleao represented another type of leader.[1] To his wide relationship connections, by birth, adoption, and through his mother's second marriage to Potik, a powerful member of the ranking gens of Pere in Peri village, Paleao added great enterprise and high organizing ability. His ease in dealing with situations had made him the government choice as village interpreter. He took great delight in running things, in upsetting existing arrangements, in taking advantage of the situation of white contact to manipulate and introduce variations into the social scene. He was extraordinarily active, outgoing, industrious, and responsive to change. When we entered the village, he immediately decided that we should have a better house than the government barracks. He organized the building of the house, doing a good proportion of the work himself, thus securing our residence in his section of the village and the payments for the house for his dependents. When the government forbade the twenty-day period of washing the corpse, Paleao invented a new ceremonial in which the American stick tobacco was used. He had a sense of the social framework as something to be played with, arranged, improved upon; he was overready to accuse other people of manipulating it for their own ends also—for example, to accuse mediums of being motivated by self-interest. He had little respect for tradition, and was not overly interested in the formal details of his culture. He was likely to introduce a skeptical, detached note into affairs, as when, in making an exchange, he called attention to the fact that the whole collection of food would be passed on almost intact to validate another and still another event. This was a mischievous thing to do. He could be said to be in the game of leadership and organizing because he enjoyed it, because he had superabundant energy, and

[1] For more details concerning Paleao see Mead, "Kinship in the Admiralty Islands," pp. 329, 324–327.

because he could keep going without feeling the same pressure of anxiety that many other men felt with far lesser responsibility.

Kemwai[1] was the one man in Peri who occupied a leading position through his wife, Isole, rather than by virtue of his personality. He was a solid, reliable, conservative, rather stupid man, and a lau. His wife, Isole, was the leading medium in Pere, and the sister of Talikai. As Talikai continued to validate his position, Kemwai rose gradually to leadership himself, spurred on by Isole's ambition as well as that of Nane, his parallel cousin, who cooperated with him.

Nane was a very aggressive, vigorous man who was tireless in journeying about keeping up trade connections. Through his mother he had powerful connections in Mbunei and he was a particularly expert turtle fisherman. He accumulated capital by disposing most advantageously of his turtle catches through fostering firm trade relationships with the land people. Although he was lau by birth, he had risen to make a *metcha*[2] by means of his strong maternal kin, his advantageous marriage, and his enormous industry and persistence. His rise was the most spectacular in Peri within the generation.

*A Dependent.*—Tanu was a dependent of Paliau's. He was the true son of the powerful man, Potik, Paliau's adopted father, whose place Paliau was taking. He was stupid, lazy, good-natured, a fair fisherman, fond of hanging about his house, and overfond of dress. He was under the domination of his wife, who was a member of a rather poor gens. As a dependent who had passed the stage of trying to assume full responsibilities, he did less work than either his leader or younger men like Saot.

*The Independents.*—The distinguishing characteristic by which the independents are grouped is the very small part they play in the complex system of exchanges. They are the nonconformists, and the reasons for their nonconformity are varied. There was Pokanau, the most intellectual man in Peri, who became Mr. Fortune's best informant on the religious system. He was a member of lapan families and by his careful attention to genealogical ramifications could boast, when he wished, of

[1] See *ibid.*, pp. 330–335. Fortune, R. F., "Manus Religion," Chap. V, subsections 13, 42.

[2] Final great exchange of property, after years of marriage, between families of wealth.

every drop of Iapan blood to which he had a claim. He preferred the amusing exercise of tracing the ways in which he could claim participation in some group in another village to actual economic participation. He tended to be overorthodox, stating the fluid Manus system in fundamentalist terms; he was interested in the structure rather than the functioning of the system. His marriage was irregular (economically) and only partially validated. He was always behind in his debts and he cooperated with no one except when he wished to make some blood claim. By his fellows he was nicknamed Crazy Man, and was frequently the butt of young men, who took advantage of the joking relationship between cross-cousins. He was litigatious, and in any clash with the supernatural always presented logical points against those of the mediums. The white administration called him a "big mouth" and a "bush lawyer." To some extent he had taken over the debts of his elder brother Seri, to whose memory he was sentimentally devoted (and for Manus, overdevoted); but the load was too heavy and he gently declined to do anything about it, beneath a heavy barrage of verbal argument.

An independent also was Ndropal, a little, undersized, shy man who had a quiet wife. He paid very little attention to anyone. His small house was the tidiest in Peri. He was an expert fisherman, and the whole thatched roof of his house was always filled with the special bait which he dried expertly. He was never seen without a tool or an implement in his hand.

Tchamutchin, who sometimes cooperated with Paliau, was almost an independent. He is a good example of the way in which the various contributory factors—economic, hereditary, and marital—are combined with personality. He was Paliau's true brother, but was adopted by Selanbelot, a much less aggressive man than Paliau's adopted father. He married a woman from a distant non-Manus village, and hence lacked affinal relatives. Neither an aggressive foster parent nor aggressive brothers-in-law pushed him forward. The fact that his father belonged to far-off Mbuke was remembered, whereas in Paliau's case it was usually forgotten. He had nine children and a hard-working wife. He was honest, interested in fishing, dogged, good-natured, and not stupid. He was thoroughly unaggressive and quite contented to work with Paliau in a simple and unexciting way. (His son Nyesa had been adopted by Paliau but too late to adopt any of Paliau's mannerisms, if he had had the capacity to do so.)

The position of old leaders has already been mentioned but as most men die before they are fifty here this is not an important problem. (The age of death is an important consideration when the competitive situation in a society is under discussion.)

## DEGREE OF INTEGRATION OF THE CULTURAL LIFE

Manus culture is singularly integrated. Every institution is bent to the single emphasis of the attainment of personal success through the manipulation of property. Behind (and below) this ideal lies the sanction of the supernatural world. The ghosts insist upon the kind of efficiency which results from the manipulation of material things, upon good houses, good exchanges, good economic planning. There is practically no art. Objects of art are bought and sold, and they have no other attribute than their value as economic counters in the system of exchanges. The religious life is completely integrated with the economic. Its main elements are magical charms and ancestral blessings which make individuals successful in handling property and ensure that they will not disrupt the peaceful exchange of valuables by sexual offenses. The religious system depends on methods of placating the ghosts with slight formal offerings and attention, and methods for discovering causes of illness and misfortune and remedying these causes.

Mediums and diviners, too, must succeed but in terms of special rules. A medium becomes one by paying another medium or by the rarer method of undergoing some abnormal nervous experience. A diviner obtains his privilege through ghostly designation in a séance and subsequent training from another diviner. Each diviner or medium judges his or her own success in terms of achievement and without reference to another medium's reputation or success. Jesting competitions between diviners, which are phrased as competition between the guardian ghosts of each diviner, are sometimes held. But in any serious matter the diviner acts alone. The diviner and medium judge their success in terms of cures. They usually throw away their power if the stated cause of an illness is rectified and still the patient dies. This throwing away of power is done on individual volition, for failure is accompanied by violent self-reproach. There are no instances on record of the community's withdrawing assent from a diviner or medium; deposition is entirely self-administered. The office of diviner is unpaid, and a medium receives for her night's work the paltry sum of two dogs' teeth. What rewards there are in these callings come from virtuosity, and a delight in political machination.

The practice of magic, charms which injure and kill and charms which undo or avert these results, is an importation into Manus. It is only slightly integrated in the economic life. Magic is invoked to explain illnesses for which all known sins have already been expiated; and also to relieve the Sir Ghost system of having to account for the deaths of infants. Between magicians there are definite competitions; a magician will threaten to kill an enemy and the enemy will employ another magician to work protective counter magic. These competitions almost uniformly end in a deadlock. They are atypical in Manus life; their only analogue is the large intervillage feasts. These feasts, which are given by each village to one or more other villages about once in every other generation, are organized by a war leader of exceptional energy. Part of their ritual is an attempt to break the dancing pole of the other village, which is done by a combination of main force and magic. These intervillage feasts are given in terms of a challenge by one village to the other villages. They are strictly competitive, and the village which breaks the pole boasts about it afterward. In this competition between individual magicians and competitions between villages, the emphasis is upon beating the competitor, rather than upon cooperating to enhance the prestige of both so that each can be successful.

### Correspondence between Actual Economic Conditions and Social Behavior

At least 50 per cent of Manus fishing, housebuilding, canoe building, and trading demands some sort of communal work. A fish drive demands from twelve to twenty men, and the larger the number, the greater is the success. Transporting logs for housebuilding and canoe building, constructing a house, manning an overseas canoe, all these activities need an efficient and large crew. Yet all these activities are organized on the basis of the obligations which one individual owes to another. It may be to a brother, a brother-in-law, an individual *vis-à-vis* in some important exchange, a financial backer, etc. Usually only the relationships which have been rendered effective by being used as a basis for the exchange pattern are used. Brothers who work in different constellations may never cooperate at all. Self-interest, the desire for success, demand cooperation with other individuals who are similarly motivated. In Manus it is most reasonable to expect cooperation from the man who owes you money and the man to whom you owe money. Every privilege and reward of cooperation is rigidly defined, whether it is the allocation of shares in a fish drive or the payments which must be made to those who help set up house posts. That is, all cooperation is paid for. Payment may be in practical immediate results (*e.g.*, if two men fish, they can engage in a more productive type of fishing), or in definite amounts of food and valuables. Cooperation is conceived of as cementing a relationship which is valuable to both parties. Brothers and sisters pay one another for all services rendered, and parents and children also pay one another. No assistance is given to anyone in Manus which is not conceived of as paid for.

There is strong emphasis on the fact that it pays to cooperate. If people do not cooperate, they fail, and to fail is a sin which merits supernatural punishment.

## DISPLACEMENT OF COMPETITIVENESS INTO THE SUPERNATURAL WORLD

The Manus ideal that everyone work together for the greater accumulation and manipulation of property exists in an atmosphere that is quarrelsome and controversial. All feuds between members of the community are disapproved and actual disagreements are moved into the ghostly sphere whenever possible. If two men quarrel, their guardian ghosts are said to have quarreled; if a man dies, the guardian ghost of someone whom he has offended is held responsible. In many cases, even when someone who has offended the possessor of black magic suffers, the magic is said to have worked without the volition of the magician. Thus a thorough fear of the evil consequences of offending one's neighbors (by default) is maintained, without the necessity of developing in the individual the attitudes necessary to administer a system of sorcery. An injured man points to the sinfulness of his neighbor to explain the disaster which diviner and medium find to be the result of his neighbor's offending him. The major offenses against one's neighbor are various forms of default. By phrasing them as sins they are thus removed—only one step, it is true, but at least one step—from individual execution.

Anxiety in Manus is always very marked. Every man is worried, irritable, apprehensive, restless, counting and recounting his debts. Every man is running an endless race with his own obligations, playing one creditor off against another, apportioning his goods among half a dozen different demands. In this there is always a chance that he may make a misstep; that he may slight one interest claim in favor of another. And should he do so, he fears that he will suffer supernatural punishment; he does not fear that his neighbor will poison him, sorcerize him, fight him, or take him to court. By attributing to the ghosts an active and rather vindictive solicitude for the moral code and an active partisan interest in their ward households, bad luck is made at once slightly impersonal and yet completely explicable.

## WAR

War in Manus had three major themes: head-hunting, following a death, which was one item in the whole exchange pattern; the capture of enemy women; and various economic considerations. Head-hunting existed but apparently was rarely undertaken. In everyday life, a man who is bereaved or grieved often expresses his anger by some violent destructive act. He may try to break the stone upon which his young son fell and cut himself, he may break down the house in which his child has just died. This same feeling could translate itself into a head-hunting vow: the bereaved person took a vow to arrange his hair a certain way until he had brought back a body. This body was not kept, however, but was sold for one hundred dogs' teeth to the cannibalistic people of the main island. The price obtained for the body played a substitute role in the subsequent ceremonies. The entrance here of trade to mute the widespread Melanesian head-hunting pattern is obvious.

The young men of a village were interested in warfare because it gave them a chance to obtain a group prostitute. Raids are said to have been sometimes organized for this purpose, and sometimes the prostitute was accidentally captured and war followed.   Girls were captured from other tribes and also from other Manus villages with whom the capturing village was temporarily on bad terms.   The most serious split in the remembered history of Peri came when the young men of half the village carried off a girl from another tribe among the members of which were important trade partners of the hereditary war leader of the village.   This permanently separated the village into two groups. Warfare with groups of other tribesmen to whom they were bound by the daily exchanges was generally regarded as more reprehensible than warfare with another Manus village to whom they were united by ties of blood and marriage as well as by common language and culture.

Similarly, in quarrels among the land people, each Manus village would often take the part of its trade friends.   Here again the Manus insist on regarding the ties which promote economic success as the most important ones.

In Peri there have been a few wars fought in which land, especially sago land, was obtained from the land people.   But the idea of conquest never reached very deep.   It is impossible to tell whether the sago lands which were the temporary spoils of war might not have been given back to the land people when peace was made, if the incidence of governmental control had not declared them to belong to the Manus by right of conquest.

In general, the Manus disapprove of war except as a way of keeping young men out of mischief.   They welcome the Pax Britannica with its compulsory resort to legal procedure.   Wars were disruptive of trade and gave no road to success.   If a man can travel widely, if he can form many firm trade friendships, he will acquire property, he can take part in more exchanges, he will be a success.   Nothing of this sort could result from war.   It was uneconomic, wasteful; it led nowhere.

### SEX AND MARRIAGE

There is a theory that women are scarce, and this is dramatized in the ghostly world by a violent scramble of all the ghosts whenever a female of any age dies.   But competition for women, except in the case of widows, has been translated into competition for desirable economic alliances.   A rich leader tries to arrange as many marriages as possible between children within his circle of influence, and children within the circle of influence of another

rich leader who is worthy to be his *vis-à-vis*. The character of
the children concerned is not considered in any way. Once the
betrothals are contracted, they become pawns in the economic
game.

To break off a marriage is a threat used to coerce one's economic
associates into a given course of action. Such threats are generally made to maintain the ordinary fabric of exchange cooperation
against the inroads of individual motives, such as friendship,
dislike, or revenge. All personal motives of this sort are thoroughly frowned upon. All motives should be wholly based upon
a valuation of a person in terms of his abilities and his value to
oneself in the game of exchange. If, then, individual A has lost
his temper with B, and wishes to do something irregular which
will injure B's exchange position, B may get C, who is an exchange
partner of his and also an exchange partner of A, to threaten A
with the breakup of an arranged marriage. Betrothals are not
broken off if it is discovered that either party to the betrothal
has had sex relations with anyone else.[1] There is tremendous
disapproval, and heavy expiation is demanded by the ghosts of
the other party to the betrothal. But the marriage arrangement,
heavily buttressed by an elaborate system of debts and credits,
proceeds. A man is never thought of as competing with another
for a wife, except in the case of a widow. A young man who has
no betrothed is in this position because some accident has inter-
vened in his relationship with the older man who might have
backed his marriage, and he must find himself another backer,
must commend himself to some financial leader. It is an individual problem, not one in which he stands over against the
other young men in the community. The fact that they have
wives and he has none determines his position; but his behavior
in righting his position is without reference to them.

The situation is somewhat different in the remarriage of a
widow or a divorced woman. The Manus approve of marriages
between people of the same age, so that in almost all cases
widowers marry widows. Usually these widowers have reached
a position of some independence, and they choose a wife not in
terms of her position as a dependent of some wealthy man, but
directly in terms of her intelligence, skill, and vigor. A man with-

[1] Two such instances are known; generalization is based on a discussion
of these.

out a wife is hardly regarded as a full member of society in Manus. So a widower says: "I will get a wife, than I will get a house, then I will set many new exchanges under way." When a widow who possesses the desirable qualifications is free to marry, a year or more after her husband's death, there is often considerable competition for her hand. But this competition is qualified by the belief that the dead husband will severely chastise and perhaps kill those who help her to remarry and the man who remarries her. The anger of the ghost becomes muted with time. These considerations serve to defer the competition as long as possible, and to decrease the machinations of different groups of relatives who favor different suitors. Remarriage for widows is always begun as an elopement, with the newly married pair fleeing to another village for several months until the dead husband's anger is entirely cooled. In this way a highly charged competitive situation, involving much strong feeling and the potentialities of intravillage feuds, is slowed down in its early stages and is finally outlawed beyond the village concerned.

The anger of ghosts seldom falls outside the community, and thus removal to another village becomes the solution for a too violently competitive situation. But a man who had offended against the moral code of the community by committing a sex offense could find no such refuge in another village. The ghosts of that village would take umbrage and scatter sickness and death if a sinner were received into their n.idst. Flight to another village is permitted the man who has married a widow, the man who has quarreled with another man over some exchange or fancied insult, the man who has temporarily overstrained the system by introducing a personal issue between himself and another man or between himself and a ghost. The communities, knit together by intermarriage and affinal exchanges, are thoroughly unstable, and this fact may be utilized by the man who cannot subordinate his personal feelings to the proper emphasis upon success at any price.

In marriage itself, husband and wife stand *vis-à-vis* to each other with their strongest interest opposed, until their children near adolescence. A man entrusts to his sister the property he is saving for a feast; it is to his sister that he looks for help in collecting property for a feast. His wife is meanwhile similarly occupied in helping her brother. In the daily household routine the wife cooks for her husband, fetches firewood and water; he brings her fish, and the proceeds of his fishing when he goes to trade at the market. But these shared activities are constantly sidetracked by demands made by the kin of each. A wife is always watchful lest her husband give his sisters too much fish; a husband is forever complaining that his wife spends more time on her brother's needs than on his. So each spouse stands in a competitive position toward the kin of the other, especially toward those of the same sex. The most competitive personal relationships in Manus are between brothers-in-law and between sisters-in-law. These relationships are surrounded with avoidance rules: brothers-in-law (or sisters-in-law) may not call each other names, may not eat together or jest in each other's presence. And yet, at the same time, these are important cooperating relationships. Manus puts a strong premium on friendship between these individuals whose interests are pointedly at variance with one another. Thus brothers-in-law are the approved fishing and trading partners; if a woman goes about with her sister-in-law, her husband will not complain as he will if she makes a companion of an unrelated woman. Conversely it may be seen that the social situation is weighted to keep those persons whose positions have been defined as hostile from ever reaching open hostility. This is comparatively easy between brothers-in-law, who have usually lived in the same village from childhood. But between sisters-in-law, one of whom is often a stranger, it is more difficult. This hostility is really a competition between a sister and a wife for the economic and practical attentions of a man. It can find expression in a formal insult, *sobalabalate*, in which the wife accuses the sister of being the husband's other wife.

This insult, which is severely punished by the ghosts, is patterned upon the violent reaction against polygamy. A man is permitted to keep two wives; very occasionally he does so. There is no sanction for monogamy except a negative one; co-wives are permitted to abuse each other publicly and obscenely. According to public opinion they have been placed in a position which is intolerable; they are forced into an open, continuous, unresolvable competition for the fish which their husband catches daily. Their quarreling offends the community and embarrasses the husband, and such ménages seldom endure. They constitute only about 4 per cent of the marriages in a community.

For the first ten to fifteen years of married life husband and wife stand allied with their own kin and opposed to each other. During those years the wife allows herself the intolerable license of visiting her brother whenever her husband is involved in some important ceremony, so that he would be embarrassed at being without a cook, and the husband takes the opportunity to beat his wife when he knows that it is to her economic advantage to stay at home rather than to run away to her own kin. Then, after all these antagonistic years, husband and wife become cooperating partners in arranging for the marriages of their own children and their dependents. The married pair can cooperate in feeling and in fact only when the all-pervading interest, exchange, is given a common focus. During the intervening years marriages break up because the wife is stupid, because the husband is stupid, or because they are both so stupid that their relatives interfere to get the stupid husband a cleverer wife. The whole community knows which women are cleverer than their husbands. In planning an exchange, it is necessary to know these two facts, the degree of cooperation to which a given marriage has attained, and which is the clever partner.

## SUMMARY

Manus is a culture in which the very exacting economic conditions and the mode of life demand group labor. The approved social personality is an aggressive, efficient individual who values success above everything else in life. Success is measured in terms of the pace of the group, not in terms of beating anyone. What cooperation exists is obtained by making cooperation the road to success. Personal motives of affection, loyalty, preference, dislike, and hatred are all barred. The only recognized, valid motivation, which is enforced by the cult of the recently dead ghosts who visit sickness and death upon those who disregard it, is the desire to succeed and to continue to succeed. A successful man must always continue the game, which is played for no fixed prize. Retirement is without honor, and means that such an individual is henceforth to be ignored as a nonentity. The whole of the social life is integrated into this one pattern; no field of social life is exempted from it. Individuals who find it uncongenial are permitted virtually to withdraw from it and to lead quiet workaday lives, whose aim is merely subsistence.

*Bibliography*

MEAD, MARGARET: *Growing up in New Guinea.* William Morrow & Company, Inc., New York, 1930. George Routledge and Co., Ltd., London, 1931.

————: " An Investigation of the Thought of Primitive Children with Special Reference to Animism," *Journal of the Royal Anthropological Institute,* Vol. 62, January–June, 1932.

————: "Kinship in the Admiralty Islands," *Anthropological Papers of the American Museum of Natural History,* Vol. 34, Part II, New York, 1934.

————: "Melanesian Middlemen," *Natural History,* Vol. 30, pp. 115–130, 1930.

FORTUNE, R. F.: "Manus Religion," *Proceedings of the American Philosophical Society,* 1935.

# CHAPTER VIII

## THE IROQUOIS[1]

### *by* B. H. QUAIN

#### INTRODUCTION

*Ethnographic Setting.*—The Jesuits were impressed with the contrast in type of culture between the nomadic Algonkians of the Atlantic Coast, who "reflect the poverty of the soil . . . live solely by hunting or fishing and through necessity fast more than half the year"[2] and the sedentary agriculturists of the Great Lakes region.[3]  The latter lived in palisaded villages of three or four hundred families,[4] cultivated extensive fields of corn which they carefully stored in large grain caches, administered the government of their communities in dignified councils, and in general ordered their lives in a manner which was relatively easy for seventeenth-century Europeans to adopt.  Characteristics of a religious and ceremonial nature were shared by both peoples, but the shared trait most pertinent to the point of inquiry was a pattern of periodic meeting of chiefs, who were chosen because of bravery and eloquence,[5] to decide upon questions of war and

[1] *Acknowledgment.*—The author is indebted to William N. Fenton whose field work has been conducted under the auspices of Yale University.  In several discussions he has also read and annotated the manuscript in the field at Tonawanda Reservation.  Jess Cornplanter, an Iroquois, became interested in the project through Fenton's efforts and suggested many valuable additions and corrections.

[2] *The Indians of North America*, edited by Edna Kenton, Vol. 2, p. 29.

[3] From the Relation of 1735: "The Iroquois and Hurons are more inclined to practice virtue than the other nations; they are the only savages capable of refined feelings; all others are to be set down as cowardly, ungrateful, and voluptuous."  *Ibid.*, pp. 458–459.

[4] *The Jesuit Relations and Allied Documents*, edited by Reuben Gold Thwaites, Vol. 10, p. 211.

[5] It is interesting that a trait upon which Morgan and others have nourished their admiration for the Iroquois should be found also among the lowly Montagnais: " . . . he who knew their language well would be all powerful among them. . . . There is no place in the world where rhetoric

peace.[1] Both divided men's and women's activities into sharp categories; men were concerned with hunting and war, women with household management and the preparation of food. But while hunting was the principal source of food among the Algonkians, it was merely a recreation[2] among the Iroquoian people, whose economic life was centered about the agricultural activities of women. This together with matrilineal inheritance and a strong tendency toward matrilocality gave women an importance and prestige among Iroquoians which they did not enjoy among the Algonkians. Since the Iroquoian tribes required large areas for careful long-time agricultural processing, the marauding Algonkians were a constant threat to their peace and material well-being and in this way may have intensified the need of the Iroquoians for intertribal coalitions.[3]

---

is more powerful . . . , it is entirely simple and yet it controls all these tribes, as the captain is elected for his eloquence alone." From le Jeune's Relation of 1632, *ibid.*, Vol. 5, p. 195.

[1] The intricacies of Iroquois political method are more comprehensible in the light of the widespread distribution of this basic element. In 1616 Father Biard said of the Eastern Algonkian: "It is principally in the summer that they pay visits and hold their state councils; I mean that several sagamores come together and consult among themselves about peace and war, treaties of friendship and treaties for the common good." Kenton, *op. cit.*, Vol. 1, p. 37.

See also F. G. Speck, "The Functions of Wampum among the Eastern Algonkian," pp. 36, 40.

[2] The consequent freedom of men from economic responsibility may have been an important factor in the political development of these tribes.

Bressani's Relation of 1653: "But the Hurons and other peoples distant from the sea, who are sedentary, hunt only for pleasure, or on extraordinary occasions; . . . " *Jesuit Relations*, Vol. 38, p. 245.

[3] Lalemant's Relation of 1643: "Although the Huron language is very widely spoken . . . it is also concentrated in the midst of a multitude of tribes . . . who all speak the Algonkian tongue, that the tribes of the Huron tongue seem only to be the center . . . of a vast circumference filled with Algonkian tribes." *Ibid.*, Vol. 27, p. 47.

That the Algonkian were at times effectively hostile is evidenced by Lalemant's Relation of 1659, in which he briefly sketches the then recent history of the Mohawks: "The Andastogehronnons [an Algonkian tribe] waged such energetic warfare against them during ten years that they were overthrown for a second time . . . rendered almost extinct . . . so that the mere name of Algonkian made them tremble, and his shadow seemed to pursue them to their very firesides." Kenton, *op. cit.*, Vol. 2, p. 135.

*Relation of the Iroquois League to Other Peoples of Iroquoian Linguistic Stock.*—Because of the amalgamation of tribes during the imperialistic epoch of the League and the resulting interchange of traits, it is difficult to ascertain precisely how the Iroquois were set off from other peoples of their linguistic stock.[1] Their material culture bears close resemblance to that of the Southeast, but ceremonial life, religious beliefs, and the cooperative patterns out of which their political machinery arose seem to have developed similar forms among all the neighboring Iroquoian-speaking tribes.[2]

The Neuters,[1] who bordered the western territory of the Iroquois, contrasted them with other tribes of the group, saying

[1] The Iroquoian linguistic family was composed of a number of politically independent tribes, who spoke dialects of the Iroquoian language. Geographically they were divided into two groups: The northern group included the Iroquois proper (the Five Nations who composed the League) in what is now central and western New York, the Huron in southern Ontario, the Neuter Nation in the region of Niagara between the Huron and western Iroquois, the Erie along the southern shore of Lake Erie, and the Susque‐hannocks in Pennsylvania; the southern group included the Tuscarora in South Carolina, who were eventually admitted to the League as a sixth nation, and the Cherokee in Georgia.

[2] With the exception of the Huron Feast of the Dead, which required far more display and destruction of wealth than Iroquois conservatism would countenance (see Horatio Hale, *The Iroquois Book of Rites*, pp. 70 *ff.*), Huron ceremonies and ceremonial games are remarkably similar to those of the Iroquois. Kenton, *op. cit.*, Vol. 1, p. 271.

The Iroquois concept of names and the role of name in determining personality existed among the Hurons and Neuters as well. *Ibid.*, Vol. 1, p. 447.

Bressani's account of Huron political succession is also descriptive of Iroquois: "These peoples have neither king nor prince, but certain chiefs, like the heads of a republic, whom we call captains—different however from those in war. These hold office commonly by succession on the side of the women, sometimes by election. They assume office on the death of a predecessor (who, they say, is resuscitated in them)." *Ibid.*, Vol. 2, p. 37.

Insofar as the scarcity of material permits judgment, method of legal control seems to have been identical among all the northern Iroquoians. The attitudes behind Huron condolence ceremonies are similar to those expressed in Hale's *Iroquois Book of Rites*. Devices for maintaining national solidarity, such as careful extension of kinship, courts to mediate intergroup conflicts, etc., were widespread. See Kenton, *op. cit.*, Vol. 1, pp. 518–521; Vol. 2, p. 120.

that their women held political offices alternately with men.[1] Though this is technically untrue, it suggests that the influential position of Iroquois women was worthy of note even to such closely allied peoples as the Neuters. To what degree the political notoriety of the League depended upon superior cultural integration, as opposed to historic accident, cannot be determined; whatever the cause, the Iroquois alone of the peoples of their area integrated widespread social forms into a political machine with definite nationalistic ideas.

*Sketch of Iroquois Culture.*—Their League, or political coalition of tribes symbolically called the Longhouse, was organized on a plan which intricately reduplicated the intricate structure of the relationship groups which existed in the family longhouse—the clan and moiety. Its five component tribes—Mohawk, Onondaga, Seneca, and Cayuga (and later Tuscarora)—were each represented in annual council by their sachems.[2] Its political policy was to expand by adopting and assimilating those tribes who would readily submit and by exterminating the recalcitrants. Its ultimate purpose, in Iroquois phrasing, was to create and maintain a large and peaceful pan-Indian state.

Men were warriors, hunters, and politicians, while women tended the fields, managed their households, and supervised the succession of family titles. Men made weapons and carved wooden ornaments.[3] Women wove mats, shaped bark utensils for household use, and beaded their garments in flowery patterns. Division of technical specialties, and secular activities in general, into male and female categories tended to place men and women in separate occupational groups. But in the domain of religion

---

[1] Kenton, *op. cit.*, Vol. 1, p. 423.

[2] Sachems were male peace chiefs whose titles were owned by, and whose succession to office was controlled by, the senior women of their matrilineal families.

The matrilineal family, "the smallest unit in Iroquois society, consisted of a head woman or matron, her immediate male and female descendants, the male and female descendants of her female descendants, and so on. Some maternal families, consisting of three or four generations living at one time, numbered fifty or less, while others had as many as one hundred and fifty or even two hundred." A. A. Goldenweiser, *Early Civilization*, pp. 73–74.

[3] Fenton adds that men peel bark for housebuilding and make bark vessels, and that old men sometimes assisted women in agricultural work.

and ceremony, categories were not so strict; ceremonial offices were divided equally between the two sexes.

The year was segmented by periodic thanksgiving festivals determined by phases in the maturation of corn, beans, and other food plants. From the planting festival in the spring until harvest in late autumn, life was concerned chiefly with agriculture and village activities. But when the harvest was complete and the supernatural powers of plant growth were dormant, families wandered off in small groups to trap and hunt; the village was deserted except for the small children and the very old. Toward the end of February they returned to prepare for the Dream Festival, at which the pent-up repressions of a year's well-ordered life were discharged in a single purge of emotional excitement.

Since important titles were owned and controlled by the matrons of influential families, status in society was partly determined by birth. Within the family itself primogeniture did not function with any degree of strictness, but long before a child was old enough to show much personal interest in his career, he was assigned to a lifelong series of names which in themselves determined his ultimate status and political function. The most venerable of names, those which entitled the bearer to a seat in the Grand Council at Onondaga, as well as lesser ceremonial and tribal titles were thus predetermined. But there were other means of obtaining a less aristocratic social position; outstanding skills in any field of activity were recognized. Especially through skills in hunting and war, which were masculine activities, one could gain the support and envy of the young men and the admiration of the girls, and thus in time become a real power in the community. The activities for which women received social recognition were concerned chiefly with life within the family; the good woman was the industrious housewife. In contrast, masculine virtues—oratory, singing, success in war, and political astuteness—constantly urged men into public life and into early adjustments with heterogeneous groups. Hence while women, steeped in the more conservative loyalties of kin, were the stabilizers of the political and social structure, men were modeled less carefully to the social ideal; and it was among men that conflicting elements arose which eventually accelerated the disintegration of their culture.

*Problems of Sources and History.*—When Morgan in 1850 attempted to reconstruct Iroquois culture, he assumed that the political structure of the League was functioning most efficiently at the time when imperialistic expansion was in the vigor of its first development—that is, during the period from 1650 to 1750. Unfortunately later investigators followed his lead so that Iroquois history has been divided into two static phases; the broken culture of today has been contrasted with a golden age in which a nation of prestige-drunk conquerors subdued their lust for individual recognition whenever national solidarity was at stake, and sat submissively outside the council house to await the unanimous decisions of their elders and the approval of their mothers and sisters. The dynamic nature of history has been slighted. Though it is generally agreed[1] that the importance of warrior chieftains as a class had so increased by the time of the Revolutionary War that sachems, or civil chiefs, were little more than honorific titles, it has not been sufficiently stressed that the rise of militarism, if not completely dependent upon European contact, at least received a powerful stimulus from it, and that the two sets of ideals, that of peaceful cooperation toward national ends and that of competition for individual war glory, are thoroughly antagonistic; the overgrowth of the latter was a symptom of the decay of the former. Investigators have marveled at the degree of cultural integration necessary to divert toward national ends the tremendous military energy displayed in the building of their empire; it is my contention that the picture becomes intelligible only when the military emphasis is considered a mutation which grew in inverse proportion to the decline of the old order.

The geographic position of the Iroquois in interior New York was a key to fur trade in North America. Not only was their own country rich in beaver but they were located at the gateway to lake routes to the distant interior. Hence as early as 1612 they had obtained firearms in trade from the Dutch with which to molest their Algonkian neighbors.[2] In 1628 Governor Bradford complained that they were intimidating the New England Indians with firearms obtained from the Dutch.[3] But it was not until

---

[1] Goldenweiser, *op. cit.*, p. 79, note; L. H. Morgan, League of the Hodenosaunee or Iroquois, Book II, Chap. VI; *et al.*

[2] Kenton, *op. cit.*, Vol. 1, p. 11; *Jesuit Relations*, Vol. 1, p. 270.

[3] William Christie MacLeod, *The American Indian Frontier*, Appendix VIII, pp. 552–557.

the 1640's that their own supply of beaver had diminished sufficiently to make them serious business rivals of the French and
Hurons for trade in the interior;[1] by this time they were already
acquainted with the virtues of firearms and rum.   Then followed
a rapid and mad period of expansion—fostered by the English
who hoped thus to weaken their French rivals in the North and
the Indian antagonists of their colonies in the South, and by the
French to divert hostilities away from their own frontier.[2]   Evidences of disruption were swift in appearing.   As early as 1666
the Jesuits lamented the frequency of drunken debauches,[3]
remarked on the depopulation of various Iroquois tribes[4] (the
Oneidas, in 1668, were estimated as two-thirds Algonkian and
Huron[5]), complained of the infusion of foreign elements and the
resultant difficulty of effectively using the Iroquois language in
the service of Christ,[6] and described the sad condition of villages
from which the entire male population had been absent for years

[1] *Ibid.*, pp. 280, 282.

[2] *Ibid.*, pp. 287, 554; Kenton, *op. cit.*, Vol. 2, p. 460.

[3] From an account of 1666: "They are drunkards only since they have
associated with the French and Dutch. . . . They have such a mania to
get possession of this baneful drink, that they do not complain of going 200
leagues, to bring three or four pots of it into their own country."   Kenton,
*op. cit.*, Vol. 2, p. 178.

   In 1670: "Drunkenness has been more general than ever, having spread
even to the women; and these debauches continue for twelve or fifteen days
after the coming of each trader.   During all this time, no food is prepared or
fire lighted in the cabins, which remain deserted day and night, . . . "
*Ibid.*, p. 179, note.

[4] The Senecas in 1657 had "depopulated their own villages to such an
extent, that they now contain more foreigners than natives of the country."
*Ibid.*, p. 88.

   Of the Mohawks in 1669: "These wars weaken the Agnieronnon
(Mohawk) terribly; and even his victories, which always cost him bloodshed, contribute not a little to exhaust him. . . . He now fears . . . those
whom he despised before. . . . " *Ibid.*, pp. 185–186.

[5] *Ibid.*, p. 178.

[6] In 1735, Nau reported from the mission at Caughnewaga: "It is very
hard to make them understand what we would have them know.   We
have had here in the mission for the last ten years a savage woman of the
Renard nation, and she does not yet know how to speak Iroquois.   All our
savages understand Huron and prefer it to Iroquois, . . . Hence it is that
they do not care to recite their prayers in their own native tongue." *Ibid.*,
p. 461.

on the warpath.[1]   This, then, is the period which has been called
the high point in Iroquois culture.   Rather it was a period in
which the identity of their culture was rapidly becoming sub-
merged in a pathologic development of military opportunism—a
development which, from the Iroquois point of view, was completely adventitious.   That there was a powerful and well-
integrated nationalistic substratum must not be minimized; it is
evidenced by the tenacity with which the Five Nations clung
together and attempted to present a united military front in
spite of opposing interests during the Revolutionary period.[2]   But
after two hectic centuries of expansion, followed by collapse, no
more than a skeleton of what had once been a healthily functioning mechanism remained for nineteenth-century investigators to
record—even in the minds of the old men.

When first reported, the Iroquois people represented an obscure
handful[3] of rather prosperous agriculturists in upper New York.
Then they rose to a height of imperialistic achievement which
was felt from the Carolinas to Ontario and from the Atlantic
Coast to the Mississippi, and their military strength maintained

---

[1] In 1657: "They go to war at a distance of two or three hundred leagues
from their country, over inaccessible rocks and through vast forests, provided solely with hope, and leaving in their villages, for whole years at a
time, only their women and little children.   But a few scalps that they
bring back, or a few prisoners of war, destined to be butchered by them, are
trophies with which they consider their labors happily rewarded." *Ibid.*,
p. 88.

[2] Even as late as 1779 the Oneidas were able to mediate with orderly
council procedure between the United States Army and other Iroquois
tribes whose position of neutrality had not only been outraged but whose
sympathies were definitely British.   W. L. Stone, *Life of Joseph Brant—
Thayendanegea*, p. 408.

[3] The estimates of recent investigators which, though more conservative
than Morgan's, place Iroquois population at about 15,000 are difficult to
accept as an index of the aboriginal native born.   Lalemant in 1659 said:
"If one should compute the number of pure-blooded Iroquois, he would
have difficulty in finding more than 1,200 of them in all the Five Nations,
since these are, for the most part, only an aggregation of different tribes
whom they have conquered." (Kenton, *op. cit.*, Vol. 2, p. 136.)   The Jesuits
in general considered the Huron country far more populous—though their
judgment may have been swayed by a desire to exaggerate the number of
their converts.   See *ibid.*, Vol. 1, p. 312.

*Cf.* also MacLeod, *op. cit.*, p. 289.

the balance of power between French, English, and Colonials for more than a hundred years. With the close of the Revolution they fell into a second obscurity on government reservations which entailed a long and arduous process of economic acculturation that has continued up to the present time. Students in their static descriptions have failed to give sufficient stress to the violent strains which must have developed at every point in this changing culture. As a result it is difficult not only to ascertain to what period descriptions relate but also to place various aspects of the culture in parallel chronological relationship.

## Cooperative and Competitive Habits

*Economic and Technological Background.*—Ends sought through cooperation over and above economic efficiency indicate a strong cultural emphasis on cooperation as such.

The principal activity concerned with maintenance of food supply was agriculture. The labor involved in processing fields gave rise to certain land values expressed in rights of use which fell into three categories—tribal, clan, and family[1]—but ownership in our sense did not exist; land was plentiful so that there was no need to draw sharp distinctions between those who owned and those who did not, privilege of disposal was limited, and ownership of agricultural products was seriously conditioned by compelling rules of generosity and hospitality. The only phase of the entire food economy in which truly owned property rights were established was that of distribution; the prestige derived from free and generous distribution of food remained permanently with the donor and his family.[2] Men often took the initiative in

---

[1] Plots of land were used communally to supply food for tribal feasts (A. C. Parker, "Iroquois Uses of Maize and Other Food Plants," p. 24). Jess Cornplanter says: "As for owning lands, it was all common. No one had title to a certain tract. Their belief is that the Great Spirit gave them land for their own use and enjoyment. So therefore each planted their share. With the community system they had plenty." Though in effect all land was commonly owned, there are evidences of individual family and clan rights of use. Parker, *op. cit.*, p. 92; Goldenweiser, "On Iroquois Work, 1912," p. 467.

[2] Cornplanter: Anyone donating to a feast gains prestige and gives incentive to others to do likewise; he also places himself in good graces with the Great Spirit.

Fenton: The names of those who have donated food for a feast are

displaying generosity but, since women controlled the food supply, hospitable gestures required the cooperation of their wives. Though perhaps interpreted subjectively as prestige gained at the expense of the rest of the community, the objective result of the custom was merely an efficient distribution of food. The prestige involved was a compliment paid by society in recognition of cooperative behavior.

In this fertile, well-watered region it would have been quite possible to engage in agriculture as an individual pursuit. But the difficult process of clearing fields of large timber made the organization of labor an important factor in increasing the efficiency of production. Though the tools used in this technique required only individual application, the process as a whole was built upon the cooperation of many individuals. Rings were cut in the bark of trees, encircling their trunks, so that the sap could not flow. The following year, when the trees were dead and dried (it was considered dangerous to allow them to stand for more than a year), fires were built at the bases of the trunks and allowed to burn until charring had penetrated deeply enough to facilitate chopping. Since crude stone axes were used, the felling of each tree was a long and tedious job. While men managed the fires and chopped away the charred wood, women brought buckets of water with which to wet the upper portions of the tree so that the fire could be kept within bounds. Though it would have been physically possible for individuals to clear their own fields in this way, it is apparent that by this cooperation more work could be accomplished. Parker and Goldenweiser suggest that a large number of people participated.[1] Though the literature gives no statement as to the composition of the laboring group, it is plausible to suppose that it corresponded to the group which held rights of use; the organization of work perhaps bore some relationship to the women's "mutual aid societies," see page 257, which functioned in all other activities concerned with agriculture.

---

announced to the assembled crowds.

Every guest expected to be fed. In case of shortage the family supply of food was almost public. Thus since prestige derived from giving was so widespread throughout the community, niggardliness would have stood out more sharply as an expression of individuality.

[1] Parker, *op. cit.*, pp. 21–29.

Goldenweiser, *Early Civilization*, pp. 72–73.

Planting, cultivating, and harvesting of crops were highly organized cooperative activities, cooperation in this instance being stimulated by the desire to enjoy the pleasure of group work.[1] Until the latter part of the nineteenth century, when United States Government pressure finally broke the emotional opposition of the men to agriculture, such work was entirely within women's sphere of activity. Champlain, who visited the Iroquois country in 1615, reported the following:

. . . They till and cultivate the soil, something which we have not hitherto observed. In place of plows, they use an instrument of hard wood, shaped like a spade. . . . Planting three or four kernels in one place they heap about it a quantity of earth with shells of signoc before mentioned. Then three feet distant they plant as much more, and thus in succession. With this corn they put in each hill three or four Brazilian beans. . . . Corn reaches to a height of five to six feet, and they keep the ground very free from weeds. We saw many squashes and pumpkins and tobacco which they likewise cultivate. . . . [2]

At harvest time the corn was husked with individually manipulated husking pins and carried to bins or storage cellars. While one group husked the ears and threw them into baskets, another group supplied transportation; a third group busied themselves in the preparation of a feast; and perhaps a fourth group braided the corn in bundles and hung it along the rafters of the longhouse. Parker emphasizes the spirit of gaiety in which the work was accomplished. The evening meal which followed the day's labor was a social occasion for the entire community—an occasion for singing, dancing, and love-making.

Though the techniques of crop growing could easily have been applied by individual workers, it was accomplished collectively by the women of the local mutual aid society. Cooperation undoubtedly permitted a degree of labor organization which

[1] Cornplanter: "It was more of a custom with the Senecas to help each other in their field work, such as planting—more like what we call 'Bee.' An old woman was chosen as leader. But clan or phratry had no part in this. All women in the village took part. They worked together and enjoyed themselves at the same time. When they finish one woman's plot they go on to the next thus accomplishing a lot in one day. They even bring their lunches. . . . Cornhusking parties are much the same way."

[2] Parker, *op. cit.*, p. 17. *Cf. Voyages of Samuel de Champlain*, Vol. 2, pp. 64–65, Prince Soc. Reprint, 1878.

resulted in greater efficiency, but desire for the stimulating effects of social intercourse was surely a strong motivating force. Individual labor responsibility was not taken carefully into account; if a woman were ill and unable to work, her fields were cared for like the rest and she received her share of the produce.[1]

Though a strip of venison or a rotten fish was desirable as a sort of condiment for the pot of succotash, hunting and fishing were not essential sources of food.[2] Fishing with traps was done by the women.[3] The trap was placed in a likely place in a stream, and the operator waited for a fish to swim into it. It was usual for two assistants to drag a vine along the bottom of the pond to drive the fish into the trap. Unless fish were very plentiful, it seems probable that the success of this technique absolutely demanded cooperation. But fishing, like children's activities of shooting birds and small animals with blowguns, played no important role in the cultural picture. Hunting, on the other hand, though it was not an essential source of food, was a formalized institution and required an economy of its own.

Family groups of four or five persons were the participating units in the fall hunt.[4] When the harvest festival was over, all able-bodied members of the community left their village houses for the forest. The women and girls managed the temporary camps while the men, assisted by their sons or nephews, stalked the game. The techniques of the hunt itself were individualistic, but the process as a whole demanded family cooperation. Though a prestige factor entered into hunting activities as a goal to be sought, its economic aspect, like that of the products of agriculture, was conditioned by the principle of hospitality; meat was at the disposal of anyone who was hungry.

Game was also secured in cooperative drives. This technique seems to have been used only upon ceremonial occasions when large numbers of animals were required. Handsome Lake said that ceremonial officials, Keepers of the Faith, were sent out in

[1] Techniques of planting are discussed most fully in Parker, *op. cit.*

[2] See p. 241, note 2; also M. R. Harrington, "Seneca Corn Foods and Their Preparations," pp. 575*ff*.

[3] Beauchamp, "Aboriginal Uses of Wood in New York."

Fenton amends the information obtained from Beauchamp. Fish traps are manipulated by men at Tonawanda Reservation. He also adds that fish spearing was men's work.

[4] Fenton and Cornplanter.

groups of four to kill the proper ceremonial number of animals.[1] Cornplanter describes the process as though it included many more participants.[2]

The sedentary life of the Iroquois was congenial to their food economy. Their agricultural methods imposed certain limits, created certain problems which they solved by building well fortified villages.[3] The process of clearing fields extended from one year into the next, crops were a constant care throughout the season; hence long-time occupancy of a single site, if not absolutely necessary, was at least convenient. Villages surrounded by three palisades with moats between them supplied a welcome sense of security from marauding Algonkian neighbors. Longhouses, several of which were contained within a village, were in themselves imposing structures of 50 to 150 feet in length. Because rotation of crops was not a part of their agricultural technique, the soil became periodically exhausted and the villages had to be rebuilt upon new sites. The organization of labor for this task is unknown; it must have required large-scale cooperation. Since tribes and villages were accustomed to assist each other in times of crisis, it is possible that one community helped another with donations of food and labor.[4] The technique for building individual houses[5] was to enlist the youth of the entire neighborhood; the occasion, like the harvest, was a time of feasting and pleasant social intercourse.[6]

Military activities, though not essentially economic, served an economic end. Since it was a favorite device of invading

[1] Parker, "The Code of Handsome Lake, the Seneca Prophet," *New York State Museum, Bulletin* 163, p. 43.

[2] Cornplanter: The communal hunt is of an entirely different nature from the individual hunt. It occurs only when Ceremonies, such as Mid-Winter, are about to begin. Then the Faith Keepers go, as they say, "hunting all abreast," meaning a sort of drive.

[3] Beauchamp, *ibid.*, pp. 99 *ff*; descriptions of villages.

[4] Parker, *op. cit.*, p. 34.

[5] Fenton adds information on the organization of labor for housebuilding: "Houses were built by cooperative effort. The community, a singing society, a man's friends, or a group of outsiders seeing that a family needs help, might organize bees to construct houses. The bark was peeled by men. Women seem to have helped bind on the outer bark and cooked for the merry workers."

[6] Morgan, *op. cit.*, (1901 ed.), Vol. 1, pp. 308–310.

enemies, especially Europeans, to burn crops,[1] it was necessary to maintain a police force for self-protection. To present a solid military front to the outside world and to keep peace between various Iroquois communities was an economic function insofar as it facilitated the practice of agriculture. Thus the policy of the League in its expansive phase, to conquer and assimilate all Indian tribes into one agricultural state, was economically sound. The Iroquois themselves considered the invasion of distant tribes an important means of procuring new vegetable food plants.[2] Slaves, too, were obtained in this way and, as their number increased during the imperialistic epoch, they must have played an increasing role in lightening the labor responsibility of Iroquois women; but there is no precise information as to how they fitted into the economic scheme.[3]

Explicit discussion of the technologies involved in maintaining armies is lacking, but there can be no doubt that war was a severe strain on the economic resources of the nation. However in early times food supply on war parties could not have been a difficult problem; expeditions were composed of very small numbers who could traverse the well-marked paths to the Cherokee country in five days.[4] On certain occasions warriors who were skilled in hunting would be detailed to supply the group with meat,[5] but this was rarely necessary because concentrated food, made from charred corn and maple sugar,[6] was carried by each warrior in sufficient quantity to last for long periods. Furthermore their sturdiness, to which warriors had been trained since early childhood, enabled them to endure strenuous physical exertion without daily nourishment. The Jesuits mentioned frequent use of captives as food on the war-

---

[1] Denonville in 1687 reported the destruction of 1,200,000 bushels of corn. Though the report is probably exaggerated, it indicates the need for protective measures. Parker, *op. cit.*, p. 18.

[2] *Ibid.*, p. 42.

[3] Despite frequent references to slaves, information as to how they were obtained or used is very unsatisfactory. Since society, in theory at least, could have functioned smoothly without them, they probably played no important role in pre-European times. See Beauchamp, *The Iroquois Trail or Footprints of the Six Nations*, p. 112; Kenton, *op. cit.*, Vol. 1, p. 445; Vol. 2, p. 79, note.

[4] Morgan, *op. cit.*, Book III, Chap. III, on communication.

[5] Fenton.

[6] Parker, *op. cit.*, p. 80.

path;[1] but this practice may have been of a ritualistic nature rather than a solution to an economic problem.

The maintenance of large armies in the field would have been a serious problem requiring carefully organized activity had it been necessary to maintain these outside the confines of their own territory.    But the large armies for which the Iroquois are famous functioned chiefly within home territory and under the influence, and probably with the economic support, of European powers.    The all-pervasive principle of hospitality required that food supply of village or longhouse be opened to all guests, especially if they happened to be fellow clan members.[2]    Hence the nearest village always offered an opportunity of eating. But feeding an army of several hundred men was a severe strain upon any village near which they might happen to be camped; and by the end of the Revolutionary period, in spite of European aid, Iroquois economy was so disrupted that the tribes no longer pretended to be economically self-sufficient.[3]

Cooperative habits were developed in fighting techniques. Despite individual desire for glory, which was a most important motive for warfare and which must have risen to competitive heights on the battlefield, military tactics indicated a well-organized cooperative effort toward group success.    In 1634 they differed from surrounding tribes in their preference for fighting in close array.    Their weapons supported this preference; in contrast to the bow and arrow of the Eastern Algonkian, which was most effective in scattered formation, they carried a javelin in one hand and a war club in the other.[4]    In 1535 Cartier described them as "an evill people, who goe all armed even to their fingers' ends.    And also they shewed us the manner of their armour, they are made of cordes and wood, finely and cunningly wrought together."[5]

Their methods of besieging walled villages indicate a high degree of military coordination.    "They defeated 2,000 men

[1] Kenton, *op. cit.*, Vol. 1, pp. 442, 446; Vol. 2, p. 152.

[2] Fenton suggests that hospitality may have helped to solve the problems of military economy.

[3] Halliday Jackson in his *Civilization of the Indian Natives* discusses the need to reestablish the Iroquois on an agricultural basis.    After the Revolution large sections of their population depended upon hunting for food.

[4] MacLeod, *op. cit.*, p. 281.

[5] Beauchamp, "Aboriginal Uses of Wood . . . ," p. 128.

of the Cat Nation in the latter's own entrenchments; and although they were only 700 in number, they nevertheless climbed the enemy's palisade, employing against it a counterpalisade which they used in place of shields and ladders, to scale the fortress, receiving the hail of shot that fell on them from every direction."[1]

During the Erie war in 1656: "They took counsel to use their canoes as bucklers; they carried them before them, and by the favor of this shelter behold them at the foot of the entrenchment. But it is needful to climb the great stakes or the trees of which it is built. They set up their same canoes and make use of them as ladders to mount upon this great palisade."[1]

Thus though there seems to have been no careful organization of military economy, the principle of hospitality, which was in itself a cooperative technique, was utilized to ease the problem of food supply. Techniques of fighting reflect the cooperative habits employed in other fields; though the application of these techniques required cooperation and is therefore not indicative of cooperative attitudes, yet the development of such technologies far surpassed that of the surrounding area and may have been stimulated by a basic cooperative emphasis in the culture.[2] Though the goals toward which military activities were directed concerned first the individual, then the war party, and finally the glory of the nation as a whole, when viewed objectively they were cooperative insofar as they maintained the peace of the community without creating undue strain upon its economic resources.

Throughout the field of economic activity, therefore, cooperative habit transcended the demands of environment and the requirements of technology. Though technologies were in most cases congenial to individual operation, the means and ends were cooperative except for the prestige factor. In spite of sharp sexual division of labor backed by strong emotional attitudes, the economic activities of men and those of women supplemented each other. Women worked the fields and thus supplied the

---

[1] *Ibid.*, p. 129.

[2] Since the problem of origin of military techniques cannot be carefully investigated, the cooperative tendency expressed in its development should not be weighed too heavily. To what degree fighting methods were dependent upon European contact is uncertain.

community with essential foods while men, by maintaining the peace, made it possible for women's work to proceed. In the very difficult tasks concerned with agriculture and village building, men and women, each performing their share of work, cooperated for the common benefit of all. Though a prestige factor entered into many activities, chiefly within men's scope, the fluidity of wealth determined by ideals of generosity made individual attempts to stand out from the group on a score of material prosperity both unnecessary and impolitic; recognition of prestige was a social function and no economic premiums were offered. (The Jesuits cite cases of Huron shamans who used their visions for material ends; in theory at least this could not have happened among the Iroquois.) Beyond the degree of cooperation required to achieve the greatest efficiency in production, there was found, especially in agricultural activity, cooperation for the purpose of experiencing the pleasures of group work.

*Social and Political Structure.*[1]—An estimate of the degree of coincidence between cooperative habit and kin-residence groupings.

Political symbolism, which uses the longhouse[2] as an emblem of kin solidarity, and the frequent occurrence of clan insignia as heraldric devices over doorways have caused a fictitious identification of clan and longhouse. But because habits of patrilocality and matrilocality were not well defined (though the theory of the League as a whole was that of matrilocality, the Senecas tended to be patrilocal and the Mohawks matrilocal), the inhabitants of longhouse and village were of mixed clan and family affiliation. Since matrilineal families varied within the clan as to influential status, a single family usually dominated the longhouse, if not in actual superiority of numbers, by the more venerable nature of its titles; the longhouse took the name and insignia of the clan of its dominant family.[3]

[1] Morgan's *League of the Hodenosaunee* describes the idealized structure of society. Information derived from Fenton has cast much light on how the system actually works. Goldenweiser's material is also valuable in attempting to estimate Morgan's oversystematization.

[2] Longhouses contained as many as twelve or thirteen fires with two or four biologic families for each fire. They were 50 to 130 feet long and had only one door at each end. This intense acquaintanceship was congenial to the extension of family loyalties. Morgan, *op. cit.*, (1901 ed.), Vol. 1, p. 308.

[3] Fenton.

The matrilineal family,[1] conditioned by factors of residence, personal friendship, and willingness to work, formed the basic cooperative group in economic, ceremonial, and local administrative affairs. Children of an influential matron tended to group themselves next to her in the longhouse, often sharing the same fire, so that the residential group comprised a biologic unit somewhat larger than our concept of family. This was the group whose women, under the direction of the head matron,[2] shared tasks and utensils of cooking and household management. If a son chose to bring up his family in his mother's household, either to avoid the inconvenience of building a new house or because his mother was especially powerful, his wife and children were included in the cooperative group, but they had no hereditary claims on the family. If friendships sprang up between members of different families, which probably happened frequently because many families lived under the same roof, these families too were included in the cooperative group. Despite the exceptions, however, the solidarity of the matrilineal family in regard to common use of utensils is still apparent on reservations today; since the pattern of family structure and housing has now been converted to that of Western civilization, the common residence factor has been removed, but if a woman needs to borrow a corn mortar or other household utensil, she may undergo considerable inconvenience in order to use her mother's, rather than borrow from a neighbor who is not a member of her matrilineal family.[3]

Mutual aid societies,[4] which functioned in agricultural activities, were usually composed of women of the entire village. The

[1] For definition of matrilineal family, see p. 243, note 2. Society as a whole was organized as follows: "each tribe was divided into two phratries [or moieties]; each phratry comprise four or more clans, and the clans were again subdivided" into two or more matrilineal families. Goldenweiser, *Early Civilization*, pp. 73–74.

[2] The head matron, though perhaps not the oldest woman of her family, was the most influential; that is, she was intelligent, energetic, and probably the possessor of medicinal power. Influence was also conditioned by nearness of kin to great titles. J. N. B. Hewitt, "A Constitutional League of Peace in the Stone Age of America," pp. 527 *ff*.

[3] Fenton has described an illustrative case among the modern Seneca, in which a young woman habitually borrowed from her mother who lived a mile away.

[4] Fenton adds that neighborhood, family, and clan were all factors which conditioned the composition of the mutual aid society.

head matron of the dominant family directed the procedure, delegating portions of the work to matrons of other family lines, who acted as lieutenants. If a community contained more than one group of this kind, the line of division probably followed that of family affiliation.[1] Though, especially in recent years, willingness to work has been the criterion of membership in the work group, family affiliation, if not the sole determinant, was formerly the basis upon which activities were organized; hence loyalties of the blood-residence group were further strengthened by common labor responsibility and the pleasure of group work.

Though common names did not remain within the confines of the family with any degree of precision, all important titles such as sachemships, tribal chief names, and names of ceremonial officials were carefully guarded within the maternal line.[2] Coming to a unanimous agreement, the women of the maternal line chose the child successors to series of names which might culminate in high administrative titles of community or nation. An important name was never bestowed upon an outsider so long as there were suitable candidates within the family. Thus pride in ownership of names was an important cohesive factor.

Fenton cites a recent Seneca case in which a religious title[3] was removed from a family and bequeathed to an entirely different clan because the women responsible for the choice of a successor "could not be of one mind"; their superior officer, who was chief of the moiety religious organization, was disgusted with their lack of unanimity and, judging them unfit to make decisions, deprived them of their privilege.[4] Though the degree to which this episode is indicative of ancient procedure is questionable, it is interesting to note that the women were angered and hurt by their loss. It is Goldenweiser's opinion that in former times women carefully watched and censured the behavior of their titled men. If a sachem expressed opinions contrary to what they con-

[1] In recent times age stratification has been a factor in determining group boundaries. Young people have broken away from the conservatism of their elders.

[2] Goldenweiser, "On Iroquois Work, 1913–1914," p. 368.

[3] The organization of religion is a replica of former political structure.

[4] Fenton has revised this clause to read: "their principal male officer, who was chief of the moiety religious organization, disgusted with their lack of unanimity, judged them unfit to make decisions and deprived them of their privilege, passing the office to the women of another clan."

sidered the general welfare, and persisted in his misbehavior, they removed him from office.[1]  This is highly indicative of the weight of responsibility that bound the women of matrilineal families into cooperative attitudes.

At marriage it was the principal matrons of each participating family who arranged and decided the matches.  Judgment of the fitness of the union was theoretically determined by its economic practicability.  Young men were married to widows and girls to mature men—to facilitate the housing problem and to insure against faulty household management.[2]  The two families cooperated in attempting to make the marriage a success.  In cases of disagreement between spouses their families tried to patch it up; but if the breach was deemed irreparable, separation was readily permitted.  There were no important affinal exchanges; no economic obligations of either party to the marriage contract interfered with the establishment of cooperative bonds between the families concerned.

In former times the moiety was[3] the exogamic unit.[4]  But there has been a gradual shrinkage of the prohibiting limits so that today clan exogamy prevails; members of the same clan do infrequently marry if they choose to face a little social antagonism (Fenton cites an instance in the Wolf clan at Tonawanda).  In Morgan's time the clan was definitely exogamous.

[1] Goldenweiser, *Early Civilization*, pp. 78–79.

[2] Morgan, *op. cit.*, Book II, Chap. VI.

[3] Fenton, in annotating the manuscript, has substituted *may have been* for *was*.

[4] Though there is difference of opinion as to the original exogamous group, Goldenweiser, Morgan, and Hewitt support the contention that it was the moiety.  Furthermore, the kin terminology does not suggest clan structure. Fenton remarks that it does not suggest moiety structure either and that it is similar to the Dakota system; though his criticism is thoroughly justifiable, there can be no question that both Iroquois and Dakota systems are congenial to moiety use, though the Dakota have no moiety structure.

Fenton, who has done special research on Iroquois social organization, adds the following information on moieties: "Moieties among the Iroquois are mainly ceremonial divisions and they may or may not have been exogamous.  I think they were only derivatively so.  I have good reason to believe that the moieties diffused to the Iroquois independently of the clans which they embrace and which may have preceded them. . . . There is always the possibility of original moieties; but unlike the Northwest Coast phratries, the Iroquois moieties are nameless, and they do not take the name of the dominant clan."  The clans, also, are essentially nontotemic.

Loyalties were intensified within the clan and secondarily within the moiety by an extension of kinship categories; all members of one's own moiety were called brothers, sisters, maternal uncles and aunts (mothers), while father, father's sister, father's brother, and cousin were applied to members of the opposing moiety. These kin groupings crosscut longhouse and village groups, extending even beyond tribal limits, but, as the individuals to whom the terms were applied became more remote, the terms had less and less familial connotation. The fact that kinship terms, rather than personal names, were customarily used in address[1] was a constant reminder of moiety distinctions.

The clan and moiety[2] now function chiefly as units in the Handsome Lake religion.[3] Titles, and the duties which they entail, are distributed equally between moieties. Ancient ceremonial activities were arranged on this basis as well—one moiety usually presented the ceremony to the other. Ceremonial officials, Keepers of the Faith, set dates for the ceremonies and divided among their henchmen in various clans the tasks of preparing the attendant feasts. Games, which usually followed ceremonies, were played by teams representing clans and moieties. Morgan emphasized the degree to which individual players subordinated interest in their own success to that of the teams on which they played; he says that even in games which demanded individual participation the score of clan and moiety was all important.[4] At the present time, however, games are never organized on a clan basis; and moiety organization is used only when the game is played as the ceremonial fulfillment of a sacred dream.[5] Teams represent each moiety

[1] Fenton adds that nicknames, which are abbreviations of clan names, are now most commonly used.

[2] Fenton describes the clan as the sociopolitical unit, the moiety as the ceremonial unit.

[3] The Handsome Lake religion is a messianic cult of nationalistic flavor initiated about 1800 by a sacred vision of Handsome Lake, "the Seneca Prophet."

[4] Morgan, *op. cit.*, Book II, Chap. V.

[5] It was considered unwise to thwart any desire of the soul, which was customarily expressed in a dream; sickness would result. Dreaming of a game of lacrosse or "dish" was quite a formalized pattern. Proper fulfillment of these dreams was an effective means of curing or preventing illness.

Fenton insists that the moiety never functions in games except when

but the individual player need not be a member of the moiety for which he plays. In contrast to Morgan's description, individuals regardless of clan or moiety affiliation seek individual prestige and recognition for brilliance of play, especially in the game of lacrosse. Hence, since Morgan did not appreciate the ceremonial function of games and assumed that they were all merely recreative, he was impressed unduly by their high degree of organization, and his intense emphasis on the role which clan and moiety played in engendering cooperative habits of recreation hardly seems creditable. The moiety, then, functions as a formal base upon which games may be organized; but the actual playing of the game is (and perhaps was in Morgan's time) independent of formal social groupings.

One of the chief functions of the moiety in the past was to condole with the other group at burial ceremonies. Wampum belts were given to the mourners to clear their throats, open their ears, and wipe away their tears so that they could participate again in practical affairs without the distraction of grief. At these times the father-son relationship between moieties was stressed.[1]

The clan functioned in adoptions. Captives were commonly adopted by families or clans to replace deceased members. A war chief considered it his duty to supply candidates for adoption to the women whose relatives had been killed under his leadership. Since the Keeper of Names was a clan official who controlled the entire set of names used by its component families, the bestowal of names fell within his sphere of activity, and to this extent at least the clan participated. Beauchamp's statement that the Iroquois, in contrast to the Huron and other Eastern Woodland tribes, did not consider adoption a sufficiently vivid resuscitation of the dead to warrant the extension of family privileges to the adoptee, suggests that the clan was the

---

directly stimulated by a dream. He cites a case where the moccasin game used at the death wake was played by moieties as the fulfillment of a death-bed request. All information concerning the role of moiety in ceremonial games was derived from Fenton.

[1] Fenton remarks that the relationship between moieties was that of *cousin*. However, in the recorded funeral ritual father and son terminology occurs frequently. If the condoler and condolee were not of the same generation, this usage of father and son would be quite regular.

primary functional unit.[1] But in 1689 the Jesuit Milet succeeded to a seat in the Oneida tribal council which should have been a carefully guarded family title.[2] Hewitt explicitly assigns the function of adoption to the matrilineal family, subject to the approval of the head matron.[3] Since Goldenweiser says that it was customary, at the time of the Green Corn or the Mid-winter Festival, for names to be bestowed by mother, maternal grandmother, or the Keeper of clan names, it is probable that the nature of the participating group was determined by the importance of the name itself.[4]

Cohesive factors within the clan were, then, common ownership of land (which is somewhat problematical), common burial ground,[5] common participation in the administration of clan affairs (important among which were acknowledgment of official titles, bestowal of ordinary names, and management of feasts and ceremonies), and common representation in tribal and national councils by official titles which, though hereditary within individual matrilineal families, were associated with the clan as a whole.

Cohesive factors within the moiety were participation as a unit in condolence and other ceremonies and common representation in ceremonial games. However, bonds across moiety divisions between affinal families were probably more effective than those existing within the moiety itself.

Goldenweiser suggests that, just as longhouses were associated with the names of important matrilineal families within them, so villages were associated with particular clans.[6] However, the village population was of heterogeneous clan and moiety affiliation. It functioned collectively in bearing the economic responsibility for the entertainment of other villages of the same tribe at tribal feasts and councils. Cooperative building habits were reestablished whenever it was necessary to change the

---

[1] Beauchamp, "Civil, Religious, and Mourning Councils and Ceremonies of Adoptions of the New York Indians."

[2] Kenton, *op. cit.*, Vol. 2, pp. 317–319.

[3] Hewitt, *op. cit.*, pp. 527 *ff.*

[4] Goldenweiser, "On Iroquois Work, 1913–1914," p. 366.

[5] Goldenweiser, "On Iroquois Work, 1912," p. 467.

[6] Goldenweiser, "On Iroquois Work, 1913–1914," p. 368.

village site. The women of the village worked their fields cooperatively in mutual aid societies.

In the old days the tribe was the limit of national loyalty. It had its own set of administrative officials who functioned at periodic councils. Residence within well-defined territorial limits, the common ownership of land to supply food for inter-tribal feasts, representation as a unit at the intertribal (League) council, a dialect different from every other tribe in the League, and military interests which were sometimes fulfilled inde-pendently of League assistance,[1] all tended to distinguish it from the nation[2] as a whole. Because of difficulties in establishing oneself as a citizen in a strange tribe, each tribe tended to be an endogamous unit;[3] for, in order to succeed to important titles or to participate in public life, it was necessary to live in the com-munity in which one's maternal family had influence. Clans and moieties crosscut tribes; but clan sets of names were owned by the tribal sector of the clan, not by the clan as a whole in its extended sense, and it is doubtful whether the fictitious kinship loyalties which were created by intertribal extension of the clan seriously rivaled loyalties resulting from tribal residence. In the maintenance of League solidarity the most conscious efforts toward unity had to be applied to gaps between tribes; divergent interests, especially between Mohawk and Seneca, were a con-stant source of chafing.

The political structure, which unified the tribes into an effective national body, reduplicated tribal organization with conscious emphasis on extended kin terminology as a unifying factor. Since the same clans were distributed throughout the region, the process of accustoming Oneida clansmen, for example, to asso-ciate themselves with a particular clan among the Senecas was

---

[1] Beauchamp, *The Iroquois Trail*, p. 96. The eastern tribes of the confederacy tended to show influence of contact with the Eastern Algonkian. The Seneca, on the other hand, were closely associated with the Neuters and Eries.

[2] The term *nation* is applied to the confederacy as a whole. Other synonymous terms are *League*, and *Five Nations*.

[3] Though marriage ties occasionally crossed tribal boundaries (Stone, [*op. cit.*, p. 307] speaks of close unity between Oneida and Onondaga because of intermarriage), Fenton is of the opinion that this was the exception and not the rule.

facilitated. The five tribes were arranged in moiety fashion and performed moiety functions:[1] Mohawk, Onondaga, and Seneca versus Cayuga and Oneida. In the national longhouse the two moiety groups sat at opposite sides of the fire, just as intratribal moieties separated themselves at tribal councils. At the nationally important condolence ceremony on the death of a sachem, the two moiety groups performed reciprocal functions and, like local moieties, washed each other's tears away with belts of wampum. Family relationships were stressed constantly in political ritual. Mohawk, Onondaga, and Seneca were father's-younger-brothers to Cayuga and Oneida who were sons.[2] Older and younger brother terms were used between tribes of the same moiety group. The familial connotation of these terms was emphasized by frequent outbursts of sentiment such as, "You whom I have so often clasped to my bosom."[3]

In the Grand Council, annually held at Onondaga to decide upon declarations of war and peace and other questions arising out of foreign relations, tribal disagreements such as boundary disputes, and any legal difficulty too large for the tribal council to cope with, fifty sachems listened to the problems under discussion until they were prepared to agree unanimously. Fourteen sachems represented the Onondaga, eight the Senecas, Mohawk nine, Oneida nine, and Cayuga ten. The sachems of each tribe were divided into classes of three or four members, each of which had one voice in the council. These classes sat apart to reach unanimous agreement before allowing their opinions to be spoken before the assembled council. A spokesman was appointed in each class to express the opinions of the others. Since no decision could be acted upon until it met with unanimous approval of the entire council, the inequality of tribal representation was meaningless. But sachems of various tribes did have varying status and function, determined by their names; the Onondagas were keepers of the council fires and of the wampum "legal docu-

[1] Though the dual arrangement of tribes had very slight bearing on habits of exogamy (see p. 726, note 1), the exceptional marriages across this moiety structure, without diminishing tribal loyalties, created many scattered ties which were an effective cement. In Iroquois phrasing, the moiety system was instituted to bind remote groups together.

[2] Morgan, op. cit. (1851 ed.), Book I, Chap. V, p. 118.

[3] See Hewitt, The Requickening Address of the League of the Iroquois, pp. 162–179. Hale and Beauchamp have also collected ritual of the council.

ments,"[1] the Senecas guarded the "western door of the Long-house," etc. Each sachem was supported by a henchman, who acted as runner and messenger.

When any group of sachems considered it necessary to call an intertribal council, a runner was sent to the nearest brother tribe with a belt of wampum to which was attached a tally stick, notched to indicate the date of the proposed meeting. The message was relayed swiftly over the well-worn forest paths to all remaining tribes of the League. The entire coutryside would move to the council site. There would be feasting, dances, and national sports; furthermore the women and warriors had discussed the problems about which their sachems would be called upon to express opinions, and they were anxious to observe the zeal and oratorical skill with which their arguments were presented. Thus the entire nation participated and every individual had opportunity to acquaint himself with his remote clan brothers in other tribes.

Each sachem also represented the groups which his tribe had conquered. Since these peoples also had similar clan totems, including them in kinship categories was relatively easy. Each Iroquois tribe assumed a big-brother relationship to the tribes it had subordinated.[2] Councils organized among the subject peoples expressed their opinions to their Iroquois brothers, who in turn relayed them to the Grand Council at Onondaga.[3]

Aside from the tremendous stress on groupings of biologic origin, expressed in the political organization, and again less clearly in economic activities, there were two classes of groups whose composition was almost fortuitous—medicine societies and war parties. Medicine societies were joined for the sake of curing illness, either upon the advice of a clairvoyant or because of a dream. Since the ceremonies were secret, little is known of their procedure. Each had songs and dances, and undoubtedly developed cooperative habits which were not coincident with kin

---

[1] In the absence of writing, wampum belts were used as a mnemonic device. Each bead connoted a prescribed bit of ritual. These belts were receptacles of tremendous supernatural power, and as such were treated with great reverence.

[2] Fenton has added the note: "The sachem was a great tree under whose branches the clan was sheltered."

[3] Most of the information used in this section was derived from Morgan, *op. cit.*, Book I, Chap. III, V.

groupings; but the degree to which they conflicted with kin loyalties is unknown. There were three categories of membership; those who kept the songs and ritual, those who had joined as fulfillment of a sacred dream, and those whose illness had been cured by the society ritual.[1] Both men and women participated; some societies were exclusively male, some of equal male and female composition, and some largely female.[2] There was probably a certain prestige attached to membership; Fenton suggests that it might have been an honor to belong to Little Water Medicine and other groups which were concerned with the supervision of war-medicine bundles.[3]

Military groups were of fortuitous composition except for locality.[4] There was a tendency for seasoned warriors to take charge of the early military training of their sons and grandsons, but anyone desirous of war glory was at liberty to join the group. Loyalties established through military participation were undoubtedly very strong, and in the imperialistic era may have superseded those of kin. In some cases relationships of the warpath were strengthened by formal "friendships" established according to the dictates of a sacred dream.[5]

[1] Fenton.

[2] Parker, "Secret Medicine Societies of the Seneca," pp. 250 *ff*.

[3] Fenton: "Only men of character may hold the bundles."

[4] Cornplanter describes war as follows: "War has always been a main factor among the Seneca because of their position as Keeper of the Western Door when the League was formed. Men were chosen as leaders on a basis of their actions in war. They were called war chiefs and are never to be classed with civil or religious chiefs or lords. To my knowledge women had no voice in war. There are legends in which a war chief takes his son on the warpath, thus giving him a chance to gain scalps. . . . The clan had no part in warfare. . . .

"War parties were recruited by a war chief who made a long speech encouraging warriors to join. . . . The war pole was struck with a tomahawk while the war chief was speaking. Then the Seneca war dance was performed as a final move. . . .

"There are instances in which one or two young Indians independently declared their intentions to go on the warpath and went out alone to attain rank and honor. They fasted, even resorted to a charm or animal for help; before going out to fight they cleansed themselves. . . . "

[5] See p. 260, note 5. Dreaming of a "friend" was also a standardized type of dream.

The obligations and loyalties involved in these relationships were strong. Note the case of Joseph Brant (Stone, *op. cit.*, Vol. I, p. 28).

Warfare was phrased as an unsuitable pursuit for men in official positions; before a sachem could participate in battle, he was required to lay aside his sachem title—even though the battle was a national necessity. Before the military pattern grew to such tremendous proportions, it may have been used as a mechanism to accommodate those individuals who could not adjust themselves to the insistently cooperative ideals of society.[1] So long as the Grand Council at Onondaga held the military activities of the nation in check,[2] it could direct the energies of prestige-seeking warriors toward cooperative ends. But when warfare, under the stimulus of European contact, became a part of the daily routine, war leaders turned military popularity to their own political advantage and assumed the principal governmental role. The balance of power between sachems and war chiefs, which seems formerly to have been strongly weighted in favor of the sachems, was shifted so that the cooperative motives of sachem government were no longer significant.

*Individual Assertion and Competition.*—There were numerous possibilities for the achievement of individual prestige without reference to inherited claims. Specialization in medicine, clairvoyance, or any of the various techniques of material culture

[1] The fact that war was given no place in the theoretical structure of society, that it was considered by the Iroquois themselves as alien to political functions, throws interesting light on Morgan's theory that the rise of military chiefs at the expense of sachems is explicable in terms of genetically degenerating influences of an hereditary caste system—a theory which Goldenweiser endorses. It is true that potential candidates for sachem titles were limited to the matrilineal family, and that war chiefships, which were available to many more persons, offered opportunity for free expression of abilities; not only was military leadership unhampered by considerations of heredity, but it was also free from the cooperative ideology which molded the attitudes of sachems. But the influence of European contacts, in presenting a material motive for using ability to advantage, must also be considered. There was no mechanism in Iroquois society by which the scramble for military leadership could be checked; hence when once stimulated, the unbridled growth in popularity of military life tipped the entire social structure. See p. 246, notes 3–6, p. 247, notes 1–3; also Introduction, pp. 245–248.

[2] In theory all military activity began with an edict of the council. Only then were tomahawks struck into the village war poles as a signal that pacifist restraints were removed, that all who were ambitious were free to seek personal honor in warfare. Morgan, *op. cit.*, Book II, Chap. VI.

resulted in respect from the community on two scores: (1) prestige derived purely from a display of technical skill; and (2) prestige derived from distributing the final products (in the case of clairvoyants, gifts received in payment for services could be distributed in place of products of material techniques). A man who married outside his own locality might deliberately try to assert himself by using any special faculty he possessed; Fenton cites a modern case of this sort in which a man used knowledge of songs and ceremonial ritual to establish himself in a strange community. But status achieved by these methods was not defined with sufficient clarity to permit the development of competitive attitudes.[1] The highest status to which an individual could rise independent of birth was that of Pine Tree Sachemship;[2] this was a purely honorary title bestowed upon men or women who were considered models of intelligent cooperation.

The war pattern offered high premiums for individual achievement, which was not so carefully measured by a social standard. Admiration of military skill was associated with an emotionally tense sex dichotomy; fighting was an expression of maleness. But here too, since positions at the top were not well defined, success, though violently sought, was not attained at the expense of other individuals; competition was not of the cutthroat variety.[3] (Though the rivals Joseph Brant and Red Jacket defamed each other publicly,[4] they both had been subjected to the flattery of drawing rooms of New York and Philadelphia and it is impossible to judge whether these attitudes grew out of Iroquois environment. It is interesting that the chief crime for which each accused the other was selfish motivation.) Successful warriors received definite social applause; they had

[1] Fenton: Among the present-day Seneca rivalries may spring up between singers who are jealous of each other's ability.

[2] Pine Tree Sachems were chosen by the tribal council and the choice was confirmed by the Grand Council at Onondaga. They were the only persons, aside from the fifty hereditary sachems, who were given seats in the council house. Though they could participate in political discussion, they had no vote. Their titles were not passed on to the next generation but "fell with the tree." (This note has been corrected by Fenton.)

[3] Fenton: There was a general tendency to pull down the man at the top. Hence the saying, "A chief's hide must be seven thumbs thick."

[4] Stone, *op. cit.*

opportunity to recite their deeds of valor publicly at the victory dance.[1] War leaders, who were elected for the occasion[2] on a basis of their past exploits, kept their valor before the public eye; each had a war post upon which he made pictographs to commemorate his deeds.[3]

Marriage was carefully arranged by the family matrons but success in hunting and especially in war[4] is said to have influenced the possibilities of winning a beautiful wife. Girls were sometimes taken on the fall hunt as consorts, and it is not improbable that famous warriors got first pick. Frequent rivalries of this sort have not been recorded; though this silence may be attributed to a cultural reticence (the Dakota, too, refuse to speak of socially unacceptable sex behavior), competition in this field could not have risen to great heights.

Opportunity for competition among shamans seems to have occurred. There were cases[5] in former times of Huron clairvoyants who, playing upon the superstitions of their tribesmen, became citizens of wealth and distinction. Materially motivated desire to maintain the position of chief seer in the community made them resent the encroachment of the Jesuits who, in their eyes, were interlopers with a new kind of magic for sale,[6] and vicious rivalries sprang up. But the Jesuits who reported the cases were violently prejudiced against these devil-worshiping enemies of the Faith, so that it is difficult to decide whether the ensuing rivalry was an aboriginal custom or a direct response to the Fathers' blasphemous attack upon native belief. Besides, the Hurons were in contact with the Ojibwa and may have inclined more toward the practices of Ojibwa sorcerers.

Among the modern Seneca old women sometimes vie with one another for local reputations as diviners or clairvoyants. Since all good clairvoyants know the techniques of black magic, it would be easy for them to use their art in checking the progress

[1] Beauchamp, "Aboriginal Uses of Wood . . . ," pp. 138 *ff*.

[2] Goldenweiser, "On Iroquois Work, 1912," p. 468.

[3] Beauchamp, *op. cit.*, p. 136.

[4] Skills of hunting and war should be classed together as insignia of masculinity.

[5] Shamanism for material ends. Kenton, *op. cit.*, Vol. 1, p. 509; Vol. 2, p. 74.

[6] Fenton: The Indians looked upon the Jesuits' communion boxes as medicine bundles.

of their rivals.[1]  But disgruntled old women are probably more anxious to maintain their own usefulness above the subsistence level of cultural requirements than to stand out as religious heroines; they may be striving simply to remain within the cooperative social picture.[2]

The supply of important titles was limited; this limitation and the prestige associated with the titles would have encouraged competition were it not for the strictness with which they were held within the matrilineal family.  Among the modern Seneca it is customary for titled persons to know to the second generation who their successors will be; "He's following me" is a common phrase.  On the other hand the case of *Z*, a modern Seneca in line for a Keeper of the Faith title but who will probably let it pass not only out of his family, but completely out of his clan because he thinks he is busy enough already, indicates that important titles are occasionally available to outsiders.  The person who eventually succeeds to the position will be judged on a basis of his socially recognized virtues and efficiencies.  But whether these situations occurred frequently enough in early times to have created that degree of expectancy among the population at large which is prerequisite to general competitive attitudes is entirely problematical.[3]

Opportunities for rivalry over titles must have occurred within the family itself.  Occasions must have arisen in which more than one child showed administrative promise.  Primogeniture would have entered as a qualifying factor, but definite decision on the

[1] Fenton.

[2] Fenton adds the following cases in which individuals attempted to maintain their own failing prestige in society:

"A certain old woman at Tonawanda still makes burden straps.  She is proud of her ability, which sets her apart and links her with the past.  She asserts that the younger generation should learn the techniques which she alone possesses; but she becomes jealous when pupils appear, and postpones teaching them.  She might come to share her status symbol, her knowledge of a specific technique, and thus dilute her prestige.

"The same attitude occurs in the case of the Songholder for the Little Water Medicine Society; he withholds one group of songs from his pupils, although he bemoans the ignorance of the ascendant generation."

[3] Fenton has added to the above: Frequently, when asked, matrons cannot name offhand the next candidate to a title.  It is apparently decided at their council.  The chief matron picks the candidate, who is usually her son, and the others confirm her choice.

inheritance of titles was postponed until the children must surely have been aware of their competitive positions. However, though active competition should result, family loyalty would act as a powerful sedative.[1]

The degree to which family solidarity withstands the disrupting influences of antagonistic subfactions within it could be investigated among the modern Seneca. Fenton speaks of a family group which has split because of a quarrel about inheritance. Attitudes toward property have been gradually affected by European influence since first contact, and quarrels about property are surely a result of acculturation. Sorcery, also, played an important role in developing the suspicions that eventually gave rise to cleavage.

Friction between groups was explicitly forbidden in the League constitution.[2] The payment of wampum, the pacific connotation of which was supernaturally sanctioned, to compensate for injury was enforced by the council under whose auspices the difficulty came for settlement. When opportunities for conflicts were observed, every effort was exerted to check their development before lesion should appear. This principle held in cases of arguments between individuals as well as those between households, villages, or tribes. Fenton suggests that fear of retaliation by the injured group is as effective as an edict of the League in preventing hostility, and that the atmosphere is tense with suspended blood feud.

*Education*[3] *and Integration.*—Small children of both sexes were under the complete charge of their mothers. During infancy they were carried to the fields in their cradleboards and hung on a near-by limb while their mothers worked.[4] Soon after

[1] Fenton adds that opportunities for conflict within the family concerning succession to titles do occur frequently among the modern Seneca. "A younger brother is sometimes promoted to sachem because his older brother is already second chief . . . (or) the latter may advance and his younger brother follow him." There has been continuous confusion since 1840 as to who are chiefs, confusion as to whether appointment by oldest woman of the clan or oldest woman of the titleholding family determines the succession.

[2] Hale, *op. cit.*, pp. 67–74. Fenton says that factional jealousies do frequently occur among the modern Seneca.

[3] Information on education was derived largely from Fenton, and through Fenton from Cornplanter.

[4] Morgan, *op. cit.*

they were old enough to walk, they were allotted small tasks which they performed under their mothers' direction. An early commentator has described the gaiety with which the entire family, mother and children, planted the cornfields.[1] That they were not busy all the time, however, is evident by a complaint in religious ritual of the prying nature of grandchildren, who got into everything.[2] Early contact with local ceremonies and councils taught children the structure of society and perhaps stimulated the first growth of patriotic sentiments. Corporal punishment was not used; instead, water was thrown in their faces. In extreme cases discipline was maintained by threats of supernatural demons.[3] Thus the parents' reputation for benevolence was kept intact; there was nothing in the child's life to alienate him from the kin group.

Boys and girls were brought up differently. Girls were occupied in household duties while boys were allowed considerably more freedom to play at war and hunting in imitation of the men. The differentiation occurred at the age of eight or nine, when boys left the strict confines of their kinship group and began to participate in large, fortuitously composed gangs. Girls remained under the careful guidance of their mothers, learning household crafts and cooperating in the work of the fields.

There were no sharp transitions in the lives of girls. On first menstruating they fasted for a few days alone in the forest, but no other ceremony marked the advent of puberty. Dreams experienced during this period were supposed to have some effect upon future personality, but there was no conscious quest for visions as among the Central Algonkians. Upon returning from the forest they resumed their tasks where they had left off.[4] Thus their entire preparation for life was centered about the family hearth and the village fields, beyond which their activities would never be socially required to extend.

When a young woman married, it was customary for her to continue living in her mother's house. According to some accounts her husband remained with his parents until she had

[1] Parker, "Iroquois Uses of Maize . . . ," p. 23.
[2] Beauchamp, "Civil, Religious, and Mourning Councils . . . ," p. 363.
[3] Beauchamp, "Iroquois Notes," pp. 214 ff.
[4] Fenton.

borne him a child. Thus even marriage was a slow transition in state, arranged by the old women of the families concerned, and accomplished with little ceremony.[1] Quite frequently, especially among the western tribes of the confederacy, a wife moved to her husband's house. But even in this instance the change was not abrupt, provided that she married within her own village. Since early childhood, the bride knew all the women of the village. She had worked with them in the local mutual aid society, knew their clan and moiety affiliations, and could readily find her own place among them. If she married into a distant village, the change might be abrupt. But because the careers of her children depended upon the titles they would inherit through her mother, it was unwise for her to marry outside the sphere of her own family's influence. However, marriages of this sort did occur; Fenton remarks that it was extremely difficult to become established in a strange community, and that the stranger rarely became adjusted to her new surroundings.[2]

The only activity engaged in by women generally which brought them outside of the immediate household group was participation in the mutual aid society; but this, too, since it was organized on a kinship basis, was a function of the matrilineal family. Other activities outside the immediate family were participation in clan councils to determine and ratify the choice of candidates for titles, or in ceremonial activities as an official or to aid in the preparation of a feast. Activities of a political nature were open to them, but these concerned chiefly the women of their own household, clan, or village. Though they determined what men should hold important titles, their interest in political matters were centered about those titles which were hereditary within their own families; they were little concerned with the activities of the sachems of other tribes. They might also join medicine societies[3] or become clairvoyants, but the only formal recognition available to them was that of a Pine Tree

[1] An exchange of small gifts of food was the only ceremonial validation of a marriage.

[2] Fenton remarks that conflicts resulting from a change of residence was greater in the case of women than of men. Since the cultural pattern for women was more closely bound to the kin-residence group than that of men, it is not surprising that women should have experienced greater difficulty in becoming adjusted to new surroundings.

[3] Fenton: Women are the managing officers of several medicine societies.

Sachemship; this title, purely honorary in nature, was bequeathed by the Grand Council in reward for thorough and intelligent conformance to the social pattern, which was, in the case of women, concerned chiefly with activities within the family and local group.

Boys, on the other hand, with the beginning of gang associations, entered upon a long process of weaning away from the family background. They had no household responsibilities, and association with their mothers became less frequent. Their fathers took no serious interest in them until they were old enough to assist on the hunt. So large groups of boys between the ages of eight and eleven played together at war and hunting or wandered in the forest for days at a time. Sometimes an older man supervised these forest excursions and taught them woodlore, but more often they managed their own adventures— sleeping in the open, eating wild roots and fruits and the small animals which they could snare or shoot with their blowguns. They may also have played lacrosse and other games in imitation of the adults, but what attitudes these games would have sponsored is somewhat questionable. Today, only when associated with ceremonies, are games organized on the kin pattern which Morgan thought to be the customary method of play. In contrast to Morgan's description in which victory was an honor for the group and not for the individual player, prestige comparable to former war honors may now be achieved by individuals who display unusual skill.[1] At any rate boys' activities had little if any relation to kinship structure.

Special "friend" relationships were sometimes formed between boys and men of their fathers' clan.[2] Though friendships thus established were essentially of a ceremonial nature, the older man often took a permanent interest in the child. He might assume personal responsibility for the child's knowledge of forest

[1] Fenton suggests that lacrosse may have been a conditioning preparation for war.

[2] Friend relationships were often a curative method for illness. If a child were sick and should dream of a person or ceremony, the fulfillment of the dream was conceived of as a curative measure. If he continued to be ill, the dreams of parents or acquaintances were also taken into account. Dreams of this sort seem to have been standardized in that they usually indicated a person of the opposite moiety, often someone of father's clan. See p. 260, note 5, and p. 266, note 5.

craft and the art of war. Though girls, too, could have ceremonial "friend" relationships, these rarely developed beyond a
purely ceremonial function. In the absence of a "friend"
the maternal grandfather, who in former times would have been
of the father's moiety, sometimes took over the function of
mentor. Close relationship between child and grandfather was
accepted by the society at large as customary.

There was no sharp transition in the boy's life at puberty.
Ceremony was even less marked than in the case of girls.[1] The
boy already had begun to sit on the men's side of the longhouse
at formal family discussions. He already identified himself
with the men of the community as opposed to any particular
kin group. His father began to show more interest in him, however, and under parental sponsoring he began to participate
more effectively in the fall hunt. Before long he would be
anxious to try his skill at winning honors on the warpath. The
Jesuits emphasize the fervor displayed by the very young men
in preparing to seek their first war honors, saying that they were
trained to cruelty from the cradle onward and marked time
impatiently until they were permitted to put their training into
practice;[2] this, however, is a somewhat exaggerated account,
inaccuracy rising not only from the shocked attitude with which
war practices were observed, but also from the fact that the
Jesuits' contact with the Iroquois occurred after the heat of
imperialistic expansion had warped military activity into far
greater prominence than was warranted by its theoretical function in society. But it is quite probable that war honors were
the major stimuli in the lives of young men.

Thus boys' activities tended to obliterate kin lines. They
broke away from the family group at an early age and participated with their village age mates, whose group organization,
if any such organization existed, was independent of kin lines.
Their interests were drawn away from cooperative family affairs;
their interest in military honors was much more immediate than
that in succession to a family title. Perhaps individual recognition to be gained as a great warrior also entailed sexual privileges.
Though participation in ceremonies which used clan-moiety

---

[1] Though young men also experienced visions in solitude, they were associated with preparation for war rather than with puberty. Cornplanter.

[2] Kenton, *op. cit.*, Vol. 2, p. 87.

organization sustained the young man's awareness of the existence of these connections, even his religion at this period was largely individualistic—he was concerned with individual quests for war medicine.[1]

In spite of the differentiation in early goals of men and women, it was men who eventually extended the loyalties of the local kinship groups to the nation as a whole. The maintenance of national solidarity was entirely within the scope of men's activities. How the sachems, to whom fell the task of maintaining cooperative relationships between tribes, were converted from individualistic warriors to group-conscious diplomats is the most interesting question that arises out of an investigation of Iroquois education, but there is no conclusive answer.

It is probable that kinship loyalties, which were firmly established at an early age, remained intact throughout the individual's life. Contact with local councils and ceremonies must have been a constant reminder of the principles of kin cooperation upon which society was based. Ceremonial games may have played a minor role. Dances seem to have been emotionally bound to ideas of nationalism; it is significant that Handsome Lake recommended, as a technique for reestablishing nationalistic spirit, a return to the practice of encouraging young men and boys to dance at ceremonies. Despite the scarcity of pertinent data, the fact remains that those men who were destined for political office were drawn away from kinship loyalties[2] at an early age and eventually required to reestablish them on a larger scale.

The Iroquois concept of names played an important role in shaping personality.[3] The thinking phase of the soul was

---

[1] Fenton adds an important note to the training process of men and women: There is marked spatial separation. There are no contact dances, and men and women usually sit apart. If a man is seen emerging from the woods before a woman who happens to be traveling the same path, he is suspected of having seduced her. Parents carefully impress their children with the importance of avoidance.

[2] Fenton remarks that men are never permitted to forget their clan, that constant joking about a particular failing for which a clan is famous (the Turtles are liars, the Wolves are braggarts, etc.) is always a reminder of clan affiliation. Nevertheless, in contrast to the consistency with which women are held within the family group, men are strikingly independent of kin bonds.

[3] Kenton, *op. cit.*, Vol. 1, pp. 342, 447, *et al.*

contained within the name[1] and at death was passed on to the next bearer; thus behavior was in part conditioned by the traditional personality which grew up around important names. Conformance to this tradition was enforced by the supernatural power in names; sachem titles, which were the greatest of names, were so powerfully imbued with sacredness that the entire nation was imperiled during the interval between the death of a sachem and the resuscitation of his name in another person. Since a series of lesser names, each of which required the expression of particular personality traits, always preceded an important title,[2] he who had progressed through such a series was thoroughly aware of the role which society expected him to fulfill. But the manner in which those young men who were slated for political titles were distinguished in the eyes of society from those who were not so destined must have been attended by far-reaching differences in treatment of the persons concerned. There is no clue in the literature as to the precise nature of this differentiation.

Thus the ideal structure of Iroquois society, as it was expressed in political theory, reflected the attitudes of women, who during their entire life span were never strongly tempted into individ-ualistic activities. Only feminine activities, which were directed toward cooperative ends and usually organized along kin lines, coincided with the cooperative and pacific principles upon which the League was built. The ritual of religious, civil, and mourning councils and the organization of ceremonial feasts constantly reiterated these principles. It is not surprising that there were devices to relieve the cooperative tension; and since men had the more precarious adjustment to make, it is to be expected that men, more frequently than women, deviated from the social ideal and that social mechanisms for utilizing male deviants were in more general use.

[1] Beauchamp, *The Iroquois Trail* . . . , p. 126; Hewitt, "The Iroquois Concept of the Soul," p. 109.

[2] As previously stated, Fenton emphasizes the surety with which young children are placed in a status-determining series of names. But the Iroquois themselves refuse to admit the fact that their officials were not chosen for the occasion for merit alone; Cornplanter: "Sachems were chosen by the housemother for merits, qualities, actions, behavior, and anything that calls for the best, because the sachem is of nobility and purity of the highest degree. He is chosen for these qualities regardless of age, rank, or any family difference."

Military activities, which were motivated by desire for individual recognition and were therefore antagonistic to the articulate ideals of the society, were in part utilized by the national council to maintain the national defense; to the degree to which military activities were so utilized, the military pattern, in which every man of the group participated during some period of his life, may have been a cultural mechanism for accommodating socially deviant attitudes.[1] Women as well as men could become clairvoyants; this field of activity, however, did not offer such vivid premiums for achievement. Compared to the warrior, the clairvoyant received but a meager allotment of social recognition. Rather than functioning as a mechanism to balance the social emphasis on cooperation, clairvoyance was merely a harmless method of preoccupying queer people with unlimited opportunity for religious experience—a kind of occupational therapy.

There was one compensatory mechanism in which everyone, even the most cooperative, might participate. This was the ceremonial expression of wishes experienced in dreams. Dream fulfillment functioned especially in the case of illness, but the mechanism was used by anyone whose individual desires conflicted with social duty. If someone were tired of cooperating with his kin, a new "friend" relationship could be established by the simple process of dreaming; or a sachem who was tired of responsibility could use a dream as an excellent excuse to retire. Though dreams were important throughout the year, the Dream or Mid-winter Festival was set apart for their special fulfillment. This ceremony was described by the Jesuits[2] as an orgiastic splurge of individualism of the most bizarre kind; houses and property were destroyed and the most useless risk of life frequently occurred.

Generally in the Woodlands and Plains regions there was a powerfully emotional belief in the virtue of maleness. There is a tale among the Western Sioux that the Iroquois once came to the Plains country arrogantly bewailing their lack of having found no "men" with whom to fight. The Sioux were duly insulted; but they strut now when they say "But we knocked the hell out of them!"—thus proving their masculinity infin-

[1] See p. 267.
[2] Kenton, *op. cit.*, Vol. 2, p. 69.

itely superior to those Eastern "women who thought they were men." This attitude, which in Iroquois culture functioned most clearly in those activities through which individual ends were sought[1]—hunting and war—was deep-seated throughout a widespread area. Hence in evaluating the particular cooperativeness of the Iroquois, the quest for prestige to be derived from expressions of masculinity must be viewed as a reflection of the cultural substratum upon which the cooperative aspects of Iroquois culture were grafted.

The fact that the governmental system required a fusion of masculine activity with feminine attitude stands out more sharply as an index of cooperativeness because of its contrast to this basic sex dichotomy. In contrast to men, who were relatively free from economic duties, women bore the responsibility for maintaining the food supply above the subsistence level. Though they frequently participated in agricultural activity with the women of the village as a whole, they were always associated intimately with the cooperative groups upon which society was organized—the family and clan. But men, who were relatively free from these associations, applied the same structural principle to an extended field. Thus men administered a government built upon an interrelation of groups whose efficacy as cooperative units depended upon the activities of women.

The degree to which kin groups were considered a basis for cooperative activity is well exemplified by the care with which all public activities, such as ceremonies, feasts, and political and religious councils, were organized upon a clan and moiety basis. In the political field, especially, these categories were deliberately used to establish national solidarity.

Other results of investigation worthy of restatement are:

[1] Prestige which was derived from distribution of goods, from skill as an artisan, clairvoyant, etc., or from knowledge of ritual was measured largely in accordance with the benefit which the community experienced as a result of the particular activity concerned. But prestige of war and hunting, though the latter was strongly affected by prestige derived from meat distribution, was not commensurable with the social value received. This margin of social admiration above value received was concerned chiefly with recognition of individual traits for their own sake. Though prestige is by definition a social phenomenon, that which depends purely upon personal attributes is individualistic when contrasted with that which is achieved through social service.

The use of extended kinship categories as a mechanism for inducing cooperation was conditioned chiefly by residential groupings.

Though individual prestige is all-pervasive, it is achieved most readily through expression of the socially beneficial virtues, generosity and hospitality. The principal exception, the quest for military honor, came during the final years of the existence of the League to exceed the requirements of society, but this was at a period when Iroquois culture had been disrupted by European influences.

No clear case of competition for a limited supply has been observed.

The importance of the rights of any component group is minimized in favor of the nation as a whole.

*Bibliography*

BEAUCHAMP, W. M.: "Aboriginal Uses of Wood in New York," *New York State Museum, Bulletin* 89, 1905.

———: Civil, Religious, and Mourning Councils and Ceremonies of Adoptions of the New York Indians, *ibid., Bulletin* 113, 1906.

———: *The Iroquois Trail or Footprints of the Six Nations*, Fayetteville, N. Y., 1892.

———: "Iroquois Notes," *Journal of American Folklore*, Vol. 8, pp. 209–221, 313–316.

GOLDENWEISER, A. A.: *Early Civilization*, Alfred A. Knopf, Inc., New York, 1922.

———: "On Iroquois Work, 1912," *Canada Geological Survey, Summary Report*, 1912.

———: "On Iroquois Work, 1913–1914," *ibid.*, 1913.

HALE, HORATIO: *The Iroquois Book of Rites*, Brinton's Library of Aboriginal American Literature, No. 11.

HARRINGTON, M. R.: "Seneca Corn Foods and Their Preparations," *American Anthropologist*, N. S., Vol. 10, pp. 575–590, 1908.

HEWITT, J. N. B.: "A Constitutional League of Peace in the Stone Age of America," *Annual Report of the Smithsonian Institution*, 1918, Washington, 1920.

———: "The Iroquois Concept of the Soul," *Journal of American Folklore*, Vol. 8, pp. 107–116, 1895.

———: "Orenda (A Definition of Religion)," *American Anthropologist*, Vol. 4, N. S., pp. 33–46, 1902.

———: *The Requickening Address of the League of the Iroquois*, Holmes Anniversary Volume, Bryan Press, Washington, 1916.

HEWITT, J. N. B., and J. CURTIN: "Seneca Myths and Fictions," *Bureau of American Ethnology*, 32d *Report*, Washington, 1918.

JACKSON, HALLIDAY: *Civilization of the Indian Natives*, J. T. Hopper, New York, and M. T. C. Gould, Philadelphia, 1830.

*The Jesuit Relations and Allied Documents*, ed. by Reuben Gold Thwaites, The Burrows Brothers Co., Cleveland, 1896–1901.

KENTON, EDNA (Editor): *The Indians of North America*, Harcourt, Brace & Company, 1927.

MACLEOD, WILLIAM CHRISTIE: *The American Indian Frontier*, Alfred A. Knopf, Inc.,New York, 1928.

MORGAN, LEWIS H.: *League of the Hodenosaunee or Iroquois*, 1851; second edition by H. M. Lloyd. Dodd, Mead & Company, New York, 1902.

PARKER, A. C.: "Certain Iroquois Tree Myths and Symbols," *American Anthropologist*, Vol. 14, N.S., pp. 608–620, 1912.

————: "Iroquois Uses of Maize and Other Food Plants," *ibid.*, *Bulletin* 144, 1910.

————: "Origin of the Iroquois as Suggested by Their Archeology," *American Anthropologist*, Vol. 18, N. S., pp. 479–507, 1916.

————: "Secret Medicine Societies of the Seneca," *ibid.*, Vol. 11, N. S., pp. 161–185, 1909.

————: "Snow Snake as Played by the Seneca Indians," *ibid.*, Vol. 11, N. S., pp. 250–256, 1909.

————: "The Code of Handsome Lake, the Seneca Prophet," *New York State Museum*, *Bulletin* 163, 1912.

SPECK, F. G.: "The Functions of Wampum among the Eastern Algonkian," *Memoirs of the American Anthropological Association*, Vol. 6, Part I, Lancaster, Pa., 1919.

STONE, W. L.: *Life of Joseph Brant—Thayendanegea*, J. Munsell, Albany, 1864.

*Voyages of Samuel de Champlain*, Vol. 2, pp. 64–65, Prince Soc. Reprint, 1878.

# CHAPTER IX

## THE SAMOANS

*by* MARGARET MEAD

The Samoan people inhabit a group of islands in the southwest of Polynesia, and are divided into three groups, the large islands of Upolu and Savai'i, the island of Tutuila, and the three small islands of Tau, Ofu, and Olosenga which constitute the Manu'a group—population 2,200. This account is based upon field work in the Manu's group in 1925 to 1926, checked against earlier manuscript records for Manu's and a large amount of published material for the entire group. Protected from the sale of their land and from indentured labor, isolated from the main impact of white contact in the Pacific, the Samoans, in spite of having been Christianized for about ninety years, have nevertheless maintained the body of their culture intact, softened somewhat in accordance with missionary teachings and to meet governmental edicts against war, intervillage brawls, feuds, etc. Their economic life has been expanded to include the growing of copra for sale, and the purchase of cloth, iron, soap, lanterns, and kerosene. But they have not lost the knowledge and control over their own methods of production, and in any emergency the native community is still self-sufficient. In a hierarchal form of government, alterations at the top do not seriously effect the functioning of the groups below, and therefore this statement of native forms is based also on a study of the present functioning of local units.

The Samoans lived in a closed universe, conceiving the some 60,000 members of the Samoan people as all members of c..e organization. Although these people lived on island groups separated by canoe voyages of several days, and the experience of the bulk of the population of each island cluster was limited to its own part of the archipelago, yet conceptually the Samoan people were one. The symbol of their unity was an ideal arrangement of all of the highest titles of the entire group. This seating plan conformed to the form of a Samoan round house, in which all councils are held. The form of this giant all-Samoan council, which was called the Great *Fono* and had never met in the history of the group, was preserved in a series of phrases called the Great Fa'alupega. (The fa'alupega were the phrases of greetings recited by the orators at the opening of a fono.) The Great Fono itself took its sanction, somewhat inarticulately, from the gods, the chief of whom was Tangola, who had delegated most of his authority to the chiefs and was himself mainly concerned with heavenly matters. When titled men died they went to become posts in the fono house of the gods.

These titles were hereditary within definite lineages within villages. Each village, each cluster of villages, each large island, or group of small islands, had its own council (fono), composed of its most exalted titles. The local village council was represented in the next largest council for the island or district by a few of its higher titles, and through them took part in deliberations affecting the larger geographical units. These deliberations were mainly concerned either with large-scale ceremonials or with war, for the great mass of judicial and legislative decisions were made within the village council in terms of the needs of that particular village.

The Great Fono represented the upper limits of Samoan society, and provided the frame into which these permanent titles were fitted in carefully noted ranking order. The other limit, the base of the society, was represented by the land, the ground plan of each village to which the family lines were firmly attached. This land was guarded by the ancestral ghosts. All individuals who were descended from those who had owned it before had a residence claim. By the exercising of that claim, of living within the village unit, they became subject to the corporate power of the village, expressed in the village fono. Each village had its own high chief, its own series of talking chiefs, its own princess, the *taupou*—a virgin of the chief's lineage who occupied a title which was an attribute of the title of the high chief—and a prince, a *manaia*, a titled youth who held another of the titles attached to the High Chief. The talking chiefs were of an order complimentary to the chiefs and made the speeches and provided food for ceremonies, while the chiefs were ornamental and executive and made presents of valuable mats and pieces of bark cloth to the talking chiefs. The village as a whole acted as the bilateral

family of the chief, reproducing on a village-wide scale the operations which surrounded the birth or marriage of an ordinary
person.   The honor of the chief was the honor of the village;
any man committing adultery with the chief's wife was put to
death by village edict.

Each household—which might range from eight to fifty
persons—was under the direct control of a *matai*, a headman.
He held a title of either chiefly or talking-chief rank, had a seat
in the village council, and was directly responsible to the council
for all those beneath his care.

Theoretically the matai had the power of life and death over
members of his own household, but this was only exercised in the
case of very delinquent minors.   The council had full authority
over the inhabitants of the village.   Usually the fullest sanction
which the council ever exercised against an adult was banishment,
in which a man's house was razed to the ground, his pigs were
killed, his breadfruit trees cut down, and he himself was chased
from the village.   Only occasionally, however, was this exile for
life.   For minor offenses the council imposed fines, work for the
village, small painful expiations like sitting all day in the sun
tossing a sting ray in the bare hands.   Such punishments were
really a test of the culprit's desire to remain in the village because
as each offence was regarded as against the village, it was only
necessary to flee to another village to find sanctuary.   The
number of villages to which a refugee could go was limited only
by the ramifications of his genealogy.   This was limited only in
the case of individuals whose ancestors had married within the
same village for generations or in the case of residents upon small
islands.   In the matter of offenses too small for the official
cognizance of the council, such as laziness or indiscreet and
complicating love affairs, the matai of the household acted.   But
again the culprit who wished to escape discipline needed only to
leave that household and attach himself to another.   His continuance within the next household depended entirely upon his
good behavior there.

The main tie which held an individual within his own household
and within his own village was his better position in the social
structure there, and the greater chance of succeeding to a title
held in his direct lineage than to one in collateral lineages.
Succession to the titles was not by primogeniture, nor even by

direct descent, nor was there a rigid insistence upon patrilineal descent. The most able youth from the entire family connection was eventually chosen by the family group to hold their matai title—and this choice was approved or vetoed by the distaff side of the family and finally ratified by the council.

The ground plan of the council, in which each position represented rank, privileges and obligations to the whole were often formulated as a duty to the High Chief, who represented the whole. This ground plan was reproduced three times in the village: The first was in the organization of wives of matais. The second was the *aumaga*,[1] the organization of the sons of matais and of all the untitled men, in which the manaia acted as the chief and the heirs of the principal talking chiefs as masters of ceremonies. The third was the *aualuma*, a less formalized group of young unmarried girls, wives of untitled men, and widows and divorcees who were gathered about the taupou. Each of these groups had a definite ceremonial life of its own, and each derived its form from that of the fono, or council.

The ceremonial meeting place of the village was the *malae*, the village plaza, the name of which was always mentioned in the fa'alupega. Additionally the chief always had a large council house, and in a sizeable village, chiefs and talking chiefs of high rank would build council houses also. The fono and the other organizations might meet in any one of these houses. The importance of the meeting place was defined by the importance of the group which met within it. When the fono was meeting, all near-by noise and casual activity were forbidden in the village. Women and young people only could approach the outer edge of the circle on specific errands and, kneeling there, present a request or deliver a message. In all its formal meetings the fono was served by the aumaga, who cooked the food for its feasts and served at the banquets. In many villages, the fono ate one large daily meal in common. The members always ate together if there was any work on foot in which they were participating. Similarly when the wives of matais gathered formally, for instance in order to carry stones for the floor of a new council house, the village was theirs and the men stayed far away from the scene of action. The evenings were the time when the aumaga gathered,

[1] g in Samoan orthography, as developed by the early missionaries, should be pronounced as *ng*.

and the members of the fono, by their absence and abstention from any interruption, expressed their respect for the integrity of the young men's groups.

The minutiae of rank is observed throughout Samoan life. It is not an attribute of the individual himself, but it is always observed as an aspect of the situation in which an individual is temporarily or sometimes permanently placed. This is in striking contrast to the Maori, among whom status is an inalienable attribute which can be lost only when one is captured and taken away in slavery from one's land. A shadow of this attitude is preserved in the special sanctity which the Samoans allowed to the first child born to the Tui Manu'a, the high chief of all Manu'a, *after* he had assumed his title. The child was allowed to have sanctity as an attribute, but this was dependent upon his father's *assumption* of a title. So the Samoans recognize status in any situation. The lover who calls on a girl is treated by the father of the girl, who may far exceed him in rank, as a chiefly visitor. In any group of untitled young girls, one will be treated as the taupou; in a traveling party in which no one has rank, some will be designated to act as talking chiefs, etc. This tendency to reinterpret each situation in terms of a heirarchy is most conspicuous in the case of skilled craftsmen. The skilled carpenter or canoe builder becomes, by virtue of his mastery and control over a given piece of work, a chief for that occasion, and must be addressed with all chiefly honors, although once the occasion is past, he may be only an untitled youth. Conversely a high chief who wishes to call upon a taupou who is visiting his village, may explicitly lay aside his title and resume the title of a young manaia. As such he may behave as he could not were he holding the title of a chief. This separation between the individual and his role is exceedingly important in the understanding of Samoan society. The whole conception is of a ground plan which has come down from ancestral times, a ground plan which is explicit in titles and remembered phrases, and which has a firm base in the land of the villages and districts. The individual is important only in terms of the position which he occupies in this universal scheme—of himself he is nothing. Their eyes are always on the play,[1] never on the players, while each individual's task is to fit his role.

[1] When I entered the village of Fitiuta under a taupou title, the people of the village spread the news that such and such a taupou with an Upolu

The circumstance that each village, and almost every family line, has more titles than it ever uses in a generation gives to this fixed pattern an expansiveness, a sense of spaciousness, and mutes competition. The custom of conferring titles within the lineage becomes stricter as the importance of the title increases. Every girl in the village is not eligible for the title of taupou, the preference goes first to the distaff line of the chief, then to his own male line; and the great majority of village girls do not come within the possibility of competition.[1] But in a large village there are lesser taupou titles also, around which small groups of related girls cluster. All these are seldom used. Competition for matai[2] titles is further muted by the fact that the matai rank is of two orders, chiefs and talking chiefs, and that the requirements and privileges of each complement the other. Every large family has titles of both kinds in its possession. If in a given generation no one measures up to the title, the title is not given, but its presence is still allowed for in the fono seating plan and the phrases which embody that plan.

Competition between holders of titles is covert and always expressed as the manipulation of the rank of a title, not as any overt alteration which affects the individual. If a holder of a title is not ineffective enough to be removed, which can be done by the fono's acting with the family line, but still does not adorn the title which he holds, the talking chiefs may, slowly over time, depress the importance of his title and rearrange the small interrelationships between titles within a village fono. This is done very slowly, without any sense of suddenness, almost in spite of the knowledge of the lackadaisical holder of the title which is being depressed. So the Samoans preserve their sense of a fixed structure but do not permit it to trammel their activities.[3]

## ECONOMIC BACKGROUND

The Samoan life is based upon an economy of plenty. They depend primarily upon agriculture, taro, bananas, yams, sweet

---

title was staying at the guest house and neglected to mention that I was white, although there had not been half a dozen white women in Fitiuta throughout the course of history.

[1] See Mead, Margaret, *Coming of Age in Samoa*, pp. 51–53.

[2] For ways in which competition within a household operates during the years before the choice for a titleholder is made, see Mead, *op. cit.*, pp. 51–53.

[3] The importance of this flexibility in relation to social change is discussed in "The Role of the Individual in Samoan Culture." See bibliography.

potatoes, breadfruit, supplemented by fish, shellfish, pigs, coconut crabs, coconuts, and greens.   There is more than enough land, even with the system of rotating garden sites over long periods of fallowness in order to restore fertility to the land. Land is owned by the household groups, and the matai is a trustee for the land, presiding over the planting and harvesting, superintending the work of all the men and women who live beneath his authority.   The gardens are worked by the household as a group, with the exception of the work which is limited to an age grade and which is performed jointly by the aumaga or the aualuma.   Men clear and fence, women plant and weed, both sexes harvest; the fruits of the harvest belong to the household, subject to the levies made upon each household by the village. Each household has to provide for its own needs, for affinal exchanges in which it may become involved during the years, either as the group of the wife, in which case gifts of bark cloth and finely woven mats will be in demand, or as the group of the husband, in which case an extra supply of food, especially pigs, and in some cases woodwork, such as kava[1] bowls, will be needed.[2] If the household plans to build a new house, provision must be made for feeding the group of carpenters.   Each household will also have to contribute during the year to village feasts, to the entertainment of guests, and to exchanges made in the name of the high chief, the taupou, and the manaia.

Whether we examine first the organization of a household cooking group or the organization of a village fishing expedition, we find the same principle exemplified, a number of individuals arranged in a hierarchical order, who contribute differentially according to their rank, age, sex, and skill, to a total result, in which the whole group share, either directly—as in eating the food from the family oven—or indirectly—as members of a household or village whose prestige has been enhanced by the result of the labor which all have expended.   All work is conceived of in this way, as something to which a number of people of different status make a contribution, which is increasingly important in proportion to the rank of the individuals involved.

[1] Kava, the ceremonial drink of Polynesia, is made by pulverizing the root of the kava plant and mixing it with water.
[2] For further discussions of the organization of affinal exchanges see Mead, "Social Organization of Manua," pp. 75–76.

So a man who builds a house for himself with the help of the young men of his household is engaged in an activity which is on the same plane as cooking in an earth oven, in which he and the members of his household participate. If, however, he calls in a master carpenter and that carpenter's associates and apprentices, then the situation immediately becomes much more important, and he as the *taufale*, "the owner of the house to be built," takes on new rank, in relation to the rank of the *tafunga fai fale*, the master housebuilder. Food must now be cooked in a more ceremonial fashion and far more etiquette observed, although the result may be a house of about the same size.

In making an oven for a household, the entire household participates; and the oven is only made about twice a week, everyone eating cold cooked food in the intervals. The matai does the most important work, butchers and stuffs the pig if there is one, if not, laces up the largest fish into coconut leaf covers; the young men grate the coconuts and mix the cocoanut puddings; the women grate the rinds off the breadfruit, peel the taro and bananas; the children fetch salt water, leaves for seasoning, etc. The smallest child assists, each performing the task to which his skill and strength and age entitle him. There is no feeling in Samoa that a task is beneath a person's dignity; the emphasis is the opposite; an individual is strong enough, or skilled enough, to do something which requires his special ability and to leave the simpler tasks to his juniors and inferiors. When the oven is opened, containing an oversupply of food for the entire household for several days, gifts of food are sent to any relatives who may be visiting in the village, or to visitors who are staying in the house of a chief. Thus even the family oven is knit into the life of the village.

If we consider the other end of the scale we find that there is the same kind of division of labor within the village.[1] But the village frequently acted as a corporate whole in economic under-

---

[1] The village is the largest effective economic unit in Manu'a and in most of Samoa. There are a few exceptions; every village in Manu'a, except Tau, where the Tui Manu'a (the High Chief of Manu'a) lived, had to contribute breadfruit to the great breadfruit pit of Tau, in which breadfruit was stored against the famine periods which followed the ten-yearly hurricanes. The villages of Ofu and Olosenga also brought fish to the Tui Manu'a.

takings, in road making, council-house building, and community fishing, in preparation for feasts, in intervillage feasts, as a village ceremonial visiting party which goes to another village, and at all the *rites de passage* of the high chief and his family. The corporate activity had various degrees of intensity. It might consist of a tabu upon the use of more than a certain number of coconuts by any household, so that there would be an adequate supply for a feast which was three months off. In some villages special titles carried with them "the power over the land"—*i.e.*, to tabu land products for a communal end, and another title would carry the "power over the sea," to tabu certain fish or shellfish so that many would accumulate. Or community control in another economic field might extend only to determining seasons; thus no one could pick breadfruit until the fono had formally eaten a feast of the first breadfruit of the year. It might be a ceremonial levy upon a large fishing catch, so that from a turtle, a shark, or any other very large fish certain parts went to the high chief, and to the taupou. Other activities were initiated by a feast and a group starting to work together. This was so for the *taloloa*, the village taro plantation which was phrased as a group activity of the aumaga, but in which each young man planted a patch which would be weeded and harvested thereafter by the women of his household. Thus for the village paper mulberry patch, from which the bark cloth was made, the aumaga cleared the ground as a group; they were then feasted by the aualuma, after which the aualuma planted the paper mulberry from which each household drew their own supplies. Village cooperation might take the form of a requisition for contributions of food, and these contributions were harvested or fished for by individuals, using individual techniques. When there were guests in the village, the talking chiefs who were masters of ceremonies would assign to each household the provision of so many baskets of food, each one of which would contain fish and shellfish, caught by individual men and women, land crabs which might have been caught by children, and various cooked foods from the family oven to which every member of the household had contributed. The emphasis was never upon what an individual did, neither upon his skill nor upon the size of his catch or harvest, but always upon its place in a larger social situation.

This emphasis is displayed most sharply in the building of a village council house or in village fishing-fleet organization. When a village council house, said to be the house of the high chief, was to be built, a fono was held and orders were given for the planting of gardens to provide food to feed the carpenters. Bark cloth and fine mats were either made or obtained by exchange or begging from relatives (in other villages) to pay the carpenters, and sennit, the coconut fiber from which the string was made to tie the house together, was braided. To each household was assigned a given amount which was often less than the largest household could provide with ease and enough to make a small household strain a little. The largest household, which was almost automatically the household of a matai of high rank, would usually make an additional contribution because the higher the rank of a man the more he had to contribute to the village, through his payments to the talking chiefs who represented the village. To each household would be assigned the task of providing a section of the round house, wood for one or two posts, wood for the rafters, the weaving of the Venetian blinds which hang between the posts, the growing of the sugar cane—this is a prerogative of married women, each one of whom has a sugar-cane patch—and the sewing of the leaf of the cane into thatch for a section of the roof. In this form of division of labor the principle of hierarchy is abandoned and the village is conceived as made up of coordinate units, which make identical contributions to the common end, but each of the identical contributions are themselves split up into sections involving contributions of both sexes, and differential strength and skill.

The continual recombination of units in a cooperative hierarchical scheme is characteristically Samoan, so two cross-cousins may have one relative rank within the fono, and a different relative rank within the descent group.[1] The fono has two kinds of divisions, one according to the classification of the title, as high chief, grouped higher chiefs, lower chiefs, high talking chiefs, supervising talking chiefs, small talking chiefs, etc., and the other according to another plan of subdivision, in which titles of different orders may be represented and the whole subdivision have a duty to perform such as the duty of acting as scouts in wartime.

[1] See Mead, "Social Organization of Manua," pp. 21 *ff.*

The organization of village fishing is carefully controlled. Both men and women do many kinds of individual fishing, contributing their catch directly to the joint meal of their household, or to their household's contribution to the village. But for fleet fishing—especially for bonito and for shark—and for the surrounding of fish in the lagoon with long woven leaf fences, the most careful organization is followed.[1] In each village, or occasionally in each section of a large village, there is a chief fisherman, who rules over the sea, both in tabuing fishing at certain periods and in organizing and leading the fishing fleet.[2] Even a high chief if he join the bonito fleet must act as a private individual under the control of the *tautai*, his rank recognized only by the ceremonial gift of the first bonito caught. The fono decides when the fleet is to set out, the tautai taking the lead in the council. He selects the fishing ground to be visited and decides on the movements at sea. When he considers the fishing over, he gives the signal to return, and before the fleet reaches the shore, he makes a levy upon each canoe, a set proportion of the catch. This levy is not for himself but for a community feast for the fishermen in which the unsuccessful member shares equally with his more fortunate fellows. The tautai makes no levy, however, on the canoes with a very bad catch. If any fisherman fails to report accurately on his catch, and this is subsequently discovered, his bonito canoe is broken up and his fishing gear is confiscated to the tautai. The specific nature of the tautai's authority is shown by the rule that if a matai sends an individual canoe out after the fleet has departed, although that canoe may subsequently join the fleet, it is not an organic part of it, and does not have to contribute to the levy for the feast. Fishermen on returning to the shore have to give a portion of their catch to anyone they meet in the lagoon or on the shore, thus further socializing the catch.

In net fishing, the whole community contributes to the finished net; for example, the rule in one village[3] was for each matai to contribute two arm spans plus an additional arm span for each male child in his household. These are then woven together

---

[1] Based on account given by Te Rangi Hiroa (Peter Buck) in "Samoan Material Culture," pp. 418–523, *passim*.

[2] *Ibid.*, pp. 517–519.

[3] *Ibid.*, p. 487.

into the net which the whole village uses.  The explicitness of this ownership of nets is revealed by the instance[1] of a village which was divided into two parts, separated by a stream.  A turtle net was owned by the two parts, and between turtle fishing seasons was kept in two sections, being reassembled for each fishing.  There is another instance[2] of a net which one village, acting as a unit, gave away to another village.

When the leaf fencing for a lagoon trap[3] is to be made, a fono is held, and a number of fathoms of leaf fencing are assigned to each matai as his household's share.  Then the head of each family sends the young men of his household to the bush to get the required number of fathoms of vine.  Meanwhile the other members of the household collect and strip coconut leaves. When the young men return, the matai ties knots in the vine, measuring off the required number of fathoms, the vine is tied between two trees, and the exact space between the two knots filled in.  Each household coils its ten fathoms, and the next day they are combined and used with a net which the tautai and a few assistants have set in the reef.  The whole village takes part in the drive that follows, and at the end of the catch the fish are divided among the households.

Bonito fishing, in which a single canoe is manned by three men, or occasionally only two, a steersman-fisherman, a bowman who is lookout, and a middleman who paddles and bails, is an example on a smaller scale of cooperative activity.[4]  The canoe is usually owned by a matai and three young men of his household, or occasionally one from another household, will make up a more or less permanent team.  In the distribution a share of the fish is given the canoe owner.

## Ownership of Property

Property may be classified into *toga*, dowry property, *oloa*, bride-price property, and *fanua*, land, which in occasional instances may be used as either toga or oloa.[5]  Toga must be given away with the bride in each marriage and is matched by a

[1] *Ibid.*, p. 488.
[2] *Ibid.*, p. 487.
[3] *Ibid.*, p. 429.
[4] *Ibid.*, p. 508.
[5] See Mead, "Social Organization of Manua," p. 71.

return of oloa.  Toga is all made by women, consisting of mats and bark cloth, while oloa is primarily made, or grown, or otherwise collected, by men, such as pigs, other food, woodwork, and, in Western Samoa, red feathers.  Not only marriage, but the birth of a child, visits of one spouse to the kin of the other, and funeral ceremonies require the exchange of the two kinds of property.  Any given household can be said to be in a fortunate or unfortunate economic position in terms of the balance which it is able to preserve between laborers of both sexes, and affinal relationships which call for the two kinds of property.  A household in which there are too many young people of one sex is in a doubly difficult position, because each time a female marries, the household becomes indebted in perpetuity in terms of the proceeds of female labor, and each time a male marries the opposite is true.  Every object in Samoa, except the crudest household utensils, the tools of a craftsman, and the simpler articles of costume, such as a grass skirt or bark-cloth G-string, is continually changing hands in these toga-oloa exchanges.  Property is valued for its mobility, for its power of validating ceremonial and increasing prestige; there is no hoarding and no great benefit given one generation by any accumulation of capital goods by the preceding generation.  There is more land than is needed, and houses last only six or seven years.

The exchange of toga and oloa between affinal relatives is reflected in the exchanges between chiefs and talking chiefs, in which the chiefs always give toga and the talking chiefs give oloa.  In intervillage alliances, in which a taupou marries a high chief or a manaia, the entire village mobilizes and contributes one kind of property.  When a matai assumed his title, if he was a talking chief he had to feast the village; if he was a chief, or a chief giving a taupou title to one of his young female relatives, he had to distribute toga to the talking chiefs.  All these interchanges were strictly reciprocal and returned in exact amounts.[1]  In intervillage exchanges following a royal marriage, the fine mats and pigs were exchanged point for point until one side ran out, a point of shame for the village which was first exhausted.

Behind these strict interchanges lay the wider kinship group, which transcended village lines and within which mutual helpfulness was the rule.  This cannot be said to be cooperation because

[1] See Mead, "Social Organization of Manua," pp. 75–76.

no individual contributes to an end in which all the contributors are interested. Instead there is a continuous begging, borrowing-lending relationship going on between all relatives to meet the strictly formalized demands for a certain kind of contribution from a given household. If fine mats are demanded for the dowry of the taupou, each household may have to contribute a given number, and it will make up its quota by borrowing in other villages, and these loans will be returned in kind, not in the opposite class of property as is the case in the formal scheme. There are always definite limits to the formal cooperating groups, the household, or the aumaga of a village or of a section of a village, or the village itself; in any case the group is defined and limited, and each individual's part is specified in terms of the whole. But within the wider relationship group the most diaphanous claims may be honored, either of blood, affinal relationship, or adoption; anyone calling another *aiga*, relative, has claims of requisition if he is of higher rank, of effective pleading if he is of lower rank. So that every Samoan may be said to live a kind of double life, one part of which is defined in terms of a social situation, the other part of which is given in terms of the multiplicity and inalienability of his kinship ties. If a Samoan is presented with a statement of a legal or social dilemma in which an individual has violated rules, or outraged his present cooperative group, the answer always is, "He will go to another relative." Only in rare instances[1] does the kinship group become exhausted. The memories of individuals are quickened in proportion to rank in Samoa, the higher a man's rank, that is, the more important his role in his cooperative political group, the greater security lies behind him in the number of aiga who will be glad to remember their relationship to him. The social organization may be said to be forms of highly cooperative but optionally composed groups. These groups are optional from the standpoint of both the individual and the rest of the group who may, if they wish, expel an uncooperative member. One of the strengths of Samoan society may lie in this dual emphasis. The commoner form of organization is that found among the Maori, in which one's membership in a cooperative group is a birth claim, and the effort of the cooperative group to discipline its members is

[1] *Coming of Age in Samoa*, pp. 173–178.

continually tempered by its inability to expel someone who is felt to have an inalienable claim to protection, sanctuary, and food. But in Samoa when an individual fails in any cooperative group, either in his own terms or in theirs, his relationship claims will always give him a new chance in a new cooperative group; if he fails in this, it is the group and not his kindred who have turned against him.

Another strength lies in the continuing redefining of the cooperative situation, so that no individual plays continuously a fixed role, except the high chief, whose role is so hedged about with etiquette, procedure, and lack of any real executive authority that he is not likely to overstep his bounds. But most individuals play a series of parts of differing importance in a series of differently organized activities; a man's attention is focused upon his behavior in relation to a situation, as host, as guest, as matai, as member of the council, as member of a matai working group, as a fisherman beneath the tautai, as a member of a war party in which his role is determined by his division membership in the village, as a giver of toga and a receiver of oloa, as a giver of oloa and receiver of toga, as the heir in his patrilineal line, as the *tamafafine*, the cross-cousin with a veto, in his mother's family, as the ranking member of one group, as the man of lowest rank in the next group he enters, as the chief to whom a young man kneels as he gives a message at noon time, and as the father of a daughter upon whom the same young man, who must now be received courteously, calls in the evening. Such a man does not develop a fixed response to others which is definitely either dominance or submission, leadership or discipleship, authoritarian insistence or meek compliance, exhibitionism or refusal to play any public part; the multiplicity and contrast between his roles prevent any commitment to one personality type from developing. Whereas in a different kind of society, it is possible to predict what a given individual A will do as compared with a given individual B, in Samoa it is much more possible to predict what a series of men, A, B, and C, will do in a given situation.

## The Place of Skill in Samoan Society

The skilled artisan in Samoa was honored, and he was permitted to defend his position, by being given a place in the fono.

There were three main types of artisans, the housebuilders and canoe builders, who were classified in a wider group as the *Sa Tangaloa*, the Household of Tangaloa, the chief high god; the tattooers; and the fishermen. All these men, however exalted their prestige within their crafts, also participated as ordinary members of the community, and most craftsmen of note were matais and administered large households, although they themselves might give most of their time to their crafts. In each craft apprenticeship was recognized, young men usually choosing to serve under a relative, and it was usually a rich relative who gave a young aspirant craftsman his first chance at a real contract. The apprentices acted as assistants to the master craftsmen and were fed by them and shared in the distributions of presents given by the contractors for houses, canoes, or tattooing. The fishermen tended to be leading matais in sections of the community. When engaged in his craft the chief craftsman occupied the rank of a chief, and the rules of that craft had to be strictly observed. Payments were made at different stages in housebuilding or canoe building, and if they were regarded as insufficient, the craftsman might refuse to continue the work. If he did so, no other craftsman could take up the unfinished job unless the contracting would-be owner started the whole series of payments again from the beginning. Any craftsman who violated this rule was severely disciplined by the young men with the approval of the fono; his tools were taken away from him and he would never be allowed to practice as a carpenter in that village again. If the final payment for a contract was unsatisfactory, the craftsman might brand the house owner as stingy by removing one rafter, or take a more insidious revenge against an owner of a canoe by leaving a concealed wedge which would render the canoe unlucky.[1] The participation of the fono in preserving the sanctity of the contract and upholding the craftsmen in disciplining either a refractory member of their craft or a man who failed to meet the contract, socializes a potentially competitive situation. The craftsmen of each village were independent of the craftsmen of other villages, except that a visiting craftsman would be invited to any feast which was being given to a member of his craft, and he would be lent tools.

[1] Te Rangi Hiroa, *op. cit.*, p. 416.

Skill in oratory is a function of the talking chiefs; if a young man discreetly displays such skill,[1] it will be regarded as a strong claim on a talking chief title.  Chiefs may not display skill in oratory without coming under the ban of social disapproval and possible loss of adherents and of prestige.  Wives of talking chiefs are forced to develop the skill after their husbands have succeeded to the title; they have no opportunity to acquire proficiency beforehand.  The sons or probable heirs of talking chiefs have a chance to display such skill in the meetings of the aumaga which is a training ground for fono life.  Good memories for genealogies and for history and proverbs are also requirements for talking chiefs, and men holding talking chief titles will start very early to train their sons or some other bright and favorite child in such lore.  The balance here between training to hold a position, recognition of skill which is followed by the award of a position, and the requirement that because a given position is held the skill must appear (as in the case of the wives of talking chiefs) or must be inhibited (as in the case of chiefs), represents in fair measure the balance in Samoan estimation between the emphasis which should be laid upon native capacity as opposed to social role.

There are a few skills which are limited to experts, midwifery, the knowledge of certain medicines, and the practice of divining by supernatural possession.[2]  Payment for all these was small, and mainly a matter of etiquette; the individual practiced through pride in virtuosity and, in the case of the *taula-aitu* (the shamans), probably for the influence which their oracular sayings yielded them.  Bark-cloth making and fine mat making, ordinary fishing, gardening, sennit making, and the simpler carpentry skills were known to everyone of the appropriate sex. Such experts as were singled out—even in the case of the tattooer, as many people could do simple tattooing—were those who were far better at the practice of a common skill than their fellows, who could make nine ornamental lashings where the average man could do only one, make ten kinds of hook where the average

[1] See Mead, *Coming of Age in Samoa*, pp. 54–56.

[2] The material on these shamans is most inadequate.  They were possessed by spirits of the dead or family deities, answered questions about causes of illness or death, and demanded amends in the name of the offended spirit or deity.

man could make only one or two; and the special position of these
men had to be defined in terms of each situation. A tautai
was of no more account than any other man of his age and village
rank, except when communal fishing was under way.

## RIVALRY ACTIVITIES

Samoa relied to a very slight degree upon group rivalry as a
cohesive force within the group. Rivalry attitudes were highest
between districts. Manu'a claimed to be more sacred than
any other part of the Samoan islands, a claim which the other
parts reluctantly admitted in various ceremonies, when they
had to exclaim: "Tui Manu'a, thou art my Lord." But such
claims were also accompanied by a great deal of mutual vituperation and abuse, by abusive songs about the other islands or
districts, and by insulting proverbs. Rivalry between districts
was therefore firmly entrenched in ceremonial usage, and when
a *malaga*—a formal traveling party—entered Manu'a from
another part of Samoa, a clubbing match between champions
was held at the beginning of the visit. Western Samoa had
worked out a scheme by which all five districts might agree to
bestow a title upon the high chief of one, who thus became a
kind of king. The Manu'a Islands were regarded as one district
in which the Tui Manu'a reigned supreme. Within one district
there theoretically should not have been war, or the theft of a
taupou—a method by which the aumaga of one village displayed
its superiority over the aumaga of another village—nor should
there have been clashes between the aumagas of two villages
within a district. All these did sometimes occur, however, but
they were regarded as rather lamentable. Standardized competitive situations between two villages in the same district might
be set up and ceremonially recognized, as in the case of the
villages of Tau and Fitiuta, both of which claimed that they were
the original capital. The two villages duplicated some of their
most important ceremonial features. Inverted rivalry may also
occur, as when the village of Ofu at present claim with pride a
talking chief title which was given it originally to symbolize a
defeat in war by the island of Tau.

All this intervillage rivalry and ceremonial—and occasionally
real hostility—lacked any basis in material circumstance, and
sprang from no scarcity of land or crowded fishing grounds.

Within the village, each individual, no matter how exalted his sense of his own importance, had to mute continually any expression of this sense in conformity to the demands of the village. Of a high chief who made his daughter taupou, it was said, "He has given her to the village. She now belongs to them to dispose of as they will." So when a high chief died, half of the watching by his corpse was done by his relatives, but the other half was the privilege of the talking chiefs, representative of the village. As one high chief phrased it to me: "The Samoan had two gods, Tangaloa and the village, and the greater of these was the village." At the same time that the expression of any individual claims ran counter to the will of the village, the craft group, the fishing fleet, or the household were sternly muted, a touchiness in regard to the honor of the group as a whole was not only permitted to develop, but was even encouraged. It was this touchiness, this sense of the group's position in regard to other groups, which formed a kind of edge about the otherwise loose and noncohesive cooperative groups, in which voluntary continuance had been substituted for any strict relationship bond. This was expressed actively in the theft of the taupou of one village by the aumaga of a rival village. The young men, once having got the taupou safely away, would go and sing the news through the injured village. This theft was not motivated by any desire for a particular girl, but was merely a village gesture. This same touchiness was expressed by the oversensitivity of any group to the hospitality which it was receiving; a ceremonial traveling party might leave a village if the coconut spines were not arranged correctly in the coconuts which they were given to drink; a group of carpenters might refuse to go on with their work because there was a stone in a fowl's gullet.[1] This touchiness, whether within the village, as between house owner and craftsmen, or between villages, was always phrased in group terms. But it was actually a way in which individuals who did not subordinate individual honor to group honor could make the group cause their own. In all these instances, it was not obligatory upon anyone to protest, there was merely a pattern within which protest was possible, just as there was a pattern within which insult was possible—for some insurgent member of the host village was responsible for mis-

[1] Buck, personal communication.

placing the spines in the coconuts originally.  That such behavior
is the overflow of individual aggressiveness into group pride is
shown by the fact that it is merely permitted to occur, whereas
all aspects of intergroup relationships which the Samoans consider essential, such as the prolonged arguments between owner
and carpenters whenever a payment is made, or the clubbing
matches between champions of host and visiting village, are
definitely provided for.  The rivalry situation in which each
village seeks to outdo the other, in some feat, in some sensitivity
to insult, in some giving of insult, is strongest between districts
and next strongest between villages; it occurs in some patterned
situations within the village, most strongly when there are two
divisions of the aumaga, based not upon age, but upon residence
in two parts of the village; and it occasionally occurs between
households.

In large villages the young people are worked into a final
group plan slowly; they grow up in small neighborhood gangs,
across which relationship ties operate more and more strongly
as they grow older, and are sometimes welded first into two
aumaga, which will sometimes but not always combine into a
whole.  These two aumaga groups perpetuate the neighborhood-
gang hostility.  They hurl insults, are rivals in their group work,
and occasionally even break out into acts of depredation such as
destroying the taro plantation of the other aumaga.  Acts such
as these are severely dealt with by the fono, on a semisuper-
natural basis in which the whole village has to celebrate an
expiatory kava ceremony, but they form the basis for village
splits.  In the dual village of Tau-Siufaga there were two well-
defined and competitive aumaga, and the fono was beginning to
split, the split increasing each year as the younger men, accustomed to the hostility of the aumaga split, assumed titles and
became members of the matai group.  Where the opposite form
of division occurs in the aumaga, into a tattooed and untattooed
group, no such rivalry can occur, because rivalry can occur by
definition only between equals, and the tattooed group are older
and so outrank the untattooed group.

These illustrations will show the two tendencies in Samoan
social organizations, the tendency to place each individual, each
household, each village, even (in Western Samoa) each district
in a hierarchy, wherein each is dignified only by its relationship

to the whole, each performs tasks which contribute to the honor
and well-being of the whole, and competition is completely
impossible.  The opposite tendency, the rebellion of individuals
within the units against this subordination to a plan and their
use of a place in a component unit to foment trouble and rivalry
with other units, while not so strong, is always present.[1]

## WAR

War in Samoa was part of the ceremonial rivalry between
villages and was fought for no gains other than prestige, nor
were there any important rewards for individual warriors.  On
the other hand, the role which one had to play in war was carefully laid down, as the people said: "How can a *Tauleá leá* (an
untitled man) be brave?  He would be killed for going ahead?"
Warfare between villages was over the theft of the taupou, over
slights delivered by one village to another, especially on traveling
parties.  It was fought at appointed spots after a great deal
of speech making and mutual exchange of courtesies, and casual-
ties were low.[2]

Households within the same village could become involved in
hostilities if the honor of one was infringed by a member of
the other, particularly if the offender was of lower rank than the
offended.  The principal cause of offense was liason between the
wife of a matai and a matai of lower rank, or a young member of

[1] This latter trend shows up sharply if compared with Tonga, an adjacent
group in which the whole people were organized in a strictly hierarchal
scheme, with a *Tui Tonga* at the top, and no village communities made any
pretense at autonomy.  Instead lineages numbering many thousands of
people, owed direct allegiance, through their chiefs—with primogeniture
and heredity—to the national kingship.  The quarrels which took place in
Tonga were quarrels between contestants for these major positions.  *Cf.*
E. W. Gifford, "Tongan Social Organization," *Bishop Museum Bulletin*,
61, 1929, *passim*.  At the other extreme is the Polynesian community of
Ontong Java, which lacks Samoa's cohesive villages and in which the joint
family was the major cohesive unit, with a late development of kingship.
*Cf.* Hogbin, I., *Law and Order in Polynesia*, passim.

[2] This applies particularly to Manu'a and to a less extent to Tutuila.
Our records for the Western Islands are complicated by the presence of white
men of different nationalities who themselves continuously incited the
natives to trouble and supplied firearms to them, so that it is difficult to
obtain any picture of the normal course of life before white interference.
The reverberations of international rivalry did not reach Manu'a impor-
tantly, so the material there can be used with more credibility.

another matai's household. In such cases, if the adultery was discovered, the principals could fight, a procedure of which the whole village disapproved but was not always able to prevent in the case of very strong households; or there might be an *ifoga*, a ceremonial reparation, in which the matai of the offending household—whether or not he was the individual who committed the offense—with his entire household, had to sit with bowed heads all day outside the house of the offended man, covered with fine mats, which the offended would finally accept as amends. Women, if one had seduced the husband of the other, could demand an ifoga also. If a matai refused to ifo or refused to accept an ifoga and inaugurated a blood feud, the fono would ultimately stop it, sometimes by exiling one or both participants.

Competition within the crafts was muted by the distribution of contracts upon a kinship basis, by the fact that all carpenters in a village participated in any large building, and by the strong sanctions against any active scabbing on the part of an individual craftsman.

## SANCTIONS

We have described the way in which any cooperative group, the village, the household, the fishing fleet, the craft guild, could take definite and summary action against a recalcitrant member so that continuance within any of these groups depended upon strict conformity to the rules of cooperation within it. There was also a series of sanctions of another order which controlled an individual's loyalty to his blood kin, and these were for the most part supernatural sanctions, but sanctions which worked indirectly rather than in producing immediate action, as in Manus. The material on Samoan religious life is very poor, but all illness and death, with the exception of diseases contracted by thieving from magically protected gardens, was laid to the spirits of the ancestors, sometimes informed by the curse of a living relative (particularly the sister), sometimes merely the result of the spirit's sense of having been wronged during life or having been given an inadequate funeral, sometimes due to ghostly wrath over quarrels among living relatives. The indications, based upon very slight hints in the literature and in the memory of informants and also upon comparative material from related cultures, seem to be that the shamans acted to interpret the cause of death, sometimes to explain illness, and demanded ceremonial, not practical, expiation. Whereas in Manus, if a quarrel were given as the explanation of an illness, the quarrel would have to be made up at once under directions given by the medium, in Samoa the cause and effect relationships were less direct. If, however, a family had many deaths and also was involved in an intrafamily conflict, these two would be connected in conversation and sometimes in shamanic possessions, and would exert gradual pressure to heal that particular quarrel and also to deter other families from entering upon or continuing quarrels in flagrant disregard of the rules of kin amity. While the cooperative groups enforced efficiency, honesty, amity, and conformity, with secular sanctions, the kin group, which underlay the cooperative groups and crosscut them and which provided each individual with his final security, took its sanction from the spirits of the ancestors.

## RELIGION

Religion played a very slight role in Samoa; the gods were conceived as having resigned their sacredness to the chiefs, who still retained enough of the divine essence so that to touch the clothing of a Tui Manu'a brought dire illness which could be removed only by the touch of his foot. Still the sanctity surrounding chiefs in Samoa was minimal for the Polynesian area, and almost every infringement of the *tapu* of a chief could be removed with a very slight ceremony. The emphasis was all upon the danger to the offender. There was no longer any sense that the chief's personal sanctity had been endangered by contact with commoners. There is some record of village gods, occasionally represented by fetishes which were carried about in war and guarded by specially titled men, whom the early missionaries described as "priests." Additionally each family had a family god, a *tupua*, which was embodied in some bird, fish, or animal. This tupua provided a convenient shamanic alibi when no family quarrel or possible curse could be invoked to explain illness. The sick person would be accused of having inadvertently insulted the tupua, through one of its embodiments, and ceremonial expiation would be demanded. But as compared with other parts of Polynesia, the Manu'a Samoans gave the slightest attention to religion; there were no temples, for the house of an officiant in a village in which a fetish was occasionally kept hardly deserved the name, and there were no religious festivals. The most important groups were the villages, and their importance was enforced by purely secular means. As a result the major dichotomy in Samoa was not between the sacred and the profane, but between work, which was solemly undertaken by a recognized group, and all other irregular, unrecognized individual activity. There was only one ceremony—the process of preparing a certain kind of dye—in which the officiant worked alone. For the rest all group activities became more solemn, in proportion to the rank of the participants; all individual activities became less important, shading off into the actually non-respectable, the less related they were to some group end.

## The Samoan Ideal Man

The ideal Samoan man is always more conscious of his position than of his personal desires or motives. He is able to make his behavior conform in the slightest details to the particular exigencies of any situation, he wears at all times an armor of courteous, reserved consciousness of social form. As will appear in the discussion of education, the great Samoan sin is *tautala lai titi*, to talk above one's age, or rank, and this is a sin which even the highest chief could commit were he, for instance, to behave like a talking chief, and make his own speeches in the fono. To know one's place and to exercise that position wisely, and above all gracefully, without any discordant note or false emphasis, is the important point. The disallowed persons are the over-violent, those who take defeat personally, those who commit themselves too violently to a given end, those who foment trouble and discord and so break through the even texture of the social pattern.

## Education

Samoan education is based upon the theory that small children are unimportant, aggressive, and in need of discipline and progressive muting, and that they become steadily more important as they grow older and display their ability to fit without friction into the social pattern. Children are desired. Under the economy of plenty and the grading of all household activities in terms of relative strength and skill, children are useful members of the household by the time they are six or so. Furthermore, conception is believed to be the result of a long period of intercourse; conception among the unmarried is a sign that the pair have loved each other enough to continue faithful for a long period, and this attitude with its accompanying affect is carried over into married life. No rigorous tabus surround pregnancy, although the old women disapprove of intercourse during the last months of pregnancy. There is no lactation tabu, and it is frequent for a woman to have to wean her child because she is pregnant again. Suckling is regarded as a pleasure for the mother, and a woman may be censured for her self-indulgence in suckling a child too long. This removes any element of guilt or strain in the mother's attitude toward weaning, which is accomplished with lemon juice or aromatic herbs. Children are frequently suckled by other women of the household or of related households and become accustomed to a number of "mothers" whom they see every day.

The training of the child from the time that it can crawl until it is five or six is conditioned by two facts, that the nurses are all little girls of from five to ten or eleven, and that *sense* or *judgment*, designated as *mafaufau*, is conceived as developing very slowly and that nothing positive can be done by the community to encourage it. Violence, aggressiveness, destructiveness, contentiousness are all qualities which show lack of judgment. These the infant is born with. The process of early education is a matter of keeping these manifestations down and waiting, with what grace one can, for the more desirable social virtues to develop. Meanwhile, the life of the community must go on in as graceful and undisturbed a fashion as possible. The children must be fed and taken care of in a way which will not interfere with the occupations of their elders. So that most of what a child learns during its first three or four years can be phrased as a series of avoidances of places, of situations, and of kinds of behavior which are frowned upon. It learns that it must never stand up in the house, that it must go outside the house to urinate or defecate, that it must not touch the pillow or possessions of the chief or the matai of the household, that it must not touch the kava bowl, that it must not go where grown people are solemnly gathered, that it must not create a fuss or disturbance. At first most of these misdemeanors are prevented by the small nurses simply dragging the child out of earshot of its elders, for when the child offends, it is the older child-nurse who is reprimanded or slapped by an adult. As a result the little nurses do everything in their power to keep the babies quiet, contented, and out of mischief. They carry them most of the time, discourage them from either crawling or walking, and do not particularly encourage them to talk. The babies are carried on the small girls' hips, often on the hips of little nurses who would not be strong enough to lift them in their arms.

Samoan children are made conscious of age from the very beginning, and even the little babies tend to be placed in an age group, because their small nurses are near of an age and cluster together. As these babies emerge from infancy, they play together under the supervision of their older sisters and cousins until they are five or six. By this time they have learned a certain number of social aptitudes; they can talk, walk, and swim well, carry loads, split open coconuts, climb coconut trees, gather land crabs, carry water, borrow fire, and carry messages— one of the most important activities of children in Samoa. They are permitted to play rough-and-tumble games among themselves and they are likely to be stopped from quarreling, not because their small nurses disapprove of quarreling but because screams will draw the unwelcome attention of the adults. The emphasis is never upon the act itself but upon the way in which it fits into a social situation; two children far away on the beach with only older children near may quarrel if they wish, or shriek and scream, but if they approach a group of matais, they must be hushed at any cost. This develops, in both mentors and charges, alertness to the social situation; even a child of three or four acts always with an eye to possible spectators.

Shame,[1] in Samoa, which is a potent force for control of individuals in the interests of conformity, is not connected with the bodily functions, nor with sex, but with social relationships, and comes from calling attention to oneself unsuitably, from speaking out of turn, from presumption, and also from awkwardness, fumbling for words, lack of skill, if these ineptitudes are specifically commented on by others. The greatest shame is aroused by the accusation tautala laititi, "talking above your age," a shame in which the parents share. For consonant with

[1] This however is much slighter than the American Indian form.

the emphasis upon form, upon each individual's slowly fitting into a decreed pattern, there is a great disapproval of haste or precocity, and the standard is the standard of the age grade. People remember the relative ages of children, and children in a neighborhood play in gangs. In these gangs the pace is always set by the slowest. This is the child to whom everyone will point with pride, and those who far exceed this slowness of pace will bring blushes to their parents' cheeks and will be constantly nagged and disapproved of by the older children.[1]

In understanding the role which age plays in the life of a Samoan child, it is necessary to bear in mind the large households in which—with the rarest exceptions, exceptions which have definite reverberations in personality development[2]—no child for long has a fixed status as the oldest, the only child, or the youngest. Rather each child begins life at the bottom spoke of a wheel which slowly revolves until in middle age he is at the top only to slowly descend again toward old age and a position near the ground. The pressure of the children whose births soon after his own rapidly rob him of the position of youngest, push him slowly upward in the relative scale, until at adolescence a girl or boy is near the center of pressure, with as many younger people who can be ordered about and disciplined as there are older people who can order him about and discipline him. What is the most difficult age in our society becomes in Samoa, because of this point of relativity, the age of maximum ease partly because it is the age of most equal pressure.

Up to adolescence, although the pressure decreases, there is a long period of discipline, which differs for boys and girls. The early years before six or so have developed children who are

[1] The attitude toward precocity in Samoa is best illustrated by the way it has affected the attempts to introduce European ideas of schooling. The missionary schools conformed to the Samoan pattern; the boy who entered first had to graduate first, regardless of how stupid he might be or how intelligent his competitors who had entered the school later. This effectually barred out competition and had a dulling and discouraging effect upon the brighter students. In the modern schools under the United States Government, ordinary American ideas of "skipping grades" had been introduced, which were resulting in a very genuine conflict. The children were taught at school to be proud of effort; when they, however, returned home to report that they had been skipped ahead of their former companions, their parents hung their heads in shame.

[2] Mead, *Coming of Age in Samoa*, pp. 141–144.

aggressive whenever the situation permits it, but who have learned never to act spontaneously, even in anger, but always after reviewing the social scene and the possibilities of disturbing their elders. These little children play hardly any group games. They play with pin wheels, make palm-leaf balls, stick little sticks in the sand, and form a parasitical group about their young nurses, about whom they surge and stumble in an unpatterned kind of play. Then, at six or so, the little girls become baby tenders, the little boys become fags for bigger boys; the girls are disciplined by responsibility for those much younger than themselves, the boys are disciplined by having to fag for an arbitrary group of adolescents. The care of the babies ties the little girls down, makes group life less possible, keeps them from wandering far afield, keeps them in the village where they are always liable to be requisitioned for some household task by any older relative, makes their play time more sporadic and precious to them. The boys on the other hand can go fishing. They can range the bush or far-away reefs with the older boys. They become more adventurous, acquire more outdoor skills, and learn to cooperate with each other, for the older boys object to having the services of their juniors interfered with by jealousies and fist fights. Similarly the earlier obstreperousness of the little girls is muted, not because the adults really care whether they fight or not, but because if they do fight their infant charges are neglected and scream with fear, which immediately brings the rage of some adult down on the little nurses' heads.

From this age on, sex differentiation is very marked. The brother and sister tabu between all siblings—blood, affinal, and foster siblings being included in this wide range—is set in motion when at about this age the young child becomes self-conscious about this point. From that time on, all the members of the opposite sex fall into two categories, tabu siblings, and members of an opposing group any one of whom may in the future be one's lover. But from six to adolescence, the opposing groups see each other only as groups. Within each household, brothers and sisters never talk to each other, nor sit near each other, nor use each other's things. In the village, if no adults are near by, the two sexes go about in play gangs and throw sticks and stones at each other. This play becomes more vigorous after dark, when opposing gangs can actually give battle without disturbing their elders. Any child who deserts these sex-solid gangs and plays with the opposite sex is regarded by adults and children with great disapproval.[1] These children's play gangs, although their hostilities are chiefly taken out upon the opposite sex, not upon other gangs of their own sex, give ample training for the rivalries and hostilities which in later life crop up between different aumagas and between village groups. The girls' solidarities are however, broken down after adolescence, when they cease to associate in neighborhood groups and turn more and more to relatives, who can be better trusted in love affairs. The breakdown into groups of twos and threes, according to degree of sex experience, is followed by marriage and the absorption of the girl into her husband's household, often in another village, where her status will depend upon his rank, not upon any affiliations of her own.

The aualuma never becomes as integrated and continually functioning a group as the aumaga, but remains a pale reflection of the women's group on the one hand and of the activities of the aumaga on the other. This whole educational situation is reflected in the behavior of the women, who are more individualistic than the men and more jealous, and who engage in more quarrels. Occasionally rivalry situations occur between young men in the free love-making which precedes marriage, but it is notable that these have the same unrealistic character as the rivalries which occur between villages. The quarrels result not because one youth wants a girl and the other youth gets her permanently, but because one youth boasts to another that he was admitted to the favors of a girl with whom the other had slept earlier the same night. It is the slight upon the first suitor's virtuosity which is resented, just as villages compete for no prize but merely defend their respective reputations and honor. Women, on the other hand, especially married women, will quarrel over the actual possession of a man, and even come to blows or bite each others' noses or ears. Men, however, do not resent a wife's leaving them and marrying another, provided that this second husband is not below them in rank. It is this latter rule which occasionally makes the castoff wives of chiefs occupy the position of prostitutes in the community, where no one is of high enough rank to marry them. Here again the chief

[1] *Ibid.*, pp. 178–180.

merely defends his honor; he does not compete for a prize which only one may have.

Throughout the whole educational system, even extending into love affairs, runs the thread of the *tautala laititi* prohibition. The girl or boy who makes love too young, or the man who has an affair with the wife of a man whose rank is higher than his, is guilty of this. Steadily the precocious, the combative, the ambitious are muted, nagged into dullness, until by the time that the household is ready to choose the matai, the slowest and steadiest man has gained self-confidence, the gayest and most brilliant has been steadied into reliability, and the choice does not in any case endanger the continuous working of the pattern. Throughout the whole educational process the Samoans wait for the development of mafaufau, judgment, they discourage any tautala laititi and they disapprove of all unusual behavior as *fua*, or uncaused, that is, occurring for an idiosyncratic and socially unrecognized reason.

## The Channeling of Opposing Tendencies

If the Samoan emphases are summed up as the subordination of the individual to the pattern, as the subordination of the younger to the older, of the commoner to the chief, and in lesser degree but no less surely, of the woman to the man, then we find in one Samoan activity—the dance—a reversal of all these attitudes. Every child learns the dance rhythms before it can walk, as it sits in its mother's lap. By the time it is three or four, its dancing is highly stylized. And in a Samoan dance, the whole usual order of society is reversed, the individual is important, and no two individuals are conceived as dancing alike. Every dance is believed to be idiosyncratic within a series of known patterns, and uniformity or mimicry of other's styles are never recognized as occurring. The taupou's dance is the most important, and the talking chiefs honor her by becoming clowns. The dance begins with the smallest toddler and ends with the chief. The dreaded tautala laititi is never heard on the dance floor. Instead each mother pushes her youngest forward and the whole group approves the baby's hesitant steps. Within the confines of a well-learned form, every individual is given a maximum chance to exhibit his own individuality and skill. There is a dance for the hunchback, for the dwarf, for the mad feeble-minded boy, for the deaf-mute. And significantly the one girl I found who suffered most from what would be designated in our society as a "feeling of inferiority" was a girl who could not dance; whose failure was in the one field in which individual display and success are permitted.[1]

### Bibliography

GIFFORD, E. W.: "Tongan Social Organization," *Bernice P. Bishop Museum Bulletin*, No. 61, 1929.

HOGBIN, IAN: *Law and Order in Polynesia*, Harcourt, Brace & Company, New York, 1934.

KEESING, FELIX: *Modern Samoa*, Stanford University Press, 1934.

MEAD, MARGARET: *Coming of Age in Samoa*, William Morrow & Company, Inc., New York, 1928.

"A Lapse of Animism among a Primitive People," *Psyche*, pp. 72–77, July, 1928.

"Social Organization of Manua," *Bernice P. Bishop Museum Bulletin*, No. 76, Honolulu, Hawaii, 1930.

"The Role of the Individual in Samoan Culture," *Journal of the Royal Anthropological Institute*, Vol. 58, 1928.

TE RANGI HIROA (P. H. Buck): "Samoan Material Culture," *Bernice P. Bishop Museum Bulletin*, No. 75, Honolulu, Hawaii, 1930.

[1] For a fuller discussion see in Mead, *Coming of Age in Samoa*, Chap. VIII, "The Role of the Dance."

# CHAPTER X

## THE ZUNI INDIANS OF NEW MEXICO

### by Irving Goldman

By the time the Spanish conquerors had come into the Southwest, the peak of pueblo civilization had already passed. At
present the culture, in spite of "white" influences, is essentially
the same as it was a number of centuries ago at the time of Coronado. The largest of the pueblos is that of Zuni. A population
of 1,900 live in compactly clustered and terraced adobe houses,
forming the familiar pueblo unit. Many of the Zuni do not
live in the main pueblo but live throughout the year scattered
in a number of farming villages to return to Zuni for the ceremonial dances and ritual observances that are held calendrically.

For a people depending entirely upon agriculture and sheep
herding for their subsistence, the physical environment is not
an easy one. The high New Mexican plateau is excessively
arid, and a good part of the country is desert or unsuitable for
agriculture and grazing. The main body of water is the Zuni
River, which for the greater part of the year is a thin trickle, but
after the summer cloudbursts in the mountains it swells to a
rushing torrent that subsides almost as quickly as it rises. Sweet
spring water is available in the neighboring mountains. The
prayer for rain dominates most of Zuni religion.

Government in Zuni is centralized in a priestly hierarchy,
which is concerned entirely with matters of religion. Civil law
is given over to a secular body that, appointed by the priests,
lacks all prestige. The mechanism of social control is not in the
hands of a centralized authority but is vested in the sanctions
of public censure. In practically all his activities, the individual
must conform to the patterns established by a number of social
groupings: the matriarchal household, which in the sharing of
food is communally organized, the matrilineal clan, and religious
societies and esoteric cults.

## Economic Background

The Zuni are primarily agriculturists and have been so since early prehistoric times. Originally they planted their maize, beans, and squash by a system of hand irrigation from the springs. At present, with the development of a system of water control in connection with a government dam, the number and extent of their crops have increased. Famine, once prevalent, is practically eliminated. In fact, in material wealth Zuni is rich. There are fruit orchards, corn and wheat fields, melon patches, peach orchards, and the greatly valued sheep herds introduced by the Spaniards, so that for the most part food is fairly abundant. Still, differences in wealth do exist, but every principle of Zuni social organization is opposed to an excessive concentration of a surplus in the hands of any one individual. Wealth is valued only for the immediate material comfort it can bring, and is highly fluid. Competition for the supply of goods is given no formal expression, and though individuals may quarrel over the ownership of sheep or peach orchards, such individuals are not the most respected in the community. It is rather the cooperative person, ready to share his food with his relatives and needy friends, ready to assist his neighbor or religious or clan colleague in agricultural labor, who is most respected in the community. Ideally, wealth that has been accumulated is redistributed among the members of the village either during the winter-solstice ceremonies or in spontaneous gifts. In the economic as well as the ceremonial field the aggressive, competitive, noncooperative individual is regarded as the aberrant type.

Such culturally fostered noncompetitive and cooperative attitudes are all the more striking in view of the actual limitation of irrigable land suitable for cultivation. In Bathonga there appeared to be some relationship between the absence of formalized rivalry for land and the abundance of suitable land. In Ifugao the land shortage correlated on the other hand with a marked competitive organization of family against family for the land. In Zuni, curiously, land shortage is not even recognized. "There is no feeling of land hunger."[1] What is felt most

[1] Ruth L. Bunzel, Mss.

sharply is the lack of labor. In Bathonga a similar emphasis upon labor resolved itself into a struggle to get more women into the kraal. The Zuni are not polygamists, but they have met the problem of land labor by organizing cooperative group labor wherever the physical conditions of the work allow it.

Fields used for cultivation belong either to an individual male or to a matriarchal household, but in either case they are worked by all the men in the household, who may be assisted by friends or relatives. All produce of the fields is pooled in one common storeroom to become the common property of all the women of the household. At hoeing and at harvesting time, when the amount of work to be done in the fields is considerable, a member of a religious fraternity asks the director for assistance and the latter then delegates a number of men to assist. The female head of the house or her daughter will also go to the men of the clan and ask them for help. The group thus assembled is of a miscellaneous composition, the men cooperating in the work for reasons of kinship, religious association, and friendship.

The next morning the men who have been summoned appear at the designated house and, without waiting for breakfast, go off together to the fields and work with "might and main" until about noon, when they stop to eat the lunch that has been brought them by the young girls of the house. The work continues with a great deal of gayety. Some men tell jokes and stories or play pranks upon one another. Others, in friendly rivalry, race at their tasks. So they work until sunset and then file back to the village, where ten or twelve great steaming bowls of stew prepared by the women have been set out in a long row on the roof of the house. All sit down and eat together.

A wealthy family that has undertaken to entertain the masked god impersonators at the winter-solstice ceremonies works very busily for a year building up vast stores of food supplies. For the entire year members of the same ceremonial group as the man preparing for the feast are obligated to work with him in the fields and in the construction of the new house where the dancers will be entertained. All other people in the village make it a point to help at one time or another during that period in order to benefit by the supernatural blessings that go with such work, or, more practically, to get the material rewards of presents and food which are sent to all those who have helped.[1]    Women, especially poor women, go about to these houses that are preparing for the festival in order to grind corn meal.    They take back bowls of stew as gifts.

Always workers who have come to help must be rewarded with gifts or with food.    Thus it is only the well-to-do who can call on their neighbors and clan kinsmen to help them in the fields. The poor families, those on the subsistence level, depend almost entirely upon the cooperative group effort of the men in the household.

Besides the fields of corn, wheat, and alfalfa that are scattered over the reservation, and the melon patches and peach orchards, the Zuni cultivate small vegetable gardens just at the edge of the village by the river.    These gardens, held in the matrilineal line, are worked exclusively by the women of the household.    The crops of beans, onions, chilis, melons are stored in the household common storeroom as common property.

After the harvest, the wheat is threshed by horses.    A common corral is constructed and the households in turn bring their wheat to be threshed.

Once food has been brought into the house it becomes the property of the women, to be used by them collectively as they see fit.    The preparation of food, the grinding of the corn into flour, is women's work.    Working in groups of three, the women crush, parch, and powder the corn grains on stone grinders.    The description by Castanada, a soldier in Coronado's army, is still true of the present method.    "Three women sit down before the stones: the first crushes the grain, the second brazes it, the third reduces it entirely to powder.    While they are at work a man seated at the doorway plays a bagpipe, so that they work keeping time; they sing in three voices."[2]    Especially when there is much food to be prepared, as at the winter-solstice ceremonies, many women and young girls come to the house that is to give the ceremonial feast and grind the corn to such music.    In any event, whether food is being prepared for festive purposes or for

---

[1] Gifts of food are given only to women, who control the food in the household.    Men are fed only for their labors.    Presents, often expensive items, go to members of the priestly body participating in the ceremonial housebuilding.

[2] Frank Cushing, "Zuni Breadstuffs," p. 389.

ordinary household use, the arrangement of three metates side by side is adhered to,[1] while the three women bend over them on their knees sharing the labor.

The major source of wealth and in that sense the most valued property is the sheep herds. Sheep herding is a foreign complex introduced at an early time by the Spanish, and the attitudes surrounding sheep economy are at present alien to basic Zuni economic concepts. Herded and, with some exceptions, owned by men, sheep represent a surplus and an important medium of exchange. They are the means with which foreign luxuries, furniture, kitchen utensils, guns, and automobiles can be bought. Sheep have been, in part at least, largely responsible for the rising standard of living of the Pueblo Indians. It is significant that the "movies of western civilization, precise ideas of property, individual ownership, acquisitiveness, prestige attached to material possessions all became focussed on this one form of property."[2] Yet prior to the establishment of trade on a firm basis, when flocks were still small and meant less in terms of Western luxuries, sheep herding was organized along lines similar to that of agriculture.

In distinction to land property, all sheep were owned by individual males, but kinsmen pooled their flocks and herded them on a cooperative basis. Though the capital was individually owned, the profits, the wool, and the newborn lambs were shared by all in the group. The owner of the most sheep was the leader, and at shearing time, when the wool was gathered, he would settle all the debts of the group. What wool was left over was divided equally. Similarly with the lambs: partners took turns claiming the lambs born in successive years. All sheep were earmarked with the brand of the owner, but so long as he kept his sheep in the group his individual ownership was but a formal phrasing.

With the increasing size of the herds and the greater purchasing value of wool, skins, and mutton, the progressive tendency is toward greater individualism in respect both to the ownership of and to the use of the profits from the sheep. As

[1] This does not imply that all grinding must be done by three women. One woman may grind by herself. But the three grindstones are always kept side by side.

[2] Bunzel, R. Mss.

far as the actual mechanics of herding are concerned, cooperation still holds. Herds are pooled together and herded cooperatively by groups of male kindred, each member taking turns in rotation at herding. At lambing time, however, each sheep owner is present to earmark each of his lambs as soon as it is born. If he is absent at this time, he will lose many lambs which will be earmarked with some other brand. Nor will he have just cause for complaint, since he should have been present to help. Lambing time begins about the end of April and lasts about three weeks, during which time the men and their wives live out on the ranch near the sheep. On the first day the men construct corrals for segregating the sheep; the women are busy grinding and preparing provisions. In the evening, after all have eaten, there is singing and dancing. "Everyone has a good time at lambing because they are living together in one big bunch."[1]

Directly after lambing, the shearing of the sheep begins. This takes from ten days to two weeks and is generally over by the middle of June, so that all can return for the summer-solstice ceremonies. If they cannot finish the job by that time, there is quarreling over who shall stay behind and complete the task. All, of course, are anxious to return to Zuni to take part in the dances, but the nonsociety members are usually prevailed upon to remain behind. If not, then the work is interrupted until after the ceremonies, when all return to finish the shearing. The actual shearing requires collective effort. Two men must hold a sheep while a third plies the shears. Two other men herd the rest of the flock. In most groups at present, all the sheep of one earmark are carefully segregated and the wool sacked and measured to become the individual property of the owner of the sheep. From the proceeds of the wool, however, he is required to provide clothing for himself, his wife, his children (including children from previous marriages), and if necessary for his mother and unmarried sisters.

Housebuilding is likewise a collective undertaking, and, since a new house is almost always built upon the occasion of the winter-solstice ceremonies, all the men of the same ceremonial group work together in cutting and hauling the lumber that will form the heavy beamed roof and in laying the adobe walls. The women, especially the old women, are the plasterers. The

[1] *Ibid.*

dedication of the house by the priestly body will bring blessings to the entire village. Each individual worker will not only gain good luck for himself and his family, but will benefit materially. Thus the labor of housebuilding is truly cooperative, the house-builder providing meals and gifts for the workers and standing the entire expense of the construction, the other men working to fulfill the necessary ceremonial requirements of the winter solstice. The end result will be gain for all. If the housebuilding is not at the instance of the Shalako masked dance ceremony, it is constructed by the men of the household. In either event it becomes the property of the women. Though the men will have done all the heavy work of construction, once they leave the house they have no further share in it. Nor do men seem to feel that they have wasted their labor when they leave a house which they have helped to construct.

The Zuni recognize and appreciate skilled craft-work. Women make the finely decorated pottery, taking pride in the skill which they have developed since early childhood. Men do work in silver and in turquoise, the latter mineral being very skillfully worked into beads. Most women are potters, and each mother stops to teach the little girls how to manipulate the clay. Bead making and silversmithing are far more restricted, the former process being long and tedious.

With the building up of the flocks, trade has become more and more important. At present, of course, a good part of the trade is with the whites, wool being traded for manufactured products. Baskets are obtained from the neighboring Hopi and Apache and blankets from the Navaho. At an earlier time it is probable that since little surplus in food was produced, this surplus was carefully stored against periods of need, and that since sheep herds were considerably smaller, trade was less common and more narrowly organized. A curious obsolete form of internal trade that appears to have existed in the last decade of the nineteenth century is described by Mrs. Stevenson.[1] This was auctioneering. When a larder became overstocked with certain foods and under-stocked in others, the head of the household would look anxiously for the auctioneer's announcement. At a certain time this man would announce a sale in the plaza, and there the women would bring their food to be displayed in bowls. The auctioneer merely

[1] Matilda C. Stevenson, "The Zuni Indians," p. 378.

stated what ware was offered and what was wanted in exchange. A sale or exchange would take place sometimes in no more than thirty seconds. For his services, in the case cited by Mrs. Stevenson, the auctioneer, an aged man with white hair, received no further recompense beyond numerous invitations to eat.

In no economic activity is competition formally sanctioned. In agricultural land there is an actual shortage of irrigable fields, as witnessed by the fact that practically no families produce enough wheat to last them to the next harvest, yet, as already mentioned, such shortage is not even phrased as a land problem; it is felt rather as a problem of labor. Of all activities, sheep herding would be expected to result in competitive relations, and to the extent that a good deal of litigation centers around the ownership of sheep this is true. Nevertheless, such litigations are more in the nature of family squabbles than the well-developed family rivalry that is found in Ifugao. In general the culture has removed all sting from a competition that might develop, by giving little weight to the possession of material goods per se. The Zuni have no interest in accumulating more property than they can use, and when an individual does become wealthy he redistributes his wealth in the great winter festival of the Shalako. The major interest of the Zuni is religious—the orderly ritual observance of the calendric ceremonies. It is in this sphere rather than in the economic that the individual gains full social recognition.

There is no information with regard to competition between skilled craftsmen, either for greater social recognition or for greater material reward.

In Ifugao the successful trader is shrewd and cunning, quick to cheat his trade opponent—if he can get him drunk all the better. Such methods are not countenanced in Zuni. The Zuni frown upon any sharpness in economic transactions. The only exception to this rule is in dealings with the Navaho, a neighboring tribe with whom the Zuni for a long time have been unfriendly. A Zuni will boast of swindling a Navaho.

## SOCIAL STRUCTURE

The individual in Zuni is fitted into an intricate and closely knit social organization. A man is born with fixed kinship and clan affiliations. As a member of the matrilineal line of his mother, in his mother's clan he assumes a number of ceremonial obligations; as a child of his father's clan he assumes still other obligations.  At marriage a man leaves the household of his mother to join the communal economic unit of his mother-in-law's household without in any way relinquishing his ceremonial obligations to his mother's house.  At approximately puberty, the boy is initiated into one of the six dance groups comprising the male tribal society.  At any time after this, or even before, he assumes membership in one or more of a great number of esoteric societies.  Thus, at all times, a man is bound to a number of groups, and the greater part of his activity is in association with a number of these, especially the ceremonial groups.  In practice, the situation of group alliance is less complicated for the women.  Primarily she is a member of a matriarchal household.  Her duties are mainly economic, though, theoretically, no woman is barred from full participation in ceremonial life.  For one thing, it is not customary, and secondly, few women care to assume the heavy responsibilities that go with belonging to a religious group.  Whether she belongs to a ceremonial society or not, the woman is still an active member of a collective household unit.  In Zuni one acts as an individual only in the sphere of sex, and "no action that is entirely personal and individual receives more than passing interest.  Births, deaths, and initiations figure largely in local gossip, marriages do not."[1]

At present the Zuni tribe is divided into thirteen matrilineal clans, varying in size from the Yellowwood, with only two members and thus faced with extinction, to the Dogwood, with several hundred individuals.  Precisely what obligations the individual has to his clan group is difficult to say.  The clan as such has no social or political function.  It is not associated with the kivas[2] of religious societies either in name, function, or membership.  It owns no property.  The clan has importance in that it is related to certain priestly offices by virtue of the fact that a number of very sacred fetishes are held by households of a particular clan.[3]  However, between an individual and the members of his clan whom he classifies under particular relationship terms,

[1] Bunzel, R. "Introduction to Zuni Ceremonialism," p. 476.
[2] Kiva, an underground ceremonial chamber.
[3] The primary association of these fetishes is with the household rather than with the clan as such.

there is a tie that enables him to call upon them to assist him in a large enterprise such as harvesting or housebuilding or at an initiation. In this respect clan members form a cooperative group, but the closest ties of the individual are to the blood relationship group.

The household is the economic unit, and is, in all economic activities, cooperatively organized. It is a group of variable composition: a mother, her husband, her daughters with their husbands and children, to which may be added a fluctuating group of males, divorced, widowed, temporarily estranged, or unmarried sons. All occupy a single house with from two to six rooms, including a large general living room in which the entire household works, eats, and sleeps, and where guests are entertained. A number of rooms serve to store food and the sacred paraphernalia. In this crowded atmosphere, children playing underfoot, women working, people chatting, the individual lacks that privacy which we seek in our own civilization.

Within the household, relations are for the most part informal. Individual authority and responsibility are almost entirely lacking. "Ordinarily the female contingent of blood relatives presents a united front. A man finding himself out of harmony with the group will withdraw quietly whenever he chooses and ally himself with another group. With his departure obligations cease, and his successor fathers his children."[1]

In the things that count most in Zuni life, in matters of ritual, the man is an outsider in the house of his wife. His most permanent ties are with the house of his sister, with whom he is united in the care of the sacred fetishes. On every occasion of moment he returns to her house. If she is in need or if her children are in need he will bring them food and gifts. If male labor is needed in the fields, a brother can be called on to assist. Similarly a woman is obligated to help her brother and her brother's children in a ceremonial and economic way. The woman, of course, as an owner of the house, is united with her own blood kin in the care of the sacred fetishes that are kept within it.

When a man marries, the ties of the blood group cut directly across the new set of obligations that are imposed on the man by marriage. He leaves his mother's house to live with his wife and mother-in-law. Here he cooperates in the economic labor of

[1] *Ibid.*, p. 477.

tilling fields that belong for the most part to his wife's household, with a group of males, his wife's sisters' husbands, who are more or less strangers to him. He lives with a group that cannot accept him completely, in which he is regarded as an outsider. Furthermore, the very stability of his marriage depends largely upon the whims of his wife, who may with little ado place his small bundle of belongings on the threshold of the home as a sign that he is no longer desired. It is not until a good many years have passed that he begins to achieve some sort of status in his wife's household, but for the most part he is regarded with suspicion as one who may, upon the dissolution of the marriage, spread slanderous bits of gossip about the household.

With regard to food, however, all in the house share equally or, rather, according to need. Yet here again it is the woman who controls the larder, who may if she sees fit trade foodstuff for some other necessities, even personal items. A man may not even enter the storeroom.

In view of the firmness of the blood tie crosscutting the economic obligations of the affinal group it is surprising that marriages show the degree of permanence which they do. Divorce, it is true, is common and simple, because the Zuni do not like bickering and quarreling, and when a situation becomes too charged it is easily remedied by the man's moving out. Still, "a very large proportion of Zuni marriages endure through the greater part of a life-time."[1] It is precisely because the Zuni dislike quarreling that most marriages tend to remain peaceful.

Originally, before the development of the sheep complex, a man was economically almost entirely dependent upon the matriarchal household into which he married. Theoretically at least, all land belonged to a matrilineal line, and the man functioned only as worker on land belonging to the household with which he was associated either through blood or by marriage. The present pattern is more complex, with regard both to sheep and to land. Sheep are essentially the property of men. Some women may own sheep, which they may have acquired through some unusual circumstance, but such cases are not usual. And through sheep the men have acquired a considerable degree of economic independence.

---

[1] Ruth Benedict, *Patterns of Culture*, p. 75.

The herding group forms a different economic unit, being composed largely of men related more or less closely through the male line. It represents another of the many crosscuttings in Zuni life.

As in our own culture, theory and practice are often disparate. In theory all members of a Zuni household should live together in amicability, yet there are many cases of conflict, not only between husband and wife, but between sisters. Such quarrels as do occur seem based largely upon problems of personal likes and dislikes, the kind of friction that may arise when a number of families live together in one room. One frequent cause of quarrels between sisters is men. *A* may dislike the husband of *B*, and the latter in anger will move out of the house in the face of the strong convention that a woman and her household are inseparable. But sisters never quarrel over the same lover. It is one of the significant points about Zuni that within a family there can be no conflict over a possible mate. No woman would even think of sleeping with a man who had slept with her sister, nor would two brothers conceivably have relations with the same woman. The affect associated with such a relationship is that of incest.

As between husband and wife, sexual jealousies appear to be a major cause of quarrels. But divorce is a simple and adequate safety valve for an untenable emotional situation and is considered preferable to a continuous state of bickering.

Marriages are very simply arranged and attract little attention. In Hopi, where marriage involves a considerable gift exchange, it is the most frequent topic of conversation. In Zuni, marriages are based largely upon sentiment and involves no property transactions beyond a formal ceremonial exchange. A young man announces his intentions to a young girl after a very brief courtship. If she is willing and her parents offer no objection, the marriage proceeds. On the fourth day the young man brings the girl a dress as a mark that he really intends to marry. The dress he gets from his mother or sister, and it is thought of as a gift from the mother-in-law. After this the girl takes corn from the boy's house to grind, in order to demonstrate her fitness as a housewife. In return for this corn she is given bowls of food. Then the girl grinds her own corn "to pay for the dress" and receives an equal amount of wheat in return so that her payment for the dress is but a formal phrasing. In fact, as a result of its scarcity, wheat is far more valuable than corn. The marriage is now completed. Beyond the formal ritual exchanges no property has been involved. Of course if a man has acquired, either by inheritance or through his own effort, a corn or wheat field he cultivates it for the benefit of his wife's household. Similarly, if he owns sheep he is in a position to contribute materially to the welfare of his family. And, as in our culture, many women prefer to marry wealthy men because of the greater luxuries the latter can give them. But this is a personal problem in Zuni. The cultural emphasis is certainly not upon wealth as a necessary condition for marriage. Moreover, if a household owns its own fields, the man is primarily valuable as an economic asset because of the labor he can contribute.

Competition for a mate is given no formal expression. There are more men than women in Zuni, and the woman is not dependent upon a husband for economic security. Girls might very well exercise personal choice in marriage. But girls who appear to be very particular and "choosy" about marrying are admonished. And Zuni mythology is full of stories about the girl who is punished by the supernaturals because she shows no inclination to take the first man who offers her marriage.

We have seen that social relations in Zuni are in great part structurally dictated. Men cooperate in agricultural work because they are members of the same household or clan group; they cooperate in sheep herding because they are united by kinship ties through the male line. In ceremonial activities the group that works together is also, though to a lesser extent, welded by clan affiliation. There are also kinship relations that invoke particular types of one-way "giving" relationship. When a boy, or a girl, is initiated into a ceremonial group, the women of his (or her) father's clan, the "aunts," must grind corn for him (or her), to be given to the initiate's ceremonial father. For this, however, the women are repaid in other foods. But a man may in addition demand gifts from these aunts, which they may not refuse. Even should a man meet his aunt on the street and ask her for her moccasins she must without further ado give them to him then and there. At marriage, as has already been observed, a man's sister or mother must provide the wedding dress for the bride.

In addition to obligations between kinsmen that are established at birth, the Zuni have institutionalized a ceremonial friendship built around economic cooperation.[1] Such friends are under obligation to lend one another assistance in all large undertakings. But the fullest development of the relationship is in the giving of presents. One never trades with a ceremonial friend, as that would be even more undignified than trading with one's own blood kinsman, and indeed one's *kihe*—as such a ceremonial friend is called—is considered a member of the family. Although the ceremonial friend is not called by the sibling term, the relationship terminology adopted toward the members of his family is the same as though that person were a brother or sister. A man calls his kihe's mother "mother" and the sister of his kihe "sister," etc. With these names go all the obligations that normally go with such a named relationship. Thus a man could no more marry his kihe's sister than he could his own.

The reasons for forming this relationship, which is formalized by the ritual washing of the hair to signify adoption into the family, are various. It may be desirable to enter into such a relationship with a man because he is rich or skillful at a particularly valued craft so that one may get fine gifts from him. Thus a number of men and women have kihe who are Navaho and Hopi because "they are such good weavers." Such material motives, however, are not the only ones involved in the formation of the friendship. The case is narrated of a man who ceremonially adopted a poor woman as his kihe because she was lonely and no one ever gave her anything. He felt sorry for her, and so at a religious dance he called her out and gave her a fine black dress.[2] Or again, children having become attached to one another have themselves adopted into each other's family. The relationship once entered upon is lifelong and may even be continued by the families after the death of one member. So close are the ties of the kihe to one another that a man not infrequently will give away part of his land to his ceremonial brother to the exclusion of the rightful heirs, and the gift will be socially sanctioned.

Strikingly characteristic of all social relations in Zuni is the relative lack of emphasis upon wealth. Property does not figure

[1] Most of the material on ceremonial friendship is from manuscript material of Dr. Ruth Bunzel.

[2] Elsie C. Parsons, "Ceremonial Friendship at Zuni," p. 5.

in marriage. Individuals do not compete for a fixed supply, and in terms of the prestige an individual may achieve, property in itself is not the determining factor. This does not at all imply that the Zuni are unmindful of the blessings of material comfort or that they are completely disinterested in the accumulation of wealth. But they do frown upon any undue interest in material possession, upon acquisitiveness, covetousness, stinginess, or sharp practice in economic transactions. If a material object has value, it has that only as a means toward a specific utilitarian end. But hoarding—the piling up of goods far beyond what is necessary for a comfortable existence—is practically unknown. Wealth circulates freely, and property rights are neither clearly defined nor strictly enforced. For one thing, material effects are never valued as a means to power and are only indirectly a source of prestige. The property that is really valued, as would be expected from the great emphasis upon ceremonial matters, is the nonmaterial property such as songs, prayers, rituals. These are the principal prestige counters; their possession gives one authority, their abuse, power.[1]

A man may possess a fine turquoise necklace which he values for its workmanship and which he likes to have people admire. "It is a badge of his economic competence and a sound investment that can be liquidated whenever he is hard pressed. But he lends it freely without recompense to members of his family, friends, people who are not friends—to any who asks. A participant in any important dance is loaded down with valuable goods and no one bothers to ask where they came from."[2]

The principles of land tenure reveal further the basic non-competitive and nonindividualistic property patterns in Zuni. Most of the reservation consists of land unsuitable, at present, for cultivation. These uncultivated areas belong communally to the tribe and any man may stake out new fields wherever he wishes. Such fields, in contrast to those held by the female line of a household, belong to him individually and may be disposed of by him at his pleasure. But so long as he remains associated with a household either by blood or by marriage he cultivates the field for a communal end, the products that he raises becoming the collective property of the women of the household. It is even

[1] Bunzel, Mss.
[2] *Ibid.*

possible to appropriate land, the title of which is held by another family providing that it is not in use. For although distinctions are made between ownership and use of a field, these are by no means clear, and it is difficult to dispossess a family that has taken possession.

It is significant, too, that litigations over the ownership of land are rare and in most cases quickly settled.[1] One might expect that disputes would arise frequently among a people whose concepts of ownership are so vaguely defined that boundaries between fields are marked only in one dimension, in width facing the road and not in depth.

The problem of sheep ownership has already been mentioned. Here evidently a new individualistic pattern seems to have developed under stimulation of white contact. Yet it is interesting to note that, although the ownership of sheep is individualistic, few Zuni know how many sheep they own.[2] Nor, in spite of the great value in which sheep are held, do men compete against one another for sheep. Rather a young man is assisted in developing a flock of his own. A boy who offers to herd for a group of his male kinsmen receives from them at the shearing season a number of sheep as gifts. These belong to him and form the nucleus of his own herd. Next season in addition to the lambs that have been born he is given more sheep by his associates until after a few seasons he has accumulated sixty sheep—a sack of wool. At this point he becomes a full-fledged member of the group and he is given no more assistance. Thus instead of attempting to acquire a monopoly, a group of men cooperate to "set up" a young relative, though this is not essential in herding.[3]

Besides accumulating sheep by working for them, a man may inherit sheep from his father or from his mother's brother. But it is most usual for a member of a herding group to inherit from

---

[1] *Ibid.*

[2] Sheep are never counted. Count is kept, though, of sacks of wool.

[3] The following case described by Dr. Bunzel illustrates the method of obtaining sheep. *C* started herding in 1920, and in 1922 he had sixty sheep. Now he has two and one-half sacks of wool. But he was a smart and hard worker. Whenever his uncles or cousins wanted to come back from camp he went to take their places and he was always nice about helping them with their work in the fields or anything else they had to do, and so they were glad to have him in their group and gave him more than they would have if he had been lazy.

someone in that group, and, since the most common group is that composed of a father and his sons, the latter stand a good chance of inheriting from their father.   There are no hard and fast rules of inheritance, however, and the ultimate bequest of sheep depends on a number of factors, with the personal desires of the owner probably decisive.

Food is shared by all in the household and is based entirely on need, with no account taken of the field it has been grown in or of who has been responsible in producing it.   If, for example, *A* should bring in some especially choice melon from his field, his wife does not feel that she has any more claim to it than her sister. A man may, however, take food from his own field to his female relatives, his mother, his sister, or a niece, providing he has not yet brought the food into the house.   For then it falls entirely under the jurisdiction of the women in the house.

Personal property is by no means negligible in Zuni.   A good string of turquoise may be worth about $700, a woman's silver necklace from $50 to $75.   A woman's ordinary dress is worth $35, and a pair of women's moccasins is valued at close to $100. Although these articles are freely loaned there is a strong sense of ownership attached to them.   Each individual has absolute control over his personal property, and even the rights of a small child are recognized.   A mother will not sell a doll or a string of beads belonging to a child without its consent, and she would insist on the money's being given to the child.   Spouses have no control over one another's possessions.

Over against the individualistically phrased ownership of personal property is the important role played by gift giving in Zuni economy.   We have emphasized before that wealth in Zuni is highly fluid, and there are any number of circumstances that make for this fluidity.   Most important of these are the ceremonial exchanges that take place at marriage, at initiations, and at the great winter-solstice ceremonies.   In none of these exchanges is any attempt made to secure an equivalent return. The emphasis is rather upon a one-way giving relationship.

When a woman comes to grind at a house where the winter-solstice Shalako is to be held, she is given a bowl of stew, several loaves of wheat bread, and a bowl of stewed peaches or some other sweet.   At the end of the Shalako the impersonators of the gods receive valuable presents from the houses they have dedicated.

A whole sheep is butchered, and each person gets several lengths of cotton cloth and one object of considerable value, such as a woman's dress, a fine black shawl, or, most valuable of all, a finely worked buckskin.   In all cases the generosity of the host makes these gifts as munificent as his means permit.   The gifts are given as payment for the work which these men have done for the host in the fields all year and in building the new house and for the prayers which they have said for him and for the entire community during the year.

Between members of the same family and in the ceremonial friendship, spontaneous giving of presents is of frequent occurrence.   Here especially no attempt is made to maintain any kind of reciprocity.   Between husband and wife it is almost always the husband who gives gifts, in addition to the necessary clothing for the household which he is required to buy.   Parents are always giving presents to their children, and a man will rarely return from a trading expedition without bringing home something for his children,[1] his wife, or even for a friend.   If reciprocity does occur, it is quite informal and dependent entirely upon the inclination of the recipient of the first gift.

Because of the fluidity of wealth and the little emphasis placed upon the accumulation of property, distinctions in wealth are highly fluctuating.   There are men who, through their industriousness and careful habits, accumulate a considerable amount of property and can therefore be considered wealthy.   But rarely can such wealth remain for long in the same family or in the same hands.   If a man has poor relatives he will feel obligated to support them with gifts of food.   Out of motives of friendship he may give expensive gifts to his kihe.   At all events he will be called upon to entertain the masked god impersonators at the Shalako. In this most of his fortune will be dissipated among the community so that by the next year he is little wealthier than the rest.   The following account given by a Zuni woman informant to Dr. Bunzel illustrates clearly the great expense of such an undertaking.

"This year we did not take the crook for the Shalako at the winter solstice, but late in the summer when they had no place to go father took the crook because he is *wole*.   So we didn't build a new house but just fixed up our front room.

---

[1] If a man has come back with many sheep he distributes a good portion of them among his children.

"They started to work in October. One morning during harvest time some girls came to work, and we didn't have a scrap of meat in the house. Se we rushed to the store and bought half a sheep. It cost five dollars. Next day *M* said, 'Now the people will start to come,' so he and *L* went to the ranch and they killed three goats and one sheep. . . . It takes two sheep each day to feed the family and five men and five women, providing many come to work. It takes a lot because women take home bowls of stew. So after two days the meat was gone and *M* said, 'I think I'll butcher a cow.' . . . this lasted five days. Everyone knew that he had butchered a cow, so all the people came just like flies to honey. The people always watch the Shalako houses and whenever they have something good there, they all come . . . of course some people come all the time, our relatives and the impersonators, but there are outsiders who come to have a good time.

"It kept up like this from this time on, and the worst of all was the day that Sayataca came in. That day we were plastering and lots of women came to help with the plastering, and old men too. . . . They had lots of fun.

"The cow lasted five days, and after it was gone *W* killed two sheep. This was for one day, and the next day *C* killed a cow and that lasted for five days again. Then *H* killed two sheep. The next day *W* killed a cow. This was the day that the Sayataca people came in, and on that night we had a big feast for the Shalako mask that stays in our house. Lots of women brought corn flour and they got wheat in return. . . . That day our whole family came and there were twelve men and fifteen women who were not relatives. They all stayed for a feast late at night when the men came to take the Shalako mask out. . . .

"Next day all the men went to the sheep camps. *W* brought back eight sheep, *M* brought six, *C*, seven. We sold all the pelts and we bought five dollars' worth of sugar, fifteen sacks of flour, twelve pounds of coffee, five gallons of gasoline for the lamps, two bolts of cotton print for decorating the house, and belts and shawls, colored blankets . . . to give as presents to the impersonators."[1]

And so it goes on. On the final days even greater quantities of food are consumed and the entire community is fed. The family

[1] Bunzel, Mss. *Note:* The men referred to, *M, C, L, W,* are husbands of four sisters in the house.

giving the Shalako need not stand the expense alone, but all the rich men and relatives are expected to come and give presents.

For the individual undertaking the feast there is a return in terms of prestige; he is looked upon as a fine man. But the motivation is nonetheless not entirely individualistic. The Shalako is an essential ceremony that has for its purpose the bringing of greater supernatural blessing upon the community as a whole, and the man who sponsors it is, therefore, contributing to the community. In addition he has put into circulation a quantity of goods which he has distributed as presents and has fed the community. Certainly there is no comparison between the motives of the Zuni in giving the Shalako and those of a man on the Northwest Coast of America in giving a potlatch. In Zuni, the emphasis upon the individual is overwhelmingly minimized as over against the great emphasis upon the collective good, and all ceremonials of any importance stress the collective good. Nor can the Shalako feast be compared to the validation of wealth and social position of the *kadangyang* in Ifugao. For, to repeat again, the only field in which the individual can seek distinction is in the ritual. Economic status is of far less importance.

The relative unimportance of property in comparison to ceremony is clearly revealed in the legal setup. The actual governing body in Zuni, the group commanding the greatest respect and prestige, is the priesthood. But these men are of too sacred a character to concern themselves with mundane problems. Their chief function is in the regulation of ceremonial dances and in the general supervision of all matters pertaining to religion. Disputes over property are left to a civil body of governor and staff appointed by the priests and subject to removal by the priests. These officers lack all prestige and have little power to enforce their decisions. That their decisions are obeyed is testimony to the willingness of the Zuni to submit to any orderly arrangement. If any principle of legal adjudication can be said to be fundamental for Zuni it is that of compromise. As an example of this there is the case described by Cushing.

"An old man died a year ago leaving a well-grown girl and two sons. The deceased, when his children were young, planted with the assistance of an old friend a large peach orchard. The orchard was now bearing fruit and had eighty-six trees. Now his sister's son claimed the entire orchard on the ground that he was the man's uterine nephew and that no other inheritance arrangements had been made. The man's children argued that the nephew had caused the old man years of anguish by his laziness, impudence, and gambling. Therefore the deceased could never have thought of leaving the orchard to him. Besides, the children argued, they had helped plant the orchard and cared for its growth. An old man was called as a witness by the court to testify that the orchard was meant to be divided half and half among the children and the nephew provided the latter did not turn out to be bad. It was finally decided that the nephew should get forty trees with the provision that he give eight to the friend who helped plant the orchard. The rest of the trees were divided between the two children."[1]

Beyond such cases of property dispute the civil court has little other business. Adultery is settled by the principals involved. A woman will either shame her husband in public by refusing to wash his hair at a ceremonial or, if she is of a more aggressive personality, fight with her rival in public so that her husband is shamed. But it is decidedly not a case for the court. Murder and assault are rare, as is theft. In none of these cases has any technique for handling the offense been developed. In connection with the absence of cases of violence and the ease with which other disputes are settled might be mentioned the aversion that the Zuni feel for any aggressive or strongly individualistic behavior. The culture stresses above all sobriety in all relations and prevents effectively the individual from setting himself apart from or against the group. The emphasis upon sobriety and upon the group comes out even more sharply in the organization of religion.

"No field of activity compares with ritual for foremost place in their attention. Probably most grown men in the western pueblos give to it the greater part of their waking life. It requires the memorizing of an amount of word-perfect ritual that our less trained minds find staggering, and the performance of neatly dovetailed ceremonies that are charted by the calendar and complexly interlock all the different cults and the governing body in endless formal procedure."[2]

The cult which is the basis for all Zuni ceremonialism is that of the *alacinawe*, the ancestors. They guide and protect and nourish human life and are beneficent beings in whose worship

---

[1] Cushing, *op. cit.*, p. 142.
[2] Benedict, *op. cit.*, p. 60.

all participate regardless of age, sex, or affiliation with special cults. At all meals it is customary to offer some food to the ancestors, and at the special ceremony held in their honor great quantities of food are sacrificed in fire and in the river. They are asked to bestow rain, seeds, life, old age, wealth, power, fecundity, health, and general happiness. In a sense the ancestors are feared because they have too great a love for their dear ones on this earth and may wish to call them to the ancestor world. Therefore it becomes necessary to cut off by ritual the recent dead from the living.

Besides this basic ancestor cult there are six major cults in Zuni. The cult of the sun, which is presided over by the *pekwin*, the most holy and revered man in Zuni, calls for the participation of all priests and appointees to ceremonial office, and many others do not neglect the ritual of offering a handful of corn meal to the sun, the source of all life, each morning. The pekwin is the man ultimately held responsible for the welfare of the community. As priest of the sun he sets by his calculations of the solstice the dates of the calendric ceremonies. In addition, "he is the active member of the priestly hierarchy and the offici- ating priest at all ceremonies at which the priests function jointly. It is he who sets up the altars for these ceremonies and even the altar for the scalp dance; it is he who meets the priests of the katcinas when they visit Zuni and 'makes their road'; it is he who installs new priests, including bow priests, and formally appoints to office the impersonators of the katcinas."[1]

The cult of the *uwanami*, the "rain makers," concerned with the worship of the supernaturals who live in all the waters of the earth, is comprised of twelve priesthoods, each with from two to six members. Membership in this priesthood is hereditary and goes always to someone in a matrilineal line that is trustee for the very sacred fetishes that are connected with the rain worship. The rain priests are very holy and must have no concern with worldly affairs. They must never quarrel. Upon the care with which they perform their rituals depends the coming of the rain. In this, their position, like the pekwin's, calls for the assumption of a great deal of responsibility. In summer, when it is important that the rain come, they go into a retreat, one group following the other. Should the rain fail on the days when a group is in

[1] Bunzel, "Introduction to Zuni Ceremonialism," p. 512.

retreat, that group will be suspected of laxness in ritual observance.

Like the ancestor cult, the worship of the katcinas, a mythical people living at the bottom of a lake and coming annually to Zuni to dance, includes a broad group in its membership. Every adult male is in the katcina society, as well as a few women. The katcina is also the most popular cult, and all the people await eagerly the coming of the masked gods. There are two kinds of masked gods: the masked gods proper and the katcina priests. The latter are the chiefs of the supernatural world and are impersonated by dancers with masks. The chief of these is Pautiwa, one who embodies the characteristics most admired in Zuni, beauty, dignity, and kindliness. His prestige is enormous. Lending dramatic contrast to Pautiwa is Kaklo, his speaker, a bustling, officious, and self-important figure. Also associated with Pautiwa is Sayatasha, who has the same characteristics but is even more austere. The second division of the katcina priests is made up of the sacred clowns, the *koyemshi*, the possessors of love charms that can make people "crazy." Upon them falls some of the severest restrictions. On the last night of their performance they must touch neither food nor drink; they must neither talk nor sleep; they may not remove their tight fitting masks from sundown to midnight of the following day. "This truly heroic act of self-denial earns them the sympathetic affection of the people, an affection manifested in the generous gifts given them on this, their last day in office."[1]

The katcina society itself is organized into six sections conforming to the six directions recognized by the Zuni. Unless one violates the sexual tabus or disagrees with the leaders, association is lifelong. Each of these groups is required to give three dances a year, the most popular public dances.

Comprising an entirely different classification of religious grouping are the medicine societies, including those devoted to the beast gods, the most dangerous and violent in the Zuni pantheon, and the bow priesthood. Membership in the former society is largely voluntary and is open to men and women. But only the men in the medicine societies hold the official positions and only they are the theurgists. The organization of the medicine society is somewhat like a guild system, each section with a

[1] *Ibid.*, p. 521.

special and carefully guarded therapy. One group cures sore throat, another epilepsy; one has a special charm for easy parturition, etc. To learn the therapeutic arts, it is necessary to buy one's way at great expense up through the different orders into which each medicine society is subdivided. But if one is ill, it is obligatory to join the society if a cure is to take place or if a cure has been effected. Because of the expense, an initiation may not be completed for many years.

While aggressiveness is strongly suppressed in all Zuni relations, the bow priesthood, the group dealing with matters of war and comprising the executive arm of the priestly hierarchy, serves to channel such aggressiveness as there is in Zuni. Members must be initiated into it to be protected from the vengeance of the ghost of an enemy they have killed. When war was still part of the Zuni pattern, the bow priests were leaders in war.

It is significant that the priesthood offices carrying the greatest responsibilities are not sought after. In fact it is only with difficulty that the priesthoods are filled. No Zuni cares to undertake the heavy obligations that go with ceremonial office. As one Zuni woman put it, "They have to catch the men young to make them priests. For if they are old enough to realize all that is required of them they will refuse. . . . Yesterday my younger brother went with his uncle to the spring for water for their altar. He was dressed in his *shiwani* costume and looked very handsome. As he went out light rain fell and everyone was happy that they had been blessed with rain. But my heart hurt and my eyes were full of tears to see my younger brother. He is so young and yet he has his mind on these serious things."[1]

Strikingly, too, all ceremonials are collective. On the western plains the Indians sought individual vision experiences; each young man attempted to obtain an individual relationship with a guardian spirit. But among the Zuni only group ritual is effective. The masked katcina dances are group dances, and it is the collective rhythmic movement of a mass of men that will bring the rain. When the priests go into retreat into the ceremonial houses, the kivas, they go in groups. Even the planting of the prayer stick fetishes to the gods, the most individual of religious acts, must be done at a fixed time. A man who plants his prayer sticks without an official announcement would be

[1] *Ibid.*, p. 543.

suspected of witchcraft. In addition to the collective performance, all the blessings asked for are collective; it is rain for the
group, fecundity for the group, long life for the group.

As relations of man to man in Zuni are supposed to be sober
and dignified, so is the relation of man to the gods. Each blessing
asked for can be obtained only through an orderly process of
painstakingly accurate ritual. It is important, too, that each
process in the complicated ritual interlock smoothly with the
total pattern. Group must cooperate with group; individuals
must cooperate with individuals within each group. One error
and the rain may not come. Crops will wilt in the sun. Misfortune may strike the community. It is not so much that
individuals do not wish to cooperate when they are reluctant to
join a priesthood, it is rather that they fear the dread possibility
of catastrophe.

To join in the katcina dances, to participate fully in the ceremonial life, involves some expense. A man should have a mask
made. But he cannot have his mask until he is married and a
man of substance. For he must pay to have his mask made;
he must feast the members of his kiva to "initiate" the mask.
Nevertheless he is not deprived from joining in the dance. If he
does not have a mask he borrows from one who has, at any time
and without payment.

Still another aspect of the close cooperation demanded between
religious groups: the bow priests have been described as the executive arm of the priestly hierarchy. The body of priests, being
too sacred to take action in a case, commands the bow priesthood
to act. If the latter refuses, nothing can be done about it. On
the other hand, no action can be taken unless it is initiated by
the rain and sun priests. It is because the Zuni are essentially
cooperative that these bodies do not checkmate each other.

In opposition to the general cooperative framework of ritual
and the fundamentally collective attitudes toward the use of
property stands the strongly institutionalized individualism with
regard to ceremonial and immaterial property, comprising sacred
songs, prayers, and ritual formulas. Whereas it is considered
despicable to be stingy with material goods, it is considered the
height of piety to be stingy with nonmaterial prerogatives. To
give away a prayer lightly would be to value the prayer lightly.
Prayers, however, may be borrowed. Thus the word *itcima*

when applied to rituals means "to cherish" and when applied to material objects means "to hoard" or "to be stingy."

Ritual also makes use of a competitive device in Zuni. Gambling games and foot races which involve a great deal of betting are common throughout North America, and are not always used for the same end. In Zuni these sports play a ritual role, chiefly for the bringing of rain. The most popular of these is foot racing, which is under the supervision of the bow priesthood, although the rain priests also officiate.

The purely ceremonial foot race involves no betting and is over a course of four miles. Any who desire to do so may participate, and no winner is announced. The races, however, which excite a most intense interest among the populace are the twenty-five-mile stick-kicking races, also conducted under religious auspices and instrumental in bringing supernatural blessings upon the community. Two men make the arrangements to hold such a race. After the details have been agreed upon, an announcement is made from a rooftop that a race will be held the next day. The swiftest runners gather at the houses of the "managers" and sides are chosen, three to six runners on each side.

By the afternoon of the day when the race is to be held the betting and excitement of the community are at a high pitch. Everything the betters can collect is placed in the plaza. Everything is wagered, from a silver button to a fine blanket.

The race begins. Each side must kick a stick representing the elder and younger gods of war across a course of twenty-five miles. The side whose stick is first carried across the finish line is the winner and the runner who kicks the stick over is the individual victor. But true to the characteristic Zuni attitude, no great prestige attaches to the winner. On the contrary, a consistent winner is prevented from running, to give others a chance. Here again, cultural attitudes stem individualism.

## EDUCATION

Out of the entire range of human behavior the Zuni have selected the nonaggressive, sober, cooperative aspects to stress. It is to this norm that the child, if he is to fit into the cultural framework set for him by his parents, must conform. He is not

broken or forcibly coerced into this pattern but is gradually fitted
to it under the most subtle stress of social sanction.  The
Bathonga regarded their children as wild, untamed animals who
had to be broken of their asocial habits before they could become
socialized members of the community.  The Zuni child, on the
other hand, grows up under little restraint; he faces no stern
disciplinarian in the house.  Rather, his parents are all kindness
to him and humor his wants.  He is rarely scolded or spanked.
But where the Zuni minimize physical force as a sanction, they
strongly emphasize shame.  The married man who is promiscu-
ous in his sex relations is shamed in public by his wife, who
chooses some public ceremonial to make her gesture of disapproval.  Or on the other hand a woman who refuses to grant her
husband a divorce is shamed into doing so by having the matter
made public.  Also there is the case of $S$, who, when he learned
that his wife was dancing in a dance in which only unmarried
women may participate, was so ashamed that he did not attend.
In the same way, throughout the period of childhood sanctions
of shame are invoked against the child that refuses to conform.

In Manus, children are not encouraged to grow up too rapidly.
Nor from their concept of adult life do the children wish to.  But
in Zuni, as is common among the North American Indians, adult
behavior is the norm that is held up to all children and to which
they must grow up as quickly as possible.  The little boy in Zuni
who can deliver the appropriate formal speech upon making a
visit is held up to praise.  "Just like a man," they say of him.
Should he be sulky, uncooperative, greedy, impolite in talking
out of his turn, or lazy, then he is reproved as being childish.
This term of opprobrium, "childish," is even applied to old men
who do not conform.

The age at which one is to graduate into adulthood is not fixed,
but it is early.  There is, however, an early period in the life of the
child, especially of the small boy, that is marked by great freedom.
Small boys of about four or five roam the country on horseback,
play games near the river just outside the village, and run in and
out of neighbors' houses.  At this age they are permitted to
break in upon adult conversation, and they are listened to respect-
fully.  If scolded, the child runs away to the house of a relative
and is coaxed back by his parents.  By the age of nine or so, the
boys may be permitted to herd their father's or big brother's

sheep, an occupation which they greatly enjoy. By entering upon an economic activity, the boy is definitely growing up. If he chooses to play rather than work, he is warned that his behavior is childish. In addition, the sanction of sex approval is invoked to keep him industrious. He is told that girls like hard workers, the man whose shirt is dirty with sweat. It is no longer proper for him to show aggressive traits; he must become socialized, an adult. At this time, too, he is drawn into the personal animosities that mark informal social relations in Zuni, and can no longer run into any house to play.

Within the household the child must learn to respect ceremonial property, and he is early conditioned to the presence of some mysteriously covered object which he is forbidden to touch, as something sacred and dangerous that might bring misfortune to the entire household if mishandled. Secular property, though, he is permitted to handle with great freedom, and he has no affect about "mine and thine," although as previously mentioned his individual ownership is always respected.

Kinship attitudes are also impressed on him very early. The child does not grow up with a fixed relationship toward one set of parents. Mother and mother's sisters are designated by the the same term, and women within a household will nurse one another's children. Men, too, enjoy fondling children, and do not concentrate their attentions on their own children. A man (or woman) showers his (or her) affection upon any child in the house, so that a child grows up to a generalized relationship with a group of parents.

In contrast with the boys, the life of the girls is far more restrained and monotonous. Little girls trail at the heels of their mothers, helping in the household, but never being given any job to complete. The mother may give the girl a bit of clay if she is making a pot so that the child may learn to handle the material, but she is not encouraged to make a pot by herself. The play of the girls is far less organized than the boys', the emphasis in their training being on the development of household skills. For a relatively brief period of her childhood, the little girl is allowed to play about with other girls, but soon she dresses in a shawl as a sign that she has grown up. She is now restricted in her going about, and is required to spend more time in the house. She is given little opportunity to meet boys, as she is always closely chaperoned. Puberty, which is regarded so widely as a significant break in the life of the girl, is passed unmarked.

For the boy, certainly, ceremonial participation begins early. All young children are taken on their mothers' backs to witness the colorful katcina dances, and they develop very soon a keen interest in religious affairs. In the families from which the hereditary priests are chosen the parents begin to watch when the boy is quite young to see whether he will be suitable for the office. They observe whether he is reserved or given to quarreling, whether or not he shows the appropriate seriousness.

Between the ages of five and nine, all boys are initiated into the katcina society. At birth the boy has already been entrusted to a ceremonial godfather, who now acts as his sponsor to initiate him into the kiva to which he, the godfather, belongs. The small boys are afraid of the imposing-looking masked "gods" who are initiating them. The climax of the initiation is reached when the impersonators of the gods strike each boy sharply on the back with yucca blades. The boy cringes and cries out, and clings the more tightly to his ceremonial father, who holds him tenderly between his knees. The whipping, though, is not meant as punishment; it is not part of a process of breaking the boy. It is to purify, to bring good luck, and is used always for that purpose. During the Shalako ceremonies, persons wishing good luck ask as a special favor to be whipped by the masked katcina dancers. With this initiation the child gains his first ceremonial status.

Traditionally at the age of fourteen the boys are initiated again, and are again ceremonially whipped. But this time, after the whipping, the masked impersonators remove their masks. It is the great revelation. The boys learn now that the katcinas are not real gods but impersonators. It is now the boy's turn to don the mask and whip the unmasked katcinas. "It is their first object lesson in the truth that they as mortals must exercise all the functions which they as initiates ascribe to the supernaturals themselves."[1] The boys are forbidden upon pain of death to reveal the secret of the katcinas to the uninitiated. They now become members of one of the six kiva societies.

Girls are weaned from an active interest in ceremonial matters at adolescence, shortly before they are expected to marry.

[1] *Benedict, op. cit.,* p. 70.

Although there is no tabu against a woman joining a katcina society, it is not considered customary. Besides there are the problems of the household which engross her interest. Few men care to have their wives belong to a religious society, membership in which implies periods of sexual continence as well as neglect of household duties.

To summarize the sanctions employed in the educational process:

Shame is used to correct what is considered bad social behavior. It is applied all through life as the most important mechanism of social control in Zuni.

Proper or good behavior is encouraged by praise. The child is told that he has acted like an adult.

Physical force is rarely applied; nor is scolding common. A child who is scolded may run away and is either coaxed back or shamed into coming back by having his behavior called childish.

Fear is employed to establish the appropriate respect attitudes toward ceremonial property, but it is fear of supernatural punishment. In adult life, though, the violation of a religious tabu that may bring misfortune to the entire community is punished by a public reprimand from the bow priests as well.

## The Role Played by the Individual in the Culture

As we have seen, the great emphasis in Zuni culture is upon the orderly, sober processes of ritual life. In comparison with the amount of time the adult male gives to ceremonial participation and the great interest that religion has for him, economics plays a definitely minor role. The ideal man is not necessarily the wealthy man, but rather the ceremonially minded individual, the man willing to devote himself to the ritual routine of bringing supernatural blessing upon the group. In this, though his position in a priestly office necessarily sets him apart from the rest, he must avoid carrying his individuality too far; he must not be too officious. Zuni stresses constantly the submergence of the individual in the group, and would frown upon the man who took advantage of his religious position to secure any undue prominence for himself. In his relations to his fellow men he must always cooperate in the work in the fields with the men of his household and with the men of his kiva in the religious performances. Toward all others within the community he may not display any competitiveness. The ideal man in Zuni is a "person of dignity and affability who has never tried to lead and who has never called forth comment from his neighbors. Any conflict, even though all right is on his side, is held against him."[1] He must cooperate readily in both the economic and the ritual field.

In our culture we have stressed the "leader," the aggressive, energetic man of will, as part of our philosophy of individualism, and it is such men that we have held up as models to the younger generation. The individualist in Zuni has little scope. Originally, when the war pattern was still in its heyday and the bow priesthood in its ascendancy, the energies of the more active, self-willed individuals could be channeled through this priesthood into socially acceptable and desirable activities. War called for aggressiveness; the bow priests acted as the executive arm of the priestly hierarchy in administering punishment to violators of ritual obligations. It was the bow priesthood, too, that dealt with people accused of witchcraft.

Economic life offers little to the individualist, for the Zuni offer no great rewards to the rich. Besides, the wealthy man is expected to expend his wealth in the communal Shalako, and though this affords him an opportunity for building prestige, he may not display that as his motive. There is the case of $N$, who sought prominence in making money but found "that was no good."

Until lately, the strong-willed and culturally aberrant individual in Zuni was faced with the danger of being accused of sorcery. Thus, $N$,[2] one of the best examples of a dominant personality type in Zuni, was hanged by the thumbs as a witch until he confessed. Sorcery is not uncommon in the primitive world, but in Zuni it actually does not exist. At least no evidences have ever been found of individuals actually practicing the black arts; nor is there any knowledge of magical techniques. Yet individuals are frequently accused as sorcerers, and almost always it is the disliked person, the culturally aberrant, who is accused. It is necessary to add in connection with witchcraft that its ideology is a cultural importation from Spain. The

[1] *Ibid.*, p. 99.
[2] See case 5, p. 349.

hanging of a witch by the thumbs from the rafter beams of the church is a European practice.

Against the sterner virtues of "initiative, ambition, an uncompromising sense of honor and justice, intense personal loyalties, the Zuni value most a yielding disposition and a generous heart."[1] It is part of the general "Apollonian" *Weltanschauung* that does not look upon the world in terms of conflict, nor of life as a striving for the unattainable. Existence should be calm and measured.[2] The individual who can adjust temperamentally to these demands is accepted and no mention is made of him; he merges into the collective stream of everyday life.

Occasionally individuals may deviate, sometimes sharply, from this norm. Wewha became a berdache and was probably accepted on that score;[3] *N* was "hanged" and finally became governor, but was always disliked. Tales of quarrelsome individuals, of people who get angry quickly, are not lacking. Nor are animosities lacking. "Grudges are cherished in Zuni. They are usually the rather generalized expression of slights and resentments in a small community."[4] If there is fighting to be done, it is curiously the women who are the protagonists. It is not considered bad form for one woman to blacken the eye of her rival for the affections of her husband. It is women, too, who will violate the strongly phrased feeling of household solidarity by running off with their husbands when the home situation becomes untenable. Kroeber estimates that from 5 to 10 per cent of women fly in the face of all tradition and leave the household for the man they love.[5]

## THE INTEGRATION OF CULTURE

The orientation of all institutions, with little exception, to a basic principle of cooperative, nonindividualistic behavior is the

[1] Bunzel, "Introduction to Zuni Ceremonialism," p. 480.

[2] It is significant to observe in this connection that suicide is unheard of in Zuni. The very notion of it is incomprehensible.

[3] According to Prof. Benedict, Mrs. Stevenson's appraisal of the attitude of the Zuni toward Wewha is not to be taken too literally. This, in reference to the statement that Wewha was "undoubtedly the most remarkable member of the tribe" and that "her" death "caused universal regret and distress in Zuni." See Case 4, p. 348.

[4] Benedict, Introduction to "Zuni Mythology," p. xix.

[5] A. L. Kroeber, "Zuni Kin and Clan," p. 105.

pattern of Zuni culture. The exceptions are sheep herding, in which individualistic concepts of property are dominant, and the bow priesthood, which allows for the expression of aggressiveness. Yet in spite of the formal phrasings of cooperation, non-aggressiveness, and affability, the Zuni are in the opinion of a number of field workers a rather "mean" people, harboring against one another personal grudges and animosities that under the influence of white contact seem to have flowered into full-blown factionalism. The Catholic adherents are ranged against the Protestants in a sharp dichotomy that cuts across even family ties and religious groupings. Both groups compete against one another to get the children to attend their school, and it is frequently the school that devises the best publicity "stunt," such as distributing free ice cream to the children, that wins the most support. In addition there are other groups, such as the prowhites and the antiwhites, each with a fixed set of attitudes, each resentful of the other. Women take less part in these more or less political factional disputes than the men, but they have developed their own antagonism around sex. A wife will attack her rival in public, pulling out her hair, blackening her eye. For somewhat different reasons sisters, after a long period of petty and even serious quarrels, resort to breaking furniture or stealing, for spite, some object from the house.

This particular discrepancy between the ideals which a culture has laid out for itself and the manner in which those ideals are put into practice is highly significant. The Zuni cooperate in all formal situations, in the economic and in the ceremonial field; they will never resort to violence, except in the few cases mentioned of quarrels between women. Nevertheless they bear no love for their fellow men, but are ready to defame anyone on the least pretext. In economics they are noncompetitive, yet they harbor resentment against the man who has become wealthy. Members of a ceremonial group may hate the priest with whom they must and do cooperate. The pekwin who by his calculations of the solstices sets the calendric ceremonial dates is opposed by one group that protests he calculated wrong and defended as hotly by another that insists he was correct. And so on. Beneath the surface of a cultural norm of benignity and of affability there appears to lie some restless irritability. It is difficult to account for it. There does appear, however, to be some relationship between these attitudes of resentment, personal dislikes, the continual malicious scandalmongering, and the fact that the chief social sanction is shame. If individuals are to be responsive to that sanction they must be made sensitive to public criticism. On the other hand, the exercise of such a sanction almost necessitates continual criticism of the actions of others. In addition, there is the problem of projection familiar enough to us in our culture. Individuals made to feel sensitive about particular aspects of their behavior are frequently quick to observe similar flaws in their neighbors'. These factors then acting together would seem to set up a vicious circle of mutual recrimination.

But this is hardly a complete explanation. Possibly, too, the Zuni have gone too far in attempting to inhibit the development of traits of aggressiveness, initiative, and what we in general call individuality without offering an adequate channeling for such traits. It may be significant, too, to point out in this connection the prevalence in Zuni mythology of the castration-phobia theme. In rape tales the sexual roles are reversed and it is the man who is afraid of the woman. There are the tales of the young husbands who are afraid of their wives and run away. The general theme running throughout most of the tales dealing with sexual relations stresses the fear of the man before the woman and of intercourse with her.

### CASE HISTORIES[1]

#### CASE 1

*W* used to sack his wool with the others in his group, and when it was sold he would settle all the bills at the store and divide up whatever was left. Now *W* never owes much at the store, but his nephews went with lots of women and used to buy all kinds of things at the store. But *W* was never like that; he was always careful with his accounts. Now all the time his nephews were complaining because *W* never goes herding, and they say he never sends provisions to the boys when they are out. Each boy is supposed to take his own provisions, but if he runs short he sends word to the headman, and he has to send something out to him. Now *W*'s nephews were quarreling all the time, and they came to *W*'s wife and told her that they did not think it was fair that *W* never went herding, and yet when it came to dividing up after wool sell he got more money than they. When *W* heard that he said, "All right. Next year I will put my wool in a separate sack and let them do what they like." So he did this and next summer he had

------

[1] From Bunzel, unpublished field notes, except as indicated.

nine sacks and his brother had four and his nephews had five between them and *C* had two and a half. So *W* did much better that way. The joke was on them. Before *W* had only about $100 after all their bills had been paid, because they always owed so much more than he, but this year he had $400 after he had paid his account, and his nephews were so disappointed.

## Case 2

A man died. He had three wives and no children. His nephew wanted all the property. He had lots of sheep. His sister's boy wanted it all. His wife cried. The man had 400 head. We talked to them. The sister's son wanted all his uncle's sheep. The officer said, "Won't you help your aunt?" He said, "No, she didn't have any children by my uncle." The officers wanted to give all the sheep to the nephew but told the boy to give his aunt plenty of mutton to eat. The boy said, "All right," but he would only give it to her once in a while, not all the time. The officer said to the governor, "What do you think?" . . . (The governor speaks to the woman.) "How long have you stayed with that man?"

"Thirty-seven years and nine months."

"Did you ever treat him bad?"

"No."

"Did you ever go with another man?" Everyone got mad. Officers and nephew asked why he asked that. The governor replied that was his business. The woman replied, "No."

Asked if she had any witnesses the woman replied that she had, her two daughters, her brother, and her son (children by a previous marriage). These were sent for. They verified the contention of the woman that she had been good to her deceased husband. They told that when her husband went to sheep camp in winter when it was cold she went with him and cooked for him.

The governor asked the woman how much sheep her husband had, she replied that he had about 461. So he turned to the nephew and told him to give the aunt 230 head of sheep, and kill a sheep giving her half the mutton. The boy wouldn't do it. He talked bad.

"How much will you give her?"

"Five head."

"No you won't, you'll give her 230."

He wouldn't do it. I tell him, "How much do you give her?" This time the boy replied 15 head. By the fourth time he was asked the same question he offered to give 20. The woman was asked how many sheep she would give the boy, but she was in tears and could not answer. The governor turned to the dead man's half brother and asked him how many sheep he thought the boy ought to have. The latter thought that the boy should not have all the sheep because the woman had been kind to her husband, and suggested that she be asked how many sheep she would give the boy. She agreed to give the boy half the flock. The governor then ordered the boy to go to the sheep camp the next morning, count his sheep, and give half to the woman. But the boy was adamant. He refused to give his aunt a single sheep, arguing that she had no children by his uncle. As a result the governor ordered two officers to accompany the boy, the woman, and her brother to the sheep camp to count the sheep and to give the boy only a quarter of the herd. They found that there were 470 head. They gave the boy 10 head and the woman took 460 head.

## CASE 3

So *J* got his sheep, and when he came back he gave some of them to his nephew and they put them in with the sheep of his father-in-law, *R*. *J* went on trading in the East and each time he gave some sheep to his nephew and they kept them with *R*'s.

Now *R* used to get angry easily. And he had lots of women and was always giving them presents. He would go to the sheep camp and butcher sheep for his women, and sometimes he took *J*'s and sometimes his nephew's sheep without asking. They were always quarreling about this, and finally *J*'s nephew decided to take his sheep out. This was in 1910.

Then *J*, and his wife, and children went to Nutria and *R* stayed behind with his other children. *J* didn't take his sheep out at that time because he was always hoping that his nephew and his father-in-law would make up, but they didn't. But *R* was angry about it, because of the quarrel with *J*'s nephew, and so he used to butcher *J*'s sheep all the time without asking, and *J* noticed that each time he got less wool, so he knew what was happening. So then he decided to take his sheep out, and he told his nephew and they both went into Latoma's bunch. They are relations and of the same clan. Now *J* had 110 sheep and his nephew 75.

Then *J* made up the quarrel with his father-in-law. They had always gotten along all right before, and he was not very well satisfied with the new arrangements, so he decided to go back with *R*. He thought it would be the way it had been before. At first everything was all right, but then it started all over again. Whenever the boys went out to camp *R* would tell them to butcher *J*'s sheep. So they quarreled all the time. *J* and his family were living out at Nutria, and when they came in for Shalako or anything else, they did not go to his wife's house but stayed with relatives.

## CASE 4[1]

A death which caused universal regret and distress in Zuni was that of Wewha, undoubtedly the most remarkable member of the tribe. This person was a man wearing a woman's dress. . . . Some declared him to be a hermaphrodite. . . .

She was perhaps the tallest person in Zuni; certainly the strongest, both mentally and physically. Her skin was much like that of the Chinese in color, many of the Zuni having this complexion. During six months' stay in Washington she became several shades lighter. She had a good memory not only for the lore of her people, but for all that she heard of the outside world. She spoke only a few words of English before coming to Washington, but acquired the language with remarkable rapidity, and was soon able to

[1] From Stevenson, *op. cit.*, p. 310.

join in conversation. She possessed an indomitable will and an insatiable thirst for knowledge. Her likes and dislikes were intense. She would risk anything to serve those she loved, but toward those who crossed her path she was vindictive. Though severe she was considered just. At an early age she lost her parents and was adopted by a sister of her father. She belonged to the Badger clan, her foster mother belonging to the Dogwood clan. Owing to her bright mind and excellent memory, she was called upon by her own clan and also by the clans of her foster mother and father when a long prayer had to be repeated or a grace was to be offered over a feast. In fact she was the chief personage on many occasions. On account of her physical strength all the household work requiring great exertion was left for her, and while she most willingly took the harder work from others of the family, she would not permit idleness; all had to labor or receive upbraiding from her. . . . (Wewha suffered from valvular heart disease.)

From the moment her family realized that Wewha was in a serious condition they remained with her, ever ready to be of assistance. The family consisted of the aged foster mother, a foster brother, two foster sisters with their husbands and children, and an own brother with his wife and children. The writer never before observed such attention as every member of the family showed her. The little children ceased their play and stood in silence close to their mothers. . . .

Wewha's death was regarded as a calamity, and the remains lay in state for an hour or more, during which time not only members of the clans to which she was allied, but the rain priests and theurgists and many others including children viewed her."

(*Note:* Pronoun *she* used by writer because she could not think of the deceased, who was a good friend of hers, as anything but a woman.)

## CASE 5

[*N*] was of a rival faction, a man of more independent activities and psychologically more aberrant than the members of the other family. He was a medicine-society headman who in his young manhood was condemned by the priests as a witch and hung by the thumbs until he confessed. He turned informant against the priests and caused the elder brother bow priest to be imprisoned in a government penitentiary. He was a person of great ability, commanding presence, and with a great personal need for achieving eminence, which he had primarily sought in the medicine societies. He knew incredible masses of ritual and song as well as tales. Earlier in his life he had sought prominence in trading and making money, but as he said, "That was no good." He had used this wealth to build one of the annually required new houses for entertaining the Shalako and he was no longer active in trading. More lately he had gained position as the Zuni representative in transactions with the whites . . . and was governor of Zuni, a secular office.[1]

[The following additional material on *N* is based on information from Dr. Ruth Bunzel:]

[1] From Benedict, Introduction to "Zuni Mythology." p. xxxix.

N came from a family that held the bow priesthood. His father had been a scalp chief. N himself belonged to two war societies—the Cactus and the Big Fire. He was no doubt influenced by the war culture. As a youth, N had worked outside of Zuni for some Mexican, and he had traveled about a bit. He lived in one of the farming communities rather than in Zuni proper. He had been governor a number of times and was heartily disliked. He was a violent person and bore numerous animosities against people and couldn't be trusted in his stories about others.

Toward his paralytic wife N showed great devotion. He was also devoted to his grandchildren. At his funeral none but a very few close friends came. True, it was the day before an important ceremonial dance and all the people were busy preparing. But that probably made little difference.

He was a rake and loved to boast of all the women he had had.

### CASE 6

He comes out of the house near the graveyards where there are witches. They caught him stealing once so probably he's the same. No one likes him. He thinks he's smart and he'll tell a person right out he doesn't like him.

He quarreled with his aunts. He took all his father's things and wouldn't let his brothers and sisters have anything or his aunts.

His father was Q. He used to be married to our aunt. He was the nicest man in Zuni. His father died in 1919. P had a few sheep—as soon as his father died he took all of his father's sheep and corn. They were at Nutria. His aunts heard it and called the officers. The officers made him give up half to his aunts and half brothers. . . . P stole sheep from the Navaho near Nutria.

### CASE 7

S was always a nice boy. Even as a child he was never naughty, and before he was grown up he was interested in working in the fields. Even as a young boy he knew how to make moccasins and do all kinds of work. He was never any trouble to his sisters; he never bothered them to wash his hair. And he would stay at home in the evenings and make dresses and moccasins and other things for the children. Everyone wanted to marry S because he was such a good worker and never gambled. Then one day his brother-in-law's friend's wife said, "I think we'll marry our sister to your brother." So when he came home he talked about it. Now S never went around with girls; he was always too busy working, and in the evenings he stayed home and made things for the children. Then all of a sudden one evening he went out, He went out to the east of the village where the girls go for water, and he met his girl. And after about three nights he married her. He was married to her for about two years, and then she got smallpox and got blind. They never had any children and when she got blind he left her, and came to his sister's house.

He didn't marry again for a long time. Then he married a girl who lived a few doors away. He was always working hard, so this girl wanted to marry him, and finally he married her. He was only married a short time.

Her mother was a cripple and so cross that *S* could not bear to live with her. So he left his wife. He had no children from her either.

About this time he used to go hunting, and he always killed lots of deer. Then he married again. He married *N*'s daughter. He was only married to her about a year. While he was away at sheep camp they started to practice for the Santu dance. He came back for the dance. He went to his sister's house and brought her meat. While he was eating his sister told him that the people were saying that his wife was in the Comanche dance. He wouldn't believe it. Only single girls dance. So they said it was true. Next day they danced. *S* wouldn't go see the dance because his wife was dancing and he was ashamed because he knew that the people would make fun of him. He had been going around with another woman, the one he later married, and his wife knew it, so that is probably why she did this to disgrace him.

After the dance he went to her house to get his clothes, and he stayed with her for a few months. Then right away he married his present wife. He never came back to his own house for a single night.

## CASE 8

*H*, married, about forty to forty-two years old. Corn clan, child of Sun clan. No society. He likes to dance. He is Koyemci in the winter, when the regular appointees do not come out. He dances in Muhewa. He used to belong to Muhewa but his father quarreled, and he resigned and went into Uptsananwa. He likes to dance and will come in from Pescado to dance in something like Buffalo or Comanche if they have it.

First he was married to a woman at Kushilowa. He had one child, a little girl. He is terribly jealous. His father-in-law was Sayataca mosona, and he didn't like all the men coming into the house all the time for their meetings. So he quarreled with his wife and left. That winter he was Koyemci. He took the part of Itsepaca, the one who is always looking for quarrels. So one night he went back to his wife. He went into the back room to go to sleep and his wife said to him, "Why don't you come every night? You are just like what you were acting." He said, "What do you mean?"

"Well, you were Itsepaca, the one who is always quarreling. You i..d better dress that way always." At that he became very angry and he got up and walked out of the house and never came back.

He stayed for a while with his people, and then he married again. After they had been married a short time she had a baby and she died and the baby died too.

The next year he married *L*. He has been living with her for seven years and they have four children. He is terribly jealous. He works hard and is very generous, and usually he is very kind to everyone. But he gets angry easily, and when he is angry he says hard words. Last year he asked his father-in-law and his brothers-in-law to come out and help him cut his wheat, because he had a b..g crop of wheat. Everyone was busy and no one could go out to Pescado to help him. So he said he would burn the field for spite, and then they would not get any of it. They told him not to say such terrible things, but just to go ahead and do the best he could, because everyone was busy. So he went ahead and cut most of it, and while it was lying in the field a heavy rain came and washed it all away. He only saved six sacks, and the field would have yielded twenty. Then everyone thought that he had been punished for his hard words, and he thought so too and was ashamed.

## CASE 9

When *H* was a young boy he married a rich girl at Hekapawa. She was a nice girl and good looking and rich, but she was terribly jealous. Whenever *H* went out after supper for a little while and came home late from his meetings she would pinch him and kick him when he went to bed. They had one child, a daughter, who died at birth. He stayed with this woman a long time, about three years. He always thought she would get over being jealous, but she never did.

Then he left her and married *Q*'s mother. Her name was *L*. She was even prettier than his first wife, and he liked her better than any woman he had ever had. They had two children, a boy *Q*, and a girl. But she was jealous too. He stayed with her a long time, about ten years.

Then he started going with *K*. She was married to *T*, the chief bow priest, and *P* was their child. He was a little boy then, and *H* was still married to *L*. Then one night *T* came home and found them sleeping together, and he left his wife. Then *K* told *H* that he would have to marry her because he had gotten her into trouble and now she had no one to take care of her. *H* did not want to marry her, he liked *L* better, but he said to her, "I know that you have no shame. You would come after me in my wife's house, so I will have to marry you." So he stayed there and never came back to his wife.

That was in the fall. He went out with *K* to bring in watermelons. In the afternoon *L* came to his mother's house. She had *H*'s two children with her. She was very angry. She said to his mother, "Where is their father? I saw him go out with that woman, and I am going to fight her." His mother tried to quiet her. She said "Don't fight her. She is strong like a man, because she is a Bear woman." Then *L* saw them coming and she left the children in the house and ran out. She was wearing a large apron, and she filled it with stones, and as they came along she pelted them with stones as they came past the corrals. *K* jumped out of the wagon without waiting for the horses to stop and went for *L*. *H* just ducked his head and laughed. All the people were watching them and laughing.

Then they came into the house. *L* said, "Now we'll fight. You are a big woman but I am not afraid of you. Whoever wins will have him." She picked up a big log from the fireplace and went for *K*. Each of them grabbed one of *H*'s arms and they began to pull him. He laughed. The children were frightened, and their grandmother took them out and took them down to the chili garden.

I don't know what happened next, but presently *L* came out of the house and came down to the chili garden and got her children and went home. *H* and *K* had already left by the back door.

After that *H* stayed with *K*. But he used to go and stay with *L* sometimes too. One spring he went there and stayed for a long time, but she married someone else and he didn't go back any more.

*Bibliography*

BENEDICT, RUTH F.: *Patterns of Culture*, Houghton Mifflin Company, Boston, 1934.

———: "Psychological Types in the Cultures of the Southwest," *Proceedings, 23d International Congress of Americanists*, pp. 572–581, New York, 1928.

———: "Zuni Mythology," *Columbia University Contributions to Anthropology*, Vol. 21, 1934.

BUNZEL, RUTH L.: "Introduction to Zuni Ceremonialism," *47th Annual Report, Bureau of American Ethnology*, pp. 467–544, 1932.

———: "Zuni Katcinas," *ibid.*, pp. 837–1086.

: "Zuni Texts," *Publications of the American Ethnological Society*, 15, New York, 1933.

———: Unpublished field notes. Case histories and material on property.

CUSHING, FRANK H.: "My Experiences in Zuni," *The Century Magazine*, N. S., No. 3, pp. 191–207, 500–511, 1883.

———: "Zuni Breadstuffs," *Publication of the Museum of the American Indian, Heye Foundation*, 8, New York, 1920.

KROEBER, A. L.: "Zuni Kin and Clan," *Anthropological Papers of the American Museum of Natural History*, Vol. 18, Part 2, New York, 1917.

PARSONS, ELSIE C.: "Ceremonial Friendship at Zuni," *American Anthropologist*, Vol. 19, No. 1, 1917.

———: "Notes on Zuni," I, II, *Memoirs of the American Anthropological Association*, Vol. 4, No. 3, 1927.

STEVENSON, MATILDA C.: "The Religious Life of the Zuni Child," *5th Annual Report of the American Bureau of Ethnology*, Washington, 1887.

———: "The Zuni Indians," *23d Annual Report of the American Bureau of Ethnology*, Washington, 1904.

In addition to the above listed sources much invaluable information about the Zuni was obtained from conversations with and from the lectures of Dr. Ruth Benedict, and from a number of discussions with Dr. Ruth Bunzel. A number of revisions were made in the text at the suggestion of Dr. Benedict and of Dr. Bunzel.

# CHAPTER XI

## THE BATHONGA OF SOUTH AFRICA

### by IRVING GOLDMAN

The Bathonga are a Bantu people settled on the eastern coast of South Africa extending from the neighborhood of St. Lucia Bay on the Natal coast up to the Sabie River to the north. These people, numbering about 750,000, represent no "true national unity" and are hardly conscious that they form a definite nation. The name Thonga or "Slave" was applied to them by the warlike Zulu in the South, who in the period between 1815 and 1830 enslaved most of the Thonga. The real unit of the Bathonga nation is the extended local group of kinsmen, "a small collectivity of some hundreds or thousands of souls,"[1] governed by a hereditary chief, the lineal descendant of an original ancestral chief to whom all members are related. A smaller unit is the family group of a patriarchal headman, his wives, his sons and their wives, his unmarried daughters, and his younger brothers, all living together in a circle of huts forming the familiar South African kraal. Though each kraal is an economically independent unit, in which each member owes implicit respect and obedience to the patriarchal headman, all the villages comprising the local group are bound to the chief by ties that are mystically phrased.

Within the circle of the low thorn fence surrounding the kraal, the family patriarch seeks to add to the number of huts by purchasing more wives; wives who will add to his material well-being by tilling the fields and bearing him children and who will bring wealth and strength to the village. To this end he must have the support of the deities (his family ancestors), who stand in intimate relationship to him as his personal gods. He purchases their support by meager sacrifices of small morsels of meat and some stale beer. When the calamities of drought and pestilence strike the country, the family gods are of no avail.

[1] Henri A. Junod, *Life of a South African Tribe*, Vol. 1, p. 339.

Then the gods of the nation are appealed to, the ancestors of the chief, in a huge national sacrifice in which all groups partici- pate. Every Thongan is tied to the capital, the kraal of the chief, by still other obligations: taxes, military service, juridical disputes, the boy's initiation school. Nevertheless the true focus of Thonga life is in the kraal; the aim of each Thongan is material well-being as represented by abundant crops, beer, and the precious oxen, for which wives can be purchased.

## Economic Background

The basis of economic life in Bathonga is in agriculture and husbandry of livestock, the latter occupation being solely the work of the boys and young men, the former chiefly the labor of women. The food supply is further supplemented by hunting and fishing. Though in the main each kraal is a self-sustaining unit, the manufacture of baskets, pottery, and ironwork is centralized in the hands of well-recognized craftsmen. Trade is important and well developed.

The principal grain products are millet (kaffir corn), used in the brewing of beer, and maize. The oldest known cereal to the Thonga, millet, is ritually treated with the juice of a magical root said to keep ants away. Only the reigning family possesses the root, and at sowing time, after the chief's fields have been planted with millet, the root is passed out among the subchiefs, who treat a quantity of seed with the root and distribute it among the villages to be mixed with the untreated seed. It is forbidden for any to sow millet before the chief and his subchiefs. Religious sanctions apply also to the growth of the kaffir pea. Thus it is forbidden for any man to enter a field in which the vegetable is growing. Pumpkins are subject to the hierarchy tabu illustrated for millet;[1] nor are girls allowed to walk among the leaves. Fruit trees are not cultivated, but the people make use of a wide variety of wild fruits plucked from trees growing in the vicinity.

In July, when the appearance of the pink and white flowered lilies over the country indicates that winter has passed, the

[1] The hierarchy prohibition is "so conscientiously believed in that, should an old man keep the people waiting and be too slow in planting his pumpkins, another will go to the field and plant some seeds in it without the old man's knowledge; then people will dare to plant in their gardens. Transgression of this tabu is said to be punished by lumbago." Junod, *op. cit.*, Vol. 2, p. 14.

women look to their hoes and prepare for the clearing of new
fields and the cultivation of marshland. The former work is
very difficult. With an ax the woman cuts down the small
trees, sparing only a few shade and fruit trees, until the field is
cleared and she can attack it with her hoe. The months of
August, September, and October are spent in this labor. If,
however, much land has been cleared in the preceding year, the
woman devotes herself to the cultivation of marshes. When the
rains begin early in September, the regular sowing begins.
The father of a family has his own field, but the mother cares
for a larger one. Every girl sows her own field. Further, each
owner of a field must sow all the principal vegetables and cereals
in it, with this exception that, because of a tabu, men may not
plant peas. The work must be done hastily to take advantage
of the last rains. To facilitate matters, a woman whose fallow
ground is beyond her own capacity to work will invite her neighbors to a *djimo* (working party). Such invitations are willingly
accepted, for not only has the woman prepared large jugs of
beer, but her neighbors know that they can depend upon her
assistance when they in turn may need it. All work rapidly to
finish the job in one morning.[1] When the grain has begun to
grow, the fields are attacked by hordes of sparrows who come
to eat the grains. Then women and children sit out in the fields
day and night, setting up a terrific clamor with tin cans, and other
"musical instruments," until the birds as a flock fly to the next
field, where they are similarly received.

At harvest time each woman and every man who owns a field
harvests his (or her) own crops, which he (or she) keeps as far
as possible in his (or her) own storehouse. The men prepare the
drying floors, and have already made the necessary repairs to
their storehouses. The women do the threshing. With the
completion of the harvest there begins a round of festivities;
beer parties and visiting between friends and relatives.

Oxen[2] are owned by any *numzane* (headman) and are kept in a
corral in the center of the kraal along with such additional head

---

[1] "One may see them, some fifty black bodies toiling vigorously, making
the sand fly . . . each one urging the other to still greater exertions and
all hurrying to finish the job." Junod, *op. cit.*, Vol. 2, p. 24.

[2] Oxen were once far more numerous among the Thonga, but the herds
have been severely decimated by Zulu raids and by plague. Oxen are

of cattle as have been entrusted to his care by his neighbors, too poor to undertake the routine of herding for themselves.[1]   Herding is entrusted to the young men of the village.   Goats, which are more common than cattle, are owned by practically everyone. They are cared for by the smaller boys, who are given the milk to drink.   (No grown person would touch goats' milk.[2])   Poultry, the most common of all livestock, is used extensively for sacrifice and for its flesh.

Big game is plentiful in Bathonga territory.   Elephants are found in various sections, hippopotamuses swarm in the Nkomati and Limpopo Rivers, sable antelope, the gnu, and the smaller varieties of antelope are still relatively abundant.   Traps and pitfalls are used to trap the animals, but most of the game is caught by regular hunters, men who have made a trade of hunting and form a special class of *phisa*, as distinguished from ordinary hunters.   The phisa have their own hunting charms and their own way of living.   "They sometimes live in particular villages, especially the hunters of hippopotamuses, and partake more or less of the nature of magicians."[3]   The art is passed on from father to son.   Apart from skill in tracking and bringing down dangerous beasts, the most important requisite is magical power.   Thus, before a man goes to hunt a hippopotamus he calls his daughter to him and has intercourse with her; he anoints himself with drugs, and keeps numerous tabus.   Generally a man and his son, armed with assagais, enter the forest to track their prey.   Upon meeting it they hurl their spears and call for help, and other hunters rush up to finish the kill.   If a hippopotamus or an elephant has been killed, the carcass is not touched until an emissary of the chief has come to do the butchering and to remove certain parts of the body that are known to possess magic.

The specialization in big-game hunting is carried even further. In certain villages there is a special group of hunters devoted

---

chiefly important as negotiable property in the purchase of a bride.   At the present time, though, iron hoes referred to as "oxen" are used in bride purchase.   This is discussed in a subsequent section.

[1] A fee of a calf is demanded by the caretaker.   Junod, *op. cit.*, Vol. 2, p. 48.

[2] They have no objection to milk from the oxen.

[3] Junod, *op. cit.*, Vol. 2, p. 56.

entirely to the hunting of the hippopotamus. A special drug, which they possess, and which they pass on only to their sons, gives them special powers over the animal; but additional sanctions are required before a hippopotamus is finally killed. One of the conditions, incest with the daughter, has already been mentioned; but in addition, as soon as the hippopotamus has been speared with a harpoon-like assagai, the hunter rushes to his house and orders his wife to shut herself into her hut and lie quietly. By homeopathic magic it is hoped that the animal will also be quiet and offer no resistance. When the animal has been finally brought down by the numerous spears of the villagers, who have been called to assist the principal hunter, the thrower of the first assagai performs the act of *lurulula*,[1] which will give him great courage. The meat is then divided among all the villagers, with a heavy portion laid aside as the chief's. The principal hunter eats the first portion of meat ritually.[2]

The organization of fishing follows both individualistic and collective patterns. In the first case, a man in his own canoe drops a hook and line and catches his fish. But most fish are probably caught in a collective enterprise.[3] At the command of the chief, all the men of the local group appear on a given day to dredge fish from the bottom of a lake that has been drying up. Each man, working as long as he chooses, scoops up the fish in a small hand basket and then attaches them to a string. At the end of the day the men compare their strings and give one fish from each string to the chief. Another method of fishing that involves some degree of collective participation is the use of the weir. Such a trap is constructed by an individual for his own use, but on the day of its inauguration he must permit all his neighbors and visitors to make use of it if they choose. The fish, however, must all be consumed on the spot.

[1] The hippopotamus is laid on its back, and the hunter crawling between its hind legs crawls up its belly to the chest. He thus partakes of the odor of the animal; future hippopotamuses will take him for one of them.

[2] The ritual of *luma*, the eating of the first flesh. The ritual is also held with the eating of the first fruits of the harvest, described in a subsequent section.

[3] This is simply my estimate. Junod does not refer to this point. However, it must be clear that the exhaustion of a dried-up lake of fish yields a considerable amount of fish.

In the handicrafts, as in big-game hunting, specialization is carried far. Pottery, though not a restricted art, in the sense that one inherits the knowledge and the right to exercise it, is nevertheless limited to those regions where potter's clay is available. From these districts comes the pottery supply of the entire country. Further, the manufacture of clay pots is essentially a woman's occupation. It is difficult work, requiring skill, patience, and above all supernatural sanction. Especially at the crucial period of firing the pot the woman must observe numerous tabus, including sexual abstention.

Similarly, the manufacture of the large *ngalu* baskets,[1] though the materials for their construction are more available, is more or less concentrated in the hands of a relatively small number of skilled male workers.

"The art of basket making is by no means commonplace. Practiced by men only, it is, in certain families, in certain villages handed down from father to son . . . children with a natural taste for such work are initiated into its mysteries by their parents. . . . In the environs of Lourenco Marques . . . lived the family of Tumbene famous for its ngalu. One of these sons inherited his father's talent . . . and, when he was but a lad, people came to him from far and wide to have their old baskets repaired."[2]

Just as in pottery, beyond the fact of its restriction to men, basket making is free to all who care to learn the techniques and are willing to devote themselves continuously and patiently for days and even weeks to such work.

The Bathonga have also developed the arts of woodcarving and metallurgy to a relatively high degree, and skilled workers in these crafts are known throughout the country.[3]

In contrast to the specialized industries of basketry, pottery woodcarving, and metallurgy, housebuilding is practiced by all

[1] These baskets measure six feet or more in circumference and are used for the storage of nuts and maize.

[2] Junod, *op. cit.*, Vol. 2, p. 109.

[3] Muhlati, a sculptor, was "famous throughout the country for his talent." Junod, *op. cit.*, Vol. 2, p. 119.

Junod mentions as well that large carved canoes are made, but gives no further information on how they are made or who makes them. It would be my guess that since woodcarving is specialized probably the canoes also are made by skilled mechanics.

men.  Each man is his own architect, but the requirements of the work demand the concerted effort of many men.  A man calls the men of his village together to construct the conical thatch roof that is then set on the house walls.  For their assistance they are liberally regaled with beer.  Also, as in the field-sowing situation, it is tacitly understood that such assistance will be reciprocated.  With the roof in place, the thatch mats, that have also been made by the men, are sewed on by two men, one outside and one inside the house, who ply a huge needle, one pushing it through from the outside, the other returning it. Finally, having made and attached the door, the men's job is done, and the woman of the house carefully plasters the walls and lays the hard clay and dung floor.[1]

Correlated with the specialization of crafts is a considerable dependence upon trade.  Barter was already well developed when the first white traders came to the country.[2]

In comparison with other cultures, absence of competitive activities is quite striking.  In the only situation where there is any suggestion of competition, the collective fishing enterprise, where the men are reported as comparing their catch, there is no indication that individuals strive to outdo one another.  On the contrary, each man stops fishing at will.  In a more definite way, the essentially noncompetitive economic organization in Bathonga can be demonstrated in the ownership of agricultural land and in the storage of food supplies.  It has been observed that each member of the family owns his or her own field,[3] and further that the food is stored "as far as possible" in individual storehouses.  Yet the individualistic display goes no further. In the use of food the Bathonga village is clearly communal, and, as will be shown later, each person in the village at a given

[1] It might be of interest to compare this sexual division of labor in the construction of a house with Zuni, where after the man has constructed the walls and laid the heavy roof beams, the wife plasters the walls.

[2] When knowledge spread that a white trading ship was in port great trading expeditions were organized by the natives to bring gold, elephant tusks, and amber from the interior to the waterways.

Unfortunately Junod gives no more than brief mention of the trading situation.

[3] Junod does not make clear whether the owner of a field is each adult, each married person, or whether even children own their own fields.  It is my guess that only married persons own agricultural land.

meal will eat a little of all the food which each housewife has prepared.

A significant correlate to the noncompetitive economic organization is the abundance of land suitable for cultivation.[1] All land is conceived of as belonging to the chief, and is freely distributed by him to all settlers[2] in return for their pledge of citizenship and their willingness to pay taxes. Indeed, each settler is a blessing to the chief, for where land is abundant labor is considered more valuable. Land under cultivation means a greater source of taxes for the chief. In addition the chief welcomes man power to swell his army and to labor for him in his own village. Once assigned, land belongs to the person to whom it is given. Though it can be inherited, it is never sold. Generally, the land allotted to a family head is far more than can be cultivated. The family head may then distribute part of such land to his kinsmen.

Thus, with land plentiful and the soil for the most part fertile, the abundance of food each individual can enjoy depends entirely upon the industry of his wives in cultivating the fields. It is not land that the Bathonga must have but women. However, in a polygamous culture women are scarce. In Bathonga they must be purchased. This might be expected to be a point of conflict among all eligible males, yet the Bathonga social organization has met this crucial situation with a minimum of competition. And each individual, depending mainly upon factors under his own control, attains at middle age all the cultural blessings he has been striving for—abundance of wealth, of wives, of children, and of friends.

## SOCIAL STRUCTURE

The Bathonga social structure is built on a hierarchy of age and rank. At the peak of the structure stand the chief and the royal family. In each kraal the headman, the father or older brother, is the individual most respected and most feared. Fol-

[1] In Ronga district 100,000 persons occupy 5,000 square miles. "The country could easily support three or four times its present population." Junod, *op. cit.*, Vol. 2, p. 5.

[2] In spite of the distribution of land according to need, it is not unusual for a "favorite at court, a clever flatterer, or one free with beer to be given the most fertile land, while a less fortunate person would be given only a barren hillside." *Ibid.*, p. 7.

lowing him in respect and responsibility is his next younger brother and so on. Among children the same age distinctions hold. The little boys must serve their elder brothers. Similarly in the capital of the local group, the village of the chief, the same distinctions as to age rank are rigidly maintained. Firmly sanctioned by religion and social custom the behavior norms set by this principle of hierarchy can be altered only in rare cases by an exceptional individual.

Though each Bathongan is tied to the capital by specific ritual and economic obligations as well as by a mystically phrased bond of union with the chief, the representative of the ancestors, the real focus of his existence is in the patriarchal village. "The Bathonga village is not a haphazard agglomeration of people. It is a social organism whose composition is well defined and which is regulated by strict laws. After all it is but an enlarged family: the headman and the old people who have fallen to his charge, his wives, his younger brothers and their wives, his married sons, his unmarried sons and daughters."[1]  In this grouping of kinsmen the Bathongan fits into a definite pattern of obligations, the most fixed of which are his relations to the headman. As the family priest, as the most mature male, as the one who has a mystical communion with the earth under him,[2] the headman is the source of administrative authority in the village. He is the magistrate in local disputes, the man who will thrash the small boys if they plunder gardens or if they allow their goats to do so. If a kraal is to be repaired or a fence built, the headman calls the younger men to do the work. At the informal councils on the men's square, when important matters, such as arrangements for the purchase of a bride, are to be discussed, the headman is the chairman. His opinion is respected. Moreover the headman is responsible for the debts of the men under him.[3]  When

---

[1] Junod, op. cit., Vol. 1, p. 280.

[2] There is a mystic tie between this man (headman) and the social organism which is under him. Should he die, the village dies also . . . it is not abandoned at once. The whole year of mourning will elapse before the moving. But as soon as the widows and the property have been distributed, the successor of the deceased will go and found his own village and the old one will remain a ruin. Should anyone else die, his hut will be merely thrown into the bush and the village will not be abandoned." Ibid., p. 289.

[3] Actually all members of the kraal are expected to assist one another financially.

a younger brother wishes to take a wife, the headman will supply the *lobola*, the bride price. Or if that brother is lax in his payments of the lobola to his parents-in-law, the indignant father-in-law will appeal to the headman. Withal the headman's control over the village under him is not autocratic, for in spite of the religious sanctions and the deeply trained habits of obedience to one's elders, any younger brother may, if dissatisfied, leave the village. In more serious cases of disaffection due to misrule, the younger brothers may appeal to their paternal uncles to have the headman removed. For the headman such drastic action is a major calamity. He is despised. People will say of him, "He is a fool! He breaks the village. He is overcome by the village."[1] But such an occurrence is rare.

The village consists of a number of round mud-plastered houses, with conical thatch roofs, arranged in a circular horseshoe. In an average small village, there may be no more than five such houses, surrounded by a low thorn fence to ward off evil witches. In the center of the horseshoe is a fenced-in circular cattle kraal. Toward the gate, shaded by spreading trees, is the men's council square, the *hubo*, where on a hot afternoon the men gather to drink beer and relate the latest gossip. Two huts on either side of the front gate are the living quarters for the young unmarried boys and girls respectively. The headman's hut is at the rear, apart from the regular circle. Each of his wives occupies one of the rear huts. The huts forming the front half (toward the front gate) of the village are the dwellings of the wives of younger brothers. The headman visits his wives in rotation, spending a month with each. When he chooses he retires to his own hut. His younger brothers, however, do not possess a private hut, but live with their wives.

Relations within the village are marked by an easy-going communal attitude toward food and by respect for age and rank. When an ox has been slaughtered the division of the meat follows a specific pattern; the best part goes to the headman and the liver is thrown to old people.[2] But at the daily evening meal

---

[1] Junod, *op. cit.*, Vol. 1, p. 303.

[2] An ox is divided in the following way: headman—breast and viscera in the breast; wives—tripe, heart, kidneys, all of which are put together in the stomach; brother—one of the hind legs; next brother—a foreleg; elder son—other hind leg; younger son—foreleg; in-laws—tail, all hind parts;

all share their food alike, except that the husband gets a larger portion. Following is Junod's excellent description of a typical evening meal. "In every yard the mistress of the hut has cooked her mealies and her sauce in different pots, and, when the sun sets, she distributes the contents in wooden or earthen plates. The largest is for the husband. He is sitting on the *bandla*[1] with his companions, the other men of the village, and the youths waiting for the meal. All these plates, generally, carried by small girls and boys, converge on the men's gathering. All do not contain the ordinary mealies pap; some are filled with manioc, some with sweet potatoes, etc. The men attack the first one, all of them taking the food with their fingers. They pass on to the second plate and so on to the last one. Meanwhile the mother has filled other small plates, one for the girls, one for the boys, one for herself. She has even sent to each of the other women of the village a little of her cooking, and others have done the same for her; so each member of the community when he or she has finished the meal will have eaten a little of all that has been cooked on all the fires. It is impossible to imagine a more perfect communism than this as regards food."[2] Such communism in food is carried even further in the village. In a case narrated by Junod, two women took ungrudgingly upon their shoulders the care of all the inhabitants of a village where the other women were incapable of doing any work.[3]

This is but one example of the closely integrated and friction-less pattern of village life, a pattern in which each individual occupies a fixed position with regard to another, and in which his social advancement follows a slow but steady pace. The small boy who watches over the goats and is bullied by his older brother, who is an ox herdsman, is recompensed, when he grows older, by the satisfaction of being able to bully his younger brother. Thus, though each younger sibling may be required to respect his elder brother, some day he will in his turn be the eldest in his group.

---

old people—the liver. The head is divided among all the men of the village. *Ibid.*, p. 298.

[1] The bandla differs from the hubo; it is a fenced-in men's sanctuary which the women may penetrate only when bringing food. Young men are responsible for keeping it clean.

[2] Junod, *op. cit.*, Vol. 1, p. 287.

[3] *Ibid.*, p. 288.

For the most part, the rule of hierarchy is only formally expressed.[1] In everyday relations, in the discussions on the hubo, in the games that occupy a good part of the man's time, and in the beer drinking there is a great deal of comradeship among all the men. Having a considerable amount of leisure they are frequently thrown together. In the council each man is given a voice. On the other hand, the women, working in their own gardens, in their own front yards over their own pots, are given far less opportunity for the expression of that sociability which is so characteristic of the men. But at night when the meal is finished, all the villagers, men, women, and children gather about one of the firesides to play games and tell stories, or ask riddles. The women are the great story-tellers, and they can amuse the company for a good part of the evening with their tales.

With the exception of conflicts arising over payments of the bride price, relations between villages follow the same easy pattern of ready hospitality. Strangers are always welcomed with food and shelter, and it is a point of pride for a man to be known as hospitable. At the great harvest feasts, the luma, when the sour wine has been brewed in quantities, there is feasting and revelry in all the villages. When one village has finished its supply of wine, all its members move on to the next one to continue the great round of drinking. And even when no such national festival is in progress, men are always visiting other villages to drink beer. Nor is it uncommon when word spreads that one village has just brewed a quantity of beer for the neighbors to gather, each bringing his own calabash. People eat and drink together as long as there is plenty in the storehouses.[2] And the more wives there are in a village, the greater will be the supply in the storehouses.

Women are, therefore, essential to the well-being of the community. Marriage, the purchase of a wife and if possible many wives, is the great goal of the male Bathonga. In the pursuit of this goal he is assisted by the village.

The Bathonga are endogamous within the local group, but a wife must be taken from another village, preferably from the village where the mother came from. When a young man has

---

[1] In addressing an elder person it is not becoming to call him by his name.
[2] Junod, *op. cit.*, Vol. 1, p. 311.

decided to get married and has accumulated the necessary lobola cattle to purchase the bride he bedecks himself with his most brilliant ornaments and his finest skins and, in the company of two friends, proceeds to the village of his mother's brother to look over the girls. Having selected the girl, he returns home and informs his parents. They send a go-between, some middle-aged man, to woo the girl. The latter makes the necessary arrangements with the girl's father, providing the girl is amenable to the marriage, and the betrothal date is set. Next there are betrothal visits, during which two or three of the groom's best friends visit the village of his fiancée and are greeted by a similar group of the girl's friends. These people spend the night together. After a return visit by the friends of the fiancée, the stage is set for the lobola feast, where the bride price is paid. On both sides there is great activity. The bride's relatives work busily to prepare the quantities of beer that will be consumed. The boy's relatives gather together the fifty or more iron hoes that will constitute the bride price.[1] On the day set the boy's relatives with the elder men who bear the hoes proceed in a long procession to the bride's village. There the girl's brothers stand watch over the gate. With sticks they attempt to repulse the young men in the procession and a sham battle in which real blows are exchanged takes place. But in the midst of this tumult the old men bearing the hoes arrive and quiet is restored.

In the village square the hoes are laid in rows and counted in the presence of many witnesses. The bride's family gather to ascertain if the number agreed upon is there. When this is done, beer is passed around. Then the old men gather together in a quiet hut to chat and drink.

When the bride is brought out, the formalized hostility between the respective families is once more resumed. The groom's men call to the bride, "As you are becoming the wife of our brother and coming into our village, try to leave all your vices behind. Do not steal any longer! Forsake your bad ways and become a good girl!" To this the bride's relatives shout in return:

"You have nothing to boast about! Give up wearying the people! She is far too good for you! Does not everybody

---

[1] Formerly the bride price was paid in oxen. Now that these animals are more scarce they are replaced by iron hoes. The iron hoes though are still called "oxen."

know the wild pranks of your son and the dishonor of your family!"[1]

So they continue, some even going so far as to bombard each other with half-chewed matter taken from a goat's stomach.

It has been suggested earlier that marriage among the polygamous Bathonga might lead to competition between men for the relatively small number of women. Actually the conflicts that do arise over women are of a somewhat different sort, though definitely related to a more basic problem, that of wife purchase. All women must be paid for, and unless the young man has collected or borrowed enough iron hoes to pay for his bride he must remain unmarried. It is this fact that makes the bride's father eager to collect the full lobola. For he uses it to purchase a bride for his son, or for a younger brother. Thus, of all the litigations appearing before the court of the chief over 90 per cent involve disputes about the payment of lobola. The competition for women, then, can be said to be between villages and is expressed in the quarrels over bride-price payment, payments which are crucial to the replacement of the girl who has been taken from the kraal.

Within a village conflicts that might arise between various males over a bride are muted by two conditions inherent in the Bathonga social structure. In the first place, a bride is viewed in the kraal as a *woman*. The material wealth which she will contribute is to the benefit of all.[2] A headman will therefore gladly assist his sons or younger brothers in acquiring wives to contribute to the general prosperity of the village. In the second place, each young man can take a wife only after his older brother has married, and according to the rules of inheritance will inherit the widows of his elder brother. A younger brother has but to wait long enough and he too will be a headman with many wives. Sex as a problem is hardly related to marriage.[3] Young men have free relations with the girls of the village.

[1] Junod, *op. cit.*, Vol. 1, p. 110.

[2] This is true in the sense that in the community of food previously described each member of the community shares in the general condition of abundance that would characterize a village in which there are many women.

[3] The two instances of suicide which Junod cites are cases which involve personal choice in sex in situations tabu in Bathonga culture. One is that of a girl forced to marry an old man (*op. cit.*, Vol. 1, p. 281), and the other,

The desire for a wife is related more closely to the desire for wealth.

Bound to one another by marriage, and by ties of kinship, the villages are themselves bound in a number of ways to the national life, to the capital of the chief. Primarily the connection between the villages and the capital is through the bond of group unity, of which the chief is the symbol. It is through the chief that the extended local group becomes conscious of its unity. "Without him it has lost its bearings; it has lost its head."[1] More specifically, the ties between the kraals and the capital can be classified as ceremonial and political. The ties are interrelated, for the chief's political power is fundamentally religious in character.

As the priest of the national gods the chief possesses the supernatural power necessary to insure the fertility of the soil and to promote the increase in crops and animals. Before certain foods can be eaten they must be ritually treated by the chief in the great national festival of *luma*. The aim of the luma is twofold. First, the food must be ritually treated with the royal drug, and, secondly, it must be enjoyed in the order of the hierarchy. Thus, in the case of the *bukanye*, a native plum, the first juice extracted from it is sacrificed to the national gods, then if, after divining bones have been cast, the gods are propitious, the chief takes the next drink. Next, the army is called to the capital and the warriors drink. In this ceremony the bravest, those who have killed an enemy, are especially honored.[2] From the army the luma rites descend to the villages. Here the subchiefs, the younger brothers of the chief, drink first. When they and the headman have tasted of the wine, the rest of the villagers succumb to an orgy of unrestrained drinking. However, the lion's share of the wine prepared for this festival must be sent to the chief

---

of a man who had committed adultery with his elder brother's wife and so could not reenter the family kraal. This latter suicide was planned but not consummated (p. 505).

[1] Junod, *op. cit.*, p. 340.

[2] For those having killed an enemy a special cask of the bukanye is mixed with a magical powder, which will restrain their warlike spirits so that they would not attack any of their own comrades during the ceremony. This group also drinks before the others. The chief, if he has killed an enemy, is also offered this prepared drink. Junod, *op. cit.*, Vol. 1, p. 371.

for his use in entertaining guests. As the culminating rite the chief visits each village and is royally feasted in each.

In an administrative sense the most important tie between the people and the capital is taxation. The chief has a right to a share of the products of the soil, and to a share of the meat from all wild beasts killed in hunting. The hippopotamus, especially, is heavily taxed, half the joints going to the chief. Further, any subject may be required to come to the capital to till a field for the chief, or for his wives, or to repair a kraal or build a hut for a newly taken wife. Fines that are collected for certain offenses also go to the chief.

To maintain control over the villages and to supervise the payment of taxes the chief appoints his sons and near relatives as subchiefs over different parts of the province. Many of his wives are scattered through the province where they are visited at regular intervals.

In addition to these ties, all ablebodied men are drafted into the military service of the extended family group,[1] and young boys at puberty attend an initiation school conducted by the chief.

In its main outlines, the organization of the capital is a direct reflection of the type of organization found in the village. The chief takes his office not through the possession of special abilities but by virtue of his being the eldest son of the reigning chief. In the village, however, the succession is in the collateral line, with brother inheriting from and succeeding brother to the position of headman. In the capital, which is faced with the problem of maintaining a direct line of descent in the elder line (to insure a lineal succession from the original ancestor chief) in harmony with the village pattern of collateral descent, a compromise solution appears to have been reached. The eldest son of the reigning chief assumes the chieftainship upon his father's death, but cannot rule until all his paternal uncles have reigned before him.[2] Under certain conditions the difficulties arising from this situation are a source of friction in Bathonga society.

[1] Warfare is not an original Bathonga pattern but has been grafted on to the culture as a result of close contact with the neighboring Zulu, who are very warlike. The army seems to function mainly as a ceremonial body.

[2] Though Junod does not make it quite clear, it appears that the younger brothers rule as regents for a time "to make the heir grow."

Thus, if a chief dies in his youth, his younger brother will reign for a long time.   Now if the latter is at all popular he may seize the chieftainship for his own family and order the tribe to crown his own son to the exclusion of the rightful heir, who will have been more or less forgotten during these years.   The heir may attempt to gather military support to fight the usurpers, but if he is weak he will keep to himself, full of bitterness and ready to seize any opportunity to assert his rights.   Brothers, also, will not uncommonly dispute the right of succession among themselves.   It was to avoid this, and to insure the succession to the throne of his own son, that Maphunga, the chief of Nondwane, killed as many as four brothers or near relatives.[1]

It is not surprising that the chieftainship should be disputed in view of the great power which the chief wields and the great wealth that he possesses.[2]   Of these, wealth is by no means the least.   For each Bathongan tries to accumulate many wives and add to his stores of beer and food, and the chief stands as the epitome of all that is desired.   He may have as many as thirty wives, great stores of beer, and a variety of food that is continually supplemented through taxation.   "Bathonga tales telling the story of someone who succeeded wonderfully in life often conclude by saying that this person was given a territory and became a chief . . . which seems to be the highest reward for virtue or wisdom."[3]

In spite of the greater wealth of the chief, and the larger size of his village, royalty makes little display.   Except for certain sacred objects possessed by the royal family there is none of the paraphernalia usually associated with royalty.   The village is accessible to visitors.   When they come to pay their respects to the chief they love to discuss the news of the day in the men's square.   There is no lack of beer.

Associated with the chief in settling the rather vague problems of government are a corps of counselors.   These include the principal counselors, the uncles of the chief, men of mature age

[1] Junod, op. cit., Vol. 1, p. 386.

[2] "Endowed with supernatural power which he owes to his magical medicines, feared and sometimes loved by his subjects, having plenty to eat and being richer than any of his people who consent to be taxed, the chief occupies an enviable position."   Op. cit., Vol. 1, p. 380.

[3] Ibid.

who meet to discuss the more serious questions involving the extended local group, and a number of lesser counselors concerned with military and magisterial affairs. Besides this official group the chief has about him a circle of his personal friends who, living near the capital, are ready to answer his every call. To complete the court there are two additional characters, a court herald and a court jester, both of whom are allowed great license in insulting the chief. It is the duty of the former to arouse the chief every morning by singing the praises of the chief's ancestors, compared to whom the present incumbent is quite insignificant. The position is not a hereditary one but open to all those gifted in the art of vituperation. The court jester, however, often inherits his place.

The life of the heir to the chieftainship does not differ very markedly from that of every other boy in Bathonga. He grows up with his age comrades, takes care of the herds, goes through the same initiation rites at pubescence. On the other hand, the dangers of chieftainship demand that certain precautions be taken with the heir. His birth is kept secret, and he is taken at an early age by his mother to live incognito in another village. However, his court training is not neglected. He is surrounded by a group of trusted companions who comprise a miniature court and who insist that his other playmates respect him. The games played are the games of all boys. Only when he is grown, and when the divining bones indicate that the time is auspicious, is the boy brought to the capital to be introduced as the heir. When his official wife[1] is chosen she must be purchased with the "pennies" of all the people, who are in this way linked more closely to the next chief, whose mother they have purchased.[2]

The chief is the source of all law. Disputes which cannot be settled locally by the headman in the village or by the chief's sons, the subchiefs, are brought to the capital for a hearing before

[1] Only after his father's death may the heir take a wife from another clan, who will be the official mother of the next heir. This does not prevent him from taking another woman before the official wife. Children born of any but the officially purchased wife cannot succeed to the throne.

[2] The significance of this purchase is made more clear by the following remark, which parents will make to a boy who chooses to live with his mother's family: "Has your mother not been bought with money?" Junod, *op. cit.*, Vol. 1, p. 226.

the chief's council. Ninety per cent of such civil cases concern the lobola.[1] We have mentioned before the great importance that is attached to the bride price, how it enables the village from which one woman has been taken to purchase another. Normally, a wise father will not allow his daughter to be taken to her husband's kraal until the full bride price has been paid. But frequently when a man is taking a second wife[2] he pays for her on what is very much like our installment plan. The father of the girl is then faced with the task of collecting the balance. Or a young man who is not yet in a position to lobola a bride may abduct her, if she is willing to go along, and pay for her later. Besides these situations in which the lobola is disputed there is, from the legal point of view, a still more perplexing problem arising from divorce. A woman found in adultery may be divorced, and the irate husband then seeks for the return of the purchase money from his father-in-law. Related also to the lobola problem are disputes arising over the collection of debts that have been incurred mainly to purchase a bride. In all these cases, once the court has handed down its decision the issue is settled, for the "Bantu are very peaceful law-abiding people."[3]

Criminal cases are far more rare and with the exception of cases of intentional murder or sorcery they are punished by fines and indemnities. Theft, in which the culprit takes food or other property, is punished by taking an equal amount from him. Similarly in manslaughter, the kin of the guilty person must give a girl to the village of the victim. Insults are common, but no cause for litigation. In none of the above cases does the Bathonga care to inflict punishment.[4] His concern is for the restitution of property that has been lost.

Murder is punished by death inflicted by the court and never results in blood feud. The most serious of all crimes is sorcery. Sorcerers are conceived to be people with an "evil eye" who from motives of hatred or jealousy plot to kill others and eat their flesh. Persons accused of sorcery are put to an ordeal test, and if found guilty are immediately killed.

[1] *Ibid.*, p. 412.

[2] That is, from the same village.

[3] Junod, *op. cit.*, Vol. 2, p. 411.

[4] In this connection, South African natives today feel that punishment of theft by imprisonment is unjust, as it involves no restitution.

Behind the orderly pattern of Bathonga life runs the thread of religion, firmly cementing the individual to the fixed structure of the hierarchy of age and rank. For behind the power of the headman in the village and the chief as the head of the kraal are the supernatural sanctions of the ancestor gods punishing any transgressions against the rule of hierarchy. Each family has its own set of ancestor gods, bothersome old people, who resent any want of respect and are always maneuvering to wheedle more offerings from their relatives on earth. When forgotten they avenge themselves by punishing the luckless relative with illness and misfortune, until they are appeased by suitable offerings of animal flesh and beer. The gods of the nation, the ancestors of the chief, are no different but their scope is wider. As guardians of the extended family group they can afflict the entire country with famine or pestilence. In each village, the headman is the officiating priest; in the capital the chief holds that office. Besides this group of priests there is a class of diviners, men having the special ability, inherited from their fathers, to determine by throwing a set of bones the nature of the ancestors' demands and the amount of sacrifice that will satisfy them. These diviners work for a fee.

Outside the orderly domain of the ancestor gods lies a more frightful realm of the supernatural. Witches, the intensely feared *buloyi*, form an unholy society of monstrous ghouls who fly about at night seeking victims whose flesh they can eat. It is against these witches that the low thorn fence surrounding the Bathonga kraal is erected; it is against these that the Bathonga seeks protective charms. In daylight, the buloyi are men and women with the "evil eye" who have had their evil power transmitted to them through their mother's milk. Only one child can get this power. Among themselves the buloyi are rivals, fighting to steal one another's charms. The stronger buloyi hope to overcome the weaker, and thus add to their own power. For jealous and hateful as they are to ordinary mortals, they are equally vindictive among themselves.

To combat the buloyi are a corps of medicine men, who do not hide their magical powers, and who have all undergone some form of initiation before attaining their particular powers. Commonly, they are drawn from men and women who have been seized with violent maniacal fits, the emotionally unstable, and psychopathic personalities. These people, who have at some time been exorcised by a school of magicians, later become practitioners themselves. But each exorcised person must belong to the society that has cured him. Between schools of magicians, there is, as among the buloyi, great rivalry. Magicians strive to steal one another's drugs. Or it may be that a disciple desires to leave his group and found a new society. This is, of course, very disagreeable to the master magician, who fears competition for fees which he would ordinarily get, so he prays that his disciples' drugs shall become ineffective. This succeeds, and the disciple returns much chastened. Only when the master is dead may the disciple take his place.

War fits but loosely into the total configuration of Bathonga culture. According to tradition they were originally peaceable but were taught the art of war from the neighboring Zulu, from whom they adopted their entire formal military pattern. Though for the Zulu war was an opportunity for glory and conquest, the Bathonga phrase their fighting as primarily defensive. In no instance did they show themselves to be able warriors.

"Bathonga, and especially Ba-Ronga, did not show themselves to be very able warriors. Want of discipline, mutual distrust, timidity resulting in frequent retreats, inability to follow up their successes, such were the main causes of their defeat. The wild soldiers of Maputju, who considered themselves to be the equals of the genuine Zulu, showed their courage only when there was no danger."[1]

To induce martial spirit in the warriors, the chief's medicine man would administer a potion to them that was designed to fill them with hatred for the enemy. They would be sprinkled with another preparation to make them invulnerable. If warriors refused to return to battle after having suffered a particularly heavy defeat, they were then subjected to the humiliation of fetching water for the chief while crawling on their knees, or of putting out a brush fire with their hands. A hero in battle was covered with glory. If he had killed an enemy he was granted the privilege of performing the war dance before the chief. But he was also considered dangerous and had to undergo ritual treatment before he could return to normal life again. Adopted also from the Zulu was the custom of counting honors in battle. Thus,

[1] Junod, *op. cit.*, Vol. 1, p. 424.

the highest honor was the killing of an enemy. Second honors went to the man who transfixed the arm of a dying enemy with his assagai. But there was little distinction attached to the killing of a helplessly wounded soldier.

## EDUCATION

Bathonga education is specifically directed toward fitting the child into the cultural framework, to develop in him the appropriate attitudes of respect to the elders, to the chief, and to the gods. Nor is the child simply permitted just to grow up. But at every stage, from the time the little boy is old enough to care for his father's goats to the time he has passed through the arduous regimen of the initiation school, he is forcibly impressed with the distinctions between older and younger, until as a man he is no longer a wild, unformed little savage but a dignified and cooperative member of his father's village. The girl will leave the village and hence she must be instructed in housewifely arts and in uncomplaining obedience to her husband.

The child is always received into the world with great joy. If it is a girl this will mean oxen to buy a wife for a son; it will mean not only increased wealth but an increased family. If it is a boy it means no material enrichment, but the family group is strengthened and the name of the father glorified and perpetuated.[1] The child is treated with great tenderness and nursed by its own mother until about the age of two and a half to three years. During the nursing period the mother allows it to take the breast at any time. For the early period of infancy the child is always with the mother, carried on her back in a soft skin baby carrier that has been presented by the mother's brother. When it is grown a bit and is more "firm" the child is put in the care of some little girl, an elder sister or a cousin. Weaning is forcible and ritually conducted. The mother either coats her breasts with pepper or sends the little boy to live with his maternal grandfather. Weaning is as significant a break for the mother as for the child. For three years she has completely abstained from sexual intercourse. After the ritual weaning, her sex life is resumed.

In the village of his great *kokwana* (maternal grandfather) the little boy is given freedom to run about and play games. His

[1] *Ibid.*, p. 43.

maternal uncle and grandfather treat him leniently and do not scold him.  With the former he may take great liberties, stealing his food, spoiling his things, even snatching the morsels of food placed by his uncle on the ancestral altar.  In the village of his father the boy must accommodate himself to a different type of behavior.  His father is stern and punishes him for his misdeeds.  Toward his father and his father's brother the boy must show respect.  They are the men in the village under whom he will live in the age hierarchy.  But from his mother's brother's village he will some day take a wife.  To them he will some day pay the lobola.  They do not fit into the hierarchical pattern, and it is not necessary that respect attitudes should be developed toward them.

From the time they are big enough to run around until the age of eleven, or so, the little boys are a sort of outlaw group, living on the fringes of a society that is quick to punish them when they have plundered some garden or stolen sweet potatoes from some storehouse.  At this time they take care of the goat herds.  A group of small boys within this general age group go out in a gang with the goats, spending their time playing games,[1] in which they take sides or in which there is an "it," but deriving most satisfaction from the outlaw life of plundering and fighting with boys from other villages.  In the gang life they are dominated by the older and stronger boys, one of whom sets himself up as a chief over them and directs their activities.  At every step the younger and weaker boy is made to serve the demands of his elder brother, who has already been promoted to the care of the oxen.  In Maputu district the big boys even scorned to drink the water brought them by the women, but preferred to be served by the younger boys.[2]  The fagging system is well established, with each older boy making a smaller youngster serve him and run errands.

During this entire period of his boyhood, the child is considered as unformed, as lacking in full intelligence, as wild.  He must be broken.  Thus, every fourth or fifth year, the chief calls all the boys between the ages of ten and sixteen to attend the circumcision school.  Here they are subjected to an extremely difficult regimen.  They are under the supervision of the young men from

[1] *Ibid.*, pp. 65 *ff.*
[2] *Ibid.*, p. 71.

the preceding circumcision class of four years ago and undergo a severe hazing from them. A group of grown-up men comprise the third group making up the school, among them being the religious teachers. As the general supervisory council these men enjoy themselves at the expense of the young novices, feasting daily on the wild game that the boys have caught for them. At their first initiation into the school the boys are made to run the gauntlet by the elder men and are whipped. Then the painful circumcision operation is performed. For three months they are kept in the school camp, made to sleep on the cold ground, given nauseating food, forbidden to taste a drop of water, continually beaten by the older boys on any pretext. Boys who are too sick to go on the daily hunting parties are attacked by their own age comrades and badly beaten. Along with these trials of the flesh, meant to develop hardihood and discipline, they are taught long ritual formulas, whose secrets they must never reveal under pain of death.

Finally, when the arduous initiation rites are completed, the boy is considered as "grown-up" and may choose a girl for a mistress, or rather he must get a girl to choose him. The boy who cannot get a girl is laughed at.

For the girl education is directed mainly toward the development of the housewifely arts and obedient submissiveness to her husband. As a little girl she trails after her mother, helping her about the house or in the fields when the birds are to be chased from the grain. The life of the little girl is by no means so wild and undisciplined as that of the boys. They play house with dolls or cat's cradle. They enjoy singing mocking songs about the women they do not like or spreading gossip. At her first menstruation the girl chooses an adoptive mother and is taken outside the village. She is secluded for a month and carefully guarded from all men. During this time she is pinched, scratched, and teased by her adoptive mother and exhorted to be polite to every grown-up person. At the end of the month she is returned to her mother. She is now an adult.

From the education of the young and more particularly from the education of the boy we can derive the Bathonga concept of personality. As we shall see the peak of Bathonga life is at maturity, at middle age. The greatest respect is showered upon men at that age. Before then individuality is still developing;

as children the boy and girl are not yet full persons. Not until the child has attained puberty has it any intelligence, can anything be done with it. At puberty formal education can be undertaken. But even before puberty, at the time when the little boy is still herding the goats in the company of his age comrades, certain indelible facts about society are firmly impressed on him. He is taught the respect for age. Very early he learns that he cannot compete with his elder brother, but that the latter is powerful and superior. The rivalry that is suppressed here later finds its expression in the games of "sides" in battles with boys of other villages, or of other clans. In the end, after the harrowing experiences of the circumcision school, the undisciplined personality is considered broken, and the individual becomes a fitting member of adult society.

### The Role Played by the Individual in the Culture

Bathongan society is essentially a man's society. For the woman the culture has no other rewards than that of early marriage and childbearing, with an additional burden of labor in the fields and in the house. For the man, on the other hand, there is the prospect of an easy life, surrounded by many relatives, possessing many wives and full storehouses. For a full nine months of the year he has the leisure to play games, drink beer, chat, and pay friendly visits to other villages.[1]

[1] To illustrate the life of a wealthy man: "Gidja's village numbered not less than twenty-four huts with beautiful shady trees behind; notice the enclosure for the cattle and for the goats on the central place, that for the pigs behind the houses. . . . There are . . . a crowd of youngsters leading the cattle, and everywhere the noise of the pestles crushing the daily mealies in the large mortars. He walks about proudly in his favorite enclosure, looking with pleasure on his prosperity. Young men are ready to do the work he will give them to do. He will treat them with beer brewed by his wives. And often the people of the neighboring villages will join his people for dances and games on the fine square, which is surrounded and enclosed on all sides by huts.

"And above all things, in the evening, each of his wives will bring him the pot which she has cooked for him. This is the essential matrimonial duty of the wife. . . . Gidja, the lord of six or seven pots of mealies, seasoned with sauce of monkey nuts, will feast and be satisfied every day. . . . He will become large and stout, quite shining, which in Africa is a sheer sign of wealth and nobility. The stouter he gets the more will he be respected. . . . The sycophants are not wanting! 'Good evening, son of so-and-so,' do they say. 'You are one of the great men of the country.' And to answer

But before a man can attain great material wealth and a life of ease he must build slowly and carefully. He must husband his goats and his oxen so that he can purchase one wife after another. He must be careful to propitiate his family gods so that they will look kindly on him and favor his oxen with increase. He must avoid any adulterous relations that will inflict a heavy fine upon him, the price of another wife. He need not compete. Neither in his own village nor in neighboring villages has he a rival either for a wife or for the stock of goods he hopes to accumulate; he need only wait, wait until he is older and his elder brother has died and left him his wives and his cattle. Then he too can be wealthy and a headman. When he has reached middle age the chief will order him to the capital, and there, in the presence of all the counselors and with the inevitable ritual, he will be permitted to plait a waxed ring into his hair as a sign that he will carry no more burdens,[1] that he is emancipated from labor.

The peak of his prestige and of his wealth is reached at middle age, after which a man faces an inexorable decline. At senility, his strength gone, he becomes a charge upon his children. He is no longer respected and can only wait the quiet release of the grave.

The role of the woman as we have already mentioned is the inferior one. If she is the first wife she is respected and called the "great one." If she is a second or third or fourth wife she has little prestige, but much hard work and possibly abuse from her higher ranking colleagues. With her husband she has few contacts. At intervals of a month he will visit her, but beyond

---

these and other compliments, the magnanimous Gidja shares his feast with his admirers!

"Strangers are crossing the country and inquire where they could be received? 'Go to Gidja,' they are told, 'he is the possessor of a harem. He is not killed by famine. He has beer to drink every day! He can give food to poor people. Even then, some of it remains on the plate and is eaten by little boys and dogs on the square. . . . '

"Thus, the man who has succeeded in life becomes famous, his advice will carry weight in the discussions in which he takes part; he will perhaps be even more esteemed than the chief himself, though he has not the special prestige which the royal family owes to the blood which runs in its veins." Junod, *op. cit.*, Vol. 1, pp. 126–128.

[1] Burdens are carried on the head in Bathonga.

that there is little intimacy. A man's social ties are with his male comrades on the hubo or the bandla. A woman may not even visit the bandla except to bring food to the men. She is never invited to the discussions of the hubo. No property in the village can be hers beyond a few despised pigs. At the death of her husband she descends as the most important item of property to his younger brother, but not before she has had interrupted intercourse with some stranger and undergone long purification rites. Old age levels out the inequalities between the sexes. Old men and old women are equally despised.

For the individual not content with the routine of acquiring wealth through the orderly process of noncompetitive accumulation, and the simple life of the agricultural village, the culture has a number of outlets. For the erratic unbalanced personality, the nervously unstable there is the role of magician. Creative, artistically minded individuals may find expression in sculpture, in poetry,[1] and in music.[2] A man can devote himself to basket making, a woman, if she comes from a district where clay is found, to pottery. And always the restless, dissatisfied man, the one who cannot stand the yoke of the hierarchy, can leave the village, if he wishes, and even go to another local group.

## The Integration of Culture

Bathonga society is highly cooperative within the bounds of the village, and in all other social and economic relations it is essentially noncompetitive. All its cultural forms promote the acquisition of wealth through noncompetitive means. In economic organization, in technology, in social relations little range is given to any expression of competition. Nevertheless the integration is not complete. In sorcery and in warfare, especially in the former, we have examples of extreme rivalry. Likewise, in a milder form, we find rivalry in games. Here the rivalry that is impossible in general social relations is given some play, but in a socially harmless way. Sorcery and witchcraft, though impinging

[1] Professional poets and singers travel about from village to village entertaining and being fed. Some ask for old rags.

[2] Trumpet players are organized in orchestras of ten men. They come to the capital to play for the chief. When there are a number of such orchestras a music tournament is held in which the best group is acclaimed. Junod, *op. cit.*, Vol. 2, p. 251.

heavily upon the culture, are definitely set apart, and the abnormal individuals, the deviants are culturally selected to follow these practices.

### Bibliography

JUNOD, HENRI, A.: *Life of a South African Tribe*, Imprimerie Attinger Frères, Neuchâtel (Switzerland), 1913; Macmillan & Company, Ltd., London.

# CHAPTER XII

## THE DAKOTA

### by JEANNETTE MIRSKY

The Teton Dakota numbered in 1910 about 14,500 persons. Their territory embraces an area which, with the Missouri River as its eastern boundary, covers the entire western part of South Dakota and goes far into Montana and Wyoming and down into Nebraska. They are divided into seven bands, of which the Oglala and Brules are the largest, together accounting for about half the entire population. They are now living on seven reservations in this area. Members of all bands are found on each reservation, though each has its headquarters where its members predominate. They all speak the same dialect of the Siouan language.

### ECONOMIC BACKGROUND

The Teton Dakota, like many others Plains Indians of North America, depended for their food, clothing, and shelter on the buffalo and other animals they hunted. They had no agriculture, but supplemented their meat diet with wild turnip, wild fruits, and berries of all kinds. During the winter and spring the people lived in encampments. These were more or less constant units composed of people from various bands who found it convenient to rove together hunting small game. There was no competition in securing food, and each family could leave the encampment freely for short periods in order to be better able to secure game.

The women dressed the skins of the animals, making them into clothes, tepee coverings, bags, and pouches, and even into containers in which cooking was done, and many of these articles they ornamented with porcupine quillwork. It was the women who prepared the food so that it could be kept and carried with them as they traveled about. Meat was jerked, dried, and cached, or it was dehydrated and pounded into pemmican. But even with these methods for preserving food, these wandering, hunting people were often faced during the winter with times of scarcity, and it was usually at such times that small units would leave the encampment to hunt.

The Dakota had horses. They were used in hunting, in warfare, and in the transportation of goods. Since no Plains Indian had any sense of ownership as regards land, they were also the most important form of property. Well-broken horses were owned by everyone and many were stolen from other tribes, this being the honorable method by which a young man was expected to make his start in life. He could not expect to inherit horses from his father, for at death a person's property was distributed outside the immediate family.

Except for the communal buffalo hunt, the technology of the Dakota pointed toward complete individualism. There was nothing that demanded the cooperation of two or more persons in handling the tools necessary to furnish them with the means of subsistence.

*The Buffalo Hunt.*—This was the one occasion upon which cooperation was demanded and enforced in the Dakota technology, and it is important not only for this fact but also because the buffalo played so vital a role in the Dakota economy. The buffalo furnished them with a large part of their food, its skins clothed and sheltered them, its sinews provided them with the perfect string for their bows. Men prayed for success in hunting, as they did for success in war and in marriage. And just as supernatural aid was an individual matter so were the more tangible requisites. Buffalo ponies, trained to run alongside a stampeding herd, to pace a particular animal, to wheel and dodge, to be sure-footed and swift, were as essential as the training a man got from boyhood on. Anyone could join in the hunt, and all men and boys did. The more active and skillful hunters carried on the more hazardous roles and shot more animals; the younger and less skillful men kept to the outside of the herd and shot the animals that had become separated from it.

The buffalo hunt was under the supervision of chosen and responsible leaders. First there were scouts, appointed by the council, who sighted a herd and reported on its size and location. It was understood that a herd was the prey of the entire community and that the chase was to be a united, group activity.

In order to be certain that no man started hunting ahead of the whole group, and thus, in order to kill one or two animals, frightened the herd away, police were designated in the camp to keep a sharp lookout to see that no man stole out to hunt before the signal was given. If he did, the police went to the man's tepee and with their pointed knives slashed it into ribbons; they also shot down a couple of his horses. He had threatened the security of the group.

When the preparations were complete, the soldier police went ahead and policed the hunt. The rest of the men, divided into two or three or four groups, as was thought best when the topography and size of the herd were considered, went out under leaders chosen for their experience and skill. All this was necessary in order to insure the greatest success in procuring the largest number of animals from the herd. Then the signal was given and the hunt was on. From this moment it was each man for himself, and each buffalo belonged to the man who killed it. There was no supervision. A bully might appropriate an animal to which he had no just claim, and a generous man assign his kill to an orphan boy. The animal could be used immediately, or given away, or kept for a while and then given away. The owner had sole right of disposal. The rules of the communal buffalo hunt insured such minimal cooperation as was necessary to secure, at the outset, maximum advantages to the whole group, and beyond this they left to every man full opportunity to exercise and profit by his own individual ability.

*Property.*—Property among the Dakota consisted of horses which were stolen from the enemy, war bonnets, weapons, pipes, pouches, wearing apparel—mocassins, robes, leggings—robes for the tepee, the tepee, parfleches, cooking utensils, and the tools necessary to make and decorate the skins. It was individually owned. It was acquired by the man's hunting and by the woman's handiwork. They had no needs and no property which could not be thus acquired. Horses were traditionally the most valuable possessions but a beautifully decorated robe or dress was as highly prized and appreciated. Since each small family was entirely self-sufficient, exchange of property was not obligatory for subsistence.

The attitude toward property was emphatically against placing any value on goods, on possessions. Social position did not depend on possessing property of any kind. This does not mean that they did not decorate objects elaborately and painstakingly, it does not mean that they did not respond to beautiful objects; there was simply a positive attitude against the accumulation and long-continued possession of material things. Such behavior was suspect. The only prestige attached to property was in giving it away. And the ways in which a person could achieve prestige by giving away property extended all the way from an informal occasion of accepting a nickname called in jest by giving the namer a present, to the highly formalized, very conspicuous intertribal giveaways. Property was given away in certain prescribed ways in order to honor an individual and incidentally the giver. It might be given directly to the one to be honored, or given to someone else in the honored person's name. In the latter case the giver, the recipient, and the one in whose name the gift was given were all honored. Furthermore the *only* way to honor someone and incidentally oneself was by a giveaway.

There was a sexual division of labor, which demanded that cooperation exist within the biological family. The men hunted and made their hunting weapons, were warriors, and assisted the women in digging the holes in which food was cached. If a family were off by itself and there was only one adult woman in the group, the man would assist in the raising of the tepee. The woman took care of everything else. It was the woman who cooked, prepared the skins, made the clothes and coverings from the hides, fetched the wood and water, and took complete charge of the tepee and all their belongings in their mobile life.

There was no trade. Each family was self-sufficing, and by its own efforts was able to secure from natural resources whatever was needed for subsistence. But that does not mean there was no exchange of commodities. All property in excess of actual wants was distributed through the giveaway; but trade where each of the two parties competed to get the better of the bargain did not exist.

The Dakota feel that property is of no importance when compared with human relations. Property achieves importance only when it is used to bring out and emphasize one's relationship to another human being. Thus if a young man was going to use his horses to pay for a wife, his uncle might add several of his best horses so that his relative would make a good showing; and it was not the number of horses the young man paid which was as important as the fact that he was of a respectable family whose members contributed to his gift. This active cooperation, expressed through the medium of property, gave a family prestige and respectability.

It is evident that when the mere possession of property has no prestige value whereas giving it away has, and when the society demands that persons publicly express their love and respect for others by either giving them property or giving it away in their name, and when the social structure rests on an active cooperation among the members of an extended family, the possession of property is an extremely fluctuating factor during any person's life.

A boy is born. His uncle or aunt may own an exceptionally fine horse, or, in modern times, a cow. "That horse stands there for my nephew," they may say. After this has been said two or three times at different occasions, it is understood that the animal belongs to the child, though it may remain to pasture where it is until the boy chooses to use it or it is given away in his honor. The boy may also be given a mare by his parents or grandparents, and in that case all the colts will be his. But whether he is given a horse or not, the young man is expected to go out and steal his own from the enemy. This is required before he is considered a man. Therefore nothing is involved in a man's accumulating riches except his own courage. If he lacks that, he is poor; if he is brave he can steal horses and fearlessly run in the buffalo hunt and acquire food. A man who has stolen horses is in a position to marry. To obtain a desirable young woman for his wife, he must pay for her. If a relative increases the payment by a gift the people will say, "That is a respectable gesture—that family does things well. The relations help each other out with gifts." A person is respectable as he demonstrates his regard for his relations by helping out with gifts.

The young man's suit is accepted. His parents arrange for him to have a new tepee. The father's sister and the mother's brother's wife cooperate to decorate the tepee and arrange the interior. They bring the best they have in robes, they bring new dishes for housekeeping, they outfit it completely. Everything the bride finds in this new tepee is hers. She keeps them and uses them. In time the young man goes to war and acquires his own things, his horses and fine apparel, war bonnets, and clubs. His wife makes fine articles from the skins of the animals he kills. And so they live. When a child is born his sisters will make the layette for the baby, and the more elaborate and numerous the various items in the layette, the greater is the respectability of the family.

On the death of a child, perhaps, the young wife will discard all her best possessions, and the man will give away a couple of horses. They may give everything away, if their grief is very great, and then they will be quite impoverished. At such a time the man's sisters will bring in the articles they see are lacking, and in time a new set will have been accumulated. Or the bereaved mother may want to "keep the ghost"[1] of her child, in which case not only her relatives but other people as well will bring her their nicest things to add to the collection she is accumulating to give away at the end of the ghost-keeping period. Again she will be impoverished, and will manage on next to nothing. She thinks, "Nothing is terrible except for human beings to die. I can manage with almost nothing. What are things compared to people?" So the couple will worry along and if they have no deaths for many years they will gradually build up their belongings again. But during that time they will be expected to contribute to the households of others who have made themselves bare at death.

When this couple have sons and daughters of their own, the father will give away lavishly in their name. A parent expresses his love for his child by giving a feast in the child's honor, at which time a horse is given to a poor old woman or a visiting stranger. The recipients, not the child, are the beneficiaries. When the children are grown up and married, the parents turn over whatever they have to the children, keeping only what is absolutely necessary. This shows that they excuse themselves from further obligations to their relatives and everyone understands and accepts it.

It is impossible to live the true Dakota life and accumulate possessions. If a person is rich all his life, the tribe is suspicious of him. As they say, death visits all families; then why all these riches? Accumulations of goods imply that the owner values

[1] See pp. 413, 414.

material objects more than relations—that goods mean more than
kin.   Such a person is greedy, such a person has no prestige in
the tribe.

In the old days most property, except horses, was perishable,
and inheritance was not a great matter.   There was absolute right
of testamentary disposal.   A woman would ask for her box to be
opened and give its contents away before her death.   But no
one, not even the children, had a prior right to anything.   If a
parent wanted a child to have something of his, he stated the
fact, and that closed the matter.   It was not regarded as a matter
of great moment, for in all probability the inheritor would not own
the article for very long.   He would part with it in the event of a
death, or someone might come and ask for it.   If a man died in
his prime, his widow gave away his best horses, and also most of
what she had.   In such cases relatives of the deceased husband
could remonstrate with her, "Keep that.   It is too much.   There
are children to consider.   With my brother (or nephew, or son)
gone, there is no one to get others for you."   The encouragement
to retain anything of value must come from the kin of the
deceased, otherwise it might appear as though the spouse's
kin thought more of property than of the life of their in-law who
had gone.   In the event of remarriage nothing belonging to the
old spouse was retained; it was considered an insult to the dead.

It will be seen that where the possession of property fluctuates
so markedly during a person's lifetime, that where cooperation
among families is so stressed, and that where the institution of the
giveaway exists to enable a person to attain prestige at every and
any point in his life, there must be a system to regulate the
passage of property from person to person.   There were two
mechanisms in operation: first, the social compulsion to cooperate
within the confines of the extended family group whenever need
arose.   This was practically self-regulating.   Second, there were
gifts.

There were three kinds of gifts recognized, with a clearly marked
etiquette for each.

1. There was the solicited gift that required repayment by
an article of greater value.

2. There was the voluntary gift that was acknowledged by
repayment of something not of the same value, but highly
personal and "from the heart."

3. There was the charity gift that was given in such a way that no return was implied in the giving.

1. If a woman were helping outfit her newly married nephew's tipi and lacked a fine robe for the bride's new home, she would send a messenger to a woman who had such a robe. The messenger would go to that woman and say, "I have come for that robe you own. It is for so-and-so's wedding. His aunt wants it." The owner would give it up. She might even say, "My aunt made this for me. I have great feeling for it. So I shall be glad that this bride will have it next. Tell her about it and ask her to keep it as long as she can." The messenger would go off with the gift, and apparently the incident would be closed. The owner now has nothing, has received nothing in place of what she gave. But she does not worry. She knows that the one who sent for the gift would not have done so unless she felt she could make a handsome return gift. And so in time, it may be after the marriage is consummated, the one who sent for the robe will bring something different and worth more to this woman who did her the honor of supplying a part of her nephew's new home. The return gift is larger because it must not only equal the gift asked for, but it must also include a sort of "interest" to cover the asker's boldness in requisitioning it and the donor's graciousness in complying. Thus the solicited gift, which is really a form of buying in an open market, is so phrased as to remove it completely from the economic field.

2. The voluntary gift is given directly to the recipient and not through a messenger. The idea here expressed is, "I don't want anything, but I wish to honor that person by this gift." Then the return gift may be anything, often much less valuable, but from the heart. There may even be no return gift, and this too is acceptable. This form is comparable to our gifts.

3. The third gift-giving requires no repayment and is in effect a form of charity, "With this I aid you." If there is someone in obvious need whom a person desires to help and yet not embarrass with the need of reciprocating, there is a method for doing it. The donor says, "With this I aid you," the receiver expresses thanks, takes the gift, and the incident is closed. The only return will be that of having befriended someone. A friend is gained, but there is no material exchange whatsoever.

## Social Structure

The social structure may be thought of as a series of circles within circles, each one complete, each like the other, varying only in the size of the circumference. The outermost circle is the tribe, the seven bands of the Teton Dakota. They are united by the same dialect of the Siouan language, by having the same heritage in the distant past, and by possessing the same ideals and way of life. Yet there are no records of the whole tribe's having come together at one place. Two or three or even four of its component bands have met in the great camp circle, but never the whole tribe. Within this great circle the members know peace with each other, and outside it is the world of enemies.

Next in size and importance is the band. A person belongs to whatever band his parents identified themselves with. A person can traditionally belong to the mother's band or the father's, depending on locality, preference, and other factors. A person counts himself a functioning member of the band in which he is raised and to that band he belongs. And yet there is nothing static about the composition of the bands. It is rather that certain localities have a preponderance of members of one band, yet in each locality every band is represented. Groups of varying sizes from each band are to be found in the midst of other bands, so that while membership in a band is determined by birth, residence is free and mobile. Sections of the band—encampments—would come together for a few days or weeks, for special occasions, usually ceremonial. These general gatherings of the encampments of any one band were announced by the chiefs. People liked these times. It meant a whole series of giveaways, seeing one's relations, an exchange of news and gossip, and general good time. It was a local arrangement. Other bands were not affected by it.

The encampment was a more or less constant unit, composed of groups of people from various bands who found it convenient to rove together. The social structure of the encampment was the model which, magnified, was to be found reflected in the band, and which on a reduced scale was present in the groups of which the encampment was made up.

In every encampment, except perhaps some in the heart of the territory occupied by the larger bands like the Oglala or Brules, in which all the people might easily be of one band, there were always several groups from other bands. Occasionally a man might come to an encampment where none of his particular band were represented, and then he was a stranger, among friends it is true, but without relations in a society where being without relations was a serious handicap. Such a stranger was classed with the old, the poor, the natural object for charity.

Each encampment had its chief, its council, its herald, and its soldier societies who performed the police duties. The encampment camped in a half-circle whose size varied with the number of tipis. The inner space was reserved for ceremonial tipis. The chief acted as administrator and judge, deciding upon the movements of the encampment, choosing the sites, and in rare cases when need arose acting as judge in murder cases. The council, composed of elderly men of experience and prestige, united the various groups within the encampment. With the chief they handled the matters that pertained to the common good: they made the plans for the communal buffalo hunt, they sent out messengers to other encampments when intraband reunions were contemplated, they settled disputes. The herald was, as his name implies, the encampment crier. The soldier-society members carried out the orders of the chief and council. It was they who saw that no individual endangered the common good by failing to cooperate with the group in the buffalo hunt. They punished all offenders, sometimes even inflicting death. In one reported case mayhem evoked this last punishment. Some encampments were large, the camp circle being about a quarter of a mile in diameter, some were much smaller. There were no set rules governing the behavior of the individuals. People cooperated by being considerate: they cautioned children and adults to be quiet so as not to be heard in the next tipi. If there was a gala day, it was scheduled, and everyone participated. Except in times of danger, as when a war party might be known to be in the vicinity, a man was free to leave the encampment without asking permission. There was a wide range of daily decisions left open to the individual, but while the individual was in the encampment he was a part of the life of the community.

The important unit in the social structure was the *tiyospaye*, the extended bilateral family group. It was composed of individual families who were related by consanguineal ties. Thus brothers and sisters and parallel cousins, who were also included in the brother-sister category, and cross-cousins and their spouses and children lived grouped together. The size of the extended family group varied from ten to twenty-odd families. At the head was a chief, usualy an elderly man of ability and dignity and prestige. The only law that regulated the smooth running of this extended group was the kinship bond with its highly specialized set of behavior attitudes clearly defined for all relationships.

To lack relatives was the great dread of the Dakota, for on kin everything depended. A man was safe as long as he had a group of relatives with whom he could cooperate and who would help him. This attitude is expressed in the form of the kinship system. By the wide use of the biological family terms to include and merge all members of the same generation, whether related by direct or collateral lines; by identifying the affinal relatives with the consanguineal, so that children who are born after a person has married into the family know such a person only by the latter terms, the Dakota insure themselves against the hazard of finding themselves destitute of a complete set of relations. In whatever extended family group a person chooses to live, and it follows that he is at home among the groups of any one of his four grandparents, he finds a complete assortment of relatives.

In the extended family group there is always an elder group, the fathers, mothers, uncles, and aunts of the generation in their prime, who constitute the principals in the group at any given time. With the passage of time these diminish, and gradually, imperceptibly, they are replaced by the next generation. All the members know exactly where they belong in relation to everyone else in the group. It is a matter of personal preference whether a man, when he marries, will live with his group or with that of his wife. Usually a man on first marrying is likely to join his wife's family group, but gradually, as he establishes himself as a householder, he will very likely gravitate toward his own brothers and sisters. As a general rule the woman who marries is not surprised to find herself in time attached to her husband's family group. So that unless a woman were a lifelong virgin or a widow she was not apt to live in the family group in which she grew up. Generally, if a woman who was living with her husband's extended family group were suddenly widowed and her children were minors without established homes of their own, she would return to her own family group; although if her husband's people were very important and provided well for her and her children, she might stay on.

There was no formality for entry into or departure from the extended family group. It was taken for granted, and everyone was aware of just how a newcomer should be placed, since this was regulated by kinship. Should a family come from a distant out-of-the-way community, they were treated kindly as strangers until some mutual, possibly very distant, relative was named, through whom a kinship term could be reckoned which would give them a place in the new group. Henceforth they were regarded as kin and were addressed by kinship terms.

An individual in the extended family group reflected that group's prestige and advanced it by all his honorable acts. All its members were equal in prestige (except the chief, who summed up in his person the collective as well as his own individual prestige). Because cooperation was viewed in terms of willingness to help rather than the amount of help given, it tended to minimize a man's inferiority or superiority within the group itself.

The family unit, which occupied a common tepee, consisted of a man, his wife, or wives, and their children; with an occasional unmarried sister or cousin of either the husband or wife, or a widowed parent of either. The Dakota family was not large, for even with plural wives the number of children was not great. This was due in part to a high rate of infant mortality and in part to the fact that children were spaced far apart. (It was regarded as shameful for a woman to have to stop nursing because she had conceived again; so that while a woman was nursing a child—up to two or three years of age—she did not have intercourse with her husband.) Five or six children were thought of as being a very large family.

The tendency was for old people to live in their own tepee, close enough to the active family so that when the man of the family hunted they could be on hand to help care for the meat, while they in turn were assured of having a vigorous man to do their hunting for them. In times of emergency families would often double up, but these were families that were well established, with children of their own. It was almost a law that newly married couples live alone as much as possible. No matter how poor a couple might be, they always were able to set up a new tepee for a newly married son apart from their own. Because of the strong son-in-law-mother-in-law and daughter-in-law-father-in-law avoidance tabu it was easier for an old, widowed mother to live with her son, for a woman could manage better with her daughter-in-law than with her son-in-law. With her daughter an awkward situation arose every time she and her son-in-law met. So it was customary for a widow to live with her son and a widower to live with his daughter, though the other arrangement also occurred. This tension between in-laws relaxed as people grew older, but it was always there.

In all these social units of the Dakota, the attitudes, obligations, and rights of kinship were the fundamental basis of all behavior, and each group of classificatory kin had its own specified obligations and rights.

*Kinship.*—All kinship categories are very widely extended. Thus the term father is used to designate one's own father, all his brothers and cross-cousins, the husbands of the mother's sisters and cross-cousins, the father's sister's husband's sister's husband, and so on through affinal extensions.

This attitude that one has for one's relatives in the classificatory extensions is heightened in the case of the member of one's own biological family, but it is not different in kind. One's social standing is rated by the nicety with which one gauges the proper nuance to different persons within the same category, observing the proper degree of duties, avoidances, respect, and joking. It is this ability to observe the proper nuance as well as wealth and achievement that makes an individual esteemed. Those individuals who have no strong drives nor outstanding abilities attain prestige on this basis as readily as those who are more gifted.

The relationship most depended upon for solid backing is that between brothers (male parallel cousins are also brothers), and the behavior toward the male cross-cousin is the same as toward the brothers.

If a man has no brothers or cousins (and this was possible in the days of wholesale death from war parties) he says, "I am related to nobody." This will be his excuse for not giving lavishly to some communal enterprise. He may have sons and daughters and uncles and aunts and mothers and fathers, but brothers are a firm support in any emergency. They constantly exchange gifts. It does not matter whether they are older or younger brothers, once they are adult the attitudes are the same. As they phrase it, "He is a part of me," and the verb used to express love between a pair of brothers or cousins is different from that used between a man and wife or a man and his children. In the universal joking they carry on toward the spouses of their sisters, and toward one another's wives and sisters-in-law, these brothers and cousins are leagued together. All the children of these men, whether brother or cross-cousin, call each other brother and sister, and they call these men father, and are called son or daughter by all of them. Strong feeling animates this relationship, and a boy is taught from earliest childhood on to regard these men of his own kind and generation—his brothers and male cross-cousins—above everything else. For a man to entice away the wife of his brother or cousin evokes the censure of the whole group, but the injured brother or cousin does nothing. He does not fight the offender either with words or with weapons. He may scold or whip the wife for her part in the matter; but there is no direct hostility toward the brother or cousin. Yet something has happened to the relationship; it is strained where once it was frank and open. The only graceful thing for the injured man to do is to step aside and let the intruder have the woman. He says, "Take her, my brother, since she means more to you than our relationship." And usually there is only one thing left for the guilty pair, for when the situation becomes public the camp ceases to be a pleasant place for them, and either the man or both flee to another group.

Sisters (this term includes the female parallel cousins) and female cross-cousins have the same frank and loyal relation as that among brothers. Sisters may criticize each other on any ground, but they must protect each other against criticism from without; and though a sister never flatters another sister to her face, she is loud in her praise to others. They stick by each other and defend each other against the brothers and cousins of the husband of any one of them. It is the sorority versus the fraternity in the joking relationship. Though the sister-female-cousin relationship mirrors that of the brother-male-cousin one, there are some differences. A brother may never refuse his brother anything he asks for; a sister is free to refuse without offense. But the main difference is in the case of a woman who steals her sister's husband—a strongly forbidden act. For this insult the sister who was loyal and devoted is justified in turning on her with the complete approval of the group. And yet a young virginal girl whose mother is dead will be given to her brother-in-law in marriage. "That she may help her sister," is the way such an arrangement is phrased. Such an arrangement is not an insult to the sister already married for the girl would live with her sister in any case. By the fact of marriage an illicit relationship is circumvented. Status is provided for both before the possibility of temptation arises.

A woman expects her sisters to show the same solicitous care of her children that she herself gives them. When sisters live close to one another it often happens that the child of one will not come home for many days. "He's over at his mother's," the real mother will say by way of explanation. This term of address, "mother," used by all the children of all the "sisters" to any one of them implies that all these "mothers" cooperate in fulfilling the maternal duties. And the same loyalty that exists between sisters as against those outside is carried over so that a "mother" will abuse anyone who abuses her "child."

This warm and loving tie between all mothers and children is heightened in the case of the own mother. The child is nursed whenever it cries, and it is not weaned until it is two or three. There is very little corporal punishment. Children are caressed and fussed over, but never in public. Kissing is indulged in only at times of great emotional stress, as when a child who was in danger is saved. Baby talk is discouraged, and by the time a child is two a mother is talking to it as though it were grown up. In fact the tendency is to talk in this way even to an infant, so that a woman says with dignity to a six-months-old, "Daughter, lie still and don't cry. I am going over to—but I will hurry right back to you. I won't be long. Don't be frightened." And upon her return the mother continues, "There, daughter, what did I tell you? That I would be right back. And here I am and I shall stay with you the rest of the day." The motivating idea is to make the children feel responsible as soon as possible.

Between daughter and mother there is the additional tie of common work. The growing girl helps the mother in her tasks, being given the less boring parts to do in housework and embroidery. It is the mother who superintends the occasion of the girl's first menstruation, though the task of getting the girl ready for a ceremony that celebrates this fact may be relegated to one of the other mothers. As the girl matures, and especially after she marries, the mother gladly takes a secondary place and the daughter adopts a kind of good-natured bossing attitude. By so doing the mother indicates that this is her daughter, whose judgment and authority are so good that she herself is willing to follow her commands. It is a consistent picture of the mother inculcating responsibility, and then at the social maturity of the daughter being the first to acknowledge that quality in her child. It is the mother's way of being responsive to her daughter's growth in various ways at progressive stages.

The good-natured scolding that the newly married daughter uses to her mother may subsequently take two forms. Either the scolding pattern will become dominant, or the good-natured one. But whatever the daughter's attitude becomes the mother remains gentle and uncomplaining, indulgent, and responsive. Until the mother is very old—past seventy—she will continue to help her daughter. She will be a second mother to her small grandchildren, do much of the outdoor work, get wood, preserve corn for the winter, pick and dry berries, dig turnips, cook—take over as much as she can so that her daughter may not be too burdened during her childbearing period. During this period the daughter takes over the pleasanter, sedentary tasks of porcupine work, while the mother tans the hides, or the daughter does the fancywork on pair after pair of mocassins while her mother sews the soles on and finishes them. If a daughter of thirty-five tans the skins while her mother does porcupine quillwork, people will say, "She tans hides at her age!" "She is still doing embroidery!"

Mothers are supposed to be indulgent to their sons, and fathers to their daughters. There is a free and easy relationship between a girl and her father, characterized by affection, trust, and dependence on the father. The only time a father will criticize his daughter is if he feels that she is not treating her husband or her child as they should be treated. That is because the father is supposed "to think the world and all" of his son-in-law. To express this he will reprimand his own child.

The father holds his children of either sex in high esteem, but once they are no longer infants he does not fondle them. There is no fear of the father; he must be indulgent either to his son or to his daughter, giving up anything he has or wants to do to make them happy.

Brothers and sisters are united in a respect relationship which is a continuing and sacred bond. A brother and sister[1] must be devoted to each other throughout life, and yet they must never talk directly to one another, nor sit together. The woman applauds his bravery in war, shares his tortures in the Sun Dance by having bits of skin cut out from her back that she might thus lessen his offering—in all ways she participates in his life as a man, except in those matters which pertain to his sex life. From these she is set apart. It is considered indecent for a girl to discuss with a brother his prospective wife, and far worse to tease him about an attachment. And yet the sister from the time she first learns to do fancywork has been making beautiful things— moccasins, beaded saddlebags, superbly decorated pillows and robes—all for whoever will become her sister-in-law. Whomever he chooses and brings home, that woman she receives and to her she gives her finest possessions. It is not that she approves or disapproves, it is not that she loves or does not love her brother's wife; it is done to show her respect and loyalty to her brother. All through her life she must retain this attitude, giving to her brother's wife the best she has. In a culture where the brother- sister tie is so strongly emphasized, it might become as in Manus a competitive one with the sister and wife vying for the man's love and attention. But because the emphasis is one of respect, carrying with it a prohibition against even considering the sexual aspects, respect is carried over to include the brother's wife and jealousy is not thought of. Reciprocally a wife is never jealous of her husband's sister—any jealousy is directed toward her own sisters and cousins—for she has been brought up to feel that a brother-sister relationship is far loftier than anything physical, and she knows this because of her own attitude toward her own brother. So strongly entrenched is this attitude between the sister and wife of a man, that often when the man has died, the sister will continue as before to honor her brother by giving to his widow without stint. If the widow remarries, such a sister will

---

[1] In the brother-sister respect relationships are included a woman to her "brothers" and her male cross-cousins; reciprocally a man to his "sisters" and female cross-cousins.

regard the second husband as though he were her brother, and the man will respond to her devotion and loyalty to his predecessor by acting to her as her brother would have acted. As for the man, he never confuses the two, his sister and his wife. Each has a place in his heart and mind that is specific, unique, and within different categories.

When a brother's child is born, his sister has a porcupine-quill embroidered cradle ready. A cradle provided by the mother's sister does not carry the same honor; it means the man has no standing, no respect relation, that the "mother" must make the child's ornaments; only if the father's sister makes it for the child to honor her brother does the gift give prestige. And reciprocally to honor the sister who thus honored him, the man will either give her, or give away in her name, the finest thing he has.

The sister will be foremost in the dancing and giveaways given to celebrate a man's distinguished act in the chase or in war, and she will recklessly throw away valuable things in his name. "Nothing I possess is as important to me as my brother. Because he is victorious and I have the chance to sing the praise of anyone so brave, my material holdings are as nothing." Likewise a brother returning with war trophies will give them to his sister, that she may carry them high in the celebration. If he brings home horses, the best goes to his sister. By all such acts they give prestige to each other and incidentally to themselves.

The attitude existing between uncle[1] and niece and uncle and nephew is the same devoted attitude that characterizes the brother-sister relationship minus its strong avoidance and respect elements. The uncle honors them throughout life because they are his sisters' children.

Aunts are the female counterpart of the uncle, and both may express their devotion not only in gifts but in a kindly teasing.

The attitude between grandchild and grandparent is that between parents and children, but magnified in its warmth and ease and indulgence to the highest degree, and with every other aspect canceled. It is impossible for a grandfather to say "That's too much" to any request made of him and so it is incumbent on the grandchild not to impose too greatly on this desire to further in every way the grandchild's requests. The grandfather speaks

[1] The brothers and cousins of the mothers and the husbands of the father's sisters and cousins. It is also extended widely through affinities.

in tender tones, comforting tones, encouraging words, as though his only remaining object in life is not to offend or sadden his grandchild. So strongly is this felt that a man will scold his own child in order to stand up for his grandchild. The grandmother has all the grandfather's attitude plus the daily care that she gives her grandchildren. "Grandparents will never turn you out; you can go there to live when all else fails, taking a dozen or more children with you, and they will turn over the best to you, and themselves sleep on the ground."

Affinal relationships contrast strongly with these extended consanguineal relationships. Within this category there are relationships that call for avoidance, those which demand respect, and those where joking is allowed. The first two attitudes are obligatory; to ignore them is to lose social standing, to be without self-respect. The joking relationship is optional, and one can joke or not as one chooses. A man of dignity may give his sisters-in-law (a joking relationship) as much respect as he does his sisters. The choice in this matter is an individual one, depending on the temperament of either the brother-in-law or the sister-in-law.

Because of the strong tie between brothers, a man does not try to take his sister-in-law while her husband is alive (see p. 395). But if a woman is widowed, then any of her brothers-in-law may make advances to her. Thus a man will say, "Her husband was a brother of Jasper's, Jasper was a cousin of my brother's wife's sister's husband. Oh, she is ours all right." This means that she is within the right relationship group for them to consider her in terms of an "affair," though there is no suggestion that she will be forced to submit.

Joking, when it is sexual joking, cannot be carried on in the presence of children or young girls, respect or avoidance relatives. Whereas brothers-in-law may joke obscenely with one another, the joking between sisters-in-law may never take this sexual turn, and with both parties the joking must cease if a spouse is present. Furthermore the joking relationship is not the only one that obtains between these affinal groups. Invariably, as has been seen in the case of a brother's sister and his wife, there are gifts given by the man or woman to the spouse of their sibling as a mark of respect for the sibling. In the old days when a warrior brought home horses he had stolen he was certain to give one to his sister's husband. This giving of gifts was a one-way matter, with the sister's husband or brother's wife always the recipient; but each person who was the recipient of such gifts gave in turn to another. Thus while there was not a direct exchange of gifts between affinal relatives, *A* gave to *B*, *B* to *C*, *C* to *D*, and so on until the circle was completed and someone gave a gift to *A*. Thus there was an even giving and receiving, and it was impossible for affinals to compete with each other for goods or prestige.

Between a woman and her daughter-in-law and a man and his son-in-law there is an absolute rule which holds as long as either lives that they must never use the other's name in talking either to or of them. During the first few years of such a relationship, they avoid each other. When a bride comes to her new home, her in-laws come and quietly shake hands with her, calling her by the relationship term, "Daughter-in-law," "sister-in-law," etc. The bride stands, eyes cast down, passive, not even offering her hand so that her in-laws have to pick it up as it hangs by her side in order to shake it. For the next few days, the mother-in-law cooks for the bride, brings the food to the new tepee, and says, "Son, or nephew, take this that my daughter-in-law may eat." The bride and her husband eat alone, and then the dishes are returned. The bride spends those days in embroidering a pair of moccasins for her father-in-law, then for her mother-in-law, and so on for the kin of her husband. And yet during those first days when a mother-in-law gives the meals and the daughter-in-law gives presents, they avoid meeting each other. Gradually the girl comes out of her strict seclusion. She will make a few comments to her sisters-in-law and her affinal sisters and cousins. Then she will begin to do her own cooking, and gradually, as time passes, she cooks for her parents-in-law. It is a gradual process. As the young wife's babies start to walk, the mother-in-law undertakes the care of them and little by little takes over an old woman's work—hauling water, gathering firewood, treating skins. They gradually adjust themselves to the duties of the household, the younger one occupied with the tasks that are easier and pleasanter and can be carried on within the confines of the tepee, the older woman cooperating by handling the heavier chores. The cooperation here is the same as between a woman and her mother, only with the mother-in-law the easy, bossing attitude assumed by the younger to the older woman is replaced by respect.

Again the fact that this relationship is a respect one, as in the case of sisters-in-law, eliminates the possibility of the mother-in-law and the wife competing with each other in any way for the affection and allegiance of the man. The parents-in-law like to receive food at the hands of their daughter-in-law and brag endlessly about it; in the same spirit they will "show off" the moccasins or dress made by her for them. This admiring, helpful attitude must be adhered to even if the women are not well suited to each other. For such women to quarrel or fight, to merit the label "She who fights with her mother-in-law" is a complete admission of loss of self-respect, of prestige. And conversely, should such women during the passage of years grow close together, they may not show this warm personal feeling by lapsing into an easy informality. A woman may not discuss with her mother-in-law anything that pertains to sex, she may not express her ideas, her philosophy of life—that is reserved for sisters and cousins. Across the affinal line no personal note may pass. The impersonality of the relationship precludes the possibility of disruption because of either a positive or a negative affect; it subordinates the individual to the relationship role.

The same cooperative, respectful attitude that exists between a woman and her mother-in-law is found between a man and his father-in-law. The strong avoidance attitude may be slightly modified as time passes; but between the woman and her father-in-law and a man and his mother-in-law the attitude of respect and avoidance reaches its highest point. They may not talk directly to each other, nor stay in the same tepee, nor look directly at one another, nor even hear anything about the other that could in the slightest way detract from the extreme respect attitude. A woman cooks and washes and cares for her husband's father, but it will be, "Go ask your grandfather for his shirt that it may be washed," using a child as an intermediary, or, "Tell your father his dinner is ready," to her husband.

To the Dakota this avoidance relationship sums up the most idealistic expression of loyalty and love. A father-in-law will, in case his son and daughter-in-law are quarreling, reprimand his son and take sides with the young wife; if his daughters or nieces complain to him about their sister-in-law, he will exonerate his daughter-in-law and scold his daughters. Even if they are right he will scold them for doing anything that might be annoying to his daughter-in-law. In the same spirit he never gives anything to his son, he gives it to him for his daughter-in-law as a mark of affection for her. He gives her gifts, but never gives or addresses her directly. If he finds her alone, he will put the gift down and say to no one in particular, "My daughter-in-law may like this," and murmuring such words look straight ahead and walk away. Or a father-in-law may be mourning for his son's wife. Instead of following the usual custom of holding the hand of the corpse while addressing it, he will stand at the head and look off in the distance as he speaks of his affection for her, telling how he will miss her, she who fed and clothed and cared for him. But he will never look at her even in death. It is a boast among old people that they are unable to describe a certain son- or daughter-in-law, as they have never looked at them.

The foundation on which the social organization rests is cooperation. Cooperation over time exists among all those who are related either by blood or by marriage; its rewards are immediate both to the group and to the individual in the attainment of prestige. The social organization with its set rules of attitudes, rights, and duties reciprocates by muting any situation within the widely extended kin group which might give rise to competition and conflict. All the competition that is allowed to exist is such as is a direct force for common good. But outside the kin group there are other roads by which a person can attain prestige, ways that take cognizance of individual differences.

Prestige can be achieved by individuals, but the ways are limited. For men there is only war and religion; for women prestige can be accorded for skill in handicrafts, for participation in religion, and for adherence to a strict code of sex behavior.

War as the Plains Indians saw it was a game governed by a few rules which were subscribed to by all the tribes who played it. It was pretty widely accepted that war parties did not scalp a man who was out alone in the wilderness fasting and seeking a vision. Such a man's condition and quest were recognized as a sanctuary, and in the one instance where such a man was killed it was regarded as an atrocity and avenged by an enraged group. War was organized as a game with points to be made and counted

—though among the Dakota there was no limit to such deeds. War parties could raid an encampment or a single isolated tipi, the scalps of defenseless women and babes could be taken as well as those of opposing braves; in this there was no difference of kind, a scalp was a scalp—only a man's boasting had a richer flavor if the scalp he had taken was that of an outstanding enemy. A war party could also go out with the sole intention of stealing horses. Any man could initiate or any man or boy could join a war party for any reason, but the most common one was to validate claims to bravery, to get glory and personal prestige. (The boys who accompanied a war party for adventure or to escape an unpleasant home situation did not participate in the actual warfare but were kept at a safe distance in the rear, where they acted as "squires" to the warriors.)

The whole point of the war game was that a warrior took a long chance and risked his life that he might achieve status among his people. It was an exciting game, in which each man had full individual expression. The party would stop just before they were about to fight or raid, and the men would prepare themselves for the attack which was supposed to be not only sudden, but also very spectacular. The warriors dressed as handsomely as possible, they painted themselves with the marks they were entitled to wear: if they were *huka* (child-beloveds) that would be fully indicated; if they had been successful in past battles—if they had stolen horses, carried off a wounded comrade under the fire of the enemy, if their horses had been shot down under them, if they had been wounded themselves—all this was indicated in their dress and the way their horses were painted. It was the occasion on which each man put on his best finery. On the very threshold of an enterprise which aimed at enhancing personal prestige each man showed by dress and mark the individual prestige "counts" to which he was entitled.

A war party might be a small informal one of from two to six men, in which a sudden, stealthy raid was made, usually for horses, and in which there was no elaborate preparation, no grand entry—just a swift attack and swifter retreat with the captured horses. But a large war party was under the direction of two or more experienced warriors who acted as leaders and advisers, a holy man who divined the future and told what was likely to happen and what precautions should be taken, and scouts, the cleverest young men, who were sharp-eyed and quick and discreet in their movements. When the party approached the enemy encampment, the scouts were sent out, and while they were gone the warriors decked themselves in their full regalia. This preparatory period contrasts sharply with the same period before the communal buffalo hunt: in the latter the end was the common good and therefore it was a punishable crime for any man to start in before the group; in the former, where the ends were individual, a young man might go forth on his own without the sanction of the leaders and either get killed outright and thus endanger the group by inviting an attack, or cover himself with glory and at the same time deprive the others of a chance to kill or steal. For such a lone warrior, if he lived, there was no punishment, only heightened glory.

Among the Dakota the highest war count or "coup" went for stealing horses, next for killing an enemy or rushing into the fray and striking a fallen man, then for bringing in a wounded or slain tribesman, then for having a horse shot down under one, etc. Any death-defying act could be counted and each coup could count for four different men—similar to our first, second, and third place in a match but without the implied grading. Thus a man might be the first to steal a fettered horse, or the third to dash into the thick of the fight and touch a fallen enemy, etc.—any and all of these coups could be counted. War insignia were standardized so that it was as easy to tell what a man had achieved in war as it is among us to know a military person's rank from the bars or stripes he wears.[1]

[1] Of coups H. S. Mekeel has said, "The man with the greatest number of points to his credit was *ipso facto* the bravest. Those having a certain number were eligible for important positions in the tribe—a redefinition of their category in the group. The points depended on specific behavior in certain situations. . . . Another count could be had for enduring the Sun Dance. In the same way there was a less formal system of counts for generous deeds. . . . In the council tent there was kept a set of one hundred or more counting sticks, so that men who wished to do so could compete with each other. A stake would often be set up with some property tied to it. The man who could count the highest took the property." *A Modern American Indian Community in the Light of Its Past.* MS.

There is nothing in the Deloria material that would suggest anything as formalized as this competitive pattern. In fact her whole material suggests that while competition was constantly present it was never, within the group, allowed clear expression.

Some war parties went out with fanfare, others left quietly. But one and all they returned dramatically. The return into camp was as planned and prescribed as the stop before the attack: if any of their number had been killed, they entered the camp wailing and singing the praises of those left on the field. Or they might come quietly leading the horses they had taken and carrying the scalps on high. The return was an exciting time for the camp. Those who had lost relatives mourned with the warriors; those who were respect or avoidance relatives of triumphant braves gave away lavishly so that the brave's name would ring out many times as befitted his prowess. The more times a man's name was heard in song the more he was honored in the tribe. Those who had lost their men in the fight put on great mourning scenes with abandoned giveaways. But the most spectacular figure in a returning war party was the wounded warrior who came limping back or one with an enemy bullet in his body. All those men who had set out to win personal glory and prestige heard their deeds acclaimed by the camp and by this acclamation achieved that for which they had ventured.

The night saw the scalp dance, in which the whole group cooperated to celebrate the bravery of their warriors—even those who were in mourning laid aside their sorrow—and they danced in vengeful delight around the pole on which hung the scalps of the enemy.

That the war pattern was a method by which an individual achieved prestige is clearly phrased by the *T' ok-o'wec' eyapi* moment in the Sun Dance. At a certain specified time each warrior prayed for the particular thing he most wanted. In general all men wanted to have a big name, and they could best achieve this by warfare. Therefore at that moment the Sun Dancers wail to the Sun asking for enemies, *i.e.*, they wail for enemies' lives.

The other way in which a man could individually seek prestige was within the field of religion. The religion of the Plains Indian was based on a highly personal relationship between the individual and the supernatural. The man who wanted to obtain some sort of relationship with the supernatural did so by going out into some lonely, barren spot to fast and pray in the hope of getting a vision. He had a mentor—a man who had had a vision—to arrange this and guide him. Or he might torture himself by fasting and thirsting, standing motionless while he gazed at the sun, cutting his flesh, or tearing his chest and back muscles out, thus trying to free himself from skewers deeply implanted under those muscles. By such techniques men sought to wring pity from the supernatural, to obtain by a vision the sign that henceforth they could rely upon the help of the supernatural to aid them in all their undertakings. The vision so obtained indicated what supernatural the individual was to have as his spirit control and with what power it endowed him; it revealed the ceremony and sacred songs by which the individual was to have communication with his spirit control— in short the vision revealed the patron saint, the entire ritual of worship, and the whole paraphernalia of religious equipment.

The means used by these deliberate seekers, the fasting and torture, served to give them power and also served as a means of thanking the supernatural. A man might fast and torture himself to fulfill a vow. "I fasted because I promised to when my child, or my father, was ill." So, if anything threatened to harm an individual or someone dear to him, a man in a moment of extremity might call upon the supernatural to aid him, promising to fast and torture himself at a later date. Were such aid vouchsafed, the deferred payment was made. There are indications that this technique of fasting and torture, prayer and weeping for a vision, which was undergone privately and alone, was the trait on which the great Sun Dance was built. The four-day Sun Dance was the way in which these individual sufferers from the different encampments or bands went through their agony together.

*The Sun Dance.*[1]—This was the most spectacular tribal ceremony. The name is derived from one aspect of the four-day ceremony in which the worshiper gazes steadily at the sun while dancing. Those who dance the Sun Dance are divided into four groups differentiated only by the amount of torture to be indulged in. The kin of the various candidates are expected to give ritual feasts on this occasion, for which they receive honor. Not only the kin groups, but all members of the candidate's band are expected at such a time to give away much property. The candidate must have a mentor to prepare and guide him through

[1] J. R. Walker, "The Sun Dance and Other Ceremonies of the Oglala Division of the Teton Dakota."

the ceremony, and the mentor receives a feast and gifts for his services, and a lifelong relationship is established between the candidate and his mentor. Once a candidate has signified his intention of dancing the Sun Dance, it is a matter for the chief and council to arrange with other groups for the united ceremony and the arrangements are carried out at their instigation by the members of the soldier-policing societies.

The time of the dance is midsummer, and the various groups, who are to foregather at a prearranged place, journey there led by the chief and council. Once they have all arrived the head chief, with the other chiefs constituting the council, direct the placing of the camp circle and the spot where the dance is to be held. The "altar" is a sacred pole around which the dancers circle, and this pole is scouted for and felled and brought to the spot as though it were an enemy. The procedure here parallels that of a war party, so that coups may be counted on the pole, and honors given for these. After three days of preparation and minor ceremonies—none of which are part of the Sun Dance but are made more significant by taking place at this time—the sufferers endure their tortures. They are attended by men who have previously gone through the identical torture and by chaste maidens. A man who has danced the Sun Dance establishes himself as a man of bravery and fortitude, the two individualistic Dakota virtues.

The Sun Dance fuses the individual vision quest with all the recognized prestige-getting patterns of the Dakota—the property giveaway, the coups counted on the sacred pole, and for women the role of proven virgins, who alone were able to serve as assistants to the sufferers. It was throughout a cooperative activity organized by the chief and the councils and by a religious council composed of the mentors of the individual sufferers.

*Societies.*—The vision could also come to those who did not seek it with fasting and torture. Such unsought visions were thought to be more potent, more lasting, of the nature of a "gift" from the supernatural, and therefore carried more honor and prestige for the recipient. They might come in dreams by day, by night, during a dizzy spell or fainting fit; but however they came, in them was imparted with great vividness the whole purport of the supernatural visitation and the way in which it was to be validated to the individual. It was by visions so imparted and so validated by some act as to demonstrate to all that the individual chosen had the cooperation of the supernatural that the various societies were founded.

The *Tok'ala*, a military policing society, was founded by a man who had a vision of the thunder giving him the elaborate details of the society. Upon the basis of his vision, the man secretly rehearsed the men and women who were to help him carry out the ceremony as he had been instructed. Whereas, when the ceremony started, a thunderstorm was so nearly on the camp that an occasional raindrop fell, as the ceremony progressed the storm cloud split in two to avoid the spot where the ceremony was going on and only joined together again when it had passed far to the east. It could be seen to travel on with greater fierceness and force than before. This was a miracle. It was a sign that the dreamer had received power from the supernatural, that he was in league with the thunder spirits. The supernatural had cooperated with him to prove his dream and by such validation to signify that a society was to be founded to carry on the ceremony which had been so given.

The various societies, acting in either a policing or advising capacity and with the vision of their founder serving them as a charter, considered it their main duty to renew the courage of their members from time to time and make the members maintain at a lofty level the highest standards of Dakota conduct. Thus a vision could serve for individual use or could serve as the basis for a cooperating group.

Once a society was organized along its supernaturally given lines its members cooperated with one another in giving feasts, going on the warpath, acting as police, and so forth. These societies were not graded, so that it was not necessary to belong to one before being eligible for another. To be invited to join a society was a sign that an individual was outstanding both by virtue of his individual prestige and as a member of a powerful extended family group. Societies, then, were a way of ensuring the cooperation of outstanding individuals of different extended family groups, and the reward they offered was heightened prestige. Once a man had been invited to join he could refuse only by sacrificing his prestige, for a refusal implied that the man was too stingy to meet the obligations involved, or too lazy to make himself able to carry on these obligations, or lacked a sufficient family backing to help him meet these obligations. Any one of these three failings was enough to cause loss of prestige.

Women could attain individual prestige by their skill in porcupine quillwork, by receiving a vision, and by adhering to a strict code of sexual behavior. Objects decorated by skilled porcupine quillworkers were highly valued and praised and were included in the important articles given at a giveaway. Such skill was regarded as outstanding as was war bravery for men. (Among the Cheyenne this was openly equated by the formation of women's societies, and their handiwork was graded in the same way men's war honors were.) Women might also, without seeking, be given supernatural visions and powers, and they had to validate their visions as did the men. But a woman who was so "gifted" by the supernatural did not marry if she acquired the power at an early age, or she acquired power only after she was widowed. She could not be a wife and mother and carry out her supernatural powers.

The other way in which a woman achieved prestige was by being chaste before marriage and faithful after. The feast of the Virgin Fire would be given by a family in honor of a girl in her early twenties who was pretty and had been courted a good deal and yet had chosen to remain single and chaste. (If a young girl so much as gave a present to a man it was regarded as a breach of chastity and would disqualify her.) A feast was given in her honor to the whole encampment by her family group. All the other virgins who could so qualify were honored guests, and presents were given them. This was not a religious occasion, it was a happy party to celebrate the individual prestige of a girl and it was made important by the giveaway of property. It was incumbent on any man to tell on any girl who tried to join the honored group if she was there falsely, and he would literally drag such a girl away. No girl was chaste who had promised a man to marry him and had then backed down, or who had given a present to a man, or who had had an affair with a man. But a girl who had had a Virgin Fire feast and had later married honorably could still qualify. For married women to know one man was honorable, whether he was alive or dead, but to know more than one was shameful. This was so strongly stressed that even if a woman were widowed and then honorably remarried it might be thrown up to her. She would forfeit by such action any claim to prestige given her by the Virgin Fire. A Virgin Fire might be given by the woman herself, and this was regarded as all the more honorable and of greater prestige. Or it might be given by a father for a daughter who repulsed all men, and in such a case the feast became a way of giving the girl honor and at the same time telling her that it was time she faced her lot as a woman. Her father would say, "My child shall now be courted, she who has repudiated her duty as a woman of the tribe and played the child too long must now be courted." The Virgin Fire then gave an individual prestige in the group; it could also be a coercive method by which the group forced an individual to participate in the role set for her by the group.

The valuation upon chastity appears clearly in the privilege accorded a man who had undergone the severest torture in the Sun Dance. This gave him the highest prestige, and this prestige was equated with that of a chaste maiden whom it was fitting that he be given in marriage. He did not have to pay for her, and such a marriage was regarded as being very honorable.[1]

Lifelong virgins were a boasted ornament of the family group and the band. They were rare, for individuals who could withstand the social pressure directed against their remaining virgins must be determined and strong-minded women.

All persons of either sex who had attained prestige in war or by skill could be reminded of their social obligations at any time. This was done by means of challenge sticks. These were small sticks made to look like a scraper, an awl, a gun, arrows, and so forth, which were thrown into the tent of a person who was skilled or brave. These sticks were a reminder of the individual's reputation, they were a device to induce him to open his heart and be generous. What the sticks seemed to say was, "You who are skilled, who are applauded by the tribe as a real woman, let us see what you can do. We are starving and you have food. Does your generosity equal your skill? Let us see!" Or, "See, this represents the gun that wounded you and yet you were brave and came home alive and did many deeds of bravery in spite of your plight. Now it is to no less a person than you that this appeal is made." No one could refuse to answer a challenge so made, and people boasted of the number of challenge sticks

[1] *Ibid.*, p. 115.

that had been sent to members of their extended family group. (Little boys unofficially took advantage of this custom to get a meal from women whom they knew liked children.)

The giveaway was the basis of several important ceremonies which gave prestige to the individual undertaking them and to the person honored. It is important to remember that in such giveaways the property was never given *to* the individual who was to be honored but was given in his name to someone else. To give to someone who could not possibly make a return gift, therefore, revealed the love and honor of the giver most clearly and freed the transaction from any involvement with property exchange. The charity gift was the most suitable way of giving "in honor of." This was institutionalized in the ear-piercing ceremony, the buffalo ceremony, the child-beloveds, and the ghost-keeping. It must be understood at the outset that none of these ceremonies could be undertaken by any individual family; only a member of an important and large extended family group could carry out such undertakings.

The first two ceremonies named were not so important or so ambitious, and, therefore, not so rare as the last two. In the ear-piercing ceremony a couple who wanted to honor their infant arranged to have an important man pierce its ears. They on their part gave the man who pierced the ears many fine presents and they gave a large feast to all who were at hand. The child bore visible signs that his parents had so honored him, and a child might be so honored and marked as many as four times. If the ceremony were done during a Sun Dance it was made more important by virtue of the greater number of persons who would be present to eat the feast. Both boys and girls had their ears pierced.

The buffalo ceremony was given at the occasion of a girl's first menstrual period. If parents had a daughter they esteemed highly and wished to obtain the respect of the tribe for her they arranged this ceremony. At the onset of the menstrual flow the girl was secluded in a special hut, where for three days she worked steadily at fancywork in order to habituate herself to industry. At the end of this time she was purified in a sweat bath. Then her father's respect relatives brought many fine things as presents —horses, beautifully worked gowns, bags, pouches, etc.—for her to give away. A woman of outstanding character—chaste, gentle, and quiet—was chosen to wash the girl ceremonially, and then she was dressed in lovely new clothes and escorted to the ceremonial tepee. A man who had dreamed the buffalo spirit was chosen to officiate, for such a man knew the proper ceremony and could also endow the girl with the blessings and aid of his spirit. Anyone could look on at the ceremony, but only those who had previously had the ceremony performed for them could take their places as honored guests. The ceremony was to insure for the girl supernatural aid from the buffalo spirit in obtaining virtues which she would have for life. At the conclusion of the ceremony the gifts were given away in the girl's name, and since she was the cause for such a giveaway those who had received gifts thanked the girl. A girl who had been so distinguished was supposed to be for life a paragon of virtues; she was supposed to be generous and hospitable, kind and chaste. In adult life if such a woman were stingy, lewd, or unkind she had obviously repudiated her prestige, and of her the people would say, "A mere fragment of one who has been sung over in buffalo style. A fine buffalo woman she turned out to be!"

Both of these ceremonies were important, but once they were enacted the giving away of property ceased. In the ghost-keeping and child-beloved ceremonies, these obligations of giving away were extended for a long period. To honor a respected person who had died, and to honor and transmit the virtues of the dead to someone in the family, an important extended family group might decide to "keep the ghost." This meant that for one year the woman who was to keep the ghost had to work steadily doing fancywork so that there would be many gifts to give away; she had to tend and watch the ghost bundle, in which a lock of the hair of the deceased was the core around which she added her fine objects; she had to "feed" this bundle daily and that meant having food always on hand to offer to anyone who passed by. In the meantime all the other members of the family group also collected and made fine things, bringing them to be added to the ghost bundle. At the end of a year the great feast and giveaway took place. Against that time all the men of the encampment had collected all the tongues of the buffalo they had killed in order to provide enough of this ceremonial food. Four young, chaste girls were chosen to be guests of honor, to eat this last meal with the dead, and thus partake of the generosity and hospitality that had characterized the deceased one. After this ceremonial meal the feast began and the possessions that had been accumulated during the year were given away, many things to each family. In the end, the family who had kept the ghost had nothing, and that was correct. The very best of the things given away went to those who had contributed fine things and to those who at some time had kept a ghost themselves. Because of the length of time involved and the huge amount of goods distributed and the necessary cooperation by the extended family group, those who kept ghosts were few in number and they were held in high esteem.

For a child to be publicly acknowledged as beloved was a very great honor for such a child and an equally strenuous undertaking for those who so honored the child. If a woman had no children and she and her husband wanted one badly and then a child came, it might be so honored. Or if a child had been born sickly, or been very ill and had then recovered, its parents might say that he, or she, was to be a child-beloved. A true child-beloved must do the community good by its very existence. If a poor person appeared in the encampment, if visiting, unrelated strangers came, if there was dire need anywhere—always the child-beloved's name was used in giving things away. The whole extended family group cooperated to give things away on any occasion, and it was always given in the name of the child. Such children had their ears pierced, and, if they were girls, had the buffalo ceremony. The name of the child thus became famous because it was much lauded by many beneficiaries. Such a child was trained from childhood to be especially generous throughout life, as a sort of obligation to his lofty position, because big things were expected of him. If such a child were to fail in the social virtues of hospitality and generosity, he was doubly liable to censure. "As though he was not a child-beloved, he is so stingy," would be said, and his prestige would suffer badly. Or if in later life such a person gave recklessly, without thought of how he was to exist, having given so much away, such a one might say, "My parents reared me thus, I cannot help but give."

Only a family who could count on an effective backing from a sufficiently important extended family group could obligate themselves to the great giveaways for a child-beloved. This intense spirit of cooperation included the child's brothers and sisters. They were supposed to understand what fortuitous circumstances had made their parents choose that particular child; they were always reminded of these circumstances; and they accepted them and assisted their parents without jealousy.

In a society like the Dakota, which depended so heavily upon the individual's deeply felt acceptance of warm and specified roles, they had to have ways in which to account for those who could not subscribe to the roles demanded of them. If after the death of a near relative a man, or especially a woman, acted in a manner contrary to the social norms, it was understood that he behaved in such a manner because of grief. A woman on the death of a child might suddenly become a loose woman, and it was said that grief had driven her to such conduct; her relatives would stand by her and hope that in time her grief would be assuaged and her behavior different.

In all the cases of marked individualism and aberrancy it was thought that such persons were endowed or touched by the supernatural. If a woman were markedly skilled in porcupine-quill embroidery, she had had the Two-women vision, and by having had a vision had learned supernaturally to excel in her craft. The Two-women vision was one which allowed of two results: either a woman might excel in embroidery and industry and generosity, or she might become the lewdest and worst woman in the band. The vision was a mark of great vitality, and this could express itself in socially approved or socially disapproved ways; but they were two expressions of the same vitality. Those who were so marked were at the extremes, the poles, of the role demanded of women. In a range going from black to white, those who were black and those who were white were grouped together over against those who were grey. Women who had had the Two-women vision acknowledged the supernatural origin of their aberrancy by having a ceremony together. In the ceremony each enacted the dream in which she had been bewitched by the Two-women. After this they all ate together. Nobody else went to this feast. In general those who were touched by the Two-women were to be pitied. Even if, when they had their vision, they chose to take the skilled, respectable way of life, nevertheless they were thought of as being under a spell. It was something they could not shake off. But openly expressed pity was kept for the lewd women who were never able to settle down to any sort of regular life, who were shiftless in their homes, interested only in sex. By phrasing this as due to the supernatural the responsibility for such behavior was lifted from the individual; such women were pitied but not outcast, they were still members of the social group.

Eccentrics of both sexes were likewise institutionalized as being supernaturally forced into such behavior. The Heyoka, or antinatural vision, gave the dreamer most powerful and valuable supernatural aid. It came to both men and women and always followed the same general line. Such a dream was announced by a soldier call sounding from the clouds, then the master Heyoka appeared accompanied by a little man or woman, fantastically marked and dressed. He would be doing all sorts of ridiculous and immodest things. The little man or woman was the dreamer, and he was the prisoner of the master Heyoka. He could never free himself until he had acted out before the whole group his dream behavior, and if he failed to do so he stood in constant danger of being killed by lightning. (Lightning storms are frequent and violent in this region.) The Heyoka dreamer was doomed to behave foolishly on pain of death. A father handed a large can of axle grease to his son who had dreamed the Heyoka saying, "Son, grease my wagon." The boy was gone a good while and then returned saying, "Father, I did all but the tongue, the grease gave out then." He had greased over the whole wagon. His mother wept. Alas, that he should be so foolish; yet she never blamed him. It was not his fault. The young man acted in that way for three years and then suddenly abandoned his foolishness. His period of service was over.

While those who dreamed the Heyoka all had the same dream, the forms of behavior within the dream varied from foolishness and consistent contrariness to acts of exhibitionism. The candidates at the Heyoka feast had to act absurdly or indecently, and either course was dreaded, especially by the women. Yet no one dared make fun of them, because no one knew when their turn to act that way might come; such action was supernaturally ordained.

Now and again there were youths in the tribe who failed to respond to what was expected of them in bravery and fortitude. Such boys as felt themselves unable to meet the requirements warfare demanded of them were forced into the position of women. They might not be homosexuals, but once they resigned from the manly role they undertook the womanly role, and with that was tied up the sexual behavior of the passive homosexual. *Wikte* was the name given to such men, and means those desirous of being women. Such men were destined from boyhood to be wiktes, and this role was made apparent at an early stage by the fact that they preferred to play with dolls, like girls. Once a boy was so marked, there was nothing to be done about it; his role was set. Little by little they took on the ways of women, using women's terms of address rather than men's, dressing like women, embroidering with exceptional skill. Wiktes are the most skillful of all in womanly arts and crafts, for they have supernatural help to bless them, as though the supernatural thus repaid them for the deficiencies and natural drawbacks they were cursed with. As they become mature they set up their own tepees and they will be accounted extra efficient because they can both hunt and do women's work. They are known for their hospitality, for their orderly, beautiful tepees filled with finery. Women pay them visits in order to get hints in embroidery, to eat an especially fine meal. The number of wiktes was very few, and those were famous. The institution of the wikte, as it was phrased among the Dakota, offered the aberrant sufficient compensations to make his role bearable; by interpreting his condition as supernaturally dictated, it removed any personal stigma from the individual, and by allowing him to excel in womanly arts it kept him within the group and did not throw him out as a pariah.

The only types of aberrance which were completely ostracized were the woman who preferred to lead a man's life and the active homosexual male. Rare cases of the former show that such women left the group and wandered by themselves. The active male homosexual was a "dog," a man without prestige, loathed despised, lacking any sanction or any compensation.

### EDUCATION

From a survey of the economic and the social structure it has been shown that certain techniques are essential for men and women in order to be able to exist; that an individual must know the attitudes, rights, and duties contained within the kinship system; that he must learn the institutionalized ways allowed the individual for expression.   An individual must be cooperative, should stay within the middle of the range of personality traits, must value relations above goods, and must confine competition to prestige outside the family or to extratribal situations.

The child is born into a world where many women cherish her[1] and tend her, and many men fondle her.   She comes into a world of mothers and fathers, aunts and uncles and grandparents, who are all warm and tender, responsive, and very tolerant.   She is not denied and she is not scolded.   Her mother is not tired out by too much childbearing, for most likely the child's older sibling is three, and the average number of children in a family will be about four.   As long as she wants to, she may nurse, for while she is nursing her mother abstains from intercourse with her husband so that she will not run the danger of losing her milk by becoming pregnant.   Grown persons boast of the fact that they nursed until three or four as a sign of how much their parents loved them, how their mother valued them above sex.   Babies were nursed or humored to keep them from crying, and this meant cooperation among the closely related adults.   "Why is she crying there like an orphan?" would be said to indicate that only where such cooperation was lacking did babies cry.   Babies were kept quiet because it might be necessary to hide from the enemy, but also because such crying disturbed the whole encampment.   This humoring of small children by a large group of adults evoked a responsive attachment from the children in return.

A baby was not named immediately after birth.   A name conferred prestige and was usually chosen from among the names offered by old men to suggest some act of bravery they had performed in the past.   Often a child was called by a nickname until the parents arranged for the property required to have its ears pierced publicly at a Sun Dance.   As soon as a child could talk she was taught the words for mother and father, aunt and uncle, to associate the terms with the proper persons, and what behavior was congruent with the term.   The correct kinship terms and attitudes were taught with a child's first words and steps.   "When my eldest half sister was married, her mother-in-

[1] I give an account of the female child first because there is more about girls than about boys in Miss Deloria's manuscript.

law assumed a respect relation to us girls, and my little sister, who was only two, was encouraged to be polite to her. She was teasing for something and crying when the woman came into the room, and my mother's sister whispered to her, 'Hush, here comes your mother-in-law, you must not cry.' My little sister did not know what it was all about, but the remark diverted her attention and she did not cry any more. That is the way the older people train the children so as to build up in them the proper attitudes toward each person. In a like manner, a child may have something said to it as a joke by a sister- or brother-in-law. Then a mother or aunt will teach her the right answer by whispering it into her ear, even though such a mother or aunt would never allow herself to say anything directly to the child's sister- or brother-in-law." Likewise by using a child to deliver a message to an avoidance relative, the child is taught what is proper to such a person.

Because each encampment presents to a child a complete set of relatives, both blood and affinal, and because the child has been taught from the very beginning the various kinship terms and the attitudes with which they correspond, by the time a child is four or five she has acquired a general understanding of these facts. From then on it is easy for the child to notice the refinements and the range allowed within a certain relationship term. This is a gradual and easy process learned by precept, observation, and comparison. In the adult world she notices that men and women are quite separate as they pursue their daily tasks, and that when they do meet her mother behaves differently with the child's fathers and uncles and grandparents, whereas among children of her own age she plays freely with girls and boys. It is obvious to the child that she need never expect discipline from her mother, for the latter never scolds, but must move circumspectly when her older sister is about. "Elder sisters can scold, they may assume the attitude of a glorified policeman, and keep a child in order. If she is given to crying too much, or whining, an elder sister will say, 'Shut her up, she gets on my nerves,' and the mothers and aunts and grandmothers are all ready to use such a sister or cousin as a kind of bugaboo, to keep the child in order."

The all-important respect attitude of a girl to her brother or male cousin has been taught the child from the very start, so that by the time she is four it will not surprise her to hear her elder sister say, "My cousin, my little brother," to a baby in arms, not a day old, with as much respect as though they were equals.

When the little girl is about six she is subtly encouraged to "cover up." There is no explanation. The mother merely pulls down the girl's skirts and tells her she is sitting like a man and shows her how girls sit. Once this has started it is followed out very consistently. It is at this age that she is made conscious of the sex dichotomy. The mother makes dolls for the girl and encourages her to make dolls too and to sew a few beads on her own little moccasins. By the time a girl is seven or eight it is usual to find her sitting beside her mother embroidering her doll's clothes while the mother does similar work on a larger scale. From then on the little girl is "self-conscious" about playing with boys. This is because she has been constantly warned not to bother her brother, not to embarrass him in any way, but always to respect him; and gradually she comes to feel, unconsciously at first, that the best way is to stay with other girls, or very young children, or older women. All play with boys of her own age is over. Along with this attitude runs another one as regards her brother. She is being constantly told "to do this, for your brother" until she gets the habit of helping him in small ways by doing tasks which do not involve her talking directly to him, or working side by side with him. "Run and gather wood for your brother, so I can cook his dinner before he comes in." "Go and call your aunt, I wish her to help me wash your brother's clothes." "Take this to your grandmother, so she can pound it into pemmican before your brother returns." And these negative and positive attitudes which a girl learns to have for her brother are not antithetical, they interlock so as to set the proper tone of respect and helpfulness, and by the time she is fifteen or so the attitude has become fixed in her.

From about ten to puberty the girls are in charge of the play group of the younger children. When she is not with her mother, the girl plays with little children of both sexes. They cluster about her, and she "mothers" them. They play house, with the young girl taking over the mother role and the little ones acting as her children. But because there is no boy of her own age in the group, there is no sex play, no playing at marriage or mates.

At the same time she has learned the necessary feminine techniques as she helped her mother with the less unpleasant tasks, she has also learned that not until she is old, a grandmother, will these unpleasant tasks be hers. Therefore there is no pressure on her to do more than fancywork. After her first menses come, at about sixteen or seventeen, she must work most industriously during each short period of seclusion.

She has now almost the entire equipment necessary to take her place as a mature member of the extended family group. She has a good grounding in all that pertains to the family and the kin group, she has learned how to do fancywork and has been introduced to industry, she has "mothered" the little children, she has seen how property is exchanged informally as gifts and formally in giveaways, she has observed that relatives are exalted and possessions minimized—and in all these patterns she has constantly rubbed shoulders with the factor of prestige. She knows the many expressions prestige may take, how inextricably it is bound up with everything at all points—how a person attains prestige and how a person loses it—and this factor of prestige is brought home to her and tied directly to her sex behavior and attitudes. From the time when she is taught to "cover up" her sex training starts. In learning to keep out of her brother's way, she also learns to stay away from all the males of her generation, she plays only with girls and works only with women, she is under female supervision all the time even when she goes berrying or swimming. As a young girl she may be an honored guest at a ghost-keeping feast or a buffalo ceremony, at which times her sex behavior is constantly the subject of admonitions and sermons. She notices the bashful behavior of the newly arrived brides, she sees older girls participate honorably in the Virgin Fire or shamedly remain away, or still worse caught trying to participate without being eligible. She contrasts the high standing of a wife who was honorably bought with the lower standing of a wife who eloped with a man; she shuns, as do all the women who surround her, any contact with loose women. She is kept from being too chummy with her sister and cousins, the only persons with whom she might be free to discuss sex or plan an affair. She hears that a certain family have left the camp circle out of shame when an unmarried daughter became pregnant. From talk and behavior and ceremonies she has learned that she must be chaste if she would have prestige, that by being chaste she brings honor to her extended family group, that her chaste behavior is the overt sign of her conformity and cooperation to raise the prestige of the group.

As for a boy, his training is the same up to the age of four or five. Until he is eight or nine, though a boy may play with bows and arrows, he is still regarded as a "baby" by his mothers, who pet him and never deny him. His aunts cherish him and give him gifts, his sisters make things easy and pleasant for him, and though he responds with affection to this, in the various ways allowed within the kinship category, yet he is taught by close contact and admonition to regard the males of his own generation as above everything else, women included. When a boy is young his father loves him, his manliness, his "maleness,"[1] but it is his uncle who assumes a peculiarly protective attitude toward him, constantly advising him in matters pertaining to safety. It is a boy's uncle who trains him gently how to meet emergencies and protect himself in them. He does not train him how to be respectable, that is done by his fathers and grandfathers; he does not train him about bravery and women, his elder brothers and cousins do that. But by the combined teaching of the uncle and father and elder brother the boy gets a rounded, though segmented, training that fits him to take his place as an adult in the society.

Up to eight or nine, then, a boy is petted and protected and without any regular discipline. The only discipline he has is in observing the correct attitudes toward his different kin. The shift from this state of childhood to that of a youth happens quite suddenly, and these new disciplinarians are the elder brothers and cousins. Not every such brother or cousin undertakes this disciplinary role; it devolves on two or three. They adopt a scolding attitude toward the little brothers, and sometimes roughly and sternly put them through a severe physical training. "There was a man who used to wake at dawn and come to the tipi where a lot of little brothers and cousins slept. 'What? Aren't these women (a term of scorn) up yet? Get up, if you call yourselves men, and jump into yonder creek.' But for such a man to do this, he had himself to be hardy, else the

---

[1] It is this emphasis on "maleness" in a son that makes the recognition of unmanly qualities, wikte potentialities, strike with such terrible affect.

boys' mothers might say, 'Never mind, what did he do himself, that he can order others to do hard things?' Sometimes a brother will encourage his younger brother to break in wild horses and take all kinds of risks. 'You are a male!' he will say to the younger boy in urging him on so that the latter will take all sorts of risks. If a boy dies as the result of such urging, nobody thinks of blaming the elder brother—he had to learn sometime, and it was his place to train him along those lines." An uncle, if he were present, would be cautious, would protect his nephew. But the brother or cousin is responsible for the younger one's bravery.

By the time a boy is in his teens he can shoot with bow and arrow, he can ride a horse and break in a wild one. He has heard old men tell of their deeds of prowess, he has been taught the meaning of the various insignia with which a man decorates himself, he has seen young warriors come home leading horses and carrying scalps, and he has seen how their bravery brought joy to all their kin. He has been honored by his uncle's giving him horses, but he has seen that only those young men who have stolen horses can honorably purchase a wife. His elder brothers have taught him how to court a girl, and his emotions have been aroused by the joking and obscene banter that takes place among male joking relatives. The time has come for him to seek a vision. In this he is taught and prepared either by an elder cousin or by a man with important supernatural power. Whether or not he succeeds in obtaining a spirit control he will begin to train as a warrior. He is taught specifically what constitutes a coup, and how coups are graded. He will enroll in his first war party.

When both the boy and the girl have reached the stage where they are ready to marry and assume their places in the adult world, the scolding and disciplinary relationship that has existed between them and their elder sibling of the same sex disappears. When they cease to be regarded as children they are accepted as equals. In reminiscent moods they may recall how they were scolded and frightened by them, and then both will laugh and be amused. Throughout their lives they will be loyal and affectionate.[1]

[1] While this is the picture as presented by Miss Deloria it seems a little too simple, too easy. It would be interesting to see what conflicts do carry over, and how they are expressed.

This is the general pattern for the early training and on this may be superimposed the various ceremonies by which a child is especially honored.   There is no hurrying of a child from stage to stage; he nurses as long as he wants to, he remains a child as long as he wants to—he is past eight before his older brother starts training him—he assumes a warrior's role only when he wants to.   Likewise the girl remains a child far into her teens—the Dakota have a late menstrual age (sixteen to eighteen)—she is given light and pleasant tasks to do, and this is carried out consistently, so that it is the women with married daughters who bear the brunt of the hard chores.   The tasks imposed upon both boys and girls are light; there is no need for driving the children, no use for precocity.   And if age carries with it the less pleasant tasks, it also is a time when an old man or woman can step outside the need for active participation in the exchanges dictated by the extended family group and, without loss of prestige, can have greater leeway to work and act as he chooses.

## SANCTIONS

The preceding picture of Dakota society is true but not complete.   These clear patterns of behavior, these lofty ideals to which both the individual and the group subscribed are set to an accompaniment of suspicion, slander, envy, and mistrust.   "As soon as a man rose among his fellows, it seems as if everyone attempted to lower him . . . there was an unstructured and ruthless attempt to pull everyone down to the same level."[1] The great god of the Dakota was respectability, and, as in our own Victorian society, every man was his brother's keeper and judge and the defender of the public good.   Each man knew his own shortcomings as measured against the social ideal, and with that as a measuring rod he marked off the shortcomings of everyone else.   Shame was the mechanism used to enforce respectability at every point, and it was used mercilessly.

I shall try to illustrate briefly and at random how this undercurrent flowed through the daily life and through every event. A woman in labor "did anything rather than cry out; she might bite her lip till it bled or moan in a low tone.   But she must never lower her dignity by screaming. . . . And when one did scream someone might comment, 'Did she think it would be as

[1] Mekeel, in a letter to the author.

pleasant at the end as at the beginning?' " The Dakota loved children and one would think, therefore, that barrenness would be pitied. But instead it is suspect. "And of them [barren women] it is often remarked that they are free to indulge without fear of pain and worry from childbearing, and that doubtless they let their passions run away with them in an orgy because they are safeguarded. They are accused of lacking in self-control. But worse yet a sterile woman is often accused of a superb technique of contraception unknown to the other women. . . . They are sometimes called murderers. . . . It is sometimes thrown up to them publicly. . . . A miscarriage of a very immature embryo was quietly disposed of by the mother. Unless she were actually seen lifting something very heavy . . . to which it would be logical to attribute the mishap, a woman was careful to keep such an event to herself because the gossips of the tribe would be sure to say she induced the miscarriage by roots or whatnot. . . . As soon as a woman knows that she is pregnant she must stop nursing it [her child]. They say the milk becomes watery then and is not good for the child. A child that grows puny and emaciated is said to have its rectum killed [diarrhea] by its parents, who through too early a resumption of intercourse have brought on another pregnancy impairing the health of the child they already have. Such parents are ridiculed or at least severely criticized. . . . The stigma attached to marrying out of one's age group is quite pronounced, and particularly if a woman marries a man younger than herself. . . . With careful families, children are not allowed to sleep away from the home. To do so indicates a fractured family life. It is only orphans who make a practice of sleeping out. . . . No 'good' child roams. A roaming child indicates negligent parents, so parents are very careful to keep them strictly near them all the time. . . . A bold, unself-conscious girl was regarded as directly on the road to perdition. A certain bashfulness was regarded as a bulwark against the advances of men. . . . Young men do not speak of women unless they find one who has submitted to them. Dakota men have been trained to regard a woman who gives herself as no good. She is then common property. Then they tell anyone they care to, and that person can also go and take advantage of her slip. Should she refuse the second man, he can and does tell about her to others until in time she is common property. Virginity is of the highest possible value. A woman who loses it never has the upper hand again. . . . Girls are taught to expect kindness and consideration and affection from a husband, but not an open display or demonstrativeness. A Dakota girl is a little ashamed if she gets a husband who does so. . . . Borrowing of anything is permissible and common, but not personal apparel or ornaments. . . . They make fun of someone who wears even her mother's shawl. 'That family lends each other shawls, you cannot tell one individual from another,' as though it were somewhat in the nature of a crime. . . . Importance of physical paternity is never lost sight of. A man is ashamed to claim a child if he thinks his wife has been with another. . . . Such a philanderer has been known to say, 'He is kind. He raises children for me, saving me considerable annoyance.' Men are deathly scared this might be said of them. . . . Confidences are out of the pattern. One lives and dies with one's secrets."

## The Ideals of the Society and the Role Played by the Individual

The Dakota have a culture that rests solidly on a constant interplay between the individual attainment and group participation, with prestige accorded a place in either. Their technological requirements are simple and individual, their manipulation of property is effected according to a manner prescribed in the kinship organization. Property is acquired noncompetitively and has no intrinsic value other than to express the loyalty and affection felt for relatives. By giving away property an individual can honor another individual; by all the kin concentrating their giveaways in one person's name, the group can honor an individual. All such honoring brings prestige, and prestige spreads to all who have a part in the honoring. The four virtues of the Dakota are generosity and hospitality, bravery and fortitude. The first two are cooperative virtues, the last two are individual. An individual may achieve prestige by bravery in war, or skill in craft, or by supernatural aid given through a vision. Marked individualism in any field is slightly suspect, and always phrased not in individual terms but in supernatural ones. The person, therefore, who does no more than conform—does the correct thing at the correct time for the correct person—can attain prestige even though he have no remarkable achievements to his credit.

The emphasis is upon mutual welfare and upon mutual and individual prestige. Overt competition is either outlawed or so muted as to be nondiscernible, but covertly it animates and gives color to both individual and group behavior. The fact that there is no grading of prestige—except in the matter of counting coups—that there is no set objective in prestige, offers a wide and open field within which each person may get the amount of prestige he wants, in the way he most desires.

*Bibliography*

DELORIA, ELLA: Unpublished manuscripts.

———: "Dakota Texts," *Publications of the American Ethnological Society*, Vol. 14, New York, 1932.

———: "Sun Dance of the Oglala Sioux," *Journal of American Folk-lore*, Vol. 42, No. 166, 1929.

WALKER, J. R.: "The Sun Dance and Other Ceremonies of the Oglala Division of the Teton Dakota," *Anthropological Papers of the American Museum of Natural History*, Vol. 16, Part 2, New York, 1917.

MEKEEL, H. S.: *A Modern American Indian Community in the Light of Its Past: A Study in Culture Change*, Yale University, New Haven, 1932. Manuscript.

———: Personal communications.

# CHAPTER XIII

## THE MAORI OF NEW ZEALAND

### *by* BERNARD MISHKIN

When and from what place the Maori arrived in New Zealand cannot be stated with perfect assurance. It is to be inferred that they journeyed from some of the tropical Polynesian islands, and more than likely they first reached the shores of their present habitat about a half-dozen centuries ago. In any event the migration to New Zealand entailed a profound and deliberate readjustment in their mode of life. Cultivable valleys, in which the bulk of the population concentrated, were acutely limited. Only birds, fish, and rats offered a respite from a purely vegetarian diet. The climate was more rigorous here, and new materials and appropriate techniques were required. In short, the Maori in their new home were confronted with a dearth of natural resources, which was an utterly new and startling context surrounding native life.

Yet the 150,000 Maori[1] were well able to cope with a hostile environment. They seldom suffered real privation, for a well-ordered economic life together with an efficient organization of production came to their defense. A rich culture was thus able to maintain itself and even prosper under relatively difficult economic conditions.

Most tribes had one dominant food-producing occupation which might be supplemented by other secondary food resources according to the location of the tribe. Along the north and east coasts of New Zealand agriculture was the chief economic pursuit; on the west coast forest products provided the tribes with a permanent food supply. All the coastal peoples depended upon

[1] This figure is a rough estimate of Maori population in 1750. "At the time of Cook's first visit the Maori population . . . approximated 150,000 souls." T. E. Donne, p. 21. It is quite possible that a peak in population was reached at an earlier time since incessant warfare among the tribes was consistently decimating the natives.

fishing either for a major or for a subsidiary source of food while the fern root was the staple for all tribes. For further variety of diet both inland and coastal tribes depended on an exchange of birds for fish and other sea foods.

This exchange of food products exemplifies the influence of the geographical distribution of raw materials on a form of economic organization. Thus trade in greenstone was important only in the area which had deposits of that mineral, a small district in the South Island. Similarly, obsidian, a mineral valuable to the natives for tools, weapons, and ornaments, was restricted in its effect on economic organization to a strip of the east coast.

In general Maori social and economic life followed essentially the Polynesian pattern. The transplanting of the society to a distinctly non-Polynesian habitat, however, left its mark on the culture.

## Social—Economic Structure

*Social Organization.*—The *whanau* or extended family group served as the social and economic unit. As members of the same household, the whanau provided a working body well suited to occupations requiring cooperation on a simple level. "Hence, rat trapping, fishing from a canoe, or the building of a small eel weir on a branch stream, were tasks for which the ordinary whanau was well adapted. In matters of organization each whanau was fairly self-reliant, the direction being taken by the headman of the group in consultation with other responsible people. As a rule it managed its own affairs without interference, except in such cases as came within the sphere of village or tribal policies."[1]

The household group consisted of a pair of grandparents and their descendants running through usually three generations. When it increased in numbers it became of sufficient importance to rank as a *hapu* and to receive a group title. The hapu was not exogamous; on the contrary, it encouraged endogamy, so long as the two parties did not have a common grandparent. Nor was it purely unilateral. Descent through one parent only was necessary and either could be counted. Since the hapu was a kinship group, its members often took the name of a common ancestor from whom they all traced descent. Sometimes

[1] Firth, p. 97.

a hapu bore the name of a woman of rank. If the parents belonged to different hapus, the children belonged to both. In such cases residence was the decisive determinant. In the main, however, an individual preferred to trace his line of descent from his most important ancestor through males alone.

The number of people in a hapu varied, but the group comprised at least several hundred members. The village sometimes was occupied by a single hapu, but a large village might contain several hapus. In such cases their respective quarters were marked off by low fences or palisades.

The hapu, too, engaged in economic activities as a unit. While certain kinds of forest work and some agricultural enterprises were adapted to the size of the whanau, fresh-water fishing and the operation of the great sieve nets required the cooperation of the membership of the hapu.

The largest kinship group among the Maori was the tribe. As in the case of the whanau and hapu the principle of descent from a common ancestor was the basis for tribal composition. The influence of the tribe as a whole was paramount over any land held by its members. For example, the sale of land by a subordinate chief could be prevented by chiefs representing the tribe. Likewise the hapu's rights took precedence over those of the whanau. And conversely, the rights, land, and fair name of the hapu were safeguarded by the tribe against all enemies.

To be sure, internal bickering was not uncommon. Among the various hapus, boundaries, violation of laws of trespass, and mutual petty insulting gave ample provocation for wrangling; nevertheless, at the first appearance of the outside enemy, these disputes were swiftly terminated.

One of the lesser features of social organization depends, in terminology at least, upon the traditional arrival of the Maori in a fleet of canoes. The *waka* or canoe was a loose political alliance of those tribes whose ancestors arrived in the same canoe.

The fundamental local group was the village, and its two constant features, around which centered the social and economic life of the natives, were the village square and the meeting house. The *marae* or square was an open space in the center of the village and served as the communal dining hall and the assembly ground for important public meetings. It was the

field on which certain religious and magical ceremonies were held—
the scene of receptions, speeches, and the chief's funeral. Food
expeditions were mobilized and their return celebrated on the
marae. The meeting house had special political significance.
In it were preserved the tribal traditions. It might have been
built to commemorate a tribal alliance, or a victorious war,
or an insult put upon the tribe, the memory of which had to be
kept alive until satisfactory revenge had been taken. The
erection of the meeting house was undertaken at the expense and
initiative of the chief but it was regarded as the common property
of all the inhabitants.

Each kinship unit, whanau, hapu, and tribe, had its particular
property rights. The one or two canoes owned by the whanau
could be taken out by any member of that family whenever he
wished; the canoe that was adzed out by one man apparently
did not admit of a special case; household membership established
equal rights to the use of the vessels. Small eel weirs were also
built and operated by a single whanau. The dwelling house was
occupied and collectively owned by the immediate kin group.
In the same way the stored food supply was held by the whanau.
On the other hand, the cooking vessels seem to have been the
private property of the women of each individual family.

The system of property relations among the Maori is not
altogether clear. Whether there existed special individual
privileges in the undifferentiated mass of collective property
is open to speculation. The material is especially remiss in
distinguishing between use or retention of property and actual
ownership. At any rate, the uncertainty at this point in itself
indicates a lack of emphasis on individual rights.

Each tribe exercised jurisdiction over a particular area.
Within the tribal bounds, the hapu held its own lands, and
inside the hapu land the whanau had its individual segments.
This is significant since in agricultural production all the people of
the village helped with the clearing and planting, while each
household owned its own bounded field and harvested its own
crops. Besides holding land rights, the hapu controlled rat runs,
fishing grounds, birding and canoe trees. Again, whanau and
private use was recognized in these resources. The hapu
furthermore owned the racing and war canoes, as well as the full-
sized eel weirs built on principal streams. To construct the latter

required complicated engineering and occupied the attention of all the men in a hapu or village.

The most clearly observable canon of Maori life is the cohesiveness of kinship groupings within the tribe. The custom of tracing descent from a common tribal ancestor and the continual breaking off of smaller kinship units from parent groups correlate perfectly with the prevalence of common economic ties. The tribe included all the hapu, and the hapu in turn embraced the many whanau. Congruently the property of the whanau was enjoyed by the hapu, and hapu rights were subordinate to the interests of the tribe.[1]

The question of whether the whanau was a self-sufficient unit can be answered by reference to the types of production. In the meantime it is obvious that property relations went hand in hand with productive techniques and the size of the labor groups. Small canoes were made, operated, and owned by the whanau; larger canoes were comparably made, operated, and owned by the hapu or village. Modest economic undertakings were conducted by the village; large-scale ventures demanded the cooperation of larger kinship units. The expenditure of labor by a group in some enterprise vested property rights in that group. The meeting house was village built and thereby village owned. Likewise, the large eel weirs followed the same manufacturing and proprietary pattern.

*Social Stratification.*—Primogeniture, major privileges being bestowed upon the first-born, is a common feature of Polynesian social organization. Several peaks in the distribution of primogeniture are found in this area, one of which is New Zealand. But even among the Maori, noble birth alone, though he was the first-born in a continuous line, did not make the chief. Rank, wealth, and leadership qualities had to be united in the person of the chief. As a responsible leader, certain personal characteristics were indispensable. He had to be (1) industrious in obtaining or cultivating food, (2) able in settling disputes, (3) brave, (4) a talented general, (5) an expert at carving, tattooing, and ornamental weaving, (6) hospitable, (7) clever at building a house or *pa* (fortified village) and in canoe making, (8) well informed as to the boundaries of tribal lands.[2] If the chief's

---

[1] *Ibid.*, p. 343.

[2] These eight *pu manawau* (innate abilities) are of course an ideal con-

first-born son did not display the necessary qualities for chieftainship the office passed to his younger brother, or failing him, to
the nearest cousin. However, in religious matters the first-born,
the *ariki*, remained supreme. Despite the loss of political
authority his own *mana* (supernatural power attendant upon
rank) was secure and he continued to act as ceremonial leader
of the community.

Wealth validated chieftainship to no mean extent. Without
well-supplied storehouses at his command a chief could not sus-
tain his reputation for liberality, which was essential to the
maintenance of his prestige. The disgrace that accompanied
his failure to distribute material goods among his guests fell
upon his people and was irreparable. This association of
interest of the whole group with that of the chief is notable.
If the chief failed to uphold his position his followers would
be deeply grieved. They would be ashamed to travel to the next
village; their pride was outraged. On the other hand the
reputation of the people for generosity mounted with the chief's
unstinted giving. It was imperative then that people actively
cooperate to keep the coffers of the chief, more properly the coffers
of the community, filled with food. The appropriation of the
entire catch of a village's fishing expedition by the chief did not
create grumbling and dissension, for it was said that the needs
of the chief could not conflict with the needs of his people.
According to a Maori proverb, "When commoner and chief
work together, the task is done."

At the same time the chief had to redistribute equitably the
goods presented to him. Otherwise he could not retain the
allegiance of his followers. The bungler and mismanager who
was unable to satisfy the needs of his people lost his office. His
dependents simply withdrew their cooperation and attached
themselves to another better fitted. No one frowned upon his
chief's prodigal feasting of friendly visitors even if the last stores
were used in the entertainment and the discomforting prospect
of frugal rations was imminent. But then it was the chief's
concern that such an event did not come to pass too often,
else his competence was called into question.

---

ception of a chief's capabilities. Not every chief possessed all eight nor
was it common for a chief to demonstrate equal ability in those accomplishments that he did practice. Best, "Beliefs of the Maori," p. 242.

In essence the chief was an entrepreneur. At the outset of his career he was not excessively wealthy. His property holdings eclipsed the possessions of lower ranking men mainly in the way of finer ornaments and garments and larger stores of food. His dwelling was not more pretentious than those of his fellow tribesmen. On the whole there were no strongly marked property distinctions. Yet by virtue of the chief's privilege of polygamy—a privilege not accorded to lesser men—and his position as community entrepreneur, he was able to manipulate the whole economic life of the people. Polygamy went a long way in buttressing his economic position, as each wife brought a dowry consisting of land and slaves. Although this was not his property to dispose of as he wished, both the land and the slaves could be used to his advantage. The wives would perhaps stay on their own land, cultivating it and acting as overseers for the chief, who visited his wives periodically.

Description of the Maori chief as an entrepreneur may be misleading unless the terms are qualified. The word "entrepreneur" has at present too many overtones of Veblen's *Captains of Industry* with his formula: to get an extension of power which will allow acquisition of greater wealth. None of the available material makes this formula strictly applicable to the Maori chief. What his followers produced and what he possessed in his storehouse automatically became communal goods of which he was the executor. It was within his domain to take the initiative in all cooperative undertakings. The erection of a public meeting house, the arrangement of large-scale fishing ventures, the conducting of wars against other tribes were all under his supervision. The power of the chief was never absolute except in the case of war. And even in time of war an entire hapu might decide that it did not wish to be involved and would refuse to lend its aid.

Those households that could not boast genuine chiefs as headmen were usually led by lesser noblemen, the junior relatives of the chiefs. These were the backbone of the chief's economic undertakings. It was with them that the chief dealt directly and they were the captains of his enterprises.

The commoners, who were the bulk of the population, were the descendants of a continuous line of the younger sons of the nobility ("younger sons of younger sons"). Since the place of each individual in the social scheme was determined by order of birth in his family, the extraction of classes from Maori social organization contains an inherent difficulty. Each individual considered himself a class unto himself, recognizing his own status in relation to that of every other individual as recorded in the tribal genealogy. It is therefore easily understandable why Best was unable to discover anyone who would admit membership in a class of commoners.[1] The commoners were by no means a dispossessed group, for they could own land and exercise individual rights to economic resources. They did not pay any exaggerated forms of obeisance to the chief. But low rank compelled the commoner to remain within his cooperative group and prevented him from even competing for leadership with members of the nobility. By his military prowess only could he rise to leadership in the community. An aggressive warrior who had distinguished himself in many battles would receive recognition for his services and might become the war leader of his group.

Slaves always belonged to individual owners and in all instances they were recruited from prisoners taken in war. They cannot be conceived of as a static class, since the offspring of the extensive intermarriages between commoners and slaves were free. Slaves owned no land, nor were they allowed to cultivate it. They performed menial tasks and occasionally were called upon to have their person provide the delicacy of a feast. Since kinship underlay all Maori social groupings, slaves, because they did not belong to the tribe and therefore did not reckon descent from the common ancestor, were outside the pale of blood obligations and privileges. The fact that they were slaves itself indicated their loss of mana, and since therefore slaves needed to observe no tabus they were invaluable workers. Slavery, then, played a key role in Maori society. The economic efficiency of the village increased with the size of the slave population. The mana and prestige of the villagers mounted in the same proportion.

Among the free men of the tribe, standing was determined by birth. The implications for competition in Maori society can at once be perceived. Caste excludes "free" competition

[1] It is also likely that the consistent decline in population due to wars and the ravages of disease gave many more individuals rank.

because it assigns to each man his role in life, prevents change of social function and position, and minutely regulates individual behavior.[1]  At most, competition is limited to an intra-caste form.  Primogeniture accordingly fixed the extent and nature of competition among the Maori.

There could be, of course, no competition between the chiefs and commoners, or between the commoners and slaves.  The mana of the first-born in a continuous line set its recipient apart and elevated him above the others.  A commoner could never become a chief.  Moreover, it would be impossible for chiefs belonging to the same tribe to vie with one another, since they traced their descent from a common ancestor with mana warranties rigidly defined in the genealogies.  Hence, competition could be effective only between chiefs of different tribes, where the genealogies were unequated and the proof of superior mana was put on an experimental or competitive basis.

A moot question can now be raised as to the amount of social dissociation occasioned by property distinctions.  It has been seen that the chief outstripped his subjects in possession of wealth.  If not the actual owner he was the beneficiary of more land resources and slave work.  The food surplus accumulated in his storehouses was greater and more dependable.  But divergent economic interest did not exist.  With primogeniture, if the wealth surplus was of a more cumulative character, and if the population increased, classes would naturally arise.  A small group of the highborn would come into vast fortunes, the entire wealth of the society polarizing toward them.  Those with a less fortunate birthright would increasingly fall into the class of the disinherited.  All commentators on Maori life unanimously agree that such a development had not occurred among these people.

The absence of important property distinctions between chief and commoner is clear.  It was not the chief alone who had considerable economic interests at stake in the event of an attack by an enemy.  The subjugation of one tribe by another might mean the payment of tribute by the vanquished—a hardship suffered equally by all members of the tribe.  The confiscation of tribal land affected the commoner as well as the chief.  The identity of interests on the economic level matched precisely the common

[1] *Cf.* Leopold von Wiese, *Systematic Sociology* (trans. by H. Becker), p. 259.

impulse to preserve the glorious mana of the original tribal ancestor. Let any chief be offended or slighted in any way and it was natural for the whole tribe to rise in his defense. More than that, if a commoner became thus embroiled with an enemy he was deserving of the same support. Manifestly Maori social stratification was not a disruptive mechanism hindering the identification of individual with group. Both the omnipresent descent factor and the common economic interests prevented the individual from ranging himself against the group.

The inevitableness with which primogeniture leads to neglect of individual capabilities for their own sake raises a different problem. Every caste society must face the prospect of reducing the value of individual contributions by encircling whole groups within unscalable walls. This inherent weakness in a caste system necessarily introduces an element of instability into the society. Fortunately for Maori society the rule of primogeniture was not rigidly interpreted except as it defined the tabus imposed by the first-born's inherited mana, as we shall see (p.452). The religious and the political powers established by birth in the nobleman's person could be disjoined, and this insured a more adequate political functioning.

*Production.*—The basic principles in the organization of work can be gleaned from an examination of the different types of productive activities. The erection of the public meeting house mentioned in the foregoing discussion offers an example of large-scale construction. A small army of unskilled labor was called upon for the hauling and setting up of timbers. Experts were called in for dressing, thatching, reed work, paneling, and carving. Some of these experts, men of wide reputation, were imported from other villages so that the structure might be a truly great achievement. A meeting house which, when completed, held fifteen hundred people might take anywhere from three to eight years to build and give employment to hundreds of men. The lavish woodcarvings alone generally took three to four years to complete. The finished hall exhibited the highest forms of technical skill and artistic expression.

The method of making great war canoes was also a protracted process. A tree selected to form the hull was cut down by relays of men aided by fires set in the trunk. A *tohunga* (priest), a specialist in forest lore, superintended the work.  The unskilled work connected with canoe making was performed by a large number of men, who cut down large trees, hollowed them out, and fitted them together.  The work of carving out the canoe and of drilling holes in the sections took months.  Usually the work was watched by two skilled men, one on each side of the canoe.  These tohunga carefully supervised the activity of the adzmen, seeing that the carving was done evenly and that the finished product was perfect.[1]

The technology involved in acquiring food illustrates still more clearly the principles of work organization.  To the Maori who lived in the vicinity of the forest lands birds were a stable source of food supply.  Trees regularly used for fowling belonged to each person or household.  No one dared to trespass on the property of another and take birds which did not belong to him.  The motive in bird snaring appears to be the acquisition of food for the community, but the keen rivalry among the young men to secure the largest catch bears evidence of the strong individualistic incentives which dominated the work.  After the catch was collected and the required ritual performed, all the gains were laid out in the village square, those of each household in separate heaps.  The chief and his people then gathered around, commenting on the success of each whanau, commending the owners of the large heaps, ridiculing the smaller contributions.  The chief publicly censured those who brought in only a few birds.  At night when the people met in the meeting house they praised the successful young men for having displayed expert craftsmanship.  After inspection and appraisement by the community, the whole was ceremonially handed over to the chief.  He might present the entire catch to a visiting chief or give it to the members of his village without keeping a single bird for himself.  He customarily turned each heap of birds back to the family group who had snared them.[2]

The Maori were familiar with several fishing techniques.  The *Koko* method of *keke* fishing demanded the cooperation of two men.  One manipulated the net; the other the pole.  While the poleman excited the fish and drove them toward the channel, the

---

[1] J. Cowan, *The Maori Yesterday and Today*, p. 154.

[2] The organization of bird snaring and the various fishing activities are further described in Firth, *op. cit.*, pp. 137–152, 210–219.

netman stood at the channel and by swift, twisting movements brought up the fish.

Fresh-water fishing necessitated the organized effort of a group of people. The fishermen entered the water with implements to drive the fish in the direction of the rapids, where a net was ready to receive them. Most often the composition of this fishing group was of a haphazard sort. If the whanau was large enough and had sufficient males it constituted such a fishing group.

A spectacular activity and one which called for a considerable amount of coordination was the deep-water fishing. The net expert dived down and set the net. Then he gave the signal to his assistants, who would dive in a prearranged formation to make their way up the channels simultaneously so as to converge and drive the fish into the net.

Fishing by means of the enormous sieve nets was performed by the whole village. Because the net was too large for a single canoe it was placed on the deck of two war canoes lashed together. A large number of men were involved in this activity; the double canoe was paddled by thirty men, the net was let out by six. The director of the enterprise sat on a high tower near by and gave orders. When he was satisfied that a good shoal had been approached he gave a signal. The net was immediately thrown out and everyone in the village gathered on the shore and helped to drag it in.

By far the largest scale economic venture was shark fishing. As a source of food supply it was unsurpassed; as a sport it was most popular. Firth describes the setting of one of these events: "In all, there were people from half a dozen villages assembled, with a muster of fifty canoes. As each had a crew of about twenty there were about at least a thousand people engaged, in addition to the many who remained in camp cooking and drying shellfish."[1] Many details had to be attended to in preparation for the festive occasion. Canoes were fitted out, platforms were erected, hooks were repaired, and bait was secured. When finally all was in readiness the crew launched the canoes. The organization of shark fishing was exceedingly complicated. The chief or an expert held the ultimate control. Under him there were a dozen captains. These captains were in control of the camp, of the preparatory bait fishing, of the various canoe fleets, etc. In this

[1] P. 216.

way the activity was thoroughly systematized, and there was a formal sequence of steps to be followed. The responsibility for the success of the coordination was centered in a few people, whose functions were clearly defined and specialized. As many as seven thousand sharks might be caught in two days of such fishing.

Rivalry was stimulated among the different crews by the great honor attached to obtaining the first fish. Rivalry here is of the form which seems to run consistently through this society. There was never competition among individuals for the economic necessities of life. There may have been wars between tribes for fertile land, but only in this connection can we speak at all of economic competition. Individual incentives were socialized because the needs of the community superseded all else. However, in meeting these needs, persons competed strenuously to gain the approval of the community, to win renown, and to acquire prestige. The needs of the individual were always best served by serving the community. The fact that a particular crew hooked the most sharks did not mean that it would have more to eat, nor did it entail disgrace for the others who did not happen to haul in the first shark.

The organization of agriculture varied with the natural possibilities of cultivation. Where productive land was scarce, a few men carried on all the diverse tasks. In those places where *kumara* planting was profitable, cooperative labor and specialization was the rule. When it was known that the owner of a plot of land was going to plant kumara, between twenty and forty men from the village would offer their services. With them came women and children.[1] "The work was carried out in what may be termed a military manner. The men were ranged in a row, a little distance apart from each other, but in echelon, and carried out the work in that peculiar formation."[2] Each man would loosen the soil, form a little mound, plant the tuber, and move on. When one row was finished, the whole line at the given command, marched one step to the rear and were ready to begin another row. The women of the village had previously brought gravel to be put on the land. It was a man's job to loosen it. As they worked, they sang in chorus and recited proverbs in unison,

---

[1] Cowan, *op. cit.*, pp. 183–184.

[2] Best, *The Maori*, Vol. 2, p. 377.

"Whilst the warrior stands insecurely the cultivator will never fall."[1]

Sometimes planting was carried on by large groups in the form of "planting bees." "If it was a working party, three men or perhaps four may be detached as breakers-up of the soil; and an equal number also to form the mounds. . . . First came the *karko* or diggers who broke up the soil with their long staves. Then came the *taugata tuaha*, who pulverized the soil and worked ashes into it, if any such were at hand, also gravel if necessary; also they formed mounds. Then came the *Kaironaki* . . . distributors of seed, who placed a seed tuber on each mound, after whom came . . . the planters."[2] When the roots ripened the women were permitted to loosen the surface of the soil while the old men frightened away the rats. Slaves did not participate in these activities since agricultural tapus were among the most powerful.

The elements of Maori technology have been described without emphasis on the division of labor. Special treatment must be given to this aspect of production, for in Maori society the division of labor both sets and solves some fundamental problems in cooperation and competition.

*Division of Labor.*—The division of labor by age distinguished between two sets of minor tasks, one reserved for children and another for the aged. Children were sent on errands to gather firewood or to collect mud with which to smear canoes. They helped in the household work and were eligible for performing a great many trivial duties connected with men's work. Since they were free from the restrictions of tapu their activities were not so specifically determined as those of adults. The first-born child of the chief, however, was compelled to observe the tapus and usually several slaves or commoners were his constant companions to see that he did not violate them. Old people passed their time in useful but leisurely labor. They made twine and cordage for nets; the old men polished stone implements; old women plaited baskets.

The division of labor between the sexes had more than biological significance. Of course the men attended to the more vigorous and arduous occupations, and the women to the routine, colorless tasks. The former were engaged in bird snaring, rat trapping,

[1] Andersen, *op. cit.*, p. 1.
[2] Best, "Maori Agriculture," pp. 158–159.

fishing, horticulture, canoe making, carving, etc. The latter preserved and prepared foods, made garments, collected forest foods, and were permitted to join in the bird snaring, a few kinds of fishing, and some of the preliminary phases of tilling the soil. But the tapu stringently defined the scope of each sex. Hence the kumara was planted, canoes and houses were built, and most of the fishing occupations were performed, by men alone, for the potent tapu of these activities prohibited women's participation.

The rules of tapu were also important in the division of labor on the basis of rank. The work of slaves among the Maori has been classified with women's work.[1] If this is to be accepted, one genuine difference in the basis for the assignment of their work should be kept in mind. Although the slaves were burdened with the household drudgery and heavy labor they were completely tapuless; this is in distinction to women, who as full-fledged members of the tribe possessed some tapu, however weak. The slaves were forced to perform unpleasant tasks because of their lack of tapu. But they also were excluded from many rigorous labors, for example, canoe making and planting, because of the powerful tapus associated with these occupations. The presence of slaves in a household thus did not mean idleness for the other occupants. Firth has remarked that "rank with all its privileges still involved a division and not a repudiation of labor."[2]

The implications of social stratification for the division of labor is apparent in the work required of men of high rank. The chiefs and *rangatira* (junior noblemen) were organizers of economic activities, skilled artisans and specialists, leaders in all pursuits. Only ranking men could practice highly tapu'd arts such as carving, tattooing, war-canoe making, meeting-house building. Each enterprise, whether it was fishing, bird snaring, forest work, or planting, had to be supervised by a tohunga, one of the noble experts. The tohunga had to have, in addition to technical knowledge in their crafts, particular religious lore to guarantee their efficacy. Specialization was consequently a function of religious power, which in turn was dependent upon rank. And just as rank was hereditary so the specialized

[1] W. von Brun, p. 23.

[2] Firth, *op. cit.*, p. 205.

occupations tended to become hereditary, passed down from father to son. Stone workers, carvers, tool makers could trace the working at their crafts directly to the ingenuity and mana of some ancestor.

Social stratification, then, in Maori society is responsible for minimizing competition; it tends also to reinforce cooperation by being fitted into the division of labor. By monopolizing a prominent place in production, high-ranking persons made themselves indispensable and laid the basis for cooperation between groups of different status.

Technological division of labor presents a problem in the relationship between leadership and forms of work organization. In the simpler occupations, where only two or three men worked together, the leader was usually a participating figure whose task in the work required greater skill or experience. So in keke fishing, the net expert was invariably the leader, the poleman acting as an assistant. In more complicated technologies the leader was a nonparticipant and purely a coordinator or director. In the case of shark fishing, the chief was an administrative officer checking on his subordinate commanders, who headed the separate phases of the activity. The intermediate stage in leadership was found in the sieve-net fishing. Here the leader was first in the position of a director selecting the proper shoal and giving the signal for action. Later he climbed out of this tower and participated in the netting.

In contrast to shark fishing, many activities required no active leadership or were entirely leaderless, for example, log hauling or catching fresh-water fish. It will be noted that where all the workers performed the same task, the leader was unimportant. Simple coordination in this case could be achieved through the accompaniment of rhythmic chants and choral recitations, special songs for each occupation. In horticulture and in the operation of the great sieve nets, where specialization of function and organization of sequence were stressed, the leader was essential. In brief, complexity of technology advanced the cooperative character of production and made the role of a leader necessary to maintain the functioning of the very cooperation which called him forth.

The procedures observed in distribution may be logically divided into two parts: whanau distribution, and those forms of

division applicable to the larger economic groups.   In the former
case a simple rule was practiced.   Each individual contributed to
the family stock and drew from it according to his needs.

The general principles underlying distribution in the collective
enterprises are explicit in the following examples.   In eel trapping, the chief apportioned the catch among the family groups
probably on the basis of their size.[1]   The gain of fishing by netting
was divided into equal portions by an old man and was handed
over to the participating families.   Buck's description of the
method of distribution employed in *inanga* fishing is perhaps
most conclusive on this point.   When the canoes were beached
the women standing around the shore had their baskets filled.
"In those communistic days nobody went away empty, but, at
the same time, a distinction was made in favor of the workers."[2]
A man who could be counted upon not to play favorites portioned
out the catch.   "More [was] given to the women of those who
had got wet skins through working.   On the other hand, when
the womenfolk of a nonworker approached with their baskets
the cry was . . . 'not deep,' hence the significance of the phrase
is easily understood.   'Not deep, not deep; a dry skin.' "   The
participants, it would seem, were rewarded for labor expended
with additional compensation proportional to their needs.

In agriculture, however, a new note was struck in the relation
between production and distribution.   It will be recalled that the
land was divided into household plots usually cultivated by
members of the community, who turned out *en masse*.   But the
crop was harvested by the whanau alone to be stored in its
common storehouse.   Evidently it was the last feature of agricultural production—harvesting—which selected the sharers in
distribution.   The communal aspect of agriculture must be
considered a technological device the operation of which did not
wholly jibe with the distributive mechanism.   Rather distribution in this sphere was adjusted to property relations.   The
whanau owned the land and hence appropriated the produce.
The fact that others had worked on the land was irrelevant.

The incomparable place of the feast in communal distribution
deserves careful analysis.   It was a vital social, political, and
economic institution among the Maori.   Certain feasts marked

[1] Best, "An Eel Fiesta," p. 108.
[2] Buck, p. 441.

births, baptisms, marriages, deaths. Others were held on such regular occasions as planting, harvesting, and first fruits. Feasts facilitated social intercourse; greeted the coming of war allies; concluded peace negotiations; constituted the first step in entertaining visitors. Then, too, there were what might be called economic feasts which initiated village undertakings.

Preparations for a feast of any sort preoccupied the whole community. As soon as the feast was proposed by the chief, the villagers began to collect food. The last reserves of the village might be tapped. New kumara land was planted; rats, birds, and fish were accumulated in incredible quantities. If the occasion happened to be an intertribal feast, preparations assumed such gigantic proportions that an entire year was necessary for their completion.

Whatever the original purpose of the feast, its social character appeared to be the only thing of moment. The native proverb says: "Should you awaken me from my sleep let it be for the purpose of eating bread [feasting]." The feast over, the community might be totally impoverished but this possibility did not deter it from lavishing its laboriously collected surplus. The noble host remained with what was more important than food—satisfaction that his reputation for generosity had been upheld. This enhancement of the chief's honor was gratification enough for his people.

The objects of distribution and remuneration were regarded as gifts. They were either given to the community by the chief in the form of shares to the household and feasts to the village, or handed to individuals for private services rendered. Carvers, tattooers, and directors of economic enterprises received individual remuneration. Besides provisions, they might be awarded greenstone, feather ornaments, adz blades, and fine cloaks.

It is thus patent that Maori distribution was fundamentally dominated by one aim: to meet the needs of the community. No one could starve so long as anything remained in the community storehouses. The barriers set up by the normal rules of distribution were broken down in time of food shortage. In the event of such a calamity, the division of a fish catch among participating households or the individual gains acquired through solitary expeditions no longer held. The chief's stores were thrown open to the community; all food brought into the village was apportioned to all who were in need. On the other hand, work was required of each individual, and the laws of distribution recognized the primacy of the participants in production. It was seen that the division of products closely followed the nature of the technology. In the highly cooperative tasks equal shares were given out except where greater needs (size of family) meant increased shares. Consistently the results of individually operated industries were claimed by the individual workers. Fish caught by the line were kept by the individual fishermen. Likewise, in the northern districts, shark catches were not divided at all, and each person marked the sharks that he himself had caught. A lucid explanation for this difference is found in the fact that in the north sharks were caught individually on hooks.

The positive correlation that exists between the complexity of technology and cooperation in production is obvious. Where productive techniques have been at all ingeniously contrived, the division of labor has necessarily been intricate, and since the division of labor in a single enterprise by definition implies cooperation there can be no doubt that the nature of the technology and cooperation in production are closely connected.

Thus sieve-net and shark fishing, planting, and constructing meeting houses in Maori society demand the diligent cooperation of individuals in order to manipulate the technologies at their command. Such technologies are characterized by a large variety of tasks performed by the working group as well as specialized roles apportioned to particular individuals within the working group. No single aspect of the work has therefore independent efficacy but must be carried out with reference to the other agents in the work organization. Hence, a task in which there is considerable division of labor cannot be successfully executed without cooperation and coordination.

The fact that increasing complexity of technology involves a higher division of labor need not be labored. A glance at the organization of Maori shark fishing will suffice to demonstrate its truth. Each working unit achieved some degree of independence from the total range of activities. And each individual cooperated in his small group to the exclusion of the other groups, although the whole enterprise was a cooperative venture. Progress in the division of labor proceeds by the reduction in size and in scope of the cooperative units. Items which are at first manufactured in a few operations are by the introduction of more refined techniques constantly broken down into more numerous operations. The point is finally reached as in our own society where the individuals who function in the productive process do not perceive the part they play in the whole and can dispense with any conscious effort at cooperation. But objectively cooperation is indeed heightened. The interdependence among all the units grows more critical and coordination is accorded an all-important place.

Psychologically speaking, the subjective state of the Maori individual in cooperative work little resembles that of the modern industrial worker. The Western individual, isolated in an obscure corner of the productive process and motivated by a standardized wage, has no reason for estimating his own activity as cooperative. On the other hand, the Maori worker, by the claims of a simpler technology, is thrust into a visible cooperative setting in which he is fully aware both of the total procedure and of his subordinate function. It is incumbent upon him to cooperate consciously or see the enterprise fail. The psychological differences arising from cooperative production exhibited by the Maori and individuals in our own society are due in part to the relative distance from the center of production; that is, the Maori individual is permitted a perspective of production that is denied to the worker in machine civilization. But the influence of what we have called distance stands in an insignificant light when we come to determine the importance of property relations in this connection.

Working together "toward an end" means one thing when the end is turned to the advantage of an individual who is not even a participant in production, and something quite different when that end is realized by a society or a group. In a society in which the means of production are privately owned and the operators in production are not the receivers of its fruits, the cooperative outlook displayed in the performance of work and the "instinct of workmanship" will be at a low ebb. Cooperation in this circumstance can be merely a mechanical reflex of the division of labor. But in Maori society, the means of production are collectively owned. The motivation for group cooperation is the knowledge that the returns of its labor will belong to the individuals in the group. The economic structure of society is in this way responsible for creating cooperative attitudes in work.

The evidence conclusively establishes the connection between cooperation in production with the nature of the technology on the one hand and the cooperative *Geist* with the distributive mechanism on the other. The presence or absence of a correlation between cooperation in production and cooperative attitudes in work will depend on the relation of distribution to production. In the Maori case a high degree of cooperation in production goes with collectivism in distribution. However collectivism in distribution need not follow automatically from cooperation in production. Too many societies with socialized productive systems, notably our own, have a strongly contrasting, nonsocialized system of distribution. It is obvious that in Maori society, where the returns of production go to the working groups and not to a few distant owners, social antagonism is obviated and conflict between the producers and the owners cannot arise to weaken the structure of society.

## THE INDIVIDUAL AND THE GROUP

The integration that was achieved in Maori society is further illuminated by a study of the motivations which were inculcated in the individual and the relation in which he stood to the mechanisms of social control. The motives which dominated him facilitated social integration, and the personality traits which were stressed were relevant to the major emphases of the society.

*Social Control.*—The tapu was a fundamental legal mechanism in Maori life. Practically every aspect of the society was clothed, to a greater or lesser degree, in this magic quality imparted by the gods to a person or thing. Things tapu were to be avoided since they were contagious and by mere contact could loose their dangerous power. The severity of the penalty for violating a tapu was directly proportionate to its intensity. Thus if a commoner were to eat food previously touched by a chief who was supremely tapu, he would surely die.[1]

---

[1] Maning cites a case in which a slave died in approximately twelve hours after the infringement of such a tapu. Reliable observers have recorded many similar cases. Undoubtedly, a kind of autosuggestion is responsible for a native's dying immediately after violating a tapu. Brill has spoken of this phenomenon as psychic suicide.

The more important the objects were to the community, the more intense the tapu. War canoes, eel weirs, and meeting houses were highly charged with tapu, whereas small fishing canoes and ordinary houses were generally tapuless. Likewise the tapu of a person increased with rank, with the chief possessing the highest grade. Many economic pursuits had strong tapu associations, especially agriculture and forest work. The pervasiveness of the tapu did not paralyze the functioning of the society; many tapus could be removed or manipulated into ineffectualness by ritual observances.

Tapu was the principal force acting for the preservation of social stratification. The position of the chief remained intact; the tapu guarding his rank was a bulwark against competitors. To the individual the tapu constituted a formidable threat: either he kept inside the impenetrable shell of his caste or he was thrust out of the society entirely.

Coupled with the tapu was the concept of mana. The latter, the magic power of the individual or group, could be lost permanently or temporarily by breaking a tapu. Mana, again, increased with the rank of the person. Yet, in contrast to the tapu, its strength was often objectively evaluated by the personal success of the bearer. A man who had achieved excellence in some activity such as war, woodcarving, executive ability, etc., had active mana. Likewise the chief who was a capable provider for his people and was also able to give great feasts and conduct successful wars was the holder of a great mana. As for the man who had the unsurpassed misfortune to be captured in war and reduced to slavery, it was self-evident that he had lost his mana.

The possessors of superior mana were obliged to maintain the dignity of their station. Hence, the *rangatira*, people of high rank, were exceedingly touchy. Any insult, no matter how slight, or any injury to their pride rendered compensation necessary. Compensation within the tribe did not create resentment and "was supposed not to cause any rupture of friendship between the persons concerned."[1] If a family had some property stolen during its absence, it might go to the house of the thief and take back as much property as it deemed compensatory for the original loss plus its outraged feelings.

[1] Donne, p. 93.

Between tribes, however, an insult aroused vicious antipathy. Although much war was economic in origin, *i.e.*, over land, it is hardly possible to separate the economic cause from insult. To attempt to expropriate another tribe's land was tantamount to questioning that tribe's mana. And only internecine war could settle the question of whose mana was superior.

At this point we are led to note a primary mechanism of social control—the pride of the individual. It has been suggested by field workers in New Zealand that every Maori was an aristocrat who knew what things were "just not done," who did not need coercion to put him in his place, and whose nobility of soul was sufficient to keep him in line. But pride never took on a competitive form within the tribe. Nothing was to be gained by shaming anyone. Even in the case of the chief's censuring a family that was recalcitrant in meeting its economic obligations, the proper thing for the community was to forget the unhappy incident. And if, by an unforgivable lack of tact, someone recalled and mentioned it, the family was shamed and justified in taking stringent action against that person. Pride in regulating behavior took precedence, in some cases, over fear of tapu. At other times pride was so preeminent that persons would carry out their own punishment, anticipating the retribution of the aggrieved parties. A man having had prohibited intercourse with a slave girl killed himself before his wife's relatives had the opportunity to punish him.[1]

The *muru* was an institution devised to remind the individual of the primacy of collective interests. It was a form of punishment that consisted in plundering a person of his property. A man who met with an accident and thereby deprived the community of his services was liable to muru. The death of a man might call for a muru against his friends, who should not have permitted him to die. Similarly, the parents of a child who had died from some natural cause were muru'd; they should have better protected it. Women, it seems, were a frequent cause of murus. If a married woman committed adultery her family usually compensated her husband with a land settlement. But the husband of a woman who eloped with another man was plundered; he should have been more discerning than to be unaware of such an affair.

[1] *Ibid.*, pp. 94–95.

A young married couple were muru'd on the evening of the day following the wedding. The friends of the couple were entertained with food and drink; they sang and danced and then became obstreperous. The couple was roughly handled and everything portable, robes, weapons, ornaments, and food, was carried off. This muru at marriage was similar to that performed on more serious occasions, but exactly what moral the punitive expedition endeavored to impress on the married pair is inexplicable.

Nothing in the marriage situation contradicted the group ideal. Premarital relations were not forbidden. In inconsequential flirtations boys visited the girls at their homes or arranged meetings in the forest near by. If the girl came to the home of the boy and stayed with him overnight the act constituted a marriage. Courting followed the pattern of our own culture, with coyness displayed by the girl and pursuit engaged in by the boy. Among the commoners of some tribes public selection of mates took place. A young man could indicate his wish to marry a girl by pointing out his choice from among the assemblage of the village inhabitants. Girls also had the right to propose to young men in this way. The slight embarrassment that might be provoked by refusals on either side was swept away in a joke. Marriage of high-ranking persons was more formally consummated. The genealogies of the two parties were carefully examined with an eye to the possible elevation in rank of the coming offspring. An exception to the customary endogamy practice obtained in marriages of noble persons belonging to different tribes to form intertribal alliances.[1] There was certainly little sign of competition in the marriage atmosphere, either in cultural phrasing or in actuality. Affinal exchanges which play a paramount role in Samoa were here practically ignored.

The sufferer's attitude toward the muru was a mixture of apprehension and delight. On the one hand, the destruction and loss of property was mortifying. However, to have been selected as a person of enough consequence to warrant raiding bolstered up his pride.

---

[1] "If a well-born member of one tribe marries into another he or she will act as a cord to draw that tribe to our assistance in war." Maori proverb.

The complete efficacy of the muru may be questioned from another aspect. Sometimes a lesser chief would feel grossly insulted by the slighting of a higher chief in the same tribe. The chief whose vanity had been wounded could not retaliate by going to war since he could not muster forces enough and, more important, a war within the tribe was beyond the realm of possibility. His only recourse lay in antagonizing an enemy tribe and precipitating war. The higher chief would then have to come to the defense of his sullen fellow tribesman, who solaced himself with the hope that his ally would be killed or ruined by the war. This is one case in which pride negated the interests of the tribe.

*Personality Traits.*—The Maori ideal in individual behavior was explicit. Their guiding proverb went, "These are the ways by which men gain influence in the world—by laboring for abundance of food to feed others, by collecting property to give to others, and by similar means by which you promote the goods of others, so that peace spreads through the world."[1] Generosity was the personal virtue most esteemed. Unless an individual displayed generosity in all his dealings with people he stood little chance of attaining social recognition.

Moreover the individualism characteristic of Maori personality was securely harnessed to the needs of the group. Stress was not laid on fulfilling one's share of a cooperative undertaking; this was taken for granted. There were no special rules for working well with people. Personal contributions were valued in a manner almost detached from the requirements of the cooperative working. Individual achievement and resourcefulness in special occupations were acclaimed by the whole group. Persons of all classes gained prestige by excelling in any endeavor. Commoners, of course, could seldom become tattooers or woodcarvers, because these callings were suited to men of high rank exclusively. But everyone could be a good warrior and there are cases of commoners being elected war chiefs. Able agriculturists were appreciated by the community; they had great mana. Directors of the special economic activities were customarily drawn from the noblemen and occasionally from the commoners. Innate

---

[1] Grey, *Polynesian Mythology* (Legend of Maui, pp. 16–58). If we substitute "tribe" for "world" at the end of the above quotation we have a more accurate description of the cultural ideal.

capacities, talents, and ambitions were respected, and although caste lines prevented them from being given unconditionally free expression, they were the determinants for the mobility between castes that did exist.

In some instances individualism passed into exhibitionism. A little notoriety was never frowned upon. Young people were able to show off by violating slight tapus. An enamored couple might take courage and exuberantly trespass on tapu ground. Young men, to flaunt their cunning, might steal tapu articles. Pranks of the latter sort were enjoyed by the members of the community and the older men did not object, recognizing that this was worthy practical training for dealing with enemy tribes. The spectacular did not go unappreciated. There were star performers in games, and solo play in connection with certain economic activity (shark fishing, deep-water fishing, etc.) delighted the villagers.

It is therefore not too difficult to trace the transition from the individualism within the tribe to the aggressive, ruthless type outside. The individual identified himself too closely with his tribe to do other than fit his personal qualities to the cultural ideals and requirements. The "chip on the shoulder" attitude was canalized outside the group. Maori war throws this into sharp relief.

Individuals who were more than normally aggressive, that is, accomplished ruffians, might prove to be great nuisances at home; and if they went into the enemy's territory on a foraging expedition and were killed, though the tribe might be secretly relieved, it nevertheless went to war. No quarter or generosity was shown between opposing sides in time of war. "A man's mana increased according as he could destroy the mana of the enemy, no matter how he did it."[1] Lying, theft, cunning, deceit, treachery, cruelty, in short, anything and everyting was legitimate. "Manslaying," said the Maori, "is one of man's most important activities, it is . . . the great game; better to die weapon in hand than by lingering sickness of old age."[2]

Individual aggressiveness could not always be deflected outside the tribe. There were times when it was inverted, causing turmoils within the tribe. Disputes between hapu over bound-

[1] Keesing, p. 29.
[2] Best, *The Maori*, Vol. 2, p. 221.

aries frequently resulted in mutual raiding. Or the village witnessed fierce internal squabbling in which murder and bloodshed was not an uncommon outcome. But basically tribal solidarity was preserved by the cooperative behavior engendered by social structure.[1]

*Education.*—The personality traits enumerated above were deliberately instilled in the young. Children were always treated with kindness.[2] They were neither shamed nor warned in the process of their education, but simply advised. They were spoken to by adults as equals. Small children were allowed to sit by their elders in tribal assembly and apparently took an interest in the proceedings. On a question that their elders were debating, children might ask questions and they were answered gravely. A boy at an early age was taken in hand by his father and grandfather. He accompanied the older people in their daily pursuits, performed minor tasks, and ran errands.[3] The attitude of the parents to their children promoted the early maturing of the latter.

Family education consisted in instructing the young in tribal traditions, genealogies, and relationships. The older kinsman who usually undertook this part of the training used effective pedagogical tricks to impress the children with the awe of traditional knowledge. He would shout in an angry tone. The children "will inquire as to the meaning of the expression, thinking that it conveys a sense of blame. And so knowledge is acquired."[4]

Precautions were taken to mold the child to the group ideal. "Sympathy and good feeling [were] the most important things in the world"[5] and they were consciously taught. When a child was given some delicacy to eat an older person might ask him

[1] With the arrival of the English in New Zealand, tribal solidarity began to weaken and the social structure to crumble (*cf.* Maning). Hapu waged war against hapu. Hapu of different tribes combined to fight their relatives allied with the English.

[2] The exception being the sporadic practice of infanticide in the time of food shortage or a long siege. Parents would then exchange children so as not to eat their own offspring. Best, *The Maori*, Vol. 1, p. 413.

[3] On bird-snaring expeditions boys were taken along to observe the snaring techniques and to learn boundaries.

[4] Best, *ibid.*, Vol. 2, p. 66.

[5] From the dying speech of a chief, quoted by Best.

for it in order to train him to be unselfish. Lessons in generosity and tribal identification were constantly given to the growing children, and no occasion was missed to impress the value of these traits upon their minds.

Young people amused themselves in countless ways. On winter evenings they would meet in a large house and play games, tell stories, sing, and dance. Some games demanded manual dexterity and agility; some required calculation, mental alertness; many were useful exercises for military training and aquatic games. Parties were arranged to visit other villages and compete for honors in kite flying, wrestling, posture dancing, canoe racing, dart throwing, etc. The older people encouraged contests which demanded agility and quickness of eye and movement in boys and young men. Running, jumping, practice in the use of weapons—all the martial sports were viewed with favor. These accentuated individualistic behavior while those that were competitive acted as an incentive for the young to become fit warriors.[1]

Young people,[2] according to the premise behind Maori education, were the property of the tribe, its future strength.[3] "Early and constant training for war was essential to the welfare of the tribe." Thus parents would encourage their boys to divide into two groups and assail each other, their light reeds being used as both striking and thrusting weapons. Not infrequently wounds were inflicted even with these light articles, as when used as a thrusting spear. Then the boys might be roused to anger, and so cast away their light implements, and procuring stones, engage in a more dangerous contest. This would bring the parents on the scene, who would interfere in behalf of their chil-

[1] Certain songs rendered in accompaniment to dances were composed for the following occasions: reception of native visitors, reception of government officials, an insulting remark made by a tribesman, ill-treatment of a woman married into another tribe, a faithless wife, an oversight in the apportioning of food, etc. Best, *ibid.*, Vol. 2, p. 177.

[2] The youngest child among the Maori was considered to be a distinct psychological type. A youngest child was spoken of as a "self-extolling or ambitious last-born" and an "adz-breaking child" referring to the mischievous boy who gets hold of his father's stone adz and spoils its sharp edge. This conception of the youngest child may have pointed significance for Adlerian theory. By action of primogeniture the youngest were disinherited and this may account for the character attributed to them.

[3] Firth, *op. cit.*, p. 173.

dren.   It sometimes occurred that the elders became excited and quarreled among themselves, the matter ending in a general affray.   Lives were occasionally lost in such an encounter.[1] Fortunately the general flow of Maori social life was not disturbed by overfrequent upset of the educational system in this way.

An interesting aspect of Maori education was the "House of Learning."   For a few months during the winter, young men of high rank and tested intelligence gathered to receive instruction in tribal lore, legends, genealogies, religious rites, and black magic. This occurred under the strictest surveillance of the tapu. Courses of a less sacred character were given to the whole community in astronomy, fishing, and agriculture.   As Best puts it: "The object of the School of Learning was to preserve all desirable knowledge pertaining to the subjects already mentioned, and other traditional lore, and to hand it down the centuries free of any alteration, omission, interpolation, or deterioration."[2]   Deviation from the accepted teaching was discountenanced and any slip in the imparting of knowledge was punished by death at the hands of the infuriated gods.[3]

Despite the great gaps in the literature pertaining to education, the development of individualistic traits in the child, their continued emphasis throughout the life of the individual, and the admission of all individualistic motivations in the framework of collective ends form a consistent whole with the society's structural imperatives.

Though Maori society insistently prescribes individual compliance with group demands, it does not submerge the individual, but, indeed, trusts its successful functioning to the full realization of individual potentialities and personality.   The individual cannot help being a pure patriot when he is bound up in a genealogy that includes every member of his group and is furthermore tied to his fellows by tangible and common economic interests.   His patriotism is a natural safeguard for the society, defending it against all enemies, and is at the same time a motive force within the society.   Pride in himself and pride in the society are two

---

[1] Best, *The Maori*, Vol. 2, p. 81.

[2] Quoted by Firth, *op. cit.*, p. 177.

[3] A young man upon the completing of his training at the House of Learning was supposed to cause the death of a close relative, father, mother, or brother, in order to give mana to his newly acquired magic.

aspects of the same feeling.   To contribute to society feeds both
the pride in himself and his pride of society.

The fact that pride can sometimes act as a boomerang against
the society is not inherent in the situation itself.   These instances
of incomplete identification with the tribe can be viewed either as
individual aberrancy, or, in the case of a whole village conspiring
against the interests of the tribe[1] as an aspect of the general
breakdown of the tribal structure.   What competition there was
for prestige at points where rank permitted it, did not undermine
the cooperative social forms.

*Bibliography*[2]

ANDERSEN, J. C.: *Maori Life in Ao-tea*, Whitcombe and Tombs Ltd.,
Melbourne and London, 1907.
BEST, E.: "An Eel Fiesta," *Journal of Science and Technology*, Vol. 5, 1922.
————: "Beliefs of the Maori," *Journal of the Polynesian Society*, Vol. 7,
1898.
————: "Maori Agriculture," *Dominion Museum Bulletin*, No. 9, Wellington,
New Zealand, 1925.
————: *The Maori*, Tombs Ltd., Wellington, New Zealand, 1924.
BRUN, W. VON: "Die Wirtschaftsorganisation der Maori auf Neuseeland,"
*Beiträge zur Kultur und Universalgeschichte*, Voigtländer Verlag, No. 18,
Leipzig, 1912.
BUCK, P. H.: "Maori Food Supplies of Lake Rotorua," *Transactions of
the New Zealand Institute*, Vol. 53, 1921.
COWAN, J.: *The Maori Yesterday and Today*, Whitcombe, Auckland, New
Zealand, 1930.
DONNE, T. E.: *The Maori Past and Present*, Seeley, Service and Company,
Ltd., London, 1927.
FIRTH, R.: *Primitive Economics of the New Zealand Maori*, E. P. Dutton &
Company, Inc., New York, 1929.
GREY, Sir G.: *Polynesian Mythology*, Murray, London, 1855.
KEESING, F. M.: *The Changing Maori*, Memoirs of the Board of Maori
Ethnological Research, Vol. 4, New Plymouth, New Zealand, 1928.
MANING, F. E.: *Old New Zealand*, Richard Bentley & Son, London, 1876.
WIESE, L. VON: *Systematic Sociology* (adapted and amplified by Howard
Becker), John Wiley & Sons, Inc., New York, 1932.

[1] This was a late development in any event.

[2] For a more comprehensive bibliography of the Maori see Firth, R.:
*Primitive Economics of the New Zealand Maori*, pp. 489–497.

# INTERPRETIVE STATEMENT

## *by* MARGARET MEAD

This is not a conclusion to this set of studies. Still less is it a set of final pronouncements on the subject of competition and cooperation. Those who have read the introduction with care and then followed through the series of studies of different cultures should be aware that this is not the type of material on the basis of which one can draw conclusions. From a survey such as this, we hope to get new insight, new illumination, suggestions for research, warnings against blind alleys, a sense of new relationships which seem genuinely worth exploring. Nor is this a conclusion meant to be read by those who would like to get a bird's-eye view of the book without troubling to read the concrete material. This chapter has no reason for being beyond its usefulness in bringing together and pointing up matters which are implicit, or disjunctive, or vague, or scattered throughout the various discussions.

Toward the end of the research, as I read over, first the shorter summaries, and later the complete accounts, I began to see that it was possible to classify each of these cultures, in terms of its major emphasis, as cooperative, competitive, or individualistic. It is important to remember that the material had not originally been organized to make any such classification; it was rather an arrangement which grew out of the material itself and gradually assumed more and more significance. It therefore seemed worthwhile to present all our interpretations in terms of this classification.

In characterizing each culture, I have attempted to view it as a social system, depending extensively for my definition of a social system upon discussions conducted by correspondence with Professor Radcliffe-Brown. According to this definition a social system consists of: (*a*) a number of individuals and (1) their intrinsic psycho-physical nature derived from heredity, and (2) their culture which they derive from their social environment;

(*b*) the interrelationships between these individuals which are dependent on (1) the actual composition of the group, in respect to age, sex, distribution of abilities and strengths, etc. and (2) the social structure prescribed by the culture; (*c*) non-human material objects involved in human interests or activities; and (*d*) relations of individuals to material objects. Now it was pointed out in the introduction that for six of the separate cultures studied, our data was not localized in time and place, and did not refer to one tribal or locality group. For those six cultures, therefore, we do not have information about the social system, but instead we possess information about a culture which was more or less characteristic of a number of social systems at different periods. Characterizing these six cultures therefore involves a large assumption: it is necessary to speak of one Ifugao system or one Maori tribe, *as if* its nature could be inferred from this wider and more general cultural data which we possess.

Looking at this material then *as if* it were data upon thirteen social systems, about which we knew all the relevant facts as outlined above, classifications as competitive, cooperative, and individualistic were made in terms of the following criteria:

(*a*) What are the principal ends to which an individual devotes his time? (*b*) What are the principal ends to which group activities are directed? (*c*) What are the proportions of time and energy devoted by individuals and by groups to ends which are (1) shared, (2) competitive, (3) individual? The ends necessarily stress the mechanisms of distribution of goods rather than techniques of production, and these do not necessarily correlate in a given society. The mechanisms of distribution are therefore primary in determining the major emphasis as cooperative, competitive, or individualistic.

The application of the criteria is admittedly rough since it involves a judgment of more or less upon data themselves incomparable. Nevertheless the range of difference in the thirteen cultures in these aspects of life was so great, and the extremes of the gamut so clear, that all those engaged upon the study were unanimous in their agreement. In a study devoted to cooperation and competition there was no doubt that the Kwakiutl were grossly competitive, the Bathonga grossly cooperative, and the Eskimo and Ojibwa grossly individualistic societies.

Nevertheless, no society is exclusively competitive or exclusively cooperative. The very existence of highly competitive groups implies cooperation within the groups. Both competitive and cooperative habits must coexist within the society. There is furious competition among the Kwakiutl at one stratum of the society—among the ranking chiefs—but within the household of each chief cooperation is mandatory for the amassing of the wealth that is distributed or destroyed. Similarly among the Manus the competitive exchanges between the wealthy entrepreneurs are dependent upon a degree of cooperation within the constellation of related persons who support the leader.

Nor did competition, as it was used in these criteria, necessarily mean conflict, and cooperation, solidarity. In the cooperative societies competition is often introduced and acts as an associative mechanism. The Maori strove to outdo one another in bird snaring and were honored publicly for their success, but the cooperative distribution of the catch was not affected; the rivalry served only to create higher productivity. The Dakota vied with one another for prestige, but the very terms in which they vied were a general giveaway to all and sundry.

Social systems can be classified from a great many points of view, and there is no reason for regarding the classifications of cooperative, competitive, and individualistic as the most significant. This must be borne in mind in the many instances where no correlation was found between the classification of societies as here presented and certain elements in the culture. Methodologically such lack of correlation generally means that these categories of cooperative, competitive, and individualistic are really only classifications of aspects of social systems to which only certain elements are relevant. Yet these classifications have proved useful in bringing to light certain interrelationships between the nature of the social structure and the kind of social life permitted within it.

Among the societies selected for study there were cultures strongly cooperative and strongly competitive, and others not so clear-cut. There were cooperative systems which tended toward individualism, and cooperative systems which tended toward competitive emphases. The thirteen systems can be arranged on a triangle. The mid-point of each side of the triangle is taken as the most intense development of that emphasis, while the places nearest the apexes stand in a more intermediate position.

With one exception, the Dakota, the placing of these social systems in such a relationship to each other can be made without reservation. The anomolies in the position of the Dakota may be due to the faultiness of the data—we know extraordinarily little about how Dakota society functions—or it may be due to some inadmissible rigorousness in the present diagrammatic arrangement. It should further be noted that the definiteness with which twelve of these thirteen societies can be classified is in all probability a function of their extreme homogeneity and integration. It is not possible to say whether this large proportion of highly integrated societies in our sample is typical or not. Certain unintegrated societies exist which present confused pictures, and it would probably not be possible to classify such societies with the same assurance.

The fact that these thirteen cultures represent only a sampling must never be overlooked in drawing any conclusions from the material.

Because no matrilineal societies are found on the competitive and individualistic sides of the triangle, it is not possible to argue that matriliny can occur only in societies with a cooperative emphasis. To invalidate a merely negative conclusion for which there is no methodological justification in any case, it would be only necessary to add the competitive matrilineal Dobuans and the individualistic matrilocal Apache. Nor can we say that because all the individualistic societies are found at a low subsistence level, that such a low level will support only individualistic societies. Again the addition of certain nonindividualistic Australian desert tribes or of the Andamanese would upset such unfounded conclusions. Furthermore, even if there were no such known instances, it would still be methodologically false to make them. We have no assurance that the primitive societies of which we have records, or even the total number of primitive societies at present in existence, have in any way exhausted the possible types of cultural adjustment which have characterized mankind through its long and diverse history.

Before discussing these classifications further, it is necessary to summarize our findings in regard to the original problems outlined in the Introduction. It proved unprofitable to attempt to isolate such an intangible as "cooperative habits" and correlate it with type of technology; it was more profitable to discuss whether or not techniques requiring overt cooperation occurred in each classification. In other words, for the vague term *cooperative and competitive habits* we have substituted *cooperative social systems* and *competitive social systems*—that is, societies in which distribution of goods is a major competitive activity and societies in which such goods enrich the whole group and contribute to its security—categories which are more subject to analysis. By doing this the original foci of inquiry—the natural environment, the state of technology, the techniques of production, the nature of the social structure, and the educational system—become possible clues to the total emphasis within each social system. If there is correspondence between the techniques of production and the degree of competition, cooperation, or individualism of the whole system, we can examine the mechanisms within these social systems by means of which such techniques either are brought into complete dependence upon the major social emphasis, or are dynamic in determining that emphasis. Even when a perfect correspondence is found between the major emphasis and, for example, the religious philosophy, it may be that the so perfectly correlated element is crucial in determining the emphasis, but it is much more likely that the element was involved in the classification that was used, and should be merely added to the definition in order to define it more completely.

Aside from the gross correspondences which exist between a very low subsistence level and very small social groups, no consistent relationship was found between subsistence level and major emphases. Well-nourished peoples were found equally among the competitive and cooperative groups, although the richest peoples—except for the Kwakiutl with their plentiful resources—were all upon the cooperative side. But the more adequate food supply of these cooperative societies, Samoa, Zuni, Bathonga, can more fairly be stated as one of the end results of the form of social organization than it can be regarded as determining their greater cooperativeness. The most desperate conditions of scarcity, furthermore, do not necessarily make different peoples handle the emergency in the same manner; the threat of starvation made the Eskimo cooperative whereas they were usually individualistic, but it did not have this effect upon the Ojibwa.

There is no correlation at all between major emphases and a classification of cultures into food-gathering, hunting, agricultural, or pastoral peoples. Among the hunting and fishing peoples are the very cooperative Dakota, the competitive Manus, the highly competitive Kwakiutl, and the individualistic Eskimo and Ojibwa. The agricultural people include the cooperative Zunis, Bathongans, and Samoans, the competitive Ifugao, and the individualistic Bachiga and Arapesh. The contrast between the individualistic Bachiga and the cooperative Bathonga, both of whom belong to one culture area and who, in addition to practicing agriculture, are also pastoral peoples, is very marked.

There is no correlation to be found by culture areas. Instead the whole gamut of organized attitudes is found within one area. Again, it is impossible to correlate the presence or absence of group work with the actual situations imposed by a particular technology. Both the Kwakiutl and the Maori build large houses which require a considerable amount of concerted group action. This is also true of their construction and method of manning canoes. Despite all this, the Kwakiutl are highly competitive in their emphasis while the Maori are cooperative. The knowledge of the usefulness of large fish-trap fences does not prevent the Manus from fitting these fences into a small partnership pattern, whereas the Samoans use the same fishing method as the basis for village-wide participation and cooperation. The economy of caring for cattle in large herds does not keep the Bachiga households from subdividing. Irrigation, which ideally is cooperative since in any case it benefits a wider group than the owners of a plot, is nevertheless one of the bases upon which the

Ifugao build their ruthless competition. The greater efficiency of the gardener's staying close to his own garden and watching his fences does not militate against the Arapesh gardener's sociable participation in an indefinite number of technologically less effective groups.

The most conspicuous instance of correspondence between the natural environment and the cultural emphases is to be found among the Ojibwa. Their highly individualistic way of life is completely congruent with the sparse distribution of game animals which makes it necessary for men to scatter widely for several months of the year. But it still remains a problem why the habits of the winter months should so completely dominate their whole outlook, rather than the habits of the summer months when they collect in villages. On the other hand, among the Dakota, it is the brief buffalo-hunting period in which everyone joins which is most congruent with the cooperative, socialized emphases of the culture.

Instances in which the dictates of the natural environment have been overridden by cultural definition are much more common. Thus the Arapesh and the Zuni, with a scarcity of good land, have succeeded in phrasing their difficulty as a scarcity of labor. In this way they have eliminated the factor of competition which arises when land is at once scarce, and a valuable for which individuals are expected to compete. Just as strikingly, the Eskimo, when they fish for capelin which come in shoals, work individualistically, each man filling his own dip net.

The problem of the division of women among the men, more than any other problem, can be discussed with comparability from one society to another. Of these thirteen cultures only the Eskimo had an exact and realistic response to a scarcity of women. The Eskimo, normally noncompetitive, become competitive whenever there are two men who desire one woman as a wife. This situation is aggravated when one of the men has no wife; yet because of the institution of polygamy and the economic advantages to a successful hunter of having two wives, both the competitors may be married. But in order to evaluate correctly the significance of this apparently logical response to a limitation in supply, it is necessary to remember that the Eskimo are conspicuously lacking in any complex social institutions for the regulation of human relations, such as inheres in clan or age-grade organization. Nor is Eskimo marriage integrated with property or with inheritance. It is a case therefore of "pure" competition, in which the actual brute facts of the situation are permitted to dominate human behavior in the absence of any socially regulative mechanism. The supply is limited, the demand exceeds the supply, more than one man wishes to obtain a woman as a wife, and in this status she can belong to only one man. This instance is particularly important because it stands out in sharp relief against the way in which more organized societies handle similar situations in which there is an equally objective limitation of women. It also stands over against the more usual Eskimo emphasis in favor of unorganized cooperativeness. This more usual emphasis is so strong that it tends to reduce drum matches, which are phrased as contests and originate in quarrels—usually over women—to friendly partnerships in which the contestants continue the match in affectionate cooperation.

Contrasting most conspicuously with the Eskimo in this matter of women are the Bathonga. Here the whole of a man's status depends upon the labor of his wives. Yet although they have an institution or numerically unlimited polygamy, among the Bathonga the male members of one kraal do not compete for women. They have met the situation in several ways. Their clearly defined hierarchical system determines that, for the best interests of both, an elder brother's interest must always precede that of a younger brother, and this cooperation of brothers in the purchase of each other's wives is enforced religiously by an active system of ancestral control. Furthermore, they have defined woman as a sexual object and woman as a worker in the opposite way from that in which the Eskimo have defined them. In Bathonga a woman's sexual favors are restricted to her husband but her labor is a cooperative activity for the benefit of the entire kraal.[1] Finally there has been a displacement of attention from the number of women to the bride price, which is conceived of as limited, although actually the same bride price may purchase many individual women. If the bride price consisted of a fixed supply of valuables this would not necessarily limit competition, but as the bride price is mainly cattle, whose

[1] Compare this adjustment with the Bachiga, where each woman works for her husband, but all the related males are permitted to share her sexual favors.

increase depends on the whim of the ancestral gods, competition is avoided. We have here then illustrations of ways in which competition, apparently inherent in the objective situation, may be prevented in a society:

1. By a social system which prevents competition by a rigidly prescribed and highly sanctioned hierarchical arrangement, so that rank is interposed between individuals who might otherwise be competitors.

2. By a social system through which the desired end is converted from an individual end into a group end.

3. By a cultural phrasing which displaces the emphasis from the objective situation to some other sphere in which competition is not so possible.[1]

On the other hand, the Manus, with their characteristic emphasis upon all life as a race in which there is a limited number of prizes, regard women as very limited in number, although polygamy is highly exceptional.

In other fields of life besides that of obtaining a wife, there is similar lack of correlation between competition for goods and the actual supply. The Ifugao base their competition upon an actual scarcity of land, the Kwakiutl in the midst of plenty build their equally fierce competition on an artificially constructed scarcity of titles and prerogatives. Here the artificial limitation of a desired good is just as powerful an element in the competitive emphases of the culture as is the actual limitation of natural resources.

In summarizing this section, we may say that while there is an occasional correspondence between the actual conditions of supply, or the technological factors, or the exigencies of the environment, and the major emphases of the culture, this correspondence is the exception rather than the rule. Cultures

[1] This last mechanism is illustrated also by the way in which the Zuni and Arapesh displace scarcity of land into scarcity of labor, and therefore into a field where they can compensate for this scarcity by cooperative activity. The Dobuans, not discussed in this study, furnish a useful contrast. They create situations in which the objectively unlimited supply is redefined as being of fixed and limited quantity. No amount of labor can therefore increase the next year's yam crop, and no man can excel another in the number of his yams without being accused of having stolen (magically) his extra yams from someone else's garden. See R. F. Fortune, *Sorcerers of Dobu*, pp. 100–101, E. P. Dutton & Company, Inc., New York, 1932.

vary greatly as to their objectively cooperative behavior, measured in such terms as the number of activities which are performed in groups and the use of techniques requiring collective work. But there is virtually no necessary relationship found between the important emphases of these cultures and the presence or absence, the frequency or infrequency, of such technologically dictated overt cooperative activities. The existence of such noncorrelations would be relevant to the discussion of such problems as the correlation of natural resources or technology with density of population, but these considerations are aside from the major problems of personality and culture which we are investigating.

We may now turn from these general considerations to a discussion of the way in which the social forms of a given society are related to its competitive, cooperative, or individual emphases.

In discussing the social structure of these thirteen social systems, *i.e.*, the cultural forms which determine the interrelationships between individuals, it is necessary to distinguish three degrees of social integration.[1] The *simplest forms* of primitive societies, represented here by the Eskimo and the Ojibwa, recognize the unity of the group but lack the political forms necessary for group action. At the next level of integration come the *corporate* societies. These may be defined as possessing (*a*) the capacity for corporate action as a group and (*b*) continuity of existence over a period such that at any moment it is possible to distinguish who is and who is not a member of the group. The most complex level of social integration is represented by those societies which may be called true *political* societies. Such a society may be defined (*a*) as being a *corporate* society as defined above; (*b*) as one in which the group maintains in some way a local or territorial continuity (usually by exercising dominion over a definite territory); and (*c*) as one in which there is some form of corporate action on the part of the group, first, in maintaining its rights against invaders from the outside and, second, in exercising control over its own members.

Regarded in terms of this definition, the Amassalik Eskimos have no permanent society. The residence groups are impermanent, fluid, and without effective sanctions. There is no set of

[1] For these distinctions I am indebted to Prof. A. R. Radcliffe-Brown.

sanctions which prevents one individual from killing another, or a husband or wife from deserting each other, or both from deserting their immature children. The Ojibwa occupy almost the same position, but they are more influenced by the possession of kinship forms congruent with a more integrated society—as for instance the social rule that a spouse must recompense the kin of the dead. But although they know of and sometimes act in reference to concepts of social behavior characteristic of adjacent societies with higher integrations, they lack effective sanctions to enforce any rule, either in mourning obligations or against incest or murder. The actual forms in both cultures call for a minimum of social cooperation. It is noteworthy that while the Ojibwa possess the idea of the extended kin group, of the Midewiwin, and of the organized war party, and though the Eskimo possess no single item of an equally complex social structure, the Eskimo nevertheless have a more cooperative total emphasis than the Ojibwa.

The Arapesh and the Bachiga represent cultures in which there has been a little more social integration. Though the Arapesh are less integrated than the Bachiga, both can be classified as corporate societies. The Arapesh function in a series of small temporary groups assembled along blood-tie lines, which participate in common tasks and common residence. They may be said to have a series of group forms, within any one of which cooperation is provided for; but they lack an effective administrative mechanism for keeping these groups permanently together and in operation. Among the Arapesh there is no closed group which can repel an outside enemy or coerce its own members. Each local group is bound to each other adjacent local group by a multiplicity of ties, and the brief and nonfatal fighting which occurs has to maintain itself across these tangled lines of reciprocity and friendliness. While the Bachiga clan is a far firmer group than any group among the Arapesh, marriage cuts across clan lines which otherwise define hostile relations, and prevents the classification of the Bachiga as a political society. But whereas the Arapesh act in ever widening circles of slight ties, the Bachiga live within cramped bounds of fear, intersected by the institution of pact brotherhood. Social interrelationships among both the Arapesh and the Bachiga are characterized more by helpfulness than by cooperation, *i.e.*, the end toward which several people bend their temporary efforts is conceived as being most relevant to one of the group whom the others help. The Arapesh tend always toward cooperation, the Bachiga toward competition.

The Kwakiutl, the Ifugao, and the Manus are corporate societies but at a higher level of integration. They are all cultures in which the individual operates through constellations of bilateral kin, with an eye to attaining prestige for himself. This goal in all three of these cultures is dependent upon the interwoven concepts of rank and wealth. Warlike hostilities among these three peoples are more organized than among the four peoples previously discussed, and take the form of active head-hunting. The most significant thing about warfare in this group of the three most competitive societies in our sample is that the group within which hostilities may not occur is so small that ties of intermarriage and trade friendships are continually being severed by internecine killing. Among the Ifugao the group within which these hostilities do not occur is relatively large and hence warfare is relatively less disruptive, but here as among the Manus and the Kwakiutl, warfare is a form of head-hunting which brings honor to the individual killer and is not carried on for conquest nor in response to pressure brought to bear by some hostile and culturally alien people.

Of the three competitive societies only in Manus do a large number of men expect to better their position as they grow older. Practically all young men begin adult life under a burden of debt incurred in their heavy marriage payment, and, since they do not fix class lines in terms of birth, an individual rises to the position of wealthy entrepreneur in terms of his ability to manipulate their economic system. Among the Kwakiutl and the Ifugao the situation is different. The class of the individual is fixed by birth and inheritance, and, though he may raise his position within his class or may be demoted, between classes there can be little vertical mobility. In Kwakiutl, under aboriginal conditions when the titles of nobility were relatively few in proportion to the population, the commoner was drastically handicapped in any attempt to set himself up as a noble. No amount of economic success could overcome the handicap of birth. Among the Ifugao the limitations upon vertical mobility were economic; only in very exceptional cases could a commoner on a margin of subsistence accumulate the money necessary for the high-interest payments necessary under their system. In both these societies class stratification served to stabilize the position of the dominant group and to limit competition.

The Dakota must be discussed in connection with these three, as they possess vertical mobility in terms of reputation, undefined, however, in fixed class terms. Rank among the Dakota was largely a matter of cumulative prestige shared between an individual and his family group. They also had warfare which was motivated by individual desire for prestige. They stand over against the other three peoples just discussed in that they fought only the outsider and had a concept of social integration which united the whole people into one society, although actually the band was the effective cooperative unit. Nevertheless, the concept was strong enough to provide for peace within the group, and cooperation in the preservation of the peace was enforced by definite administrative institutions like the buffalo soldiers. Each of the four societies has a single scale of success: possession and validation of status among the Ifugao; numbers of feasts and validation of names, Kwakiutl; participation in numbers of exchanges, Manus; attainment of war counts and distribution of wealth among the Dakota.

In the three competitive cultures there is a basic recognition of discrepancies in status among individuals. Status is felt to be important, and there is a possibility of improving one's status on the one hand, and losing it completely on the other. There is no way of measuring success except by comparison with another's, and there are no fixed positions to which an individual can attain without fear of subsequent loss.

In these respects these three cultures can be described under one rubric. But it is notable that among the Ifugao there is no limit to the number of feasts which a kadangyang can give. He has no need to exchange only with equals, and so there is no premium whatsoever upon permanent ties outside the small blood and affinal group who are associated with a "center" of importance. Thus there is no tendency to form a permanent aristocracy which might crystallize the group along firmer lines of stratification and form the basis for wider cooperative units. Instead each family group competes with each other, and the only mechanism of law and order is the threatened or actual dueling between these small cooperating groups within the highly competitive total system. It is also important to note that membership within these groups is not entirely fixed. Outside the immediate family, allegiance may follow different blood and affinal ties according to choice. This introduces a new element of competition into the situation, competition for adherents. Among the Kwakiutl there seem to be tendencies which make for greater coherence among the members of the ranking group. One of these is the need of near equals with whom to compete, which makes a rival valuable; another is a strong concept of rank, under which the chiefly class can unite against the upstart and about which all the members of the tribe can rally in planning a cooperative food supply and for intertribal raids. Among the Ifugao the aim of each man is to acquire and hold firmly to wealth, which will mean power and status, and the game is played in terms of the means of subsistence. The Kwakiutl play a more phantom game in which the handling and destruction of surplus wealth replace the attempt to gain power and security through holding fast to necessary wealth. The Manus, by giving very little recognition to rank and by emphasizing instead the constellations of individuals related either by blood or marriage and gathered round an enterprising and wealthy leader, lack a ruling class and group leadership almost as completely as the Ifugao. But they have compensated for this by stressing heavily the value to each other of those who are institutionally opposed within the economic system. One can engage in satisfactory exchange only with a worthy equal. Also they have removed the one fixed position of rank, that of war leader, from the competitive game. They have overlaid the highly competitive nature of the social system with a religiously sanctioned cooperation, in which a man's own Sir Ghost punishes him and his partners for failure to meet their financial obligations. As compared with the Kwakiutl, the Manus have made their system less competitive by outlawing rivalry and making it impossible to destroy goods or to eliminate a successful person. While the Kwakiutl ideal of success has as its end the gradual elimination of rivals, the Manus ideal calls for more and more equals. These checks upon unlimited self-aggrandizement among the Manus are made possible by the submission of each individual to the oracularly expressed will of the ancestral ghosts, each of whom stands in a chastening but cooperative relationship to his mortal ward. The Ifugao on the other hand conceive themselves as fighting a losing battle of bribery with their capricious ancestors, and the Kwakiutl relationship to his supernaturals is that of violent attack and acquisition of power over them.

The Dakota stand over against these three societies in that their ideal is cooperation, and prestige is attached to an inverted pride in giving instead of in getting from others. They have succeeded in eliminating warfare within their own cultural limits, which the three competitive societies have never done. They have muted competition within the group, so that concerted communal action—as within the buffalo hunt—is possible. But by their insistence upon variable status and a common scale of success they introduce a strain into the social order. This can be compensated for only by very heavy group sanctions, administered in terms of shame, against the indulgence of the very qualities which the system is designed to stimulate— pride, acquisitiveness, high self-valuation, and individual initiative. They represent the most confused picture from the standpoint of this study, but it is worth while bearing this in mind and seeking to find what elements in their culture are incompatible and produce these contradictions.

Zuni and Samoa may be discussed together as corporate societies in which each individual acts cooperatively in reference to the whole, but in which strong central authority with effective sanctions is peculiarly lacking. In both any concerted action against outside societies is virtually impossible. The position of the Samoans on islands fortunately protected them from the necessity of combining against the threats of invaders, but Zuni was not so fortunate, and six of the seven original Zuni pueblos were wiped out by enemies. Both are cooperative and in both the form and extent of the cooperation of any individual is determined by fixed categories: partly determined by birth, which defines the kin constellations with which one will cooperate and the importance of the role which one will play, and partly dependent upon age, sex, and ritual considerations.

One of the most illuminating contrasts in social structure between the two is in the emphasis of the sanctions; Zuni relies upon unorganized negative sanctions against the kinds of personality which are fostered by competitive behavior—assertiveness, aggression, pride, conspicuousness. They depend upon individual response to group needs to carry out the calendric ritual of the society within which houses are built, surplus food collected, and ritual objects manufactured. To the extent that the Zuni function in terms of fixed status, such as membership in one of the kiva societies, in a dancing society, in a priesthood, the individual has merely to discharge a role which had been defined for him. There is no way in which these interwoven, overlapping groups can become competitive, for each one winds its way in and out of the lineages of Zuni, which are the only fixed groups who might tend to vaunt themselves upon their position as bundle owners. Operating upon a very adequate food supply and without any strong central authority, Zuni ceremonial life is interwoven in a complex network. Its form is set by the calendar and it is maintained by the faithful discharge of customary obligations by all the members of the society. The Zuni use as their sanction the vigilance of public opinion, which shames an individual who shows either aggressiveness or pride. This is the same type of sanction which occurs among the Dakota, a sanction *against* the competitive type of personality. Thus while Zuni is highly cooperative to the extent that each individual directs all his activities toward an end which others share, there is no set of terms in which it is possible to appeal continuously to every Zuni, so that faced with any outside problem such as adjustment to the white man they break up into factions.

The Samoan system presents a contrasting picture. Where each Zuni is a member of a series of cooperating groups, his maternal household, his wife's household, his kiva, his curing society, and perhaps his priesthood, which crosscut and overlap and prevent his attaining any fixed and antagonistic allegiances, the allegiances of the Samoan do not crosscut each other in the same way. A man is a member of a household, and according to his position in the household so is his position in the village structure. The whole scheme is hierarchical as opposed to the Zuni system, which Dr. Benedict has described as a system of "interlocking wheels." And in contrast to Zuni, the Samoan system, which relies upon fitness for office rather than upon pure hereditary transmission, permits a certain amount of competition within the household.   Freedom of movement from household to household and from village to village prevents this competition from becoming acute, as does the mechanism by which the assumption of position is postponed until middle age.   The Samoan village presents a strongly cooperative picture, in which each individual works for group ends and is subject to group sanctions for failure to cooperate.   Where the Zuni sanction is against competitiveness, the Samoan sanction is against noncooperativeness.   Where the Zuni are articulate in their disapproval of self-assertion, the Samoans give their approval to pride in the accurate discharge of the privileges and obligations of one's status.

Pride, in Samoa, is permitted an outlet through the high valuation which is put upon the village, its honor, its prestige. Because of the intricate kin ties between villages, and the freedom of choice which makes membership in each cooperative group ultimately voluntary, competitiveness between villages usually does not reach important heights of intervillage aggressiveness. But intervillage warfare was a possibility which increased with the number of people who lived within easy reach of each other. Thus warfare was far more frequent in Savaii and Upolu than in tiny Manu'a.   At the same time there was a high value placed upon cooperative ties between villages in terms of feasts and intervillage borrowing, and these served to diminish warfare. But actually although the great Fa'alupega provided a ground plan for a dignified view of society, it could not make two hostile villages cooperate with each other.   So, when faced with outside problems or attempts to impose authority from the top,[1] Samoa displays the same tendencies toward factionalism as does Zuni, although their actual day-by-day cooperative mechanisms are so different.   It is significant, however, that one would not even consider discussing the problem of factionalism among the Manus or the Ifugao for these societies lack the amount of integration necessary to provide true factionalism.

The Bathonga are an example of a cooperative political society, integrated on a far larger scale than Samoa or Zuni, into groups of 30,000 and 40,000 people.   Here the structure is strictly hierarchical, each local group administers only its local affairs,

[1] Cf. Felix Keesing, Modern Samoa, passim, Allen and Unwin, London, 1934, and his discussion of European contact.

and there is always a possible appeal to a higher authority. All are bound together into a national unity in which the position of the king is not the mere delicate pinnacle of a flimsy structure of titles, as in Samoa, but is instead the basis of national organization. In Bathonga the ancestral gods of the king are the gods of the nation. Whereas the Samoan hierarchical organization was confined to the village, within which it insured cooperation, the Bathonga hierarchical organization extended from child to king. Within the kraal, cooperation was insured by a fixed succession in order of birth and a strict rule of the ancestor gods, who insisted upon its preservation. Success was defined merely by the attainment of dignified status, by becoming one of a group of householders, not by position within that group. All dissensions between individuals were referred to an orderly judiciary based on the theory that individuals had no right to exercise their individual wills at the expense of the state. The cooperative groups were fixed enough for easy administration and flexible enough to permit an individual to leave and join another cooperative group if he was under too great pressure.

An examination of one highly discrepant note in the Bathongan social structure is instructive. This is the struggle for the kingship which occurred after the death of each king and in which competition was very keen and fierce. The kingship, the capital, the position of the Great Wife, etc., all reproduced the structure of an ordinary kraal, with its headman and his circle of wives. (The Samoan Great Fono, on the other hand, was an elaboration of the titular superstructure of the village, not of the organization of the household.) This similarity in structure from the smallest unit of the society to the largest, while it is the strength of the Bathonga organization, is also its chief weakness. The analogy is pushed to the breaking point at the death of a king. When the ordinary headman of a kraal dies, there is a year's period of mourning before the new headman assumes authority. This familiar interregnum passes off without trouble because peaceful relationships between brothers are socially insured and guaranteed by the existence of the state, personified in the king. But for the king himself, this is impossible. The attempt to hide the king's death and, after an interval, to announce the accession of the new king simultaneously with the death of the old king has not prevented the Bathonga from being periodically involved in civil wars between rival claimants to the throne from among the king's sons and brothers.

Inheritance in the kraal is entirely regular and passes from brother to brother before the lineal descendants of the eldest brother are considered, and thus each adult male of the family has the possibility of eventually being headman of his own kraal. No such firm rule is in existence for the kingship, but there is an attempt to recognize lineal descent, which is at variance with the descent of chieftainship from elder to younger brother in the kraal. Nor can the conflict among the claimants for the throne be solved as it is in the kraal by the founding of another village, for the claimants to the throne forfeit every hope if they retire peacefully, and the conflict among them can only be satisfied by one of them obtaining the prize. The resolution of this conflict in many monarchies makes it clear that the dynastic wars of the Bathonga are not the inevitable outcome of a monarchial system, but an instance of a flaw in the social system due to reliance upon conflicting social mechanisms.

This is an instance of defective structure in the society which relies most completely upon structure to ensure its cooperativeness. The Bathonga neither suppress aggressiveness as overtly as the Samoans and the Zuni, nor use strong social disapproval of non-conformity like the Dakota. They simply rely upon a firm structure within which each man's place is defined. The civil-war picture is the more conspicuous because the Bathongans were an unwarlike people, without warlike ambitions, who yielded quickly and without loss of social integration, to conquest by the Zulus. This clearly shows that the cohesiveness and cooperativeness of the Bathonga is a function of the internal integration of the society and not a cohesiveness based upon opposition to outside groups, as among the Iroquois, the Dakota, and to some extent, the Maori.

There remain only two peoples to discuss, the Iroquois and the Maori, two peoples who have commanded the respect of the white invader. The League of the Iroquois and the Maori tribe[1] were

---

[1] It must be borne in mind that while the Iroquois were one closed politically autonomous people, the dominant and most integrated society within fighting distance of themselves, the Maori were a great number of closed politically autonomous groups warring with other similar groups.

both political societies, but the Iroquois represented a more elaborate political organization, consisting as they did of five, and later, six tribes, all combined in a federation of mutual peace and cooperation. In degree of political integration the Iroquois stand midway between the Samoans and the Bathonga: like the Samoans the basic functioning group for ordinary economic and social cooperation was one of the components of a larger political unity, and that unity was a superstructure which functioned independently of the family; like the Bathongans, the League had a certain amount of central authority for regulating intra-League clashes, so that to some slight extent authority could be said to be centralized at the top. But the cooperation of the member tribes in the League Council was of a negative nature; they were pledged not to compete with or fight one another, they were not pledged to fight for or in the interests of one another nor of the whole League. The primary interest of Iroquois political organization was *against* war, not *for* peace. So the Iroquois, having a social structure which was constructed to prevent warfare within the society and to continue warlike activities outside the society, stands over against the Bathonga, organized as a nation which owed allegiance to a king, each member of which was precious to that king in a social structure which required peace. Furthermore, whereas the Bathonga, when they did fight, organized their army along national lines into a coherent whole in which each individual served because it was his duty to his king, the Iroquois kept the familiar North American pattern of the individually organized war party, in which individual war honors and individual prestige were sought for primarily. The structure of the society, the sachem titles, the orderly inheritance of these titles within family lines, all these were socialized mechanisms to preserve order, but the need for individual initiative in war was a discrepant and explosive element in this imperfectly realized social synthesis. Here again we find a fundamental flaw in integration; this society attempted to preserve an ideal of peace while still devoting the bulk of every male's time to war so that whole villages were depopulated for months at a time. The Iroquois had not succeeded in reorganizing the warpath institutions of the North American continent into a form more in consonance with their major emphases. They had proceeded far in political invention in the development of their federation of tribes, but the important individual war-party pattern still remained to confuse their development.

The Maori on the other hand present the picture of a completely integrated political society which is cooperative; they lack the diffuseness and unregulated individualism of the Arapesh, the Eskimo, the Ojibwa, and the Bachiga, and the competitiveness and internal dissensions and rivalries of the Kwakiutl and the Ifugao, the pressure and competitive striving of the Manus, the political flaws of the Iroquois and the Bathonga. The Maori obtained cooperation on the basis of virtually inalienable and unalterable status, by which the rank of an individual and the form of his obligations were fixed by birth. Authority and the adequate regulation of conflicts within the tribe were made possible by the existence of inalienable rank. The lack of economic stratification and the absence of the idea of altering and validating status by economic means prevented competition within the group. Individual skill or bravery was recognized as enhancing both the position of the individual and the importance of his tribe but such recognition did not alter the individual's position in relation to others. There was no need to suppress the individual since his sphere of activity was well defined and his individual pride tied up with the maintenance of his own position. The only underprivileged class was external to the system, slaves captured in war, and therefore no man had to face loss of caste and continue living within his own society. Death in battle and capture by the enemy were the risks which a man ran for the tribe with which he was completely identified. There was no need to stress sanctions for cooperation, for cooperation, like the absence of competition, was implied in the structure of the group. The only field for rivalry was in terms of skill or bravery, and the attainment of that skill was its own reward and was not expressed in some common denominator such as dogs' teeth or blankets or war counts. Viewed from the standpoint of perfection of social structure, the Maori had obtained the most complete integration of any of the societies which we have studied. They secured this by a complete identification of the individual with his tribe, but they had to keep the tribe relatively small to make this possible. The disintegrative potentiality in the Maori form of organization was this factor of size; when the society grew too large it was not possible to maintain this complete identification, and a subgroup would split off and become another autonomous, closed, cooperative unit, competing without and cooperating within.

With this brief review of the larger social structure, we may turn to some smaller details. In the cooperative societies, the family group is the important local unit within a wider social structure which permits the more removed kinship obligations to be relatively neglected. The competitive cultures are not closed societies, and an individual may fight tomorrow with his ally of today without having changed in any way his "national status," *i.e.*, his membership in a closed group. In these societies, the main integrating forces are the widespread network of kinship paths along which a man may seek temporary assistance in his persistent struggle to maintain or better an unstable position.

The permanence or fluidity of primary groups has important repercussions. In the two most stable cooperative societies, Maori and Bathonga, the composition of the cooperative group was determined by blood alone, for males among the Bathonga and for both sexes, with an emphasis upon endogamy, among the Maori. In Samoa and Zuni membership in cooperative groups was much less absolutely defined and less stable. In Samoa the highest rewards were offered a man who remained continuously in the same village with his close blood kin. In Zuni the domestic arrangements provided that a woman remain permanently in the household of her birth, but a man's allegiances were divided. His only real rewards came from his own blood kin, but the results of his daily labor went to this wife's household. Whereas the possibility of shifting from one household cooperative group to another made for cooperation in Zuni and Samoa and to a lesser extent in Bathonga, among the competitive societies the possibility of shifting kin allegiances made for increased competitiveness. In the individualistic societies, those with shifting allegiances—Arapesh and Eskimo—were more cooperative than those with fixed ones—Ojibwa and Bachiga. These considerations suggest that it is the larger structure of the society which is determinative and not the organization of the subgroups, although, as was demonstrated in the cases of the Samoans, the Iroquois, and the Bathonga, any discrepancy between the different elements in the social structure will produce strain in the whole society.

It is possible to summarize the main structural difference between the competitive and cooperative cultures. In the cooperative cultures, there are real closed groups within which the individual's status is defined, and within which he is given security in relation to his fellows; the society depends upon the structure for its perpetuation, not upon the initiative and ambition of individuals. In the competitive cultures, there is no closed society; fighting exists within the group of loosely integrated lineages; no individual is secure in relation to his fellows because success is defined as the maintenance of a status which can be lost or as the attainment of higher relative status; and the culture is organized around the initiative of individuals.

It is significant that all the competitive societies depend upon the initiative of individuals for the motive force behind the accumulation and distribution of property, while in the cooperative societies social life goes on in response to a structural form expressed in a calendar, a court ritual, or a seasonal rhythm, and there is far less dependence upon individual initiative.

Among the cooperative societies, there are systems within which status is inalienable, like the Maori, and systems within which there is no status, like the Zuni, and systems with somewhat movable status, like the Samoans. But in all these systems, the status of the individual is not measured as shifting up or down on some one common scale, a characteristic of the three competitive societies.

The degree of diversification of individual goals is relevant to the problems of cooperation and competition in societies of all types. In the most purely competitive societies, as has been said, all achievement is measured upon a common scale, though for the Ifugao more diversity of achievement is permitted than for the other two. In the individualistic societies one of the most important structural clues to organization is the fact that achievements are individual, different, and incomparable. In the cooperative societies, where there is one common goal, the diversified achievements of the individual participants are related to each other through this shared end relationship, and the craftsman and the fisherman in Samoa both contribute to the honor of the village.

It is also necessary to discuss the relations of these cultures to the tribes surrounding them, for a social system cannot be considered in isolation. We have seen that in the competitive cultures war exists practically within the cultural group itself, while in the cooperative and individualistic cultures this is not so. Among the cooperative societies, we find the warlike Iroquois, Maori, and Dakota, the slightly warlike Samoans and Bathongans, and the relatively unwarlike Zuni. The Samoans owe their very existence in part to isolation, in part to a premium on cooperation between imperfectly integrated groups. The Zuni owe theirs in part to isolation, in part to historical accident; one Pueblo village after another has been destroyed when attacked and still the peaceful Pueblo cultures have not developed offensive war patterns commensurate with the situation. The Bathonga owed theirs to the cohesiveness of their social structure which even survived conquest. To the Maori the preservation of absolute cohesion within was a function of presenting a definite offensive to the outside world. (This tendency appears in the Samoan village structure and, being less compatible with the wider political structure, is internally disruptive.) It may also be said that the League of the Iroquois received much of its impetus from the exposed position of the Iroquois, agriculturists among raiding peoples, but that owing to a less perfect integration than the Maori, their individualistically organized warfare was not an integrating force on the inside. From this we may infer that unorganized peacefulness can occur only under conditions of at least partial isolation and freedom from attack, and also that a war pattern must be firmly integrated into the social structure as a part of its very existence or it is disintegrative inside the group even while protecting the society against outside enemies.

Judging from our three competitive societies, internecine warfare is characteristic of competitive societies. It occurs even where food is plentiful and danger of attack from outside and differently organized societies nonexistent, as in Manus and Ifugao.

Under the heading of social structure we have discussed those cultural factors which seem most relevant to the problem of competitive and cooperative emphasis. We have seen that it is not the actual supply of a desired good which decrees whether or not the members of a society will compete for it or cooperate and share it, but it is the way the structure of the society is built up that determines whether individual members shall cooperate or shall compete with one another.  Imperfect functioning of the cooperative societies can be laid to flaws in the structure, such as the unreconciled conflict in the rules of the royal descent among the Bathonga or the imperfect integration of villages into a wider district pattern in Samoa, the lack of a system which could integrate large groups of people among the Maori, and the failure among the Iroquois to rework the North American Indian war pattern to suit a more cooperative structure.  The cooperative societies depend upon the existence of a well-defined, well-integrated social structure within which the individual can play a cooperative role, whereas the competitive societies lack a closed structure and depend upon institutionalized individual initiative. We saw further that among the individualistic societies, helpfulness takes the place of cooperation because of the lack of structure within which real cooperative behavior could occur.  The extent to which a society will be cooperative is primarily a function of the social forms themselves, and does not depend upon the physical environment nor upon the level of technological development.

But from the standpoint of the problem of personality and culture, there is another set of factors to consider.  Are there any other terms in which we can explain why the Eskimo and Arapesh tend toward cooperation while the Ojibwa and Bachiga tend toward competitiveness?  We may now consider the educational system and the type of character which is favored and rewarded by the culture.  These are of course one aspect of the total social system, but they are nevertheless of a different order from, let us say, the presence of clans or the concept of a king.  Still less are they dependent upon the state of economic and technological development—parallels in character formation can be found in the Manus adult and in the puritan New Englander of the last generation.  This problem of the culturally produced character formation has to be viewed from several different angles:

1. The articulate cultural ideal of human character.

2. The educational system which is in operation in that society.

3. The congruence and incongruence between the cultural ideal and the educational system, and the results for the character formation of individuals and for the functioning of the society.

It is a tenable assumption that if a group of people were permitted to live isolated from all foreign influence and free from all cataclysms such as epidemics and famines, in time all the different aspects of the culture would be integrated and harmonious. Even under such circumstances of isolation, however, there is every probability that stresses and strains would develop within the culture. Conflicts might arise from such endogenous factors as an overdependence upon the constancy of the sex ratio or upon a nonselective death rate, or from an insistence on culturally linking such unrelated phenomena as order of birth and intelligence. Many such cultural dependences upon fictitious relationships between phenomena which are actually unrelated would produce discrepancies and changes within the culture. If such changes did not proceed at a proportionate rate in all fields of life certain aspects of the culture would be increasingly dissonant with others.

Since such maladjustments may be postulated even for isolated societies, they must be constantly reckoned with in any discussion of societies in contact. Different aspects of culture spread at different rates; imported technological and social inventions alter parts of the culture, leaving others for the time unaffected. As a result the delicate mechanisms for character formation in a culture may be more or less well adjusted to the chief cultural emphasis, more or less congruent with the structure, more or less adapted to producing the ideal personality type. Yet the character formation of individuals in a society may itself become a definite force for change as it finds expression in the *ethos* of the culture.

Here it becomes again necessary to point out the limitations imposed by our material. In only seven of these studies is there any material on education; in only three of them were a series of individual children studied so as to obtain some understanding of the variation within the cultural norm. Furthermore, as we saw in the introduction, the use of the cross-sectional method gives us only an external picture of character formation, an artificial construction composed of layers, each being an average of a series of the individuals in that age group. In no instance is there material to show how this character formation is laid down in a single individual over a period of years within the molds decreed by the culture. The importance of such material for a final understanding of the relationship between the personalities of individuals and the culture within which that personality was formed has been fully discussed by Dr. Dollard.[1] And there is a second requirement to a full understanding of this problem. That is the necessity of following a group of individuals through time, so that the way in which their actual interrelationships are patterned and in turn pattern each personality may be known. This approach has been most fully stated by Dr. Moreno.[2] It is reasonably unlikely that either one of these requirements will be met fully by researches in primitive societies. Conditions of living in primitive society do not make it possible to set up a twenty-year longitudinal study, and no retrospective versions of their own lives by individuals can be substituted for the actual record of those lives as they are lived. Students of primitive society will probably have to be content to regard their results as exploratory work through which clues are provided, assumptions are preliminarily tested out, and new hypotheses are formed. Then more precise work can be done under controlled conditions. This is not as limited a possibility as it sounds. Although we may never be able to study the Zuni character formation as fully as we can study the western European character formation, the knowledge that the Zuni personality exists and that any generalizations which we draw from the European material must be such as to include the Zuni material will in itself expand and develop and qualify those generalizations.

The following discussion of some aspects of character formation in these selected cultures is offered from this standpoint, to indicate problems and suggest new lines of research. Again the material itself has been the guide just as it was in the discussion of the social structure. I have chosen those aspects of character formation which seemed most pertinent to the problem of competition and cooperation and on which there were relevant data in these studies. The two most promising focusing points seemed to be (1) the development of the ego, and (2) the strength of the sense of security.[3] I have taken these two focusing points as

[1] J. Dollard, *Criteria for the Life History*, Yale University Press, New Haven, 1935.

[2] F. Moreno, "Shall We Survive?" *Nervous and Mental Disease Monographs*, John Wilkes and Company, Baltimore, 1934.

[3] For a full recognition of the importance of these two aspects of the character I am indebted to discussions with Dr. Caroline B. Zachry and Miss Wilma Lloyd.

points of reference about which to arrange a rather meager body of material. I am using the ego in the sense in which Freud used it in his earlier work, as the ego drives which he opposes to the sexual drives. A satisfactory short definition for the purposes of this analysis has been given by Dr. Kenworthy: "In the use of our term *ego needs* is implied the self-protective, self-maximating tendencies so often described under the caption of the self-preservative instinct."[1]

By a sense of security I mean an individual's freedom to act in human situations without fear or uncertainty, with a sure sense of an unthreatened place in the world in which he lives. The way in which such a sense of security is related to the strength or weakness of the ego seems almost entirely a function of the social system within which the characters are formed. It depends upon whether individual security is based on achievement measured against the achievement of others, or whether it is phrased in quite different terms; it also depends upon the presence and vividness of warm libidinal ties.

In order to systematize this discussion,[2] I have selected for treatment those phases of the culture which seem particularly relevant to the development of these two aspects of character, as they themselves are related to competititive and cooperative behavior. These aspects are summarized in parallel columns[3] so that they may be more conveniently consulted.

1. In connection with ego development I have selected (a) the attitude toward achievement and the terms in which achievement is phrased, (b) the attitude toward property, (c) the external sanctions in effect in the society, (d) the presence or absence of suicide.

*a. The attitude toward achievement.* Achievement seems to be definitely an ego value. It is the way in which the society provides for the expression of the self-maximating tendencies of the

[1] P. L. Lee and M. Kenworthy, *Mental Hygiene and Social Work*, Chap. III, p. 66, The Commonwealth Fund, New York, 1932.

[2] I have confined the discussion to males, as the material on females is much too inadequate for comparative treatment. Similarly in societies with strong vertical mobility, where individuals of high status show behavior different from those of low status, for the same reasons discussion centers around the personality traits of the higher classes.

[3] Pp. 497–505. The following discussion is comment upon these summaries.

individual. In a society which disallows those self-maximating tendencies, achievement vanishes as an ego value, and achievement itself is likely to be minimized. This is the case in both Zuni and Arapesh, the two societies where the lowest development of self-maximating tendencies are found. In the three competitive societies achievement is strongly emphasized and so defined that each individual can measure his achievement against that of his fellows. In these societies the culture provides a definite channel for this form of ego expression and it is not surprising to find strong ego development sought for and valued in all three of these societies.

Among the individualistic societies, achievement is defined in several ways. Among the Bachiga it is phrased as getting out from under the power of others; among the Ojibwa as excelling in any activity and having most power; among the Eskimo as the optimum ability to preserve the self; and among the Arapesh as maintaining a slow-tempoed participation in the impersonal adventure of growing things. Where achievement is defined in reference to the achievement of others, Ojibwa and Bachiga, there is a tendency toward competitiveness in the total system; and where it is defined either with minimum reference to others, as among the Eskimo, or in terms of an unprecise abstract goal, as among the Arapesh,[1] there is a trend toward cooperation.

*b. The attitude toward property.* Property is one of the most concrete ways in which ego values can be expressed. The importance of property is high in the corporate and political societies and much lower in the four individualistic societies. In the three competitive societies, property is definitely an aspect of the ego. (The individual's sense of his own importance is increased through what he has, can acquire, can manipulate, can destroy, or can give away.) Here it is interesting to notice the different ways in which the attitude toward property supports the ego. Among the Ifugao, property is a necessity for any individual who would achieve success; among the Kwakiutl, the possession of property not only defines one's ability to compete,

---

[1] For instance an Arapesh will boast of the yams he has grown and fed to the children of the community, but he will not count his children, and he is as likely to boast of the number of times he has made an abullu as of the size of the abullu, and failing either he can boast of his abstention from acts which would interfere with growth.

but its destruction is a symbolic proof of the strength of the ego to stand even these extreme, self-inflicted hurts; among the Manus, where the ego is threatened more by a sense of sin than by any material threat, the possession and handling of property is a proof of individual moral character.

Among the cooperative societies, the two which value property as an end in itself and not merely as a means of group subsistence are the Bathonga and the Dakota. Had the Bathonga placed their high valuation upon property which was not subject to a natural increase, it would possibly have been incompatible with their cooperative emphases. As it was, a man's position depended upon the increase of herds, not upon property which he took from others in trade or struggle. The Dakota have reconciled their emphasis on property with their insistence upon the partial submission of the self-maximating tendencies of the individual to group ends, by inverting the emphasis. Here a man's sense of self-maximation depends upon the amount of property that he gives away. It is interesting to compare this with the Kwakiutl attitude and see how slight is the difference in overt behavior. The Kwakiutl gives to shame his rival, the Dakota to honor someone else.

The neighbors of the Iroquois all emphasize conspicuous destruction of property in connection with mortuary rites. The Iroquois made one plank in their platform of political cooperation the interdictic of this type of destruction, so that property assumed a social value. The Maori and Samoans both use property to validate the cooperative social system.

In none of the societies studied is a surplus ever accumulated in a short enough period of time for it to effect the equilibrium of the society. It is interesting, however, to note that the competitive societies have the least reliable mechanisms for redistributing the surplus. By permitting property to be used for the glorification of individuals, they open the way to the accumulation of property by individuals, and very possibly for the use of that property as capital.[1] A similar possibility of potentially capitalistic accumulation is less probable in the cooperative societies, which refuse to permit the ego of the individual to attach itself

---

[1] This observation was the result of applying a suggestion of Dr. Erich Fromm to these discussions. Dr. Fromm suggested asking the questions: "Is there a surplus? If so, who gets it?"

to property at the expense of the group. It would seem, in fact, that cooperation in these societies is based upon cooperative consumption rather than upon cooperative production, and that the way the individual is harmoniously devoted to the interests of his group is by emphasizing his position as a coconsumer. This suggests that within this sample, at least, production of the sort which might turn into capital investment occurs, if at all, in cases of display of wealth and power, *over against some other*, either another individual, clan, village, or nation, while production for shared consumption can be organized along less aggressive lines. It is possible to suggest that the societies which combine strong ego development with marked aggressive tendencies, and are nevertheless cooperative, Iroquois and Maori and to a lesser extent Dakota, achieved this only because warfare was ever present to hold the society together; but that the other cooperative societies, which did not permit the development of strong egos and aggressive tendencies, would also not have had the aggressive forces necessary to produce and utilize a surplus.

I shall postpone the discussion of (c) external sanctions until later, discussing external and internal sanctions together.

*d. The presence or absence of suicide.* Here I am discussing not a statistical statement about the actual occurrence of suicide in a given year, but rather whether or not the society institutionalizes suicide as a practice. Here there is a certain correspondence between those societies with strong ego development and the presence of institutionalized suicide. The two exceptions are the Manus, where suicide is not recognized at all, and the Bachiga, whose ego development is strong but unchanneled and among whom suicide is rare and uninstitutionalized. An individual in Manus is judged only against a pace set by a group, and failure for him is never in absolute terms; so also among the Bachiga, there is a paucity of situations to which an all-or-none response is necessary.

2. In discussing the individual's sense of security, I have regarded as relevant (a) the factors on which security depends, (b) the importance of the individual's relation to the immediate kin group, (c) the religious view of the universe, (d) the nature of the internal sanctions, (e) the attitude toward children and toward the aged.

*a. The factors on which security depends.* The factors on which security depends in any given culture may well be inextricably linked to the problem of competition and cooperation. If, as among the Arapesh, the individual feels completely insecure unless surrounded by helpful kin, this need for security is channeled into making him a helpful person in his turn so as to assure to him the helpfulness of others. This, in the absence of strong ego demands, is the principal social drive. In Manus the individual is secure only when he has discharged his economic obligations, which are defined as a continual race toward an unreachable goal. Here his need for security as well as his ego demands lie behind his social participation; and the double stake provides a unified drive toward approved social behavior. Among the Ojibwa, on the other hand, the individual has no sense of security unless he is convinced of his own unchallenged superiority. His ego demands force him into achievement, and his demand for security, threatened by the most casual knowledge of or reference to any defeat, keeps him away from others.

*b. The relationship to the immediate kin group.* This is important in several ways. Where this group is very narrow, and the culture lacks mechanisms for extending it, as among the Eskimo, the ability of the individual to develop a dependence upon others is almost automatically limited. Beyond the narrow and fragile circle of his own immediate family there is no one upon whom he can depend; he is thrown back upon himself, and his security lies in his ability to maintain that isolated position. Here the desire for security is combined, not so much with the self-maximating tendencies of the individual as with the self-preservative, in such a way as to reduce his social ties to a minimum.

An opposite situation is presented by the Samoans, the Bathongans, the Zuni, the Maori, the Dakota, and the Iroquois. In these cultures the warm ties to the own kin group are extended to include many persons; one relative can easily be substituted for another within a classificatory system, and the satisfaction of ego demands is closely tied up with the preservation of extended kinship ties. The individual is not encouraged to turn in upon himself nor to pin his sense of security to isolated performance. His sense of security and the ego demands of both self-preservation and self-maximation are centered in the wide kin group, and in the village or tribe or state which may be variously held as extensions of this kin group.

In the competitive societies, the ties to the own kin group are complicated by the way in which the individual's kin are involved in his self-maximation. Where self-maximation is defined in terms of one individual over against another, the dependence upon the same persons to give one security and to advance one's isolated achievements sets up a situation which is not conducive to security. It is notable that of these three societies, the Manus seem to have the highest sense of security; that they phrase achievement with the least reference to others; and that they regard their achievement as depending less upon the approval of living kin than upon the approval of the dead.

The Arapesh and the Bachiga are perhaps the most interesting cultures in this respect. The Arapesh have developed strong ties to their own kin which have been extended to include the whole locality, and they have set up no strong ego demands to diminish their strength. They have developed a character formation which allows of security only when an individual is receiving a maximum of warmth from everyone defined as a relative, but they have failed to develop an ability to maintain this warmth toward all the members of the locality. It may also be maintained that the exceedingly low ego development among the Arapesh, the denial of all aggression, of any individual right to self-aggrandizement, and the insistence that self-preservation is dependent upon the suppression of self-maximation, may in itself produce a state of anxiety in the individual which is partly responsible for the low sense of security. It is noteworthy that in Zuni, where there is a similar dissociation between self-preservation and self-maximation, the men also show many symptoms of anxiety. But because of the tighter and more adequate form of social organization, the Zuni have a far higher sense of security than the Arapesh.

The Bachiga dependence upon their kin is particularly illuminating. The own group is essentially unreliable and likely to turn hostile, and the individual is forced to transfer the ties developed within the own group to the pact brother, who belongs to a group regarded as enemies. Thus the sense of security is outraged at two points: the original ties prove unreliable and the greatest security must be sought in a formerly distrusted spot.

*c. The religious view of the universe.* Relevant to the problem of individual security is the view a culture holds of the universe, the nature of the cosmic laws, the way in which these laws can be influenced, the extent to which they are internally consistent and harmonious or arbitrary and capricious. Perhaps the two most important considerations are whether man is conceived of as able to influence the supernatural or whether he must conform to its rules, and whether his means of influencing the supernatural are orderly or not.

Of the individualistic societies, the Arapesh believe in an ordered universe, a system of balance between male and female potencies supernaturally maintained, within which an individual has only to keep the rules in order to be safe. They have not, however, incorporated death into this scheme. This exclusion of death from the orderly universe with which they are otherwise able to deal leaves them vulnerable and insecure before the sorcerer. The Eskimo believe in a supernatural world which is subject to systematic manipulation by human individuals for their own ends, and which imposes certain tabus which must be obeyed. The faith in the tabus provides them with a sense of order, the performance of rituals gives them a sense of channeled power, and the individual supernatural feats of the angakut reaffirm their sense of individual power and importance. Their attitude toward death is fatalistic and secular. The Ojibwa phrase the supernatural world as a source of power which the strong individual can tap for his own ends; supernatural contests, therefore, become just another way of testing an individual's achievement and are a potential source of insecurity whenever he himself fails or another succeeds.

The Bachiga conceive an arbitrary system of powers controlled by priests for their own ends. As such it gives no security to anyone except the priests. It reinforces the individual's sense of being up against other human beings who wish to limit and control his movements. Both the Eskimo and the Arapesh may be said to have a partially systematic view of the universe with rules which everyone must keep; whereas the Ojibwa and the Bachiga supernaturals are a series of somewhat isolated and unrelated powers who act as capriciously as living individuals and do not impose their will in a continuous, consecutive, and impersonal fashion.

None of the three competitive societies rely upon a religious system which is integrated and impersonal. Their supernaturals are ancestors or spirits which man may control, the Ifugao by bribery, the Kwakiutl by a sort of spiritual attack and by privilege of rank, and the Manus by economic achievement and by subduing the lusts of the flesh. The capricious Bachiga ancestral spirits fall somewhat into this class also. It is notable that the Manus, who approach most closely to a cooperative emphasis, have an ethical code individually administered, but still approaching, although not reaching, a system which is impersonal and automatic in its operation. In all three societies man's relationship to the supernatural is prevailingly antagonistic; a tug of war with a competitor, not trust in and submission to a higher power.

When we turn to the cooperative societies we find perhaps one of the most suggestive generalizations from this study. All these societies, with again the least complete inclusion of the Dakota, have an ordered view of the universe. They conceive of a supernatural system which operates on its own rules and which man may propitiate and influence in an orderly way. The Iroquois combine a calendrical round of ceremonies which absolve the individual from his sins with secret societies in which individual relationships with the supernatural are possible. The Bathonga make a similar double provision. The ordinary round of life is controlled by offerings to a hierarchy of ancestors, from the ancestors of the king to the ancestors of the lowest kraal, and by a meticulous use of magical prescriptions which invoke impersonal magical forces in the universe. For those who wish a more personal relationship to the supernatural, where also, it will be remembered, indulgence in phantasy competition and aggression within the group are permitted, there are the witch societies. It has already been pointed out that the Iroquois attempt to preserve a balance between the demands of the individual and the demands of the group was not always successful. The double system of the Bathonga might have been equally unsuccessful if it were not for the firm African convention that sorcery is a criminal offense.

The Zuni devote most of their time to the loving performance of an elaborate ritual by which the society of men is infused with the blessings of the gods. Although there is great difference in the emphasis placed on religion by the Samoans and the Maori, the systems are essentially similar; the universe is an orderly one within which man is safe if he does not break the rules. Man walks safely under strong impersonal gods.

*d. Internal and external sanctions.* One of the most crucial aspects in the problem of character structure is that of the sanctions by which the individual is controlled. The term sanctions is used to denote the mechanisms by which conformity is obtained, by which desired behavior is induced and undesired behavior prevented. The development in the growing child of a responsiveness to the peculiar sanctions of his society is the essence of character formation. "Exercising control over its own members" was an element in the definition of a political society. And even in the nonpolitical societies, where the power of the society over its members is much weaker, there are also mechanisms of control by which the behavior of one individual is made to conform to the behavior of the others. The sanctions may be internal or external. The individual child may be so educated that he internalizes the standards of his society and obeys them in the absence of force exerted upon him from the outside, as in obeying a tabu for fear of death or disease, or in abstaining from illicit sex activities for fear of punishment by the ghosts. Once these are established within the character of the individual they operate automatically. When, on the other hand, the growing individual is not so delicately impressed with his society's standards, and has merely developed a responsiveness to forces which must be set in motion by others, whether these be ridicule, abuse, or execution by a royal decree, such sanctions are external. So the devout Catholic who alone on a desert island would still abstain from meat on Friday may be said to be responding to an *internal* sanction, which we customarily call conscience; whereas the businessman from a middlewestern city who regards a visit to New York as a suitable occasion for a debauch in which he would never indulge at home conducts his exemplary home behavior in response to an *external* sanction.

As much specific education is necessary to train a child to respond to external as to internal sanctions. But the education is of a different order and herein probably lies one of the keys to the culture and personality problem.

Whether a society principally relies upon external or internal sanctions, however, does not correlate with whether it is individualistic, competitive, or cooperative.

The individualistic Arapesh and the competitive Manus are the only cultures in our sample which have a character structure which can be roughly compared with our own Western European forms, and both of them rely upon guilt as an internal control. Guilt differs from fear in that it represents a disordered state within the psyche which can be righted only by atonement. Guilt is a response to past threat; for the Arapesh to the threat of loss of love if aggression has been manifested, for the Manus to the threat of loss of support if the emotions have not been controlled and socially directed. This early threat seems to be internalized in the character, and reenactment of analogous situations throughout life invokes the earlier fears and makes it necessary to reestablish the internal balance of the personality. In societies in which the individual is controlled by fear of being shamed, he is safe if no one knows of his misdeed; he can dismiss his misbehavior from his mind. In societies which are regulated by tabu, the individual who breaks a tabu is safe if he can invoke a stronger magical force. But the individual who feels guilt must repent and *atone* for his *sin*.

The use of shame as a principal external sanction is, as we have seen, characteristic of all the North American Indian cultures in the sample whether they are individualistic, competitive, or cooperative. The development in North American Indian children of an enormous sensitivity to the opinion of others seems to be fundamental for this culture area. Among the cultures with a strong development of the ego, the exercise of the sanction may result in suicide. Shame may also, when it is very strongly developed, become a relatively internal sanction. For example, among the Ojibwa the group takes a comparatively passive part in defining the situation as shameful but permits the vulnerable ego of the individual to declare itself shamed before them.

The competitive societies combine an internal sanction of fear of loss of position, and the invocation by the society of that fear for purposes of social control. On the other hand, in the cooperative societies, except those of North America, the sanction is not negative, *i.e.*, the fear of loss, but positive, *i.e.*, the individual's pride in participation. Even in North America this is to a large extent true for the Iroquois and the Dakota, though they invoke also the usual North American sanction of shame. Zuni, however, is an extreme example of a cooperative society in which individuals are not motivated by pride in social participation. Zuni sanctions are extraordinarily negative, the fear of being shamed. Nor are Zuni individuals controlled by *organized* external sanctions, such as execution, banishment, official plunder, etc., which are characteristic of the cooperative political societies. In Bathonga, Samoa, and Maori it is not sufficient for the group to jeer at or frighten its members; it has to use central authority against them. The lack of such sanctions in Zuni is probably related to the extreme sensitivity to shame which is built up in the individual. It is possible that the highly sensitive ego is easier to control than one that is permitted to develop with a more positive attitude toward others, and that the absence of organized social mechanism in Zuni is feasible because of this strong development of shame.

*e. The attitude toward children and the aged.* The last point to examine among the elements contributing to a sense of security is the attitude toward children and toward the old. Here the most significant point is that in all the competitive societies children are hurried toward adulthood; in only two of the cooperative societies, Zuni and Dakota, does this occur, and this again is part of the widespread American Indian custom of treating children like adults. In the other cooperative societies children are permitted, even encouraged, to grow up very slowly. It is possible that here again in the cases of Zuni and Dakota we are looking at a flaw in the structure, of the type which Prof. Radcliffe-Brown[1] calls *dysnomia*, that hurrying children toward adulthood is incompatible with their full participation in a society whose chief emphases are cooperative. While the flaws in Bathonga, Iroquois, Samoa, and Maori were, as we have seen, in political organization, the flaws in Zuni and Dakota are rather flaws in the educational system. A similar example of incompatibility between major emphasis and the educational system is found among the Bachiga. Their social system relies upon the initiative of individuals, and, by failing to hurry or train or direct

[1] Radcliffe-Brown, A. R., "On the Concept of Function in Social Science." American Anthropologist, N.S. Vol. 37, 1935, pp. 394–402.

their children, they produce an adult character that does not cope adequately with the demands of individualistic enterprise.

The examination of the position of the aged brings out one other aspect of this whole inquiry which must be borne in mind. There was found to be no correspondence between attitudes toward the old and either the degree of security itself or the major emphases. The cooperative, secure Bathonga treat their old people far worse than do the competitive Manus and Kwakiutl.

In addition to analyzing the ego development and the security of the members of these societies, it is also instructive to look at the presence of the will to power over persons. This does not occur among the cooperative societies unless we include the dysnomic Bathonga war among claimants for the throne. The absence of will to power over persons among the cooperative societies correlates with the presence in these societies of shared ends among all members of the group. Since all individuals work together toward these ends, no individual requires servile individuals to do his bidding. The fact that interest in power over persons is also absent among the highly competitive Kwakiutl makes it abundantly clear that this is the significant correlation. The Kwakiutl are interested in victory over a rival and this is pushed to extreme competitive lengths, but this victory which is sought is a shared victory which will accrue, by the reflected glory of their chief, to all the members of the numaym or the tribe. In this respect the competitive Kwakiutl resemble the cooperative Maori, and in neither society does the chief command a servile group of dependents. Among the Ifugao and the Manus, on the other hand, the two other competitive societies, the poor attach themselves to wealthy men to whom they are in debt and who become richer by exploiting them. Among the Ifugao the stratification between rich and poor approaches that with which we are familiar in our own society, but among the Manus the poor are an age group, those who are in debt to an entrepreneur for their marriage payments, and an able person has the opportunity to work his way up to an honored position. But in both societies the man who attains high status depends upon exploitation of others who are in debt to him and who do not share in the glory of his successful exploits.

In the individualistic societies shared ends are reduced to a minimum, but the two individualistic societies, Arapesh and Eskimo, which approach most nearly the social mechanisms of the cooperative societies with their shared ends are without an interest in power over persons, and the two, Ojibwa and Bachiga, which approach the competitive emphasis rely upon power over persons. These two societies both have strongly buttressed institutions of private property though actually property is of little economic moment, and among the Ojibwa the only great power in the society is wielded by the sorcerer, who has in his hands supernaturally sanctioned means of exploitation.

In all the societies in which the will to power is obviously developed, there is a low degree of security for the individual, and in none of the societies with a high degree of security is there a will to power over persons. It is striking that will to power does not necessarily occur where there is strong ego development, for it is absent in Eskimo, Maori, and Iroquois.

## TABULAR SUMMARY OF CHARACTER FORMATION

| Tribe | EGO DEVELOPMENT, *achievement, attitude toward property, external sanctions, attitude toward suicide* | SECURITY, *relationship to kin group, dominant emphasis in religion, internal sanctions, attitude toward children and the aged* |
|---|---|---|
| I. Arapesh... | Weak development of the ego. | Security dependent upon receiving the help and love of every member of the community; easily disturbed. |
| | Achievement in terms of activities directed toward others, feeding and cherishing plants and persons. | Warmth toward immediate kin merged in a similar attitude toward the whole community. |
| | Property of slight importance. | |
| | External sanction: the withdrawal of help and affection by all the members of the community; symbolic destruction of the property of a recalcitrant. Sorcery administered outside the group. | Faith in an ordered universe, which does not include an acceptance of death. |
| | | Internal sanction: guilt; anxiety over loss of love and over loss of health; both conceived as the penalty of aggression toward others. |
| | No suicide. | |

| Tribe | EGO DEVELOPMENT, *achievement, attitude toward property, external sanctions, attitude toward suicide* | SECURITY, *relationship to kin group, dominant emphasis in religion, internal sanctions, attitude toward children and the aged* |
|---|---|---|
| | | Children cherished and held back from adulthood. Aged treated tenderly. |
| II. Eskimo.... | Marked development of ego. Achievement phrased in terms of individual strength and skill, ability to survive. | Security given only by confidence in one's own strength. Only immediate relatives give any security; lack of relatives means complete insecurity for immature child. |
| | Property of very slight importance. | |
| | External sanction: threat of starvation induces effort and efficiency; fear of murder makes individual essay his own strength before he acts. | Belief in individual power and a universe with which individual can deal, through acquisition of supernatural power, and the keeping of tabus. |
| | Suicide at loss of strength through age or ill-health. (*Note:* This is brought about by others' recognizing this loss, not completely on individual initiative.) | Internal sanction: fear of loss of strength. |
| | | Low position of all persons without strength, but the child, who will obtain it later, is valued above the old, who have lost it permanently. |
| III. Ojibwa.... | Strong development of ego. Achievement phrased in terms of individual ability to succeed in every venture, and to remain physically and psychically independent of others. | Security given only by confidence in one's power to stand alone. Close kin are important because identification with them is possible. Religion is a system of obtaining individual power for individual ends, originally dependent upon the individual's ability to obtain it. |
| | Property of slight importance in itself, but used symbolically, with strong emphasis on individual ownership for ego gratification. | Internal sanction: fear of being shamed by *any* failure |

| Tribe | EGO DEVELOPMENT, *achievement, attitude toward property, external sanctions, attitude toward suicide* | SECURITY, *relationship to kin group, dominant emphasis in religion, internal sanctions, attitude toward children and the aged* |
|---|---|---|
| | External sanction: sorcery and threat of punitive attacks on the person and property of a dissenter; threat of insult to which the individual will react by suicide or leaving group. | or *any* insult, which will result in violent self-repudiation. |
| | | Children trained to be independent and the old forgotten in the extreme individualism of the adult life. |
| | Suicide of angry shame. | |
| IV. Bachiga... | Fairly strong ego drive but directed toward no definite goals. | Low security and reliance upon pact brotherhood (*i.e.*, upon the mitigation of omnipresent hostility). |
| | Achievement phrased in terms of escaping dependence upon others, possible in a variety of ways. | Unstable and shifting kin group combined with low degree of individual's ability to shift entirely for himself. |
| | Property valued as a means toward independence and not considered to be worth sustained effort on the part of everyone in order to acquire it. | Religion: an arbitrary system of powers controlled by priests for their own ends, and cult of own ancestors. |
| | External sanctions: very slightly developed, but an antisocial man would be forced to flee to a pact brother under threat of being killed. An informal judiciary enforced by the supernatural powers of the priests who act as referees. | Internal sanctions: fear of loss of security and health automatically resulting from neglect of kin duties. Belief in an arbitrarily penalizing universe. |
| | | Children treated casually, and the aged with the same gamut of behavior as that shown toward the adult. |
| | Rare uninstitutionalized suicide. | |
| V. Ifugao..... | Strong development of the ego. Achievement attached to keeping or bettering one's position on the status scale, | Security based upon trust in kin group and trust in self, plus sufficient possessions to buy security in |

| Tribe | EGO DEVELOPMENT, *achievement, attitude toward property, external sanctions, attitude toward suicide* | SECURITY, *relationship to kin group, dominant emphasis in religion, internal sanctions, attitude toward children and the aged* |
|---|---|---|
| | by means of possessions and a fierceness which readily breaks into violence. (In lowest class makes for recklessness, which upper classes must reckon with.) | terms of food, health, or safety. |
| | Property highly valued as the platform from which an individual can attain both achievement and security. | Kin-group solidarity blurred by bilateral organization, by conflict between generations and between individual and group interest. |
| | External sanction: threat of force from other kin groups and of failure of own group not to use force and spend property in one's favor. | Religion: belief in ancestral spirits who arbitrarily penalize and impoverish their descendants. |
| | Suicide by way of murderous running amok. | Internal sanction: fear of loss of status one attribute of which is ability to intimidate others. |
| | | Children pushed toward adulthood, especially so for upper-class children. Aged were demoted but retained some religious and advisory powers. |
| VI. Kwakiutl.. | Strong development of the ego. Achievement attached to ability to outdistance and beat down equals in the endless race for prestige by potlatching. | Low sense of security in a shifting structure. Kin-group security mitigated by individualistic striving within the group. |
| | Property highly valued; its dissipation and destruction a proof of the strength of the ego to stand these self-inflicted hurts. | Religious system: belief in a series of powers over which man could obtain control. |
| | External sanctions: public shaming for failure in competitive economic situations or exposure in shamanism; killing or expelling under | Internal sanction: fear of shame, loss of position in others' eyes. |
| | | Children pushed toward adulthood and hurried into |

| Tribe | EGO DEVELOPMENT, *achievement, attitude toward property, external sanctions, attitude toward suicide* | SECURITY, *relationship to kin group, dominant emphasis in religion, internal sanctions, attitude toward children and the aged* |
|---|---|---|
| | threat of killing the dissenter. | the competitive game. Aged demoted but treated with respect. |
| | Suicide of angry shame. | |
| VII. Manus..... | Strong ego development. Achievement consists of constructive and continuous activity measured against the pace of the group, with no point of rest. | Security given by own kin and by the religious system is conditional upon moral character. Extended blood and affinal kin bound together in reciprocal services which justify affection, rather than vice versa. |
| | Property highly valued as evidence of individual virtuous activity. | |
| | | Religion: reliance upon a compact with a highly personal, just, and exacting supernatural guardian. |
| | External sanction: administered almost entirely through the invocation of the internal sanction, but by mediums and diviners representing the community, to invoke guilt and shame. | Internal sanction: guilt; anxiety over failure to achieve, or over any self-indulgence which will result in *loss* of supernatural and mortal *support*. |
| | No suicide. | |
| | | Children highly valued, their care one of the chief goals of acitivity. Aged cared for, but without justifying their existence by activity. |
| VIII. Iroquois[1].. | Strong ego development. Insistence upon social virtues which are defined as bravery and initiative on the one hand and support of the established order on the other. | Security achieved by firm structure of society. |
| | | Well-organized cohesive kin group. |
| | | Religious system combined an externalized system |

[1] So little material on personality is available for this group that the analysis has to be upon another, less immediate level.

| Tribe | EGO DEVELOPMENT, *achievement, attitude toward property, external sanctions, attitude toward suicide* | SECURITY, *relationship to kin group, dominant emphasis in religion, internal sanctions, attitude toward children and the aged* |
|---|---|---|
| | Valuation of property was moderate and social control was exercised at such points as their prohibition of the destruction of property at death, which is characteristic of surrounding peoples. | whereby the individual was blessed and exonerated from personal responsibility, with a validation of idiosyncratic behavior. Essentially a system which could be operated by society for everyone's good. |
| | External sanction: ritual scolding and ridicule. | Internal sanction: pride and fear of loss of status. |
| | Suicide of hurt pride, grief, and by children who feel themselves abused by parents.[1] | |
| IX. Samoa .... | Socially directed suppression of ego development which is nevertheless marked. Achievement phrased in terms of fitting into the social pattern, success or failure being measured by the degree to which the individual measures up to his age and sex groups. | High degree of security based on wide extension of unconditional kinship ties and a marked valuation of sex. |
| | | Wide kin group with undifferentiated attitude toward all members, supported by ghostly sanction in favor of helping kin. |
| | Property conceived in terms of social usefulness for groups, not for individuals. | Religion: little emphasis on supernatural; faith in an ordered universe within which an individual can walk safely and without supernatural aid, if he keeps the rules. |
| | External sanctions: expulsion from cooperative groups which could be done summarily because the individual was always given shelter elsewhere; social invocation of internal sanction. | Internal sanction: pride in playing well one's socially dictated role and mild shame if individual overreaches himself. |
| | Practically no suicide. | |

[1] See *The Jesuit Relations and Allied Documents*, trans. by Reuben Gold Thwaites, vol. XLIII, p. 271.

| Tribe | EGO DEVELOPMENT, *achievement, attitude toward property, external sanctions, attitude toward suicide* | SECURITY, *relationship to kin group, dominant emphasis in religion, internal sanctions, attitude toward children and the aged* |
|---|---|---|
| | | Children regarded as potentially good material for society and so all treated well, but disciplined. Aged given honor until death, but removed if they are unfit to exercise it. |
| X. Zuni | Suppressed ego development, with emphasis on shame, and no channel permitted for pride. | High security tempered with a continual fear of shame. |
| | Achievement phrased in terms of selfless participation in the pattern. Success measured in terms of others' lack of assertiveness. | Compact and reliable kin group, walled about with suspicion toward outsiders. |
| | Property not highly valued; socialized. | Religion: faith and happy trust in the efficacy of the gods and an impersonal externalized ritual. |
| | External sanction: invocation of shame, accusation of witchcraft and sorcery. | Internal sanction: extreme fear of being shamed before others. |
| | No suicide. | Children hurried toward adulthood, shamed by accusal of childishness. Aged treated well. |
| XI. Batonga | Balanced ego development, blending organized aggression with organized submission. | Strong sense of security in an ordered society, inalienable social bonds, and freedom of the individual to leave a cooperative group within which he was too pressed. |
| | Achievement phrased in terms of the attainment of a propertied status within defined lines in the hierarchy, the acquisition of which was ultimately dependent upon fate which | Well-organized, well-defined kin groups with definite mutual obligations and affection, reinforced by |

Tribe

| EGO DEVELOPMENT, *achievement, attitude toward property, external sanctions, attitude toward suicide* | SECURITY, *relationship to kin group, dominant emphasis in religion, internal sanctions, attitude to children and to the aged* |
| --- | --- |
| could only partially be influenced. | ancestor cult. |
| Property valued but dependent upon increase of herds, not upon alienation of property from others. | Religious system: great dependence on magic, combined with a submissive and hopefully bargaining attitude toward the somewhat arbitrary ancestors.[1] |
| External sanction: a well-enforced judicial system, under the power of the king, and a clan discipline enforced by the ancestral cult. | Internal sanction: very slightly developed, mainly fear of offending against the system. |
| Suicide by individuals trapped by the pattern. | Position of middle-aged is highest with lower position of children and aged. Aged sometimes almost abandoned. |

XII. Dakota....

| Marked ego development. Achievement is phrased as attainment and maintenance of prestige relative to prestige of other members of the group, and of own group relative to other groups; some identification of ego with kin group. Suppression, within the group, of competitiveness, acquisitiveness, and will to power produces in individuals a determination to keep others from committing these congenial sins. | Relatively high security; strong kin group but emphasis upon bettering one's own position within it and upon bettering its relative position. |
| --- | --- |
| | Religion: supernatural power sought by all individuals for personal ends; elaborate esoteric formulation of an ordered universe. |
| | Internal sanction: fear of being shamed. |
| Property highly valued in inverted fashion with emphasis upon ability to give it away. | Children pushed toward adulthood. Aged respected. |

[1] Great externalization of religious system balanced by baloyi cult.

| Tribe | EGO DEVELOPMENT, *achievement, attitude toward property, external sanctions, attitude toward suicide* | SECURITY, *relationship to kin group, dominant emphasis in religion, internal sanctions, attitude toward children and the aged* |
|---|---|---|
| | External sanction: mechanism to shame individual, permanently divest him of reputation. | |
| | Institutionalized indirect suicide in war-bravery pattern. | |
| XIII. Maori..... | Strong development of ego but complete identification of the individual with his group. | High degree of security based on an inalienable position which the individual was given every opportunity to validate by achievement. |
| | Achievement is in terms of adding to the honor of the group either by individual or collective acts; the maintenance of the individual's position in the group is a necessary part of maintaining his own and the group's honor. | Very strong kin group, conceptually coterminous with the tribe; endogamous emphasis. |
| | Property valued only for social uses. | Religious system which identifies social and religious order within which an individual walked safely and with honor. Failure to obey the rules was fatal. |
| | External sanction: invocation of pride and of hierarchical rank in which pride was involved. | Internal sanction: sense of one's own position which must be kept inviolate. |
| | Suicide in mourning and when honor was lost. | |

Note on relative character formation in men and women:

Zuni: neither men nor women allowed pride, only shame.

Dakota: women allowed less pride than men, and far more shame and overt suicide found among them.

Bachiga: no shame for men, but in women ego is suppressed, given no possible outlet, and there is high development of shame.

## DIAGRAMS

These diagrams can be profitably used only with reference to the extended discussions. Cultures can rarely be placed unequivocably in a fixed category, *e.g.*, the high or medium security of the individual under a given social system allows of different answers. These diagrams are presented only as possibly useful summaries of the discussions.

DIAGRAM SHOWING THE RELATIONSHIP BETWEEN MAJOR
CULTURAL EMPHASES AND THE PRINCIPAL
TECHNIQUES FOR SECURING FOOD

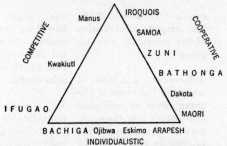

Capitals—Agricultural cultures.    Spaced capitals—Agricultural plus herding. Lower case letters—Cultures which depend upon hunting, fishing, and food gathering.[1]

This diagram shows the lack of correlation between these factors and competitive and cooperative societies.

DIAGRAM SHOWING THE CORRELATION
WITH CLOSED SOCIETIES

[1] The Manus are anomalous here as they depend upon trade with agricultural peoples.    They also raise pigs.

DIAGRAM SHOWING THE CORRELATIONS WITH THE PRESENCE OR
ABSENCE OF STATUS, EMPHASIS UPON RISING IN STATUS, AND
AN EDUCATIONAL SYSTEM WHICH PRODS CHILDREN
TOWARD ADULTHOOD

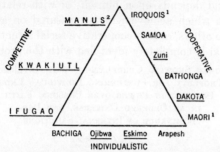

Spaced capitals—Concept of status, and emphasis upon rising in status.
Capitals—Status, but less emphasis upon rising in status. Lower case letters—
No status concepts of importance. Underlining—An educational system which
prods children toward adulthood.

This analysis reveals the anomalous position of Zuni with
their absence of a status concept and their prodding of children.
It also reveals the contrastingly anomalous position of the Bachiga
who with a competitive emphasis and a certain recognition of
status fail to prod their children or to develop any premium
upon achievement.

DIAGRAM SHOWING THE INCIDENCE OF STRONG DEVELOPMENT OF
THE EGO, LESS DEVELOPMENT OF THE EGO, PRESENCE OF A
HIGH SENSE OF SECURITY AND SUICIDE AS A CULTURALLY
RECOGNIZED INSTITUTION

* Culturally institutionalized suicide. Double underlining—High development of the ego. Single underlining—Medium development of the ego. No
underlining—Low development of the ego. Capitals—Presence of high security
for individuals.

[1] Iroquois and Maori material does not provide sufficient data to determine satisfactorily in how far they prodded their children toward adulthood.

This correlation shows that a strong development of the ego may occur in all three types of cultures, correlated with almost complete absence of social structure under which circumstances the individual depends upon himself, or with relativistic social structures in which achievement is measured on a single scale in relation to others, or in a cooperative social structure in which the individual is completely identified with the group.

DIAGRAM SHOWING CORRELATIONS WITH INTEREST IN
PROPERTY FOR FURTHERING INDIVIDUAL ENDS,
INTEREST IN POWER OVER PERSONS, FAITH
IN AN ORDERED UNIVERSE, AND PRE-
DOMINANCE OF INTERNAL SANCTIONS

Capitals—Interest in property for individual ends. Single underlining—Interest in power over persons. Double underlining—Faith in an ordered universe. * Predominance of internal sanctions.

The anomalous position of the Manus here is striking with their internal sanctions, and of the Dakota who cannot be said to have a concept of an ordered universe in the same sense that this can be said of the other cooperative societies. Note also the lack of interest in power over persons among the Kwakiutl (see p. 496).

DIAGRAM SHOWING COMMON ELEMENTS IN THE CULTURES AT
THE APEXES OF THE TRIANGLE

To test whether the relative position of cultures as placed on these diagrams is meaningful, the cooperative culture which most closely approaches the competitive emphasis was compared with the competitive culture which most closely approaches the cooperative emphasis, etc.

Bachiga and Ifugao both share strong ego drive, differentiation of goals, and *fear of loss of independence.*

Manus and Iroquois are both societies organized around *the regulation and limitation of competition* rather than the suppression of the ego or harnessing the ego to social ends, but the Manus depend more upon the individual, the Iroquois more upon the social structure.

Maori and Arapesh represent two contrasting systems by which the *distinction between the self and the good of others is eliminated,* in Maori by a structure which identified others with the own ego, in Arapesh by an educational emphasis which relies upon warm dependence upon others, and does not permit the ego to develop.

## SUMMARY OF CHARACTER FORMATION

It is possible to regard the educational procedure of a social system just as we would regard any other of its component subsystems, as, for example, the economic adjustment to the environment or the form of political integration. The components of a social system may or may not work harmoniously together, regardless of whether the main emphasis of the system is sufficiently clear to characterize it as primarily cooperative, competitive, or individualistic. Changes from one form of social system to another may be laid theoretically to shifts within the internal equilibrium of the social system, either in its numbers, in its natural environment, or in a disproportionate change in some part of the culture. It is probable that such complete correspondences as the strong ego, a high valuation of property, and a belief in arbitrary supernatural powers, which occur in all our competitive examples, may well represent essentials in the equilibrium of competitive societies.

In attempting to utilize these findings for further research or as a basis for constructive planning, the most important finding is the interrelation and interdependence of all these factors. It is impossible to interpret any one factor alone. Considering any one factor without regard to the others is as one-sided an approach to the problem of personality and culture as it would be to describe an isolated individual removed from the political and economic aspects of the social system within which he lives.

These correspondences raise several problems. As emphasized earlier in this discussion, they are significant only when they are positive. Even then they must be taken not in any absolute sense but rather as indicating possible optimum cohesions of traits or trends toward the formation of constellations of traits. Nevertheless when there is a complete correspondence, as between a single scale upon which success is reckoned and the competitive emphasis in society or between a high sense of security and a cooperative emphasis in society, the problems raised are very challenging. The more immediate the connection between the aspect of character formation and the social structure, the more readily the correspondence may be accepted as meaningful. Traits which are ranged over against each other without apparent relevance may become significant when we refer them back to their respective social structures, *e.g.*, strong emphasis upon private property used for personal ends is congruent with the competitive emphasis and a faith in an ordered universe with cooperative emphasis, although their mutual compatibility ranged alone might not appear on the surface.

These correspondences can be used further to point problems. When an incongruity is observed between one culture and all the other cultures classified with it in major emphases, this incongruity will bear further examination. So we find that the competitive Kwakiutl with their lack of interest in power over persons emphasize the fact that the significant correlation here is with shared ends and not with competition per se; the glory in victory which a member of a group shares with his chief takes the place of the exploitation of dependants which occurs in the other competitive societies. Again, the presence of relativistic status in Dakota and of relativistic judgment on persons in Zuni, a society without status, are aberrant in cooperative societies and may perhaps explain the great exploitation of shame to demote individuals to a common level. Similarly the fact that the Zuni and Dakota push their children toward adulthood puts them in line with the educational policy of the most strongly competitive cultures and out of line with the educational methods used by most cooperative cultures. Again the Bachiga, with an individualistic competitive emphasis, fail to push or direct their children toward adult goals, and the adult Bachiga shows a lack of aim and ambition which can be explained more readily by this factor than by the structure of the society.

Certain conspicuous absences of correspondence were observable which can be used to counsel caution and the need for check material from many cultures before conclusions in the field of personality are attempted. Public shame used as a principal sanction is a function not of competitive or cooperative emphases nor yet of the development of the ego, but of the North American Indian culture area. This example demonstrates vividly the way in which the cultural exploitation of a human potentiality may be actually a cultural invention characteristic of one geographical area. Another type of lack of correspondence, and perhaps the most significant one for this study, is the lack of correspondence between strong ego development and cultural emphasis upon competitive, cooperative, or individualistic behavior. Although no competitive society was found without strong ego development, strong ego development is possible within a social structure which provides adequately for cooperation.

The most significant specific conclusions which can be drawn from the sample and used for further research are:

Strong ego development can occur in individualistic, competitive, or cooperative societies.

Whether a group has a minimum or a plentiful subsistence level is not directly relevant to the question of how cooperative or competitive in emphasis a culture will be.

The social conception of success and the structural framework into which individual success is fitted are more determinative than the state of technology or the plentifulness of food.

There is a correspondence between: a major emphasis upon competition, a social structure which depends upon the initiative of the individual, a valuation of property for individual ends, a single scale of success, and a strong development of the ego.

There is a correspondence between: a major emphasis upon cooperation, a social structure which does not depend upon individual initiative or the exercise of power over persons, a faith in an ordered universe, weak emphasis upon rising in status, and a high degree of security for the individual.

# Bibliography on the Problem of Culture and Personality

BENEDICT, RUTH: "Culture and the Abnormal," *Journal of General Psychology*, Vol. 10, No. 1, pp. 59–82, January, 1934.

——: *Patterns of Culture*, Houghton Mifflin Company, Boston, 1934.

BURGESS, E. W.: *Personality and the Social Group*, University of Chicago Sociological Series, University of Chicago Press, Chicago, 1929.

DOLLARD, J.: *Criteria for the Life History*, Yale University Press, New Haven, 1935.

——: "Psychotic Personality Seen Culturally," *American Journal of Sociology*.

FRANK, L. K.: "The Concept of Inviolability in Culture," *American Journal of Sociology*, Vol. 36, No. 4, pp. 607–615, January, 1931.

——: "Management of Tensions," *American Journal of Sociology*, Vol. 33, No. 5, pp. 705–736, March, 1928.

——: "Personality and Rank Order," *American Journal of Sociology*, Vol. 35, No. 2, pp. 177–186, September, 1929.

——: "Physiological Tensions and Social Structure," *Proceedings of the American Sociological Society*, Vol. 22, Dec. 20–30, 1927.

——: "Society as the Patient," *American Journal of Sociology*, Vol. 42, November, 1936.

FROMM, ERICH: "Über Methode und Aufgabe einer analytischen Sozialpsychologie," *Zeitschrift für Sozialforschung*, C. L. Hirschfeld, Leipzig, Jahrgang I, 1932.

——: "Die psychoanalytische Charakterologie und ihre Bedeutung für die Sozialpsychologie," *Zeitschrift für Sozialforschung*, C. L. Hirschfeld, Leipzig, Jahrgang I, 1932.

——: Sozialpsychologischer Teil der Studien über "Autorität und Familie," Librarie Alcand, Paris, 1936, herausgegeben von Max Horkheimer, pp. 77–135.

HORNEY, K.: "Culture and Neurosis," *American Sociological Review*, Vol. 1, No. 2, pp. 221–230, April, 1936.

——: "The Subject of Female Masochism," *Psychoanalytic Review*, Vol. 22, pp. 241–257, July, 1935.

LEWIN, K.: *A Dynamic Theory of Personality*, McGraw-Hill Book Company, Inc., New York, 1935.

MEAD, MARGARET: "On the Institutionalized Role of Women and Character Formation," *Zeitschrift für Sozialforschung*, Vol. 5, pp. 69–76.

——: *Sex and Temperament in Three Primitive Societies*, William Morrow & Company, Inc., New York, 1935; George Routledge & Sons, Ltd., London, 1935.

——: "The Use of Primitive Material in the Study of Personality," *Character and Personality*, Vol. 3, pp. 3–16, September, 1934.

MORENO, F.: *Who Shall Survive?* Nervous and Mental Disease Publishing Company, 1934, *Nervous and Mental Disease Monograph Series*, No. 58, Washington, D. C.

SAPIR, EDWARD: "Cultural Anthropology and Psychiatry," *Journal of Abnormal and Social Psychology*, Vol. 27, No. 132, pp. 229–242.

————: "Emergence of the Concept of Personality in the Study of Culture," *Journal of Social Psychology*, Vol. 5, pp. 408–415, 1934.

*Further Sources*

FRANK, L. K.: "Art and Living," *American Magazine of Art*, May, 1932.

————: "An Institutional Analysis of the Law," *Columbia Law Review*, Vol. 24, No. 5, pp. 480–499, May, 1924.

————: "The Principle of Disorder and Incongruity in Economic Affairs," *Political Science Quarterly*, Vol. 47, No. 4, pp. 515–525, December, 1932.

————: "Social Change and the Family," *Annals of the American Academy of Political and Social Science*, Vol. 160, March, 1932.

————: "Social Planning and Individual Ideals," *International Journal of Ethics*, Vol. 45, No. 1, October, 1934.

————: "Social Problems," *American Journal of Sociology*, Vol. 30, No. 4, pp. 462–473, January, 1925.

————: "Structure, Function and Growth," *Journal of Philosophy of Science*, Vol. 2, No. 2, April, 1935.

"Hanover Outline on Personality and Culture" (ms.) drafted by conference group composed of following: Lura Beam, John Dollard, Earl T. Engle, Mary Fisher, Willis Fisher, Hugh Hartshorne, Robert S. Lynd, Mark A. May, Margaret Mead, James Plant, V. T. Thayer, Lloyd Warner, Edna N. White, L. K. Frank, Chairman.

MEKEEL, H. S.: "Clinic and Culture," *Journal of Abnormal and Social Psychology*, Vol. 30, No. 3, pp. 292–300, October-December, 1935.

*Proceedings* of the First Colloquum on Personality Investigation, held under the Joint Auspices of the American Psychiatric Association, Committee on Relations of Psychiatry and the Social Sciences, and of the Social Science Research Council, Dec. 1 and 2, 1928. Published by the Lord Baltimore Press, 1928.

*Proceedings* of the Second Colloquum on Personality Investigation, held under the Joint Auspices of the American Psychiatric Association, Committee on Relations of Psychiatry and the Social Sciences, and of the Social Science Research Council, Nov. 29 and 30, 1929. Published by the Lord Baltimore Press, 1930.

RANK, O.: *Modern Education*, Alfred A. Knopf, Inc., New York, 1932.

————: "Psychology and Social Change," *News-Letter of the American Association of Psychiatric Social Workers*, Vol. 4, No. 3, January, 1935.

Seminar on the Impact of Culture on Personality, Yale University, 1932–33; Dr. Edward Sapir, Director, and Dr. John Dollard, Assistant Director; organized by the Committee of this name under the Social Science Research Council. The advisory committee was as follows: E. W. Burgess, F. L. Wells, W. I. Thomas, Clark Wissler, James S. Plant, Edward Sapir, L. K. Frank, Chairman. The Seminar group was composed of thirteen men from twelve foreign countries, including the Orient and India, who spent a year in discussion of problems and methodologies in the field of personality and culture.

"Sociological Research in Adolescence," Report of Committee composed of E. B. Reuter, H. Blumer, E. W. Burgess, E. F. Frazier, Margaret Mead, Ruth Shonle Cavan, John Dollard, Eleanor Wembridge, R. G. Foster, L. K. Frank, J. B. Maller, F. B. Shuttleworth, and F. M. Thrasher, *American Journal of Sociology*, Vol. 42, No. 1, pp. 81–93, July, 1936.

Thomas, W. I., editor: Committee on Personality and Culture, Social Science Research Council; Edward A. Bott, Chairman. Report prepared by W. I. Thomas.

Note:

In addition to the comments and references in my new concluding chapter (p. 516), I should like to refer the reader to the following bibliographies in this field:

Honigman, J. J.: *Culture and Personality,* Harper & Brothers, New York, 1954.

May, M. A. and Doob, L. W.: *Competition and Cooperation:* A report of the sub-committee on competitive-cooperative habits, of the committee on personality and culture, based on analyses of research achievement and opportunity by members of the committee. Social Science Research Council, Bulletin 25, New York, 1937.

Mead, M.: "Research on Primitive Children" in *Manual of Child Psychology,* L. Carmichael, ed., Ch. 13, 2nd ed., pp. 667–706, 1953.

"The study of national character" in *The Policy Sciences,* D. Lerner and H. D. Lasswell, eds., Stanford Univ. Press, Stanford, pp. 70–85, 1951.

"L'étude du caractère national," trans. by J. G. and P. H. Maucorps, in *Les "sciences de la politique" aux Etats-Unis,* Cahiers de la fondation des sciences politiques, Vol. 19, pp. 105–132, 1951, Librairie Armand Colin, Paris.

Mead, M. and Métraux, R.: *The Study of Culture at a Distance,* Univ. of Chicago Press, Chicago, 1949.

# APPRAISAL 1961

## *by* MARGARET MEAD

The interpretative statement gives us a landmark for measuring the state of our conceptualizations twenty-five years ago. As materials to work with, we had voluminous information about primitive societies but no theoretical framework about their structure, such as was later provided by the British structural anthropologists,[1] by Gregory Bateson,[2] and by Claude Lévi-Strauss.[3] We knew the kinds of information that were needed to understand the socialization of the infant and young child but had no systematic way of relating chronological age and zonal involvement, such as was later provided by Gesell and Ilg,[4] Dollard,[5] Erikson,[6] and Gorer,[7] by which information about feeding and weaning, training and prohibitions could be integrated. John Dollard's *Criteria for the Life History*,[8] a part of this same research enterprise, was published just as our work was

---

[1] A. R. Radcliffe-Brown and Daryll Forde, editors, *African Systems of Kinship and Marriage,* Oxford University Press for the International African Institute, London, 1950.

[2] Gregory Bateson, *Naven,* Cambridge University Press, Cambridge, 1936; second edition: Stanford University Press, Stanford, California, 1958.

[3] Claude Lévi-Strauss, *Les structures élémentaires de la parenté,* Presses Universitaires de France, Paris, 1949.

[4] Margaret Mead, "On the Implications for Anthropology of the Gesell-Ilg Approach to Maturation," *American Anthropologist,* Vol. 49, No. 1, pp. 69-77, January-March, 1947.

[5] John Dollard, *Criteria for the Life History,* Yale University Press, New Haven, 1935. Reprinted: Peter Smith, New York, 1949.

[6] Erik H. Erikson, *Childhood and Society,* W. W. Norton & Company, Inc., New York, 1950.

[7] Geoffrey Gorer, "National Character: Theory and Practice," in *The Study of Culture at a Distance,* Margaret Mead and Rhoda Métraux, editors, pp. 57-82, The University of Chicago Press, Chicago, 1953. Also: "The Concept of National Character," *Penguin Science News,* No. 18, pp. 105-122, Penguin Books, Harmondsworth, 1950.

[8] John Dollard, *op. cit.*

finished. Bateson was working on the concept of schizmogenesis;[9] Gorer was working with Ruth Benedict on the Report of Psychological Leads for Field Workers.[10] He left New York for a short trip to Russia, where, on the basis of the *Cooperation and Competition* hypothesis, he persuaded Barton to make a more thorough investigation into the character structure of his Ifugaos, whom Barton in his popular book[11] had painted as warm, generous lovers, but whose institutions suggested quite different kinds of motivations. Barton went back to the Philippines, and the result was *Philippine Pagans, the Autobiographies of Three Ifugaos,*[12] which demonstrated that the same motives that operated in the rest of life also came into play in love affairs. Fenton, whose help we had enlisted on the Iroquois, writes, January 5, 1961,

> I remember attending the seminar, meeting Quain and then working with him at the American Museum. We were both very young and it was exciting. I was fresh from the field and was about to return to Tonawanda for the U. S. Indian Service. I returned and read Quain's manuscript to Jesse Cornplanter and a committee of informants in Jesse's kitchen near the Tonawanda Longhouse, where Morgan had worked ninety years before me, and I wager it was the exception, not the rule, to have a Columbia University Seminar report criticized by a committee of informants. Quain raised most of the important theoretical questions and we tried to get answers even when there was no data. The time had long gone when most of these could be probed. But it was a good thing to have done because it put me on the *qui vive* for information on these points, and gradually some of it has emerged. Jesse J. Cornplanter, himself, tired of such enquiries, borrowed my typewriter and wrote his own *Legends of the Long House.*[13]

[9]Gregory Bateson, "Culture Contact and Schismogenesis," *Man,* XXXV, pp. 178-183, December, 1935.

[10]Geoffrey Gorer, A National Research Council Committee Report, unpublished, 1936.

[11]R. F. Barton, *The Half-Way Sun,* Brewer & Warren, Inc., New York, 1930.

[12]———, *Philippine Pagans, the Autobiographies of Three Ifugaos,* George Routledge & Sons, Ltd., London, 1938.

[13]Jesse J. Cornplanter, *Legends of the Long House,* J. B. Lippincott Company, New York, 1938.

What we had done in our research method was to assemble a group of workers, chosen not because of any arbitrary disciplinary allegiances, but from knowledge and interest and competence, and we drew upon our own colleagues — Ruth Bunzel, William Fenton, Ella Deloria; our seniors — Ruth Benedict and Radcliffe-Brown; and our colleagues in other fields — Erich Fromm, John Dollard, Abraham Edel — where we knew that we needed the illumination and help they could provide. I believe that our different degrees of competence and experience, and the contrasts among our temperaments and special interests, were in themselves fruitful.

It was a new kind of seminar — we all shared each other's written reports and reacted, individually and as a group, to the same shared materials. This is a method that has stood the test of time in getting cooperative intellectual work done — work that is related to the materials and not to disciplinary stances and postures.

There are two specific problems raised by the study which have continued to arouse discussion and interest. The first is the question of sanctions — which sanctions are invoked by a society in the education of the children and the disciplining of the adults. In this study we identified only two, shame and guilt, and used relatively simple definitions, and we made some use of the idea of external and internal sanctions.

The second problem was an attempt to relate the type of sanction used to stages of development, processes of character formation, and to types of social structure. In addition to the Piers and Singer study,[14] a whole literature has now grown up about these problems. The most ambitious of these formulations is that of Erikson, who has gone on from his original chart relating modes of behavior, zones to which these modes were most appropriate, and stages of development, to distinguishing eight stages of ego tasks: (1) for infancy, trust versus basic mistrust (corresponding to the oral stage and the receptive and incorporative modes), in which he also recognizes a deep pervading sense of sin as the religious accompaniment; (2) autonomy versus shame and doubt (corresponding to the two anal stages of con-

[14]Gerhard Piers and Milton B. Singer, *Shame and Guilt: A Psychoanalytic and Cultural Study,* Charles Thomas, Springfield, Illinois, 1953.

trol of elimination and retention); (3) initiative versus guilt (corresponding to the phallic and oedipal stage); (4) industry versus inferiority (corresponding to latency or late childhood); (5) identity versus role diffusion (corresponding to puberty and early adolescence); (6) intimacy versus isolation as the problem of the young adult; followed by (7) a mature stage of generativity versus stagnation; and (8) a final stage of ego integrity versus despair.[15]

From the cultural side these may be expressed as (1) early infancy, in which fear is the major emotion invoked, fear of loss of support, of being overwhelmed by impulse or attack, fear empathetically communicated, and in which the basis is laid for a sense of sin in which there is no content to prohibition or admonition; (2) the period of learning autonomy, in which shame-pride are the major emotions invoked, which range from the extreme of a shame sanction — the disapproval of those who are themselves disapproved or despised — to the extreme of a pride sanction — delight in the approval of the admired (Gorer has suggested the use of the term "concern with renown" to cover the range of adult behaviors which fall within this category);[16] (3) the oedipal stage in which the principal task is controlling initiative towards adults and the sanctions range from guilt — a self-generated response to anticipated punishment if admonitions of parents or parental surrogates are disregarded, which includes the type of religious sense of sin related to the content of the sinful acts committed — to responsibility — the establishment of self-generated enjoyment of fulfilling parental expectations (this is sometimes called "good guilt," which raises semantic difficulties). Riesman,[17] in working with comparable problems of character formation and society, described the character in which this third stage — the guilt component — predominates as "inner directed," and his less fully defined autonomous man corresponds to a preponderance of responsibility and free choice

[15]Erik H. Erikson, *op. cit.* Also: "On the Sense of Inner Identity," *Clinical and Theoretical Papers, Austen Riggs Center,* Vol. I, Robert Knight, editor, pp. 324-341, International Universities Press, New York, 1954.

[16]Margaret Mead, "Some Anthropological Considerations Concerning Guilt," *Feelings and Emotions, The Mooseheart Symposium,* Martin L. Reymert, editor, pp. 362-373, McGraw-Hill, New York, 1950.

[17]David Riesman, *The Lonely Crowd,* Yale University Press, New Haven, 1950.

over guilt. Djilas' *Land Without Justice*[18] presents us with the fullest account of a character structure in which pride was the major sanction.

Although a great deal of new, more detailed work has been done in specifying the interplay between cultural sanctions and stage of development in infancy, particularly on Russian character,[19] and on the second stage, particularly in Germany,[20] and a slight beginning has been made on the importance of adolescence in France,[21] relatively little has yet been done relating adult character, character formation, cultural institutions, and psychoanalytical theory.[22]

There is a third development of this type of inquiry which parallels the emerging new concern with the growth of the mind, almost forgotten in the half century of concern with man's rediscovered early childhood complexities. The types of thought which are appropriate to the chronological stages of childhood are now being explored. Studies of character structure now combine knowledge of primary process thinking with studies of the way thinking itself develops, thus providing a new synthesis between psychoanalytic and child development insights, cultural

[18]Milovan Djilas, *Land Without Justice,* Harcourt Brace, New York, 1958. See also W. Goldschmidt, "Ethics and the Structuring of Society," *American Anthropologist,* Vol. 53, pp. 506-524, October-December, 1951.

[19]Geoffrey Gorer, *The People of Great Russia,* The Cresset Press, London, 1949, and Chanticleer Press, New York, 1950. Also "Swaddling and the Russians," *New Leader,* pp. 19-20, May 21, 1951; and Margaret Mead, "The Swaddling Hypothesis: Its Reception," *American Anthropologist,* Vol. 56, pp. 395-409, June, 1954.

[20]Rhoda Métraux, "Parents and Children: An Analysis of Contemporary German Child-Care and Youth-Guidance Literature," "A Portrait of the Family in German Juvenile Fiction," and "The Consequences of Wrongdoing: An Analysis of Story Completions by German Children," in *Childhood in Contemporary Cultures,* Margaret Mead and Martha Wolfenstein, editors, pp. 204-228; pp. 253-276; pp. 306-323, The University of Chicago Press, Chicago, 1955.

[21]Rhoda Métraux and Margaret Mead, *Themes in French Culture, Preface to a Study of French Community,* Stanford University Press, Stanford, California, 1954; Françoise Dolto, "French and American Children as seen by a French Child Analyst," in *Childhood in Contemporary Cultures,* Margaret Mead and Martha Wolfenstein, editors, pp. 408-423, The University of Chicago Press, Chicago, 1955.

[22]Margaret Mead, "Cultural Contexts of Puberty and Adolescence," The Freud Memorial Lecture, presented May 1, 1959, *The Bulletin of the Philadelphia Association for Psychoanalysis,* Vol. 9, pp. 59-79, September, 1959.

insights, and studies like those of Piaget.[23] In retrospect, the lack of attention to the style of thought of our thirteen cultures is very striking. *Ethos* as compared with *Eidos* was the predominant interest.

In social organization analysis, although the idea of role was used, there was no attempt to relate role behavior generated from a structural position, for example, behavior of succoring parent to dependent child, to the development of patterns of interpersonal relationships, such as initiative-response or exhibition-spectatorship. These were to wait upon the development of the interaction studies of Chapple and Arensberg,[24] and Oliver,[25] and upon the integration of Bateson's types of interaction — complementary, symmetrical, and reciprocal — with fixed and flexible role positions (end linkage).[26] Temperament, innate behavioral style, was treated as a given, with allowance for deviant temperaments. There had been as yet no attempt to really measure either constitutional factors, such as Chapple's invariant factors,[27] or deeply patterned personality types, such as that provided by projective tests,[28] where the position of the individual in the socio-cultural structure was fully specified.

The other special emphasis in the original study was the rela-

---

[23]————, "Some Relationships between Social Anthropology and Psychiatry," *Dynamic Psychiatry*, Franz Alexander and Helen Ross, editors, pp. 401-448, The University of Chicago Press, Chicago, 1952. J. M. Tanner and Barbel Inhelder, editors, *Discussions on Child Development*, Meetings of the World Health Organization Study Group on the Psychobiological Development of the Child, 1953, 1951, 1955, 1956, Tavistock Publications, Ltd., London. Vol. I, 1956, Vol. II, 1956, Vol. III, 1958, Vol. IV, 1961. Also, Edith Cobb, "The Ecology of Imagination in Childhood," *Daedalus*, pp. 537-518, Summer 1959.

[24]Eliot D. Chapple and C. M. Arensberg, "Measuring Human Reactions: An Introduction to the Study of the Interaction of Individuals," *Genetic Psychology Monographs*, XXII, pp. 3-147, 1940.

[25]Douglas L. Oliver, *A Solomon Island Society*, Harvard University Press, Cambridge, 1956.

[26]Gregory Bateson, "Morale and National Character," *Civilian Morale*, Goodwin Watson, editor, pp. 71-91, Houghton Mifflin, Boston, 1942; Margaret Mead and Rhoda Métraux: *The Study of Culture at a Distance*, Part Nine: "End Linkage: An Analytic Approach," pp. 365-393, The University of Chicago Press, Chicago, 1953.

[27]Eliot D. Chapple, "The Interaction Chronograph: Its Evaluation and Present Application," *Personnel*, XXV, pp. 295-307, 1949.

[28]These projective tests were collected by T. Schwartz in the American Museum of Natural History Admiralty Island Expedition, 1953-54.

tionship between institutions and character formation, represented today by the whole field of social class studies, Dollard,[29] Davis,[30] Havinghurst,[31], Fromm,[32] Gorer;[33] changing character under conditions of social change,[34] Thompson,[35] Riesman,[36] Birdwhistell,[37] Mead;[38] caste character, Carstairs;[39] and by the whole field of national character in which the relationships of regularities in character to national institutions are analyzed.[40] However, although these later developments have drawn upon anthropological materials and methods, most of the work has been on materials from modern complex societies rather than from primitive societies.

Comparative studies of the type that we did are still rare. In the 1930's coincidentally with the inauguration of the studies in Cooperation and Competition, Yale University was beginning to build up the classified cross referencing system now known as the Human Relations Area Files. Interest shifted to using as

[29]John Dollard, *Caste and Class in a Southern Town,* Yale University Press, New Haven, 1937.

[30]Allison Davis and John Dollard, *Children of Bondage,* American Council on Education, Washington, D. C., 1940.

[31]W. A. Davis and R. J. Havinghurst, *Father of the Man,* Houghton Mifflin, Boston, 1947.

[32]Erich Fromm, *Escape from Freedom,* Farrar and Rinehart, New York, 1941.

[33]Geoffrey Gorer, *Exploring English Character,* The Cresset Press, London, 1955.

[34]Melford E. Spiro, *Children of the Kibbutz,* Harvard University Press, Cambridge, 1958; William Caudill, "Psychological Characteristics of Acculturated Wisconsin Ojibwa Children," *American Anthropologist,* Vol. 51, pp. 409-427, July-September, 1949.

[35]Laura Thompson, "Attitudes and Acculturation," *American Anthropologist,* Vol. 50, pp. 200-215, April, 1948.

[36]David Riesman, *op. cit.*

[37]Ray L. Birdwhistell, "Family Structure and Social Mobility," *Transactions of the New York Academy of Sciences,* Series II, Vol. 21, pp. 136-145, December, 1958; and *Border Country: A Study in Socialization and Mobility Potential,* Doctoral Dissertation (in microfilm), University of Chicago Press, Chicago, 1951.

[38]Margaret Mead, *New Lives for Old, Cultural Transformation — Manus, 1928-1953,* William Morrow & Company, Inc., New York, 1956.

[39]Morris Carstairs, *The Twice-Born,* Hogarth, London, 1957.

[40]Margaret Mead, "National Character" in *Anthropology Today,* A. L. Kroeber, editor, pp. 642-667, University of Chicago Press, Chicago, 1953. Also Margaret Mead and Rhoda Métraux, editors, *The Study of Culture at a Distance,* The University of Chicago Press, Chicago, 1953.

large a number of cultures on which information on a few variables, theoretically regarded as crucial, could be obtained, as the basis for cross cultural studies like those of Whiting and Child,[41] or Ford and Beach.[42] Parallel to these studies based on biological regularities, studies of areal political forms continued, but with very little inclusion of studies of character structure. Fundamentals of kinship style or political organization were treated like patterns which had no intimate connection with the developed and developing personalities of those who embodied the patterns.[43]

There have been two related evolutionary approaches, those of White[44] and Steward,[45] which flatly maintain that personality is not a relevant variable in the study of culture change. Two recent studies, both areal and comparative, and both ignoring any factors of cultural character are Goldman's[46] study of social stratification in Polynesia and Sahlins'[47] contrasting theory. These researches and Lehman's study of cultural evolution in India[48] are all conducted at a macrocultural level where the specification of human characteristics except in specied and demographic terms are regarded as irrelevant.

But the design of our study was based on an assemblage of a set of whole cultures, not chosen at random, nor in order to get a large number for the purpose of statistical manipulations, but chosen purposefully so that each culture would in some

[41]J. W. M. Whiting and I. L. Child, *Child Training and Personality: A Cross Cultural Study,* Yale University Press, New Haven, 1953.

[42]C. S. Ford and F. A. Beach, *Patterns of Sexual Behavior,* Paul B. Hoeber, Inc., New York, 1951.

[43]G. P. Murdock, *Social Structure,* The Macmillan Company, New York, 1949.

[44]Leslie White, *The Evolution of Culture,* McGraw-Hill Book Company, Inc., New York, 1959.

[45]Julian Steward, *Theory of Culture Change,* University of Illinois Press, Urbana, 1955. Julian Steward, *et. al.: The People of Puerto Rico,* University of Illinois Press, Urbana, 1956.

[46]Irving Goldman, "Variations in Polynesian Social Organization," *Journal of the Polynesian Society,* Vol. 66, No. 4, pp. 374-390, December, 1957.

[47]Marshall D. Sahlins, "Differentiation by Adaptation in Polynesian Societies," *Journal of the Polynesian Society,* Vol. 66, No. 3, pp. 291-300, September, 1957.

[48]Frederic Lehman, *Some Anthropological Parameters of a Civilization: The Ecology and Evolution of Indian High Culture,* a Columbia University Ph.D. Dissertation, 1959.

specific way highlight the problem under investigation. We were making not a probabilistic study but working with a specially constructed organized complexity.[49] The criteria of choice were those of relevance to the problem. The cultures thus assembled formed a universe within which hypotheses could be developed, which, although valid only within that universe, were still one step closer to cross cultural validity.

This method, where the purpose was the demonstration of relevant conditions rather than the investigation of a problem was used also in *Cultural Patterns and Technical Change*.[50] In my *Male and Female*[51] I was able to treat the seven Oceanic cultures that I had studied myself, in a somewhat similar way. But because this limited me to one area and my own field work, certain significant variables were omitted — for example, I had no society in which age grading was important.[52]

Yehudi Cohen's comparative work[53] has taken us a further step forward. He has devised a method which derives both from the quantitative style of the Human Relations Area File analysis, as he uses a large sample of societies, and from our Cooperation and Competition style of comparing whole societies while focusing on a few key subjects — child rearing, distribution of food, localization of kin group, types of legal responsibility, etc. However he does select his sample without reference to his particular problem, in the belief that this demonstration of lack of bias is more important than specific structural relevance, and he counts occurrences and tests the statistical reliability of his results. In our study we worked slowly, selecting our cultures one by one for the contrasts that seemed most essential, building in effect a structure that was ever more intimately related to the central problem. This method is an exploratory, hypothesis-generating

[49]Warren Weaver, "Science and People," *Science,* Vol. 122, No. 3183, pp. 1255-1259, December 30, 1955.

[50]Margaret Mead, editor, *Cultural Patterns and Technical Change,* UNESCO, Paris, 1953; also The New American Library (A Mentor Book), New York, 1955.

[51]———, *Male and Female,* William Morrow and Company, New York, 1949; also The New American Library (A Mentor Book), New York, 1955.

[52]Bruno Bettelheim, *Symbolic Wounds: Puberty Rites and the Envious Male,* The Free Press, Glencoe, Illinois, 1954.

[53]Yehudi Cohen, *Social Structure and Personality, A case book,* Holt, Rinehart and Winston, New York, 1961. See especially pp. 312-350.

method. Yehudi Cohen's method is designed for testing hypotheses, and also, because of the inclusion of whole cultures and not merely selected variables, for generating new hypotheses. In an expansion of his earlier cross cultural studies, Whiting[54] is collecting material in ways that will assure a lack of bias, recording for short periods at stated intervals within cultures which have been previously studied, so that details are available for further cross testing of the results.

I believe that the light that our study threw upon the central problem of the nature of cooperative and competitive habits was more a matter of demonstrating the extent to which these behaviors — in the biological and psychological sense — have to be examined in the fullest possible cultural contexts, than upon the specific phrasing of the possible cultural determinants. That the problem is still a lively one is attested to by the recent claims of such an eminent biologist as H. J. Müller,[55] that traits like cooperativeness are genetically determined, a claim which flies in the face of our available cultural evidence on the extent to which such behavior is dependent upon socio-cultural forms. Furthermore the hypothesis that an ordered view of the universe and clear-cut boundaries to social group may facilitate cooperative behavior still seems useful. I would, today, lay more stress upon the exceedingly standardizing effect of competition in the reduction of range in behavior and the production of uniformity and conformity.[56]

Examination of the state of our knowledge both then and now demonstrates how far we have come and how far we still have to go in building a satisfactory theory of the relationships of cultural character and socio-cultural forms.

[54]John W. M. Whiting, "Personality as a Mediator in the Patterning of Culture," in Francis Hsu, editor, forthcoming volume on culture and personality. (Work in progress.)

[55]H. J. Müller, "The Guidance of Human Evolution," *The Evolution of Man, Mind, Culture and Society*, Vol. II of *Evolution After Darwin*, The University of Chicago Centennial, Sol Tax, editor, pp. 423-462, The University of Chicago Press, Chicago, 1960. See also Julian Steward, discussion in *Issues of Evolution*, Vol. III of *Evolution After Darwin*, Sol Tax and Charles Callender, editors, pp. 240-241.

[56]L. K. Frank, *Society as the Patient*, Rutgers University Press, 1948, see Chapter 3, "The Cost of Competition," pp. 21-36; Margaret Mead, "Our Documentary Culture," *The American Scholar*, Vol. 25, pp. 401-409, Autumn, 1956.

# COOPERATION AND COMPETITION IN GEOMETRIC-VECTORIAL SYMBOLISM

*A Note Provided by* WALTER ZESSNER, *Engineering Department of the Canadian Broadcasting Corporation, Toronto, Canada*

Graphic configurations compared to descriptive language symbolism offer an inherent advantage for concise demonstration and understanding. This is readily perceived through the application of an equilateral triangle that depicts Cooperation, Competition, and Individuality as a means for cultural comparisons of various characteristics (Fig. 1). Besides graphical

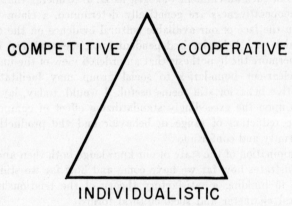

COMPETITIVE     COOPERATIVE

INDIVIDUALISTIC

*Fig. 1.* The equilateral triangle as graphical simplification for demonstrating the Competitive, Cooperative and Individualistic characteristic. Maximum intensity for each trait has been designated at the mid-point of every side (1-p. 461).

comprehension there arise possibilities in deriving abstract symbolization for hypothetical and methodical evaluations.

Such a tentative attempt is demonstrated by locating the triangular sides of cooperation and competition in parallel and in center division in order to develop four geometric-vectorial elements. These vector lengths being of equal magnitude estab-

lish perfect equilibrium (Fig. 2). In assuming proportional
relations for opposing vector forces, the fixed and static configuration transforms into a flexible and dynamic operational
concept that permits the constellation of an infinite number of
behavioristic variations and modifications and consequently of
definitial values (1x). In linking various related character traits
symbolically, unconditional competition (e.g. independent strife)
may diminish at the expense of conditional competion (e.g. goal
expectation) and a dominance of unconditional cooperation (e.g.
unorganized cooperation) is obtained by a recessed vector
orientation of conditional cooperation (e.g. organized cooperation [Fig. 3]) or vice versa. Such imbalanced symmetry as perfect horizontal orientation would normally not be expected since
either cooperation or competition will occur emphasized either
positively (+) or negatively (—), which could cause a corresponding angular shift of the symbolic pattern (2x). While a
maximum imbalance would demand greater determination, tension (in-tension), or ego-strength (1-p. 511), a minimum imbalance would tend to obliterate cooperative/competitive as
well as masculine/feminine qualities that may give rise to a
predominant relativistic, subjective or indvidualistic valuation
(3x). By implication it may very well be asked what constitutes
optimum balance?

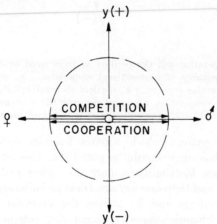

*Fig. 2.* Cooperation and Competition as four equal vector elements in
opposition and therefore hypothetical suspension or absolute equilibrium
(zero).

It should be pointed out that under the given assumption the principles of (a) equilibrium, (b) compensation, (c) complementarity, and (d) psycho-bisexuality, may be said to be simultaneously effective. It becomes evident that as for individuals " . . . , no society is exclusively competitive or exclusively cooperative" (1-p. 460) and similar assumptions are extended to the male-female bipolarity (4x). Contrary to the exemplified

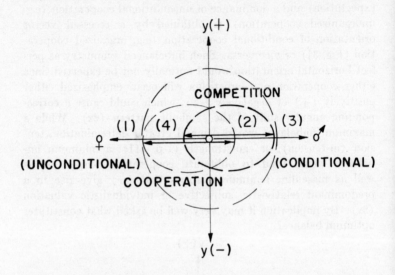

*Fig. 3.* Cooperation and Competition as imbalanced or complementary symmetry. Dominance of unconditional cooperation, e.g., unorganized cooperation (1) invokes recessed, e.g., required cooperation (2), and dominating conditional competition, e.g., goal directed (3) recesses the opposite element of unconditional competition, e.g., independent orientation (4).

hypothetical pattern which equates feminine-masculine symmetry as balanced, it should be noted that this does not occur naturally since bisexuality is normally either male or female predominant and therefore asymmetrical or imbalanced. Besides other shortcomings and limitations the vectorial elements or variables as dynamic somewhat paradoxical interaction remain, without justifications for the circular and ellipsoidal areas, at all times only a one-dimensional orientation, taken from or imposed upon a multi-dimensional and complex human and social reality.

# ADDITIONAL NOTES TO CHAPTERS
## AND BIBLIOGRAPHIES

Each of these chapters has been handled individually in accordance with the best judgment of the author of the chapter, or where the author is no longer living, by other consultants combined with my own addenda. Each note will be signed by the initials of the writer who prepared it. Wherever there is a publication with an adequate, up-to-date bibliography, we have listed this as a principal reference, sometimes with certain special additions, either because they were not included in the bibliography, are the work of the original author, or principal source, etc. The variation in the number of bibliographical references for any chapter is no indication of the volume of research or publication in that area since 1935.

M.M.

### CHAPTER I   THE ARAPESH OF NEW GUINEA

#### *Bibliography*

Full bibliography to subsequent publications can be found in:
MEAD, M.: *Male and Female,* Mentor edition, William Morrow, New York, 1949; New American Library, New York, 1955; Victor Gollancz, London, 1950; Diana Verlag (under the title *Mann und Weib*), Zurich and Stuttgart, 1955.

M.M.

### CHAPTER II   THE ESKIMO OF GREENLAND

I am grateful to Charles C. Hughes, who in his article, "Anomie, the Ammassalik, and the Standardization of Error" (*Southwestern J. of Anthropology,* Vol. 14, No. 4, pp. 352-377, 1956), pointed out the inexactitude of the title as printed. As implied in the first paragraph, the study is limited to the Ammassalik Eskimo and applies only to that group.

A quarter of a century after this study was written, it is well to recall why the Ammassalik were chosen. Their isolation from the main body of Eskimo whose habitat stretches from Point Barrow in Alaska to the West Coast of Greenland, and the special quality of their terrain makes their cultural idiom unique. Among the last of the Eskimo groups to be encountered by Europeans (1883-1884), and among the first to have case histories included in descriptions of Eskimo groups, the Ammassalik invited this pioneer attempt in extrapolating their social structure from such individual case studies. These, slight and impressionistic, remind us of the social structures compressed into a *Spoon River Anthology*, rather than those documented in a *Middletown*.

## Bibliography

A good bibliography on the Eskimo can be found in:

BIRKET-SMITH, KAJ: *The Eskimos,* revised ed., Methuen & Co., Ltd., London, 1959.

For specific works on the Ammassilik, see also:

Arctic Institute of North America: *Arctic Bibliography,* prepared for and in cooperation with the Department of Defense, Government Printing Office, Washington, D.C., Vol. 1-, 1953-.

And see also:

MIRSKY, JEANETTE: *To the Arctic, the Story of Northern Explorations from Earliest Times to the Present,* Alfred A. Knopf, New York, 1948.

J.M.

## CHAPTER III THE OJIBWA OF CANADA

Aggressively self-sufficient individualism gave an integrating focus to Canadian Ojibwa culture of the 1930's. Individualism was greatly honored in males but, despite lip service to a separate female world and standard, there was no comparable system for females. However, some women displayed high skills in the male pursuits of hunting, warfare and competitive games, engaging in these activities at whim or under special temporary circumstances, when they were honored as if they were men. The tribe's techniques of hunting and trapping were closely adapted to the demand for individualistic strength in all — Ojibwa's enduring pattern. Southern branches of Ojibwa readily adopted from neighboring tribes and white Americans some alterations in family structure, functions and terminology, and some economic techniques. Yet responses to projective tests reveal the perseverance of the traditional individualistic character.

## Bibliography

DUNNING, R. W.: *Social and Economic Change among the Northern Ojibwa.* University of Toronto Press, Toronto, 1959. Has a good bibliography.

BOGGS, S. T.: "Culture change and personality of Ojibwa children," *Amer. Anthropol.,* Vol. 60, No. 1, pp. 47-58, 1958.

BROWN, P.: "Changes in Ojibwa social control," *Amer. Anthropol.,* Vol. 54, No. 1, pp. 57-70, 1952.

LANDES, R.: "Personality of the Ojibwa," *Character and Personality,* Vol. 6, pp. 51-60, 1937.

——— "The abnormal among the Ojibwa Indians," *J. abnorm. soc. Psychol.,* Vol. 33, pp. 14-33, 1938.

——— "The Ojibwa Woman," *Columbia University Contributions to Anthropology 31.* Columbia University Press, New York, 1938.

TEICHNER, M. I.: "Windigo Psychosis: A Study of a Relationship between Belief and Behavior among the Indians of Northeastern Canada," *Proc.* of the 19th Annual Spring Meeting of the American Ethnological Society, ed. V. F. Ray. Seattle, Washington, American Ethnological Society, pp. xi-129, 1960.

R.L.

## CHAPTER IV    THE BACHIGA OF EAST AFRICA

The official orthography that has now been settled upon is Kiga. The terms "extraordinary" and "peculiar to them," appearing in this account are no longer appropriate, in the light of materials which have appeared since this account was written. The fissioning lineage, with segments at different levels of genealogical depth which are in what Evans-Pritchard has called "complementary opposition" to each other, has now been described for quite a number of African peoples. The tension within the patrilineal extended family, the division of brothers' households after the father's death, the importance of the feud, the existence of mechanisms to minimize it within some limited spheres, particularly between different lineage segments of a larger lineage or clan, all appear to be common features of such systems. Some of the others do, however, have more contexts of required cooperation among siblings, and more effective moral and ritual sanctions for implementing the common ideal of sibling solidarity.

## Bibliography

OTTENBERG, S. and P.: *Culture and Societies of Africa,* Random House, New York, 1960. Excellent regional comparative references in very full bibliography.

BAXTER, P. T. W.: "The Kiga," in RICHARDS, A. I. (ed.): *East African Chiefs,* Faber and Faber, London, 1960.

EDEL, M. M.: *The Chiga of Western Uganda,* Oxford University Press, Oxford and New York, 1957.

MIDDLETON, J. and TAIT, D.: *Tribes Without Rulers,* Routledge and Kegan Paul, London, 1958.

M.M.E.

### CHAPTER V    THE IFUGAO OF THE PHILIPPINE ISLANDS

Professor Harold Conklin of Columbia University who has done field work in the Philippines has been kind enough to call my attention to some errors of fact and to misrepresentations. The most serious error is my observation in a footnote that the Ifugao lack the institution of friendship. Friendship is described by Barton in his *Philippine Pagans,* published in 1938, after this chapter had been written. Other corrections to be made are that houses are not located at the base of mountains but farther up the slopes among the rice terrace lands. The statement in my text that "the division of land into small holdings is not very productive, for rats, wild pigs, monkeys and deer wreak havoc with the border fields" is unclear. The point to be made is that the owners of very small border fields suffer disproportionate losses. As Barton has explained, "Heads of rice are laid in the middle of a field — in the middle in order to prevent them being stolen by .rats or crows." (*Ifugao Economics,* p. 402). Finally, the note on the comparative food values of camotes and of rice could be stated more precisely by noting that the protein content of Asiatic rice is roughly between seven and nine percent while that of Philippine potatoes is about 65 percent.

## Bibliography

BARTON, R. F.: *Philippine Pagans: The Autobiographies of Three Ifugao.* George Routledge & Sons, London, 1938.

———: "The Religion of the Ifugaos," *Amer. Anthropol.,* Vol. 48, No. 4, Memoir No. 65, pp. 1-219, 1946. Menasha: the American Anthropological Association.

———: *The Kalingas: their institutions and custom law.* 275 pp., biblio., glossary, index, map, 29 plates. Introduction by E. A. Hoebel. University of Chicago Press, Chicago, 1949.

———: *The mythology of the Ifugaos.* 244 pp., Appendix, notes, biblio. Memoirs of the American Folklore Society 46, Philadelphia, 1955.

BEYER, H. O.: "Origin myths among the Mountain peoples of the Philippines." *Philippine Journal of Science.* Vol. 8D, pp. 85-116, Manila, 1913.

———: "An Ifugao Burial Ceremony." *Philippine Journal of Science,* Vol. 6D, pp. 227-252, Manila, 1911.

LAMBRECHT, F.: "Ifugao villages and houses." *Publications of the Catholic Anthropological Conference,* Vol. 1, No. 3, pp. 117-141. Maps, figs., photos. The Catholic University of America, Washington, 1929.

———: "Ancestors' knowledge among the Ifugaos and its importance in the religious and social life of the tribe." *J. East. Asiat. Stud.,* Vol. 3, pp. 366-369, Manila, 1954.

SCOTT, W. H.: "A preliminary report on upland rice in northern Luzon," *Southwest J. Anthropol.,* Vol. 14, No. 1, pp. 57-105, Albuquerque, 1958.

I.G.

## CHAPTER VI THE KWAKIUTL OF VANCOUVER ISLAND

The Kwakiutl are one of a group of Wakashan-speaking tribes. The Kwakiutl proper consist of a northern division and a southern division. Present estimates, according to a communication from Professor Helen Codere, indicate a population in 1835 of about 10,000 for both divisions. Kwakiutl culture as here described refers in the main to the climactic period when the potlatch had begun to assume major importance, sometime after the 1830's, in the opinion of Professor Codere. When Franz Boas visited the Kwakiutl during the 1890's the culture had already begun to pass its peak. By then the population decline had left vacant many titles of nobility.

Students of North Pacific Coast societies are not agreed on the interpretation of the potlatch, which seemingly had different connotations in each tribe. It is my present view that the Kwakiutl potlatch and its associated complex of status rivalry and honorific displays is to be regarded as essentially sacred in character, and as related to a religion that sanctifies aggressive powers. Kwakiutl secular life is much more cooperative and, as Professor Codere has observed, far more amiable.

## Bibliography

MÜLLER, W.: *Weltbild und Kult der Kwakiutl-Indianer*, F. Steiner, Wiesbaden, 1955. Contains the most complete bibliography. See also:

CODERE, H.: "Kwakiutl society: rank without class," *Amer. Anthropol.*, Vol. 59, No. 3, pp. 473-486, June 1957.

FORD, C. S.: *Smoke from Their Fires*, Yale University Press, New Haven, 1941.

HAWTHORN, H. B., BELSHAW, C. S., and JAMIESON, S. M.: "The Indians of British Columbia: A Study of Contemporary Social Adjustment," University of California Press, Berkeley, 1958.

I. G.


CHAPTER VII   THE MANUS OF THE ADMIRALTY ISLANDS

The Manus were intensively restudied in 1953-54, so that we have an additional check on the accuracy of the 1928-29 observations.

The population estimate is wrong, present estimates place the population of the Admiralties in the 1920's as closer to 14,000.

## Bibliography

MEAD, M.: *New Lives for Old.* William Morrow and Company, New York, 1956. New American Library, 1961. Contains the most complete bibliography to 1955. See also:

———: *Continuities in Cultural Evolution. The Dwight H. Terry Lectures, 1957.* Yale University Press, New Haven, (in press).

——— and SCHWARTZ, T.: "The cult as condensed social process" in *Group Processes. Transactions,* 5th Conference, Josiah Macy Jr. Foundation. Madison Printing Company, Inc., New Jersey, 1960.

SCHWARTZ, L.: "Cultural Influence on Perception." M.A. essay. Temple University, Philadelphia, 1959 (ms.).

SCHWARTZ, T.: "The Paliau Movement of the Admiralty Islands, 1946-1954." Ph.D. dissertation. University of Pennsylvania, Philadelphia, 1957 (ms.).

M. M.

## CHAPTER VIII   THE IROQUOIS

Dr. Fenton has very kindly checked over the chapter again and in addition to the remarks quoted above, page 517, indicated that the most satisfactory bibliography at present available is in Fenton, W. N. and Gulick, J., eds., *Symposium on Cherokee and Iroquois Culture,* Bur. Amer. Ethnol. B. 180, 1961 (in press). (This contains the latest summaries of Iroquois research by Lounsbury, Ritchie, Chafe, Shimony Kurath, Sturtevant, Wallace, Fenton, and a group of Cherokee scholars.)

Dr. Fenton has supplied the following bibliographical annotations with page references to Quain's original chapter.

## Bibliography

p. 242. *Relation . . . to other peoples . . .*
FENTON, W. N.: "Problems Arising from the Historic Northeastern Position of the Iroquois," *Essays in Historical Anthropology of North America,* published in honor of John R. Swanton, Smithsonian Msc. Coll. Washington, D. C., Vol. 100, pp. 159-251, 1940.

HUNT, G. T.: *The Wars of the Iroquois*, The University of Wisconsin Press, Madison, Wisconsin, 1940. (See Fenton's review in the *American Anthropologist*, Vol. 42, No. 4, pp. 662-664, October-December, 1940.)

On Huron culture, see:

KINIETZ, W. V.: *The Indians of the Western Great Lakes 1615-1760*. Occasional Contributions from the Museum of Anthropology of the University of Michigan, 10, Ann Arbor, Michigan, 1940.

QUIMBY, G. I.: *Indian Life in the Upper Great Lakes*, the University of Chicago, 1960.

p. 243. On general Iroquois culture:

SPECK, F. G.: "The Iroquois: A Study in Cultural Evolution," Cranbrook Institute of Science, Bloomfield Hills, Mich. Bull. 23, 1955. (Material culture, economics, art.)

WILSON, EDMUND: *Apologies to the Iroquois*, Farrar, Straus & Cudahy, New York, 1960.

fn. 3: Men made fishnets, and all the gear that they used except burden straps and clothing.

The questions that Quain raised about Iroquois women have been answered in a series of studies, notably by:

RANDLE, M. C.: "Iroquois Women, Then and Now," Symposium on Local Diversity in Iroquois Culture, N.8. [W. N. Fenton, editor,] Bur. Amer. Ethnol. Bull. 149, Smithsonian Institution, Washington, D. C., pp. 167-180, 1951.

RICHARDS, C. B.: "Matriarchy or Mistake: The Role of Iroquois Women Through Time," *Cultural Stability and Cultural Change, Proc.* of the 1957 Spring Meeting of the Amer. Ethnol. Soc., V. F. Ray, editor, pp. 36-45, Seattle, 1957.

SHIMONY, A.: "Conservatism on the Six Nations Reserve," Doctoral Dissertation at Yale University, 1958. (To be published by Yale University Publications in Anthropology.)

On problems of sources and history, see:
HUNT, G. T.: *op. cit.*
FENTON, W. N.: *op. cit.*
————: *American Indian and White Relations to 1830: Needs and Opportunities for Study*, The University of North Carolina Press, Chapel Hill, 1957.

ADDITIONAL NOTES AND BIBLIOGRAPHIES 537

TRELEASE, A. W.: *Indian Affairs in Colonial New York: The Seventeenth Century*, Cornell University Press, Ithaca, New York, 1960.

On the population of the Iroquois and the reasons behind their warfare, see:

HUNT, G. T.: *op. cit.*

FENTON, W. N.: "An Outline of Seneca Ceremonies at Coldspring Longhouse," Yale University Publications in Anthropology No. 9, 1936.

On dreams and religion:

WALLACE, A. F. C.: "Dreams and the Wishes of the Soul: A Type of Psychoanalytic Theory Among the Seventeenth Century Iroquois," *American Anthropologist*, Vol. 60, pp. 234-248, April, 1958.

p. 264 Mohawk — Onondaga — Seneca are Elder brothers, Fathers, Uncles, *Agadoni* to Oneida-Cayuga (Delaware, Tuscarora, Tutelo), Younger brothers, Offspring, Nephews in the Condolence Council. See:

FENTON, W. N.: "The Roll Call of the Iroquois Chiefs," Smithsonian Msc. Coll. Washington, D. C., Vol. III, No. 15, pp. 1-73, 1950.

————: "An Iroquois Condolence Council for Installing Cayuga Chiefs in 1945," *Journ. Wash. Acad. Sci.*, Vol. 36, No. 4, pp. 110-127, 1946.

Morgan's classes of chiefs are committees.

Asher Wright, the New England Missionary at Buffalo Creek and Cattaraugus, left an excellent description of the levels of political structure from family to League and down again:

WRIGHT, ASHER: "Seneca Indians (1859)," W. N. Fenton, editor, *Ethnohistory*, Vol. 4, No. 3, pp. 302-321, 1957.

p. 266. The whole concept of medicine societies is set forth in:

FENTON, W. N.: *The Iroquois Eagle Dance: An Offshoot of the Calumet Dance*, Bur. Amer. Ethnol. Bull. 156, 1953.

p. 271. On factions:

FENTON, W. N.: "Factionalism in American Indian Society," Actes des IVᵉ Congrès International des Sciences Anthropologiques et Ethnologiques, Vienne, t.2, pp. 330-340, 1952.

SCHEELE, R.: "Warfare of the Iroquois and Their Northern Neighbors in the Seventeenth Century," Doctoral Dissertation at Columbia University, 1949.

SNYDERMAN, G. S.: "Behind the Tree of Peace: A Sociological Analysis of Iroquois Warfare," *Pennsylvania Archaeologist*, Bull. of the Soc. for Pennsylvania Archaeology, 18, pp. 1-93, 1948.

Economic and technological background (Quain failed to use two important studies then available):

STITES, S. H.: *Economics of the Iroquois*, Bryn Mawr College Monographs, Vol. 1, No. 3, Bryn Mawr, 1905.

WAUGH, F. W.: *Iroquois Food and Food Preparation*, Canada Geol. Surv. Anthrop. Ser. 12, Mem. 86, Ottawa, 1916.

Social and political structure:

FENTON, W. N., editor: *Symposium on Local Diversity in Iroquois Culture*, Bur. Amer. Ethnol. Bull. 149, 1951. See especially Fenton's introduction and references and his "Locality as a Basic Factor in the Development of Iroquois Social Structure," pp. 35-54.

NOON, JOHN A.: *Law and Government of the Grand River Iroquois*, Viking Fund Publications in Anthropology 12, pp. 1-186, 1949.

On the number of chiefs, their education and installation Fenton published a whole series in the *Journal of the Washington Academy of Sciences*, 1944-46. These are listed in the bibliography to:

FENTON, W. N.: "The Roll Call of the Iroquois Chiefs," Smithsonian Msc. Coll., Washington, D. C., Vol. III, No. 15, pp. 1-73, 1950.

On the ceremonies of the Handsome Lake Religion:

DEARDORFF, M. H.: "The Religion of Handsome Lake: Its Origin and Development," *Symposium on Local Diversity*, N.5. Bur. Amer. Ethnol. Bull. 149, pp. 77-107, 1951.

Finally, the problem of learning, seemingly haphazard, is explored in:

RAY, V. F., editor: *Cultural Stability and Cultural Change*, Proc. of the 1957 Spring Meeting of the Amer. Ethnol. Soc., Seattle, 1957. See especially, "Long-term Trends of Change Among the Iroquois," pp. 30-35.

p. 273. Footnote 2 . . . conflicts . . . were . . .

W. N. F.

CHAPTER IX    THE SAMOANS

*Bibliography*

MEAD, M.: *Male and Female.* William Morrow and Company, New York, 1949. New American Library, New York, 1955. Contains most complete bibliography to 1949. See also:

COOK, P. H.: "The application of the Rorschach test to a Samoan group," Rorschach Research Exchange 6, pp. 1151-60, 1942.

COPP, J. D.: *The Samoan Dance of Life,* Beacon Press, Boston, 1950.

EMBER, M.: "The nonunilinear descent groups of Samoa." *Amer. Anthropol.* Vol. 61, No. 4, 1959.

GRAY, CAPT. J. A. C.: *Amerika Samoa: A history of American Samoa and its United States Naval Administration,* U. S. Naval Institute, Annapolis, Md., 1960.

HOLMES, L.: *Ta'u: Stability and Change in a Samoan Village.* Wellington, New Zealand, The Polynesian Society, 1958.

————: "The restudy of Manu'an culture: A problem in methodology, Ph.D. dissertation. Northwestern University, Evanston, Ill., 1957 (ms.). A restudy of Ta'u in Manu's on which this chapter was based.

KEESING, F. M.: "The Ta'upo System of Samoa. A study of institutional change," *Oceania,* Vol. VIII, No. I, pp. 1-14, Sept., 1937.

———— and KEESING, M. M.: *Elite Communication in Samoa. A Study of Leadership.* Stanford University Press, Stanford, California, 1956.

MEAD, M.: "Cultural factors in community-education programs," *Community Education, National Society for the Study of Education,* 58th Yearbook, part I, pp. 66-96, 1959.

M.M.

CHAPTER X    THE ZUNI OF NEW MEXICO

Errata:

p. 316, line 20.  *Castanada* should be *Castañeda.*

p. 317, line 14.  *movies* should be *motives.*

Dr. Ruth Bunzel, whose field work on the Zuni was the principal source for this chapter, has been kind enough to call my attention to some errors of fact and to misstatements. First, the time to which the study refers, in the main, is the period between 1924-1930. This has particular reference to the case histories. On economics, my statements on Zuni wealth were exaggerated. The Zuni are not rich, but well-to-do: they do not sacrifice "great quantities" of food to their ancestors, but the equivalent of a family meal. The Zuni gardens are not "small"; they are minuscule. Melons are not grown in separate patches but in the corn fields. In aboriginal days flood farming was probably more important than hand irrigation. Lambing time is an occasion when young and poor helpers are given ewe lambs by their more well-to-do fellows. Finally, I had given the impression that ceremonial absorbs more of a man's time than economics. The reverse, of course, is true. The point is that ceremonial commands more of a man's *interest*. Much ceremonial, moreover, has an economic motive.

On social life, the dichotomy between Catholic and Protestant is not "sharp" as I had said. As Dr. Bunzel observes, "It is rather bland. Individuals transfer their allegiance from one group to another, some go to both churches, adhering to neither." Similarly, my comment that the Zuni may "hate" a priest is too strong. Dislike is the more accurate term. As to household quarrels, I gave the impression that these were for personal reasons only. A common source of quarrels, Dr. Bunzel notes, is "over cooperation in work and contributions to the larder." My statement that sacred fetishes are held by households of a clan should actually read, "lineages of a clan."

Finally, on childhood disciplines, a most serious omission was to ignore the role of corporal punishment and of the "scare" Katcinas who go from house to house frightening unruly children.

## Bibliography

SMITH, W., and ROBERTS, J. M.: *Zuni Law*, with appendix by Stanley Newman, *Papers of the Peabody Museum, Harvard University*, Vol. 43, No. 1, Harvard University Press, Cambridge, 1951. This volume contains a good bibliography. See also:

GOLDFRANK, E.: "The Linguistic Note to Zuni Ethnography." *Word*, Vol. 2, pp. 191-196, 1946.

———— "Socialization, Personality and the Structure of Pueblo Society." *Amer. Anthropol.,* Vol. 47, pp. 516-539, 1945.

GOLDMAN, I.: "The Morals of the Zuni Indians" in *The Encyclopedia of Morals,* Philosophical Library, New York, 1957.

KAPLAN, B.: "A Study of Rorschach Responses in Four Cultures," *Papers of the Peabody Museum, Harvard University,* Cambridge, Vol. 52, No. 2, 1954.

WILSON, E.: *Red, Black, Blond and Olive. Studies in four civilizations: Zuni, Haiti, Soviet Russia, Israel,* Oxford University Press, New York, 1956.

I.G.

## CHAPTER XI   THE BATHONGA OF SOUTH AFRICA

This chapter stands as written based on Junod's work.

A recent paper by Dr. Marvin Harris brings Thongan social structure more closely in line with current terminology and concepts, and corrects what has been an overly idealized view of Thongan social unity and cooperation. Of particular relevance to the present chapter is the point that all Thongan political units were kin-unified. Some were held together by more ephemeral ties. In this connection, A. Rita-Ferreira's criticism ("Labour Emigration Among the Moçambique Thonga: Comments on a Study by Marvin Harris," *Africa,* Vol. XXX, No. 2, pp. 141-152, April, 1960) of Harris' views ("Labour Emigration Among the Moçambique Thonga. Cultural and Political Factions," *Africa,* Vol. XXIX, No. 1, pp. 50-66, January, 1959) should be read.

### Bibliography

For supplementary references see:

CAILLOIS, R.: *Man and the Sacred,* The Free Press, Glencoe, Ill., 1959.

SCHAPERA, ISAAC, ed.: *The Bantu-speaking Tribes of South Africa,* edited for the (South African) Inter-University Committee for African Studies, George Routledge & Sons, Ltd., London, 1937.

I.G.

## Chapter XII  The Dakota

A principal source for the Dakota chapter was the unpublished manuscripts of Dr. Ella Deloria, who had been working for many years with Dr. Boas and Dr. Benedict on linguistics. Dr. Deloria's manuscripts are still unpublished as she is still in the process of gathering more material from the oldest living informants. I wrote her when this reprinting was planned and asked for comments, but received none.

### Bibliography

ERIKSON, ERIK H.: "Childhood in Two American Indian Tribes," Part Two of his *Childhood and Society,* pp. 93-160, W. W. Norton & Company, Inc., New York, 1950.

GOLDFRANK, E. S.: "Historic Change and Social Character: A Study of the Teton Dakota," *American Anthropologist,* n.s., Vol. XIV, pp. 67-83, 1943.

LANDES, RUTH: "Dakota Warfare," *Southwestern J. of Anthropology,* Vol. 15, pp. 43-52, 1959.

LESSER, ALEXANDER: *Siouan Kinship,* A Doctoral Dissertation at Columbia University, 1958; University Microfilms Dissertation Abstracts V. 19:2, p. 208, 1958.

MACGREGOR, GORDON: *Warriors Without Weapons; a Study of the Society and Personality Development of the Pine Ridge Sioux,* University of Chicago Press, Chicago, 1946.

THOMPSON, LAURA: "Personality and Government, *Part III,*" *America Indigena,* Vol. 10, No. 3, 1950.

M.M.

## Chapter XIII  The Maori of New Zealand

I am indebted to Dr. Andrew P. Vayda for the following comments:

p. 428 n.l. Some authorities have estimated pre-European Maori population to be somewhat greater. See Lewthwaite, *op. cit.*

p. 428, par. 2. They may well have suffered real privation. Cf. p. 454, ft. 2.

p. 428-429. The north-south differences in economic pursuits were much more important than the east-west ones. See Cumberland . . .

p. 430. The swift termination of internal disputes at the first appearance of an outside enemy is an exaggeration. On how hard it was for related *hapu* to act together see Vayda, *op. cit.*

p. 432. Leader in war would be a more appropriate term than general.

p. 435. I am not at all sure that the economic efficiency of the village did increase with the size of the slave population. See Vayda, 1961, "Prisoners and Slaves in the 19th Century," *Ethnohistory,* Vol. 8, 1961.

p. 436. The paragraph on the chief's being a beneficiary of more land resources is misleading, since he was expected eventually to distribute most of the wealth he "possessed."

p. 436-437. All references to tribal cohesion, impulses common to fellow tribesmen, etc., are suspect. Members of a *hapu* acted together readily; members of the larger unit (the tribe) did not.

p. 450. Donne an untrustworthy source here.

p. 451. "Customary endogamy practice" may be exaggeration. The most recent work on Maori marriage is Biggs, *op. cit.*

p. 452. My impression is that warfare within the tribe was fairly common. See Dr. Vayda's "Expansion and warfare among Swidden agriculturists," *Amer. Anthropol.,* April, 1961.

p. 454, footnote. Not supported by the evidence. Tribal solidarity may well have grown as intratribal mobility increased and *hapu* boundaries became blurred. The statement at the top of the page that "basically tribal solidarity was preserved by the cooperative behavior engendered by social structure" is without foundation.

p. 478, 505. Maori individuals identify, I think, with the *hapu,* not with the tribe.

I do not find that these comments alter the way in which Maori culture, on which our information was and is poor, was placed in the study.

## Bibliography

FIRTH, R.: *Economics of the New Zealand Maori*. Revised edition of his 1929 edition used in the preparation of this chapter. For most complete bibliography to 1958. And Vayda, Andrew P., 1961. *Maori Warfare*, Maori Monograph 2, The Polynesian Society, R. E. Owen, Wellington, N. Z., 1960.

See also:

AGINSKY, B. W. and BUCK, P. H.: "Interacting forces in the Maori Family," *Amer. Anthropol.* Vol. 42, pp. 195-210, 1940.

BEAGLEHOLE, ERNEST and PEARL: *Some Modern Maoris*, New Zealand Committee of Educational Research, Wellington, 1946.

—— and RITCHIE, J.: "The Rakan studies," *J. polynes. Soc.* Vol. 67, pp. 132-154, 1958.

BIGGS, BRICE: *Maori Marriage*, Maori Monograph 1, The Polynesian Society, Wellington, N. Z. (in press).

CUMBERLAND, K. B.: "Aotearoa Maori: New Zealand about 1780." *Geographical Review*, Vol. 39, pp. 401-24, 1949.

LEWTHWAITE, G.: "The Aotearoa: Its number and distribution." *New Zealand Geographer*, Vol. 6, pp. 35-52, 1950.

VAYDA, ANDREW P.: "Expansion and warfare among Swidden agriculturists," *Amer. Anthropol.* Vol. 63, No. 2, April, 1961.

——: "Prisoners and slaves in the 19th century." *Ethnohistory*, Vol. 8, 1961.

M.M.

# INDEX

## A

Aberrant, 42, 43, 73, 74, 83, 85, 225, 277, 278, 305, 314, 343, 344, 348, 349, 373, 380, 381, 415–417, 457, 510

Achievement, 485
(*See also* Goals)

Age, attitude toward, 495, 496
food categories, 38
goals, 13
groups, 8
growth, 39
(*See also* Cultures)

Allport, Prof. Gordon, 3

Andamanese, 462

Apache, 461

Arapesh, 4, 13
aberrant, 42, 43
*abullu*, 29, 49, 486
age, 28, 38, 44, 49
*ano' in*, 41
Beach, 20, 22, 23, 36
behavior, 39, 41, 47
boys, 25, 26, 37–39, 47, 48
"brother" trade friend, 21
*buanyin*, 32–34, 37, 42
child, 44–47
clan, 21, 25, 26, 27, 36
clothing, 22, 25
competition, 41, 48
cooperation, 27, 28, 33, 36, 37, 49, 468, 469, 482
cult, 24, 26, 36, 38
culture, 468, 509
curse, 44
dance complex, 22, 23, 32, 36, 47
dead, use of bones of, 41, 50
debt, 33
disease, 24
"dogs" in feast, 33, 39

Arapesh, dual organization, 21
economic obligations, 25–27
economics, 22–25, 28–32
education, 38, 43, 44–49, 494
environment, 23, 31, 464
feasts, 24, 26, 27, 29, 30, 32, 33, 36, 37
food, 24, 29, 30, 33, 38
gardening, 21, 24, 25, 28–31, 40, 464
ghosts, 21, 26
gifts, 22, 26, 29, 42
girls, 26, 46, 47, 48
goals, 37, 38, 40, 43, 50, 486
group activity, 36, 46, 468
"growth," meaning of, 26, 37–40, 43, 44
habit, 45
hospitality, 30
housing, 24, 25, 29, 30, 31
hunting, 21, 23, 25, 26, 30, 31, 41
ideal man, 38, 40, 48
incest, 35
individual, 27, 31, 36, 38, 478
individualistic culture, 461, 463
infants, 25, 40, 44, 45, 47
kinship, 25, 27, 31, 34, 35, 42, 44, 45, 46, 479, 489, 490
labor, 22, 24, 25, 28–32, 37, 40, 47, 463, 464
leadership, 32, 33, 40, 41, 43
magic, 28, 36, 41, 43
marriage, 25, 26, 35, 39, 41, 48
*marsalai*, 21, 26
moiety, 32
Mountain, 20–23, 29, 43
murder, 35
offenses, 31, 34, 35, 42, 43;
ownership, 21, 25, 29, 30, 31, 36
Plains, 20–23, 34, 36, 38, 39, 40, 43–45

Manus, ownership, 222
   personality, 213, 222, 225, 226, 229, 233
   political structure, 211
   prestige, 216–218
   property, 217, 218, 221, 226, 228, 232, 487
   quarrels, 222, 232, 237
   rank, 213, 216, 228
   religion, 220, 230, 492
   sanctions, 212, 214–220, 224, 230, 237, 471, 494
   sex, 221, 223, 235
   sin, 232, 233, 236, 487
   *sobalabalate*, 237
   social classes, 216;
   social structure, 213, 238, 469
   sorcery, 232
   status, 217, 496
   success, 214, 216, 218, 221, 230, 234, 238
   tabu, 212, 221, 223
   Tabular Summary, 501
   technology, 210–212, 230, 231
   trade, 210–212, 216–218, 226, 233, 234
   unit, the village, 211–213
   war, 210, 212, 216, 233, 234, 469, 481
   wealth, 214, 216, 228
   widow, 235, 236
   wife, 219, 236–238
   women, 215, 219–221, 234, 238, 466
Maori, 4, 7, 18, 286, 295, 459
   age, 441
   behaviour, 436, 450, 453, 454
   boys, 454, 455
   chief, 432–436, 438, 443–445, 449
   child, 445, 454
   competition, 436, 443, 455, 460
   cooperation, 430, 433, 439, 440, 443, 446–448, 460, 461, 476, 478, 488
   dance, 455
   economics, 428–433, 437, 449, 452
   education, 454–457
   environment, 428

Maori, family, 428, 429, 438
   feast, 435, 444, 445
   fishing, 429, 433, 438, 443
   food, 428, 429, 438
   games, 453, 455
   gifts, 445
   *hapu*, 429, 432, 454
   hospitality, 433
   housing, 430
   hunting birds, 438
   ideal, 452
   individual, 440, 450, 456, 478
   infanticide, 454
   kinship, 429–432, 450, 457, 479, 489
   labor, 435, 437–446
   leadership, 432, 435, 442, 443, 452
   magic, 449, 456
   *mana*, 433, 449
   marriage, 434, 435, 450, 451
   *muru*, 450, 451
   offenses, 449, 450
   ownership, 431, 434
   personality, 452–454
   prestige, 440, 452
   property, 432, 434, 436, 444–448
   quarrels, 430, 450, 453, 456
   rank, 432, 435, 442, 449
   religion, 433, 437, 442
   residence, 430
   ritual, 438, 449
   rivalry, 478
   sanctions, 449
   slaves, 434, 435, 441, 442, 449, 478
   social classes, 434, 435
   social structure, 432, 443
   status, 478, 480
   suicide, 448, 450
   *tabu*, 435, 437, 441, 442, 448, 449, 453, 456
   Tabular Summary, 505
   technology, 429, 432, 437, 442–448, 463
   trade, 429
   tribe, 430, 432, 450, 457
   village, 430
   war, 434, 435, 453, 455, 478, 481
   wealth, 433, 434

M